Literacies
Second Edition

Ken Smith
Indiana University South Bend

Terence Brunk
Rutgers University

Suzanne Diamond
Rutgers University

Priscilla Perkins
Cameron University

McGraw-Hill, Inc.
College Custom Series

*New York St. Louis San Francisco Auckland Bogotá
Caracas Lisbon London Madrid Mexico Milan Montreal
New Delhi Paris San Juan Singapore Sydney Tokyo Toronto*

McGraw-Hill's College Custom Series consists of products that are produced from camera-ready copy. Peer review, class testing, and accuracy are primarily the responsibility of the author(s).

Literacies

1 2 3 4 5 6 7 8 9 0 DOC DOC 9 0 9 8 7 6 5 4

ISBN 0-07-058982-8

Editor: J.D. Ice
Cover Photo: *Homage to Outerbridge II* by Robert Sulkin
Back Cover Photo: Detail of *Homage to Outerbridge II* by Robert Sulkin
Manuscript Preparation: Architext
Permissions Supervisor: Carla Keever
Printer/Binder: R. R. Donnelly & Sons Company

 This book is printed on recycled, acid-free paper containing 10% postconsumer waste.

Acknowledgements

Like the first edition of *Literacies*, this second edition has been nourished by the fertile atmosphere of the Writing Program community at Rutgers. We have been guided in our revisions and additions by the feedback we have received from many recent teachers of the English 100 course. We are especially grateful to Mike Williamson, Ann Rea, April Lidinsky, Carol Allen, Priti Joshi, and other instructors whose thoughtful evaluations of the book helped us to re-imagine the directions we might take with it.

The essays by David Gilmore and Susan Brownmiller come to us from Marilyn Rye, who assembled a packet of challenging "supplementary" readings during her time as English 100 course coordinator; after a while, the kinds of texts which had once seemed to supplement our classroom work began to look pivotal, and we thank her for pointing us toward them. Kurt Spellmeyer's influence and example will be important to us wherever we are. Finally, we need to recognize Eleanor Creedon, Susan Mayer, Judy Karwowski, Maribel Gill, and Emma Rumen; their work is central to the Writing Program at Rutgers.

We wish to thank our editor, J.D. Ice, Karen Slothower, Carla Keever, and the rest of the College Custom Series team at McGraw-Hill, for their consistently creative responses to our needs and ideas.

Priscilla Perkins
Terence Brunk
Suzanne Diamond
Ken Smith

July 4, 1994

Contents

A Preface...For Students and Teachers

Literacies contains three forms of study materials or "apparatus" that can be used to help make our work with the readings more productive. A collection of Invitations to Write and a brief guide to a Systematic Approach to Error appear at the end of the book, and study questions appear before and after each reading. The Invitations to Write provide brief, informal opportunities to reflect (in writing) upon the things we do when we read and write. The Invitations encourage us to become more aware of the procedures that work effectively for each of us as individual writers; they also help us recognize aspects of our writing that require particular attention. In their emphasis upon the writer's awareness about his or her own methods of reading and writing, the Invitations not only offer a unique and beneficial strategy for making our writing more effective, they also encourage writers to practice the same kinds of self-awareness evident in so many of the selections in *Literacies*.

The guide to a Systematic Approach to Error provides techniques for proofreading and revising that help each writer identify the kinds of language errors she or he tends to make repeatedly as well as offer suggestions about how each of us can develop personal strategies for correcting these errors. By assisting us to engage constructively and confidently with our errors, the systematic approach is more useful and more effective than many other approaches to error, which tend to stress the memorization of rules rather than the development of effective ways to understand and enact those rules. The study questions, described in greater detail below, offer initial paths of investigation into individual readings and suggest possibilities to explore as we bridge from one reading to another. Additionally, a short guide to the MLA citation method appears at the end of the book.

The editors designed all the study materials for *Literacies* to be flexible enough for use with a variety of teaching styles and classroom situations. At the same time, we sought to maintain a certain degree of theoretical consistency across the different forms of apparatus, since we wanted the apparatus to reflect our shared perceptions of reading/writing processes. The Introduction outlines a number of the theoretical concerns that guided us as we prepared the apparatus, particularly the study questions that go with each reading. These concerns include, among others, the meaningful incorporation of personal experience into our interpretive practice as readers and writers; the use of our own writing as sites for weaving together several texts, literacies, and perspectives so that we can better explore them in relation to each other and to our own thoughts; a willingness to view such weavings of texts as opportunities to construct our arguments and ask questions about our ideas; the development of our own "writerly" authority (to invoke Roland Barthes) to engage actively and responsibly with a wide range of issues and ways of speaking (from Michelle Cliff's thoughts on colonialism to James Clifford's ideas about tourism) and to work with those discourses in ways appropriate to our own thoughts, values, and positions. The study questions for each reading address these concerns by asking us—as communities of readers and writers—to be sensitive to them in our own interrelated work as readers of and writers about the selections in *Literacies*.

There are four types of study questions for each reading: *Before Reading*, *Dynamics*, *Critical Tools*, and *Draft One/Draft Two*. Each category of questions reflects a specific set of the theoretical issues which have governed the genesis and development of *Literacies*. These sets of issues are "discrete" (to echo Amy Tan) only in the most provisional sense. Although each type is somewhat distinctive, the process of writing the questions consistently reminded us as editors that the categories cross into one another with the same energizing—and occasionally perplexing—fluidity as do the readings in the anthology. In many classes, the questions and categories will work effectively as they are written; we hope, nonetheless, that teachers and students will put the fluidity of the study questions to their own best uses through revision, reconceptualization, and experimentation.

Before Reading questions invite us to explore our own knowledge of and expectations about some of the strategies of interpretation, methods of argument, and issues important to the text we are preparing to read. These explorations foreground our own ideas and experiences so that we may become more active players in the interpretive process and have a greater sense of our own authority to converse with the authors as "experts" on a breadth of issues. Many of us might never have heard of the Ilongot people of the Philippines, let alone know anything of the spiritual-psychological foundations of their mourning practices. But investigating our own preconceptions about death, anger, and mourning can make us more comfortable with—and more competent at—responding to anthropologist Renato Rosaldo's evaluation of Ilongot culture in his essay, "Grief and a Headhunter's Rage." As we read Rosaldo's and other texts in *Literacies*, *Before Reading* questions will help us be more sensitive to the ways our own positions support, contest, or otherwise complicate the arguments of the readings. In short, these questions remind us of our own "texts"—of experience, of knowledge, of belief systems—texts we can put into meaning-making conversations with the readings.

Dynamics questions ask us to become more self-conscious about the dynamic or "unstable" qualities of language and interpretation by encouraging us to trace variations in meaning as terms, experiences, and concepts reappear in a variety of slightly (or sometimes significantly) different contexts throughout a reading. This self-consciousness enhances our interpretive possibilities by highlighting the "dialogic" (Mikhail Bakhtin's term for the competition among numerous voices or perspectives within a single text) elements of a reading. For instance, it aids us as we trace the different class perspectives at play in Liliana Heker's "The Stolen Party." With an awareness of the dynamic qualities of a reading, we can locate clues about some of the tensions, assumptions, and values that inform a text. As we increase our appreciation for the dynamic qualities of language, we open up new points of contact with the readings, further our capacity to critically evaluate what a reading offers us, and better position ourselves to create new meanings.

Critical Tools questions offer another approach to the relationship between meaning and context. Writers choose analytic methods or strategies from one or more texts or bodies of experience and apply them to other texts and contexts. Through our own acts of recontextualization, we as writers appropriate, revise, and actively use the same writerly techniques that characterize the readings in *Literacies*. Just as we might understand something new about a puzzling math theorem when we see how a physicist uses it to hypothesize about the relationship between mass and energy, we frequently can gain a foothold on difficult readings (or discover new aspects of familiar ones) by viewing them in different lights. Paul Harrison, for instance, borrows the concept of "reference-group behavior" from sociology and uses it as a critical tool to clarify what he calls "cultural imperialism." We, in turn, might work with both of these concepts to understand and respond to the decisions Richard Rodriguez makes about his cultural heritage in "Complexion." This process invites us to become more subtle in our understanding and management of different methods of argument.

Draft One / Draft Two questions provide a broader forum for the same kinds of interpretive acts writers develop with the other categories of questions. When working with a two-draft structure, writers can produce both a detailed, well-developed analysis (in draft one) and a reconsideration in a new context of the meanings produced by that initial analysis (in draft two). These questions, with their emphasis on revision and on the writer's self-consciousness about her or his own work, give writers the opportunity to speculate about the significance of this double or layered act of interpretation.

We intend these study questions to be as flexible as they are fluid. *Dynamics*, *Critical Tools*, and *Draft One / Draft Two* questions are generally appropriate for the standard essay assignments which structure the course. Questions from the two latter categories generally call for writers to move back and forth between readings and so contain possibilities for the effective "sequencing" of assignments. With minor revisions, most *Dynamics* questions should accommodate sequencing as well. All the categories of questions are open to a range of uses, just a few of which are suggested below:

Class Discussion: Readers might use any of the study questions to prepare for class discussion of a reading. *Before Reading* questions should be particularly useful in preparing for the first discussion of a reading, while the other questions could be used for later discussions. When sequencing with a reading from earlier in the course, study questions can provide new avenues of inquiry into a text that has already been discussed.

Journals: Writers frequently keep journals as on-going records of their developing ideas about events, experiences, and material they read and write. Some writers might compose one or two pages per week, others might commit themselves to an hour or two of writing each week. Whatever approaches we adopt, when we prepare journal entries we practice a form of writing that maintains at least some of the academic, critical focus of regular essay assignments but in a more "relaxed," self-paced, and perhaps exploratory setting. Journals provide material for class discussion, class exercises, revision sessions, and are good sources of ideas for early drafts of more formal essays. As running accounts of our development as readers and writers, journals frequently prove useful to students and teachers alike.

Peer Group Exercises: Although we often picture reading, writing, and interpretation as solitary activities (as the image from Foucault's "Fantasia of the Library" implies in Barbara Christian's essay), these processes are inevitably social in that they always come into contact—directly or indirectly—with our experiences of other people. Peer group exercises take advantage of the various knowledge and experiences different writers bring to the group. In one model for these exercises, each member of the peer group might write for 20-30 minutes in response to one of the study questions. At the end of that time, students could exchange papers and spend another 20-30 minutes writing an evaluation of their colleague's work. After reading over this second set of written responses, the group might collectively discuss questions and ideas raised by the exercise. In a second model, the group could select a particular argument or idea that appears at several places in an essay. Each member of the group might then explore in writing a different instance of that idea. Afterwards, the group could discuss its findings. Whatever form these exercises take, when we share our insights and our confusions we can open up more opportunities for meaning-making.

Terence Brunk

Introduction
Experience, Ratification, and Reading

Experience is necessary for growth and survival, but experience is not simply what happened. A lot may happen to a piece of stone without making it any wiser. Experience is what we are able and prepared to do with what happens to us.

—Chinua Achebe, Preface,
Morning Yet on Creation Day

In this course we might take Chinua Achebe's words as advice about the experience we acquire in reading. We could ask what it would mean to make reading important or even necessary for our growth and survival as individuals or as a community. We might consider what the experience of reading is, if, as Achebe would probably advise us, reading is not simply what the pages say. We might think about times when reading has left us unchanged, as events often leave a piece of stone unchanged, and we could ask why this happens to a reader. But following Achebe's advice, we could also practice being readers who "are able and prepared to do [something] with what happens to us" when we read. While making something new of the experience of reading, we could, if Achebe is right, make something new of ourselves.

But what does that really mean for you or me or for this course, since we have all sometimes put down a piece of reading no more changed than a stone would be? We know that this common event speaks powerfully against Achebe's noble advice. Here at the start of a semester of reading and writing, what are we to make of the contradiction between what he says about experience and what we have experienced ourselves as readers? As with any important question, we each look for our own answers. I found some help composing *my* answer as I read some of the essays in this book, and in the next few pages I have tried to work on my ideas with those writers as partners, just as you will work with the writers on *your* ideas as you compose your essays. I turned to "Communication in a Global Village," for example, where Dean C. Barnlund describes "how powerfully human beings are drawn to those who hold the same beliefs and how sharply they are repelled by those who do not" (42). Barnlund helps me explain certain empty reading experiences when he says that this common human trait "converts many human encounters into rituals of ratification, [with] each person looking to the other only to obtain endorsement and applause for his own beliefs" (43). If we approach reading as a "ritual of ratification," an opportunity for "endorsement and applause," where we seek only to confirm what we already know, then Achebe's noble possibilities cannot come true. Something riskier than that has to happen, it seems to me.

Yet I don't mean simply to criticize rituals of ratification. While with some experiences, and some *reading* experiences, we do much more than endorse commonly held beliefs (as Barnlund and Achebe would no doubt agree), I think many important experiences and ceremonies *are*, at least in part, rituals of ratification. Certain religious services—many funerals, for example—repeat and ratify beliefs of the community, rather than analyze or question those beliefs. I think most people would accept that some rituals of ratification are important for "cultural reinforcement," a term used by Robert Scholes, another of the writers in this book (479). It's not hard to discover practices of cultural reinforcement in our daily lives, where people confirm their community's values and traditions for the sake of continuity and an orderly life. For centuries some Christian religious services, for example, have included a recital of a list of central beliefs, called a "creed" or "credo" from the Latin word meaning "I believe." In "On Reading a Video Text," Scholes says that cultural reinforcement can, however, become a series of more extreme "recipes for the indoctrination of young people" (482). But Scholes accepts cultural reinforcement as a necessary part of reading, in spite of this danger. He believes that good readers *must* read a text closely and openly enough to risk being influenced or even shaped by it. He calls this aspect of reading "surrender," a word that indicates how much readers give themselves over, for a time, to a text. But good readers, Scholes believes, do not stop there. Having submitted for a while to someone else's meanings in a text, they step back and reconsider the experience from their own context. They find ways to evaluate based on what *they* bring to the reading and what they know of the world. Having only temporarily "surrendered," good readers use their critical skills to "recover" their own integrity and meanings, according to Scholes. Most importantly, by doing so they create an opportunity for new understanding of themselves and of others. Foregoing ratification, they *risk* the experience of reading in exchange for the opportunities it offers, as Achebe might say, for change, for survival and growth.

The ideas of surrender and recovery help me understand how reading can involve a person in the evolving life of a wider community. If we practice only rituals of ratification, then institutions (like schools and colleges) can easily turn the truths of a previous generation into "fixed recipes" and "frozen monuments of Greatness," as Scholes calls them, the vital truth of which "can only die" along the way (482). But in the process Scholes calls surrender we engage ourselves with the portions of that old truth that have been fixed into a text by a writer. In that way we get to know something of a community's history and its ideas of itself. Then in the process Scholes calls recovery we each have a chance to save ourselves from the "fixed recipes," to assert ourselves, as well as to contribute our perspectives to the remaking of the community's truths. Reinvigorating a society's "frozen monuments" by the process of critical recovery is, he says, the interpretive work of every community and every person, including me and you. Seen in this way, reading can become a personal and social act of great importance, as is the writing that comes of it. The writers in this book are excellent guides to this kind of interpretive work.

In this course you, your classmates, and your teacher will have a chance to make reading a personal and social act. You will share many reading experiences and work together through conversation and writing to create a small community whose interpretive practices take on Achebe's advice as well as attend to the practical goals of the course. You will also take a good deal of responsibility for your own authority as a reader and writer, perhaps more than you have in your school career so far. As a result, you will be able to judge for yourself the claims I make here about the personal and social value of reading and writing.

Literacies, the title of this book, introduces some of the opportunities you may encounter as you write your papers. The editors chose this name to acknowledge the many types of essays and stories in these pages, the many kinds of specialist-writers represented here, and the specialized kinds of language and knowledge used to compose these readings. In the late twentieth century it is not possible to assume that there is one general sort of literacy that suits all experiences, all audiences, and all occasions. Our society is made up of many social voices, many kinds of expertise, many contexts and languages, and the editors believe that a reading anthology that includes many of those voices offers a more realistic sense of the complex lives we are all leading. Furthermore, our world of contesting social voices offers special opportunities for a person to go beyond ratification to shape her own meanings. Each person can try out some of the ways of interpreting used by these different social voices—learning from many of them, rather than ratifying one of them. Your course's sequence of writing assignments will ask you to explore those possibilities throughout the semester.

But a common barrier still may arise as you read the work of these specialists in different fields. We are all in the habit of granting specialists a good deal of authority over their subject matter, and, as a result, we may fail to question their ideas even when our own experience says otherwise. This course offers you a chance to overcome this problem by bringing many kinds of literacy together for *your use*. By this I mean that your teacher's assignments will ask you to use the special terms, the ways of thinking and talking from these different readings, by bringing them into a conversation with each other and with what you know from your own experience. Those assignments will invite you to speak with these other writers and to speak back. That may be a challenging, exciting, and even risky difference between this course and reading and writing courses you have taken before.

In her essay, "The Anthropological Looking Glass," Nancy Scheper-Hughes points out that anthropologists' books are ordinarily "shielded" from responses by non-experts, and especially by the people they study and write about. Often anthropologists don't write in the same language spoken by the people they study, so their subjects cannot dispute or even add to what the anthropologists say about them. Accustomed to having their authority shielded in this way, anthropologists find it "most unsettling" when their subjects do speak back, as in the case of Scheper-Hughes's own book about a village in Ireland. This is an example of "the anthropological looking glass," a practice of critical analysis, being "reflected back" on the anthropologist, she says (460). When *Saints, Scholars, and Schizophrenics* was first published, villagers read it avidly, saw how their society was portrayed, and came to their own angry conclusions about the book's value and truthfulness. They disputed the book, though quietly, in the village's own customary ways. More importantly, perhaps, they *used* the book. One man was pleased to see some of his witty sayings quoted there, and he memorized them so he could say them again—a very curious example of ratification, perhaps. One group began to examine the social problems the book revealed, and one woman reported that she and her friend were able to discuss common problems as they never could before. "A great burden has been lifted," that villager said (463).

All of this new thinking was made possible by crossing Scheper-Hughes's anthropological language with what she calls the "commonsense world" of the village. As these two realms intersect in the book and in the lives of the readers in the village, a "hitherto unchallenged native interpretation" of their experience comes up for fresh thought and discussion, that is, for the benefits and risks of revision (461). Crossing over from one kind of literacy to another, from one area of experience and language to another, as Scheper-Hughes does in her book and as the villagers do again (in a different way) when they read her book, they all undo the limits of ratification. As they surpass the "hitherto unchallenged native interpretation" (of the village, of anthropology), they compose a new understanding that corresponds to their own contexts and desires. By reading the anthropology, the villagers are able to read their experience again, freshly. When they encounter this outsider's voice, written in a strange, specialized language, they discover that they have to reread their own lives in order to read the anthropology. They discover that experience can be read—that is, reinterpreted rather than merely ratified—just as a book can be. They also have a chance to discover one of the important aspects of this course—the opportunities for revision that are created when we bring different social voices together. If the villagers of Ballybran come to see reading as a risky chance for crossing boundaries, as a valuable chance for revision, then I believe they have grasped the promise of Achebe's quotation and made the experience of reading part of their own process of "growth and survival." They have also proven something very important: when mere ratification stops, the authority to interpret can belong to anyone—villagers, college students, anthropologists—who dares to use it.

This book invites you to be a reader and writer who crosses boundaries, who dares to speak within and across disciplines and areas of experience, and who composes essays that go beyond ratification. In order to do that, you will need to make a study of what it means to bring another person's language into a conversation with your own. This means much more than quoting an author to "back up" or "prove" your point—we recognize that as ratification. While you might hear someone refer to the conversational writing process as "quoting" (since it does involve placing someone else's words in quotation marks in your paper), "quoting" itself is not an adequate explanation of the process of crossing boundaries, of bringing together literacies that are strangers to each other, of composing as you read and write. When you turn to the readings in *Literacies* you will find many voices to work with, and at first they will be very strange in each other's company. But that strangeness is your chance to see your subject freshly, just as it was for Nancy Scheper-Hughes's friends and acquaintances in the Irish village and for Scheper-Hughes herself. These diverse literacies have the power to make things strange, to make things visible in a new way, and you can use that special power as a partner in your work this semester. As you read, as you participate in class discussions, and as you write your drafts and revisions this semester, bring these voices into the conversation. Let their words, their terms, their phrases and sentences, their ideas and experiences, aid and influence you as you revise *your* ideas.

Readers and writers who know how to work conversationally with what they read can find ways to continue their thinking almost anywhere. For example, although you *might* find the terms I've borrowed from Scholes and others useful as you think about reading and writing and the goals of this course, perhaps some of the other authors will speak more directly to your experience. This book is full of possibilities. For example, does James Baldwin's idea of a society's stultifying "labyrinth of attitudes" help explain something about the problems of interpretation that "ratification" does not (32)? Could readers and writers make use of his idea of "[renewal] at the fountain of their own lives" (32)? Does Robert Bellah hint at something important about reading and writing, about "ratification" and "recovery," when he describes a person's need to "invent a second language out of the failing fragments of his usual first language" (62)? Can we protect ourselves from the dangers of ratification by creating what he calls "a community of memory and hope" (62)? What can the anger in Audre Lorde's essay tell us about what is at stake in reading and writing? No matter which writers you bring into the conversation this semester, they, like Lorde, are all concerned with what is at stake when we interpret experience. They can become resources and guides as you fashion your own reading and writing practices based on a conversational model that includes but does not end with quotation. As you make your own study of these practices they will give you more authority as a reader and writer in a world of many competing literacies. I hope you will find this important and exciting work.

Ken Smith
New Brunswick, New Jersey

Literacies

❖ ❖ ❖

Before Reading Maya Angelou . . .

1. Write informally about an experience you have had in which you felt that your contribution to a group effort was not sufficiently noticed. Describe the circumstances as fully as you can. How did you explain the lack of recognition you received and how did you resolve the problem? Explain why you would or would not offer your experience as a model for handling similar situations.

2. How significant is a name? Discuss your various—even conflicting—ideas about the importance of names. If you like, use your own name as an example.

"Mary"

Maya Angelou

Recently a white woman from Texas, who would quickly describe herself as a liberal, asked me about my hometown. When I told her that in Stamps my grandmother had owned the only Negro general merchandise store since the turn of the century, she exclaimed, "Why, you were a debutante." Ridiculous and even ludicrous. But Negro girls in small Southern towns, whether poverty-stricken or just munching along on a few of life's necessities, were given as extensive and irrelevant preparations for adulthood as rich white girls shown in magazines. Admittedly the training was not the same. While white girls learned to waltz and sit gracefully with a tea cup balanced on their knees, we were lagging behind, learning the mid-Victorian values with very little money to indulge them. (Come and see Edna Lomax spending the money she made picking cotton on five balls of ecru tatting thread. Her fingers are bound to snag the work and she'll have to repeat the stitches time and time again. But she knows that when she buys the thread.)

We were required to embroider and I had trunkfuls of colorful dishtowels, pillowcases, runners and handkerchiefs to my credit. I mastered the art of crocheting and tatting, and there was a lifetime's supply of dainty doilies that would never be used in sacheted dresser drawers. It went without saying that all girls could iron and wash, but the finer touches around the home, like setting a table with real silver, baking roasts and cooking vegetables without meat, had to be learned elsewhere. Usually at the source of those habits. During my tenth year, a white woman's kitchen became my finishing school.

Mrs. Viola Cullinan was a plump woman who lived in a three-bedroom house somewhere behind the post office. She was singularly unattractive until she smiled, and then the lines around her eyes and mouth which made her look perpetually dirty disappeared, and her face looked like the mask of an impish elf. She usually rested her smile until late afternoon when her women friends dropped in and Miss Glory, the cook, served them cold drinks on the closed-in porch.

The exactness of her house was inhuman. This glass went here and only here. That cup had its place and it was an act of impudent rebellion to place it anywhere else. At twelve o'clock the table was set. At 12:15 Mrs. Cullinan sat down to dinner (whether her husband had arrived or not). At 12:16 Miss Glory brought out the food.

It took me a week to learn the difference between a salad plate, a bread plate and a dessert plate.

Mrs. Cullinan kept up the tradition of her wealthy parents. She was from Virginia. Miss Glory, who was a descendant of slaves that had worked for the Cullinans, told me her history. She had married beneath her (according to Miss Glory). Her husband's family hadn't had their money very long and what they had "didn't 'mount to much."

As ugly as she was, I thought privately, she was lucky to get a husband above or beneath her station. But Miss Glory wouldn't let me say a thing against her mistress. She was very patient with me, however, over the housework. She explained the dishware, silverware and servants' bells. The large round bowl in which soup was served wasn't a soup bowl, it was a tureen. There were goblets, sherbet glasses, ice-cream glasses, wine glasses, green glass coffee cups with matching saucers, and water glasses. I had a glass to drink from, and it sat with Miss Glory's on a separate shelf from the others. Soup spoons, gravy boat, butter knives, salad forks and carving platter were additions to my vocabulary and in fact almost represented a new language. I was fascinated with the novelty, with the fluttering Mrs. Cullinan and her Alice-in-Wonderland house.

Her husband remains, in my memory, undefined. I lumped him with all the other white men that I had ever seen and tried not to see.

On our way home one evening, Miss Glory told me that Mrs. Cullinan couldn't have children. She said that she was too delicate-boned. It was hard to imagine bones at all under those layers of fat. Miss Glory went on to say that the doctor had taken out all her lady organs. I reasoned that a pig's organs included the lungs, heart and liver, so if Mrs. Cullinan was walking around without those essentials, it explained why she drank alcohol out of unmarked bottles. She was keeping herself embalmed.

When I spoke to Bailey[1] about it, he agreed that I was right, but he also informed me that Mr. Cullinan had two daughters by a colored lady and that I knew them very well. He added that the girls were the spitting image of their father. I was unable to remember what he looked like, although I had just left him a few hours before, but I thought of the Coleman girls. They were very light-skinned and certainly didn't look very much like their mother (no one ever mentioned Mr. Coleman).

My pity for Mrs. Cullinan preceded me the next morning like the Cheshire cat's smile. Those girls, who could have been her daughters, were beautiful. They didn't have to straighten their hair. Even when they were caught in the rain, their braids still hung down straight like tamed snakes. Their mouths were pouty little cupid's bows. Mrs. Cullinan didn't know what she missed. Or maybe she did. Poor Mrs. Cullinan.

For weeks after, I arrived early, left late and tried very hard to make up for her barrenness. If she had had her own children, she wouldn't have had to ask me to run a thousand errands from her back door to the back door of her friends. Poor old Mrs. Cullinan.

Then one evening Miss Glory told me to serve the ladies on the porch. After I set the tray down and turned toward the kitchen, one of the women asked, "What's your name, girl?" It was the speckled-faced one. Mrs. Cullinan said, "She doesn't talk much. Her name's Margaret."[2]

"Is she dumb?"

"No. As I understand it, she can talk when she wants to but she's usually quiet as a little mouse. Aren't you, Margaret?"

I smiled at her. Poor thing. No organs and couldn't even pronounce my name correctly.

"She's a sweet little thing, though."

"Well, that may be, but the name's too long. I'd never bother myself. I'd call her Mary if I was you."

I fumed into the kitchen. That horrible woman would never have the chance to call me Mary because if I was starving I'd never work for her. I decided I wouldn't pee on her if her heart was on fire. Giggles drifted in off the porch and into Miss Glory's pots. I wondered what they could be laughing about.

Whitefolks were so strange. Could they be talking about me? Everybody knew that they stuck together better than the Negroes did. It was possible that Mrs. Cullinan had friends in St. Louis who heard about a girl from Stamps being in court and wrote to tell her. Maybe she knew about Mr. Freeman.[3]

My lunch was in my mouth a second time and I went outside and relieved myself on the bed of four-o'clocks. Miss Glory thought I might be coming down with something and told me to go on home, that Momma would give me some herb tea, and she'd explain to her mistress.

I realized how foolish I was being before I reached the pond. Of course Mrs. Cullinan didn't know. Otherwise she wouldn't have given me the two nice dresses that Momma cut down, and she certainly wouldn't have called me a "sweet little thing." My stomach felt fine, and I didn't mention anything to Momma.

That evening I decided to write a poem on being white, fat, old and without children. It was going to be a tragic ballad. I would have to watch her carefully to capture the essence of her loneliness and pain.

The very next day, she called me by the wrong name. Miss Glory and I were washing up the lunch dishes when Mrs. Cullinan came to the doorway. "Mary?"

Miss Glory asked, "Who?"

Mrs. Cullinan, sagging a little, knew and I knew. "I want Mary to go down to Mrs. Randall's and take her some soup. She's not been feeling well for a few days."

Miss Glory's face was a wonder to see. "You mean Margaret, ma'am. Her name's Margaret."

"That's too long. She's Mary from now on. Heat that soup from last night and put it in the china tureen and, Mary, I want you to carry it carefully."

Every person I knew had a hellish horror of being "called out of his name." It was a dangerous practice to call a Negro anything that could be loosely construed as insulting because of the centuries of their having been called niggers, jigs, dinges, blackbirds, crows, boots and spooks.

Miss Glory had a fleeting second of feeling sorry for me. Then as she handed me the hot tureen she said, "Don't mind, don't pay that no mind. Sticks and stones may break your bones, but words . . . You know, I been working for her for twenty years."

She held the back door open for me. "Twenty years. I wasn't much older than you. My name used to be Hallelujah. That's what Ma named me, but my mistress give me 'Glory,' and it stuck. I likes it better too."

I was in the little path that ran behind the houses when Miss Glory shouted, "It's shorter too."

For a few seconds it was a tossup over whether I would laugh (imagine being named Hallelujah) or cry (imagine letting some white woman rename you for her convenience). My anger saved me from either outburst. I had to quit the job, but the problem was going to be how to do it. Momma wouldn't allow me to quit for just any reason.

"She's a peach. That woman is a real peach." Mrs. Randall's maid was talking as she took the soup from me, and I wondered what her name used to be and what she answered to now.

For a week I looked into Mrs. Cullinan's face as she called me Mary. She ignored my coming late and leaving early. Miss Glory was a little annoyed because I had begun to leave egg yolk on the dishes and wasn't putting much heart in polishing the silver. I hoped that she would complain to our boss, but she didn't.

Then Bailey solved my dilemma. He had me describe the contents of the cupboard and the particular plates she liked best. Her favorite piece was a casserole shaped like a fish and the green glass coffee cups. I kept his instructions in mind, so on the next day when Miss Glory was hanging out clothes and I had again been told to serve the old biddies on the porch, I dropped the empty serving tray. When I heard Mrs. Cullinan scream, "Mary!" I picked up the casserole and two of the green glass cups in readiness. As she rounded the kitchen door I let them fall on the tiled floor.

I could never absolutely describe to Bailey what happened next, because each time I got to the part where she fell on the floor and screwed up her ugly face to cry, we burst out laughing. She actually wobbled around on the floor and picked up shards of the cups and cried, "Oh, Momma. Oh, dear Gawd. It's Momma's china from Virginia. Oh, Momma, I sorry."

Miss Glory came running in from the yard and the women from the porch crowded around. Miss Glory was almost as broken up as her mistress. "You mean to say she broke our Virginia dishes? What we gone do?"

Mrs. Cullinan cried louder, "That clumsy nigger. Clumsy little black nigger."

Old speckled-face leaned down and asked, "Who did it, Viola? Was it Mary? Who did it?"

Everything was happening so fast I can't remember whether her action preceded her words, but I know that Mrs. Cullinan said, "Her name's Margaret,
goddamn it, her name's Margaret." And she threw a wedge of the broken plate at
me. It could have been the hysteria which put her aim off, but the flying crockery
caught Miss Glory right over her ear and she started screaming.

I left the front door wide open so all the neighbors could hear.

Mrs. Cullinan was right about one thing. My name wasn't Mary.

NOTES
1. Bailey is Angelou's brother.
2. Angelou's name as a child was Marguerite Johnson.
3. Angelou had been raped by a Mr. Freeman, and she had testified in court against him.

Dynamics

1. Trace the evolution in Marguerite's thoughts and behavior that culminates in
    her scene in the Cullinan kitchen. How would you characterize and/or explain
    the transition(s) in Marguerite's behavior? Be sure to describe Marguerite's acts
    and feelings in a way that she has not done already.

Critical Tools

1. Angelou's first-person narrative begins in the present moment and then
    switches to her childhood. Look closely at passages where Angelou's reading of
    the past seems to be affected by her understanding in the present, and vice
    versa. How does her use of different "times" contribute to the meanings you find
    in her story? Apply your insights about Angelou's techniques to discuss another
    narrative writer's uses of the present and past.

Draft One/Draft Two

Draft One: An old expression holds that "sticks and stones may break my bones, but
names will never hurt me." Look back at your responses to the second Before Reading question, and write an essay in which you explain how your own experiences
with naming contribute to your interpretation of Marguerite's actions.

Draft Two: Apply some of the observations in your first draft to another text from
Literacies in which naming is an issue. Where do you see Angelou and the second
writer's theories of naming overlap? How do you explain the differences you see?

❖ ❖ ❖

Before Reading Gloria Anzaldúa. . .

1. Anzaldúa, a Chicano woman, writes about feeling "invisible" in mainstream culture. Have you ever had the experience of "invisibility"? Write informally about a time when you felt that you were not being "seen" by people around you. How do other essays in *Literacies* help you to talk about the experiences you describe?

2. Anzaldúa's text is in the form of a letter, one addressed to people she may not know personally. What are some of the reasons why people choose to use letters to communicate? Make a list of words or phrases that come to mind when you think of letters or letter-writing.

Speaking In Tongues: A Letter To 3rd World Women Writers*

Gloria Anzaldúa

21 mayo 80

Dear mujeres de color, companions in writing—

I sit here naked in the sun, typewriter against my knee trying to visualize you. Black woman huddles over a desk in the fifth floor of some New York tenement. Sitting on a porch in south Texas, a Chicana fanning away mosquitos and the hot air, trying to arouse the smouldering embers of writing. Indian woman walking to school or work lamenting the lack of time to weave writing into your life. Asian American, lesbian, single mother, tugged in all directions by children, lover or ex-husband, and the writing.

It is not easy writing this letter. It began as a poem, a long poem. I tried to turn it into an essay but the result was wooden, cold. I have not yet unlearned the esoteric bullshit and pseudo-intellectualizing that school brainwashed into my writing.

How to begin again. How to approximate the intimacy and immediacy I want. What form? A letter, of course.

My dear *hermanas*, the dangers we face as women writers of color are not the same as those of white women though we have many in common. We don't have as much to lose—we never had any privileges. I wanted to call the dangers "obstacles" but that would be a kind of lying. We can't *transcend* the dangers, can't rise above them. We must go through them and hope we won't have to repeat the performance.

Unlikely to be friends of people in high literary places, the beginning woman of color is invisible both in the white male mainstream world and in the white women's feminist world, though in the latter this is gradually changing. The *lesbian* of color

---

*Originally written for Words In Our Pockets (Bootlegger: San Francisco), the Feminist Writers' Guild Handbook.

is not only invisible, she doesn't even exist. Our speech, too, is inaudible. We speak in tongues like the outcast and the insane.

Because white eyes do not want to know us, they do not bother to learn our language, the language which reflects us, our culture, our spirit. The schools we attended or didn't attend did not give us the skills for writing nor the confidence that we were correct in using our class and ethnic languages. I, for one, became adept at, and majored in English to spite, to show up, the arrogant racist teachers who thought all Chicano children were dumb and dirty. And Spanish was not taught in grade school. And Spanish was not required in High School. And though now I write my poems in Spanish as well as English I feel the rip-off of my native tongue.

I lack imagination *you say.*

No. *I lack language.*
The language to clarify
my resistance to the literate.
Words are a war to me.
They threaten my family.

To gain the word
to describe the loss
I risk losing everything.
I may create a monster
the word's length and body
swelling up colorful and thrilling
looming over my mother, *characterized.*
Her voice in the distance
unintelligible illiterate.
These are the monster's words.[1]

—Cherríe Moraga

Who gave us permission to perform the act of writing? Why does writing seem so unnatural for me? I'll do anything to postpone it—empty the trash, answer the telephone. The voice recurs in me: *Who am I, a poor Chicanita from the sticks, to think I could write?* How dare I even considered becoming a writer as I stooped over the tomato fields bending, bending under the hot sun, hands broadened and calloused, not fit to hold the quill, numbed into an animal stupor by the heat.

How hard it is for us to *think* we can choose to become writers, much less *feel* and *believe* that we can. What have we to contribute, to give? Our own expectations condition us. Does not our class, our culture as well as the white man tell us writing is not for women such as us?

The white man speaks: *Perhaps if you scrape the dark off of your face. Maybe if you bleach your bones. Stop speaking in tongues, stop writing left-handed. Don't cultivate your colored skins nor tongues of fire if you want to make it in a right-handed world.*

"Man, like all the other animals, fears and is repelled by that which he does not understand, and mere difference is apt to connote something malign."[2]

I think, yes, perhaps if we go to the university. Perhaps if we become male-women or as middleclass as we can. Perhaps if we give up loving women, we will be worthy of having something to say worth saying. They convince us that we must cultivate art for art's sake. Bow down to the sacred bull, form. Put frames and metaframes around the writing. Achieve distance in order to win the coveted title "literary writer" or "professional writer." Above all do not be simple, direct, nor immediate.

Why do they fight us? Because they think we are dangerous beasts? Why *are* we dangerous beasts? Because we shake and often break the white's comfortable stereotypic images they have of us: the Black domestic, the lumbering nanny with twelve babies sucking her tits, the slant-eyed Chinese with her expert hand—"They know how to treat a man in bed," the flat-faced Chicana or Indian, passively lying on her back, being fucked by the Man *a la* La Chingada.

The Third World woman revolts: *We revoke, we erase your white male imprint. When you come knocking on our doors with your rubber stamps to brand our faces with DUMB, HYSTERICAL, PASSIVE PUTA, PERVERT, when you come with your branding irons to burn MY PROPERTY on our buttocks, we will vomit the guilt, self-denial and race-hatred you have force-fed into us right back into your mouth. We are done being cushions for your projected fears. We are tired of being your sacrificial lambs and scapegoats.*

I can write this and yet I realize that many of us women of color who have strung degrees, credentials and published books around our necks like pearls that we hang onto for dear life are in danger of contributing to the invisibility of our sister-writers. "La Vendida," the sell-out.

The danger of selling out one's own ideologies. For the Third World woman, who has, at best, one foot in the feminist literary world, the temptation is great to adopt the current feeling-fads and theory fads, the latest half truths in political thought, the half-digested new age psychological axioms that are preached by the white feminist establishment. Its followers are notorious for "adopting" women of color as their "cause" while still expecting us to adapt to *their* expectations and *their* language.

How dare we get out of our colored faces. How dare we reveal the human flesh underneath and bleed red blood like the white folks. It takes tremendous energy and courage not to acquiesce, not to capitulate to a definition of feminism that still renders most of us invisible. Even as I write this I am disturbed that I am the only

Third World woman writer in this handbook.[3] Over and over I have found myself to be the only Third World woman at readings, workshops, and meetings.

We cannot allow ourselves to be tokenized. We must make our own writing and that of Third World women the first priority. We cannot educate white women and take them by the hand. Most of us are willing to help but we can't do the white woman's homework for her. That's an energy drain. More times than she cares to remember, Nellie Wong, Asian American feminist writer, has been called by white women wanting a list of Asian American women who can give readings or workshops. We are in danger of being reduced to purveyors of resource lists.

Coming face to face with one's limitations. There are only so many things I can do in one day. Luisah Teish addressing a group of predominantly white feminist writers had this to say of Third World women's experience:

> *"If you are not caught in the maze that (we) are in, it's very difficult to explain to you the hours in the day we do not have. And the hours that we do not have are hours that are translated into survival skills and money. And when one of those hours is taken away it means an hour not that we don't have to lie back and stare at the ceiling or an hour that we don't have to talk to a friend. For me it's a loaf of bread."*

> *Understand.*
> *My family is poor.*
> *Poor. I can't afford*
> *a new ribbon. The risk*
> *of this one is enough*
> *to keep me moving*
> *through it, accountable.*
> *The repetition like my mother's*
> *stories retold,* each *time*
> *reveals more particulars*
> *gains more familiarity.*

> *You can't get me in your car so fast.*[4]

—Cherríe Moraga

"Complacency is a far more dangerous attitude than outrage."[5]

—Naomi Littlebear

Why am I compelled to write? Because the writing saves me from this complacency I fear. Because I have no choice. Because I must keep the spirit of my revolt and myself alive. Because the world I create in the writing compensates for what the real world does not give me. By writing I put order in the world, give it a handle so I can grasp it. I write because life does not appease my appetites and hunger. I write to record what others erase when I speak, to rewrite the stories others have miswritten about me, about you. To become more intimate with myself and you. To discover myself, to preserve myself, to make myself, to achieve self-autonomy. To dispell the myths that I am a mad prophet or a poor suffering soul. To convince myself that I am worthy and that what I have to say is not a pile of shit. To show that I *can* and that I *will* write, never mind their admonitions to the contrary. And I will write about the unmentionables, never mind the outraged gasp of the censor and the audience. Finally I write because I'm scared of writing but I'm more scared of not writing.

Why should I try to justify why I write? Do I need to justify being Chicana, being woman? You might as well ask me to try to justify why I'm alive.

The act of writing is the act of making soul, alchemy. It is the quest for the self, for the center of the self, which we women of color have come to think as "other"— the dark, the feminine. Didn't we start writing to reconcile this other within us? We knew we were different, set apart, exiled from what is considered "normal," white-right. And as we internalized this exile, we came to see the alien within us and too often, as a result, we split apart from ourselves and each other. Forever after we have been in search of that self, that "other" and each other. And we return, in widening spirals and never to the same childhood place where it happened, first in our families, with our mothers, with our fathers. The writing is a tool for piercing that mystery but it also shields us, gives a margin of distance, helps us survive. And those that don't survive? The waste of ourselves: so much meat thrown at the feet of madness or fate or the state.

24 mayo 80
It is dark and damp and has been raining all day. I love days like this. As I lie in bed I am able to delve inward. Perhaps today I will write from that deep core. As I grope for words and a voice to speak of writing, I stare at my brown hand clenching the pen and think of you thousands of miles away clutching your pen. You are not alone.

Pen, I feel right at home in your ink doing a pirouette, stirring the cobwebs, leaving my signature on the window panes. Pen, how could I ever have feared you. You're quite house-broken but it's your wildness I am in love with. I'll have to get rid of you when you start being predictable, when you stop chasing dustdevils. The more you outwit me the more I love you. It's when I'm tired or have had too much caffeine or wine that you get past my defenses and you say more than what I had intended. You surprise me, shock me into knowing some part of me I'd kept secret even from myself.
—Journal entry.

In the kitchen Maria and Cherríe's voices falling on these pages. I can see Cherríe going about in her terry cloth wrap, barefoot washing the dishes, shaking out the tablecloth, vacuuming. Deriving a certain pleasure watching her perform those simple tasks, I am thinking *they lied, there is no separation between life and writing.*

The danger in writing is not fusing our personal experience and world view with the social reality we live in, with our inner life, our history, our economics, and our vision. What validates us as human beings validates us as writers. What matters to us is the relationships that are important to us whether with our self or others. We must use what is important to us to get to the writing. *No topic is too trivial.* The danger is in being too universal and humanitarian and invoking the eternal to the sacrifice of the particular and the feminine and the specific historical moment.

The problem is to focus, to concentrate. The body distracts, sabotages with a hundred ruses, a cup of coffee, pencils to sharpen. The solution is to anchor the body to a cigarette or some other ritual. And who has time or energy to write after nurturing husband or lover, children, and often an outside job? The problems seem insurmountable and they are, but they cease being insurmountable once we make up our mind that whether married or childrened or working outside jobs we are going to make time for the writing.

Forget the room of one's own—write in the kitchen, lock yourself up in the bathroom. Write on the bus or the welfare line, on the job or during meals, between sleeping or waking. I write while sitting on the john. No long stretches at the typewriter unless you're wealthy or have a patron—you may not even own a typewriter. While you wash the floor or clothes listen to the words chanting in your body. When you're depressed, angry, hurt, when compassion and love possess you. When you cannot help but write.

Distractions all—that I spring on myself when I'm so deep into the writing when I'm almost at that place, that dark cellar where some "thing" is liable to jump up and pounce on me. The ways I subvert the writing are many. The way I don't tap the well nor learn how to make the windmill turn.

Eating is my main distraction. Getting up to eat an apple danish. That I've been off sugar for three years is not a deterrent nor that I have to put on a coat, find the keys and go out into the San Francisco fog to get it. Getting up to light incense, to put a record on, to go for a walk—anything just to put off the writing.

Returning after I've stuffed myself. Writing paragraphs on pieces of paper, adding to the puzzle on the floor, to the confusion on my desk making completion far away and perfection impossible.

26 mayo 80

Dear mujeres de color, I feel heavy and tired and there is a buzz in my head—too many beers last night. But I must finish this letter. My bribe: to take myself out to pizza.

So I cut and paste and line the floor with my bits of paper. My life strewn on the floor in bits and pieces and I try to make some order out of it working against time, psyching myself up with decaffeinated coffee, trying to fill in the gaps.

Leslie, my housemate, comes in, gets on hands and knees to read my fragments on the floor and says, *"It's good, Gloria."* And I think: *I don't have to go back to Texas, to my family of land, mesquites, cactus, rattlesnakes and roadrunners. My family, this community of writers. How could I have lived and survived so long without it. And I remember the isolation, re-live the pain again.*

"To assess the damage is a dangerous act,"[6] writes Cherríe Moraga. To stop there is even more dangerous.

It's too easy, blaming it all on the white man or white feminists or society or on our parents. What we say and what we do ultimately comes back to us, so let us own our responsibility, place it in our own hands and carry it with dignity and strength. No one's going to do my shitwork, I pick up after myself.

It makes perfect sense to me now how I resisted the act of writing, the commitment to writing. To write is to confront one's demons, look them in the face and live to write about them. Fear acts like a magnet; it draws the demons out of the closet and into the ink in our pens.

The tiger riding our backs (writing) never lets us alone. *Why aren't you riding, writing, writing?* It asks constantly till we begin to feel we're vampires sucking the blood out of too fresh an experience; that we are sucking life's blood to feed the pen. Writing is the most daring thing I have ever done and the most dangerous. Nellie Wong calls writing "the three-eyed demon shrieking the truth."[7]

Writing is dangerous, because we are afraid of what the writing reveals: the fears, the angers, the strengths of a woman under a triple or quadruple oppression. Yet in that very act lies our survival because a woman who writes has power. And a woman with power is feared.

> *What did it mean for a black woman to be an artist in our grandmother's time? It is a question with an answer cruel enough to stop the blood.*
>
> —Alice Walker[8]

I have never seen so much power in the ability to move and transform others as from that of the writing of women of color.

In the San Francisco area, where I now live, none can stir the audience with their craft and truthsaying, as do Cherríe Moraga (Chicana), Genny Lim (Asian American), and Luisah Teish (Black). With women like these, the loneliness of writing and the sense of powerlessness can be dispelled. We can walk among each other talking of our writing, reading to each other. And more and more when I'm alone, though still in communion with each other, the writing possesses me and propels me to leap into a timeless, spaceless no-place where I forget myself and feel I am the universe. *This* is power.

It's not on paper that you create but in your innards, in the gut and out of living tissue—*organic writing* I call it. A poem works for me *not* when it says what I want it to say and *not* when it evokes what I want it to. It works when the subject I started out with metamorphoses alchemically into a different one, one that has been discovered, or uncovered, by the poem. It works when it surprises me, when it says something I have repressed or pretended not to know. The meaning and worth of my writing is measured by how much *I* put myself on the line and how much nakedness I achieve.

> *Audre said we need to speak up. Speak loud, speak unsettling things and be dangerous and just fuck, hell, let it out and let everybody hear whether they want to or not.*[9]
> —Kathy Kendall

I say mujer magica, empty yourself. Shock yourself into new ways of perceiving the world, shock your readers into the same. Stop the chatter inside their heads.

Your skin must be sensitive enough for the lightest kiss and thick enough to ward off the sneers. If you are going to spit in the eye of the world, make sure your back is to the wind. Write of what most links us with life, the sensation of the body, the images seen by the eye, the expansion of the psyche in tranquility: moments of high intensity, its movement, sounds, thoughts. *Even though we go hungry we are not impoverished of experiences.*

> *I think many of us have been fooled by the mass media, by society's conditioning that our lives must be lived in great explosions, by "falling in love," by being "swept off our feet," and by the sorcery of magic genies that will fulfill our every wish, our every childhood longing. Wishes, dreams, and fantasies are important parts of our creative lives. They are the steps a writer integrates into her craft. They are the spectrum of resources to reach the truth, the heart of things, the immediacy and the impact of human conflict.*[10]
> —Nellie Wong

Many have a way with words. They label themselves seers but they will not see. Many have the gift of tongue but nothing to say. Do not listen to them. Many who have words and tongue have no ear, they cannot listen and they will not hear.

There is no need for words to fester in our minds. They germinate in the open mouth of the barefoot child in the midst of restive crowds. They wither in ivory towers and in college classrooms.

Throw away abstraction and the academic learning, the rules, the map and compass. Feel your way without blinders. To touch more people, the personal realities and the social must be evoked—not through rhetoric but through blood and pus and sweat.

Write with your eyes like painters, with your ears like musicians, with your feet like dancers. You are the truthsayer with quill and torch. Write with your tongues of fire. Don't let the pen banish you from yourself. Don't let the ink coagulate in your pens. Don't let the censor snuff out the spark, nor the gags muffle your voice. Put your shit on the paper.

We are not reconciled to the oppressors who whet their howl on our grief. We are not reconciled.

Find the muse within you. The voice that lies buried under you, dig it up. Do not fake it, try to sell it for a handclap or your name in print.

Love,
Gloria

NOTES

1. Cherríe Moraga's poem, "It's the Poverty" from *Loving In The War Years*, an unpublished book of poems.

2. Alice Walker, editor, "What White Publishers Won't Print," *I Love Myself When I am Laughing—A Zora Neale Hurston Reader*, (New York: The Feminist Press, 1979), p. 169.

3. [The author is referring to the original publication of the essay. *The Editors*]

4. Moraga, *Ibid.*

5. Naomi Littlebear, *The Dark of the Moon*, (Portland: Olive Press, 1977) p. 36.

6. Cherríe Moraga's essay, see "La Güera."

7. Nellie Wong, "Flows from the Dark of Monsters and Demons: Notes on Writing," *Radical Woman Pamphlet*, (San Francisco, 1979).

8. Alice Walker, "In Search of Our Mother's Gardens: The Creativity of Black Women in the South," *MS*, May, 1974, p. 60.

9. Letter from Kathy Kendall, March 10, 1980, concerning a writer's workshop given by Audre Lorde, Adrienne Rich, and Meridel LeSueur.

10. Nellie Wong, *Ibid.*

Dynamics

1. Locate the points in her text where Anzaldúa describes being or becoming naked. For each of these passages, try to determine the values that are associated with "nakedness," first for what Anzaldúa calls the "mainstream" culture, and then for Anzaldúa herself. What kind of development do you note in the values Anzaldúa assigns to "nakedness"?

2. Anzaldúa's text includes quotations from many sources. Select two or three passages where you see Anzaldúa using quoted material in different ways. Write or talk about the strategies you see at work in her use of quotation. Why do certain ways of "quoting" appear where they do?

Critical Tools

1. In response to the poet Cherrie Moraga, who wrote that "to assess the damage is a dangerous act," Anzaldúa argues that "to stop there is even more dangerous." After defining what she and Moraga mean by "damage," pick some passages where Anzaldúa is engaged mainly in acts of "assessment." Explain how this process works for her. At what points do you see Anzaldúa going beyond "damage assessment" to a new form of analysis? Working with the insights you have gained, apply the idea of "damage assessment" to another essay you have read this semester. What are the strengths and limitations of this critical tool?

2. Anzaldúa claims that "what validates us as human beings validates us as writers." Using a critical tool from another reading, explore Anzaldúa's use of personal experience in two or three passages from her essay. How does the critical tool you have chosen need to be adapted to fit Anzaldúa's context?

Draft One/Draft Two

Draft One: Respond to Anzaldúa's letter/text with a letter of your own. Decide what you think are her most important or troubling observations and use your own experience to explore their possible significance. Discuss the ways that your emotional reactions to Anzaldúa's text fuel your written response.

Draft Two: Anzaldúa claims that "we start writing to reconcile this other within us." Working with another essay that addresses the idea of "the other," explain your understanding of how "otherness" operates in both Anzaldúa's and your own letters. Then "turn around" and consider how the expressions of "otherness" that you find in the letters affect the way you understand this concept in the new essay.

❖ ❖ ❖

Before Reading James Baldwin. . .

1. According to your experiences or observations, what are the uses of religion?

2. In his essay, Baldwin writes about certain contradictions he sees between his country's moral standards and its beliefs and practices of racism. Based on your observations of life in the United States, what are the contradictions?

3. Discuss an institution you know of that fails to carry out some of its social purposes. Why does it fail, and what are the consequences for those involved?

Down at the Cross

James Baldwin

Letter from a Region in My Mind

Take up the White Man's burden—
Ye dare not stoop to less—
Nor call too loud on Freedom
To cloak your weariness;
By all ye cry or whisper,
By all ye leave or do,
The silent, sullen peoples
Shall weigh your Gods and you.

—Kipling

Down at the cross where my Saviour died,
Down where for cleansing from sin I cried,
There to my heart was the blood applied,
Singing glory to His name!

—Hymn

I underwent, during the summer that I became fourteen, a prolonged religious crisis. I use the word "religious" in the common, and arbitrary, sense, meaning that I then discovered God, His saints and angels, and His blazing Hell. And since I had been born in a Christian nation, I accepted this Deity as the only one. I supposed Him to exist only within the walls of a church—in fact, of *our* church—and I also supposed that God and safety were synonymous. The word "safety" brings us to the real meaning of the word "religious" as we use it. Therefore, to state it in another, more accurate way, I became, during my fourteenth year, for the first time in my life, afraid—afraid of the evil within me and afraid of the evil without. What I saw around me that summer in Harlem was what I had always seen; nothing had changed. But now, without any warning, the whores and pimps and racketeers on the Avenue had become a personal menace. It had not before occurred to me that I could become one of them, but now I realized that we had been produced by the same circumstances. Many of my comrades were clearly headed for the Avenue, and my father said that I was headed that way, too. My friends began to drink and smoke, and embarked—at first avid, then groaning—on their sexual careers. Girls, only slightly older than I was, who sang in the choir or taught Sunday school, the children of holy parents, underwent, before my eyes, their incredible met-amorphosis, of which the most bewildering aspect was not their budding breasts or their rounding behinds but something deeper and more subtle, in their eyes, their heat, their odor, and the inflection of their voices. Like the strangers on the Avenue, they became, in the twinkling of an eye, unutterably different and fantastically *present*. Owing to the way I had been raised, the abrupt discomfort that all this aroused in me and the fact that I had no idea what my voice or my mind or my body was likely to do next caused me to consider myself one of the most depraved people on earth. Matters were not helped by the fact that these holy girls seemed rather to enjoy my terrified lapses, our grim, guilty, tormented experiments, which were at once as chill and joyless as the Russian steppes and hotter, by far, than all the fires of Hell.

Yet there was something deeper than these changes, and less definable, that frightened me. It was real in both the boys and the girls, but it was, somehow, more vivid in the boys. In the case of the girls, one watched them turning into matrons before they had become women. They began to manifest a curious and really rather terrifying single-mindedness. It is hard to say exactly how this was conveyed: something implacable in the set of the lips, something farseeing (seeing what?) in the eyes, some new and crushing determination in the walk, something peremptory in the voice. They did not tease us, the boys, any more; they reprimanded us sharply, saying, "You better be thinking about your soul!" For the girls also saw the evidence on the Avenue, knew what the price would be, for them, of one misstep, knew that they had to be protected and that we were the only protection there was. They understood that they must act as God's decoys, saving the souls of the boys for Jesus and binding the bodies of the boys in marriage. For this was the beginning of our burning time, and "It is better," said St. Paul —who elsewhere, with a most unusual and stunning exactness, described himself as a "wretched man"—"to marry than to burn." And I began to feel in the boys a curious, wary, bewildered despair, as though they were now settling in for the long, hard winter of life. I did not know then what it was that I was reacting to; I put it to myself that they were letting themselves go. In the same way that the girls were destined to gain as much weight as their mothers, the boys, it was clear, would rise no higher than their fathers. School began to reveal itself, therefore, as a child's game that one could not win, and boys dropped out of school and went to work. My father wanted me to do the same. I refused, even though I no longer had any illusions about what an education could do for me; I had already encountered too many college-graduate handymen. My friends were now "downtown," busy, as they put it, "fighting the man." They began to care less about the way they looked, the way they dressed, the things they did; presently, one found them in twos and threes and fours, in a hallway, sharing a jug of wine or a bottle of whisky, talking, cursing, fighting, sometimes weeping: lost, and unable to say what it was that oppressed them, except that they knew it was "the man"—the white man. And there seemed to be no way whatever to remove this cloud that stood between them and the sun, between them and love and life and power, between them and whatever it was that they wanted. One did not have to be very bright to realize how little one could do to change one's situation; one did not have to be abnormally sensitive to be worn down to a cutting edge by the incessant and gratuitous humiliation and danger one encountered every working day, all day long. The humiliation did not apply merely to working days, or workers; I was thirteen and was crossing Fifth Avenue on my way to the Forty-second Street library, and the cop in the middle of the street muttered as I passed him, "Why don't you niggers stay uptown where you belong?" When I was ten, and didn't look, certainly, any older, two policemen amused themselves with me by frisking me, making comic (and terrifying) speculations concerning my ancestry and probable sexual prowess, and for good measure, leaving me flat on my back in one of Harlem's empty lots. Just before and then during the Second World War, many of my friends fled into the service, all to be changed there, and rarely for the better, many to be ruined, and many to die. Others fled to other states and cities—that is, to other ghettos. Some went on wine or whisky or the needle, and are still on it. And others, like me, fled into the church.

For the wages of sin were visible everywhere, in every wine-stained and urine-splashed hallway, in every clanging ambulance bell, in every scar on the faces of the pimps and their whores, in every helpless, newborn baby being brought into this danger, in every knife and pistol fight on the Avenue, and in every disastrous bulletin: a cousin, mother of six, suddenly gone mad, the children parcelled out here and there; an indestructible aunt rewarded for years of hard labor by a slow, agonizing death in a terrible small room; someone's bright son blown into eternity by his own hand; another turned robber and carried off to jail. It was a summer of dreadful speculations and discoveries, of which these were not the worst. Crime became real, for example—for the first time—not as a possibility but as *the* possibility. One would never defeat one's circumstances by working and saving one's pennies; one would never, by working, acquire that many pennies, and, besides, the social treatment accorded even the most successful Negroes proved that one needed, in order to be free, something more than a bank account. One needed a handle, a lever, a means of inspiring fear. It was absolutely clear that the police would whip you and take you in as long as they could get away with it, and that everyone else—housewives, taxi-drivers, elevator boys, dishwashers, bartenders, lawyers, judges, doctors, and grocers—would never, by the operation of any generous human feeling, cease to use you as an outlet for his frustrations and hostilities. Neither civilized reason nor Christian love would cause any of those people to treat you as they presumably wanted to be treated; only the fear of your power to retaliate would cause them to do that, or to seem to do it, which was (and is) good enough. There appears to be a vast amount of confusion on this point, but I do not know many Negroes who are eager to be "accepted" by white people, still less to be loved by them; they, the blacks, simply don't wish to be beaten over the head by the whites every instant of our brief passage on this planet. White people in this country will have quite enough to do in learning how to accept and love themselves and each other, and when they have achieved this—which will not be tomorrow and may very well be never—the Negro problem will no longer exist, for it will no longer be needed.

People more advantageously placed than we in Harlem were, and are, will no doubt find the psychology and the view of human nature sketched above dismal and shocking in the extreme. But the Negro's experience of the white world cannot possibly create in him any respect for the standards by which the white world claims to live. His own condition is overwhelming proof that white people do not live by these standards. Negro servants have been smuggling odds and ends out of white homes for generations, and white people have been delighted to have them do it, because it has assuaged a dim guilt and testified to the intrinsic superiority of white people. Even the most doltish and servile Negro could scarcely fail to be impressed by the disparity between his situation and that of the people for whom he worked; Negroes who were neither doltish nor servile did not feel that they were doing anything wrong when they robbed white people. In spite of the Puritan-Yankee equation of virtue with well-being, Negroes had excellent reasons for doubting that money was made or kept by any very striking adherence to the Christian virtues; it certainly did not work that way for black Christians. In any case, white people, who had robbed black people of their liberty and who profited by this theft every hour that they lived, had no moral ground on which to stand. They had the judges, the juries, the shotguns, the law—in a word, power. But it was a criminal power, to be feared but not respected, and to be outwitted in any way whatever. And those virtues preached but not practiced by the white world were merely another means of holding Negroes in subjection.

It turned out, then, that summer, that the moral barriers that I had supposed to exist between me and the dangers of a criminal career were so tenuous as to be nearly nonexistent. I certainly could not discover any principled reason for not becoming a criminal, and it is not my poor, God-fearing parents who are to be indicted for the lack but this society. I was icily determined—more determined, really, than I then knew—never to make my peace with the ghetto but to die and go to Hell before I would let any white man spit on me, before I would accept my "place" in this republic. I did not intend to allow the white people of this country to tell me who I was, and limit me that way, and polish me off that way. And yet, of course, at the same time, I *was* being spat on and defined and described and limited, and could have been polished off with no effort whatever. Every Negro boy—in my situation during those years, at least—who reaches this point realizes, at once, profoundly, because he wants to live, that he stands in great peril and must find, with speed, a "thing," a gimmick, to lift him out, to start him on his way. *And it does not matter what the gimmick is.* It was this last realization that terrified me and—since it revealed that the door opened on so many dangers—helped to hurl me into the church. And, by an unforeseeable paradox, it was my career in the church that turned out, precisely, to be my gimmick.

For when I tried to assess my capabilities, I realized that I had almost none. In order to achieve the life I wanted, I had been dealt, it seemed to me, the worst possible hand. I could not become a prizefighter—many of us tried but very few succeeded. I could not sing. I could not dance. I had been well conditioned by the world in which I grew up, so I did not yet dare take the idea of becoming a writer seriously. The only other possibility seemed to involve my becoming one of the sordid people on the Avenue, who were not really as sordid as I then imagined but who frightened me terribly, both because I did not want to live that life and because of what they made me feel. Everything inflamed me, and that was bad enough, but I myself had also become a source of fire and temptation. I had been far too well raised, alas, to suppose that any of the extremely explicit overtures made to me that summer, sometimes by boys and girls but also, more alarmingly, by older men and women, had anything to do with my attractiveness. On the contrary, since the Harlem idea of seduction is, to put it mildly, blunt, whatever these people saw in me merely confirmed my sense of my depravity.

It is certainly sad that the awakening of one's senses should lead to such a merciless judgment of oneself—to say nothing of the time and anguish one spends in the effort to arrive at any other—but it is also inevitable that a literal attempt to mortify the flesh should be made among black people like those with whom I grew up. Negroes in this country—and Negroes do not, strictly or legally speaking, exist in any other—are taught really to despise themselves from the moment their eyes open on the world. This world is white and they are black. White people hold the power, which means that they are superior to blacks (intrinsically, that is: God decreed it so), and the world has innumerable ways of making this difference known and felt and feared. Long before the Negro child perceives this difference, and even longer before he understands it, he has begun to react to it, he has begun to be controlled by it. Every effort made by the child's elders to prepare him for a fate from which they cannot protect him causes him secretly, in terror, to begin to await, without knowing that he is doing so, his mysterious and inexorable punishment. He must be "good" not only in order to please his parents and not only to avoid being punished by them; behind their authority stands another, nameless and impersonal, infinitely harder to please, and bottomlessly cruel. And this filters into the child's consciousness through his parents' tone of voice as he is being exhorted, punished, or loved; in the sudden, uncontrollable note of fear heard in his mother's or his father's voice when he has strayed beyond some particular boundary. He does not know what the boundary is, and he can get no explanation of it, which is frightening enough, but the fear he hears in the voices of his elders is more frightening still. The fear that I heard in my father's voice, for example, when he realized that I really

believed I could do anything a white boy could do, and had every intention of proving it, was not at all like the fear I heard when one of us was ill or had fallen down
the stairs or strayed too far from the house. It was another fear, a fear that the
child, in challenging the white world's assumptions, was putting himself in the path
of destruction. A child cannot, thank Heaven, know how vast and how merciless is
the nature of power, with what unbelievable cruelty people treat each other. He
reacts to the fear in his parents' voices because his parents hold up the world for
him and he has no protection without them. I defended myself, as I imagined,
against the fear my father made me feel by remembering that he was very old-
fashioned. Also, I prided myself on the fact that I already knew how to outwit him.
To defend oneself against a fear is simply to insure that one will, one day, be conquered by it; fears must be faced. As for one's wits, it is just not true that one can
live by them—not, that is, if one wishes really to live. That summer, in any case, all
the fears with which I had grown up, and which were now a part of me and controlled my vision of the world, rose up like a wall between the world and me, and
drove me into the church.

As I look back, everything I did seems curiously deliberate, though it certainly
did not seem deliberate then. For example, I did not join the church of which my
father was a member and in which he preached. My best friend in school, who
attended a different church, had already "surrendered his life to the Lord," and he
was very anxious about my soul's salvation. (I wasn't, but any human attention was
better than none.) One Saturday afternoon, he took me to his church. There were no
services that day, and the church was empty, except for some women cleaning and
some other women praying. My friend took me into the back room to meet his
pastor—a woman. There she sat, in her robes, smiling, an extremely proud and
handsome woman, with Africa, Europe, and the America of the American Indian
blended in her face. She was perhaps forty-five or fifty at this time, and in our world
she was a very celebrated woman. My friend was about to introduce me when she
looked at me and smiled and said, "Whose little boy are you?" Now this, unbeliev-
ably, was precisely the phrase used by pimps and racketeers on the Avenue when
they suggested, both humorously and intensely, that I "hang out" with them. Perhaps part of the terror they had caused me to feel came from the fact that I unquestionably wanted to be *somebody's* little boy. I was so frightened, and at the mercy of
so many conundrums, that inevitably, that summer, *someone* would have taken me
over; one doesn't, in Harlem, long remain standing on any auction block. It was my
good luck—perhaps—that I found myself in the church racket instead of some other,
and surrendered to a spiritual seduction long before I came to any carnal knowledge.
For when the pastor asked me, with that marvellous smile, "Whose little boy are
you?" my heart replied at once, "Why, yours."

The summer wore on, and things got worse. I became more guilty and more
frightened, and kept all this bottled up inside me, and naturally, inescapably, one
night, when this woman had finished preaching, everything came roaring, scream-

ing, crying out, and I fell to the ground before the altar. It was the strangest sensation I have ever had in my life—up to that time, or since. I had not known that it
was going to happen, or that it could happen. One moment I was on my feet, singing
and clapping and, at the same time, working out in my head the plot of a play I was
working on then; the next moment, with no transition, no sensation of falling, I was
on my back, with the lights beating down into my face and all the vertical saints
above me. I did not know what I was doing down so low, or how I had got there. And
the anguish that filled me cannot be described. It moved in me like one of those
floods that devastate counties, tearing everything down, tearing children from their
parents and lovers from each other, and making everything an unrecognizable
waste. All I really remember is the pain, the unspeakable pain; it was as though I
were yelling up to Heaven and Heaven would not hear me. And if Heaven would not
hear me, if love could not descend from Heaven—to wash me, to make me clean—
then utter disaster was my portion. Yes, it does indeed mean something—something
unspeakable—to be born, in a white country, an Anglo-Teutonic, antisexual country,
black. You very soon, without knowing it, give up all hope of communion. Black
people, mainly, look down or look up but do not look at each other, not at you, and
white people, mainly, look away. And the universe is simply a sounding drum; there
is no way, no way whatever, so it seemed then and has sometimes seemed since, to
get through a life, to love your wife and children, or your friends, or your mother
and father, or to be loved. The universe, which is not merely the stars and the moon
and the planets, flowers, grass, and trees, but *other people*, has evolved no terms for
your existence, has made no room for you, and if love will not swing wide the gates,
no other power will or can. And if one despairs—as who has not?—of human love,
God's love alone is left. But God—and I felt this even then, so long ago, on that
tremendous floor, unwillingly—is white. And if His love was so great, and if He
loved all His children, why were we, the blacks, cast down so far? Why? In spite of
all I said thereafter, I found no answer on the floor—not *that* answer, anyway —and
I was on the floor all night. Over me, to bring me "through," the saints sang and
rejoiced and prayed. And in the morning, when they raised me, they told me that I
was "saved."

Well, indeed I was, in a way, for I was utterly drained and exhausted, and
released, for the first time, from all my guilty torment. I was aware then only of my
relief. For many years, I could not ask myself why human relief had to be achieved
in a fashion at once so pagan and so desperate—in a fashion at once so unspeakably
old and so unutterably new. And by the time I was able to ask myself this question, I
was also able to see that the principles governing the rites and customs of the
churches in which I grew up did not differ from the principles governing the rites
and customs of other churches, white. The principles were Blindness, Loneliness,
and Terror, the first principle necessarily and actively cultivated in order to deny
the two others. I would love to believe that the principles were Faith, Hope, and
Charity, but this is clearly not so for most Christians, or for what we call the Christian world.

I was saved. But at the same time, out of a deep, adolescent cunning I do not pretend to understand, I realized immediately that I could not remain in the church merely as another worshipper. I would have to give myself something to do, in order not to be too bored and find myself among all the wretched unsaved of the Avenue. And I don't doubt that I also intended to best my father on his own ground. Anyway, very shortly after I joined the church, I became a preacher—a Young Minister—and I remained in the pulpit for more than three years. My youth quickly made me a much bigger drawing card than my father. I pushed this advantage ruthlessly, for it was the most effective means I had found of breaking his hold over me. That was the most frightening time of my life, and quite the most dishonest, and the resulting hysteria lent great passion to my sermons—for a while. I relished the attention and the relative immunity from punishment that my new status gave me, and I relished, above all, the sudden right to privacy. It had to be recognized, after all, that I was still a schoolboy, with my schoolwork to do, and I was also expected to prepare at least one sermon a week. During what we may call my heyday, I preached much more often than that. This meant that there were hours and even whole days when I could not be interrupted—not even by my father. I had immobilized him. It took rather more time for me to realize that I had also immobilized myself, and had escaped from nothing whatever.

The church was very exciting. It took a long time for me to disengage myself from this excitement, and on the blindest, most visceral level, I never really have, and never will. There is no music like that music, no drama like the drama of the saints rejoicing, the sinners moaning, the tambourines racing, and all those voices coming together and crying holy unto the Lord. There is still, for me, no pathos quite like the pathos of those multicolored, worn, somehow triumphant and transfigured faces, speaking from the depths of a visible, tangible, continuing despair of the goodness of the Lord. I have never seen anything to equal the fire and excitement that sometimes, without warning, fill a church, causing the church, as Leadbelly and so many others have testified, to "rock." Nothing that has happened to me since equals the power and the glory that I sometimes felt when, in the middle of a ser-mon, I knew that I was somehow, by some miracle, really carrying, as they said, "the Word"—when the church and I were one. Their pain and their joy were mine, and mine were theirs—they surrendered their pain and joy to me, I surrendered mine to them—and their cries of "Amen!" and "Hallelujah!" and "Yes, Lord!" and "Praise His name!" and "Preach it, brother!" sustained and whipped on my solos until we all became equal, wringing wet, singing and dancing, in anguish and rejoicing, at the foot of the altar. It was, for a long time, in spite of—or, not inconceivably, because of—the shabbiness of my motives, my only sustenance, my meat and drink. I rushed home from school, to the church, to the altar, to be alone there, to commune with Jesus, my dearest Friend, who would never fail me, who knew all the secrets of my heart. Perhaps He did, but I didn't, and the bargain we struck, actually, down there at the foot of the cross, was that He would never let me find out.

He failed His bargain. He was a much better Man than I took Him for. It happened, as things do, imperceptibly, in many ways at once. I date it—the slow crumbling of my faith, the pulverization of my fortress—from the time, about a year after I had begun to preach, when I began to read again. I justified this desire by the fact that I was still in school, and I began, fatally, with Dostoevsky. By this time, I was in a high school that was predominantly Jewish. This meant that I was surrounded by people who were, by definition, beyond any hope of salvation, who laughed at the tracts and leaflets I brought to school, and who pointed out that the Gospels had been written long after the death of Christ. This might not have been so distressing if it had not forced me to read the tracts and leaflets myself, for they were indeed, unless one believed their message already, impossible to believe. I remember feeling dimly that there was a kind of blackmail in it. People, I felt, ought to love the Lord *because* they loved Him, and not because they were afraid of going to Hell. I was forced, reluctantly, to realize that the Bible itself had been written by men, and translated by men out of languages I could not read, and I was already, without quite admitting it to myself, terribly involved with the effort of putting words on paper. Of course, I had the rebuttal ready: These men had all been operating under divine inspiration. *Had* they? *All* of them? And I also knew by now, alas, far more about divine inspiration than I dared admit, for I knew how I worked myself up into my own visions, and how frequently—indeed, incessantly—the visions God granted to me differed from the visions He granted to my father. I did not understand the dreams I had at night, but I knew that they were not holy. For that matter, I knew that my waking hours were far from holy. I spent most of my time in a state of repentance for things I had vividly desired to do but had not done. The fact that I was dealing with Jews brought the whole question of color, which I had been desperately avoiding, into the terrified center of my mind. I realized that the Bible had been written by white men. I knew that, according to many Christians, I was a descendant of Ham, who had been cursed, and that I was therefore predestined to be a slave. This had nothing to do with anything I was, or contained, or could become; my fate had been sealed forever, from the beginning of time. And it seemed, indeed, when one looked out over Christendom, that this was what Christendom effectively believed. It was certainly the way it behaved. I remembered the Italian priests and bishops blessing Italian boys who were on their way to Ethiopia.

Again, the Jewish boys in high school were troubling because I could find no point of connection between them and the Jewish pawnbrokers and landlords and grocerystore owners in Harlem. I knew that these people were Jews—God knows I was told it often enough—but I thought of them only as white. Jews, as such, until I got to high school, were all incarcerated in the Old Testament, and their names were Abraham, Moses, Daniel, Ezekiel, and Job, and Shadrach, Meshach, and Abednego. It was bewildering to find them so many miles and centuries out of Egypt, and so far from the fiery furnace. My best friend in high school was a Jew. He came to our house once, and afterward my father asked, as he asked about everyone, "Is he a Christian?"—by which he meant "Is he saved?" I really do not know whether my answer came out of innocence or venom, but I said coldly, "No. He's Jewish." My father slammed me across the face with his great palm, and in that moment everything flooded back—all the hatred and all the fear, and the depth of a merciless resolve to kill my father rather than allow my father to kill me—and I knew that all those sermons and tears and all that repentance and rejoicing had changed nothing. I wondered if I was expected to be glad that a friend of mine, or anyone, was to be tormented forever in Hell, and I also thought, suddenly, of the Jews in another Christian nation, Germany. They were not so far from the fiery furnace after all, and my best friend might have been one of them. I told my father, "He's a better Christian than you are," and walked out of the house. The battle between us was in the open, but that was all right; it was almost a relief. A more deadly struggle had begun.

Being in the pulpit was like being in the theater; I was behind the scenes and knew how the illusion was worked. I knew the other ministers and knew the quality of their lives. And I don't mean to suggest by this the "Elmer Gantry" sort of hypocrisy concerning sensuality; it was a deeper, deadlier, and more subtle hypocrisy than that, and a little honest sensuality, or a lot, would have been like water in an extremely bitter desert. I knew how to work on a congregation until the last dime was surrendered—it was not very hard to do—and I knew where the money for "the Lord's work" went. I knew, though I did not wish to know it, that I had no respect for the people with whom I worked. I could not have said it then, but I also knew that if I continued I would soon have no respect for myself. And the fact that I was "the young Brother Baldwin" increased my value with those same pimps and racketeers who had helped to stampede me into the church in the first place. They still saw the little boy they intended to take over. They were waiting for me to come to my senses and realize that I was in a very lucrative business. They knew that I did not yet realize this, and also that I had not yet begun to suspect where my own needs, *coming up* (they were very patient), could drive me. They themselves did know the score, and they knew that the odds were in their favor. And, really, I knew it, too. I was even lonelier and more vulnerable than I had been before. And the blood of the Lamb had not cleansed me in any way whatever. I was just as black as I had been the day that I was born. Therefore, when I faced a congregation, it began to take all the strength I had not to stammer, not to curse, not to tell them to throw away their Bibles and get off their knees and go home and organize, for example, a rent strike. When I watched all the children, their copper, brown, and beige faces staring up at me as I taught Sunday school, I felt that I was committing a crime in talking about the gentle Jesus, in telling them to reconcile themselves to their misery on earth in order to gain the crown of eternal life. Were only Negroes to gain this crown? Was Heaven, then, to be merely another ghetto? Perhaps I might have been able to reconcile myself even to this if I had been able to believe that there was any loving-kindness to be found in the haven I represented. But I had been in the pulpit too long and I had seen too many monstrous things. I don't refer merely to the glaring fact that the minister eventually acquires houses and Cadillacs while the faithful continue to scrub floors and drop their dimes and quarters and dollars into the plate. I really mean that there was no love in the church. It was a mask for hatred and self-hatred and despair. The transfiguring power of the Holy Ghost ended when the service ended, and salvation stopped at the church door. When we were told to love everybody, I had thought that that meant *everybody*. But no. It applied only to those who believed as we did, and it did not apply to white people at all. I was told by a minister, for example, that I should never, on any public convey-ance, under any circumstances, rise and give my seat to a white woman. White men never rose for Negro women. Well, that was true enough, in the main—I saw his point. But what was the point, the purpose, of *my* salvation if it did not permit me to behave with love toward others, no matter how they behaved toward me? What others did was their responsibility, for which they would answer when the judgment trumpet sounded. But what *I* did was *my* responsibility, and I would have to answer, too—unless, of course, there was also in Heaven a special dispensation for the benighted black, who was not to be judged in the same way as other human beings, or angels. It probably occurred to me around this time that the vision people hold of the world to come is but a reflection, with predictable wishful distortions, of the world in which they live. And this did not apply only to Negroes, who were no more "simple" or "spontaneous" or "Christian" than anybody else—who were merely more oppressed. In the same way that we, for white people, were the descendants of Ham, and were cursed forever, white people were, for us, the descendants of Cain. And the passion with which we loved the Lord was a measure of how deeply we feared and distrusted and, in the end, hated almost all strangers, always, and avoided and despised ourselves.

But I cannot leave it at that; there is more to it than that. In spite of every-thing, there was in the life I fled a zest and a joy and a capacity for facing and surviving disaster that are very moving and very rare. Perhaps we were, all of us—pimps, whores, racketeers, church members, and children—bound together by the nature of our oppression, the specific and peculiar complex of risks we had to run; if so, within these limits we sometimes achieved with each other a freedom that was close to love. I remember, anyway, church suppers and outings, and, later, after I left the church, rent and waistline parties where rage and sorrow sat in the dark-ness and did not stir, and we ate and drank and talked and laughed and danced and forgot all about "the man." We had the liquor, the chicken, the music, and each other, and had no need to pretend to be what we were not. This is the freedom that one hears in some gospel songs, for example, and in jazz. In all jazz, and especially in the blues, there is something tart and ironic, authoritative and double-edged. White Americans seem to feel that happy songs are *happy* and sad songs are *sad*, and that, God help us, is exactly the way most white Americans sing them—sound-ing, in both cases, so helplessly, defenselessly fatuous that one dare not speculate on the temperature of the deep freeze from which issue their brave and sexless little voices. Only people who have been "down the line," as the song puts it, know what this music is about. I think it was Big Bill Broonzy who used to sing "I Feel So Good," a really joyful song about a man who is on his way to the railroad station to meet his girl. She's coming home. It is the singer's incredibly moving exuberance that makes one realize how leaden the time must have been while she was gone. There is no guarantee that she will stay this time, either, as the singer clearly knows, and, in fact, she has not yet actually arrived. Tonight, or tomorrow, or within the next five minutes, he may very well be singing "Lonesome in My Bedroom," or insisting, "Ain't we, ain't we, going to make it all right? Well, if we don't today, we will tomorrow night." White Americans do not understand the depths out of which such an ironic tenacity comes, but they suspect that the force is sensual, and they are terrified of sensuality and do not any longer understand it. The word "sensual" is not intended to bring to mind quivering dusky maidens or priapic black studs. I am referring to something much simpler and much less fanciful. To be sensual, I think, is to respect and rejoice in the force of life, of life itself, and to be *present* in all that one does, from the effort of loving to the breaking of bread. It will be a great day for America, incidentally, when we begin to eat bread again, instead of the blasphemous and tasteless foam rubber that we have substituted for it. And I am not being frivolous now, either. Something very sinister happens to the people of a country when they begin to distrust their own reactions as deeply as they do here, and become as joyless as they have become. It is this individual uncertainty on the part of white American men and women, this inability to renew themselves at the fountain of their own lives, that makes the discussion, let alone elucidation, of any conundrum—that is, any reality—so supremely difficult. The person who distrusts himself has no touchstone for reality—for this touchstone can be only oneself. Such a person interposes between himself and reality nothing less than a labyrinth of attitudes. And these attitudes, furthermore, though the person is usually unaware of it (is unaware of so much!), are historical and public attitudes. They do not relate to the present any more than they relate to the person. Therefore, whatever white people do not know about Negroes reveals, precisely and inexorably, what they do not know about themselves.

White Christians have also forgotten several elementary historical details. They have forgotten that the religion that is now identified with their virtue and their power—"God is on our side," says Dr. Verwoerd—came out of a rocky piece of ground in what is now known as the Middle East before color was invented, and that in order for the Christian church to be established, Christ had to be put to death, by Rome, and that the real architect of the Christian church was not the disreputable, sun-baked Hebrew who gave it his name but the mercilessly fanatical and self-righteous Saint Paul. The energy that was buried with the rise of the Christian nations must come back into the world; nothing can prevent it. Many of us, I think, both long to see this happen and are terrified of it, for though this transformation contains the hope of liberation, it also imposes a necessity for great change. But in order to deal with the untapped and dormant force of the previously subjugated, in order to survive as a human, moving, moral weight in the world, America and all the Western nations will be forced to reexamine themselves and release themselves from many things that are now taken to be sacred, and to discard nearly all the assumptions that have been used to justify their lives and their anguish and their crimes so long.

"The white man's Heaven," sings a Black Muslim minister, "is the black man's Hell." One may object—possibly—that this puts the matter somewhat too simply, but the song is true, and it has been true for as long as white men have ruled the world. The Africans put it another way: When the white man came to Africa, the white man had the Bible and the African had the land, but now it is the white man who is being, reluctantly and bloodily, separated from the land, and the African who is still attempting to digest or to vomit up the Bible. The struggle, therefore, that now begins in the world is extremely complex, involving the historical role of Christianity in the realm of power—that is, politics and in the realm of morals. In the realm of power, Christianity has operated with an unmitigated arrogance and cruelty—necessarily, since a religion ordinarily imposes on those who have discovered the true faith the spiritual duty of liberating the infidels. This particular true faith, moreover, is more deeply concerned about the soul than it is about the body, to which fact the flesh (and the corpses) of countless infidels bears witness. It goes without saying, then, that whoever questions the authority of the true faith also contests the right of the nations that hold this faith to rule over him—contests, in short, their title to his land. The spreading of the Gospel, regardless of the motives or the integrity or the heroism of some of the missionaries, was an absolutely indispensable justification for the planting of the flag. Priests and nuns and schoolteachers helped to protect and sanctify the power that was so ruthlessly being used by people who were indeed seeking a city, but not one in the heavens, and one to be made, very definitely, by captive hands. The Christian church itself—again, as distinguished from some of its ministers—sanctified and rejoiced in the conquests of the flag, and encouraged, if it did not formulate, the belief that conquest, with the resulting relative well-being of the Western populations, was proof of the favor of God. God had come a long way from the desert—but then so had Allah, though in a very different direction. God, going north, and rising on the wings of power, had become white, and Allah, out of power, and on the dark side of Heaven, had become—for all practical purposes, anyway—black. Thus, in the realm of morals the role of Christianity has been, at best, ambivalent. Even leaving out of account the remarkable arrogance that assumed that the ways and morals of others were inferior to those of Christians, and that they therefore had every right, and could use any means, to change them, the collision between cultures—and the schizophrenia in the mind of Christendom—had rendered the domain of morals as chartless as the sea once was, and as treacherous as the sea still is. It is not too much to say that whoever wishes to become a truly moral human being (and let us not ask whether or not this is possible; I think we must *believe* that it is possible) must first divorce himself from all the prohibitions, crimes, and hypocrisies of the Christian church. If the concept of God has any validity or any use, it can only be to make us larger, freer, and more loving. If God cannot do this, then it is time we got rid of Him.

❖ ❖ ❖

Dynamics

1. Make a list of the different social groups and institutions that influenced James Baldwin during the years he describes in his text. What does each group or institution contribute to his understanding of himself as a young man? What does each one contribute to his understanding years later as he reflects upon those experiences in order to write this essay? What surprises do you find as you answer these questions?

2. James Baldwin writes about the desire for "safety" as well as the desire for "communion." In the context of his experiences growing up, what do these two terms mean, and what do they have to do with each other?

Critical Tools

1. Baldwin writes about a "labyrinth of attitudes" that helps him explain some of the workings of racism. Prepare a working definition of that term, based on Baldwin's use of it, and then consider another text you have read this semester where someone's life is influenced by a similar labyrinth. What does the second text allow you to add to your definition of the term?

2. At one point Baldwin says that some people of his community "achieved with each other a freedom that was close to love." What do you think he means by "love," if the example he offers here is only "close to love"? (You might also look at the final section of Baldwin's book, *The Fire Next Time*, where he occasionally continues the discussion of love that he starts in our text.)

Draft One/Draft Two

Draft One: Baldwin suggests that people may have the ability to "renew themselves at the fountain of their own lives." For draft one, use this text and another you have read this semester to explain how that process of renewal might work.

Draft Two: For draft two, consider another text from *Literacies* that you feel makes a social criticism of one kind or another. Relate the criticism made in that text to ideas about renewal you generated in your first draft. How does your first draft reflect upon the criticism of that third text, and how does that third text reflect on the ideas in your first draft?

❖ ❖ ❖

Before Reading Dean Barnlund. . .

1. Describe a system of thought with which you disagree, perhaps strongly (codes of morality, political philosophies, and cultural practices are some possibilities). Explore the reasons for your disagreement: what, specifically, troubles you about this practice or system of thought? Why? Evaluate how this system of thought relates to your fundamental assumptions about the world.

2. What ideas come to mind when you think about the term "communication"? Explore your understanding of "communication" as a process. Define the specific steps required for effective communication, and explain how you believe effective communication can be achieved.

3. Barnlund writes about the "global village." What does this phrase mean to you? As you explore your ideas about the "global village," describe what you see as its major benefits and challenges. Consider how some of the essays you've read might contribute to your response to this concept.

Communication in a Global Village

Dean C. Barnlund

Nearing Autumn's close.
My neighbor—
How does he live, I wonder?

　　　　　　—Basho

These lines, written by one of the most cherished of *haiku* poets, express a timeless and universal curiosity in one's fellow man. When they were written, nearly three hundred years ago, the word "neighbor" referred to people very much like one's self—similar in dress, in diet, in custom, in language—who happened to live next door. Today relatively few people are surrounded by neighbors who are cultural replicas of themselves. Tomorrow we can expect to spend most of our lives in the company of neighbors who will speak in a different tongue, seek different values, move at a different pace, and interact according to a different script. Within no longer than a decade or two the probability of spending part of one's life in a foreign culture will exceed the probability a hundred years ago of ever leaving the town in which one was born. As our world is transformed our neighbors increasingly will be people whose life styles contrast sharply with our own.

The technological feasibility of such a global village is no longer in doubt. Only the precise date of its attainment is uncertain. The means already exist: in telecommunication systems linking the world by satellite, in aircraft capable of moving people faster than the speed of sound, in computers which can disgorge facts more rapidly than men can formulate their questions. The methods for bringing people closer physically and electronically are clearly at hand. What is in doubt is whether the erosion of cultural boundaries through technology will bring the realization of a dream or a nightmare. Will a global village be a mere collection or a true community of men? Will its residents be neighbors capable of respecting and utilizing their differences, or clusters of strangers living in ghettos and united only in their antipathies for others?

Can we generate the new cultural attitudes required by our technological virtuosity? History is not very reassuring here. It has taken centuries to learn how

Barnlund, Dean C. *Public and Private Self in Japan and the United States,* Yarmouth, Maine: Intercultural Press. Used by permission.

to live harmoniously in the family, the tribe, the city state, and the nation. Each new stretching of human sensitivity and loyalty has taken generations to become firmly assimilated in the human psyche. And now we are forced into a quantum leap from the mutual suspicion and hostility that have marked the past relations between peoples into a world in which mutual respect and comprehension are requisite.

Even events of recent decades provide little basis for optimism. Increasing physical proximity has brought no millennium in human relations. If anything, it has appeared to intensify the divisions among people rather than to create a broader intimacy. Every new reduction in physical distance has made us more painfully aware of the psychic distance that divides people and has increased alarm over real or imagined differences. If today people occasionally choke on what seem to be indigestible differences between rich and poor, male and female, specialist and non-specialist within cultures, what will happen tomorrow when people must assimilate and cope with still greater contrasts in life styles? Wider access to more people will be a doubtful victory if human beings find they have nothing to say to one another or cannot stand to listen to each other.

Time and space have long cushioned intercultural encounters, confining them to touristic exchanges. But this insulation is rapidly wearing thin. In the world of tomorrow we can expect to live—not merely vacation—in societies which seek different values and abide by different codes. There we will be surrounded by for-eigners for long periods of time, working with others in the closest possible relation-ships. If people currently show little tolerance or talent for encounters with alien cultures, how can they learn to deal with constant and inescapable coexistence?

The temptation is to retreat to some pious hope or talismanic formula to carry us into the new age. "Meanwhile," as Edwin Reischauer reminds us, "we fail to do what we ourselves must do if 'one world' is ever to be achieved, and that is to de-velop the education, the skills and the attitudes that men must have if they are to build and maintain such a world. The time is short, and the needs are great. The task faces all men. But it is on the shoulders of people living in the strong countries of the world, such as Japan and the United States, that this burden falls with special weight and urgency."

Anyone who has truly struggled to comprehend another person—even those closest and most like himself—will appreciate the immensity of the challenge of intercultural communication. A greater exchange of people between nations, needed as that may be, carries with it no guarantee of increased cultural empathy; ex-perience in other lands often does little but aggravate existing prejudices. Studying guidebooks or memorizing polite phrases similarly fails to explain differences in cultural perspectives. Programs of cultural enrichment, while they contribute to curiosity about other ways of life, do not cultivate the skills to function effectively in the cultures studied. Even concentrated exposure to a foreign language, valuable as it is, provides access to only one of the many codes that regulate daily affairs; human understanding is by no means guaranteed because conversants share the same dictionary. (Within the United States, where people inhabit a common territory and possess a common language, mutuality of meaning among Mexican-Americans, White-Americans, Black-Americans, Indian-Americans—to say nothing of old and young, poor and rich, pro-establishment and anti-establishment cultures—is a sporadic and unreliable occurrence.) Useful as all these measures are for enlarging appreciation of diverse cultures, they fall short of what is needed for a global village to survive.

What seems most critical is to find ways of gaining entrance into the assumptive world of another culture, to identify the norms that govern face-to-face relations, and to equip people to function within a social system that is foreign but no longer incomprehensible. Without this kind of insight people are condemned to remain outsiders no matter how long they live in another country. Its institutions and its customs will be interpreted inevitably from the premises and through the medium of their own culture. Whether they notice something or overlook it, respect or ridicule it, express or conceal their reaction will be dictated by the logic of their own rather than the alien culture.

There are, of course, shelves and shelves of books on the cultures of the world. They cover the history, religion, political thought, music, sculpture, and industry of many nations. And they make fascinating and provocative reading. But only in the vaguest way do they suggest what it is that really distinguishes the behavior of a Samoan, a Congolese, a Japanese or an American. Rarely do the descriptions of a political structure or religious faith explain precisely when and why certain topics are avoided or why specific gestures carry such radically different meanings according to the context in which they appear.

When former President Nixon and former Premier Sato met to discuss a growing problem concerning trade in textiles between Japan and the United States, Premier Sato announced that since they were on such good terms with each other that the deliberations would be "three parts talk and seven parts 'haragei.' " Translated literally, "haragei" means to communicate through the belly, that is to feel out intuitively rather than verbally state the precise position of each person.

Subscribing to this strategy—one that governs many interpersonal exchanges in his culture—Premier Sato conveyed without verbal elaboration his comprehension of the plight of American textile firms threatened by accelerating exports of Japanese fabrics to the United States. President Nixon—similarly abiding by norms that govern interaction within his culture—took this comprehension of the American position to mean that new export quotas would be forthcoming shortly.

During the next few weeks both were shocked at the consequences of their meeting: Nixon was infuriated to learn that the new policies he expected were not forthcoming, and Sato was upset to find that he had unwittingly triggered a new wave of hostility toward his country. If prominent officials, surrounded by foreign advisers, can commit such grievous communicative blunders, the plight of the ordinary citizen may be suggested. Such inter-cultural collisions, forced upon the public consciousness by the grave consequences they carry and the extensive publicity they receive, only hint at the wider and more frequent confusions and hostilities that disrupt the negotiations of lesser officials, business executives, professionals and even visitors in foreign countries.

Every culture expresses its purposes and conducts its affairs through the medium of communication. Cultures exist primarily to create and preserve common systems of symbols by which their members can assign and exchange meanings. Unhappily, the distinctive rules that govern these symbol systems are far from obvious. About some of these codes, such as language, we have extensive knowledge. About others, such as gestures and facial codes, we have only rudimentary knowledge. On many others—rules governing topical appropriateness, customs regulating physical contact, time and space codes, strategies for the management of conflict— we have almost no systematic knowledge. To crash another culture with only the vaguest notion of its underlying dynamics reflects not only a provincial naïvete but a dangerous form of cultural arrogance.

It is differences in meaning, far more than mere differences in vocabulary, that isolate cultures, and that cause them to regard each other as strange or even barbaric. It is not too surprising that many cultures refer to themselves as "The People," relegating all other human beings to a subhuman form of life. To the person who drinks blood, the eating of meat is repulsive. Someone who conveys respect by standing is upset by someone who conveys it by sitting down; both may regard kneeling as absurd. Burying the dead may prompt tears in one society, smiles in another, and dancing in a third. If spitting on the street makes sense to some, it will appear bizarre that others carry their spit in their pocket; neither may quite appreciate someone who spits to express gratitude. The bullfight that constitutes an almost religious ritual for some seems a cruel and inhumane way of destroying a defenseless animal to others. Although staring is acceptable social behavior in some cultures, in others it is a thoughtless invasion of privacy. Privacy, itself, is without universal meaning.

Note that none of these acts involves an insurmountable linguistic challenge. The words that describe these acts—eating, spitting, showing respect, fighting, burying, and staring—are quite translatable into most languages. The issue is more conceptual than linguistic; each society places events in its own cultural frame and it is these frames that bestow the unique meaning and differentiated response they produce.

As we move or are driven toward a global village and increasingly frequent cultural contact, we need more than simply greater factual knowledge of each other. We need, more specifically, to identify what might be called the "rulebooks of meaning" that distinguish one culture from another. For to grasp the way in which other cultures perceive the world, and the assumptions and values that are the foundation of these perceptions, is to gain access to the experience of other human beings. Access to the world view and the communicative style of other cultures may not only enlarge our own way of experiencing the world but enable us to maintain constructive relationships with societies that operate according to a different logic than our own.

Sources of Meaning

To survive, psychologically as well as physically, human beings must inhabit a world that is relatively free of ambiguity and reasonably predictable. Some sort of structure must be placed upon the endless profusion of incoming signals. The infant, born into a world of flashing, hissing, moving images, soon learns to adapt by resolving this chaos into toys and tables, dogs and parents. Even adults who have had their vision or hearing restored through surgery describe the world as a frightening and sometimes unbearable experience; only after days of effort are they able to transform blurs and noises into meaningful and therefore manageable experiences.

It is commonplace to talk as if the world "has" meaning, to ask what "is" the meaning of a phrase, a gesture, a painting, a contract. Yet when thought about, it is clear that events are devoid of meaning until someone assigns it to them. There is no appropriate response to a bow or a handshake, a shout or a whisper, until it is interpreted. A drop of water and the color red have no meaning, they simply exist. The aim of human perception is to make the world intelligible so that it can be managed successfully; the attribution of meaning is a prerequisite to and preparation for action.

People are never passive receivers, merely absorbing events of obvious significance, but are active in assigning meaning to sensation. What any event acquires in the way of meaning appears to reflect a transaction between what is there to be seen or heard, and what the interpreter brings to it in the way of past experience and prevailing motive. Thus the attribution of meaning is always a creative process by which the raw data of sensation are transformed to fit the aims of the observer.

The diversity of reactions that can be triggered by a single experience—meeting a stranger, negotiating a contract, attending a textile conference—is immense. Each observer is forced to see it through his own eyes, interpret it in the light of his own values, fit it to the requirements of his own circumstances. As a consequence, every object and message is seen by every observer from a somewhat different perspective. Each person will note some features and neglect others. Each will accept some relations among the facts and deny others. Each will arrive at some conclusion, tentative or certain, as the sounds and forms resolve into a "temple" or "barn," a "compliment" or "insult."

Provide a group of people with a set of photographs, even quite simple and ordinary photographs, and note how diverse are the meanings they provoke. Afterward they will recall and forget different pictures; they will also assign quite distinctive meanings to those they do remember. Some will recall the mood of a picture, others the actions; some the appearance and others the attitudes of persons portrayed. Often the observers cannot agree upon even the most "objective" details—the number of people, the precise location and identity of simple objects. A difference in frame of mind—fatigue, hunger, excitement, anger—will change dramatically what they report they have "seen."

It should not be surprising that people raised in different families, exposed to different events, praised and punished for different reasons, should come to view the world so differently. As George Kelly has noted, people see the world through templates which force them to construe events in unique ways. These patterns or grids which we fit over the realities of the world are cut from our own experience and values, and they predispose us to certain interpretations. Industrialist and farmer do not see the "same" land; husband and wife do not plan for the "same" child; doctor and patient do not discuss the "same" disease; borrower and creditor do not negotiate the "same" mortgage; daughter and daughter-in-law do not react to the "same" mother.

The world each person creates for himself is a distinctive world, not the same world others occupy. Each fashions from every incident whatever meanings fit his own private biases. These biases, taken together, constitute what has been called the "assumptive world of the individual." The world each person gets inside his head is the only world he knows. And it is this symbolic world, not the real world, that he talks about, argues about, laughs about, fights about.

Interpersonal Encounters

Every communication, interpersonal or intercultural, is a transaction between these private worlds. As people talk they search for symbols that will enable them to share their experience and converge upon a common meaning. This process, often long and sometimes painful, makes it possible finally to reconcile apparent or real differences between them. Various words are used to describe this moment. When it involves an integration of facts or ideas, it is usually called an "agreement"; when it involves sharing a mood or feeling, it is referred to as "empathy" or "rapport." But "understanding" is a broad enough term to cover both possibilities; in either case it identifies the achievement of a common meaning.

It would be reasonable to expect that individuals who approach reality similarly might understand each other easily, and laboratory research confirms this conclusion: people with similar perceptual styles attract one another, understand each other better, work more efficiently together and with greater satisfaction than those whose perceptual orientations differ. Research done by Donn Byrne and replicated by the author demonstrates how powerfully human beings are drawn to those who hold the same beliefs and how sharply they are repelled by those who do not. Subjects in these experiments were given questionnaires requesting their opinions on twenty-six topics. After completing the forms, each was asked to rank the thirteen most important and least important topics. Later each person was given four forms, ostensibly filled out by people in another group but actually filled out to show varying degrees of agreement with their own answers, and invited to choose among them with regard to their attractiveness as associates. The results were clear: people most preferred to talk with those whose attitudes duplicated their own exactly, next chose those who agreed with them on all important issues, next chose those with similar views on unimportant issues, and finally and reluctantly chose those who disagreed with them completely. It appears that most people most of the time find satisfying relationships easiest to achieve with someone who shares their own hierarchy of beliefs. This, of course, converts many human encounters into rituals of ratification, each person looking to the other only to obtain endorsement and applause for his own beliefs. It is, however, what is often meant by "interpersonal under-standing."

It must be emphasized that perceptual orientations, systems of belief, and communicative styles do not exist or operate independently. They overlap and affect each other. They combine in complex ways to determine behavior. What a person says is influenced by what he believes and what he believes, in turn, by what he sees. His perceptions and beliefs are themselves partly a product of his manner of communicating with others.

There is an underlying narcissistic bias in human societies that draws similar people together. Each seeks to find in the other a reflection of himself, someone who views the world as he does, who interprets it as he does, and who expresses himself in a similar way. It is not surprising, then, that artists should be drawn to artists, radicals to radicals, Jews to Jews—or Japanese to Japanese and Americans to Americans.

The opposite seems equally true: people tend to avoid those who challenge their assumptions, who dismiss their beliefs, and who communicate in strange and unintelligible ways. When one reviews history, whether he examines crises within or between cultures, he finds people have consistently shielded themselves, segregated themselves, even fortified themselves, against wide differences in modes of perception or expression. (In many cases, indeed, have persecuted and conquered the infidel and afterwards substituted their own cultural ways for the offending ones.) Intercultural defensiveness appears to be only a counterpart of interpersonal defensiveness in the face of uncomprehended or incomprehensible differences.

Intercultural Encounters

Every culture attempts to create a "universe of discourse" for its members, a way in which people can interpret their experience and convey it to one another. Without a common system of codifying sensations, life would be absurd and all efforts to share meanings doomed to failure. This universe of discourse—one of the most precious of all cultural legacies—is transmitted to each generation in part consciously and in part unconsciously. Parents and teachers give explicit instruction in it by praising or criticizing certain ways of dressing, of thinking, of gesturing, of responding to the acts of others. But the most significant aspects of any cultural code may be conveyed implicitly, not by rule or lesson but through modelling behavior. The child is surrounded by others who, through the mere consistency of their actions as males and females, mothers and fathers, salesclerks and policemen, display what is appropriate behavior. Thus the grammar of any culture is sent and received largely unconsciously, making one's own cultural assumptions and biases difficult to recognize. They seem so obviously right that they require no explanation.

In *The Open and Closed Mind*, Milton Rokeach poses the problem of cultural understanding in its simplest form, but one that can readily demonstrate the complications of communication between cultures. It is called the "Denny Doodlebug Problem." Readers are given all the rules that govern his culture: Denny is an animal that always faces North, and can move only by jumping; he can jump large distances or small distances, but can change direction only after jumping four times in any direction; he can jump North, South, East or West, but not diagonally. Upon concluding a jump his master places some food three feet directly West of him. Surveying the situation, Denny concludes he must jump four times to reach the food. No more or less. And he is right. All the reader has to do is to explain the circumstances that make his conclusion correct.

The large majority of people who attempt this problem fail to solve it, despite the fact that they are given all the rules that control behavior in this culture. If there is difficulty in getting inside the simplistic world of Denny Doodlebug—where the cultural code has already been broken and handed to us—imagine the complexity of comprehending behavior in societies whose codes have not yet been deciphered. And where even those who obey these codes are only vaguely aware and can rarely describe the underlying sources of their own actions.

If two people, both of whom spring from a single culture, must often shout to be heard across the void that separates their private worlds, one can begin to appreciate the distance to be overcome when people of different cultural identities attempt to talk. Even with the most patient dedication to seeking a common terminology, it is surprising that people of alien cultures are able to hear each other at all. And the peoples of Japan and the United States would appear to constitute a particularly dramatic test of the ability to cross an intercultural divide. Consider the disparity between them.

Here is Japan, a tiny island nation with a minimum of resources, buffeted by periodic disasters, overcrowded with people, isolated by physical fact and cultural choice, nurtured in Shinto and Buddhist religions, permeated by a deep respect for nature, non-materialist in philosophy, intuitive in thought, hierarchical in social structure. Eschewing the explicit, the monumental, the bold and boisterous, it expresses its sensuality in the form of impeccable gardens, simple rural temples, asymmetrical flower arrangements, a theatre unparalleled for containment of feeling, an art and literature remarkable for their delicacy, and crafts noted for their honest and earthy character. Its people, among the most homogeneous of men, are modest and apologetic in manner, communicate in an ambiguous and evocative language, are engrossed in interpersonal rituals and prefer inner serenity to influencing others. They occupy unpretentious buildings of wood and paper and live in cities laid out as casually as farm villages. Suddenly from these rice paddies emerges an industrial giant, surpassing rival nations with decades of industrial experience, greater resources, and a larger reserve of technicians. Its labor, working longer, harder, and more frantically than any in the world, builds the earth's largest city, constructs some of its ugliest buildings, promotes the most garish and insistent advertising anywhere, and pollutes its air and water beyond the imagination.

And here is the United States, an immense country, sparsely settled, richly endowed, tied through waves of immigrants to the heritage of Europe, yet forced to subdue nature and find fresh solutions to the problems of survival. Steeped in the Judeo-Christian tradition, schooled in European abstract and analytic thought, it is materialist and experimental in outlook, philosophically pragmatic, politically equalitarian, economically competitive, its raw individualism sometimes tempered by a humanitarian concern for others. Its cities are studies in geometry along whose avenues rise shafts of steel and glass subdivided into separate cubicles for separate activities and separate people. Its popular arts are characterized by the hugeness of Cinemascope, the spontaneity of jazz, the earthy loudness of rock; in its fine arts the experimental, striking and monumental often stifle the more subtle revelation. The people, a smorgasbord of races, religions, dialects and nationalities, are turned expressively outward, impatient with rituals and rules, casual and flippant, gifted in logic and argument, approachable and direct yet given to flamboyant and exaggerated assertion. They are curious about one another, open and helpful, yet display a missionary zeal for changing one another. Suddenly this nation whose power and confidence have placed it in a dominant position in the world intellectually and politically, whose style of life has permeated the planet, finds itself uncertain of its direction, doubts its own premises and values, questions its motives and materialism, and engages in an orgy of self criticism.

It is when people nurtured in such different psychological worlds meet that differences in cultural perspectives and communicative codes may sabotage efforts to understand one another. Repeated collisions between a foreigner and the members of a contrasting culture often produce what is called "culture shock." It is a feeling of helplessness, even of terror or anger, that accompanies working in an alien society. One feels trapped in an absurd and indecipherable nightmare.

It is as if some hostile leprechaun had gotten into the works and as a cosmic caper rewired the connections that hold society together. Not only do the actions of others no longer make sense, but it is impossible even to express one's own intentions clearly. "Yes" comes out meaning "No." A wave of the hand means "come," or it may mean "go." Formality may be regarded as childish, or as a devious form of flattery. Statements of fact may be heard as statements of conceit. Arriving early, or arriving late, embarrasses or impresses. "Suggestions" may be treated as "ultimatums," or precisely the opposite. Failure to stand at the proper moment, or failure to sit, may be insulting. The compliment intended to express gratitude instead conveys a sense of distance. A smile signifies disappointment rather than pleasure.

If the crises that follow such intercultural encounters are sufficiently dramatic or the communicants unusually sensitive, they may recognize the source of their trouble. If there is patience and constructive intention the confusion can sometimes be clarified. But more often the foreigner, without knowing it, leaves behind him a trail of frustration, mistrust, and even hatred *of which he is totally unaware.* Neither he nor his associates recognize that their difficulty springs from sources deep within the rhetoric of their own societies. Each sees himself as acting in ways that are thoroughly sensible, honest and considerate. And—given the rules governing his own universe of discourse—each is. Unfortunately, there are few cultural universals, and the degree of overlap in communicative codes is always less than perfect. Experience can be transmitted with fidelity only when the unique properties of each code are recognized and respected, or where the motivation and means exist to bring them into some sort of alignment.

The Collective Unconscious

Among the greatest insights of this modern age are two that bear a curious affinity to each other. The first, evolving from the efforts of psychologists, particularly Sigmund Freud, revealed the existence of an "individual unconscious." The acts of human beings were found to spring from motives of which they were often vaguely or completely unaware. Their unique perceptions of events arose not from the facts outside their skins but from unrecognized assumptions inside them. When, through intensive analysis, they obtained some insight into these assumptions, they became free to develop other ways of seeing and acting which contributed to their greater flexibility in coping with reality.

The second of these generative ideas, flowing from the work of anthropologists, particularly Margaret Mead and Ruth Benedict, postulated a parallel idea in the existence of a "cultural unconscious." Students of primitive cultures began to see that there was nothing divine or absolute about cultural norms. Every society had its own way of viewing the universe, and each developed from its premises a coherent set of rules of behavior. Each tended to be blindly committed to its own style of life and regarded all others as evil. The fortunate person who was able to master the art of living in foreign cultures often learned that his own mode of life was only one among many. With this insight he became free to choose from among cultural values those that seemed to best fit his peculiar circumstances.

Cultural norms so completely surround people, so permeate thought and action, that few ever recognize the assumptions on which their lives and their sanity rest. As one observer put it, if birds were suddenly endowed with scientific curiosity they might examine many things, but the sky itself would be overlooked as a suitable subject; if fish were to become curious about the world, it would never occur to them to begin by investigating water. For birds and fish would take the sky and sea for granted, unaware of their profound influence because they comprise the medium for every act. Human beings, in a similar way, occupy a symbolic universe governed by codes that are unconsciously acquired and automatically employed. So much so that they rarely notice that the ways they interpret and talk about events are distinctively different from the ways people conduct their affairs in other cultures.

As long as people remain blind to the sources of their meanings, they are imprisoned within them. These cultural frames of reference are no less confining simply because they cannot be seen or touched. Whether it is an individual neurosis that keeps an individual out of contact with his neighbors, or a collective neurosis that separates neighbors of different cultures, both are forms of blindness that limit what can be experienced and what can be learned from others.

It would seem that everywhere people would desire to break out of the boundaries of their own experiential worlds. Their ability to react sensitively to a wider spectrum of events and peoples requires an overcoming of such cultural parochialism. But, in fact, few attain this broader vision. Some, of course, have little opportunity for wider cultural experience, though this condition should change as the movement of people accelerates. Others do not try to widen their experience because they prefer the old and familiar, seek from their affairs only further confirmation of the correctness of their own values. Still others recoil from such experiences because they feel it dangerous to probe too deeply into the personal or cultural unconscious. Exposure may reveal how tenuous and arbitrary many cultural norms are; such exposure might force people to acquire new bases for interpreting events. And even for the many who do seek actively to enlarge the variety of human beings with whom they are capable of communicating there are still difficulties.

Cultural myopia persists not merely because of inertia and habit, but chiefly because it is so difficult to overcome. One acquires a personality and a culture in childhood, long before he is capable of comprehending either of them. To survive, each person masters the perceptual orientations, cognitive biases, and communicative habits of his own culture. But once mastered, objective assessment of these same processes is awkward since the same mechanisms that are being evaluated must be used in making the evaluations. Once a child learns Japanese or English or Navaho, the categories and grammar of each language predispose him to perceive and think in certain ways, and discourage him from doing so in other ways. When he attempts to discover why he sees or thinks as he does, he uses the same techniques he is trying to identify. Once one becomes an Indian, an Ibo, or a Frenchman—or even a priest or scientist—it is difficult to extricate oneself from that mooring long enough to find out what one truly is or wants.

Fortunately, there may be a way around this paradox. Or promise of a way around it. It is to expose the culturally distinctive ways various peoples construe events and seek to identify the conventions that connect what is seen with what is thought with what is said. Once this cultural grammar is assimilated and the rules that govern the exchange of meanings are known, they can be shared and learned by those who choose to work and live in alien cultures.

When people within a culture face an insurmountable problem they turn to friends, neighbors, associates, for help. To them they explain their predicament, often in distinctive personal ways. Through talking it out, however, there often emerge new ways of looking at the problem, fresh incentive to attack it, and alternative solutions to it. This sort of interpersonal exploration is often successful within a culture for people share at least the same communicative style even if they do not agree completely in their perceptions or beliefs.

When people communicate between cultures, where communicative rules as well as the substance of experience differs, the problems multiply. But so, too, do the number of interpretations and alternatives. If it is true that the more people differ the harder it is for them to understand each other, it is equally true that the more they differ the more they have to teach and learn from each other. To do so, of course, there must be mutual respect and sufficient curiosity to overcome the frustrations that occur as they flounder from one misunderstanding to another. Yet the task of coming to grips with differences in communicative styles—between or within cultures—is prerequisite to all other types of mutuality.

Dynamics

1. Barnlund writes that "It is differences in meaning, far more than mere differences in vocabulary, that isolate cultures...." Consider several passages in which Barnlund attempts to define some aspect of "meaning": where it comes from, how it is produced and transmitted, the factors upon which it depends, etc. How well do his efforts to make meaning of "meaning" work?

2. What relationship(s) does Barnlund see between interpersonal communication and intercultural communication? Focus on a few passages in which Barnlund's discussion moves back and forth between these two modes of communication. How do the similarities and contrasts between these modes complicate Barnlund's overall argument?

Critical Tools

1. Explore a couple of passages that help you understand what Barnlund means by "the assumptive world." Use your understanding to investigate what lies "behind" some of the arguments Barnlund makes in his essay. What do you discover about the "private biases" of Barnlund's "distinctive world" by applying his concept of "the assumptive world" to his own essay?

2. How would you define Barnlund's term, "universe of discourse"? Investigate one of your own "universes": any community to which you belong that has its own ways of looking at the world. Consider the ways that community fosters and transmits its values and perspectives to the members of the group.

3. To overcome "blind[ness] to the sources of [our] meanings," Barnlund says we need experiences which "might force people to acquire new bases for interpreting events." Evaluate your response to another essay you've read that challenged your usual means of interpretation. How might this reading experience help you discover something new about the sources of your meanings?

Draft One/Draft Two

1. *Draft One:* Barnlund says we need to "inhabit a world that is relatively free of ambiguity." Examine how the author of another essay manages ambiguous evidence, arguments, or signals. How do you think the author minimizes or makes use of ambiguity? Use your discussion to help you consider your own response to Barnlund's claim.

    Draft Two: Based on your ideas from draft one, evaluate your own thoughts about ambiguity. How might your analysis of Barnlund and a second essay help you to investigate your management of ambiguous incidents in your own experience?

2. *Draft One:* According to Barnlund, "each society places events in its own cultural frame and it is these frames that bestow the unique meaning...they produce." Use your responses to an essay that makes use of "cultural frames" different from your own. Write an essay in which you examine the kinds of meaning that contrasts in cultural frames can produce.

    Draft Two: Barnlund asserts that "perceptual orientations, systems of belief, and communicative styles do not exist or operate independently." Use some of the specific arguments Barnlund makes about these three elements of meaning-making in order to reevaluate your insights from draft one. What relationships do you see between these three elements in your own process of meaning-making?

❖ ❖ ❖

Before Reading Simone de Beauvoir. . .

1. Consider some of the pressures—direct and indirect—you experience as a woman or as a man. What are some of the gendered expectations placed upon you by your family, peers, co-workers, or other groups to which you belong? Explore your responses to these expectations.

2. Investigate your understanding of the term "feminism." What are some of the values and characteristics you associate with feminist ideas and practices? Use another essay or two to relate your own ideas about gender to your understanding of "feminism."

The Second Sex

Simone de Beauvoir

For a long time I have hesitated to write a book on woman. The subject is irritating, especially to women; and it is not new. Enough ink has been spilled in the quarreling over feminism, now practically over, and perhaps we should say no more about it. It is still talked about, however, for the voluminous nonsense uttered during the last century seems to have done little to illuminate the problem. After all, is there a problem? And if so, what is it? Are there women, really? Most assuredly the theory of the eternal feminine still has its adherents who will whisper in your ear: "Even in Russia women still are *women*"; and other erudite persons—sometimes the very same—say with a sigh: "Woman is losing her way, woman is lost." One wonders if women still exist, if they will always exist, whether or not it is desirable that they should, what place they occupy in this world, what their place should be. "What has become of women?" was asked recently in an ephemeral magazine.[1]

But first we must ask: what is a woman? "*Tota mulier in utero,*" says one, "woman is a womb." But in speaking of certain women, connoisseurs declare that they are not women, although they are equipped with a uterus like the rest. All agree in recognizing the fact that females exist in the human species; today as always they make up about one half of humanity. And yet we are told that femininity is in danger; we are exhorted to be women, remain women, become women. It would appear, then, that every female human being is not necessarily a woman; to be so considered she must share in that mysterious and threatened reality known as femininity. Is this attribute something secreted by the ovaries? Or is it a Platonic essence, a product of the philosophic imagination? Is a rustling petticoat enough to bring it down to earth? Although some women try zealously to incarnate this essence, it is hardly patentable. It is frequently described in vague and dazzling terms that seem to have been borrowed from the vocabulary of the seers, and indeed in the times of St. Thomas it was considered an essence as certainly defined as the somniferous virtue of the poppy.

But conceptualism has lost ground. The biological and social sciences no longer admit the existence of unchangeably fixed entities that determine given characteristics, such as those ascribed to woman, the Jew, or the Negro. Science regards any characteristic as a reaction dependent in part upon a *situation*. If today femininity no longer exists, then it never existed. But does the word *woman*, then, have no specific content? This is stoutly affirmed by those who hold to the philosophy of the enlightenment, of rationalism, of nominalism; women, to them, are merely the human beings arbitrarily designated by the word *woman*. Many American women particularly are prepared to think that there is no longer any place for woman as such; if a backward individual still takes herself for a woman, her friends advise her to be psychoanalyzed and thus get rid of this obsession. In regard to a work, *Modern Woman: The Lost Sex*, which in other respects has its irritating features, Dorothy Parker has written: "I cannot be just to books which treat of woman as woman.... My idea is that all of us, men as well as women, should be regarded as human beings." But nominalism is a rather inadequate doctrine, and the antifemininists have had no trouble in showing that women simply *are not* men. Surely woman is, like man, a human being; but such a declaration is abstract. The fact is that every concrete human being is always a singular, separate individual. To decline to accept such notions as the eternal feminine, the black soul, the Jewish character, is not to deny that Jews, Negroes, women exist today—this denial does not represent a liberation for those concerned, but rather a flight from reality. Some years ago a well-known woman writer refused to permit her portrait to appear in a series of photographs especially devoted to women writers; she wished to be counted among the men. But in order to gain this privilege she made use of her husband's influence! Women who assert that they are men lay claim none the less to masculine consideration and respect. I recall also a young Trotskyite standing on a platform at a boisterous meeting and getting ready to use her fists, in spite of her evident fragility. She was denying her feminine weakness; but it was for love of a militant male whose equal she wished to be. The attitude of defiance of many American women proves that they are haunted by a sense of their femininity. In truth, to go for a walk with one's eyes open is enough to demonstrate that humanity is divided into two classes of individuals whose clothes, faces, bodies, smiles, gaits, interests, and occupations are manifestly different. Perhaps these differences are superficial, perhaps they are destined to disappear. What is certain is that right now they do most obviously exist.

If her functioning as a female is not enough to define woman, if we decline also to explain her through "the eternal feminine," and if nevertheless we admit, provisionally, that women do exist, then we must face the question: what is a woman?

To state the question is, to me, to suggest, at once, a preliminary answer. The fact that I ask it is in itself significant. A man would never get the notion of writing a book on the peculiar situation of the human male.[2] But if I wish to define myself, I must first of all say: "I am a woman"; on this truth must be based all further discussion. A man never begins by presenting himself as an individual of a certain sex; it goes without saying that he is a man. The terms *masculine* and *feminine* are used symmetrically only as a matter of form, as on legal papers. In actuality the relation of the two sexes is not quite like that of two electrical poles, for man represents both the positive and the neutral, as is indicated by the common use of *man* to designate human beings in general; whereas woman represents only the negative, defined by limiting criteria, without reciprocity. In the midst of an abstract discussion it is vexing to hear a man say: "You think thus and so because you are a woman"; but I know that my only defense is to reply: "I think thus and so because it is true," thereby removing my subjective self from the argument. It would be out of the question to reply: "And you think the contrary because you are a man," for it is understood that the fact of being a man is no peculiarity. A man is in the right in being a man; it is the woman who is in the wrong. It amounts to this: just as for the ancients there was an absolute vertical with reference to which the oblique was defined, so there is an absolute human type, the masculine. Woman has ovaries, a uterus; these peculiarities imprison her in her subjectivity, circumscribe her within the limits of her own nature. It is often said that she thinks with her glands. Man superbly ignores the fact that his anatomy also includes glands, such as the testicles, and that they secrete hormones. He thinks of his body as a direct and normal connection with the world, which he believes he apprehends objectively, whereas he regards the body of woman as a hindrance, a prison, weighed down by everything peculiar to it. "The female is a female by virtue of a certain *lack* of qualities," said Aristotle; "we should regard the female nature as afflicted with a natural defectiveness." And St. Thomas for his part pronounced woman to be an "imperfect man," an "incidental" being. This is symbolized in Genesis where Eve is depicted as made from what Bossuet called "a supernumerary bone" of Adam.

Thus humanity is male and man defines woman not in herself but as relative to him; she is not regarded as an autonomous being. Michelet writes: "Woman, the relative being...." And Benda is most positive in his *Rapport d'Uriel*: "The body of man makes sense in itself quite apart from that of woman, whereas the latter seems wanting in significance by itself....Man can think of himself without woman. She cannot think of herself without man." And she is simply what man decrees; thus she is called "the sex," by which is meant that she appears essentially to the male as a sexual being. For him she is sex—absolute sex, no less. She is defined and differentiated with reference to man and not he with reference to her; she is the incidental, the inessential as opposed to the essential. He is the Subject, he is the Absolute—she is the Other.[3]

The category of the *Other* is as primordial as consciousness itself. In the most primitive societies, in the most ancient mythologies, one finds the expression of a duality—that of the Self and the Other. This duality was not originally attached to the division of the sexes; it was not dependent upon any empirical facts. It is revealed in such works as that of Granet on Chinese thought and those of Dumézil on the East Indies and Rome. The feminine element was at first no more involved in such pairs as Varuna-Mitra, Uranus-Zeus, Sun-Moon, and Day-Night than it was in the contrasts between Good and Evil, lucky and unlucky auspices, right and left, God and Lucifer. Otherness is a fundamental category of human thought.

Thus it is that no group ever sets itself up as the One without at once setting up the Other over against itself. If three travelers chance to occupy the same compartment, that is enough to make vaguely hostile "others" out of all the rest of the passengers on the train. In small-town eyes all persons not belonging to the village are "strangers" and suspect; to the native of a country all who inhabit other countries are "foreigners"; Jews are "different" for the anti-Semite, Negroes are "inferior" for American racists, aborigines are "natives" for colonists, proletarians are the "lower class" for the privileged.

Lévi-Strauss, at the end of a profound work on the various forms of primitive societies, reaches the following conclusion: "Passage from the state of Nature to the state of Culture is marked by man's ability to view biological relations as a series of contrasts; duality, alternation, opposition, and symmetry, whether under definite or vague forms, constitute not so much phenomena to be explained as fundamental and immediately given data of social reality." These phenomena would be incomprehensible if in fact human society were simply a *Mitsein* or fellowship based on solidarity and friendliness. Things become clear, on the contrary, if, following Hegel, we find in consciousness itself a fundamental hostility toward every other consciousness; the subject can be posed only in being opposed—he sets himself up as the essential, as opposed to the other, the inessential, the object.

But the other consciousness, the other ego, sets up a reciprocal claim. The native traveling abroad is shocked to find himself in turn regarded as a "stranger" by the natives of neighboring countries. As a matter of fact, wars, festivals, trading, treaties, and contests among tribes, nations, and classes tend to deprive the concept *Other* of its absolute sense and to make manifest its relativity; willy-nilly, individuals and groups are forced to realize the reciprocity of their relations. How is it, then, that this reciprocity has not been recognized between the sexes, that one of the contrasting terms is set up as the sole essential, denying any relativity in regard to its correlative and defining the latter as pure otherness? Why is it that women do not dispute male sovereignty? No subject will readily volunteer to become the object, the inessential; it is not the Other who, in defining himself as the Other, establishes the One. The Other is posed as such by the One in defining himself as the One. But if the Other is not to regain the status of being the One, he must be submissive enough to accept this alien point of view. Whence comes this submission in the case of woman?

There are, to be sure, other cases in which a certain category has been able to dominate another completely for a time. Very often this privilege depends upon inequality of numbers—the majority imposes its rule upon the minority or persecutes it. But women are not a minority, like the American Negroes or the Jews; there are as many women as men on earth. Again, the two groups concerned have often been originally independent; they may have been formerly unaware of each other's existence, or perhaps they recognized each other's autonomy. But a historical event has resulted in the subjugation of the weaker by the stronger. The scattering of the Jews, the introduction of slavery into America, the conquests of imperialism are examples in point. In these cases the oppressed retained at least the memory of former days; they possessed in common a past, a tradition, sometimes a religion or a culture.

The parallel drawn by Bebel between women and the proletariat is valid in that neither ever formed a minority or a separate collective unit of mankind. And instead of a single historical event it is in both cases a historical development that explains their status as a class and accounts for the membership of *particular individuals* in that class. But proletarians have not always existed, whereas there have always been women. They are women in virtue of their anatomy and physiology. Throughout history they have always been subordinated to men, and hence their dependency is not the result of a historical event or a social change—it was not something that *occurred*. The reason why otherness in this case seems to be an absolute is in part that it lacks the contingent or incidental nature of historical facts. A condition brought about at a certain time can be abolished at some other time, as the Negroes of Haiti and others have proved; but it might seem that a natural condition is beyond the possibility of change. In truth, however, the nature of things is no more immutably given, once for all, than is historical reality. If woman seems to be the inessential which never becomes the essential, it is because she herself fails to bring about this change. Proletarians say "We"; Negroes also. Regarding themselves as subjects, they transform the bourgeois, the whites, into "others." But women do not say "We," except at some congress of feminists or similar formal demonstration; men say "women," and women use the same word in referring to themselves. They do not authentically assume a subjective attitude. The proletarians have accomplished the revolution in Russia, the Negroes in Haiti, the Indo-Chinese are battling for it in Indo-China; but the women's effort has never been anything more than a symbolic agitation. They have gained only what men have been willing to grant; they have taken nothing, they have only received.

The reason for this is that women lack concrete means for organizing themselves into a unit which can stand face to face with the correlative unit. They have no past, no history, no religion of their own; and they have no such solidarity of work and interest as that of the proletariat. They are not even promiscuously herded together in the way that creates community feeling among the American Negroes, the ghetto Jews, the workers of Saint-Denis, or the factory hands of Renault. They live dispersed among the males, attached through residence, housework, economic condition, and social standing to certain men—fathers or husbands—more firmly than they are to other women. If they belong to the bourgeoisie, they feel solidarity with men of that class, not with proletarian women; if they are white, their allegiance is to white men, not to Negro women. The proletariat can propose to massacre the ruling class, and a sufficiently fanatical Jew or Negro might dream of getting sole possession of the atomic bomb and making humanity wholly Jewish or black; but woman cannot even dream of exterminating the males. The bond that unites her to her oppressors is not comparable to any other. The division of the sexes is a biological fact, not an event in human history. Male and female stand opposed

within a primordial *Mitsein*, and woman has not broken it. The couple is a fundamental unity with its two halves riveted together, and the cleavage of society along
the line of sex is impossible. Here is to be found the basic trait of woman: she is the
Other in a totality of which the two components are necessary to one another.

One could suppose that this reciprocity might have facilitated the liberation of
woman. When Hercules sat at the feet of Omphale and helped with her spinning, his
desire for her held him captive; but why did she fail to gain a lasting power? To
revenge herself on Jason, Medea killed their children; and this grim legend would
seem to suggest that she might have obtained a formidable influence over him
through his love for his offspring. In *Lysistrata* Aristophanes gaily depicts a band of
women who joined forces to gain social ends through the sexual needs of their men;
but this is only a play. In the legend of the Sabine women, the latter soon abandoned
their plan of remaining sterile to punish their ravishers. In truth woman has not
been socially emancipated through man's need—sexual desire and the desire for
offspring—which makes the male dependent for satisfaction upon the female.

Master and slave, also, are united by a reciprocal need, in this case economic,
which does not liberate the slave. In the relation of master to slave the master does
not make a point of the need that he has for the other; he has in his grasp the power
of satisfying this need through his own action; whereas the slave, in his dependent
condition, his hope and fear, is quite conscious of the need he has for his master.
Even if the need is at bottom equally urgent for both, it always works in favor of the
oppressor and against the oppressed. That is why the liberation of the working class,
for example, has been slow.

Now, woman has always been man's dependent, if not his slave; the two sexes
have never shared the world in equality. And even today woman is heavily handicapped, though her situation is beginning to change. Almost nowhere is her legal
status the same as man's,[4] and frequently it is much to her disadvantage. Even
when her rights are legally recognized in the abstract, long-standing custom prevents their full expression in the mores. In the economic sphere men and women can
almost be said to make up two castes; other things being equal, the former hold the
better jobs, get higher wages, and have more opportunity for success than their new
competitors. In industry and politics men have a great many more positions and
they monopolize the most important posts. In addition to all this, they enjoy a
traditional prestige that the education of children tends in every way to support, for
the present enshrines the past—and in the past all history has been made by men.
At the present time, when women are beginning to take part in the affairs of the
world, it is still a world that belongs to men—they have no doubt of it at all and
women have scarcely any. To decline to be the Other, to refuse to be a party to the
deal—this would be for women to renounce all the advantages conferred upon them
by their alliance with the superior caste. Man-the-sovereign will provide woman-the-
liege with material protection and will undertake the moral justification of her
existence; thus she can evade at once both economic risk and the metaphysical risk
of a liberty in which ends and aims must be contrived without assistance. Indeed,

along with the ethical urge of each individual to affirm his subjective existence, there is also the temptation to forgo liberty and become a thing. This is an inauspicious road, for he who takes it—passive, lost, ruined—becomes henceforth the creature of another's will, frustrated in his transcendence and deprived of every value. But it is an easy road; on it one avoids the strain involved in undertaking an authentic existence. When man makes of woman the *Other*, he may, then, expect her to manifest deep-seated tendencies toward complicity. Thus, woman may fail to lay claim to the status of subject because she lacks definite resources, because she feels the necessary bond that ties her to man regardless of reciprocity, and because she is often very well pleased with her role as the *Other*.

NOTES

1. *Franchise,* dead today.

2. The Kinsey Report [Alfred C. Kinsey and others: *Sexual Behavior in the Human Male* (W. B. Saunders Co., 1948)] is no exception, for it is limited to describing the sexual characteristics of American men, which is quite a different matter.

3. E. Lévinas expresses this idea most explicitly in his essay *Temps et l'Autre.* "Is there not a case in which otherness, alterity [*altérité*], unquestionably marks the nature of a being, as its essence, an instance of otherness not consisting purely and simply in the opposition of two species of the same genus? I think that the feminine represents the contrary in its absolute sense, this contrariness being in no wise affected by any relation between it and its correlative and thus remaining absolutely other. Sex is not a certain specific difference...no more is the sexual difference a mere contradiction....Nor does this difference lie in the duality of two complementary terms, for two complementary terms imply a pre-existing whole....Otherness reaches its full flowering in the feminine, a term of the same rank as consciousness but of opposite meaning."

I suppose that Lévinas does not forget that woman, too, is aware of her own consciousness, or ego. But it is striking that he deliberately takes a man's point of view, disregarding the reciprocity of subject and object. When he writes that woman is mystery, he implies that she is mystery for man. Thus his description, which is intended to be objective, is in fact an assertion of masculine privilege.

4. At the moment [1952] an "equal rights" amendment to the Constitution of the United States is before Congress.—TRANSLATOR

Dynamics

1. For the purposes of her essay, de Beauvoir wants to "admit, provisionally, that women do exist." Look at several passages in which de Beauvoir works with "provisional" arguments about "women." Explore the advantages and disadvantages of working "provisionally." How does provisionality complicate her arguments about gender?

2. De Beauvoir claims that "along with the ethical urge of each individual to affirm his subjective existence, there is also the temptation to forego liberty and become a thing." Respond to this claim by examining a few passages in which you see this tension between affirming one's "self" and asserting one's "thingness." What do you think about her use of this tension in developing her argument?

Critical Tools

1. Locate some of the dualities of "self" and "other" de Beauvoir makes use of. How does she revise the general concept of "duality" in order to make it appropriate for examining different groups of people? Choose an essay that you believe can be read usefully in terms of "duality," and consider the kinds of revisions you have to make as you apply this critical tool to the second essay. What insights do you produce?

2. De Beauvoir suggests that women lack the "definite resources" needed to claim status as "subjects" rather than "others." Work with another essay that broaches issues of "othering" (even if it doesn't use that term). How do the perspectives from the second essay help you evaluate de Beauvoir's suggestion? Explore your ideas in terms of your own experience of gender.

Draft One/Draft Two

1. *Draft One:* Define your understanding of "reciprocity" in de Beauvoir's essay. Examine the degrees and kinds of reciprocity in one or two relationships you have with other people. How does the issue of reciprocity in these interactions affect the way you see them?

   Draft Two: What are some of the reasons different kinds of relationships are marked by different kinds of reciprocity, or perhaps none at all? Use your analysis of reciprocity from your own experience to reconsider an important relationship in another reading. Why do you believe that relationship takes the forms it does?

2. *Draft One:* De Beauvoir asserts that "the nature of things is no more immutably given, once for all, than is historical reality." Consider the ways she employs the tension between the "natural" and the "historical" in her discussion of gender. What does it mean to view something as either natural or historical? Relate her use of these concepts to your own ideas about what can or cannot be altered in gender relationships.

   Draft Two: Reconsider your ideas about the "natural" and the "historical" in light of another reading that addresses a similar issue. How might your juxtaposition of these readings encourage you to investigate something that you had accepted as natural?

❖ ❖ ❖

Before Reading Robert Bellah et al. . . .

1. In this essay Robert Bellah and his colleagues speculate on different meanings
    for the terms *community*, *individuality*, *private life*, and *public life*. Based on
    your experience and observations, what range of meanings can each of these
    terms have? What outcomes might follow for individuals and communities that
    define these concepts differently? What is the relation between the terms?

2. In this essay Bellah challenges one fairly common notion of individualism. What
    evidence would you need to see to find a criticism of individualism persuasive?
    Why?

Community, Commitment, and Individuality

Robert Bellah, et al.

Les Newman, very much a middle-class American, has found a home in the church, one that allows him to take a critical view of the environing society. He says that "American society is becoming very self-oriented; or very individual-oriented: what's in it for me, how much do I get out of it, am I getting everything I'm entitled to in my life? It is tearing down a lot that is right about the country. People don't look at the repercussions of their individual actions outside of themselves."

For this evangelical Baptist, reared in the South, just graduated from a well-known business school, and now working as an executive in the California suburbs, such sweeping criticism becomes more specific in characterizing his fellow-alumni. Most of them "felt they didn't need God, didn't need religion. There was a strong impression in business school, the self-made individual, being able to do it all yourself if you just work hard enough and think hard enough, and not having to rely on other people." It is precisely because such self-made individuals don't appreciate their need for God that they don't appreciate their need for other people, Les Newman observes. He experiences both needs in the active life of his church congregation. Its members aren't "the standard go-to-church-Sunday-morning people" who practice "a ritual as opposed to a lifestyle." For them religion is more than just saying "Here's a set of morals to live by and here's this great example of 2,000 years ago." The heart of their shared life and teaching "is that Jesus Christ is a person. He's alive today, to relate to today. He works in your life today, and you can talk to Him through the week in prayer." Church for this believer, therefore, "isn't just a place, it's a family" that has given him the closest friends he has. Despite leaving home, moving to California, and entering the competitive world of business, he has found a new family-like anchor for his life, a new bond to other people through the shared celebration of a "personal relationship with Jesus Christ."

In this traditional Christian view, what connects one self to another is the objectively given reality of their creation as God's children and God's own continuing presence in the world in Jesus Christ. This reality is one each person freely accepts, thus establishing the bonds of the Christian congregation while affirming individual identity. Reflecting on this process of self-integration, the Baptist businessman testifies, "I got my personal Christian relationship with Jesus and that has sort of been the ongoing thing that has tied together a whole bunch of different things. That relationship with Christ has changed me somewhat as an individual when it comes to my outlook on the world. He is the person who has steadied my emotion. Before, I was kind of unstable, and I've had some pretty good lows, and now I find that doesn't happen. It has strengthened my commitment in my marriage, and it's had a great deal of impact on the way I relate to other people at work. My life is such a combination of disjointed events. My childhood was just a whole series of moves." Relating oneself to Christ, even in the disjointed course of social uprooting and cultural conflict, yields an experience of the self's integrity.

His church community has helped Les Newman find a language and a set of practices that have strengthened his marriage, aided him in dealing with his work situation, and given him a more coherent sense of self, as well as providing him with some critical distance from the environing society. Ted Oster, whom we met in chapter 4, has no such community and seems much more at ease in the first language of modern individualism, a language he uses to explain most of what goes on around him. Yet when pressed to explain why he remains in a long marriage, his several attempts to do so in cost/benefit terms finally break down. His happiness with his wife comes from "proceeding through all these stages of life together. . . . It makes life meaningful and gives me the opportunity to share with somebody, have an anchor, if you will, and understand where I am. That for me is a real relationship." Here Ted Oster seems to be groping for words that could express his marriage as a community of memory and hope, a place where he is not empty, but which essentially defines who he is. It is as though he had to invent a second language out of the failing fragments of his usual first language.

Although we did not see it in the case of Ted Oster, and only tentatively in the case of Les Newman, communities of memory, though often embedded in family experiences, are an important way in which individuals are led into public life. Angelo Donatello, a successful small businessman who has become a civic leader in a suburb of Boston, tells how a reluctant concern for the ethnic heritage rooted in his family finally led him into public life: "One of the important things that got me into politics was that I was a confused individual. I came from a real old-fashioned Italian family in East Boston. We spoke both languages at home, but I was more Americanized than my brothers or sisters, so to speak. We were forgetting our heritage—that meant becoming more free, more liberal, being able to express myself differently. Thirteen or fourteen years ago, there was a group of people in town who talked about forming a chapter of the Sons of Italy. I would not have been one of the first ones to propose such a thing. My wife was Irish—I was one of the first ones in my family to marry out. But I went to these meetings. Before I had gotten into this I had forgotten my heritage." What catalyzed Angelo's involvement was the unexpected appearance of prejudice when the group tried to buy a piece of land for the Sons of Italy hall. In fighting the opposition, which seemed to focus on the belief that Italians are drunken and rowdy, Angelo became involved with the town government. Remembering his heritage involved accepting his origins, including painful memories of prejudice and discrimination that his earlier efforts at "Americanization" had attempted to deny.

The experience of ethnic prejudice helped Angelo see that there is more to life than leaving behind the past, becoming successful on his own, and expressing himself freely. But as he became more involved with the community he had tried to forget—more active, that is, in the Sons of Italy—he also became more involved with his town. Elected a selectman, he saw it his duty to represent not only Italian-Americans but also the welfare of the town as a whole. Abandoning one kind of individualism, he was led toward a civic individualism that entailed care for the affairs of his community in both the narrower and wider senses. While leaving behind "Americanization," he became American.

Marra James provides an interesting contrast to Angelo Donatello. Born in a small town in West Virginia, she has lived for some years in a Southern California suburb, where she has become active in a variety of causes focussing around environmental issues such as saving wild land from development. Marra was raised in the Catholic church and was active in her parish when she first came to California. She does not go to church anymore as she has gone beyond what she calls "structural religion." Yet she has carried a sensitivity to ritual over into her new concerns. She dates her involvement in the environmental movement from the celebration of the first Earth Day at a local college, and she was, when interviewed some ten years later, actively planning the local tenth anniversary celebration.

Marra has a strong and explicit understanding of the importance of community: "Many people feel empty and don't know why they feel empty. The reason is we are all social animals and we must live and interact and work together in community to become fulfilled." But she sees serious impediments to the realization of community in America: "Most people have been sold a bill of goods by our system. I call it the Three C's: cash, convenience, consumerism. It's getting worse. The reason you don't feel a part of it is that nobody is a part of it. Loneliness is a national feeling." But Marra has not reacted to this realization with despair. She is intensely active and returns to the fray whether she wins or loses. In her years as city council member and chair of a county planning commission, she has suffered plenty of defeats. "I sometimes describe myself as a rubber ball," she says. "I've been pushed down sometimes to where I've almost been pressed flat, but I've always been able to bounce back." For Marra, politics is a worthwhile educational endeavor, win or lose, perhaps especially when you lose.

Marra James is remarkable in the scope with which she defines her community: "I feel very much a part of the whole—of history. I live in a spectrum that includes the whole world. I'm a part of all of it. For what I do impacts the whole. So if I'm going to be wasteful, misuse resources—that will impact the whole world."

Marra identifies herself as a moderate Republican, but her politics go beyond any such label. For her, the "whole world" is a community of memory and hope and entails practices of commitment that she assiduously carries out. Undoubtedly, there has been involvement in many communities along the way, each one important in constituting her as the person she is—her family, the church, the network of her fellow environmental activists. In trying to give substance to what is as yet an aspiration by defining her community as the whole world, she runs the risk of becoming detached from any concrete community of memory.

Finally, let us consider the example of Cecilia Dougherty, in whose life a series of communities of memory have played a part in leading to her present political commitment in ways even clearer than in the case of Marra James. Cecilia lives in a part of Santa Monica whose landscape is shaped by shade trees, schools, and churches. She, like Wayne Bauer, is an active member of the Campaign for Economic Democracy. At present she works for a local attorney involved in progressive causes, and in addition serves as an elected official of city government. Despite these rather daunting commitments, Cecilia is the single mother of four teenagers, her husband having died several years ago, an event that was for her at once traumatic and transformative.

Cecilia Dougherty began her political activism in her forties following the great break caused in the continuity of her life by her husband's death. She started out by working on the congressional campaign of a local candidate, in part because his opponent supported many things she opposed, but also to try out her capacities to engage in political life on her own. Cecilia had begun to think about taking more public initiative while her husband was living.

The critical event was meeting a colleague of her husband, a woman of their age, who told Cecilia that having heard good things about her from her husband, she was eager to learn more about her. Cecilia says that she began, "I have four children . . ." but the woman persisted, saying, "Wait just a minute. I didn't ask about your children, I asked about you. Where are *you* coming from?" At this Cecilia was stunned. "I mean, my role was a housewife and I didn't quite grasp what she was really talking about." But the woman told her: "I'm not talking about your identity as Greg's wife. I'm concerned with your identity as a human being, as a person, and as an individual, and as a woman." She invited Cecilia to join a consciousness-raising group, "a turning point in my life, a real change for me."

Once into the consciousness-raising group, Cecilia Dougherty experienced herself as waking up as if from a sleep, reaching back to hopes and aspirations she had had as a girl, before becoming a wife and mother. Cecilia rediscovered that she had wanted to become a teacher, and at first thought about going to college to fulfill that dream. She was already working as a clerk for a labor union, however, and she decided to tailor her educational aspirations around that. "I decided that I would work with what I had already." Whatever earlier "gut feelings" Cecilia may have discovered in consciousness raising, her decision to build on the past, on what she "had already," is characteristic of the way she has acted on her new sense of freedom and efficacy.

In fact, for all their importance as catalysts, contact with feminist consciousness raising and discovering her identity "as a person and as an individual" have not been the determining factors in Cecilia Dougherty's activist commitments. Rather, as she describes it, the new sense of efficacy that she learned from consciousness raising in a real sense returned her to earlier commitments and an identification with the cause of the dignity of working people that was deeply rooted in her family's experience. Her sense of purpose in political involvement is not based simply on radical individualism but grounded in the continuity of generations: "I want to see the have-nots have power that reflects their numbers, and I want to protect the future of my children and my grandchildren. I feel a historical family responsibility for continuing to be working for progressive causes."

When Cecilia was asked to explain her commitment to activism, she responded, characteristically, with the story of how her ideals of self developed through the experience of her family. That is, she employed a "second language" that organizes life by reference to certain ideals of character-virtues such as courage and honor—and commitments to institutions that are seen as embodiments of those values. For example, Cecilia's feminism is in part emulation of her mother in a different context. Her mother was an Italian immigrant who married at eighteen and did not go to college, but became the first woman in her county to be elected chair of the state Democratic Central Committee. "So," commented Cecilia, "she made me realize a commitment at a very early age. By eight years old, I was working in party headquarters, licking stamps and answering the phone."

But the paradigmatic event that gave Cecilia a deep sense of identity with the labor movement and its goals of a more just and inclusive society involved her father. When Cecilia was fourteen, her father, an Irish Catholic immigrant working for an energy corporation, went on strike. This was shortly after World War II. Cecilia vividly recalls the weeks of the strike, especially the union solidarity that got the family through it. "We went every night to the town where the union hall was," she recounted, "for dinner in the soup kitchen kind of thing, and my mother would help cook." However, the decisive event occurred six weeks into the strike, when her father was arrested on charges of throwing rocks at strikebreakers.

The shock was that Cecilia's father "who'd been such a good citizen; so honest, and so conscientious, the American-way type person" should be not only arrested, but attacked in court as a communist and rabble-rouser. The revelation of the low tactics of the corporation's lawyers had a strong impact on her, resulting in a sense of moral outrage that continues to frame her political concerns. She was also deeply impressed by her father's courage and sense of honor under attack by the "company attorneys, with their suits and everything." Most of all, she was impressed by the strength of the solidarity in the labor movement. "I realized then the value of the union and how we were utterly dependent on the union for our very sustenance."

Thus when Cecilia Dougherty returned to politics in the Democratic party, and when she decided to become heavily involved in local activism, she could, and did, draw upon a considerable heritage. She describes her transition from working wife and mother to her present, much more public involvements not so much as a choice—in the sense that one might choose to take up painting versus taking up bowling—but as a response to part of her identity, as fulfilling a responsibility to which her life, her heritage, and her beliefs have called her.

Asked what she sees her activism achieving, Cecilia responded by saying that she hopes to "bring people away from concern only about their own lives, to a sense of much, much broader, greater responsibility. It sounds very grandiose! Probably the most I'm going to be able to do is sustain and build better community in Santa Monica, you know, and that's certainly a life's work." The image of community contained in Cecilia's account of the strike is quite different from the association of like-minded individuals advocated by others we talked to.

The fundamental contrasts between Cecilia Dougherty's self-understanding and the first language of modern individualism can be narrowed to three. First, Cecilia articulates her sense of self by reference to a narrative illustrative of long-term commitments rather than desires and feelings. While she sees certain breaks with her past as crucial "turning points" in her life, she interprets the resulting freedom as an opportunity for new commitments, often "working from what I had already." Thus, unlike the radical individualistic notion of a life course based on leaving home in order to become a free self, Cecilia's self-image is rooted in a concept of the virtues that make an admirable life, especially those exemplified in the lives of her mother and father. This is the second contrast: that her sense of self is rooted in virtues that define a worthwhile life and have been passed on and modeled by others who have shared that tradition, not in a contentless freedom attained by leaving concrete commitments behind.

The third distinguishing feature of Cecilia's "second language" is her notion that community means a solidarity based on a responsibility to care for others because that is essential to living a good life. She describes her solidarity with working people and "the have-nots" as an expression of a concern for human dignity, the violation of which sparked her first anger at the abuse of power. This sense of a community of solidarity recalls the classical civic contrast between the private person who thinks first of himself alone and the citizen who knows himself to be a participant in a form of life through which his own identity is fulfilled. The civic vision is quite different from the image of a gathering of like-minded individuals whose union depends entirely on their spontaneous interest. Indeed, thinking about this contrast tends to confirm Tocqueville's claim that public order and trust cannot spring from individual spontaneity alone, but require the kind of cultivation that only active civic life can provide.

The lived source of the civic language in Cecilia Dougherty's life is not hard to identify: it was her and her parents' lifelong commitments to the labor movement. It was probably reinforced by a similar emphasis on solidarity in the Catholicism she shared with parents and husband. It is this that she has been able to expand into a general concern for "economic democracy."

It is characteristic of Cecilia Dougherty and the others we have just considered that they define themselves through their commitments to a variety of communities rather than through the pursuit of radical autonomy. Yet Cecilia, like the others, exhibits a high degree of self-determination and efficacy. She exemplifies a form of individualism that is fulfilled *in* community rather than against it. Conformism, the nemesis of American individualism, does not seem to be a problem for Cecilia and the others. Their involvement in practices of commitment makes them able to resist pressures to conform. On occasion, they show great resilience in so doing, as when Marra James bounces back after being "pressed flat." Our examples suggest that Tocqueville was probably right in believing that it was isolation, not social involvement, that led to conformism and the larger danger of authoritarian manipulation.

There are authoritarian groups in the United States, sometimes devoted to destructive ends. What makes them different from genuine communities is the shallowness and distortion of their memory and the narrowness of what they hope for. A radically isolating individualism is not a defense against such coercive groups. On the contrary, the loneliness that results from isolation may precipitate the "hunger for authority" on which such groups feed.

Sometimes Americans make a rather sharp dichotomy between private and public life. Viewing one's primary task as "finding oneself" in autonomous self-reliance, separating oneself not only from one's parents but also from those larger communities and traditions that constitute one's past, leads to the notion that it is in oneself, perhaps in relation to a few intimate others, that fulfillment is to be found. Individualism of this sort often implies a negative view of public life. The impersonal forces of the economic and political worlds are what the individual needs protection against. In this perspective, even occupation, which has been so central to the identity of Americans in the past, becomes instrumental—not a good in itself, but only a means to the attainment of a rich and satisfying private life. But on the basis of what we have seen in our observation of middle-class American life, it would seem that this quest for purely private fulfillment is illusory: it often ends in emptiness instead. On the other hand, we found many people, some of whom we introduced earlier in this chapter, for whom private fulfillment and public involvement are not antithetical. These people evince an individualism that is not empty but is full of content drawn from an active identification with communities and traditions. Perhaps the notion that private life and public life are at odds is incorrect. Perhaps they are so deeply involved with each other that the impoverishment of one entails the impoverishment of the other. Parker Palmer is probably right when he says that "in a healthy society the private and the public are not mutually exclusive, not in competition with each other. They are, instead, two halves of a whole, two poles of a paradox. They work together dialectically, helping to create and nurture one another."

Certainly this dialectical relationship is clear where public life degenerates into violence and fear. One cannot live a rich private life in a state of siege, mistrusting all strangers and turning one's home into an armed camp. A minimum of public decency and civility is a precondition for a fulfilling private life. On the other hand, public involvement is often difficult and demanding. To engage successfully in the public world, one needs personal strength and the support of family and friends. A rewarding private life is one of the preconditions for a healthy public life.

For all their doubts about the public sphere, Americans are more engaged in voluntary associations and civic organizations than the citizens of most other industrial nations. In spite of all the difficulties, many Americans feel they must "get involved." In public life as in private, we can discern the habits of the heart that sustain individualism and commitment, as well as what makes them problematic.

❖ ❖ ❖

Dynamics

1. Bellah notices certain tensions or dichotomies or even contradictions in the lives of the people he studies. Marra James, for example, has come to resist regular church attendance, part of what she calls "structural religion," yet she remains interested in public rituals like the Earth Day celebration. Locate several tensions in the individuals Bellah discusses, and discuss them. What do they suggest to you about the psychology of these individuals, or about the issues that interest Bellah? What role do these tensions ordinarily play in people's lives?

2. Compile one or more details from the story of each person Bellah describes that help you understand what a "community of memory and hope" is. Are you as satisfied with this kind of community as a social value as Bellah seems to be? Discuss your reactions.

Critical Tools

1. More than once in this essay Bellah notes that an individual has found a way to "take a critical view of the environing society." Locate several individuals in this essay who manage to "take a critical view," and examine passages where this critical view is described or implied. Compose a theory of "criticism" that addresses these questions: what makes it possible for an individual to take a critical view? what is the social value of criticism?

2. Bellah places much emphasis on the idea that a person may "invent a second language out of the failing fragments of his usual first language." Compile a list of phrases and sentences from different parts of the essay that show this process in action, and then discuss what each of them tell you about the process by which a person may invent a second language out of the fragments of the first.

Draft One/Draft Two

Draft One: Choose another text you have read this semester that explores the relation between an individual and a wider community, such as the essays by Shirley Brice Heath or Maxine Hong Kingston. Use several of Bellah's main terms or ideas to explore the events of that other text. Which details of the narrative would Bellah find important, and why? What does Bellah help you say about this other text?

Draft Two: Consider the concluding paragraphs of Bellah's essay in light of the most troubling aspects of the other text. What events or ideas in the other text most successfully challenge Bellah's argument about the proper relation of public and private life, of individual and community? Can you extend Bellah's theory to meet these challenges, or must his theory be replaced? Compose the revision to Bellah that will address the challenges you located in the other text.

❖ ❖ ❖

Before Reading Bruno Bettelheim. . .

1. What strategies do you use to cope with difficult psychological and emotional experiences? As you evaluate your management of one or two such experiences, investigate which strategies effectively contributed to some kind of resolution and which strategies seem to have served some other purpose(s).

2. Think about some books or movies you have encountered recently. How do the different kinds of endings (for instance, happy, tragic, unresolved, etc.) affect your responses to them? Explore why you find certain kinds of endings satisfying and others dissatisfying.

The Ignored Lesson of Anne Frank

Bruno Bettelheim

When the world first learned about the Nazi concentration and death camps, most civilized people felt the horrors committed in them to be so uncanny as to be unbelievable. It came as a severe shock that supposedly civilized nations could stoop to such inhuman acts. The implication that modern man has such inadequate control over his cruel and destructive proclivities was felt as a threat to our views of ourselves and our humanity. Three different psychological mechanisms were most frequently used for dealing with the appalling revelation of what had gone on in the camps:

> (1) its applicability to man in general was denied by asserting—contrary to evidence—that the acts of torture and mass murder were committed by a small group of insane or perverted persons;
>
> (2) the truth of the reports was denied by declaring them vastly exaggerated and ascribing them to propaganda (this originated with the German government, which called all reports on terror in the camps "horror propaganda"—*Greuelpropaganda*);
>
> (3) the reports were believed, but the knowledge of the horror repressed as soon as possible.

All three mechanisms could be seen at work after liberation of those prisoners remaining. At first, after the discovery of the camps and their death-dealing, a wave of extreme outrage swept the Allied nations. It was soon followed by a general repression of the discovery in people's minds. Possibly this reaction was due to something more than the blow dealt to modern man's narcissism by the realization that cruelty is still rampant among men. Also present may have been the dim but extremely threatening realization that the modern state now has available the means for changing personality, and for destroying millions it deems undesirable. The ideas that in our day a people's personalities might be changed against their will by the state, and that other populations might be wholly or partially exterminated, are so fearful that one tries to free oneself of them and their impact by defensive denial, or by repression.

The extraordinary world-wide success of the book, play, and movie The *Diary of Anne Frank* suggests the power of the desire to counteract the realization of the personality-destroying and murderous nature of the camps by concentrating all attention on what is experienced as a demonstration that private and intimate life can continue to flourish even under the direct persecution by the most ruthless totalitarian system. And this although Anne Frank's fate demonstrates how efforts at disregarding in private life what goes on around one in society can hasten one's own destruction.

What concerns me here is not what actually happened to the Frank family, how they tried—and failed—to survive their terrible ordeal. It would be very wrong to take apart so humane and moving a story, which aroused so much well-merited compassion for gentle Anne Frank and her tragic fate. What is at issue is the universal and uncritical response to her diary and to the play and movie based on it, and what this reaction tells about our attempts to cope with the feelings her fate— used by us to serve as a symbol of a most human reaction to Nazi terror—arouses in us. I believe that the world-wide acclaim given her story cannot be explained unless we recognize in it our wish to forget the gas chambers, and our effort to do so by glorifying the ability to retreat into an extremely private, gentle, sensitive world, and there to cling as much as possible to what have been one's usual daily attitudes and activities, although surrounded by a maelstrom apt to engulf one at any moment.

The Frank family's attitude that life could be carried on as before may well have been what led to their destruction. By eulogizing how they lived in their hiding place while neglecting to examine first whether it was a reasonable or an effective choice, we are able to ignore the crucial lesson of their story—that such an attitude can be fatal in extreme circumstances.

While the Franks were making their preparations for going passively into hiding, thousands of other Jews in Holland (as elsewhere in Europe) were trying to escape to the free world, in order to survive and/or fight. Others who could not escape went underground—into hiding—each family member with, for example, a different gentile family. We gather from the diary, however, that the chief desire of the Frank family was to continue living as nearly as possible in the same fashion to which they had been accustomed in happier times.

Little Anne, too, wanted only to go on with life as usual, and what else could she have done but fall in with the pattern her parents created for her existence? But hers was not a necessary fate, much less a heroic one; it was a terrible but also a senseless fate. Anne had a good chance to survive, as did many Jewish children in Holland. But she would have had to leave her parents and go to live with a gentile Dutch family, posing as their own child, something her parents would have had to arrange for her.

Everyone who recognized the obvious knew that the hardest way to go underground was to do it as a family; to hide out together made detection by the SS most likely; and when detected, everybody was doomed. By hiding singly, even when one got caught, the others had a chance to survive. The Franks, with their excellent connections among gentile Dutch families, might well have been able to hide out singly, each with a different family. But instead, the main principle of their planning was continuing their beloved family life—an understandable desire, but highly unrealistic in those times. Choosing any other course would have meant not merely giving up living together, but also realizing the full measure of the danger to their lives.

The Franks were unable to accept that going on living as a family as they had done before the Nazi invasion of Holland was no longer a desirable way of life, much as they loved each other; in fact, for them and others like them, it was most dangerous behavior. But even given their wish not to separate, they failed to make appropriate preparations for what was likely to happen.

There is little doubt that the Franks, who were able to provide themselves with so much while arranging for going into hiding, and even while hiding, could have provided themselves with some weapons had they wished. Had they had a gun, Mr. Frank could have shot down at least one or two of the "green police" who came for them. There was no surplus of such police, and the loss of an SS with every Jew arrested would have noticeably hindered the functioning of the police state. Even a butcher knife, which they certainly could have taken with them into hiding, could have been used by them in self-defense. The fate of the Franks wouldn't have been very different, because they all died anyway except for Anne's father. But they could have sold their lives for a high price, instead of walking to their death. Still, although one must assume that Mr. Frank would have fought courageously, as we know he did when a soldier in the first World War, it is not everybody who can plan to kill those who are bent on killing him, although many who would not be ready to contemplate doing so would be willing to kill those who are bent on murdering not only them but also their wives and little daughters.

An entirely different matter would have been planning for escape in case of discovery. The Franks' hiding place had only one entrance; it did not have any other exit. Despite this fact, during their many months of hiding, they did not try to devise one. Nor did they make other plans for escape, such as that one of the family members—as likely as not Mr. Frank—would try to detain the police in the narrow entrance way—maybe even fight them, as suggested above—thus giving other members of the family a chance to escape, either by reaching the roofs of adjacent houses, or down a ladder into the alley behind the house in which they were living.

Any of this would have required recognizing and accepting the desperate straits in which they found themselves, and concentrating on how best to cope with them. This was quite possible to do, even under the terrible conditions in which the Jews found themselves after the Nazi occupation of Holland. It can be seen from many other accounts, for example from the story of Marga Minco, a girl of about Anne Frank's age who lived to tell about it. Her parents had planned that when the police should come for them, the father would try to detain them by arguing and fighting with them, to give the wife and daughter a chance to escape through a rear door. Unfortunately it did not quite work out this way, and both parents got killed. But their short-lived resistance permitted their daughter to make her escape as planned and to reach a Dutch family who saved her.[1]

This is not mentioned as a criticism that the Frank family did not plan or behave along similar lines. A family has every right to arrange their life as they wish or think best, and to take the risks they want to take. My point is not to criticize what the Franks did, but only the universal admiration of their way of coping, or rather of not coping. The story of little Marga who survived, every bit as touching, remains totally neglected by comparison.

Many Jews—unlike the Franks, who through listening to British radio news were better informed than most—had no detailed knowledge of the extermination camps. Thus it was easier for them to make themselves believe that complete compliance with even the most outrageously debilitating and degrading Nazi orders might offer a chance for survival. But neither tremendous anxiety that inhibits clear thinking and with it well-planned and determined action, nor ignorance about what happened to those who responded with passive waiting for being rounded up for their extermination, can explain the reaction of audiences to the play and movie retelling Anne's story, which are all about such waiting that results finally in destruction.

I think it is the fictitious ending that explains the enormous success of this play and movie. At the conclusion we hear Anne's voice from the beyond, saying, "In spite of everything, I still believe that people are really good at heart." This improbable sentiment is supposedly from a girl who had been starved to death, had watched her sister meet the same fate before she did, knew that her mother had been murdered, and had watched untold thousands of adults and children being killed. This statement is not justified by anything Anne actually told her diary.

Going on with intimate family living, no matter how dangerous it might be to survival, was fatal to all too many during the Nazi regime. And if all men are good, then indeed we can all go on with living our lives as we have been accustomed to in times of undisturbed safety and can afford to forget about Auschwitz. But Anne, her sister, her mother, may well have died because her parents could not get themselves to believe in Auschwitz.

While play and movie are ostensibly about Nazi persecution and destruction, in actuality what we watch is the way that, despite this terror, lovable people manage to continue living their satisfying intimate lives with each other. The heroine grows from a child into a young adult as normally as any other girl would, despite the most abnormal conditions of all other aspects of her existence, and that of her family. Thus the play reassures us that despite the destructiveness of Nazi racism and tyranny in general, it is possible to disregard it in one's private life much of the time, even if one is Jewish.

True, the ending happens just as the Franks and their friends had feared all along: their hiding place is discovered, and they are carried away to their doom. But the fictitious declaration of faith in the goodness of all men which concludes the play falsely reassures us since it impresses on us that in the combat between Nazi terror and continuance of intimate family living the latter wins out, since Anne has the last word. This is simply contrary to fact, because it was she who got killed. Her seeming survival through her moving statement about the goodness of men releases us effectively of the need to cope with the problems Auschwitz presents. That is why we are so relieved by her statement. It explains why millions loved the play and movie, because while it confronts us with the fact that Auschwitz existed it encourages us at the same time to ignore any of its implications. If all men are good at heart, there never really was an Auschwitz; nor is there any possibility that it may recur.

The desire of Anne Frank's parents not to interrupt their intimate family living, and their inability to plan more effectively for their survival, reflect the failure of all too many others faced with the threat of Nazi terror. It is a failure that deserves close examination because of the inherent warnings it contains for us, the living.

Submission to the threatening power of the Nazi state often led both to the disintegration of what had once seemed well-integrated personalities and to a return to an immature disregard for the dangers of reality. Those Jews who submitted passively to Nazi persecution came to depend on primitive and infantile thought processes: wishful thinking and disregard for the possibility of death. Many persuaded themselves that they, out of all the others, would be spared. Many more simply disbelieved in the possibility of their own death. Not believing in it, they did not take what seemed to them desperate precautions, such as giving up everything to hide out singly; or trying to escape even if it meant risking their lives in doing so; or preparing to fight for their lives when no escape was possible and death had become an immediate possibility. It is true that defending their lives in active combat before they were rounded up to be transported into the camps might have hastened their deaths, and so, up to a point, they were protecting themselves by "rolling with the punches" of the enemy.

But the longer one rolls with the punches dealt not by the normal vagaries of life, but by one's eventual executioner, the more likely it becomes that one will no longer have the strength to resist when death becomes imminent. This is particularly true if yielding to the enemy is accompanied not by a commensurate strengthening of the personality, but by an inner disintegration. We can observe such a process among the Franks, who bickered with each other over trifles, instead of supporting each other's ability to resist the demoralizing impact of their living conditions.

Those who faced up to the announced intentions of the Nazis prepared for the worst as a real and imminent possibility. It meant risking one's life for a self-chosen purpose, but in doing so, creating at least a small chance for saving one's own life or those of others, or both. When Jews in Germany were restricted to their homes, those who did not succumb to inertia took the new restrictions as a warning that it was high time to go underground, join the resistance movement, provide themselves with forged papers, and so on, if they had not done so long ago. Many of them survived.

Some distant relatives of mine may furnish an example. Early in the war, a young man living in a small Hungarian town banded together with a number of other Jews to prepare against a German invasion. As soon as the Nazis imposed curfews on the Jews, his group left for Budapest—because the bigger capital city with its greater anonymity offered chances for escaping detection. Similar groups from other towns converged in Budapest and joined forces. From among themselves they selected typically "Aryan" looking men who equipped themselves with false papers and immediately joined the Hungarian SS. These spies were then able to warn of impending persecution and raids.

Many of these groups survived intact. Furthermore, they had also equipped themselves with small arms, so that if they were detected, they could put up enough of a fight for the majority to escape while a few would die fighting to make the escape possible. A few of the Jews who had joined the SS were discovered and immediately shot, probably a death preferable to one in the gas chambers. But most of even these Jews survived, hiding within the SS until liberation.

Compare these arrangements not just to the Franks' selection of a hiding place that was basically a trap without an outlet but with Mr. Frank's teaching typically academic high-school subjects to his children rather than how to make a getaway: a token of his inability to face the seriousness of the threat of death. Teaching high-school subjects had, of course, its constructive aspects. It relieved the ever-present anxiety about their fate to some degree by concentrating on different matters, and by implication it encouraged hope for a future in which such knowledge would be useful. In this sense such teaching was purposeful, but it was erroneous in that it took the place of much more pertinent teaching and planning: how best to try to escape when detected.

Unfortunately the Franks were by no means the only ones who, out of anxiety, became unable to contemplate their true situation and with it to plan accordingly. Anxiety, and the wish to counteract it by clinging to each other, and to reduce its sting by continuing as much as possible with their usual way of life incapacitated many, particularly when survival plans required changing radically old ways of living that they cherished, and which had become their only source of satisfaction.

My young relative, for example, was unable to persuade other members of his family to go with him when he left the small town where he had lived with them. Three times, at tremendous risk to himself, he returned to plead with his relatives, pointing out first the growing persecution of the Jews, and later the fact that transport to the gas chambers had already begun. He could not convince these Jews to leave their homes and break up their families to go singly into hiding.

As their desperation mounted, they clung more determinedly to their old living arrangements and to each other, became less able to consider giving up the possessions they had accumulated through hard work over a lifetime. The more severely their freedom to act was reduced, and what little they were still permitted to do restricted by insensible and degrading regulations imposed by the Nazis, the more did they become unable to contemplate independent action. Their life energies drained out of them, sapped by their ever-greater anxiety. The less they found strength in themselves, the more they held on to the little that was left of what had given them security in the past—their old surroundings, their customary way of life, their possessions—all these seemed to give their lives some permanency, offer some symbols of security. Only what had once been symbols of security now endangered life, since they were excuses for avoiding change. On each successive visit the young man found his relatives more incapacitated, less willing or able to take his advice, more frozen into inactivity, and with it further along the way to the crematoria where, in fact, they all died.

Levin renders a detailed account of the desperate but fruitless efforts made by small Jewish groups determined to survive to try to save the rest. She tells how messengers were "sent into the provinces to warn Jews that deportation meant death, but their warnings were ignored because most Jews refused to contemplate their own annihilation."[2] I believe the reason for such refusal has to be found in their inability to take action. If we are certain that we are helpless to protect ourselves against the danger of destruction, we cannot contemplate it. We can consider the danger only as long as we believe there are ways to protect ourselves, to fight back, to escape. If we are convinced none of this is possible for us, then there is no point in thinking about the danger; on the contrary, it is best to refuse to do so.

As a prisoner in Buchenwald, I talked to hundreds of German Jewish prisoners who were brought there as part of the huge pogrom in the wake of the murder of von Rath in the fall of 1938. I asked them why they had not left Germany, given the utterly degrading conditions they had been subjected to. Their answer was: How could we leave? It would have meant giving up our homes, our work, our sources of income. Having been deprived by Nazi persecution and degradation of much of their self-respect, they had become unable to give up what still gave them a semblance of it: their earthly belongings. But instead of using possessions, they became captivated by them, and this possession by earthly goods became the fatal mask for their possession by anxiety, fear, and denial.

How the investment of personal property with one's life energy could make people die bit by bit was illustrated throughout the Nazi persecution of the Jews. At the time of the first boycott of Jewish stores, the chief external goal of the Nazis was to acquire the possessions of the Jews. They even let Jews take some things out of the country at that time if they would leave the bulk of their property behind. For a long time the intention of the Nazis, and the goal of their first discriminatory laws, was to force undesirable minorities, including Jews, into emigration.

Although the extermination policy was in line with the inner logic of Nazi racial ideology, one may wonder whether the idea that millions of Jews (and other foreign nationals) could be submitted to extermination did not partially result from seeing the degree of degradation Jews accepted without fighting back. When no violent resistance occurred, persecution of the Jews worsened, slow step by slow step.

Many Jews who on the invasion of Poland were able to survey their situation and draw the right conclusions, survived the Second World War. As the Germans approached, they left everything behind and fled to Russia, much as they distrusted and disliked the Soviet system. But there, while badly treated, they could at least survive. Those who stayed on in Poland believing they could go on with life-as-before sealed their fate. Thus in the deepest sense the walk to the gas chamber was only the last consequence of these Jews' inability to comprehend what was in store; it was the final step of surrender to the death instinct, which might also be called the principle of inertia. The first step was taken long before arrival at the death camp.

We can find a dramatic demonstration of how far the surrender to inertia can be carried, and the wish not to know because knowing would create unbearable anxiety, in an experience of Olga Lengyel.[3] She reports that although she and her fellow prisoners lived just a few hundred yards from the crematoria and the gas chambers and knew what they were for, most prisoners denied knowledge of them for months. If they had grasped their true situation, it might have helped them save either the lives they themselves were fated to lose, or the lives of others.

When Mrs. Lengyel's fellow prisoners were selected to be sent to the gas chambers, they did not try to break away from the group, as she successfully did. Worse, the first time she tried to escape the gas chambers, some of the other selected prisoners told the supervisors that she was trying to get away. Mrs. Lengyel desperately asks the question: How was it possible that people denied the existence of the gas chamber when all day long they saw the crematoria burning and smelled the odor of burning flesh? Why did they prefer ignoring the exterminations to fighting for their very own lives? She can offer no explanation, only the observation that they resented anyone who tried to save himself from the common fate, because they lacked enough courage to risk action themselves. I believe they did it because they had given up their will to live and permitted their death tendencies to engulf them. As a result, such prisoners were in the thrall of the murdering SS not only physically but also psychologically, while this was not true for those prisoners who still had a grip on life.

Some prisoners even began to serve their executioners, to help speed the death of their own kind. Then things had progressed beyond simple inertia to the death instinct running rampant. Those who tried to serve their executioners in what were once their civilian capacities were merely continuing life as usual and thereby opening the door to their death.

For example, Mrs. Lengyel speaks of Dr. Mengele, SS physician at Auschwitz, as a typical example of the "business as usual" attitude that enabled some prisoners, and certainly the SS, to retain whatever balance they could despite what they were doing. She describes how Dr. Mengele took all correct medical precautions during childbirth, rigorously observing all aseptic principles, cutting the umbilical cord with greatest care, etc. But only half an hour later he sent mother and infant to be burned in the crematorium.

Having made his choice, Dr. Mengele and others like him had to delude themselves to be able to live with themselves and their experience. Only one personal document on the subject has come to my attention, that of Dr. Nyiszli, a prisoner serving as "research physician" at Auschwitz.[4] How Dr. Nyiszli deluded himself can be seen, for example, in the way he repeatedly refers to himself as working in Auschwitz as a physician, although he worked as the assistant of a criminal murderer. He speaks of the Institute for Race, Biological, and Anthropological Investigation as "one of the most qualified medical centers of the Third Reich," although it was devoted to proving falsehoods. That Nyiszli was a doctor didn't alter the fact that he—like any of the prisoner foremen who served the SS better than some SS were willing to serve it—was a participant in the crimes of the SS. How could he do it and live with himself?

The answer is: by taking pride in his professional skills, irrespective of the purpose they served. Dr. Nyiszli and Dr. Mengele were only two among hundreds of other—and far more prominent—physicians who participated in the Nazis' murderous pseudo-scientific human experiments. It was the peculiar pride of these men in their professional skill and knowledge, without regard for moral implications, that made them so dangerous. Although the concentration camps and crematoria are no longer here, this kind of pride still remains with us; it is characteristic of a modern society in which fascination with technical competence has dulled concern for human feelings. Auschwitz is gone, but so long as this attitude persists, we shall not be safe from cruel indifference to life at the core.

I have met many Jews as well as gentile anti-Nazis, similar to the activist group in Hungary described earlier, who survived in Nazi Germany and in the occupied countries. These people realized that when a world goes to pieces and inhumanity reigns supreme, man cannot go on living his private life as he was wont to do, and would like to do; he cannot, as the loving head of a family, keep the family living together peacefully, undisturbed by the surrounding world; nor can he continue to take pride in his profession or possessions, when either will deprive him of his humanity, if not also of his life. In such times, one must radically reevaluate all of what one has done, believed in, and stood for in order to know how to act. In short, one has to take a stand on the new reality—a firm stand, not one of retirement into an even more private world.

If today, Negroes in Africa march against the guns of a police that defends *apartheid*—even if hundreds of dissenters are shot down and tens of thousands rounded up in camps—their fight will sooner or later assure them of a chance for liberty and equality. Millions of the Jews of Europe who did not or could not escape in time or go underground as many thousands did, could at least have died fighting as some did in the Warsaw ghetto at the end, instead of passively waiting to be rounded up for their own extermination.

NOTES
1. Marga Minco, *Bitter Herbs* (New York: Oxford University Press, 1960).
2. Nora Levin, *The Holocaust* (New York: Thomas Y. Crowell, 1968).
3. Olga Lengyel, *Five Chimneys: The Story of Auschwitz* (Chicago: Ziff-Davis, 1947).
4. Miklos Nyiszli, *Auschwitz: A Doctor's Eyewitness Account* (New York: Frederick Fell, 1960).

Dynamics

1. Look at some of the different ways Bettelheim characterizes choices made by the Franks. How effectively do you think he balances his opinions about their decisions against his view that they had "every right to arrange their life as they wish[ed]"? Choose some passages from his essay that help you to evaluate Bettelheim's reading of the Franks' story in light of your own ideas about their situation.

2. What does "survival" seem to mean at different points in Bettelheim's argument? Consider some of the different meanings the concept has when applied to individuals, families, and communities. Discuss the ways Bettelheim places certain kinds of "survival" in relation to other kinds. What do you make of Bettelheim's use of this concept?

Critical Tools

1. Bettelheim outlines some psychological mechanisms he believes people use when faced with information which threatens "our views of ourselves and our humanity." Explore his analysis of these mechanisms by using them to read another essay in which someone attempts to cope with such information. How might your application of these tools to a second reading create new implications for Bettelheim's use of them?

2. Think about the kinds of knowledge you have developed out of your own experiences of psychological strain. In what ways might your knowledge complicate Bettelheim's arguments about the Franks? Consider how the differences between your experiences and those of the Franks might shape your interpretation of their story.

Draft One/Draft Two

1. *Draft One:* Writing analytically--even critically--about events like the holocaust, events "so uncanny as to be unbelievable," can feel extremely risky, perhaps sacrilegious. What kinds of authority and evidence does Bettelheim appeal to in making his arguments about so sensitive an issue? Show how you see Bettelheim negotiating the tension between his desire to make what he believes to be an important argument, on the one hand, and his desire to respect his subject matter, on the other.

   Draft Two: Discuss an instance in which you felt you lacked the authority, experience, or justification to address a particular issue in your writing. How did you manage this experience? Use your analysis of Bettelheim in draft one to give you insight about the degree and kinds of authority you possess as a writer.

2. *Draft One:* Bettelheim raises the "dim but extremely threatening realization that the modern state now has available the means for changing personality...." According to Bettelheim, what are these means and how do they operate? Explore your response to this "realization" by reading it in terms of another essay.

   Draft Two: Bettelheim also refers to the way that gradually "yielding to the enemy" can lead either to "a commensurate strengthening of the personality" or "an inner disintegration." Investigate how a personal experience led to one or both of these results. How might you relate your experience(s) of these possibilities to your views about "the means for changing personality" you discussed in Draft One?

❖ ❖ ❖

Before Reading Howard Brody. . .

1. What, in your experience, does it mean to be a "patient"? List some of the social factors that help to determine the kind of relationship a patient has with his or her physician. Where does your own knowledge about patient/doctor relationships come from?

2. What role do "experts" play in the decisions you make about your life? Talk about some of the people or groups whose advice you take seriously. Where do you think their authority comes from? Write about the kind of power you have in your relationships with these experts.

The Social Power of Expert Healers

Howard Brody, M.D.

So far I have addressed the power that physicians possess by virtue of being physicians. In this chapter I wish to argue that the physician's social power (and, to a lesser extent, cultural power) derives not only from physicianhood per se but also from membership in a particular social class, that of the affluent, professionally trained expert. I will suggest further that some ethical analyses in medicine will be flawed or incomplete unless this source of power (and of the abuse of power) is taken into account.

The Case of Opal

Opal, now two and a half, suffers from microcephaly, extreme developmental delay, grand mal seizure disorder, regurgitation with aspiration (partially corrected by surgery), feeding by jejunostomy tube, and recurrent respiratory infections requiring eight to ten hospitalizations a year. She was delivered by emergency cesarean section at four weeks past her due date. Her teenage mother was a heavy user of drugs throughout the pregnancy; her father (unmarried) also used drugs and was in prison by the time Opal was born. Opal's mother had only sporadic prenatal care and showed up at the hospital in labor, initially unsure of her due date. The fetal monitor showed loss of fetal heart tones requiring emergency cesarean section.

Opal was in the nursery for six weeks and required respirator support. She also developed her seizure and reflux problems at that time. (Microcephaly did not become evident until Opal was eight months of age.) Her teenage mother initially took her home and cared for her with the help of the maternal grandmother. After a short time, the mother dropped Opal off at grandmother's house with a request to "take care of her for a while I get a break." She stayed away three weeks. Finally, the grandmother suggested that she assume legal custody of Opal; the mother and the father (contacted in prison) both agreed. Grandmother now takes care of Opal full-time; Opal's mother comes by to visit once a week or so.

The grandmother lives in a farmhouse in a rather isolated area. The house belongs to her male companion, who is a truck driver; he occasionally helps out by taking care of Opal for short periods. Opal also has an uncle in his early twenties who is seldom seen; once he came home for a while with a broken leg (suffered in a fight over drugs) and demanded that his mother take care of him while he was disabled. Income for Opal and the grandmother consists primarily of Social Security, state Crippled Children's funds, and Aid to Dependent Children. These cover most medical care but still leave grandmother with many unpaid bills. For example, as the previous summer was unusually hot, Opal had great difficulty with perspiration and secretions, and the grandmother and her male companion installed air conditioning in the house; they were unable to get the welfare grant for the added utility expenses and currently are in arrears to the power company for seven hundred dollars.

Grandmother spends almost her entire day taking care of Opal, who needs fairly constant attention for clearing secretions in her throat, feeding her, and administering range-of-motion exercises prescribed by the physical therapist. There are some school programs for handicapped children Opal's age, but the grandmother has not utilized them; she claims that Opal's frequent infections have made this impossible but also admits that she thinks she can take care of Opal better than anyone else can.

The primary physician and other members of the crippled children's team who make occasional home visits as well as see Opal in the hospital have noted that they consider the grandmother to be pathologically attached to Opal. The grandmother has virtually no interests or human contacts outside of Opal's care. She is totally unwilling to engage in any discussion of Opal's poor long-term prognosis, saying, "She won't die until I die." Although she generally uses denial to avoid the subject, she has said specifically on several occasions that if Opal did die she would not want to go on living herself. Dealing with these issues is also complicated by distrust toward the hospital and toward at least some caregivers. The grandmother has contacted a lawyer to discuss whether "mistakes" made by the physician who did the cesarean section caused any of Opal's problems (highly unlikely). During one hospitalization, Opal suffered a burn on the hand from the efforts of an inexperienced phlebotomist to warm the extremity before blood drawing, and this incident has also led grandmother to threaten the hospital with legal action. She does, however, seem to trust the primary-care pediatrician and the crippled children's team.

That group is now meeting in their weekly family assessment conference. They wish to try to intervene to do something about grandmother's clinging relationship with Opal, thinking in part that Opal could benefit from some school programs and that the grandmother could also benefit from giving up some of Opal's care and finding other interests. They hypothesize that this clinging relationship is meeting some deeply felt needs of the grandmother. She seems to feel guilty for having been unable to control her daughter better during the pregnancy, to keep her off drugs and get her to accept regular prenatal care. (Hence, presumably, the displaced anger in trying to blame the obstetrician.) Moreover, Opal, despite her inability to do any of the things that a normal two-year-old would, is in many ways, the perfect child. She will remain forever in a totally dependent status and will never challenge the grandmother's authority or control. ("Opal is the only kid in the family the grandmother knows will never do drugs," is how one of the team members put it.)

The discussion among the medical staff turns to mechanisms to accomplish the desired changes. One person suggests that legal pressure could be applied if there is a school program that could benefit Opal and the grandmother refuses to cooperate. "Is it illegal not to send a two-year-old to school?" another wonders. And a third says, "Look, we have a kid that is being well cared for and a grandmother who is happy. Who are we to mess with this?"

Power, Interests, and Experts

There are a variety of ways to approach this case ethically. Surely it could be asked what the plans ought to be if Opal suffers a crisis, is hospitalized, and questions of aggressive life-prolonging treatment come up. More to the point now, should the staff intervene regarding school placement and the overly clinging relationship between the child and the grandmother?

Both these issues will no doubt be addressed first by asking what would be in Opal's "best interests." Does grandmother reflect Opal's best interests in her decisions? Or is she so preoccupied with her own interests that she is a poor surrogate decision-maker for Opal? Is it in Opal's interests to be deprived of the training and stimulation that the school could provide? What about the additional infections she would be exposed to at school? Or the risk of upsetting the major caregiving relationship in Opal's life—perhaps the only thing that stands between Opal and the back ward of a state hospital?

How should the team resolve disputes about what is truly in Opal's interest? I have argued that the term *best interests,* if not actually meaningless, is at least extremely difficult to specify with any operational precision (Brody 1988a). As Humpty Dumpty would have it, the question is not what the term means, but who is to be master.[1] I suggest that almost any effort to state what would be in Opal's best interests is really a disguised way to promote some specific *adult* agenda, which entails a variety of value judgments about how "good" people ought to lead their lives.[2]

One such agenda is that of the particular social class and subculture to which Opal's family belongs. This is a way of life shaped by chronic financial inadequacy, uncertain employment, and constant battles with social bureaucracies designed by the middle class to treat the lower class as adversaries.[3] This way of life is further shaped by the relative inability to control one's environment or plan for the future and by the pervasive temptation of alcohol and other drugs as escapes from this grim realization. In this setting, certain kinds of human relationships make sense which would be dysfunctional in a middle-class world. And an infant like Opal may indeed have a value that would be unthinkable in social world that prizes good looks, mental proficiency, and accomplishments. According to this agenda, the decisions involving Opal ought to be made by those who are of her world and who have the closest family and emotional ties.

A quite different agenda is that of the upper-middle-class, professionally trained healers, or "experts." This is the group to which the physicians and the crippled children's team belong. They are committed to a worldview that prizes specialized, scientifically based knowledge and the dividing up of all human experience into problems for which one must consult the correct expert if one is to have any chance of being happy.[4]

Moreover, if these experts have psychological training, then of course they know the motives and intentions of the average citizen better than he does; and if he is so impertinent as to reject their advice, they can state precisely which mental pathology is responsible for his aberrant behavior. According to this agenda, what is best for Opal is what this group of experts says is best, and indirectly it is whatever creates the greatest chance of future employment for all members of the expert class, including special-education teachers, physical therapists, social workers, family counselors, and of course physicians.[5]

A quite different agenda would be that of the conservative group which has become increasingly vocal in U.S. politics during the 1980s. Their reaction to Opal's case would be one of disgust for all family members, whom they would censure as unemployed junkies ripping off the welfare system and having sex outside of marriage. Presumably this group would favor using any medical technology to keep Opal alive regardless of her prognosis; fight against using tax dollars to create any supportive services to aid her when she is well; call for locking up both her parents for as many years as possible; and blame the grandmother for her failure to discipline her daughter properly and teach her the proper values.[6]

Each of these three agendas has a different status within American society. The third has managed to rise several notches during the 1980s, with the success of a federal administration committed to it. But for our purposes the most important agenda is the second one. If anyone in the United States runs afoul of administrative or legal rules—particularly within the school or court systems—it is this agenda which is most likely to be forcibly imposed by the state apparatus. It is this class of experts which is likely to decide who should go to jail, who should be committed to a mental hospital, who should be enrolled in this or that school program, and for how long, and what counts as having achieved benefit from being there; and judges, teachers, and school boards are likely to acquiesce in whatever course of action the experts suggest.

Of course, all this has been heard before. It has become the stock criticism against medicine more generally and psychiatry particularly (Szasz 1974). The argument goes that these disciplines have almost no scientific credence but function simply as a means of social control imposed by the ruling class for its own benefit. To these critics, the Chief of Medicine is correct in assessing the real Aesculapian power of the physician as very limited.* They contend that social power is the primary

---

* Brody is referring here to a story from the first chapter of his book. Aesculapins is the Greco-Roman god of medicine.—*The Editors*

element of physician power and that the myth of Aesculapian power is used as a smoke screen lest the lower classes catch on.

This line of criticism may seem trite and simplistic, but it is also occasionally on target. Numerous examples could be given; for now it may be sufficient to consider the question of psychiatric testimony regarding the future potential of criminals for violence. It seems difficult to dispute that there is hardly any scientific basis for making confident prediction of future violent behavior. Rather, there seems to have arisen an unholy alliance between the courts and certain psychiatrists. The courts benefit by passing off difficult decisions about length of sentence and the sort of facility to which prisoners should be sent; they get to pretend that these decisions derive from objective criteria instead of from irreducibly subjective judgments for which the judges themselves would be held accountable. A few psychiatrists, who have made a career out of giving such testimony, would find their income and prestige in jeopardy were the lack of scientific validity for their conclusions ever discussed. A larger group of psychiatrists, who may have genuine sympathy for individual prisoners or patients and want to view themselves as aiding them, offer testimony of low potential for violence altruistically; and so they too, though for better motives, acquire an interest in obscuring the scientific basis of their predictions. The rest of us, who can be relied upon most of the time not to want to know what really goes on in courtrooms or in prisons are inclined to leave this unholy alliance to its own devices and not to question it.[7]

Yet focusing on these examples of the use of pseudo-Aesculapian power for social control will obscure the more subtle message of the Chief of Medicine story about the fine line between the use and the abuse of physician power. It is one thing for people to view themselves as victims of the abuse of power by physicians and other powerful groups in society; it is another for them to view themselves as active collaborators in that abuse of power. But ultimately the public must acknowledge their role, as the more thoughtful critics of physician power make clear.

As Lasch (1979) has eloquently stated, we Americans seem to have become, as a society, profoundly uncomfortable with and estranged from a set of functions and behaviors that our forebears viewed as natural and manageable. We have adopted an ideology of personal happiness which holds that life consists of a series of snares to be avoided and problems to be solved, and that only by getting the advice and aid of specialist experts can we solve those problems in such a way as to assure happiness. I view this as an ideology rather than a rational belief because the more experts we consult, the more unhappy we get. But of course we tell ourselves, in that case, that we went to the wrong experts or did not properly follow their advice: ideology always wins out over facts.

The power of this ideology can be seen in that efforts to reject it end up re-creating it in a different form. Many in American society view physicians as too powerful and call for a return of power over one's health to the individual. Among some groups involved in holistic cancer self-help, for instance, it is an article of faith that cancer is easily preventable and curable and that physicians have a selfish interest in avoiding and suppressing these preventive and curative measures in order to make more money off cancer sufferers. But the movements dedicated to overturning the power of the expert healers—notably the so-called holistic or alternative medicine movement—tend to re-create the structure of the system they reject. People appear to become every bit as dependent on the counsel of these "alternative" experts as they were on that of the more traditional healers.

It is doubtful that we can replace this ideology with another, less dysfunctional and less neurotic one. It is therefore especially important to see how it feeds the temptation to abuse the power of the class of experts either for social control or for the personal gain of the expert class. *Personal gain* must here be construed as including the expansion of employment opportunities for like-minded experts by systematically expanding the number of experts that must be consulted before a "problem" can be declared "solved."

The difficulty of doing away with this ideology, however, can itself be used as a rationalization to avoid change, even where individual experts can make small modifications for the better. This difficulty requires a hard look at how physicians might abuse power in this fashion and what can be done to avoid that abuse.

Abuses of Expert Power

The abuses of power attached to membership in the expert class cut across all guidelines for judging the responsible use of power. Owned power becomes a problem when the role of the expert and the need to consult experts over every detail of day-to-day living are taken for granted. It is easy for the physician to deny under these circumstances that she has any such power since the self-image of the expert healer is to be helpful, not manipulative for selfish ends.[8] But power that is unrecognized is hard to channel into responsible uses.

Similarly, aimed power is resisted so long as the self-image of benevolent helper remains untarnished. If the power tends both to respond to the needs and desires of individuals and to cement the social authority of the expert class, the first aim of the power may be confused with the total aim. Justifications for the use of power will be offered which miss the problematic features of the case but sound superficially compelling. Worse, alternative strategies may be denounced in the name of the individual autonomy they are supposed to promote. Since the public willingly complies with the expert ideology, refusal by the expert to accept the assigned role could be seen as a violation of the autonomy of the client or patient and as an attempt to impose a new ideology on them out of paternalistic arrogance: "we know better than they do what they really need."[9]

Shared power is difficult to achieve so long as the physician occupies this expert role.[10] To empower the patient might, in some ways at least, threaten the social hegemony of the expert class and put experts out of their jobs. Despite this pull, most experts genuinely want to be helpful and see an overdependence as unhelpful to their clients. But the more subtle problem is that even given the urge to empower, the ideology may be so strong that the empowerment itself becomes a reinforcement of helpless dependence. It may, in the end, seem as if one can get power only by going to the right expert and following his advice precisely; one cannot get power simply by choosing to exercise it. In an age when people pay lots of money to attend seminars that purport to teach assertiveness and self-esteem, this danger seems real.

In chapter 3, I argued that some abuses of power might be called playing God. The expert may be tempted to use the power attached to his role not simply to carry out his role functions and assist those who seek his aid but to try to redesign the world—often by rewarding the "good" and punishing the "bad." Of course, if the power were appropriately aimed and owned, the expert would have to take explicit responsibility for doing this—and by implication would have to defend publicly his judgments as to who the good and the bad are and what gives him the right to decide their fate. The net result is that some patients get approved for disability or other benefits while others get turned down; some needy persons have opportunities and assistance opened up to them while others face a brick wall of bureaucratic inertia. No expert has to own responsibility for making any value-laden judgments because each of these acts can be justified in terms of the professional judgments within a particular field of expertise.

The challenge for physicians (and other experts) is to find ways to make their patients feel genuinely more powerful to control their own lives and health; to be more aware of the actual ends of their social and cultural power, not only the ends that bear the most benign interpretation; and to be willing to accept responsibility for the use of power with a realistic understanding of all its facets.

The Rabkin Explosion

It is of little use to analyze the power of the healing experts in our society if the only conclusion is that the experts are bad people (or else that the society is bad). A further case study may help at this point to illustrate how complex the issues around power and expertise can be.

This case comes from an unusual source. People are by now used to the idea that books and articles on medical ethics might present controversial cases, which become the subject of heated debate. But it is a bit out of the ordinary for controversial cases to arise in literature and medicine journals.[11] Nevertheless, the growing field of literature and medicine now has one "hot" case study to its credit, and it may prove instructive here.

David Barnard, a professor of medical humanities trained in religion and psychology, contributed a case study which he titled, "A Case of Amyotrophic Lateral Sclerosis" (Barnard 1986). As a participant-observer, he followed "Dr. Valerie Walsh" in a series of visits with "Mr. and Mrs. Baker." Mr. Baker was seventy-seven when he developed progressive weakness and was diagnosed as having ALS. Mrs. Baker, seventy-three, became his caretaker in spite of her own medical problems of angina, diabetes, and arthritis. Dr. Walsh came to bond closely with the Bakers, who were in turn deeply and openly grateful for the care that she provided. But she also struggled with two ongoing problems. The first was her desire to clarify Mr. Baker's wishes regarding intensity of medical treatment, particularly the eventual question of intubation and mechanical ventilation. The signals given by both Bakers strongly suggested their desire to hold onto hope and not to face the grim prognosis. The second was the Bakers' insistence on remaining in their own home, at some distance from needed social and nursing services, and their resistance to efforts to place aides or other workers in the home following an unfortunate incident with an uncaring person. These limitations conflicted with Dr. Walsh's desire to provide the best care possible for Mr. Baker and to spare the strain on Mrs. Baker's health.

Eventually, after months of home visits that left Dr. Walsh feeling both isolated and frustrated, she was able to get Mr. Baker to articulate his desire not to receive mechanical ventilation; she also was able to arrange for a health aide to visit the home to help with the most burdensome physical chores. Within a month, however, Mrs. Baker was dead of a sudden heart attack. Mr. Baker then had to be placed in a nursing home, where he died six weeks later.

When the case study was solicited for the journal *Literature and Medicine*, the issue editor, Joanne Trautmann Banks, had some questions about the case history format. To what extent was the study an "objective" account of events, and to what extent was it fiction? With this in mind, she requested a commentary from an authority on narrative theory, Eric Rabkin. Rabkin's commentary (1986) is perhaps most notable for violating one of the norms of commentaries in scholarly journals: it is markedly uncivil, even angry.[12] He concluded that Barnard had elected to ignore the needs of the Bakers in order to write a manuscript that glorified the caring physician; that Dr. Walsh had been driven more by a need to see herself as a hero-martyr than by a realistic appraisal of the Bakers' needs; and that between them Barnard and Walsh had lied to Mr. Baker about his disease and its prognosis and probably hastened Mrs. Baker's death.

Not unnaturally, given his background, Rabkin chose to analyze Barnard's text as a piece of fiction, and indeed Rabkin offered much internal evidence to justify that way of looking at the material. His analysis led him to conclude that Barnard was too self-effacing as narrator; if he was actually present in the home during some of the highly emotional exchanges he described, then his being there was a part of the narrative, and it was not honest to act as if he were merely the reader's window onto events. Rabkin also identified a number of passages that hinted at Dr. Walsh's personal needs—to do battle against a dread disease; to protect Mr. Baker from demoralizing news by being the sole judge of what he was ready to hear and when; to keep other potential team helpers out of the case while complaining that she was left to deal with the Bakers all by herself; and especially to accept the frequent and forceful expressions of gratitude and praise bestowed on her by the Bakers.

Rabkin suggested that two things should have been done. First, Mr. Baker should have been confronted earlier with his poor prognosis so that open planning could have taken place; and second, Dr. Walsh should have insisted on getting the Bakers to move closer to the center of the city, where more services were close at hand. Banks thus felt obligated to call for another commentary on the ethics of these recommendations, and that was supplied by David H. Smith (1986). Smith faulted Rabkin for ethical inconsistency. Presumably the need to tell Mr. Baker the truth was rooted in respect for his autonomy. How, then, could Rabkin recommend violating Mr. Baker's autonomy by forcing him to leave the home that meant so much to him and his wife?[13]

These are the basic facts of the case and the central issues in the controversy that erupted around its publication. What light can the case shed on the question of experts' power?

An interesting role reversal developed in this controversy. Walsh is the physician, and Barnard seems to have accepted the role of the physician's apologist. It would therefore seem natural for them to impose their own views on the Bakers, paying scant attention to what the Bakers themselves say they want. And Rabkin, as defender of the patient against the power of the experts, might have been expected to call the experts to task. But the reality of the case is quite different. Dr. Walsh is the one who seems to be listening to the Bakers, telling them what they want to hear, backing off when they indicate they do not wish to deal with certain issues, and supporting their oft-stated wish to remain in their own home. It is Rabkin, by contrast, who urges Dr. Walsh to push her expert opinion of the matter onto the Bakers and force them to move to a more convenient location for sending a crowd of like-minded experts into the Baker home to take care of them. This observation by itself does not establish who is right and who is wrong (if anyone is either). But it does suggest that things may be muddier than they first appear. Taking sides with or against the experts is not enough to assure moral purity.

What should have been done in this case? Rabkin's telling observations suggest that Dr. Walsh's course was not driven by the most appropriate needs. But neither is it clear that Rabkin's suggestions are wise: people cannot be forced to move, accept home services, or face a harsh prognosis squarely.

It is always much easier to be wise or creative in retrospect in such cases. What would have happened, though, if Dr. Walsh had paid more attention to her own conflicts about the Bakers earlier in the course of treatment? She was defending their rights and their privacy, she was having their praise and gratitude heaped on her, yet she still felt frustrated and fearful that things would not go well. This led to her increasing isolation from her medical team. What if she had seen this isolation and had decided to get the team more involved and to consult other physicians as to what her own feelings meant?[14]

Through this consultation, Dr. Walsh may have learned more about her own psychological needs and how they were influencing her treatment decisions. In addition, she might have evolved a positive plan for confronting the Bakers with the difficult care issues. Ideally, the confrontation would lead each faction—the Bakers and the healing experts—to own the part of the problem that only they could solve.

Dr. Walsh might have arranged for some colleagues on her medical team to accompany her on a home visit to make a less biased assessment of the home situation and of Mr. Baker's present and future needs. If after that visit no new plans could be formulated, the next step might be to return to the Bakers' home and tell them something like the following:

"Our team is frustrated. We are getting mixed messages about you and your situation and don't know how to interpret them.

"On the one hand, we know that you love each other, that you value your home life and your privacy, that Mrs. Baker is dedicated and unselfish in providing care, and that Mr. Baker has shown great emotional strength in coming to grips with a serious disease. These are all very important, and it ought to be our job as a health-care team to support and reinforce them.

"On the other hand, we know that a good deal of help is available for families in situations like yours, and we are puzzled as to why we have not been able to get you linked up with such help. We have heard Mrs. Baker express her own frustration with how things are going, and we know that she fears that her own health will be affected by the strain. And we are not sure that we have yet had a frank discussion about what Mr. Baker's future needs are going to be.

"We are frustrated because we have these two sets of messages—one saying that things are going well and the other that things are going badly. Until we get our own problem solved, we are afraid we will not provide for you the high-quality care you deserve. Can you help us work toward a resolution?"

If this approach seems like a reasonable alternative to the trap Dr. Walsh sensed herself falling into, it may be because the message is a complicated mix of owned power and owned powerlessness. The powerlessness is admitted: the health team cannot remake the Baker family into their image of the ideal client and cannot force the Bakers to place a higher value on receiving certain sorts of technical assistance than on remaining together in their own home without outside interference. The team cannot even get a clear idea of what the problem is without their participation. The power is stated more subtly: there is a clear threat that if the Bakers do not discuss these matters and in the process talk about things that they have heretofore been unwilling to talk about, assistance will be withdrawn at some level. But this threatened use of power does not seem inappropriate, for professionals should be able to avoid giving care under circumstances in which they feel strongly that they cannot do a good job.[15]

If this team conference approach to the Bakers' situation represents an ethically superior alternative to what actually occurred, then why was it not done or even considered? One hypothesis is that the three parties—Mr. Baker, Mrs. Baker, and Dr. Walsh—were locked in a serious but unrealized power struggle. Indeed, one might conclude that all three were guilty of the unowned, unaimed, and unshared use of the power that they possessed, thereby producing a tangle of cross-purposes.[16]

Dr. Walsh never examined the types of power she did and did not possess in relation to the Bakers. For example, she agonized over her power to destroy Mr. Baker's hope by being too candid in discussing the prognosis of ALS, but she paid scant attention to the power she was assuming by taking it upon herself to decide how much he wanted to hear and when. She worried about an eventual bad outcome and several times referred to the Bakers as a "time bomb," but continued to make her routine home visits without asking whether they might be reinforcing the impression that no additional help was needed. She paid no attention to the potential for a power struggle between her and Mrs. Baker that was inherent in a female physician's making house calls.

Without having examined the power issues, Dr. Walsh could never be sure what she was trying to do with her power. How much was aimed at doing battle with ALS, which had killed a previous patient of hers just before she met the Bakers? How much was aimed at keeping up her own hopes, in the guise of keeping up Mr. Baker's hopes? (When she finally did bring up the subject of mechanical ventilation, Mr. Baker responded promptly and thoughtfully, with appropriate sadness; there was no clue from that exchange that the subject could not have been safely broached six months earlier.) How much was aimed at maintaining herself in the role of sole caregiver, the only one who could meet the needs of the Bakers?

Power is almost impossible to share when one does not know that one has it and does not know what one is doing with it. Therefore Dr. Walsh lost opportunities to empower the Bakers through her visits and her care. This failure assured that any power the Bakers exercised themselves had as much chance of being in conflict as in collusion with Dr. Walsh's power. The Bakers were in a bind: they were quite socially isolated and needed the comfort that Dr. Walsh's visits provided. They could not bring the power struggle out in the open without threatening that relationship. And so on the surface, all of Dr. Walsh's efforts were met with expressions of praise and gratitude, but no one looked critically at those statements to see what issues might lie concealed below them.

The Bakers, on their side, had similar problems with power. Mr. Baker seems to have become quite absorbed in his illness. His calm resignation in the face of weakness and loss of independence was commendable. But there is almost no hint, in the passages recorded by Barnard, of any real concern for the toll the illness must be taking on Mrs. Baker. At one point Mrs. Baker complains bitterly that her husband is not trying to help himself. His reaction is to defend his efforts: it's not that he isn't trying, but his muscles simply will not respond. Any reaction from him like, "I know how hard it is on her, and I worry about her health," is absent from the record. Neither wish to admit that Mr. Baker is going to die soon. This means they cannot address the subject of what life will be like for Mrs. Baker after he is gone— whether she will be able to function well or whether his illness will have taken such toll on her that she will have to go into a nursing home. There is thus a sense in which Mr. Baker's power to cope with his illness is being directed against his wife, not just against the effects of the ALS.

Mrs. Baker's efforts to use her power mirror Dr. Walsh's. Mrs. Baker also has a strong need to be seen as the sole caregiver, even at the cost of being the hero-martyr. At one point she proclaims, pointing at her husband, "I'm going to get ten more years out of this if it kills me!" (Barnard 1986, p. 29). This statement is a tragic foreshadowing of the actual outcome of the case. Mrs. Baker also has a strong need to buoy her own hopes by not facing the serious prognosis of ALS. A statement by Mr. Baker that suggests resignation and acceptance is likely to be followed by an aggressively optimistic interruption from his wife. In retrospect, when Dr. Walsh withheld frank discussions about prognosis because she felt that her patient was not ready to hear them, we may wonder whether it was actually Mrs. Baker she was protecting. It is thus possible that Mrs. Baker used her power to maintain control and sustain her own sense of her role instead of trying to achieve the best outcomes for Mr. Baker and meet his real needs. This also made it inevitable that Mrs. Baker would become locked in a power struggle with Dr. Walsh.[17]

The way all parties used their power at cross-purposes makes it understandable why a better resolution was not reached—and why the outcome of the case might have been the best that could *practically* have been achieved. Still, when it comes to the appropriate use of power, the professional must assume a deeper responsibility than the client. It is perfectly excusable for the Bakers to be unclear on what their power consisted of and how it was being employed; it is less excusable for Dr. Walsh. My analysis suggests that all three guidelines on the responsible use of power would need to be consulted to avoid this sort of outcome in future cases.

The analysis suggests a further clue. If Dr. Walsh went wrong, it may be due in part to an inappropriate and unrealized *self-preoccupation*. She may have been too wrapped up in her needs to vanquish the disease, decide what should be told to the patient, and see herself as a certain kind of compassionate physician. Thus an important character trait for physicians to cultivate would be a way of avoiding, or at least identifying, self-preoccupation. I will discuss this under the heading of the physician's virtues and character in chapter 16.

NOTES

1. For more on problems with the term *best interests*, see the extended discussion of decisions on behalf of incompetent patients in chapter 10.

2. This assertion must of course be qualified. It could be determined to be contrary to Opal's best interests right now to cause her such sensations as pain and hunger. But these basic and obvious interests of all sentient beings say little about the important decisions that must be made about Opal's care.

3. I am indebted to Leonard Fleck for pointing out the peculiar injustice of the bureaucracy Americans have created as a result of a patchwork of health-care entitlement programs. Many of those who lack health insurance in the United States are among the working poor and therefore pay taxes. These taxes go to support systems like Medicaid, which hire staff to make sure that only those truly eligible get benefits. Therefore, the working poor effectively pay taxes to make sure that they are excluded from the health-care system. Likewise, private insurance companies hire extra staff to make sure that only those eligible receive benefits; and that practice adds to the cost of private insurance, helping to price insurance out of the market for the smaller companies that employ most of the working poor. As noted in chapter 12, some have calculated that Americans could pay for health care for all citizens now excluded from coverage if they saved the money they now spend on administering this crazy quilt of systems (Himmelstein and Woolhandler 1986).

4. A caricature of this view is that the ideal citizen is one who on getting up in the morning immediately checks whether any of the American Cancer Society's seven early warning signs of cancer has appeared overnight, runs the precise number of miles at precisely the target pulse rate that his sports

medicine specialist has recommended after his graded exercise electrocardiogram, and then phones his nutritionist to see how much fiber he should eat for breakfast.

5. My analysis here draws heavily on Lasch 1979 and to a lesser extent on Freidson 1970; see also Illich 1976. On the irony of a society that is increasingly preoccupied with its health and as a result feels a decreased sense of well-being, see Barsky 1988. No doubt this paragraph in the text presents a vicious caricature of "experts"; but since many of my readers, like me, are among them, it is wise occasionally to remind ourselves how foolish we can look to those who do not share our comfortable presuppositions.

6. William B. Weil, in commenting to me on this case, has suggested that there is a fourth agenda, one of rights of the disabled. I would argue that that agenda is actually a hybrid, adopting sanctity-of-life elements from the third agenda and elements of liberal do-gooderism from the second. A common observation in the wake of the Baby Doe controversies in the early 1980s is that the movement for the rights of the disabled, previously a creature of the political left (because it advocated reallocating tax revenues to aid a self-proclaimed minority group), had suddenly made an uneasy alliance with the conservative right in espousing a sanctity-of-life ethic for the treatment of seriously deformed newborns.

7. For representative views on psychiatrists' predictions of violent behavior, see Peszke 1975; Ewing 1983; Monahan 1984; Chiswick 1985.

8. "The elite cannot truly be thought of as men who are merely 'doing their duty.' In considerable part they are the ones who determine their duty, as well as the duties of other men. They do not merely follow orders; they give orders. They are not merely bureaucrats; they command bureaucrats. They may try to disguise these facts from others and from themselves by appealing to traditions of which they imagine themselves to be the instruments, but there are many traditions, and they must choose which ones they will serve. And now they face decisions for which there simply are no traditions" (Ladd 1981, citing Mills 1959).

9. An oft-cited example of this phenomenon is the clash between the modern physician, who has been trained to believe in patient autonomy, and the old-fashioned patient, who expects and indeed values paternalistic treatment from the doctor. To the extent that one can autonomously choose to be treated paternalistically, the physician's efforts to promote the patient's autonomy can themselves be denounced as unwarranted paternalism.

10. Ladd (1981) indicates that the sharing of power is a useful antidote to the possible abuses of social and political power by physicians. He fails to address, however, the problem of sharing when the power has been rendered culturally invisible. In this regard, shared power requires owned power as a prior condition.

11. "Literature and medicine" refers to an emerging field within the medical humanities. Professors of literature have turned to the study of medical themes, teaching various works of fiction that portray medical themes and examining how language is used within the practice of medicine itself. The journal *Literature and Medicine* is the primary compendium of work in this field.

12. An example of the tone that runs throughout the article is an early sentence, "I must stress that I personally believe Barnard and Walsh in no *conscious* way acted to harm the Bakers" (Rabkin 1986, p. 43; emphasis in original). In context, this sentence can best be interpreted as saying: not only did they do evil things, but they were also too stupid to know what they were doing.

13. Smith's commentary on patient autonomy seems correct as far as it goes; but it also appears to be a cheap shot in the context of the case. It seems reasonable that a more active confrontation with the Bakers, focused on the eventual need for additional home services and the threats to Mrs. Baker's own health, would have caused them to revise their initial views on accepting help or even on moving (after all, they did eventually accept an aide, after saying consistently that they would refuse). And in turn, insisting on being more forthright about Mr. Baker's actual prognosis would seem to be a vital element in this process of confrontation. Although Rabkin openly admitted his lack of clinical experience and skills, his recommendations nevertheless seem to have a clinical cohesion which Smith fails to recognize.

14. A family physician found herself taking care of a close friend during a terminal illness. This physician feared that the personal ties could lead her to mistakes in judgment, but she did not use that as an excuse to withdraw. Instead she made special efforts to consult regularly with her colleagues to be sure that her management of the case was reviewed regularly by more impartial observers. I am grateful to Elizabeth Alexander, M.D., for this illustration. See the discussion in chapter 16 on compassion and the widespread fear that too much compassion will cause the physician to lose objectivity.

15. Of course, if professionals claimed that they could do a good job only in those circumstances where they were given enough control unilaterally to define both the problem and the solution in their own terms, then professional help would be too much of a threat to individual autonomy for American society to tolerate. My assumption, by contrast, is that professionals define respect for individual autonomy as part of what it means to do a good job (compare the patient-centered primary-care model discussed in chapter 4); and that the conclusion, "I can't do a good job in this case," is reached only after extensive dialogue with the would-be client.

16. I here omit the fourth party, Barnard, from consideration. For one thing, Rabkin has already given him sufficient grief to render him an unappealing target for further criticism. For another, Barnard's lapse was primarily in the area of owned power, in that he tried to efface himself as the narrator rather than acknowledge and reveal the role he played in the unfolding of the case. He portrayed himself at the start of his article (Barnard 1986) as a "participant-observer" but then went on to write as all observer and no participant. It is perhaps revealing that Barnard's purported misstatement of the issues found an echo in the editorial comments of the issue editor of the journal. Rabkin took Barnard to task for calling his article, "A Case of Amyotrophic Lateral Sclerosis," as if this locution would guarantee the scientific objectivity of what followed—and as if what really mattered was Mr. Baker's disease, not Mr. Baker. In her brief editorial note that introduced the series of three articles, Joanne Trautmann Banks used the title, "A Controversy about Clinical Form." This again runs the risk of leaving out the human dimension of the account in favor of a comfortable scholarly analysis. If we are to take Rabkin seriously (even to disagree with him), the controversy is not over clinical form; it is over whether some professionals abused the people they were supposed to be helping.

17. A revealing statement by Dr. Walsh, toward the end of the case, is, "I feel like I have no control over what's happening right now. I'm completely dependent on [Mrs. Baker] and she's doing an *excellent* job" (Barnard 1986, p. 40). An undercurrent in this passage is that Dr. Walsh thinks that she herself should have control and feels badly for not having it. (The obvious rejoinder is: the caregiver who is actually in the home should be the central figure, and the doctor should not feel threatened in her role by the strength and power of the caregiver.) Although Dr. Walsh implies that she resents Mrs. Baker's power, she lauds her work, thereby mirroring the praise and gratitude that the Bakers feel obliged to heap on Dr. Walsh at every opportunity.

❖ ❖ ❖

Dynamics

1. Brody offers several different perspectives on the case of Mr. and Mrs. Baker. Using Brody's and the other observers' interpretations of the Baker case as your model, comment on the way Brody presents the situation of Opal and her grandmother. How do Brody's theories help you to talk about his own "agenda" in describing Opal's case?

2. In one of his footnotes, Brody describes the difficulty of sharing power "when the power has been rendered culturally invisible." Which passages in his essay might help you to explain how power becomes "culturally invisible"? Find some passages which show Brody or his subjects making power "visible."

3. Brody writes about an "unholy alliance between the courts and certain psychiatrists." Use his description of these relationships to come up with your own definition of an "unholy alliance." Of the many relationships Brody analyzes in his essay, which ones have some of the characteristics of an unholy alliance (as you have defined the term)? Consider the role that social position plays in influencing the kinds of alliances Brody's subjects create.

Critical Tools

1. Brody introduces the concepts of "owned," "aimed," and "shared" power without defining them in an explicit way. Locate passages in his essay that allow you to define these terms. What relationship do you see between these three kinds of power? Use one or more of these concepts to re-read a power relationship in another essay you have read this semester.

2. In his presentation of Opal's case, Brody suggests that the idea of acting in another person's "best interests" is more complicated than most people usually admit. Find a critical tool from another reading that helps you to analyze what might be at stake in discussions of other people's "interests." How does your use of the tool affect the way you understand this concept in Brody's essay?

Draft One/Draft Two

Draft One: Use your own experience of an illness or injury which required medical attention as the starting point for a reading of Brody's essay from a *patient's* point of view. In your essay, explain which of his terms are relevant to your own experience and why.

Draft Two: Using your own draft one, Brody's essay, and another essay in *Literacies* which treats relationships between "experts" and "subjects," explain your theory of how power works in unequal relationships. In each of the relationships you analyze, what would have to change in order for the power you describe to be more fairly distributed?

❖ ❖ ❖

Before Reading Susan Brownmiller. . .

1. What does it mean to be feminine? Does this definition hold for all historical periods? For all classes? For all cultures? Offer the most specific details and examples you can.

2. What are the advantages and disadvantages of conducting oneself in a "feminine" manner? List some of the benefits and risks involved in questioning or challenging this category.

Femininity and Ambition

Susan Brownmiller

If prettiness and grace were the extent of it, femininity would not be a puzzle, nor would excellence in feminine values be so completely at odds with other forms of ambition. In a sense this entire inquiry has been haunted by the question of ambition, for every adjustment a woman makes to prove her feminine difference adds another fine stitch to the pattern: an inhibition on speech and behavior, a usurpation of time, and a preoccupation with appearance that deflects the mind and depletes the storehouse of energy and purpose. If time and energy are not a problem, if purpose is not a concern, if the underlying submissiveness is not examined too closely, then the feminine esthetic may not be a handicap at all. On the contrary, high among its known satisfactions, femininity offers a welcome retreat from the demands of ambition, just as its strategic use is often good camouflage for those wishing to hide their ambition from public view. But there is no getting around the fact that ambition is not a feminine trait. More strongly expressed, a lack of ambition—or a professed lack of ambition, or a sacrificial willingness to set personal ambition aside—is virtuous proof of the nurturant feminine nature which, if absent, strikes at the guilty heart of femaleness itself.

When applied to women, nurturance embraces a love of children, a desire to bear them and rear them, and a disposition that leans toward a set of traits that are not gender-specific: warmth, tenderness, compassion, sustained emotional involvement in the welfare of others, and a weak or nonexistent competitive drive. Nurturant labor includes child care, spouse care, cooking and feeding, soothing and patching, straightening out disorder and cleaning up dirt, little considerations like sewing a button on a grown man's raincoat, major considerations like nursing relationships and mending rifts, putting the demands of family and others before one's own, and dropping one's work to minister to the sick, the troubled and the lonely in their time of need.

When nurturance is given out of love, disposition or a sense of responsible duty, the assumption exists that whatever form it takes—changing a diaper or baking a tray of raisin-nut cookies—the behavior expresses a woman's biological nature. When nurturing acts are performed by men, they are interpreted as extraordinary or possibly suspect. When nurturance is provided by maids, housekeepers, kindergarten teachers or practical nurses, its value in the marketplace is low.

Are women the nurturing sex by anatomical design? In the original sense of nurture, what the body can do to support new life, of course the answer is yes. Femaleness in humans and other mammals is defined by the manner of reproduction: gestation and nourishment inside the womb followed by nursing the dependent young upon birth. Few would deny that the nurturant responsibilities of motherhood begin as a biological process, and that suckling connects the labor of birth to the social obligation of continuing care. Or so the rhythms of nature undisturbed by human civilization suggest.

In the depths of the forest or on the grassy plains of the savanna, wherever groupings of mammals exist in the wild, milk is the crucial lifeline from mother to infant. Cleaning, carrying and protecting from danger are closely related acts, although the indifferent mother is not unknown. Active maternal nurturance is the stable core of the social order for animals that live in groups, marked by strong bonds of kinship and positions of high rank and power (for some) that frequently pass to the next generation. Behavior that appears more pronounced in the male of some species—fighting, displays of dominance, defense against predators, grabbing the best and largest portion—does not compare in social cohesion to the bond of maternal relation. In hunting and gathering bands, the earliest form of human society that was once universal, the dual purpose of female work was central to group survival. Responsible for bearing and rearing the next generation, as well as for collecting and preparing the basic foods for everyday needs, woman the mother and gatherer matched the productive labor and communal importance, at least, of man the hunter, as she does today in the Kalahari desert where remnant foraging groups, the !Kung San, continue their traditional ways.

It was no fault of women or men, or even of their ambitious yearnings, that as civilization advanced, the unchanging nature of biologically determined work became increasingly tangential to societal progress. To gain dominion over nature and bend it to human will, the restless intelligence of the Homo sapiens brain required a carefree reproductive system and physical strength, attributes that were characteristically male. With the cultivation of land and permanent towns, with the unleashing of competitive drives and personal ambitions that led to the accumulation of property and the rise of stratified classes, the necessary tasks of reproduction and nurture were no longer at the vital center of human endeavor. Inexorably and conclusively, the logic of femaleness with its inherent capacity for two kinds of purposeful labor, reproductive and "other," became a less powerful force in the social order than the single-minded capabilities of males.

Examining the social contribution of women's work in four pre-industrial economies (foraging, slash-and-burn horticulture, animal herding and intensive farming), the anthropologist Sharon Tiffany suggests that the perception of motherhood as woman's sole valuable function goes hand in hand with severe prohibitions on other opportunities for work, and with a devaluation of womanhood in general, in economic systems where men unquestionably dominate the means of production and the balance of power. When motherhood, child tending and housekeeping chores become a socioeconomic and cultural ideal that excludes the performance of income-producing work, female sexuality in turn becomes a male concern that reflects male interests. The right to free sexual expression, the right to control fertility and to choose whether or not to be a mother, and the right to value a girl child and her promise as much as a boy and his are determined by considerations that are male-defined.

Thousands of years ago in the pantheistic religions of the Eastern and Western worlds, worship of the Mother Goddess (Astarte, Isis and many others) was a reverent acknowledgment of the life-giving powers of woman and nature. Reflective of patriarchal domination over woman and land, monotheistic belief turned away from the concept of primordial birth and superimposed the divine will of a male deity on the act of procreation. Motherhood plays no part in the Genesis myth of creation. Adam is not born of woman; he is fashioned directly by the hand of God. Eve, his helpmate, is fashioned in turn from man's proverbial rib. With this unusual reordering of biological birth, the submission of woman to man was given a firm theological basis. The historic terms under which motherhood was sanctioned (only in marriage, to insure inherited wealth) further eroded maternal power and placed upon pregnancy elements of coercion, punishment and shame. As Christianity spread and suppressed the pagan religions, gestation in the womb was reduced to a caretaker function; and the pain and peril of childbirth, ironically a consequence of the large human head and its capacity for knowledge, came to be seen as the wages of original sin.

As the means of survival shifted perceptibly from agricultural systems to industrial economies, the traditional scope of women's work suffered new forms of attrition. The hearth, the broom, the spinning wheel and the cradle had been honored symbols of the female share in the household partnership of productive family labor, but the home itself as a central place of work was diminished in importance when spinning and weaving, among other skills, were gradually supplanted by mass production. Developing technology, mechanized power, specialization of labor and a system of wages increased the mobility and status of men in the economy at large, but the isolated performance of women's domestic work remained "free," except when performed by servants. Even milk from the breast suffered a drastic loss in status when a wet nurse of the peasant class or milk from a cow or goat (and later a powdered formula) were found to suffice, and moreover to improve the chance for infant survival when maternal breastfeeding was unavailable, insufficient or discouraged by social custom.

While the power of law and religion combined to prohibit a woman from seeking out income-producing work that was stamped as male, an appeal to her feminine nature was duly employed to assuage her ambitions and keep her content. In a poignant example of feminine sentiment used as a wedge against female ambition, childbirth itself was placed under male supervision when the skills of midwifery were surpassed by medical study from which women were barred as unfit by their delicate nature. Armed with the newest antiseptic and surgical knowledge, a doctor in the nineteenth century did have more to offer than a midwife limited to traditional skills, a sorry fact that did much to destroy a historic bond of sisterhood at the urgent moment of new life. Yet a woman doctor, or a woman who wished to become a doctor, was typically caricatured as unwholesomely mannish or likely to faint at the sight of blood—fated to fail one way or another in her foolish attempt to transgress the limits of her sex. Only the soft, unchallenging aspects of human behavior remained in the female province—a sweet disposition, the habits of neatness, a gentle desire to care for others—and these were enshrined as the superior values of unspoiled femininity as a moral ideal: the dutiful daughter, the good little wife and the virtuous mother who were grateful to live within the protected enclosure of their shrinking domestic sphere.

Refinement of one's feminine nature by staying at home in love and devotion was not meant for women of the working poor who labored side by side with their men on the land, or those who came to the city with their families to put in twelve hours a day at the mills. Neither did women at the upper levels of society need instruction in the feminine impropriety of labor. Born to a fashionable life of esthetic indulgence and a continual round of social engagements, they showed the usual eagerness of their privileged station to hand over all practical work, including the rearing of children, to the care of servants. It took the scrambling ambitions of a powerful new middle class—hardworking, ingenious, acquisitive and insecure—to impose the ideal of the aristocratic, leisured lady on women of its own kind as a hallmark of upward direction. It took a bourgeois value system propelled by industrious struggle and material gain to pridefully create a woman of total economic dependency in a home in which she now ranked as an ornamental possession, and to see her as a reward of free enterprise, a tribute to the virile success of men.

Marxist theoreticians of the nineteenth century might analyze reproduction as the means by which the exploited masses provided their oppressors with cannon fodder and factory hands, but they could find no place within their strict definitions of work and class for motherhood and nurturance as genuine forms of productive labor. Viewing the new rich in a kinder light, Social Darwinians attempting to explain the human struggle developed the concept of survival of the fittest as an exclusive matter of male-against-male competition. In the first half of the twentieth century it fell to the Freudians to puzzle over the unhappiness of middle-class women with their suppressed ambitions, and to offer the solution of marriage and motherhood as full-time work. The goal of a healthy, mature and adjusted woman was to rid herself of mannish, competitive drives, as she was to transcend her immature, mannish clitoral pleasure. Complete fulfillment and sexual satisfaction could reside only in her vagina, her uterus and her feminine role.

Two centuries before the Christian era, the moral goodness of motherhood was extolled by the Romans in the story of the widow Cornelia, mother of the noble Gracchi, who sacrificed the chance of remarriage and wealth to devote her life to raising her sons, whom she proudly called her "jewels." Cornelia's example soon was surpassed, however, by another mother whose impact on the feminine ideal has been felt for nearly two thousand years. Created by the Catholic Church on a few scant references in the Gospels, not always favorable at that, the story of Mary, mother of Jesus, is a moral exhortation to the high purpose of motherhood as the pinnacle of feminine ambition that excludes the reality of sex.

As Marina Warner reminds us in her brilliant treatise, *Alone of All Her Sex*, the Virgin is not tainted by worldly desires. She never gets angry or seeks to impose her will. She prayerfully intercedes with the difficult Father, but she does not interfere with His commands or wishes, nor with the commands or wishes of His Son. The Madonna's perfection resides in her simplicity, her chastity, her gentle devotion, her merciful compassion, her modest humility and her dutiful submission, and her luck in having been chosen as the Holy Womb and Comforting Breast for the Son of God. For these humble qualities she is ultimately rewarded as a Queen in Heaven. Alone among women, she has pleased the Lord. (The suckling goddess was an important fixture in religious iconography as far back as discovered civilization. In Roman legend the Milky Way was created when Juno, who was nursing Hercules, squirted her milk across the night sky. Warner records that the one female biological function permitted the Virgin in Christian faith was the act of nursing, yet by the sixteenth century contemporary prudishness and the upper-class custom of employing a wet nurse led to the virtual disappearance from art of the suckling Madonna.)

Collected and told by the brothers Grimm, German folklore in the eighteenth century put forward another vision of motherhood that was also a moral lesson. In *Hansel and Gretel, Cinderella* and the tale of *Snow White*, the story turns on a mother who is not really a mother at all. She is, instead, an uncaring stepmother, a stock figure of selfishness, overweening pride and personal ambition. Unmindful of her nurturant duties or actively plotting to get rid of her children (her husband is either too busy, too weak or too blinded by love to notice), the Wicked Stepmother is a cautionary example of maternal negligence and rejection who always gets her comeuppance in the end.

By the mid-twentieth century another negative parable of motherhood had assumed the proportions of popular myth. Stereotyped in modern American folklore as the nagging Jewish Mother, although hardly restricted to one ethnic type, she was a melodramatic matriarch past her childbearing years who could not accept that her job was over and done. A caricature of overbearing nurture, this mother belittled and bossed her husband, scrubbed the floor on her hands and knees when the maid had finished, overcooked the food in her efforts to provide a nourishing meal, and made her son feel guilty for not calling home. In psychoanalytic thinking, the "domineering" or "suffocating" or "overprotective" mother was held responsible for humankind's problems (homosexuality and criminal behavior, including rape, among them) as much as the "rejecting" mother who refused to accept her feminine role.

The point is this: While the sentiments of motherhood are designed to collect the ambitions a woman might hold in her heart and direct them toward the goal of nurture, even the nurturing woman can be too ambitious and powerful for the public good. Aggressive nurturance looms as yet another unfeminine fault, or perhaps as a contradiction in terms. Although managerial direction of the career of a husband or child has produced some important reputations in art, music and literature, the Stage Mother who encourages her offspring's talent and the Professional Widow who works tirelessly to keep her husband's work in the public eye are still perceived as unpleasantly pushy.

When it comes to her own success, it has never been becoming for a woman to try hard. Sweat under the arms, a clenched jaw, an unladylike grunt—these are, after all, the unavoidable signs of straining effort. A man may keep his nose to the grindstone, but a woman had better stop now and again to powder hers. Appearance, we are told, is more feminine than result. Unremarkably, the tiny handful of ambitious careers with certified feminine allure remain those glamorous big dreams with a slim chance for realization (actress, singer, model, interviewer on television) in which looking attractive is a part of performance, so the desire to be noticed can be partly excused.

But not totally excused. Not long ago a lady was someone whose name appeared in the papers only at birth, marriage and death, and a castrating bitch was a woman whose competence equaled a man's. Despite the celebrity mania of the last few decades, unreserved approval of an outstanding woman is still debatable in the public mind, and when asked, she is expected to profess as an article of faith that her husband and children come first, or would come first were she lucky enough to have them. Talent, ability and intellectual promise integrate uneasily with a feminine ideal romantically connected to the superior accomplishments of husband or lover. A lust for power, status, money or immortal fame stands outside the framework of womanly values on the grounds of brash immodesty and selfish indulgence, if not high romance.

Metaphoric reminders of the feminine ideal are doubly instructive when they cast the ambitions of women in a monstrous light. Think of the glamorous facade on a chilling Faye Dunaway in *Network*, the sugary frosting on a poisonous Anne Baxter in *All About Eve*. As a frightening image of femininity abandoned, the ugly witch with her crooked nose and hairy chin is all the more satanic when she rides her broomstick at midnight, subverting the trusty symbol of loyal housewifery, the moral goodness of sweeping clean, to nefarious ends. In *A Tale of Two Cities* Madame Defarge makes sinister use of a nurturant task, her knitting, to implement her vengeance. Childless and driven, she embodies the terrifying excesses of the French Revolution. Lady Macbeth and Hedda Gabler, possibly the two most ambitious and destructive females in theatrical history, are childless women; a third, Medea, destroys her children in an act of revenge. Well into the Sixties, before the new feminist movement, it was conventional in books, movies, plays and psychoanalytic writing to ascribe success, achievement and, especially, destruction, in women to motherhood denied and nurturance thwarted.

By contrast, as we are forever reminded, the ambitions of men, their manly striving and competitive struggles, find inspiring metaphors in the acts of erection, copulation, ejaculation, in seminal fluid itself, and in a fairy-tale picture of the physiology of conception in which eager, aggressive, adventurous sperm are imagined to elbow each other out of the way in their dash to reach an impassive egg. (As it happens, the swimming motions of sperm are random, not directed. They are actively transported upward through the female tract by estrogen-induced secretions, cervical filaments and muscular contractions along the passage. Sperm of unusual size and shape are shunted aside, destroyed and discarded. Scientific information, however, is slow to catch up with popular myth, particularly when it contradicts a cherished bias.)

Motherhood and ambition have been seen as opposing forces for thousands of years. Largely because of the new feminist movement, the internalized conflict as well as the external reality recently have become a subject of renewed attention. For many women, perhaps most, motherhood versus personal ambition represents the heart of the feminine dilemma. In the work of psychologist Carol Gilligan, ambivalence in making and sticking to some hard decisions (abortion, career choice), long considered a feminine weakness, has been shown to stem from the ethics and responsibilities of motherhood—the importance of "caring relationships"—as women perceive their role.

But if ambition and motherhood have been in conflict, femininity and motherhood have not had a happy conjunction either. The swollen belly, edema in legs and feet, the heaving flood tide of birth, the breast as a lactating organ, and the fatiguing chores of child care are not glamorous, sexy, delicate, romantic, refined or passive, as these words are usually defined.

The desire to be a mother can be a powerful ambition, too, especially when the opportunity is slow in coming. Responsive to the ticking of the biological clock, the motivation to produce and raise a child of one's own (for whatever reason, and the reasons are legion) and the gratifications that a child may bring are spurred by an urgency that is as unique to femaleness as motherhood itself. On the other hand, motherhood is so universally perceived as the ultimate proof of the feminine nature and the intended purpose of female existence that few women have the courage to admit that they do not have the gift for it, or that given a choice, they would rather marshal their energies, their sensitivities and their gratifications in other directions.

Duality of purpose is built into female biology in ways that are hard to resist (and without the freedom of contraceptive choice, in ways that are hard to avoid). The single-mindedness with which a man may pursue his nonreproductive goals is foreign not only to the female procreational ability, it is alien to the feminine values and emotional traits that women are expected to show. The human sentiments of motherhood (goodness, self-sacrifice and a specialty in taking care of the wants of others) are without question desirable characteristics for the raising of children, but I would argue strenuously that women do not possess these traits to a greater degree by biological tendency than men.

Without a radical restructuring of a social order that works well enough in its present form for those extremely ambitious, competitive men whose prototypical ancestors arranged it, and who have little objective reason, just yet, to change the rules, what hope is there for a real accommodation of dual-purpose ambition? The corporate hierarchy has no compelling motivation to modify what it demands of its career employees, and the prizes at the top of the heap go to those who pursue them with single-minded devotion. Pursuit of achievement in literature, science and the arts is a single-minded ambition that will never be restructured, for the competition, understandably, is fierce. Whatever form it takes, satisfying work that earns a decent income is always in short supply, and men are right when they say that the required expenditure of time and effort leaves little room for life's other rewards. Yet a man, if he wishes, may acquire a woman, or a succession of women, to provide him with the rewards of emotional support, practical nurturance, a home and a family. A woman responding to the same needs and desires must split in two and become the traditional reward herself, at least that part which is firmly rooted in biological fact.

Is it unfair for a woman to expect that her desire to be a full-time mother should be accommodated for an unspecified number of years? Should another woman avoid motherhood entirely in order to secure the full chance that any man might have for economic autonomy and satisfying work? Does a society that under-stands the need for successive generations have a moral obligation to ease the way for a third woman intent on fulfilling both aspects of her dual-purpose ambition? Should one set of expectations be viewed as a predictable retreat into a feminine tradition of dependence, another as a singular expression of unfeminine aspirations, and the third as an admirable solution possible only for the extremely ambitious, extremely energetic few, or for those who are lucky to live with more mildly ambi-tious, nurturing partners?

There are no easy answers to these questions.

Epilogue

My aim is not to propose a new definition of femininity, one that better suits the coming decade or one that lays claim to moral (or physical) superiority as some sort of intrinsic female province, but to invite examination of a compelling esthetic that evolved over thousands of years—to explore its origins and the reasons for its perseverance, in the effort to illuminate the restrictions on free choice.

Historically, as I have attempted to show, the fear of not being feminine enough, in style or in spirit, has been used as a sledgehammer against the collective and individual aspirations of women since failure in femininity carries the charge of mannish or neutered, making biological gender subject to ongoing proof. The great paradox of femininity, as I see it, is that a judicious concession here and there has been known to work wonders as protective coloration in a man's world and as a means of survival, but total surrender has stopped women point-blank from major forms of achievement. However femininity is used—and if one fact should be clear, it is that femininity *is used*—all approaches toward what men have defined as proper masculine pursuits are set up with roadblocks and detours that say, "For Femininity, Turn Here," or "For Femininity, Turn Back," and the lonesome traveler who wishes to ignore the signs still proceeds at her own risk.

During femininity's own cautious movement through centuries of social upheaval, at least three nostalgic objectives—woman as symbolic aristocrat, woman as humble servant, and woman as glamorous plaything—became melded into a prettified composite that understandably shows its strains. In whatever terms the divisions are cast—the lady and the whore; the provocative and the chaste; noble, altruistic nurturance and childlike dependency—the embedded contradictions leave every woman uncertain: Has she correctly followed all the instructions? Additionally, the conflicts that are rife in ladylike refinement, a submissive demeanor and dazzling allure guarantee that women will be divided among themselves, suspicious of other women as they seek to master an impossible formula to win the approval of men.

There is no denying that femininity's dependence on established traditions, be they styles of dress or codes of behavior, offers a psychological grip on one's sexual identity, particularly for those whose dimorphic characteristics fall within the statistical overlap that is biologically normal, yet far from the cultural ideal. (This holds true for masculinity as well. An androgynous appearance may be fine for a person of androgynous persuasion; it is not so fine—and can be devastating—when androgyny is not the intention.) What happens next is that certain arbitrary cues and symbols—a hair style, an inflection, an attitude toward work—become the social determinants of gender, and they in turn act as conservators of outworn social values and as levers against social change. In the great cultural need to differentiate one sex from the other with absolute clarity, there are burdens of proof on each side of the aisle, but while the extremes of masculinity can harm others (rape, wife beating, street crime, warfare and a related inability to concede or admit defeat), the extremes of femininity are harmful only—only!—to women themselves in the form of a self-imposed masochism (restraint, inhibition, self-denial, a wasteful use of thought and time) that is deliberately mistaken for "true nature."

Most hurtfully, perhaps, femininity is not something that improves with age, for girlishness, with its innocent modesty, its unthreatening impudence and its promise of ripe sexuality in the rosy future, typifies the feminine principle at its ephemeral best. Women who rely on a feminine strategy as their chief means of survival can do little to stop the roaring tide of maturity as they watch their advantage slip by. No doubt a sociobiologist would argue that this female misfortune is, after all, the way things are supposed to be, for the cultural clock merely reflects the biological clock and ticks off the years of reproductive readiness that are finite in number.

This will not do. Gender does ultimately rest on how the species reproduces, but while femaleness will continue to be defined by the XX chromosomal count and its reproductive potential, many women have ceased to define themselves by their reproductive role. (Men were never constrained, anatomically or philosophically, to see themselves primarily as fathers, for reproductive biology is not demanding of the time and energies, and consequently the commitment, of males.) Earning a living, however much the neo-Darwinians would like to frame it as male-against-male competition and survival of the fittest, has become something other than that. Increasingly it is a necessity for both of the sexes, with parenthood fitted in optionally as a gratifying interest, not as service to the species or moral duty (or perpetuation of one's genes). The post-reproductive years grow longer and longer, putting into perspective an emerging truth: the problem is not that some women are feminine failures, but that femininity fails as a reliable goal.

So much for theory. Women still remain emotionally and financially needy, and understandably they will grasp at strategies that seem to have worked in the past and that appear to be working for some right now. Even as they reintroduce themselves to the higher heel, the shorter skirt, the thinner brow, the longer lash, and step back with that inimitable, feminine self-conscious absorption to admire the effect and scrutinize for imperfection, they are thankful they need not put up with the full armature of deceits and handicaps of earlier generations. For things do improve, and progress is made, and they are, in their awareness if not yet in their freedom to choose, a little closer to being themselves.

❖ ❖ ❖

Dynamics

1. Trace Brownmiller's use of the term "feminine" in her essay, and explain the revisions she proposes as she redefines this term in the course of her essay. How do Brownmiller's definitions relate to the ways you have been accustomed to using the term.

Critical Tools

1. Brownmiller asks:

   without a radical restructuring of a social order that works well enough in its present form for those extremely ambitious, competitive men whose prototypical ancestors arranged it, and who have little objective reason, just yet, to change the rules, what hope is there for a real accommodation of dual-purpose ambition?

   Use some of Brownmiller's own key terms to write a detailed answer to her question, and offer examples from contemporary culture to illustrate your points.

Draft One/Draft Two

Draft One: Discuss the role of social class in Brownmiller's account of women's lives. How do her findings relate to your own experience?

Draft Two: Choose another text from *Literacies*, such as Scott Russell Sanders's essay, and explore the relations between that text and your own observations in draft one. What is the significance of your findings?

❖ ❖ ❖

Before Reading Barbara Christian. . .

1. Think about some of the activities you engage in: the work you do, your fields of study, or your hobbies, for example. How do you explain or justify your participation in these activities? What different kinds of evidence do you use to evaluate how significant or worthwhile these activities are?

2. What forms of expression or strategies of communication do you use when trying to explain an idea to someone who has less knowledge of or experience with that idea? What strategies of communication do you find useful when someone is trying to explain an unfamiliar idea to you? Discuss how you feel these varying strategies work.

Black Feminist Process: In the Midst of . . .

Barbara Christian

I am sprawling at the low table I work at, surrounded by books and plants, a pad and pencil in front of me. Brow knit, sometimes muttering, sometimes reading or staring out the window, I am engrossed. My 10-year-old daughter touches me.

"Come play a game," she implores.

"I'm working," ending the discussion, I think. Her skeptical face bends down.

"You're not teaching," she retorts, "You're just reading a story."

I see an image from Foucault's "Fantasia of the Library," at the center of which is a European male reader, surrounded by books, which comment on books, his posture rapt. Not too long ago I'd read Marcelle Thiebaux's commentary on Foucault's "Fantasia," in which she proposed replacing the male reader with a woman reader. She reminds us that her reader would occupy a different space; her reading would be seen as time away from her main work. Interruptions would be normal and she would likely be reinterpreting the book she is reading without even being aware of it, reinventing herself in the midst of patriarchal discourse, as to who she is supposed to be.

Quite true, I think, but most of my black sisters *and* brothers would not even have gotten in the library, or if some of them did, like the parlour maid in *Jane Eyre*, they'd be dusting the books. *Their* libraries in Alexandria and elsewhere had been burnt long ago in the wake of conquest and slavery.

Not wishing to prolong the discussion by reminding my daughter that 100 years ago, I would not even have been conceived of as a reader, might in fact have been killed for trying, I notice the Nancy Drew book she has in her hand, her finger still tucked in her place. She's probably solved the mystery already.

"Why are you reading?" she presses.

I know the words that come to my mind—"If I don't save my own life, who will?"—are triggered by the Walker essay I'd been reading and the book under her arm. I dodge her question.

"That would involve a long discussion. I'm working."

But her comment has set my mind on a different track. She knows it, sees the shift, and pulls out her now-constant refrain.

"I'm old enough to know." As indeed she is.

I remember as a young girl in the Caribbean gobbling up Nancy Drew books, involved in the adventures of this intrepid white teenage girl, who solved mysteries, risked danger, was central to her world. I know their pull for a young girl—the need to see oneself as engaging the dangerous world in a fiction protective enough to imagine it, the need to figure out the world, the need to win. And I remember the privileges of Nancy's world—pretty, intelligent, well taken care of, white, American, she had winning allies. What girl actually lives in that universe? What black girl protagonist competed with her? My daughter has read about Harriet Tubman, Mary McLeod Bethune; she has even met Rosa Parks. Historical personages, they are still too awesome for her.

Alice Walker notes in her essay that when Toni Morrison was asked why she wrote the books she did, she replied because she wanted to read them. And Marcelle Thiebaux makes the same comment in the *lit crit* language of our day: "The only possible library for a woman is one invented by herself, writing herself or her own discourse into it."

My daughter is waiting for an answer. If I'd been reading a how-to manual, a history book, or even a cookbook, she'd have accepted the answer about work.

Leaving momentous questions aside, I respond: "I enjoy it."

Abandoned for the moment by her friends, having solved the Nancy Drew mystery, she sees a long boring afternoon ahead. She asks one of her whoppers:

"What good does it do?" Knowing that the reading will turn into writing, she looks at the low table, books, pen, and pencil: "What *are* you doing?"

A good question, I think. But she is not finished. Knowing she's got me in the grip of a conversation, she rallies:

"Why is it that you write mostly about black women's books? You read lots of other books. Is it because you like what they say best?"

Art is not flattery, I think, trying to remember if I'd read that in the Walker essay.

What my daughter was asking is not a new question. It's one I often ask myself. What is a literary critic, a black woman critic, a black feminist literary critic, a black feminist social literary critic? The adjectives mount up, defining, qualifying, the activity. How does one distinguish them? The need to articulate a theory, to categorize the activities is a good part of the activity itself to the point where I wonder how we ever get around to doing anything else. What do these categories tell anyone about my method? Do I do formalist criticism, operative or expressive criticism, mimetic or structuralist criticism (to use the categories I'd noted in a paper by a feminist colleague of mine)? I'm irked, weighed down by Foucault's library as tiers of books written on epistemology, ontology, and technique peer down at me. Can one theorize effectively about an evolving process? Are the labels informative or primarily a way of nipping the question in the bud? What are the philosophical assumptions behind my praxis? I think how the articulation of a theory is a gathering place, sometimes a point of rest as the process rushes on, insisting that you follow. I can see myself trying to explain those tiers of books to my daughter as her little foot taps the floor.

"Well, first of all," I say, having decided to be serious, "I'm a reader," stressing my activeness, as I try to turn her comment, "You're just reading," on its head. As I state that simple fact, I think of the many analyses of the critic's role that bypass reading and move immediately to the critic's role as performer, as writer. I continue, "Reading is itself an involved activity. It's a response to some person's thoughts, and language, even possibly their heart."

When I read something that engages me, my reaction is visceral: I sweat, get excited, exalted or irritated, scribble on the edges of the paper, talk aloud to the unseen writer or to myself. Like the Ancient Mariner, I waylay every person in my path, "Have you read this? What about this, this, or this?" This reaction is no news to my daughter. She and her friends get that way about Michael Jackson, TV shows, stickers, possibly even Judy Blume. But that response, of course, is not so much the accepted critical mode, despite Barthes's *plaisir*. It's too suspect, too subjective, not grounded in reality.

Still, when I read much literary criticism today, I wonder if the critic has read the book, since so often the text is but an occasion for espousing his or her philosophical point of view—revolutionary black, feminist, or socialist program. The least we owe the writer, I think, is an acknowledgment of her labor. After all, writing is intentional, is at bottom, work.

I pause, trying to be as clear as possible to Najuma in my description of what I am doing.

"Right now," I say, "I'm listening to the voice, the many voices created by Alice Walker in this book and looking at the way she's using words to make these voices seem alive, so you believe them." (Aha, I think, formalist criticism, expressive criticism, operative criticism.) My daughter does not know these referents.

"Why," she inquires, "So you can write something?" She is now focused on the pencil and pad, which may take my attention away from her.

I try again, this time using a comparison. "Everybody wants to be understood by somebody. If you want somebody to know you, who you are, what you think and feel, you've got to say something. But if nobody indicates they heard you, then it's almost as if you never said anything at all. African people are wise when they say 'speech is knowledge.' "

My last sentence tells me my teaching instinct has been aroused. I'm now intent on her understanding of this point, the Nancy Drew book still in my mind.

"If black women don't say who they are, other people will and say it badly for them," I say, as I remember Audre Lorde's poem about the deadly consequences of silence. "Silence is hardly golden," I continue. "If other black women don't answer back, who will? When we speak and answer back we validate our experiences. We say we *are* important, if only to ourselves." Too hard for her, I think, but she's followed me.

"Like when you and your friends talk on the phone about how politicians don't understand what it means to be a mother'?" she quips. "Then, why don't you just call Alice Walker on the phone and tell her what you think about her book?"

She has seen Alice. She's flesh and blood—a pretty brown-skinned woman with a soft voice. But I'm not finished.

"I am a black woman, which means that when I read I have a particular stance. Because it's clear to me that black people, black women, women, poor people, despite our marvelous resilience, are often prevented from being all they can be, I am also a black feminist critic."

I think of literary criticism as a head detaching itself from the rest of a body, claiming subjectivity only in one part of the brain. "Everybody has a point of view about life and about the world, whether they admit it or not," I continue.

"Then," she ventures, "why do you have all these other books around you?" (questioning my definite point of view). "And why can't you just tell Alice Walker what you think?"

While she's talking, she notices, on the low table, Paule Marshall's essay, "Poets in the Kitchen." Seeing that our discussion is getting her nowhere, she changes the subject.

"Isn't it funny," she says, "that whenever your friends come over, whether you're cooking or not, you all end up in the kitchen?"

"That's what Paule is talking about." I shift back to our original conversation. "That's why I need all these other books. She's telling us how she learned about language and storytelling from her mother and her mother's friends talking in the kitchen" (rather than just in Foucault's library or Rochester's drawing room, I think).

"Are your friends poets too?" she smiles, amused by the thought. "They're in the kitchen because they're used to it," says Najuma as her face shows that she's begun thinking about the delights of food.

Yes, I think, but it's also because communities revolve around food and warmth, at least until they generate enough surplus to have women or blacks or some other group do it for them and they can retire to the library. (Ah, Marxist criticism?)

"That's true, Najuma, sometimes, we are forced to be there. But even then, human beings often make an opportunity out of a constraint. If we don't recognize what we're doing, the value of what we are doing . . . ? That's part of what a writer does. And as a critic (I now use the ponderous word), I call attention to the form, show how it comes out of a history, a tradition, how the writer uses it. If we, and others don't understand Paule's form, that it *is* a form, we can't even hear what she's saying or how meaningful it is."

My being from the Caribbean helps me to recognize that people invent their own forms. I think of Ellison's discussion of the mask Afro-Americans use, of Elaine Showalter's analysis of the double-voiced discourse of women. But I've lost her—my daughter's face puckers. Wondering if interrupting me has been worth it, she looks out the window.

Of course, I think, following my own train of thought, it's even more complicated than that. For in illuminating her kitchen poets, Paule is also calling attention to the constraints imposed on them. In denying her expression as art, those who control the society can continue their cultural hegemony. What's published or seen as central has so much to do with the cultural reproduction of the powerful.

But Najuma has interrupted my thoughts. Intently she asks: "Why do you write it down, why not just tell Alice about her book?" Writing, she knows, is even more private than reading, which separates her from me and has many times landed her in bed before she wanted to go.

I smile. Barthes's comment, "Writing is precisely that which exceeds speech" comes to mind. I pause. "Well," I say, again searching for a clear way out. "Writing is another way of ordering your thoughts. You write things differently from the way you say them, if only because you can look back at what you write, at what other people have written, and can look forward to what you may write. A blank piece of paper is an invitation to find out what you think, know, feel, to consciously make connection."

Medium criticism, I think. Is she going to ask about tape recorders or TV shows? No, I've lost her. But if she had asked, I'd remind her that tape recordings are transcribed and edited; even TV shows, as instant as they seem, are based on scripts.

Seeing her perplexity, I try again. "Sometimes," I say, "I haven't the slightest idea what I'm thinking. There's so much rushing through my mind. Don't you feel that way sometimes?" I ask as I look at her stare out the window. "Writing helps to form that chaos, (I change the word) all that energy."

I can see she's heard me.

"But what good is it besides knowing a little better what you are thinking. Who cares?"

"Hmm," I mutter, "if you don't care, who will?" But I refrain from this flippant comment and decide to take a leap. "Najuma, do you know why you worry about your kinky hair? Why there are so many poor people in this rich country? Why your friends sometimes tease you about reading too much?"

She pauses, then surprises me: "For the same reason, my school wasn't sure that a jazz class, instead of classical music, would be good music training," she says imitating a grown-up's voice.

She does notice things; I feel triumphant: "And that has to do with ideas," I continue, "and how they affect consciousness." Does she know the meaning of that word? I use it so often; do I know what it means? "People *do* things, one of which might be writing, to help themselves and other people ask questions about who they are, who they might be, what kind of world they want to create, to remind ourselves that we do create the world." (I am now being carried away by my own rhetoric.) "I teach too, go to conferences, support organizations I believe in, am a mother," I emphasize, as I begin to worry about whether I've exalted writing too much.

But the writing point holds her: "So," she says, "writers tell people what to do?"

My mind winces. "Well, not so much as they ask questions, try to express reality as they see it, feel it, push against what exists, imagine possibilities, see things that might not yet exist," I say, as I think of Wilson Harris's discourse on vision as a historical dimension.

"Anyway," she says, clearly wanting to end this too serious conversation, "I know what a critic is, because I saw it in the newspaper. You say what's good and what's bad," she says in triumph, knowing that I will finally agree with her.

"Literature is not a horse race," I mutter, as I remember Doris Lessing's response to such a statement. Foucault's library looms again.

Calmly I state: "First you've got to know what it *is* you're reading. What the writer, the person speaking, is doing, which may be unfamiliar since no two of us are, fortunately, alike. Remember how you told me that I didn't understand your way of dressing, that it had a way of its own?" (I see her combining colors I wouldn't even dream of, but when I calm down, they certainly do make their own statement.)

"Then, how do you judge what's good or bad," she says, "since everybody has their own way?"

From the past, I hear R. P. Blackmur's words, "the critic will impose the excellence of something he understands on something he doesn't understand." All those texts from Plato and Aristotle through Northrop Frye, the rationalist critics, the structuralists begin to fall on me. I relax by breathing deeply.

"You play the piano," I remind her. "Sometimes, something you're learning doesn't sound quite right at first, until you begin to see the way it's put together, how it works, what it's trying to do. Then you hear it, something new perhaps, something you just didn't know about before. It sounds beautiful. Writing is like that too. It's got its own workings. At least you need to understand the workings before you can say whether it's done well, which is not the same, I think, as whether you like it or not." I think of the Latin American writers whose work I find beautiful but whose tradition I know little about.

"There's no absolute way to tell what's good or bad," I continue, wondering how I got into this conversation. "I try to hear a writer's voice, or more precisely the one she's gotten on the page in comparison to the one she might have in her head. Then I try to situate that in a tradition that has evolved some approximate ways of how that gets written down best." My thoughts go faster than my speech. I think the best writers are often the ones that break the tradition to continue it. Baraka's comment on art, "hunting is not those heads on the wall," though male, is true.

"In any case," I emphasize, as she retreats to the kitchen, this conversation having become too heavy for her, "every critic knows one thing—writing is a complex activity. That's one of the reasons, I suppose, why we too must write." By now, I'm talking to myself. "And oh, how we write, as we invent our own vocabularies of mystification. Sometimes, things ought to be switched around and writers should get a chance to judge us."

Munching an apple, Najuma passes through the room, sweetly ending the conversation: "It sounds to me like too much work. Why don't you get involved with the airlines, so we can travel free." For her, traveling is the most pleasurable activity humankind has invented. "Or if that's too much, try gardening," she continues, compromising on my fetish for plants. "At least you'd look like you're having fun," she concludes as she turns to her collection of airline flyers.

"But I do have fun doing this," I respond, though, humbled again by the terror of the blank page in front of me, it's a mystery to me why.

❖ ❖ ❖

Dynamics

1. Locate some of the different ways Christian defines the processes of reading and writing. What kinds of significance do these definitions take on at various stages in her essay? Consider how your own thoughts about reading and writing influence your responses to her ideas about these processes.

2. Christian presents us with her conversation with her daughter and with her running commentary about that conversation. What different ways of speaking does she use as she moves back and forth between conversation and commentary? Evaluate how these different modes of presentation inform your understanding of and response to her arguments.

Critical Tools

1. Christian frequently refers to other writers and other texts. What use does she make of these references? Think about a second essay which, in your view, does interesting things with quotation. How do Christian's models of quotation relate to those in the second essay? Consider what new strategies for quotation—the kinds of material you might quote and the uses to which you would put those quotes—you might develop out of your analysis.

2. Christian raises the idea of "reinventing" oneself. What do you think this concept means in her essay? As you examine how this idea operates for Christian, think about some experiences in which you might claim to have "reinvented" yourself. How do your experiences relate to Christian's?

Draft One/Draft Two

Draft One: In her title, Christian suggests she is "in the midst of...." Identify the things she is "in the midst of" in her essay and explore how she responds to doing her "work" in the midst of these other things. How might this analysis help you examine the ways in which your own "work" is situated in the midst of other things?

Draft Two: Based on your analysis in draft one, try to discover some of the different processes at work in another reading. How are this second author's ideas situated "in the midst" of other processes? Consider the significance of this situatedness for the author's arguments, as well as for your response to those arguments.

❖ ❖ ❖

Before Reading Michelle Cliff. . .

1. Identify the power and authority you have in two or three roles you play in life: as a child, sibling, parent, employee, student, member of a team or organization, to name some of your many possible roles. Then identify some of the ways each role makes you responsible to someone of greater authority. How do the powers and limitations of each role work with or against each other? How do the powers and limitations you describe make you feel about playing these roles?

2. Analyze some of the ideas or images that come to mind when you hear the word "colonization." What have you learned about colonization from your own cultural background, from books, or in school? As you develop your ideas, think about the values and assumptions you associate with "colonizers" and "colonized." How do you position yourself in relation to these values? Why?

3. Consider some of the significant beliefs—about yourself, about "life," about the way the world works, or other issues important to you—you hold now that you did not hold in the past. Write about your experience of changing your perspective on these issues. What inspired you to revise your positions? How do you account for your former beliefs, and how do you feel about having changed them?

If I Could Write This in Fire, I Would Write This in Fire

Michelle Cliff

I

We were standing under the waterfall at the top of Orange River. Our chests were just beginning to mound—slight hills on either side. In the center of each were our nipples, which were losing their sideways look and rounding into perceptible buttons of dark flesh. Too fast it seemed. We touched each other, then, quickly and almost simultaneously, raised our arms to examine the hairs growing underneath. Another sign. Mine was wispy and light-brown. My friend Zoe had dark hair curled up tight. In each little patch the riverwater caught the sun so we glistened.

The waterfall had come about when my uncles dammed up the river to bring power to the sugar mill. Usually, when I say "sugar mill" to anyone not familiar with the Jamaican countryside or for that matter my family, I can tell their minds cast an image of tall smokestacks, enormous copper cauldrons, a man in a broad-brimmed hat with a whip, and several dozens of slaves—that is, if they have any idea of how large sugar mills once operated. It's a grandiose expression—like plantation, veran-dah, out-building. (Try substituting farm, porch, outside toilet.) To some people it even sounds romantic.

Our sugar mill was little more than a round-roofed shed, which contained a wheel and woodfire. We paid an old man to run it, tend the fire, and then either bartered or gave the sugar away, after my grandmother had taken what she needed. Our canefield was about two acres of flat land next to the river. My grandmother had six acres in all—one donkey, a mule, two cows, some chickens, a few pigs, and stray dogs and cats who had taken up residence in the yard.

Her house had four rooms, no electricity, no running water. The kitchen was a shed in the back with a small pot-bellied stove. Across from the stove was a mahogany counter, which had a white enamel basin set into it. The only light source was a window, a small space covered partly by a wooden shutter. We washed our faces and hands in enamel bowls with cold water carried in kerosene tins from the river and poured from enamel pitchers. Our chamber pots were enamel also, and in the morning we carefully placed them on the steps at the side of the house where my grandmother collected them and disposed of their contents. The outhouse was about thirty yards from the back door—a "closet" as we called it—infested with lizards capable of changing color. When the door was shut it was totally dark, and the lizards made their presence known by the noise of their scurrying through the torn newspaper, or the soft shudder when they dropped from the walls. I remember most clearly the stench of the toilet, which seemed to hang in the air in that climate.

But because every little piece of reality exists in relation to another little piece, our situation was not that simple. It was to our yard that people came with news first. It was in my grandmother's parlor that the Disciples of Christ held their meetings.

Zoe lived with her mother and sister on borrowed ground in a place called Breezy Hill. She and I saw each other almost every day on our school vacations over a period of three years. Each morning early—as I sat on the cement porch with my coffee cut with condensed milk—she appeared: in her straw hat, school tunic faded from blue to gray, white blouse, sneakers hanging around her neck. We had coffee together, and a piece of hard-dough bread with butter and cheese, waited a bit and headed for the river. At first we were shy with each other. We did not start from the same place.

There was land. My grandparents' farm. And there was color.

(My family was called *red*. A term which signified a degree of whiteness. "We's just a flock of red people," a cousin of mine said once.) In the hierarchy of shades I was considered among the lightest. The countrywomen who visited my grandmother commented on my "tall" hair—meaning long. Wavy, not curly.

I had spent the years from three to ten in New York and spoke—at first—like an American. I wore American clothes: shorts, slacks, bathing suit. Because of my American past I was looked upon as the creator of games. Cowboys and Indians. Cops and Robbers. Peter Pan.

(While the primary colonial identification for Jamaicans was English, American colonialism was a strong force in my childhood—and of course continues today. We were sent American movies and American music. American aluminum companies had already discovered bauxite on the island and were shipping the ore to their mainland. United Fruit bought our bananas. White Americans came to Montego Bay, Ocho Rios, and Kingston for their vacations and their cruise ships docked in Port Antonio and other places. In some ways America was seen as a better place than England by many Jamaicans. The farm laborers sent to work in American agribusiness came home with dollars and gifts and new clothes; there were few who mentioned American racism. Many of the middle class who emigrated to Brooklyn or Staten Island or Manhattan were able to pass into the white American world—saving their blackness for other Jamaicans or for trips home; in some cases, forgetting it altogether. Those middle-class Jamaicans who could not pass for white managed differently—not unlike the Bajans in Paule Marshall's *Brown Girl, Brownstones*—saving, working, investing, buying property. Completely separate in most cases from Black Americans.)

I was someone who had experience with the place that sent us triple features of B-grade westerns and gangster movies. And I had tall hair and light skin. And I was the granddaughter of my grandmother. So I had power. I was the cowboy, Zoe was my sidekick, the boys we knew were Indians. I was the detective, Zoe was my "girl," the boys were the robbers. I was Peter Pan, Zoe was Wendy Darling, the boys were the lost boys. And the terrain around the river—jungled and dark green—was Tombstone, or Chicago, or Never-Never Land.

This place and my friendship with Zoe never touched my life in Kingston. We did not correspond with each other when I left my grandmother's home.

I never visited Zoe's home the entire time I knew her. It was a given: never suggested, never raised.

Zoe went to a state school held in a country church in Red Hills. It had been my mother's school. I went to a private all-girls school where I was taught by white Englishwomen and pale Jamaicans. In her school the students were caned as punishment. In mine the harshest punishment I remember was being sent to sit under the *lignum vitae* to "commune with nature." Some of the girls were out-and-out white (English and American), the rest of us were colored—only a few were dark. Our uniforms were blood-red gabardine, heavy and hot. Classes were held in buildings meant to recreate England: damp with stone floors, facing onto a cloister, or quad as they called it. We began each day with the headmistress leading us in English hymns. The entire school stood for an hour in the zinc-roofed gymnasium.

Occasionally a girl fainted, or threw up. Once, a girl had a grand mal seizure. To any such disturbance the response was always "keep singing." While she flailed on the stone floor, I wondered what the mistresses would do. We sang "Faith of Our Fathers," and watched our classmate as her eyes rolled back in her head. I thought of people swallowing their tongues. This student was dark—here on a scholarship—and the only woman who came forward to help her was the gamesmistress, the only dark teacher. She kneeled beside the girl and slid the white web belt from her tennis shorts, clamping it between the girl's teeth. When the seizure was over, she carried the girl to a tumbling mat in a corner of the gym and covered her so she wouldn't get chilled.

Were the other women unable to touch this girl because of her darkness? I think that now. Her darkness and her scholarship. She lived on Windward Road with her grandmother; her mother was a maid. But darkness is usually enough for women like those to hold back. Then, we usually excused that kind of behavior by saying they were "ladies." (We were constantly being told we should be ladies also. One teacher went so far as to tell us many people thought Jamaicans lived in trees and we had to show these people they were mistaken.) In short, we felt insufficient to judge the behavior of these women. The English ones (who had the corner on power in the school) had come all this way to teach us. Shouldn't we treat them as the missionaries they were certain they were? The creole Jamaicans had a different role: they were passing on to those of us who were light-skinned the creole heritage of collaboration, assimilation, loyalty to our betters. We were expected to be willing subjects in this outpost of civilization.

The girl left school that day and never returned.

After prayers we filed into our classrooms. After classes we had games: tennis, field hockey, rounders (what the English call baseball), netball (what the English call basketball). For games we were divided into "houses"—groups named for Joan of Arc, Edith Cavell, Florence Nightingale, Jane Austen. Four white heroines. Two martyrs. One saint. Two nurses. (None of us knew then that there were Black women with Nightingale at Scutari.) One novelist. Three involved in whitemen's wars. Two dead in whitemen's wars. *Pride and Prejudice.*

Those of us in Cavell wore red badges and recited her last words before a firing squad in W. W. I: "Patriotism is not enough. I must have no hatred or bitterness toward anyone."

Sorry to say I grew up to have exactly that.

Looking back: To try and see when the background changed places with the foreground. To try and locate the vanishing point: where the lines of perspective converge and disappear. Lines of color and class. Lines of history and social context. Lines of denial and rejection. When did *we* (the light-skinned middle-class Jamaicans) take over for *them* as oppressors? I need to see when and how this happened. When what should have been reality was overtaken by what was surely unreality. When the house nigger became master.

"What's the matter with you? You think you're white or something?"
"Child, what you want to know 'bout Garvey for? The man was nothing but a damn fool."
"They not our kind of people."
Why did we wear wide-brimmed hats and try to get into Oxford? Why did we not return?

Great Expectations: A novel about origins and denial, about the futility and tragedy of that denial, about attempting assimilation. We learned this novel from a light-skinned Jamaican woman—she concentrated on what she called the "love affair" between Pip and Estella.

Looking back: Through the last page of *Sula.* "And the loss pressed down on her chest and came up into her throat. 'We was girls together,' she said as though explaining something." It was Zoe, and Zoe alone, I thought of. She snapped into my mind and I remembered no one else. Through the greens and blues of the riverbank. The flame of red hibiscus in front of my grandmother's house. The cracked grave of a former landowner. The fruit of the ackee which poisons those who don't know how to prepare it.

"What is to become of us?"
We borrowed a baby from a woman and used her as our dolly. Dressed and undressed her. Dipped her in the riverwater. Fed her with the milk her mother had left with us: and giggled because we knew where the milk had come from.

A letter: "I am desperate. I need to get away. I beg you one fifty-dollar."

I send the money because this is what she asks for. I visit her on a trip back home. Her front teeth are gone. Her husband beats her and she suffers blackouts. I sit on her chair. She is given birth control pills which aggravate her "condition." We boil up sorrel and ginger. She is being taught by Peace Corps volunteers to embroider linen mats with little lambs on them and gives me one as a keepsake. We cool off the sorrel with a block of ice brought from the shop nearby. The shopkeeper immediately recognizes me as my grandmother's granddaughter and refuses to sell me cigarettes. (I am twenty-seven.) We sit in the doorway of her house, pushing back the colored plastic strands which form a curtain, and talk about Babylon and Dred. About Manley and what he's doing for Jamaica. About how hard it is. We walk along the railway tracks—no longer used—to Crooked River and the post office. Her little daughter walks beside us and we recite a poem for her: "Mornin' buddy/Me no buddy fe wunna/Who den, den I saw?" and on and on.

I can come and go. And I leave. To complete my education in London.

II

Their goddam kings and their goddam queens. Grandmotherly Victoria spreading herself thin across the globe. Elizabeth II on our t.v. screens. We stop what we are doing. We quiet down. We pay our respects.

1981: In Massachusetts I get up at 5 A.M. to watch the royal wedding. I tell myself maybe the IRA will intervene. It's got to be better than starving themselves to death. Better to be a kamikaze in St. Paul's Cathedral than a hostage in Ulster. And last week Black and white people smashed storefronts all over the United Kingdom. But I really don't believe we'll see royal blood on t.v. I watch because they once ruled us. In the back of the cathedral a Maori woman sings an aria from Handel, and I notice that she is surrounded by the colored subjects.

To those of us in the commonwealth the royal family was the perfect symbol of hegemony. To those of us who were dark in the dark nations, the prime minister, the parliament barely existed. We believed in royalty—we were convinced in this belief. Maybe it played on some ancestral memories of West Africa—where other kings and queens had been. Altars and castles and magic.

The faces of our new rulers were everywhere in my childhood. Calendars, newsreels, magazines. Their presences were often among us. Attending test matches between the West Indians and South Africans. They were our landlords. Not always absentee. And no matter what Black leader we might elect—were we to choose independence—we would be losing something almost holy in our impudence.

WE ARE HERE BECAUSE YOU WERE THERE
BLACK PEOPLE AGAINST STATE BRUTALITY
BLACK WOMEN WILL NOT BE INTIMIDATED
WELCOME TO BRITAIN ... WELCOME TO SECOND-CLASS CITIZENSHIP
(slogans of the Black movement in Britain)

Indian women cleaning the toilets in Heathrow airport. This is the first thing I notice. Dark women in saris trudging buckets back and forth as other dark women in saris—some covered by loosefitting winter coats—form a line to have their passports stamped.

The triangle trade: molasses/rum/slaves. Robinson Crusoe was on a slave-trading journey, Robert Browning was a mulatto. Holding pens. Jamaica was a seasoning station. Split tongues. Sliced ears. Whipped bodies. The constant pretense of civility against rape. Still. Iron collars. Tinplate masks. The latter a precaution: to stop the slaves from eating the sugar cane.

A pregnant woman is to be whipped—they dig a hole to accommodate her belly and place her face down on the ground. Many of us became light-skinned very fast. Traced ourselves through bastard lines to reach the duke of Devonshire. The earl of Cornwall. The lord of this and the lord of that. Our mothers' rapes were the things unspoken.

You say: But Britain freed her slaves in 1833. Yes.

Tea plantations in India and Ceylon. Mines in Africa. The Cape-to-Cairo Railroad. Rhodes scholars. Suez Crisis. The white man's bloody burden. Boer War. Bantustans. Sitting in a theatre in London in the seventies. A play called *West of Suez*. A lousy play about British colonials. The finale comes when several well-known white actors are machine-gunned by several lesser-known Black actors. (As Nina Simone says: "This is a show tune but the show hasn't been written for it yet.")

The red empire of geography classes. "The sun never sets on the British empire and you can't trust it in the dark." Or with the dark peoples. "Because of the Industrial Revolution European countries went in search of markets and raw materials." Another geography (or was it a history) lesson.

Their bloody kings and their bloody queens. Their bloody peers. Their bloody generals. Admirals. Explorers. Livingstone. Hillary. Kitchener. All the bwanas. And all their beaters, porters, sherpas. Who found the source of the Nile. Victoria Falls. The tops of mountains. Their so-called discoveries reek of untruth. How many dark people died so they could misname the physical features in their blasted gazetteer. A statistic we shall never know. Dr. Livingstone, I presume you are here to rape our land and enslave our people.

There are statues of these dead white men all over London.

An interesting fact: The swear word "bloody" is a contraction of "by my lady"—a reference to the Virgin Mary. They do tend to use their ladies. Name ages for them. Places for them. Use them as screens, inspirations, symbols. And many of the ladies comply. While the national martyr Edith Cavell was being executed by the Germans in 1915 in Belgium (called "poor little Belgium" by the allies in the war), the Belgians were engaged in the exploitation of the land and peoples of the Congo.

And will we ever know how many dark peoples were "imported" to fight in white men's wars. Probably not. Just as we will never know how many hearts were cut from African people so that the Christian doctor might be a success—i.e., extend a white man's life. Our Sister Killjoy observes this from her black-eyed squint.

Dr. Schweitzer—humanitarian, authority on Bach, winner of the Nobel Peace Prize—on the people of Africa: "The Negro is a child, and with children nothing can be done without the use of authority. We must, therefore, so arrange the circumstances of our daily life that my authority can find expression. With regard to Negroes, then, I have coined the formula: 'I am your brother, it is true, but your elder brother.'" (*On the Edge of the Primeval Forest,* 1961)

They like to pretend we didn't fight back. We did: with obeah, poison, revolution. It simply was not enough.

"Colonies . . . these places where 'niggers' are cheap and the earth is rich." (W. E. B. Du Bois, "The Souls of White Folk")

A cousin is visiting me from Cal Tech where he is getting a degree in engineering. I am learning about the Italian Renaissance. My cousin is recognizably Black and speaks with an accent. I am not and do not—unless I am back home, where the "twang" comes upon me. We sit for some time in a bar in his hotel and are not served. A light-skinned Jamaican comes over to our table. He is an older man—a professor at the University of London. "Don't bother with it, you hear. They don't serve us in this bar." A run-of-the-mill incident for all recognizably Black people in this city. But for me it is not.

Henry's eyes fill up, but he refuses to believe our informant. "No, man, the girl is just busy." (The girl is a fifty-year-old white woman, who may just be following orders. But I do not mention this. I have chosen sides.) All I can manage to say is, "Jesus Christ, I hate the fucking English." Henry looks at me. (In the family I am known as the "lady cousin." It has to do with how I look. And the fact that I am twenty-seven and unmarried—and for all they know, unattached. They do not know that I am really the lesbian cousin). Our informant says—gently, but with a distinct tone of disappointment—"My dear, is that what you're studying at the university?"

You see—the whole business is very complicated.

Henry and I leave without drinks and go to meet some of his white colleagues at a restaurant I know near Covent Garden Opera House. The restaurant caters to theatre types and so I hope there won't be a repeat of the bar scene—at least they know how to pretend. Besides I tell myself, the owners are Italian *and* gay; they *must* be halfway decent. Henry and his colleagues work for an American company which is paying their way through Cal Tech. They mine bauxite from the hills in the middle of the island and send it to the United States. A turnaround occurs at dinner: Henry joins the white men in a sustained mockery of the waiters: their accents and the way they walk. He whispers to me: "Why you want to bring us to a battyman's den, lady?" (*Battyman = faggot* in Jamaican.) I keep quiet.

We put the whitemen in a taxi and Henry walks me to the underground station. He asks me to sleep with him. (It wouldn't be incest. His mother was a maid in the house of an uncle and Henry has not seen her since his birth. He was taken into the family. She was let go.) I say that I can't. I plead exams. I can't say that I don't want to. Because I remember what happened in the bar. But I can't say that I'm a lesbian either—even though I want to believe his alliance with the whitemen at dinner was forced: not really him. He doesn't buy my excuse. "Come on, lady, let's do it. What's the matter, you 'fraid?" I pretend I am back home and start patois to show him somehow I am not afraid, not English, not white. I tell him he's a married man and he tells me he's a ram goat. I take the train to where I am staying and try to forget the whole thing. But I don't. I remember our different skins and our different experiences within them. And I have a hard time realizing that I am angry with Henry. That to him—no use in pretending—a queer is a queer.

1981: I hear on the radio that Bob Marley is dead and I drive over the Mohawk Trail listening to a program of his music and I cry and cry and cry. Someone says: "It wasn't the ganja that killed him, it was poverty and working in a steel foundry when he was young."

I flash back to my childhood and a young man who worked for an aunt I lived with once. He taught me to smoke ganja behind the house. And to peel an orange with the tip of a machete without cutting through the skin—"Love" it was called: a necklace of orange rind the result. I think about him because I heard he had become a Rastaman. And then I think about Rastas.

We are sitting on the porch of an uncle's house in Kingston—the family and I—and a Rastaman comes to the gate. We have guns but they are locked behind a false closet. We have dogs but they are tied up. We are Jamaicans and know that Rastas mean no harm. We let him in and he sits on the side of the porch and shows us his brooms and brushes. We buy some to take back to New York. "Peace, missis."

There were many Rastas in my childhood. Walking the roadside with their goods. Sitting outside their shacks in the mountains. The outsides painted bright—sometimes with words. Gathering at Palisadoes Airport to greet the Conquering Lion of Judah. They were considered figures of fun by most middle-class Jamaicans. Harmless—like Marcus Garvey.

Later: white American hippies trying to create the effect of dred in their straight white hair. The ganja joint held between their straight white teeth. "Man, the grass is good." Hanging out by the Sheraton pool. Light-skinned Jamaicans also dredlocked, also assuming the ganja. Both groups moving to the music but not the words. Harmless. "Peace, brother."

III

My grandmother: "Let us thank God for a fruitful place."
My grandfather: "Let us rescue the perishing world."

This evening on the road in western Massachusetts there are pockets of fog. Then clear spaces. Across from a pond a dog staggers in front of my headlights. I look closer and see that his mouth is foaming. He stumbles to the side of the road—I go to call the police.

I drive back to the house, radio playing "difficult" piano pieces. And I think about how I need to say all this. This is who I am. I am not what you allow me to be. Whatever you decide me to be. In a bookstore in London I show the woman at the counter my book and she stares at me for a minute, then says: "You're a Jamaican." "Yes." "You're not at all like our Jamaicans."

Encountering the void is nothing more nor less than understanding invisibility. Of being fogbound.

Then: It was never a question of passing. It was a question of hiding. Behind Black and white perceptions of who we were—who they thought we were. Tropics. Plantations. Calypso. Cricket. We were the people with the musical voices and the coronation mugs on our parlor tables. I would be whatever figure these foreign imaginations cared for me to be. It would be so simple to let others fill in for me. So easy to startle them with a flash of anger when their visions got out of hand—but never to sustain the anger for myself.

It could become a life lived within myself. A life cut off. I know who I am but you will never know who I am. I may in fact lose touch with who I am.

I hid from my real sources. But my real sources were also hidden from me.

Now: It is not a question of relinquishing privilege. It is a question of grasping more of myself. I have found that in the real sources are concealed my survival. My speech. My voice. To be colonized is to be rendered insensitive. To have those parts necessary to sustain life numbed. And this is in some cases—in my case—perceived as privilege. The test of a colonized person is to walk through a shantytown in Kingston and not bat an eye. This I cannot do. Because part of me lives there—and as I grasp more of this part I realize what needs to be done with the rest of my life.

Sometimes I used to think we were like the Marranos—the Sephardic Jews forced to pretend they were Christians. The name was given to them by the Christians, and meant "pigs." But once out of Spain and Portugal, they became Jews openly again. Some settled in Jamaica. They knew who the enemy was and acted for their own survival. But they remained Jews always.

We also knew who the enemy was—I remember jokes about the English. Saying they stank. saying they were stingy. that they drank too much and couldn't hold their liquor. that they had bad teeth. were dirty and dishonest. were limey bastards. and horse-faced bitches. We said the men only wanted to sleep with Jamaican women. And that the women made pigs of themselves with Jamaican men.

But of course this was seen by us—the light-skinned middle class—with a double vision. We learned to cherish that part of us that was them—and to deny the part that was not. Believing in some cases that the latter part had ceased to exist.

None of this is as simple as it may sound. We were colorists and we aspired to oppressor status. (Of course, almost any aspiration instilled by Western civilization is to oppressor status: success, for example.) Color was the symbol of our potential: color taking in hair "quality," skin tone, freckles, nose-width, eyes. We did not see that color symbolism was a method of keeping us apart: in the society, in the family, between friends. Those of us who were light-skinned, straight-haired, etc., were given to believe that we could actually attain whiteness—or at least those qualities of the colonizer which made him superior. We were convinced of white supremacy. If we failed, we were not really responsible for our failures: we had all the advantages—but it was that one persistent drop of blood, that single rogue gene that made us unable to conceptualize abstract ideas, made us love darkness rather than despise it, which was to be blamed for our failure. Our dark part had taken over: an inherited imbalance in which the doom of the creole was sealed.

I am trying to write this as clearly as possible, but as I write I realize that what I say may sound fabulous, or even mythic. It is. It is insane.

Under this system of colorism—the system which prevailed in my childhood in Jamaica, and which has carried over to the present—rarely will dark and light people co-mingle. Rarely will they achieve between themselves an intimacy informed with identity. (I should say here that I am using the categories light and dark both literally and symbolically. There are dark Jamaicans who have achieved lightness and the "advantages" which go with it by their successful pursuit of oppressor status.)

Under this system light and dark people will meet in those ways in which the light-skinned person imitates the oppressor. But imitation goes only so far: the light-skinned person becomes an oppressor in fact. He/she will have a dark chauffeur, a dark nanny, a dark maid, and a dark gardener. These employees will be paid badly. Because of the slave past, because of their dark skin, the servants of the middle class have been used according to the traditions of the slavocracy. They are not seen as workers for their own sake, but for the sake of the family who has employed them. It was not until Michael Manley became prime minister that a minimum wage for houseworkers was enacted—and the indignation of the middle class was profound.

During Manley's leadership the middle class began to abandon the island in droves. Toronto. Miami. New York. Leaving their houses and businesses behind and sewing cash into the tops of suitcases. Today—with a new regime—they are returning: "Come back to the way things used to be" the tourist advertisement on American t.v. says. "Make it Jamaica again. Make it your own."

But let me return to the situation of houseservants as I remember it: They will be paid badly, but they will be "given" room and board. However, the key to the larder will be kept by the mistress in her dresser drawer. They will spend Christmas with the family of their employers and be given a length of English wool for trousers or a few yards of cotton for dresses. They will see their children on their days off: their extended family will care for the children the rest of the time. When the employers visit their relations in the country, the servants may be asked along—oftentimes the servants of the middle class come from the same part of the countryside their employers have come from. But they will be expected to work while they are there. Back in town, there are parts of the house they are allowed to move freely around; other parts they are not allowed to enter. When the family watches the t.v., the servant is allowed to watch also, but only while standing in a doorway. The servant may have a radio in his/her room, also a dresser and a cot. Perhaps a mirror. There will usually be one ceiling light. And one small square louvered window.

A true story: One middle-class Jamaican woman ordered a Persian rug from Harrod's in London. The day it arrived so did her new maid. She was going downtown to have her hair touched up, and told the maid to vacuum the rug. She told the maid she would find the vacuum cleaner in the same shed as the power mower. And when she returned she found that the fine nap of her new rug had been removed.

The reaction of the mistress was to tell her friends that the "girl" was backward. She did not fire her until she found that the maid had scrubbed the teflon from her new set of pots, saying she thought they were coated with "nastiness."

The houseworker/mistress relationship in which one Black woman is the oppressor of another Black woman is a cornerstone of the experience of many Jamaican women.

I remember another true story: In a middle-class family's home one Christmas, a relation was visiting from New York. This woman had brought gifts for everybody, including the housemaid. The maid had been released from a mental institution recently, where they had "treated" her for depression. This visiting light-skinned woman had brought the dark woman a bright red rayon blouse and presented it to her in the garden one afternoon, while the family was having tea. The maid thanked her softly, and the other woman moved toward her as if to embrace her. Then she stopped, her face suddenly covered with tears, and ran into the house, saying, "My God. I can't. I can't."

We are women who come from a place almost incredible in its beauty. It is a beauty which can mask a great deal and which has been used in that way. But that the beauty is there is a fact. I remember what I thought the freedom of my childhood, in which the fruitful place was something I took for granted. Just as I took for granted Zoe's appearance every morning on my school vacations—in the sense that I knew she would be there. That she would always be the one to visit me. The perishing world of my grandfather's graces at the table, if I ever seriously thought about it, was somewhere else.

Our souls were affected by the beauty of Jamaica, as much as they were affected by our fears of darkness.

There is no ending to this piece of writing. There is no way to end it. As I read back over it, I see that we/they/I may become confused in the mind of the reader: but these pronouns have always co-existed in my mind. The Rastas talk of the "I and I"—a pronoun in which they combine themselves with Jah. Jah is a contraction of Jahweh and Jehova, but to me always sounds like the beginning of Jamaica. I and Jamaica is who I am. No matter how far I travel—how deep the ambivalence I feel about ever returning. And Jamaica is a place in which we/they/I connect and disconnect—change place.

❖ ❖ ❖

Dynamics

1. Locate several passages in Cliff's essay in which colors or shades of light and dark seem to be important. Discuss your response to the connections Cliff makes between color and different ideas, values, or beliefs. How do you understand her use of color in each of these passages? Consider the ways her use of color in one passage might challenge or extend her use of color in other passages.

2. Cliff concludes that "Jamaica is a place in which we/they/I connect and disconnect—change places." Analyze some of the different "identities" Cliff takes on throughout her essay. Work with specific passages to explore how she makes use of these connections and disconnections; consider also the challenges these shifting identities present to her. What conclusions might you draw about her strategy for coping with these shifts?

Critical Tools

1. Many of us have had little exposure to the style of writing Cliff employs in her essay; even after several readings, we might remain confused, perhaps frustrated. Scholes, Scheper-Hughes, and other authors offer us strategies for reading and interpretation. Work with one or two strategies from another reading or readings to examine a few passages from Cliff's essay. How do these strategies help us move past our initial confusion? Work with your new insights about Cliff's arguments to discuss why Cliff might have chosen to write in this style.

2. Cliff frequently punctuates her essay with emotionally-charged references to memories, people, and historical events. How do your emotional reactions to these passages shape your responses to Cliff's arguments? Use some passages from Cliff's essay to help you re-think the role that your emotions played in your interpretation of another essay. How do you feel about "emotion" as a tool for making an argument?

3. Use the passages in Cliff's essay that pertain to Zoe in order to evaluate the arguments Cliff makes about herself, her past, and her beliefs. How does Cliff account for the various ways in which she and Zoe relate to each other at different points in time? Working with the kind of self-analysis Cliff uses in her essay, explore how changes in your ideas about an issue important to you have affected your relationship with someone.

Draft One/Draft Two

1. *Draft One:* Cliff asserts that she is "trying to write [her essay] as clearly as possible" but she runs into difficulty because what she has to say is "insane." Referring to a couple of passages from Cliff's essay in which the tension between "clarity" and "insanity" seems especially pronounced, discuss an experience in which you struggled to write about an idea, issue, or argument that continually escaped your efforts. What does your reading of Cliff allow you to say about your own experience?

    Draft Two: Use your new insights to review one or two similarly tense sections from another essay you've read. How does your understanding of the experience you describe in draft one help you affect the ways you now understand these passages? Consider how your new views about these passages might help you to revise your response to the essay as a whole.

2. *Draft One:* Evaluate the specific ways Cliff characterizes and responds to her varied experiences as a woman of color in England and America. How do these experiences relate to the life she lives in Jamaica? Consider your ideas about "assimilation" and "cultural identity" as you analyze her experiences.

    Draft Two: According to Cliff, "the whole business is very complicated." Based upon your analysis in draft one, identify and evaluate some of the ways Cliff sorts through the issues which make her "business" so complex. How might Cliff's coordination of issues help you to discover something new about the way "complicated" issues are managed in a second essay?

❖ ❖ ❖

Before Reading James Clifford. . .

1. What stereotypes of the tourist are you familiar with? What problems do you associate with these stereotypes?

2. Tell a story from your own experience that helps explain why and how an expert and a novice look at the same event differently. What can you say about expertise and perception, based on that story?

3. Look up Chiapas at the library. What has been happening there in recent years?

Incidents of Tourism in Chiapas & Yucatan

James Clifford

Notes in memory of Michel Leiris, 1901-1990

Arrival.

Leaving Mexico City, our plane flies close to volcanoes. Then, under a low sky in the streets of San Cristóbal de las Casas. Scattered smiles. What there is to see.

[falling on; as, an *incident* ray]

Dusk, wandering around. Impressions of San Cristóbal. Streets full of accelerating cars close to narrow sidewalks. Anxiety. Constantly watching out for a tired three-year-old. Ben's disoriented, dragged through a noisy labyrinth. Wants to run. But where?

City coming to life. People moving in all directions.

Clatter of bells from a church somewhere in the dark. People's indifference to us, a relief. Only the other tourists, looking away, seem displeased by our presence, as we are by theirs.

Glances into bright doorways, color coded rooms. Each a side altar, small collection, museum, Cornell box, universe, store.

Beyond the tourist experience: Explorer? Writer? Pilgrim? Scientist? Aesthete? Ecologist? Initiate? Poet? Politico? All the established routes/roots.

Available.

＊

Collection.

Tourist "herds" in buses. Safe in their literal bubble.
Taking pictures, buying postcards.

From James Clifford," Incidents of Tourism in Chiapas & Yucatan." Appeared in *Sulfur,* Fall 1991. Reprinted by permission of the publisher.

We think we can speak (English) freely without being understood.
Safety of food consumed, streets walked on, sheets slept in.
The somehow inspiring colors of walls and houses.
Pleasures of ignorance. The nameless plants. Displeased by Muzak.
Invisible birds crying in the palms at the Zócalo.
Rolling drums and a cacophonous school band.

❋

Incident.

Since Ben is in no shape for a restaurant, we decide to have dinner served in our hotel room. It's old fashioned and chilly, but with a fireplace that we were told could be used. Dinner beside a roaring blaze! However Judith's a little embarrassed to ask someone to lay the fire since today the weather in San Cristóbal turned warm. I prevail. We're tourists. So what if we want a fire on a warm night? The cozy atmosphere will be nice.

Two telephone calls. Finally a man appears with a half dozen sticks and a gas can. Glum, none of the usual banter. He douses the wood, throws on a match, watches a minute and leaves. The fire flares, fades. (We've paid 3,000 pesos—$1.25.) I look everywhere for paper to revive the flames, but none is to be found (the hotel staff are endlessly tidying up). Should we complain? (But for $1.25?) And we probably shouldn't have asked anyway. Still, the room *is* chilly. (A fire wouldn't have helped much.) And how could he bring just six sticks? (Is wood so hard to come by here?) Our cozy fire's only contribution to the room's atmosphere is a strong odor of gas.

Outside, crowds of people stroll in the warm evening. We're famished. More delays. Dinner comes at last, and it's delicious. The wine tastes good. We go to sleep.

❋

Through a Doorway.

Photographs strictly forbidden, by order of the Indian municipal government.

> *The San Loranzo [Zinacantán] church is remarkable mainly for its saints, many of whom wear Zinacanteco robes. It also has a wooden cross, twenty feet tall, swathed in blue cloth and decked with streamers like the ones on the Indians' hats. When we come out, copal smoke is billowing from the chapel door and the men who were drinking have gone inside. Three musicians on a bench to the right of the altar are playing a harp, a violin, and a guitar. The instruments, like the alcohol, are homemade; they produce a reedy, off-key dirge of fathomless sadness. Three other men in full regalia dance slowly, swaying to the maudlin songs. Hats and bottles are on the table, and behind those you see a dark Christ wreathed in arum lilies, chrysanthemums, and clouds of incense.*

—Ronald Wright,
Time Among the Maya: Travels in Belize, Guatemala, and Mexico, 1989

When we visit the church of San Lorenzo, a basketball tournament is in progress outside. Bright uniforms and a squawking loudspeaker.

＊

Apprentice traveller.

For Ben, every day is a series of arbitrary moves. He's jerked from place to place, a lot of different faces, things, sounds. He works to invent routes and routines. Visits to a favorite place atop the Zócalo bandstand, retreats to the hotel room and a small collection of toys.

Ben shouts across the street to a grim looking soldier (helmet, automatic rifle) who's guarding a bank. White gloved fingers on the gun barrel ripple. A grin spreads beneath the reflecting sunglasses.

Collecting pats on the head.

A local boy plays with cheap plastic cars, a cowboy, an Indian. Ben contributes his matchbox rocketmobile. Things are set up, knocked down. A trade negotiated.

＊

Incident.

Ben and I explore the hotel's long halls. On the third floor, a passage leads up to the roof. Suddenly the whole city of San Cristóbal is visible. A full 360° ringed by mountains. Immense, variegated dome of sky—an area of intense blue here, rain laden clouds there. Light filtering in at the edges. Exhilarating. We count all the churches.

Later, I remember what Mary Pratt, writing on the history of travel literature, calls the "monarch of all I survey scene." From a hilltop, promontory, balcony. . .the "whole" is grasped, usually as a natural (unpopulated) landscape. On our hotel roof, everything that made us feel strangers down in the streets (language, looks, gestures, fear of being cheated, of falling ill, of seeming stupid) is gone. Replaced by an expanded range of sight, a feeling of centrality.

Isn't some moment of power, of emptying/opening, part of any "good trip?"

＊

We fly to Yucatan.

＊

Incident.

Obligatory contretemps with *taxista* at Cancún Airport. We bargain him down to the going rate. Hey, no hard feelings. In the course of a pleasant conversation it emerges that our driver is a school teacher. Salary hasn't gone up in ten years. *No importa.* Our job is to make you feel welcome. His wife sells Fuller Brush products. He drives a dilapidated cab. The governments of Latin America are all corrupt, he says, with plenty of help from the USA. What counts is to be honest, to sleep well at night. My wife always has to wake me; I sleep too well.

Forty minutes down the coast to our resort, La Posada del Capitán Lafitte. (Its billboard features a pirate with eye patch.) At the end of a long bumpy driveway, stucco cabins and a perfect white beach.

✳

Resort.

Idyllic community. No money openly changes hands. "Sign, Sign, Sign. Pay, Pay, Pay!" laughs the young man taking us to our *cabaña*. The poolside bar seems to be always open. Empty pockets. Bare feet. We relax. Every morning a couple of guys sweep the sand, clearing the debris thrown up by the waves.

Perfect white beach.

First night: a "floor show." The emcee, a waiter with pretty good English, asks us to be patient, to wait just "five Mexican minutes!" The manager's wife who operates the gift shop and a couple of waiters dance in costume, *típico*, beer bottles balanced on heads. (They seem to be having fun.) Music is provided by a trio of guitarists. Then a *piñada* for the kids, candy flying, balloons popping. Ben wild with excitement. Finally, an elimination broom dance. Young and old. Family ambiance. We drop our skepticism (it's a tourist trap, phoney, too windy, drinks expensive. . .) and begin to feel at home.

By breakfast the next day everybody seems to know "Ben."

Unlike the international tourist scene at San Cristóbal, every guest at the Posada Capitán Lafitte speaks North American English. We have all booked our cabañas through the same 800 number in Colorado. No averted looks. We are here to have fun with people just like us.

✳

Virtuous tourists.

Adjoining the Posada Lafitte, another ideal community—"Kai Luum." There the guests rough it, in tents along the beach (covered by thatch canopies). Eco-tourism. Meals taken together in a big tent, sand floor. "Save the tortugas." "Honor system" bar. Diving shop. Adult castaways in athletic communion with nature. No kids under 16.

We visit Kai Luum for Thanksgiving dinner. (Children OK this once.) Turkey with all the trimmings. Lantern lit and festive. The waiters are silent, anonymous. At Kai

Luum the "staff" are young North American men and women who stop for a moment at our table to chat. But the lack of any contact, even brief, with the non-White people working here feels oppressive. . .after the very friendly scene at Lafitte.

The Posada Capitán Lafitte and Kai Luum were founded together and still share some facilities. But the former is owned and managed by Mexicans, the latter by North Americans. The waiters, cleaners, beach sweepers, at both places are largely (Yucatec) Mayans.

How many different homes away from home are there in the tourist universe? "Authentic" San Cristóbal; the hotel scene at Cancún ("Miami Beach gone wild," someone called it). Kai Luum, Lafitte,. . .Are some of these places less exploitative than others? Could we choose to be good tourists? Staying at the smaller establishments? Locally owned? (But what hierarchies of class, race, or ethnicity are hidden by the word "local?") Worth a try perhaps.

With help from the Colorado 800 number (serving both Lafitte and Kai Luum) we have selected the "good" community, the one best suited to our liberal, family values. But our choice was based on a short paragraph in the guide book. And without Ben we would probably have picked Kai Luum!

✻

Voice.

> *That the native does not like the tourist is not hard to explain.... Every native would like to find a way out, every native would like a rest, every native would like a tour. But some natives—most natives in the world—cannot go anywhere. They are too poor. They are too poor to go anywhere. They are too poor to escape the reality of their lives; and they are too poor to live properly in the place where they live, which is the very place you, the tourist, want to go—so when the natives see you, the tourist, they envy you, they envy your ability to leave your own banality and boredom, they envy your ability to turn their own banality and boredom into a source of pleasure for yourself.*

—Jamaica Kincaid, *A Small Place*, 1988.

✻

Ruin.

In travel guides and publicity, "Maya" is almost always attached to the adjective "ancient." Ancientmaya.

> *The ground was entirely new; there were no guide-books or guides; the whole was a virgin soil. We could not see yards before us, and never knew what we would stumble upon next. At one time we stopped to cut away branches and vines which concealed the face of a monument, and then to dig around and bring to light a fragment, a sculptured corner of which protruded from the earth. I leaned over with breathless anxiety while*

the Indians worked, and an eye, an ear, a foot, or a hand was disentombed; and when a machete rang against the chiselled stone, I pushed the Indians away, and cleared out the loose earth with my hands.

—John L. Stephens, *Incidents of Travel in Central America. Chiapas and Yucatan,* 1841.

Cobá. Fabulous stone stairs rising up through trees, strewn with the small, bright-colored bodies of tourists. Tallest pyramid in Yucatan. Halfway up, a cigarette butt squashed against old rock. Then a view of *la selva*, distant lakes, electricity pylons, some mysterious bumps in the surrounding green—structures of a Mayan city.

Twelve stories up, and still no overview. Forest. At the more famous ruins (Tulum, Chichen Itza, Palenque) you get a "map" at ground level. Here, only a few patches of green have been scraped off. No way to know where you are in the large city. No way at Cobá to step back, or up. In a proper ruin you magically experience the space of another civilization and time. You expand to fill the blanks left by (produced by) excavation.

Here, we find indifferent forest. Faceless.

❋

The desire.

To excavate and complete. Establish names. Redeem the lost city.

Watch out for kids! Some nasty speed bumps on the straight road to Cobá almost bring us to a halt in a couple of Indian settlements.

> *No doubt there were men living in Yucatan and its adjacent areas before the Mayan occupation of that space. They took sustenance from the land and their labors and when the Mayan civilization came they contributed their labor and allegiance to it and when the Mayan civilization was broken they continued to live there, as indeed they do now, centuries later. But it was the Mayan civilization that occupied that space, and so effectively that the mark of the occupation has outlasted the civilization. The present inhabitants hardly occupy it, and are largely indifferent to its former occupation. But there are others who come there to locate and study the old sites, to clear away the vegetation and debris from them, and to rename those whose old names have been lost. The old occupation still asserts itself even though the force of its assertion is now in contrast to the surrounding desolation.*

—William Bronk, *The New World,* 1974.

Atop the smallest excavated pyramid at Cobá, a stone house. Ben takes possession, asks us in, kicks us out.

According to the guide book, Cobá is a preferred place for "independent travellers," hardy souls looking for real exploration. There's a luxury hotel nearby, belonging to a Club Med chain of "Archaeological Villas." Full library (ask concierge for key). Also a sophisticated gift shop selling artistic reproductions of Maya glyphs, "quality" Indian crafts. Gourmet restaurant.

> *I leaned over with breathless anxiety while the Indians worked, and an eye, an ear, a foot or a hand was disentombed...*

❋

Sophisticated travellers.

> *...when a machete rang against the chiselled stone, I pushed the Indians away, and cleared out the loose earth with my hands.*

Judith (who studies Mayan linguistics) talks in Spanish with Luis, a waiter at the Posada Capitán Lafitte. A Mayan, he was emcee at the evening "floor show." They discuss Yucatec. Judith recognizes words and sounds that are reminiscent of Tzotzil (the language she works on in San Cristóbal). Luis wants his children to speak Yucatec, but his wife is not a Mayan. How? Visits to grandparents and other kin? Or...?

The waiters are all young men, living away from their families (5 days a month home leave). They have Mexican first names (Luis, Manuel, Ricardo . . .) and Mayan last names. At Lafitte they study English with an elderly "regular" (guest/employee) from the States. Pay is low, compared with the earnings of a full-time taxi driver. But room and board are provided. With English, there's a prospect of mobility to a higher paid job. Maybe in Cancún.

The young men are travelers—part of the same transnational economy that made it possible for us to get from New York to highland Chiapas in less than 24 hours, that built the straight road to Cobá, that ensured our pleasant sojourn on this bit of pure coast. Different travelers—intersecting routes/ roots—we spend some amiable time together. But the Mayans living at the Posada del Capitán Lafitte are working. We're on holiday. They go home for vacation. We go abroad. Everyone dresses casually. But their flowered shirts are uniforms.

The Mayans in the dining room have first hand knowledge of our language and culture. We know little of theirs.

Judith's "expertise" begins to emerge in conversations with our fellow guests. They're surprised to hear that the waiters and cooks are Indians speaking Yucatec to one another. (Yet it sounds very different from Spanish.) And they're fascinated to learn there are thirty living Mayan languages with millions of speakers.

We begin to feel different, with superior knowledge (morality?). Our fellow guests are just "tourists." (But some have been in the area much longer and more often than we have. . .) Isn't this sense of a special experience, sensibility, or knowledge an essential part of any good trip? The sophisticated traveller's "other" is the tourist.

And the distinction is a routine production.

✳

Incident.

We hover in unclenched fetal positions over throngs of fish. Every imaginable color. No language for this but cliché. Voyeurs gazing. They notice us, hide sideways in the fire-coral. Sounds of heavy breathing. And a kind of participation. As we float the fish slide off, according to the same wave. Enormous, blatant strangers. (During a shower, we might have taken shelter together, without words.)

✳

Incident.

Airplane travel: heavily disciplined and anesthetized. Little individuality or interaction. Why are these people, this collection, traveling north from Mexico? Hard to read who's who. Some dress up, others down (like me) for a flight. Signs of class? The poorest aren't here. At least that's obvious. "We" cross borders with travel agents, "they" use *coyotes*.

The tourist, political refugee, anthropologist, picture bride, journalist, grandchild, missionary, technician, *opère*, diplomat, poet, scholar, soldier of fortune, physician, athlete, cook, student, sales rep...each in a numbered seat.

And hitting the runway, our brakes take hold. The entire molded plastic environment vibrates uncontrollably.

Lucid moment of fear, of homecoming.

❖ ❖ ❖

Dynamics

1. Located two or three passages where Clifford describes an event that allows him to distinguish between different kinds of travellers. What values are at work in these passages? Describe what you think is at stake in the passages you have chosen.

2. Discuss some ways in which Clifford's son Ben is typical of the many tourists described in this essay. In what ways is a specialist in cultural studies, like Clifford himself, typical of the tourists described in this essay?

Critical Tools

1. Identify some of the terms Clifford uses in the final pages, such as "distinction," "routine production," "uniforms," or "discipline," or choose some others that interest you. Which of these terms are implicitly present in the way Clifford describes some of the events in the early and middle parts of the essay? What is the significance of your findings?

2. What does Clifford mean by "authentic" and what social problems does he suggest are sometimes hidden by "authenticity"? Turn to another text in *Literacies*, such as the short story by Alice Walker, and expand upon Clifford's ideas about authenticity with the help of what you find there.

Draft One/Draft Two

Draft One: Expand upon your answer to the second Before Reading question by discussing one or two additional examples of expertise and perception taken from Clifford's essay. What is the significance of your findings?

Draft Two: Expand the discussion from draft one by relating it to another text from *Literacies* that is not written by an anthropologist, such as the essays by Robert Scholes or Czeslaw Milosz. What happens to the ideas you have generated about perception and expertise when you carry them across the boundary into another academic discipline or area of experience?

❖ ❖ ❖

Before Reading Nancy Fienup-Riordan. . .

1. What are some of the ideas or theories you have heard about how a human community should best interact with the natural environment? What complications arise with each of these ideas or theories? Which historical human community do you believe has had the best understanding of nature? How can you tell?

2. Think of a book or movie you know that represents an encounter between two cultures. Describe it briefly, and then speculate about how members of each culture would react to the ways their people are portrayed there.

3. What are the common barriers to a community's understanding of its own history?

Yup'ik Lives and How We See Them

Ann Fienup-Riordan

The Ideology of Subsistence

In descriptions of the coastal Yup'ik Eskimos, as well as of other Eskimo groups, their ability to survive in a frigid and inhospitable environment has often been emphasized to the exclusion of a comprehensive account of the value system that makes such survival meaningful. In fact, by idealizing their survival ability, we emphasize that aspect of their way of life most comprehensible within our own cultural system. Small wonder the students of Malthus and Darwin are continually drawn to the contemplation of the life ways of the inhabitants of the Arctic, whose cultural adaptation seems to epitomize the necessary fit between natural constraints and human response.

Yet a close look at the value system and ritual exchanges that characterize their elegantly efficient, traditional technology reveals less common-sense environmental determinism than cultural imagination. Certainly the fact that the traditional distributions of seal meat serve to feed the aged and the needy cannot be denied. In fact, the periodic random distribution of the products of the chase may well be ecologically required, something on the order of give now so that in your turn you may receive and so survive. Yet how this redistribution is accomplished, through an exchange of gifts between male cousins or between married women who are not related, is culturally determined and not nearly as preordained as one might suppose.

As the whole of symbolic anthropology is definitely an interpretive endeavor, and as the bulk of my work as an anthropologist has been directed toward this interpretation, I would like to relay in narrative fashion the experiences that taught me the significance of traditional and contemporary systems of exchange. I say *experiences* instead of *evidence* because anthropologists, just like other humans, are notorious for finding what they are looking for. I am under no illusion that what I "saw" while in the field was not at least partially a product of what I sought.

Ann Fieup Riordan, *Eskimo Essays*, © 1990 by Rutgers, the State University. Reprinted by permission of Rutgers University Press.

Further, and more important, I hope that by speaking through my own experiences I may help introduce the reader to a cultural logic that is difficult to convey through abstractions alone (such as, "the traditional Yup'ik Eskimos respected animals; they believed these animals had souls"). Thus, I take the tack of the seasoned hunter who requires the attention of the uninitiated while I tell a story of what it means to subsist.

In 1974 I was working in Anchorage, without experience of bush Alaska and without wish or desire to seek out such experience. I was studying anthropology and going off to investigate the mainland Chinese, and that was that. Then I was hired by the Nelson Islanders under a grant from the Alaska Humanities Forum to see what I could locate pertaining to the history and archaeology of pottery production in western Alaska. Whatever information I was able to find I was asked to take to Nelson Island in the spring of 1975. At that time I was to make a trip to Toksook Bay, the location of the Nelson Island School of Design, a production pottery that had recently been constructed in the village as a means of encouraging local industry and employment.

When I arrived on Nelson Island, I was initially impressed with how modern and Western the village of Toksook Bay seemed. It had electricity and running water, and most of the people I met during the first few days spoke English. Maybe they had once been exotic, but they certainly were not any more.

While I stayed in the village, I slept in the pottery workshop on an old army cot brought down from the National Guard armory. Every morning at about 7:30, with no knock or courteous inquiry as to whether I was presentable, several older village men would come into the building, turn up the stove, turn on the coffee pot, and take their places on the benches along the wall. From the back room where I had my cot, I could hear them talking slowly, softly. One might begin to mend an *uluaq*,[1] while another continued an ivory carving that he had started a few days before. Later during the morning, and again after the midday meal, younger men would drift into the pottery workshop, stand around, and silently watch what the older men were doing. No one paid any attention to me, although several of the older men were interested in the pictures I had brought of traditional Eskimo pottery from other parts of the Arctic. Also, no one paid any attention to the new pottery wheels and equipment that filled the workshop area.

At first I was bewildered by this apparent apathy in the face of government largesse. Community Enterprise Development Corporation had put up a substantial amount of money for the facility. Why were the old men here? Why was no one making pottery? I soon found that no one was making pottery because they were too busy doing everything else. It was spring, seal hunting was about to begin, and what little pottery production had taken place during the winter was at a standstill. Wages could not lure workers into the pottery. Hunting came first.

That old men gathered in the warmest communal space available (the community hall had no heat) was no surprise. In their youth most of them had lived together in the traditional *qasgiq*, or men's house. What better use to make of this new building, which had quickly proved itself incapable of housing Western industry as a design school. So the old men had taken over. Before I left the village, several snow machines were also moved in for repair, and there was talk by one village elder of using the building to cover the construction of a new boat.

The upshot of finding that my bedroom was in the modern version of the traditional men's house was that I didn't spend much time in it. Rather, I visited the houses and talked to the women. They said that I had come at the best time of the year, that the seal parties were about to begin.

Seal parties? What were they? I'd never read about seal parties. I'd never even heard of them. Well, my new friends told me, seal parties were given when the men and boys of the village brought home the first seals of the season. They were very exciting and lots of fun, as not only was the meat and blubber of every man's first-caught seal given away, but lots of other things as well. I was intrigued and waited eagerly for the parties to commence.

They began the next day—three parties in a row. I was just up and having a cup of tea when a little girl ran in the door and said to come quick. There, right next door, a woman was standing in her porch throwing Pampers and packs of gum into the waiting hands of a large group of women. I joined the fun and followed the group to the next house for a repetition of the event. I noticed that not all the same women attended, but other women joined the group. I asked about this later and was told that when a woman gives her seal party, her relatives could not attend; only her nonrelatives received the gift of meat.

By this time I was extremely excited. Here was a distribution of goods through which social relations were articulated. My interest in anthropology had originally been in the study of kinship systems. Also, I was convinced that one could not learn much about people's social relations simply by asking them genealogical questions such as "Who is your sister?" or "Who is your cousin?" Rather, to learn anything important about kinship, one must see it in action and witness what it means to be a sister or mother. The seal party provided a wonderful window into how the people of Nelson Island still thought about and acted out their ideas of what it meant to be related.

I found out later that while the explicit rule was that only nonrelatives attend one's seal party, in fact only sisters, mothers, mothers-in-law, and parallel cousins were excluded. More important, the hostess of the seal party normally "gave away" the privilege of throwing the gifts to an older woman, who in her turn singled out one individual in the audience to receive a special gift. These women were usually cross-cousins, the mothers of children who would be, or had already been, married. Also, it was significant that what they gave each other was raw meat, for the gift of raw meat was traditionally the exchange that marked the marriage relationship between a man and a woman. Thus, the seal-party exchange paralleled the marriage exchange. During the event a woman gave away the products of the hunt of her husband and sons, the symbolic proof of their potency, not just to anybody, but to women who could eventually give their daughters to the hosting family as brides.

Much more might be said on the metaphorical marriage between cross-cousins that the seal party represents. What is important is that, as I found later on, the seal party is not an isolated relic of traditional culture but rather is part of an annual cycle of ritual distribution. Pieces of this cycle are no longer practiced, but other parts are still alive and well and still express coastal villagers' attitudes toward their land and their lives.

The immediate counterpart of the seal party on Nelson Island is the men's and women's exchange dance (*Kevgiruaq*), in which men and women are said to fight through the dance. This sequence takes a slightly different form in the lower Yukon villages of Emmonak and Alakanuk, but the message is comparable. On the first night of the exchange dance, all the women in the village pair up as married couples, one woman taking the part of the husband and the other the part of the wife. Then, together, the women dance a multitude of gifts into the community hall and on the following morning give them out to the men of the village. The men perform for the women on the following evening, and the next morning the women receive gifts in their turn. The entire sequence of dances and gift-giving takes hours and hours, as everyone in the community has a turn on the dance floor. As each mock married couple comes out to dance, they are greeted by much laughing and teasing from the audience. The particular dance that is performed is always the same, but each couple vies with the others to make its rendition particularly hilarious. Young men put mop ends on their heads for hair. Fur parkas are turned inside out to imitate age and senility, and fake muscles are pushed into the dresses of the women who are playing the role of husband.

Even if one knew nothing about Yup'ik cultural configurations, the exchange dance would still be a splendid and exuberant performance to behold. Seen in the light of the seal party, its eloquence becomes apparent. Whereas in the seal party gifts are thrown out the doors of the individual houses, in the exchange dance gifts are danced in the door of the community hall. In the seal party these gifts consist of strips of cloth and bits of string, in fact bits and pieces of every conceivable household commodity. In the exchange dance, whole cloth is given, whole skeins of yarn, and sometimes quilts or bedspreads made from the very bits of cloth given away during the seal party. The length of cloth that a woman receives in the exchange dance she usually tears into strips for her seal party distribution. With the strips of cloth that she has collected from the various seal parties she has attended, she fabricates a quilted cover that she will then give away during the next year's exchange dance. If all that was required was a cover for the bed, the Yup'ik people have certainly taken a circuitous route to ensure its provision. In fact, after all the giving and receiving has been accomplished, no one is much the richer or poorer in material goods. Their world view, their whole cultural mode of being, has, however, been put on stage along with the dancers, acted out, and so reestablished and reaffirmed.

Social relations are also articulated in the dance. When I asked women how their dance partners were related to them, they said to me simply, "They are my relatives." In itself this was certainly an acceptable answer, but these so-called relatives were, in fact, the same persons who had been designated as nonrelatives at the seal parties! Cross-cousins who had stood on opposite sides as host and guest in one event joined together to host the entire community as a "married couple." As with the cycling of goods between the two events, relatives seemed to be cycling as well. Instead of a moral on the order of "never the twain shall meet," the Yup'ik celebrations seemed to imply that always that which is separated (socially, physically, and, as we shall see, metaphysically) will in the end be reunited.

As this ideological program is somewhat abstruse, let me detail a few more experiences to show how this point of view pervades village life today. In the spring of 1978 I made a visit to Nelson Island while I was pregnant with my first child. I was, of course, quite proud of my condition and sure that with the proper food and exercise the pregnancy and birth would go well. My Yup'ik friends, however, were not so blasé and proceeded to teach me an elaborate set of dos and don'ts that still accompanies pregnancy and childbirth in the village. I was to sleep with my head toward the door. As soon as I got up every morning, I was to run outside as fast as I could. Only then might I come in, sit down, and drink tea. In fact, any time during the day that I left the house I was to do it quickly without stopping in the doorway. If I were to pause in my exiting, the baby was sure to get stuck during delivery.

This series of prescriptions draws an obvious parallel between the womb in which the unborn baby lives and the house in which the expectant mother resides. Analogically, the throwing of gifts out of the house through the doorway at the time of the seal party is comparable to their birth. Analogous relationships exist between the progress of the souls of the human dead and the return of gifts into the community hall at the time of the exchange dance. In fact, imagery of birth and rebirth pervaded the system of symbols and meanings that was beginning to become apparent. The finality of death was everywhere averted, in both action and ideal.

Another anecdote will help make the significance of this cultural framework clear. During the time I lived on Nelson Island I had hoped in my heart of hearts that someone would give me a real Yup'ik name. No one ever did. They gave me a nickname that translated loosely as "big piece of fat." But that was as close to a traditional name as I got. Certainly I had asked about naming procedures, just as I had asked about pregnancy taboos, but with little solid response. I was made to feel acutely nosey. And, in fact, part of the message of this story is how little progress one can make in understanding the coastal Yup'ik people if one confines oneself to information acquired through a questionnaire approach. It certainly never worked for me, and in fact my best friends used to lie to me, in a good-natured way, to show me how foolish and misguided my occasional bouts of verbal curiosity were. Watching and listening, however, were different matters. And so it was with my understanding of the significance of naming.

Although I had never been given a name, when I returned to the village with my newborn daughter in the fall of 1978, she was immediately named. The older woman who had been my real teacher while I had lived on the island had had a cousin. That man had drowned not three weeks before. No sooner had my daughter and I come into the village than she came to where we were staying and gave my daughter the name of her dead cousin. Then, in every house in which we visited, people would ask me what my daughter's name was. When I told them, they would laugh and say such things as "Oh, he's come back a *kass'aq* [white person]!" or "He always did want to learn English!" or "To think now he has red hair!"

All this verbal play on the baby's name was a kind way of welcoming my daughter into their midst. But, as important, these endearments were wonderfully explicit expressions of the belief that in the newborn child the soul of the recently dead is born again. In the Yup'ik world, no one ever finally passes away out of existence. Rather, through the naming process, the essence of being human is passed on from one generation to the next.

This cycling of human souls is especially interesting when considered in light of the traditional belief that the souls of the seals must be cared for by the successful hunter in order that they, too, will be born again. Seals as well as other animals and fish are believed to give themselves to men voluntarily. A seal, for instance, is said to sense, and in fact to see, the merits of a hunter. If the hunter is seen to be "awake" to the rules of the proper relationship between humans and animals, and between humans and humans, then the seal will allow the hunter's harpoon or bullet to kill it. When the seal is hit, if the seal is likewise awake, its soul will retract to its bladder. Although its body will die and so provide life to humans, its soul will stay alive and await return to the sea. In fact, traditionally, the coastal Yup'ik Eskimos held a Bladder Festival every winter. At the Bladder Festival the bladders of the seals caught during the year along with the bladders of other animals were inflated, hung at the back of the men's house, and feasted and entertained for five days. Then, on the fifth day, each family took the bladders of the animals they had killed to the sea and pushed them down through a hole in the ice so that the souls of the seals might be born again.

Through these events the circle is completed. Not only do goods cycle, as do the seasons, but human and animal souls likewise are continually in motion. The birth of a baby is the rebirth of a member of its grandparental generation. The death of the seal means life to the village. The same people and the same seals have been on this earth from the beginning, continually cycling and recycling through life and death. Through this generational cycling, a life-celebrating system is put forward. The coastal Yup'ik Eskimos are not simply surviving on the resources of their environment but are living in a highly structured relationship to them. This relationship is important to comprehend, not as an exercise in Eskimo esoterica, but as the key to why they act and feel the way they do.

In light of the current subsistence debate,[2] the focus of present cultural consciousness on the coast and an issue that is not likely to be quickly resolved, one final anecdote is worth relating. In the spring of 1979 I revisited Nelson Island. It had been a good spring, and numerous seals and walrus had been taken. But Alaska Department of Fish and Game officials had unfortunately found several walrus carcasses at Cape Vancouver. Head hunters had taken the valuable ivory and left the rest of the meat to rot. Nelson Islanders accused Nunivak Islanders of the infraction and vice versa. Talking to an old man about the incident, I played devil's advocate and queried, "What difference does it make who killed them? Dead is dead and nothing can bring them back now, can it?" That I should have been so cavalier even now amazes me. The old man never lifted his eyes from the bench. "No," he said, "if they had been properly cared for they would have been able to return. Now they are gone forever."

Can these experiences help you to see the significance, in Yup'ik eyes, of the threat of an oil spill or game mismanagement? Although active shamanism and the celebration of the Bladder Festival are no more, too many embodiments of the traditional cosmology remain to be casually catalogued as superstition or to allow the scientific attitude toward species extinction to hold sway. Even the youngest child is still instructed in a code of etiquette toward natural surroundings that is as important as any code of etiquette toward other human beings (see also Nelson 1977). Given this cultural framework, it is possible but altogether inappropriate to deduce subsistence activities to mere survival techniques and their significance to the conquest of calories. Their pursuit is not simply a means to an end but an end in itself.

In what little literature exists on western Alaska, authors often comment that, even given alternatives, living off the land is still the preferred pattern. This preference is explicable only if being a hunter has intrinsic value. What Richard Nelson says of the Iñupiat is equally true of the coastal Yup'ik Eskimos: "One of the things that continually amazes me when I go back there is that people are still out there hunting, dedicated—sometimes almost passionately dedicated—to continuing this way of life" (quoted in Schiller 1981:16).

Small wonder the words of the Nelson Island elders were echoed by their children and more sophisticated contemporaries during testimony in Bethel in the spring of 1981 on the repeal of the subsistence legislation. Everywhere the emphasis was on the real kinship between the people and their environment. Stewardship, not to mention ownership, of resources is taken with a grain of salt, as the real power is not in people, but in the continuing relationship between humans and the natural world on which they depend.

NOTES

1. An *uluaq* is a woman's traditional semilunar knife set in a handle opposite the arc-shaped edge. It is also sometimes referred to as *ulu* in English from the Iñupiaq name for this type of knife (Jacobson 1984:391).

2. Since the passage of the Alaska Native Claims Settlement Act (ANCSA) in 1971, regulatory control over land and sea resources has become as big an issue as landownership and the closely related issue of the retention of subsistence hunting and fishing as priority activities. The d(2) section of ANCSA mandated legislation passed in 1980 as the Alaska National Interest Land Conservation Act (ANILCA). Although ANILCA is nearly 450 pages long, it sets down only general guidelines for the U.S. Fish and Wildlife Service to follow in managing land. The Fish and Wildlife Service has begun to implement broad provisions of the bill, and its regulations will ultimately determine the bill's success or failure. As they say on the delta, "You can't eat a regulation;" but, what's worse, regulations can make it so you can't eat, period.

Legislative actions and administration policies have already begun to tie the concept of subsistence use as a priority activity into the fabric of management—for example, the issuing at a reduced fee of resident permits to hunt musk oxen on Nelson Island. Yet the villagers' continuing concern is that when resources dwindle and competition from other users increases, the political process will undercut their subsistence rights. As political battles in Alaska have made abundantly clear, their fears are justified.

Robert Redford, Apanuugpak, and the Invention of Tradition

A project is currently under way to produce a full-length feature film in the western Alaska village of Toksook Bay on Nelson Island. The screenplay, appropriately enough, focuses on a traditional hero—Apanuugpak—and epic tales of bow-and-arrow warfare that are still very much a part of the oral tradition of the Yup'ik Eskimos who make Nelson Island their home. There are, however, discrepancies between Yup'ik history as it can be read from oral tradition and as both the scriptwriter and the people of Toksook Bay choose to present it in the film. These discrepancies relate to both the making and the marketing of tradition, on Nelson Island and beyond.

The current rethinking of ethnographic inquiry has focused on the need for anthropological writing to reflect the dialogic character of ethnographic interaction. It follows that the dialogic character of other native/non-native encounters also merits scrutiny. Far from reducing the ethnographic enterprise to fiction, the current reevaluation of the role of the ethnographer lends support to the development of a more critical view of situations of cross-cultural exchange already under way.

My acquaintance with the Apanuugpak film project began in the summer of 1985, when I was living at Toksook Bay working on an oral history project sponsored by the Toksook Bay City Council, a project intended to help villagers record their history.[1] While sharing tea and conversation with friends, I was told that Robert Redford was coming to Toksook to play the part of the famous warrior Apanuugpak in a film that was to be made on Nelson Island in the near future. People proudly announced that this film would soon air on one of the fourteen cable channels that had recently been made available in the community. A standing joke soon developed. Every time we heard a plane pass over (which was often), friends teased that I should hurry and put on lipstick, dress up, and run over to the airport. There I would be the first to greet Mr. Redford, take the part of Mrs. Apanuugpak, and what a fine film that would be!

The apparently farfetched juxtaposition of Robert Redford and Apanuugpak that provided the material for so many jokes that summer had a factual basis and already a very interesting history. The idea for a film based on the Apanuugpak stories was the brainchild of Dave Hunsaker, a Juneau playwright who first came to Nelson Island in 1984 seeking support for a play he had written entitled *Inuit Antigone*. This play was an English adaptation of Sophocles' Greek drama into an Eskimolike genre. Hunsaker was searching for native actors for the production. He met with the Toksook Bay City Council and received their approval of his project with two conditions. The first was that the title of the production be changed from *Inuit* to *Yup'ik Antigone*. The second was that the play be performed in the Yup'ik language.

Yup'ik Antigone was well received from Bethel to New York City and eventually all the way to Greece. The farther the troop traveled from home, the more exotic they appeared. The critical acclaim given to the play was simultaneously refreshing and revealing. The most impressive feature of *Yup'ik Antigone* was not the success of its international debut but the local enthusiasm it engendered. Applause was loudest closest to home. Nelson Islanders clearly enjoyed their introduction to Sophocles. The local production in the village high school was the first masked performance on the island since the missionaries' suppression of indigenous ceremony forty years before. Village elders both approved of and admired the dramatic staging, which shared elements with their traditional performance style.

Although the local enthusiasm *Yup'ik Antigone* elicited is commendable, it was not a factor in the response of the non-native audience. In the final analysis, the rave reviews the play received are telling examples of our Western objectification of culture and the fact that we are for the most part willing to take the other only on our terms—that is, translated through the Greeks. The play was constructed on the flawed assumption of a fundamental similarity between the Yup'ik Eskimos and the ancient Greeks. The face-to-face parent/child confrontations central to Sophocles' *Antigone* illustrate how different these two views of the world are. The Yup'ik pattern of conflict resolution prescribes both diffusion and extreme care in order not to injure the "mind" of the offender (Fienup-Riordan 1986a). One actor later commented on how embarrassed he was by so much "scolding" in the production. Another observer pointed out that a Yup'ik translation of an Italian sex comedy, with all its banter and innuendo, would have been culturally more appropriate than this translation of a Greek tragedy. While bestowing their applause, most of the audience persisted in using the Yup'ik people to define themselves and then concluded that they had witnessed a cultural universal.

Although supportive of *Yup'ik Antigone* and the sympathy it generated for Eskimo people, Nelson Islanders criticized its conflation of Yup'ik and Greek tradition. Villagers maintained that if Hunsaker wanted to produce a really fine play, he should forsake Greek drama and look to Yup'ik oral tradition. Hunsaker was receptive, and soon after *Yup'ik Antigone* completed its foreign tour, he visited Nelson Island to start work on a new production.

The stories that emerged as best suited for such a transformation were those concerning Apanuugpak, the famous warrior-hero of Nelson Island. Dealing as they do with the period of bow-and-arrow warfare in Yup'ik oral tradition, they are full of action and adventure and seemed ideally suited to the production Hunsaker and his Yup'ik coworkers had in mind. In Yup'ik narrative tradition, the Apanuugpak stories form but one set within a larger group of stories concerning the period of bow-and-arrow warfare in western Alaska during the seventeenth and eighteenth centuries. These stories can be divided roughly into four major sets, each pertaining to a different group of regional confrontations. They include the longstanding dispute between the people of Pastolik, at the mouth of the Yukon Delta, and the coastal people around Hooper Bay; the hostility separating the inhabitants of the lower coast and those of modern Quinhagak; confrontations between the lower Kuskokwim Eskimos (*Aglurmiut*) and the people of the middle Kuskokwim living near modern Kalskag; and, finally, the historic animosity between the people of the Kuskokwim drainage and the residents of Nunivak Island.

Aside from scattered references (Michael 1967:281; Nelson 1899:327-330), nineteenth-century explorers and ethnographers largely ignored evidence of Eskimo warfare, content to foster the stereotype of Eskimos as never hostile, not to mention warlike. Not until recently have the details of their bloody feuds and battles come into focus for outside investigators (Burch 1974; Burch and Correll 1972; Fienup-Riordan 1984a; VanStone 1967; VanStone and Goddard 1981). For the local population these dramatic orations have been a staple of narrative tradition for at least 150 years and probably much longer. The turn-of-the-century Moravian missionary John Kilbuck was among the first to record accounts of all the major confrontations (Fienup-Riordan 1988d:32-34, 43-50, 390-392). Moreover, contemporary oral accounts still exist concerning specific battles won and lost in all four of these major "wars" (for example, Fienup-Riordan 1986b:359-365).

Within this elaborate oral tradition stories of the exploits of the warrior-hero Apanuugpak, defender of Nelson Island, are told up and down the coast of western Alaska from Dillingham in the south all the way to Nelson Island and beyond. Depending on where the stories are recorded, Apanuugpak is depicted as a villain or a hero. In the Togiak area he is said to have been so powerful that no warrior could stand up to him. To protect themselves the Togiak people employed a powerful shaman to put a curse on Apanuugpak. As a result, on his return from a raid in the Togiak area, it is said that he was turned into a rock, which can still be seen when sailing along the coast.

For the people of Nelson Island, however, Apanuugpak is the embodiment of all that is powerful and cunning in a warrior. From his infancy, he is said to have been trained by his grandfather to be tough and strong. Stories recount the strict regimen of his youth, the storyteller often opposing this upbringing to the easy time young people have today. According to oral accounts, his grandfather would wake him up early every morning and have him run to the top of Nelson Island. On his return he would be given only one drop of water from the tip of the feather of a snowy owl to quench his thirst. Similarly, he was taken down to the beach every day and told to roll naked over mussel shells to toughen both his body and his mind.

Along with numerous stories concerning the rigors of Apanuugpak's training, other tales recount his exploits. In all these Apanuugpak emerges victorious by virtue of superior strength, courage, and ingenuity. The hallmark of his cunning is the mussel-shell armor that he wore under his parka, which rendered useless the arrows of his enemies. This "secret weapon" so annoyed his antagonists that, in one account, an opponent is said to have cried out in frustration, "Where in tarnation can we hit this Apanuugpak so that the arrow head can find its deadly mark?" To this, Apanuugpak answered, "Your arrows do not hit my body. Rather they land on the beaches at Engel'umiut!", referring enigmatically to the mussel shells that protected him (Billy Lincoln, Jan. 26, 1987, NI).

Significantly, the Yup'ik Eskimos categorize the Apanuugpak stories as histori-cal narratives (*qanemcit*) rather than mythical tales (*qulirat*). Whereas the narra-tives are grounded in the experience of a particular person, whether that person is living or dead, the tales are part of the experience of ancient ancestors and never involve particular individuals definitely believed to have existed. In the 1980s the Yup'ik people became more interested in recording and transcribing, although not necessarily translating, both literary genres.

This interest is part of a growing general self-consciousness in western Alaska brought on by intense efforts at cultural conversion, including new and often com-mercial interests in their traditional dances, carving, and storytelling. During the last decade Nelson Island has been the focus of a great deal of attention from outside writers, photographers, filmmakers, ornithologists, fish biologists, archaeologists, bureaucrats, and cultural anthropologists. Public hearings, held on an almost weekly basis, regularly confront villagers with the responsibility of reacting to proposed developments and changes in the regulatory systems that increasingly constrain their lives. In the face of this massive and unprecedented inquiry, some Nelson Islanders may view their past as inadequate to vindicate present positions. As a result, many are in the process of inventing a new past to meet the situation. At least some view Hunsaker's project as a vehicle for such re-creation. For both natives and non-natives, the dramatization of history becomes a viable mechanism for distancing oneself from the distress of the current political situation, albeit in different ways.

As the project gained momentum during the winter of 1985, Hunsaker spent several weeks on Nelson Island listening to English glosses on a multitude of differ-ent versions of the Apanuugpak stories. To reduce confusion the village council advised him to work with only one village elder (Billy Lincoln) and to develop his script primarily from Lincoln's version of the narratives in Yup'ik. A translator accompanied him, and through him Hunsaker heard the tales. Hunsaker was also able to ask Billy Lincoln questions about what he had heard, and he made notes. No detailed transcriptions or translations were made of the interviews. Although the film was to be based on the oral traditions, it was not intended to be a precise enactment of them.

Notes in hand, Hunsaker returned to Juneau, where he wrote a screenplay entitled *Winter Warrior*. He created a storyboard for the film, scene by scene. Sev-eral months later, Hunsaker took this picture sequence back to Nelson Island for review. Again he visited Billy Lincoln, to whom he showed the drawings. Through an interpreter Lincoln approved the script. The process was one of negotiation, not simple acceptance, as exemplified by one proposed scene that Hunsaker agreed to strike early in the going. Significantly, the scene depicted Apanuugpak's opponent confronting him with a gun. Here Hunsaker was attempting a commentary on the devastation and imbalance of power wrought by Alaska natives' acquisition of elements of Western technology. However, given the fact that oral tradition places Apanuugpak before the arrival of the first *kass'aq*, or white man, in western Alaska, Lincoln found the gun unacceptable.

The screenplay takes on a new dimension from the point of view of what the scriptwriter omitted and what Nelson Islanders chose to represent tradition. Just as Lincoln required the deletion of the gun scene because of its misleading reference to the period of historic contact, Hunsaker balked at including evidence of cold-blooded murder on the part of his hero. Rather, Apanuugpak's escalating lust for blood needed to appear consistently motivated by his obsession with revenge. For example, in traditional accounts of Apanuugpak's confrontation with an unarmed Bristol Bay native, Apanuugpak routinely dispatches the man for no reason more obvious than the fact of the encounter. In order not to jeopardize audience sympathy for the warrior-hero by the appearance of unmotivated violence, Hunsaker changed the story and let the man live. Responding differently than he did to the scene with the gun, Lincoln accepted this explanation and approved the change. Clearly, history was viewed as neither totally sacred nor wholly profane but in specific instances open to alteration.

Given the current reflexive mood in anthropology, Hunsaker's dismissal of the perils of translation seems somewhat suspect. Admittedly his intent to collaborate, to make himself the vehicle for a Yup'ik story, is in line with the noblest recent attempts to do away with the power relationship inherent in traditional ethnographic/native relations. Moreover, the ability of film in general and Hunsaker's film in particular to employ traditional dramatic forms, including dance scenes and shamanic performances, has intriguing advantages over discursive ethnography.

The creation of film, like the creations of the written word, can empower a community by manipulating knowledge, but it can also be impoverishing. We cannot dismiss the irony that the film is based on stories no longer familiar to young people on Nelson Island, in part because they are so fully engaged by the movie channel on local cable television. Like ethnography, film might document oral tradition while contributing to its demise, as it is part of a cultural context in which oral literature rarely survives. Like the ethnographers criticized by Clifford (1983) and Rosaldo (1986), the filmmaker has confined to private conversation discussion of the circumstances that shaped his knowledge. In public-relations descriptions of the project, he depicted the story he created out of his encounters with Lincoln as a mirror image of the memory of the tradition bearer himself, thereby validating his creation as authentic and historically accurate. The first page of the screenplay precisely dates the historical drama as occurring in 1650. In the venerable tradition of anthropological realism, Hunsaker asks his audience to view his creation as a "true outline" (Rosaldo 1986:93).

Just as the ethnographer might adopt the trappings of ethnographic authority and proceed under the assumption that one can apprehend native life in unmediated fashion, the filmmaker strikes a collaborative pose that creates the illusion of the direct apprehension of historically and culturally distant acts and meanings. One possible response to this ploy by the anthropologist well versed in Yup'ik oral tradition is to dismiss the film as a variety of Western humanism artfully dressed in traditional Yup'ik fur clothing—a film that tells us more about the meaning people seek to see in their own history than about Yup'ik history itself. Even more interesting than the disjunction between "authentic" oral tradition and "inauthentic" cinematic representation, however, is the creative interchange enacted between filmmaker and Nelson Islanders, each re-creating themselves in terms of the history of the other.[2]

After undergoing the review process on Nelson Island, Hunsaker's next step was to submit his script to the Script Development/Film Laboratory Workshop of the Sundance Institute. Robert Redford founded the institute in 1980 to support and encourage films by independent filmmakers that reflect the richness and diversity of American life. Hunsaker's script was one of nine chosen for detailed review from among more than six hundred entries. At Sundance, a number of nationally known directors and scriptwriters gave the script a thorough critique and helped Hunsaker bring the Yup'ik narrative in line with Western dramatic concepts. At Sundance Hunsaker also had the opportunity to test special effects in filming scenes involving shamanic activity. During this period, Hunsaker remarked that he was especially impressed by the techniques employed by the Japanese cinematographer Akira Kurosawa and hoped to achieve the visual of Kurosawa's films in his own finished product.

During the summer before Hunsaker approached Robert Redford's Sundance organization, I was living at Toksook, working on their oral history project and waiting to become Mrs. Apanuugpak. Along with enjoying the joking and storytelling that were a part of that period, I was both surprised and delighted when, at the end of July and the close of the summer fishing season, the people of Toksook began building the set for the Apanuugpak film. Two dozen men and boys were employed in the construction of four sod houses, located on a point of land half a mile down the coast from the modern village. Pits were dug and driftwood hauled to the site. Within a week, the wooden skeletons of three of the houses had been completed and were ready to receive the grass insulating mats that women had been busy weaving back in the village. I visited the site every day and was impressed with how much people were enjoying the work. Older men boasted that they had seen nothing like this since their youth, and, clearly, for everyone under forty years of age this was a new and exhilarating experience.

Lincoln acted as foreman in the work. As the sod houses neared completion, he began directing work on the large *qasgiq*, or communal men's house, which formed the center of the new "old" community. This *qasgiq*, I was told, would never be left to rot as in times past. Instead, after the completion of the film, it would be preserved as a "permanent replica" and used as a shelter for the valuable gut parkas, wooden masks, and other artifacts that would also be produced for and used in *Winter Warrior*. This "living museum" would then function for western Alaska as a tourist attraction comparable to colonial Williamsburg.[3] Here Nelson Islanders' enjoyment in recreating their past is somewhat reminiscent of the pleasurable sentiments expressed by Kwakiutl natives involved in Edward Curtis's famous fictive reconstruction *In the Land of the War Canoes* (1914).

As much as I felt the immediate excitement engendered by the building project, I was particularly interested in rumors that were circulating concerning a celebration villagers planned to hold when they completed the *qasgiq*. I was told that traditionally the building or refurbishing of a men's house in late summer or early fall was marked by an *Ingulaq*, later referred to by the missionaries as a berry festival. This celebration was characterized by slow ceremonial dancing, also known as *ingulaq*, as well as the presentation of and feasting upon bowls of *akutaq*, a festive mixture of berries, oil, and snow. Islanders had not held such a performance for more than forty years and greatly anticipated the impending celebration.

Suddenly, two weeks later, both the construction of the old village and the plans for the *Ingulaq* were called to a halt. Apparently there had been a misunderstanding about the film's funding. Although the filmmaker had promised to pay workers if and when the film was funded, as yet no backers had been found and villagers had begun construction on the site without the filmmaker's knowledge. When the anticipated paychecks did not arrive, disgruntled workers refused to continue what they had begun spontaneously with such goodwill.

I was disappointed, as were many other people in the village. The turn of events was not without its irony. Here were men and women working to re-create a model of a bygone age, which they firmly maintained was more valuable to them than anything money could buy and representative of a way of life they held superior to modern cash-driven society. Nevertheless, without the promised paychecks, they would stop work rather than continue it for its own sake. They had come to place a price on their priceless heritage, which their actions, if not their words, treated as a commodity.

After my summer in Toksook, I continued to monitor the progress of the film project. Not until the fall of 1986 did I have the opportunity to read a draft of the script. What I read was far removed from Apanuugpak narratives I had heard on Nelson Island. I was reminded that the script was an adaptation for a commercial film, not an attempt at documentary, and that Hunsaker had based his work on the Apanuugpak stories with no intention of merely restating them.

In brief, the screenplay that I read in the fall of 1986 developed as follows. A young man (Apanuugpak) is being educated in the rules for right action by his grandfather. Although talented, he is presented as naive and immature. A neighboring group soon visits his village and seeks its support in a territorial struggle. Apanuugpak is troubled by this overture, having asserted in an earlier confrontation, "The waters don't belong to anybody" (Hunsaker 1986b:11). Moreover, in a fight he accidentally causes the death of the headstrong brother of the chief of the visiting group. To atone for this sin, Apanuugpak leaves the village to seek spiritual renewal. However, during his quest he is captured by a witch-woman who keeps him a prisoner and through daily copulation gradually saps his strength. Fortunately, Apanuugpak is rescued from this predicament by a young woman he subsequently marries. The couple lives happily for a brief time. Yet trouble is already brewing. The feud that began with the accidental killing of the chief's brother escalates into warfare between the two groups, and in the course of the next four dozen scenes, forty-one additional individuals are dispatched on screen and reference is made to numerous others killed off screen. As the killing escalates, so does Apanuugpak's obsession with revenge. Finally, returning to his village to find all its inhabitants, including his grandfather, burned alive in the *qasgiq* (this disaster constitutes the previous scene), Apanuugpak realizes that war is wrong. He then confronts his enemies and declares that weapons are for killing animals, not human beings. Presumably he then rejoins his wife, through whom he begins to rebuild his shattered world.

The cinematographic "present," like its ethnographic counterpart, is given as one step removed from the contemporary world. In the film's closing scene, a young Yup'ik woman views with concern the photograph of her boyfriend, who has the face of Apanuugpak and is dressed in a National Guard uniform. The scene is set in a village on Nelson Island in the 1940s, a period during which the rights and duties of citizenship were introduced in quick succession in the coastal communities of western Alaska. This scene brings the film full circle. The film opened with a scene in which the villagers were gathered in a wood-frame community hall. There the voice and person of Lincoln were introduced, and in turn introduced the life and times of Apanuugpak. Thus, the entire film is framed as a narration concerning the distant past told in the immediate past. In this story within a story the other is represented not altogether accurately but as a trope for a cultural possibility other than our own. The filmmaker's decision to remove his message is new neither to ethnographic nor to cinematic representation. However, it is significant that Hunsaker's predecessors, including both Curtis and Robert Flaherty (*Nanook of the North*) used no such framing scenes. True to the period in which they worked, they were more content with the fiction of realism and less self-conscious in their use of material.

It is noteworthy that another recent attempt at indigenous dramatic representation in western Alaska was framed in a similar way. The play, produced by the village of Chevak (located less than one hundred miles up the coast from Nelson Island), was performed statewide. The main body of the play was a re-creation of the traditional Bladder Festival; five days of feasts were collapsed into an intense three-hour performance that included audience participation. As in *Winter Warrior*, an element of tradition was taken as the focus, in this case a ceremonial enactment of the belief in an endless cycle of birth and rebirth of human and animal souls. Also like *Winter Warrior*, the play was framed in the present, once removed. In the opening scene a "Brooks Brothers" native moves forward to the sound of disco music and takes a long pull from a flask of whiskey drawn out of a leather briefcase.

From the beginning, the Chevak players neatly juxtaposed the material success of this native Everyman to his spiritual decline; however, the spirits of his past engage him in the Bladder Festival, through which he is reborn along with the souls of the animals. It is perhaps appropriate that the ceremony that traditionally had the power to re-create the past in the future was chosen to represent tradition itself in the present. The Chevak production, just like Hunsaker's, looks to the past to supply the concrete symbolic forms that Western social symbolism has failed to provide. Apparently ethnography is not alone in its propensity to turn to "other times, other customs" (Sahlins 1985: 32) to more clearly understand its own.

To return to *Winter Warrior*, the script as summarized here is both carefully developed and dramatically successful by Western standards. Fast paced, it clearly works as an adventure story. To achieve the dramatic force that is its strong point, however, the screenplay has moved far from the Nelson Island oral traditions and Yup'ik dramatic style on which it was based.

This shift is telling. First of all, in oral accounts Apanuugpak was born into warfare and from his earliest youth was trained as a virtual "killing machine." Although the filmmaker heard stories about Apanuugpak's early years, at least in reference, he did not use them because they were not part of Lincoln's account. This omission highlights the problems associated with using Lincoln as sole tradition bearer. Lincoln was born and raised north of Nelson Island, not on Nelson Island proper. Although he knew the stories of Apanuugpak's childhood, they may not have been part of his personal repertoire and consequently part of what he felt he had a right to communicate.

Second, in his screenplay Hunsaker adds substantially to the traditional stories of Apanuugpak's adult years. In Nelson Island oral tradition these narratives all revolve around the battles Apanuugpak fought and won and the tricks he played on his enemies. There are no stories of whom or how he married. However, at the end of his life he is seen surrounded by his grandsons telling stories in the *qasgiq*. Thus the witch-woman scenes, as well as the subplot of Apanuugpak's twofold "salvation" by the woman who becomes his wife, are dramatic inventions. A more troublesome alteration concerns Apanuugpak's social role. As a warrior (*anguyaq*), Apanuugpak occupied a social position distinct from that of either a great hunter (*nukalpiaq*) or a shaman (*angalkuq*). In Yup'ik oral tradition, warriors are viewed as men apart, hunters of men rather than men who are hunters in either the animal or spirit worlds. In the screenplay these categories are collapsed, and Apanuugpak is presented as the quintessential embodiment of all three.

Third, in the screenplay Apanuugpak is depicted as the unwitting cause of the onset of warfare. He is also presented as the sadder but wiser restorer of the peace through his ultimate recognition of the evils inherent in warfare. This message is, in fact, a critical part of the meaning of the film and is epitomized in Apanuugpak's dramatic concluding statement: "Weapons are meant for killing animals, not humans." Here Hunsaker is using Yup'ik oral tradition to state what he considers a universal truth: War is wrong and through war a man risks losing his soul. Whatever the merits of this statement, it is ironic that Yup'ik stories celebrating the preeminent war hero of their past should be used as its vehicle.

In the final analysis, Hunsaker's most significant revision is the invention of the beginning and end of warfare and the placement of these accomplishments in the hands of a single human being, however famous. Yup'ik oral tradition does, in fact, have an explanation for the beginning and the end of warfare in general, as well as specific wars. For example, in perhaps the best-known account of the beginning and end of the Yukon Delta/coastal conflict, an unskilled hunter from Pastolik who had married into the village of Hooper Bay killed his hunting companions one after the other and claimed their catch as his own. When the people of Hooper Bay discovered his crime, he fled north to Pastolik. There he sowed the seeds of distrust among the Yukon Eskimos, who subsequently took the offensive against their coastal neighbors. Many battles took place during the ensuing years. However, during a period of extreme food shortage, a man from the Yukon and a man from Hooper Bay formed an unlikely partnership out on the ice while stalking a seal. They shared their catch and consequently saved each other's lives. From that time on the hostilities between the Yukon and coastal areas began to subside (Fienup-Riordan 1986b:38, 359-365).

This complete rendition of the beginning and end of the famous Yukon Delta/coastal conflict is revealing in several respects. It begins in theft and the refusal to cooperate; it ends in food-sharing and trading. Whereas the original conflict divides a group united by marriage, the resolution brings about the rapprochement of two originally distinct regional groups. In addition, the breach pivots around the food quest and a conflict over resources in one region. Although it does not originate as a boundary dispute, in the intervening war episodes men are depicted as defending a range or a site or a kill (Fienup-Riordan 1984a:76-77).

Nelson Islanders have their own account concerning the end of wars (Fienup-Riordan 1983:247). In brief, two survivors approached their enemies seeking revenge after their own village had been destroyed. As they drew closer in their kayaks, they broke the spears they had intended to kill with and instead used them to beat the sides of their kayaks like drums. Then the women of the opposing village walked down to the shore to meet them and, standing in front of their men, began to dance. So it is said, from that time forward, Yup'ik people have never fought with bows and arrows but rather through the dance. Anyone who has seen Yup'ik dancing will know that this is indeed still the case!

Although Hunsaker had viewed Yup'ik dance, he had neither asked for nor received this origin story. He was likewise unaware of the cycle of narratives recounting the beginning and ending of warfare. His invention of such a sequence was thus not based on a considered rejection of these narratives but on limited information. Although sensitive to known issues, he was not told enough to realize his omission. What the narratives had in common was the motif of an endless cosmological cycling between birth and rebirth. In the traditional accounts of warfare, the primary issue was not death but rather in what manner life would be maintained in perpetuity. For Hunsaker, as for Sophocles before him, the inevitability of death becomes focal. On the contrary, within Yup'ik cosmology the narratives depicting warfare are about death's impossibility not its finality. This divergence in part explains the differences between Hunsaker's and Lincoln's views regarding the motivation and meaning behind Apanuugpak's acts of violence.

Finally, in replacing traditional accounts of the beginning and end of warfare, Hunsaker also transformed the traditional and contemporary Yup'ik concepts of territoriality. In the beginning of *Winter Warrior*, Apanuugpak exclaims, "The waters do not belong to anyone." This sentiment is brought full circle when, in the final scene of the film, the young woman views with concern the portrait of her boyfriend in his National Guard uniform. Here, along with the message "war is wrong," Hunsaker attempts to make the point that with the emergence of the modern nation-state in western Alaska, the same "foreign" issues of landownership and water rights that brought on the wars of the past are resurfacing in the present.

In fact, the traditional Yup'ik Eskimos possessed a well-developed sense of territory; however, rights to land and water use were not based on, or reduced to, possession of a particular site by an individual or group at any one point in time. Rather the concept of ownership was relational; a man had a right, and in fact an obligation, to use a site because of his relationship to previous generations of people who had a defined relationship to the species taken at that same place. In other words, a man had a right to use a site not because he owned the land but because his grandparent (by name and by birth) hunted there and had a relationship with the animals of that area. A man was his grandfather incarnate, and therefore the animals that gave themselves to him were those that gave themselves to his grandfather. A man's right to resource extraction was thus relational rather than possessive. In this sense ownership was and continues to be tied to defined territories insofar as these reflect social boundaries. This traditional understanding of territoriality does not correspond to the capitalist notion of property that the scriptwriter has the Yup'ik people reject.

In the fall of 1986 I discussed with the scriptwriter the differences between his screenplay and Yup'ik history as I understood it, arguing for changes in his script that would bring it closer to the form and meaning of Yup'ik oral tradition. His answer was simple and straightforward: We were talking about two different films. From my point of view the interchange was less than satisfactory as, like the native on whom the anthropologist relies, I was put in the uncomfortable position of being asked to give information without the requisite power to control its subsequent use. Within the context of our differences, however, two issues of broad significance emerged that merit consideration here.

It should be clear that Hunsaker and I hold different views of what is important about Nelson Island. As in *Yup'ik Antigone*, in *Winter Warrior* the scriptwriter chose to focus on the universality of the human condition. This is a venerable theme in the Western tradition, and much of anthropology has been framed as an attempt to speak to this issue. My chief concern, however, is that Yup'ik Eskimos in general, and Nelson Islanders in particular, have a unique way of looking at and acting in the world. From my perspective it makes no sense to override significant and instructive differences between the seventeenth-century Yup'ik Eskimos and contemporary American culture to present the ways in which Yup'ik people were in essentials "just like us" (Fienup-Riordan 1985:9).

The dialogue between Hunsaker and me was further constrained by the fact that we have different agendas. Both of us must have the support of our peers for our work to succeed. On the one hand, to find backing for his film, Hunsaker had to convince the Sundance Institute that his script had broad dramatic appeal, not that his facts were correct. On the other hand, I must convince research agencies that there is something special but not necessarily of universal appeal about the Yup'ik people that merits detailed inquiry.

Along with and related to the different practical constraints on our work, Hunsaker and I hold very different views about the meaning of history and tradition. When Hunsaker visited Nelson Island to discuss *Winter Warrior*, in addition to gathering Apanuugpak stories, he kept his ears open to the current state of affairs. The years during which he visited Nelson Island brought dramatic challenges to the political and cultural integrity of the region. Numerous state and federal agencies had become increasingly involved in the management and regulation of the fish and game on which Nelson Islanders depend for their livelihood. New regulations challenged the islanders' ability to freely harvest the geese, halibut, herring, and musk oxen that, among other species, inhabit the area. In addition, outside pressure on these resources had also escalated. At the same time that they were feeling increased pressure on these resources, their right to the use and "ownership" of ancestral lands was threatened by the approach of 1991, when village and regional corporation land becomes transferable under the 1971 Alaska Native Claims Settlement Act.

In the context of this political situation Hunsaker carried out his "fieldwork" on Nelson Island. Perhaps not surprisingly, native suspicion and resentment of current non-native forms of regulation colored his interviews and history lessons. Nelson Islanders told him that in the past no one had specific rights over the land or the resources, and no one could restrict another's use. In fact, this is not an accurate presentation of the past, as already indicated. However, this was the view of Yup'ik history that Hunsaker took home with him, and he developed his script based on this history. Thus the "tradition" on which Hunsaker's screenplay rests, and that may well appear to be old, is quite recent in origin and has in fact been intentionally invented by Nelson Islanders to establish continuity between their present political position and a suitable historic past. Although they desire free use of their land "as in the past," unrestricted movement and unregulated access to resources were not a part of the nineteenth-century Yup'ik way of life.

The phenomenon of "invented traditions" is not unique to Nelson Island. Hobsbawm and Ranger (1983) make it the subject of detailed inquiry. Invented tradition, as distinguished from noninvented tradition and custom, is said to be a set of practices governed by accepted rules and of a symbolic nature that seeks to inculcate certain values implying continuity with the past. Insofar as there is reference to a historic past, Hobsbawm and Ranger note, the continuity with it is largely fictitious. Moreover, this phenomenon may in part be attributed to the contrast between the constant innovation of the modern world and the attempt to find some part of it invariant. Thus, increasingly, old materials (like the Apanuugpak stories or the Bladder Festival) are used to construct invented traditions of a novel type to establish a people's legitimacy through history.

Furthermore, Hobsbawm and Ranger (1983: 8) distinguish between the adaptability of genuine traditions and the "invention of tradition." They contend that where old ways are alive, traditions need be neither revived nor invented. Where they are invented, it is often not because the old ways are no longer available or viable, but because those ways are deliberately not used or adapted. In the case of *Winter Warrior*, a double invention is in process, with Hunsaker inventing a trope for the condition of modern man based on a tradition of nonownership and an absence of territorial concepts that the people of Nelson Island have themselves invented to validate their contemporary relationship to the land. Hunsaker moves from the misinterpretation of tradition to its "invention" in his claim that the people of Nelson Island regard his screenplay as acceptable history. He already has a strong following for his project.

Hunsaker vacillates between naturalizing the Yup'ik as paragons of simplicity and virtue and historicizing them as victims of Western imperialism. Nowhere is he encumbered by the specificity of Yup'ik concepts of space, time, or personhood. He has responded instead to their contemporary plea for the severing of a connection with a white man's world they view as having gone awry. Hunsaker was told essentially, "We have always been a peaceful people living in harmony with our land. Boundaries have been imposed from without, and the constraint is unacceptable." In fact, the nineteenth-century Yupiit were preoccupied with the creation of boundaries and passages in a world perceived as formless without them (Fienup-Riordan 1987). Today the Yupiit are intent on breaking externally imposed constraints and are doing so in the name of tradition.

Hunsaker was finally forced to face the claim that his "invention" conflicts with other traditions still adhered to on Nelson Island. There was danger that the bow-and-arrow wars of the past were to be fought again in the regional newspaper, the *Tundra Drums*. An exchange of letters (Hunsaker 1987; Oscar 1987) concerning the use of explicit sexual imagery in the witch-woman scene undercut local support for the project. This "paper war" was doubly ironic in that the stated goals of the film project are "to advance public understanding of a little known traditional American culture" (Hunsaker 1986a) and to be as "authentic" and historically accurate as possible. However, filmmakers (just like anthropologists), whatever else their objectives, are engaged in the process of "inventing traditions" inasmuch as they "contribute, consciously or not, to the creation, dismantling, and restructuring of the images of the past" (Hobsbawm and Ranger 1983:8).

Moreover, the push for the film is forcing more and more Nelson Islanders to expand their concept of what is and is not marketable within their own world. As in the case of the aborted construction of the old village, their oral traditions have begun to take on market value. Whereas they still value the oral traditions for what they can teach about proper living, Nelson Islanders are recognizing the monetary value they have in the contemporary world. Also, for the younger generation, the prospect of being an actor, not just a viewer, in a movie drama draws them toward what for many is the clearinghouse if not the creator of Western reality—the media.

The younger villagers are the ones most interested in acting in the film. These would-be actors are the same generation of men and women made inactive in their own culture in part by the unreality of American television. In the 1940s Nelson Islanders were more in touch with their own past than with the national present in which they were nominally included. Today, that historical reality as constructed in myth and story has dimmed to the point where its preservation on the silver screen represents true re-creation.

To date, the community continues to support the film project over the voices of individual dissidents. Among villagers, however, support remains contingent on the filmmaker's ability to find funding for his project. Although their realities are not identical, the interests of the Nelson Islanders and the filmmaker in the film overlap, and they are not at odds. Nelson Islanders are not replacing their version of history with Hunsaker's, and they retain a measure of ironic distance from cinematic concessions to Western audiences in the name of profit.

Nevertheless, winning on Hunsaker's terms may be a form of losing if stories once told to provide moral guidance and to preserve tradition become equated with monetary gain. In the film project's relationship with the community, money has talked in the past and will again in the future. Although the filming will be done in the native language, the fact that the actors will be paid in cash, in the language of venture capitalism, elicits local support for the project. Whatever Hunsaker's view of his creation and its worth, Nelson Islanders are currently content to view it as a finite resource to be harvested if and when it arrives, in contrast to the infinitely renewable resources they harvested in the past.

Beyond the invention and reevaluation of history, the question arises concerning the extent to which the collection of Yup'ik artifacts and oral tradition constitutes an invention of heritage—by the filmmaker or by anthropologists in general. By his own admission, Hunsaker's selective recording and organization of Yup'ik material is an act of creation. Although finding support within the community, the impetus for making the film comes not only from within Nelson Island but from without. The farther away the film moves, the greater the interest it elicits. The product will be an ethnic display, not an act of Eskimo self-representation.

Just as the historicism of the nineteenth century and the belief that it was necessary to collect before it was "too late" made possible the ethnological collecting associated with the "museum movement" (Cole 1985:48; Dominguez 1986:549), so the social and political climate in Alaska enables the cinematographic invention of a new Yup'ik tradition. Similarly, the collections of Eskimo artifacts and the Eskimos themselves were and remain objects of interest not because of their intrinsic value but because of their perceived contribution to our understanding of our own history. The value of *Winter Warrior* will lie not in its "true" representation of the Yup'ik Eskimos, the proverbial "others," but in the degree to which it can be read as a referential index of ourselves.

At its best *Winter Warrior* may rise above the accusation of cultural imperialism. Just as cultural order is not immediately given but constantly achieved through the process of negotiation between symbolic structures and historical circumstances, a film is a marriage between script and actors, who in this case will be Yup'ik Eskimos acting in their own language in their own time and place. Although the city council has given permission to the filmmaker to pursue his project, they do not view their agreement as writ in stone but as contingent on continued goodwill and agreement on essentials between the filmmaker and the community. The filmmaker has developed a script that both he and they view as open to alteration as they begin to play it out in the filming process. Thus, the community feels in control of the production, to the credit of all concerned.

In the enthusiasm of Nelson Islanders to use their history to talk about their present, the distinction between "authentic," lived culture and "inauthentic" invented tradition loses its force. Rather the screenplay may be viewed as performing the role of mediator in Wagner's (1986) sense, insofar as its negotiation of cultural conceptions results in a re-creation of them. *Winter Warrior* as presently conceived will not represent the traditional Yup'ik way of life any more accurately or inaccurately than *Road Warrior* represents modern American culture. Rather, like *Road Warrior*, *Winter Warrior* will re-present it, complete with strategic omissions and additions. Although the film may provoke the purist, it is valid in its own right. In the best anthropological tradition, the text that is the film is more than description (accurate or inaccurate) of the Yup'ik past. Rather it embodies an act of translation, of re-creation, where both Yup'ik and non-Yup'ik audiences may learn something about themselves by means of the other.

Limits exist in our ability to apprehend the other. This point has been made in myriad ways, from Sahlins's (1976) dictum that no ethnography exists without ethnology to Wagner's (1975) exegesis on the invention of culture to Clifford and Marcus's (1986) grim conclusion that constructed truths are made possible only by lies of exclusion. Accepting these limits to its own enterprise, anthropology cannot fairly condemn the filmmaker, who faces challenges similar to those of ethnographic writing, including problems of narrative and focus, of editing, and of reflexivity.

As in the case of ethnography, although we can recognize the limits of the cinematographic enterprise, we do not have to reject it in toto. With ethnography's own authority in question, anthropology's chief use is not in standing up for the accurate representation of the pure culture of the past but in clarifying the significance of action in the present. The question of the differences between the ethnographic and cinematographic enterprise appears to be a reinvention of the Mead-Freeman debate in a colder clime.[4] Following Clifford's (1986) analysis of this debate, I would argue that if anthropology's response is dismissal on the grounds of inaccuracy or inauthenticity, it misses the point of the attempt to depict the Yup'ik past so as to provide a moral lesson for the present. Just as Mead went to Samoa and Hunsaker to Nelson Island, the Yup'ik Eskimos are visiting another time within their own world to frame a present as both inherited and in the process of being reinvented.

NOTES

1. As of fall 1989, this project was still under way. It has involved primarily a group of Nelson Island men and women working to record traditional narratives and oral history from the oldest living Nelson Islanders. Some of these accounts are now being transcribed into Yup'ik and translated into English for use by students in the local elementary and high schools.

2. Anthropologists continue to debate the extent to which writing and for that matter filmmaking are inevitable corruptions (for example, Derrida 1973, 1974; Ong 1977, 1982). Although something may be sacrificed in such textualization, what is lost is not the power of a culture to re-create itself, which is at issue here (for example, Sahlins 1985; Wagner 1975).

3. A science fiction magazine published a story about Nelson Island. In it a man awakens in a traditional Eskimo village, dresses himself in fur clothing, and leaves the sod house to walk down the beach. His destination, however, is not a kayak but the modern village of Toksook Bay. He had paid cash to experience the past. His time was up and he was returning home.

4. Whereas Margaret Mead (1928) selectively described aspects of Samoan culture to demonstrate that the stressful adolescence of American teenagers was not a universal phenomenon, Derek Freeman (1983) marshaled examples of Samoan anxiety and violence to show where Mead's conclusions were wrong. Freeman's criticism talked past the value of Mead's initial enterprise and ignored the fact that his account of the "real" Samoa was as much a framed construction determined by his point of view as Mead's had been before him.

Dynamics

1. In "The Ideology of Subsistence" Fienup-Riordan chooses to write a narrative rather than a more traditional ethnographic description, yet she continues to use some of the special terms of anthropology. Choose a few passages where she uses narrative as well as anthropological terms, and discuss the roles they both play as she constructs her portrait of the Yup'ik Eskimos.

2. Early in her first essay Fienup-Riordan mentions "cultural imagination," but she does not define it in much detail. Find several passages in this piece that are examples of cultural imagination, and compose a detailed definition of the term.

3. In her second essay Fienup-Riordan discusses "the dialogic character of native/non-native encounters." Trace the meaning of this concept through several incidents in her essays. Compose a fuller definition of the phrase, and discuss the significance of your findings.

4. The author speaks supportively of the "process of inventing a new past." How is such a thing possible, and why does Fienup-Riordan support it? Choose several incidents from her writing to help compose your answer.

Critical Tools

1. Fienup-Riordan mentions the "eloquence" of the exchange dance and notes that "social relations are articulated" in its performance, both ways of saying that the dance "speaks." What does it mean to say that a cultural custom speaks, judging from "The Ideology of Subsistence"? How do those ideas help explain events or customs from another *Literacies* text you have read?

2. Fienup-Riordan describes "the rules of proper relationship" as a central element of Yup'ik Eskimo culture. Consider another text from *Literacies* and describe the role of "the rules of proper relationship" that you find there. Do such rules work similarly in different cultures?

3. In her second essay the author mentions "the circumstances that shaped...knowledge." Make a catalog of as many of those circumstances as you can find in her essays, and explain your current understanding of the shaping of knowledge. Is she talking about prejudice when she uses this phrase?

Draft One/Draft Two

Draft One: Use Fienup-Riordan's experiences in these two essays to consider the author's theory that her encounters with the Yup'ik might be called a "creative interchange" through which anthropologist and subject peoples "each [recreate] themselves in terms of the history of the other." What are the requirements for that creative interchange?

Draft Two: Turn to another text in *Literacies* and discuss whether the parties described there manage to "[recreate] themselves in terms of the history of the other." What does that other text help you add to the discussion of draft one, and what does it allow you to say about the meeting of different cultural groups?

❖ ❖ ❖

Before Reading Barbara Garson. . .

1. What are the most significant challenges and difficulties facing American
    workers right now? How does the situation of American workers compare to
    that of workers in other parts of the world? In your answer to this question,
    consider where your knowledge about workers in both the U.S. and other coun-
    tries comes from.

2. Based on your own knowledge, what are some forces that make it difficult for
    people to change the circumstances of their lives? Try to list these forces in the
    order of their importance, but consider also the ways in which these forces are
    interrelated. How does your list reflect your own experiences and values?

McDonald's—We Do It All for You

Barbara Garson

Jason Pratt

"They called us the Green Machine," says Jason Pratt, recently retired McDonald's griddleman, " 'cause the crew had green uniforms then. And that's what it is, a machine. You don't have to know how to cook, you don't have to know how to think. There's a procedure for everything and you just follow the procedures."

"Like?" I asked. I was interviewing Jason in the Pizza Hut across from his old McDonald's.

"Like, uh," the wiry teenager searched for a way to describe the all-encompassing procedures. "O.K., we'll start you off on something simple. You're on the ten-in-one grill, ten patties in a pound. Your basic burger. The guy on the bin calls, 'Six hamburgers.' So you lay your six pieces of meat on the grill and set the timer." Before my eyes Jason conjures up the gleaming, mechanized McDonald's kitchen. "Beep-beep, beep-beep, beep-beep. That's the beeper to sear 'em. It goes off in twenty seconds. Sup, sup, sup, sup, sup, sup." He presses each of the six patties down on the sizzling grill with an imaginary silver disk. "Now you turn off the sear beeper, put the buns in the oven, set the oven timer and then the next beeper is to turn the meat. This one goes beep-beep-beep, beep-beep-beep. So you turn your patties, and then you drop your re-cons on the meat, t-con, t-con, t-con." Here Jason takes two imaginary handfuls of reconstituted onions out of water and sets them out, two blops at a time, on top of the six patties he's arranged in two neat rows on our grill. "Now the bun oven buzzes [there are over a half dozen different timers with distinct beeps and buzzes in a McDonald's kitchen]. "This one turns itself off when you open the oven door so you just take out your crowns, line 'em up and give 'em each a squirt of mustard and a squirt of ketchup." With mustard in his right hand and ketchup in his left, Jason wields the dispensers like a pair of six-shooters up and down the lines of buns. Each dispenser has two triggers. One fires the premeasured squirt for ten-in-ones—the second is set for quarter-pounders.

"Now," says Jason, slowing down, "now you get to put on the pickles. Two if they're regular, three if they're small. That's the creative part. Then the lettuce, then you ask for a cheese count ('cheese on four please'). Finally the last beep goes off and you lay your burger on the crowns."

"On the *crown* of the buns?" I ask, unable to visualize. "On top?"

"Yeah, you dress 'em upside down. Put 'em in the box upside down too. They flip 'em over when they serve 'em."

"Oh, I think I see."

"Then scoop up the heels [the bun bottoms] which are on top of the bun warmer, take the heels with one hand and push the tray out from underneath and they land (plip) one on each burger, right on top of the re-cons, neat and perfect. [The official time allotted by Hamburger Central, the McDonald's headquarters in Oak Brook, Ill, is ninety seconds to prepare and serve a burger.] It's like I told you. The procedures make the burgers. You don't have to know a thing."

• • •

McDonald's employs 500,000 teenagers at any one time. Most don't stay long. About 8 million Americans—7 per cent of our labor force—have worked at McDonald's and moved on. Jason is not a typical ex-employee. In fact, Jason is a legend among the teenagers at the three McDonald's outlets in his suburban area. It seems he was so fast at the griddle (or maybe just fast talking) that he'd been taken back three times by two different managers after quitting.

But Jason became a real legend in his last stint at McDonald's. He'd been sent out the back door with the garbage, but instead of coming back in he got into a car with two friends and just drove away. That's the part the local teenagers love to tell. "No fight with the manager or anything...just drove away and never came back....I don't think they'd give him a job again."

• • •

"I would never go back to McDonald's," says Jason. "Not even as a manager." Jason is enrolled at the local junior college. "I'd like to run a real restaurant some-day, but I'm taking data processing to fall back on." He's had many part-time jobs, the highest-paid at a hospital ($4.00 an hour), but that didn't last, and now dishwashing (at the $3.35 minimum). "Same as McDonald's. But I would never go back there. You're a complete robot."

"It seems like you can improvise a little with the onions," I suggested. "They're not premeasured." Indeed, the reconstituted onion shreds grabbed out of a container by the unscientific-looking wet handful struck me as oddly out of character in the McDonald's kitchen.

"There's supposed to be twelve onion bits per patty," Jason informed me. "They spot check."

"Oh come on."

"You think I'm kiddin'. They lift your heels and they say, 'You got too many onions.' It's portion control."

"Is there any freedom anywhere in the process?" I asked.

"Lettuce. They'll leave you alone as long as it's neat."

"So lettuce is freedom; pickles is judgment?"

"Yeah but you don't have time to play around with your pickles. They're never gonna say just six pickles except on the disk. [Each store has video disks to train the crew for each of about twenty work stations, like fries, register, lobby, quarter-pounder grill.] What you'll hear in real life is 'twelve and six on a turn-lay.' The first number is your hamburgers, the second is your Big Macs. On a turn-lay means you lay the first twelve, then you put down the second batch after you turn the first. So you got twenty-four burgers on the grill, in shifts. It's what they call a production mode. And remember you also got your fillets, your McNuggets...."

"Wait, slow down." By then I was losing track of the patties on our imaginary grill. "I don't understand this turn-lay thing."

"Don't worry, you don't have to understand. You follow the beepers, you follow the buzzers and you turn your meat as fast as you can. It's like I told you, to work at McDonald's you don't need a face, you don't need a brain. You need to have two hands and two legs and move 'em as fast as you can. That's the whole system. I wouldn't go back there again for anything."

June Sanders

McDonald's french fries are deservedly the pride of their menu; uniformly golden brown all across America and in thirty-one other countries. However, it's difficult to standardize the number of fries per serving. The McDonald's fry scoop, perhaps their greatest technological innovation, helps to control this variable. The unique flat funnel holds the bag open while it aligns a limited number of fries so that they fall into the package with a paradoxically free, overflowing cornucopia look.

Despite the scoop, there's still a spread. The acceptable fry yield is 400 to 420 servings per 100-lb. bag of potatoes. It's one of the few areas of McDonald's cookery in which such a range is possible. The fry yield is therefore one important measure of a manager's efficiency. "Fluffy, not stuffy," they remind the young workers when the fry yield is running low.

No such variation is possible in the browning of the fries. Early in McDonald's history Louis Martino, the husband of the secretary of McDonald's founder Ray Kroc, designed a computer to be submerged in the fry vats. In his autobiography, *Grinding It Out*, Kroc explained the importance of this innovation. "We had a recipe...that called for pulling the potatoes out of the oil when they got a certain color and grease bubbles formed in a certain way. It was amazing that we got them as uniform as we did because each kid working the fry vats would have his own interpretation of the proper color and so forth. [The word "kid" was officially re-placed by "person" or "crew person" in McDonald's management vocabulary in 1973 in response to union organizing attempts.] Louis's computer took all the guesswork out of it, modifying the frying to suit the balance of water to solids in a given batch of potatoes. He also engineered the dispenser that allowed us to squirt exactly the right amount of catsup and mustard onto our premeasured hamburger patties...."

The fry vat probe is a complex miniature computer. The fry scoop, on the other hand, is as simple and almost as elegant as the wheel. Both eliminate the need for a human being to make "his own interpretation," as Ray Kroc puts it.

Together, these two innovations mean that a new worker can be trained in fifteen minutes and reach maximum efficiency in a half hour. This makes it economically feasible to use a kid for one day and replace him with another kid the next day.

June Sanders worked at McDonald's for one day.

"I needed money, so I went in and the manager told me my hours would be 4 to 10 P.M." This was fine with June, a well-organized black woman in her early twenties who goes to college full time.

"But when I came in the next day the manager said I could work till 10 for that one day. But from then on my hours would be 4 P.M. to 1 A.M. And I really wouldn't get off at 1 because I'd have to stay to clean up after they closed.... Yes it was the same manager, a Mr. O'Neil.

"I told him I'd have to check first with my family if I could come home that late. But he told me to put on the uniform and fill out the forms. He would start me out on french fries.

"Then he showed me an orientation film on a TV screen all about fries.... No, I still hadn't punched in. This was all in the basement. Then I went upstairs, and *then* I punched in and went to work.... No, I was not paid for the training downstairs. Yes, I'm sure."

I asked June if she had had any difficulty with the fries.

"No, it was just like the film. You put the french fries in the grease and you push a button which doesn't go off till the fries are done. Then you take them out and put them in a bin under a light. Then you scoop them into the bags with this thing, this flat, light metal—I can't really describe it—scoop thing that sits right in the package and makes the fries fall in place."

"Did they watch you for a while?" I asked. "Did you need more instruction?"

"Someone leaned over once and showed me how to make sure the fry scooper was set inside the opening of the bag so the fries would fall in right."

"And then?"

"And then, I stood on my feet from twenty after four till the manager took over my station at 10:35 P.M.

"When I left my legs were aching. I knew it wasn't a job for me. But I probably would have tried to last it out—at least more than a day—if it wasn't for the hours. When I got home I talked it over with my mother and my sister and then I phoned and said I couldn't work there. They weren't angry. They just said to bring back the uniform.... The people were nice, even the managers. It's just a rushed system."

"June," I said, "does it make any sense to train you and have you work for one day? Why didn't he tell you the real hours in the first place?"

"They take a chance and see if you're desperate. I have my family to stay with. That's why I didn't go back. But if I really needed the money, like if I had a kid and no family, I'd have to make arrangements to work any hours.

"Anyway, they got a full day's work out of me."

Damita

I waited on line at my neighborhood McDonald's. It was lunch hour and there were four or five customers at each of the five open cash registers. "May I take your order?" a very thin girl said in a flat tone to the man at the head of my line.

"McNuggets, large fries and a Coke," said the man. The cashier punched in the order. "That will be—."

"Big Mac, large fries and a shake," said the next woman on line. The cashier rang it up.

"Two cheeseburgers, large fries and a coffee," said the third customer. The cashier rang it up.

"How much is a large fries?" asked the woman directly in front of me.

The thin cashier twisted her neck around trying to look up at the menu board.

"Sorry," apologized the customer, "I don't have my glasses."

"Large fries is seventy-nine," a round-faced cashier with glasses interjected from the next register.

"Seventy-nine cents," the thin cashier repeated.

"Well how much is a *small* fries?"

As they talked I leaned over the next register. "Say, can I interview you?" I asked the clerk with glasses, whose line was by then empty.

"Huh?"

"I'm writing a story about jobs at fast-food restaurants."

"O.K. I guess so."

"Can I have your phone number?"

"Well...I'll meet you when I get off. Should be sometime between 4 and 4:30."

By then it was my turn.

"Just a large fries," I said.

The thin cashier pressed "lge fries." In place of numbers, the keys on a McDonald's cash register say "lge fries," "reg fries," "med coke," "big mac," and so on. Some registers have pictures on the key caps. The next time the price of fries goes up (or down) the change will be entered in the store's central computer. But the thin cashier will continue to press the same button. I wondered how long she'd worked there and how many hundreds of "lge fries" she'd served without learning the price.

• • •

Damita, the cashier with the glasses, came up from the crew room (a room in the basement with lockers, a table and a video player for studying the training disks) at 4:45. She looked older and more serious without her striped uniform.

"Sorry, but they got busy and, you know, here you get off when they let you."

The expandable schedule was her first complaint. "You give them your availability when you sign on. Mine I said 9 to 4. But they scheduled me for 7 o'clock two or three days a week. And I needed the money. So I got to get up 5 in the morning to get here from Queens by 7. And I don't get off till whoever's supposed to get here gets here to take my place.... It's hard to study with all the pressures."

Damita had come to the city from a small town outside of Detroit. She lives with her sister in Queens and takes extension courses in psychology at New York University. Depending on the schedule posted each Friday, her McDonald's paycheck for a five-day week has varied from $80 to $114.

"How long have you worked at McDonald's?" I asked.

"Well, see I only know six people in this city, so my manager from Michigan...yeah, I worked for McDonald's in high school...my manager from Michigan called this guy Brian who's the second assistant manager here. So I didn't have to fill out an application. Well, I mean the first thing I needed was a job," she seemed to apologize, "and I knew I could always work at McDonald's. I always say I'm gonna look for something else, but I don't get out till 4 and that could be 5 or whenever."

The flexible scheduling at McDonald's only seems to work one way. One day Damita had arrived a half hour late because the E train was running on the R track.

"The assistant manager told me not to clock in at all, just to go home. So I said O.K. and I left."

"What did you do the rest of the day?" I asked.

"I went home and studied, and I went to sleep."

"But how did it make you feel?"

"It's like a humiliating feeling 'cause I wasn't given any chance to justify myself. But when I spoke to the Puerto Rican manager he said it was nothing personal against me. Just it was raining that day, and they were really slow and someone who got here on time, it wouldn't be right to send them home."

"Weren't you annoyed to spend four hours traveling and then lose a day's pay?" I suggested.

"I was mad at first that they didn't let me explain. But afterwards I understood and I tried to explain to my sister: 'Time waits for no man.' "

"Since you signed on for 9 to 4," I asked Damita, "and you're going to school, why can't you say, 'Look, I have to study at night, I need regular hours'?"

"Don't work that way. They make up your schedule every week and if you can't work it, you're responsible to replace yourself. If you can't they can always get someone else."

"But Damita," I tried to argue with her low estimate of her own worth, "anyone can see right away that your line moves fast yet you're helpful to people. I mean, you're a valuable employee. And this manager seems to like you."

"Valuable! $3.35 an hour. And I can be replaced by any [pointing across the room] kid off the street." I hadn't noticed. At a small table under the staircase a manager in a light beige shirt was taking an application from a lanky black teenager.

"But you know the register. You know the routine."

"How long you think it takes to learn the six steps? Step 1. Greet the customer, 'Good morning, can I help you?' Step 2. Take his order. Step 3. Repeat the order. They can have someone off the street working my register in five minutes."

"By the way," I asked, "on those cash registers without numbers, how do you change something after you ring it up? I mean if somebody orders a cheeseburger and then they change it to a hamburger, how do you subtract the slice of cheese?"

"I guess that's why you have step 3, repeat the order. One cheeseburger, two Cokes, three..."

"Yeah but if you punched a mistake or they don't want it after you get it together?"

"Like if I have a crazy customer, which I do be gettin' 'specially in this city, and they order hamburger, fries and shake, and it's $2.95 and then they just walk away?"

"I once did that here," I said. "About a week ago when I first started my research. All I ordered was some french fries. And I was so busy watching how the computer works that only after she rang it up I discovered that I'd walked out of my house without my wallet. I didn't have a penny. I was so embarrassed."

"Are you that one the other day? Arnetta, this girl next to me, she said, 'Look at that crazy lady going out. She's lookin' and lookin' at everything and then she didn't have no money for a bag of fries.' I saw you leaving, but I guess I didn't recognize you. [I agreed it was probably me.] O.K., so say this crazy lady comes in and orders french fries and leaves. In Michigan I could just zero it out. I'd wait till I start the next order and press zero and large fries. But here you're supposed to call out 'cancel sale' and the manager comes over and does it with his key.

"But I hate to call the manager every time, 'specially if I got a whole line waiting. So I still zero out myself. They can tell I do it by the computer tape, and they tell me not to. Some of them let me, though, because they know I came from another store. But they don't show the girls here how to zero out. Everybody thinks you need the manager's key to do it."

"Maybe they let you because they can tell you're honest," I said. She smiled, pleased, but let it pass. "That's what I mean that you're valuable to them. You know how to use the register. You're good with customers."

"You know there was a man here," Damita said, a little embarrassed about bragging, "when I was transferred off night he asked my manager, 'What happened to that girl from Michigan?' "

"Did your manager tell you that?"

"No, another girl on the night shift told me. The manager said it to her. They don't tell you nothing nice themselves."

"But, see, you are good with people and he appreciates it."

"In my other McDonald's—not the one where they let me zero out but another one I worked in in Michigan—I was almost fired for my attitude. Which was helping customers who had arthritis to open the little packets. And another bad attitude of mine is that you're supposed to suggest to the customer, 'Would you like a drink with that?' or 'Do you want a pie?'—whatever they're pushing. I don't like to do it. And they can look on my tape after my shift and see I didn't push the suggested sell item."

McDonald's computerized cash registers allow managers to determine immediately not only the dollar volume for the store but the amount of each item that was sold at each register for any given period. Two experienced managers, interviewed separately, both insisted that the new electronic cash registers were in fact slower than the old mechanical registers. Clerks who knew the combinations—hamburger, fries, Coke: $2.45—could ring up the total immediately, take the cash and give change in one operation. On the new registers you have to enter each item and may be slowed down by computer response time. The value of the new registers, or at least their main selling point (McDonald's franchisers can choose from several approved registers), is the increasingly sophisticated tracking systems, which monitor all the activity and report with many different statistical breakdowns.

"Look, there," said Damita as the teenage job applicant left and the manager went behind the counter with the application, "If I was to say I can't come in at 7, they'd cut my hours down to one shift a week, and if I never came back they wouldn't call to find out where I was.

"I worked at a hospital once as an X-ray assistant. There if I didn't come in there were things that had to be done that wouldn't be done. I would call there and say, 'Remember to run the EKGs.' Here, if I called and said, 'I just can't come by 7 no more,' they'd have one of these high school kids off the street half an hour later. And they'd do my job just as good."

Damita was silent for a while and then she made a difficult plea. "This might sound stupid, I don't know," she said, "but I feel like, I came here to study and advance myself but I'm not excelling myself in any way. I'm twenty years old but—this sounds terrible to say—I'm twenty but I'd rather have a babysitting job. At least I could help a kid and take care. But I only know six people in this city. So I don't even know how I'd find a babysitting job."

"I'll keep my ears open," I said. "I don't know where I'd hear of one but..."

Damita seemed a little relieved. I suppose she realized there wasn't much chance of babysitting full-time, but at least she now knew seven people in the city.

Jon DeAngelo

Jon DeAngelo, twenty-two, has been a McDonald's manager for three years. He started in the restaurant business at sixteen as a busboy and planned even then to run a restaurant of his own someday. At nineteen, when he was the night manager of a resort kitchen, he was hired away by McOpCo, the McDonald's Operating Company.

Though McDonald's is primarily a franchise system, the company also owns and operates about 30 percent of the stores directly. These McOpCo stores, including some of the busiest units, are managed via a chain of command including regional supervisors, store managers and first and second assistants who can be moved from unit to unit. In addition, there's a network of inspectors from Hamburger Central who make announced and unannounced checks for QSC (quality, service, cleanliness) at both franchise and McOpCo installations.

Jon was hired at $14,000 a year. At the time I spoke with him his annual pay was $21,000—a very good salary at McDonald's. At first he'd been an assistant manager in one of the highest-volume stores in his region. Then he was deliberately transferred to a store with productivity problems.

"I got there and found it was really a great crew. They hated being hassled, but they loved to work. I started them having fun by putting the men on the women's jobs and vice versa. [At most McDonald's the women tend to work on the registers, the men on the grill. But everyone starts at the same pay.] Oh, sure, they hated it at first, the guys that is. But they liked learning all the stations. I also ran a lot of register races."

Since the computer tape in each register indicates sales per hour, per half hour or for any interval requested, the manager can revv the crew up for a real "on your mark, get set, go!" race with a printout ready as they cross the finish line, showing the dollars taken in at each register during the race.

The computer will also print out a breakdown of sales for any particular menu item. The central office can check, therefore, how many Egg McMuffins were sold on Friday from 9 to 9:30 two weeks or two years ago, either in the entire store or at any particular register.

This makes it possible to run a register race limited to Cokes for instance, or Big Macs. Cashiers are instructed to try suggestive selling ("Would you like a drink with that?") at all times. But there are periods when a particular item is being pushed. The manager may then offer a prize for the most danish sold.

A typical prize for either type of cash register race might be a Snoopy mug (if that's the current promotion) or even a $5 cash bonus.

"This crew loved to race as individuals," says Jon of his troubled store, "but even more as a team. They'd love to get on a production mode, like a chicken-pull-drop or a burger-turn-lay and kill themselves for a big rush.

"One Saturday after a rock concert we did a $1,900 hour with ten people on crew. We killed ourselves but when the rush was over everyone said it was the most fun they ever had in a McDonald's."

I asked Jon how managers made up their weekly schedule. How would he decide who and how many to assign?

"It comes out of the computer," Jon explained. "It's a bar graph with the business you're going to do that week already printed in."

"The business you're *going* to do, already printed in?"

"It's based on the last week's sales, like maybe you did a $300 hour on Thursday at 3 P.M. Then it automatically adds a certain percent, say 15 percent, which is the projected annual increase for your particular store.... No, the person scheduling doesn't have to do any of this calculation. I just happen to know how it's arrived at.

Really, it's simple, it's just a graph with the numbers already in it. $400 hour, $500 hour. According to Hamburger Central you schedule two crew members per $100 hour. So if you're projected for a $600 hour on Friday between 1 and 2, you know you need twelve crew for that lunch hour and the schedule sheet leaves space for their names.

"You mean you just fill in the blanks on the chart?"

"It's pretty automatic except in the case of a special event like the concert. Then you have to guess the dollar volume. Scheduling under could be a problem, but over would be a disaster to your crew labor productivity."

"Crew labor productivity?"

"Everything at McDonald's is based on the numbers. But crew labor productivity is pretty much *the* number a manager is judged by."

"Crew labor productivity? You have to be an economist."

"It's really simple to calculate. You take the total crew labor dollars paid out, divide that into the total food dollars taken in. That gives you your crew labor productivity. The more food you sell and the less people you use to do it, the better your percentage. It's pretty simple."

Apparently, I still looked confused.

"For example, if you take an $800 hour and you run it with ten crew you get a very high crew labor percent."

"That's good?"

"Yes that's good. Then the manager in the next store hears Jon ran a 12 percent labor this week, I'll run a 10 percent labor. Of course you burn people out that way. But . . ."

"But Jon," I asked, "if the number of crew you need is set in advance and printed by the computer, why do so many managers keep changing hours and putting pressure on kids to work more?"

"They advertise McDonald's as a flexible work schedule for high school and college kids," he said, "but the truth is it's a high-pressure job, and we have so much trouble keeping help, especially in fast stores like my first one (it grossed $1.8 million last year), that 50 percent never make it past two weeks. And a lot walk out within two days.

"When I was a first assistant, scheduling and hiring was my responsibility and I had to fill the spots one way or another. There were so many times I covered the shifts myself. Times I worked 100 hours a week. A manager has to fill the spaces on his chart somehow. So if a crew person is manipulable they manipulate him."

"What do you mean?"

"When you first sign on, you give your availability. Let's say a person's schedule is weeknights, 4 to 10. But after a week the manager schedules him as a closer Friday night. He calls in upset, 'Hey, my availability isn't Friday night.' The manager says, 'Well the schedule is already done. And you know the rule. If you can't work it's up to you to replace yourself.' At that point the person might quit, or he might not show up or he might have a fight with the manager."

"So he's fired?"

"No. You don't fire. You would only fire for cause like drugs or stealing. But what happens is he signed up for thirty hours a week and suddenly he's only scheduled for four. So either he starts being more available or he quits."

"Aren't you worried that the most qualified people will quit?"

"The only qualification to be able to do the job is to be able physically to do the job. I believe it says that in almost those words in my regional manual. And being there is the main part of being physically able to do the job."

"But what about your great crew at the second store? Don't you want to keep a team together?"

"Let me qualify that qualification. It takes a special kind of person to be able to move before he can think. We find people like that and use them till they quit."

"But as a manager don't you look bad if too many people are quitting?"

"As a manager I am judged by the statistical reports which come off the computer. Which basically means my crew labor productivity. What else can I really distinguish myself by? I could have a good fry yield, a low M&R [Maintenance and Repair budget]. But these are minor."

As it happens, Jon is distinguished among McDonald's managers in his area as an expert on the computerized equipment. Other managers call on him for cash register repairs. "They say, 'Jon, could you look at my register? I just can't afford the M&R this month.' So I come and fix it and they'll buy me a beer."

"So keeping M&R low is a real feather in a manager's cap," I deduced.

"O.K., it's true, you can over spend your M&R budget; you can have a low fry yield; you can run a dirty store; you can be fired for bothering the high school girls. But basically, every Coke spigot is monitored. [At most McDonald's, Coke doesn't flow from taps that turn on and off. Instead the clerk pushes the button "sm," "med" or "lge," which then dispenses the premeasured amount into the appropriate-size cup. This makes the syrup yield fairly consistent.] Every ketchup squirt is measured. My costs for every item are set. So my crew labor productivity is my main flexibility."

I was beginning to understand the pressures toward pettiness. I had by then heard many complaints about slight pilferage of time. For instance, as a safety measure no one was allowed to stay in a store alone. There was a common complaint that a closer would be clocked out when he finished cleaning the store for the night, even though he might be required to wait around unpaid till the manager finished his own nightly statistical reports. At other times kids clocked out and then waited hours (unpaid) for a crew chief training course (unpaid).

Overtime is an absolute taboo at McDonald's. Managers practice every kind of scheduling gymnastic to see that no one works over forty hours a week. If a crew member approaching forty hours is needed to close the store, he or she might be asked to check out for a long lunch. I had heard of a couple of occasions when, in desperation, a manager scheduled someone to stay an hour or two over forty hours. Instead of paying time-and-a-half, he compensated at straight time listing the **extra** hours as miscellaneous and paying through a fund reserved for things like register race bonuses. All of this of course to make his statistics look good.

"There must be some other way to raise your productivity," I suggested, "besides squeezing it out of the kids."

"I try to make it fun," Jon pleaded earnestly. "I know that people like to work on my shifts. I have the highest crew labor productivity in the area. But I get that from burning people out. Look, you can't squeeze a McDonald's hamburger any flatter. If you want to improve your productivity there is nothing for a manager to squeeze but the crew."

"But if it's crew dollars paid out divided by food dollars taken in, maybe you can bring in more dollars instead of using less crew."

"O.K., let me tell you about sausage sandwiches."

"Sausage sandwiches?" (Sounded awful.)

"My crew was crazy about sausage sandwiches. [Crew members are entitled to one meal a day at reduced prices. The meals are deducted from wages through a computerized link to the time clocks.] They made it from a buttered English muffin, a slice of sausage and a slice of cheese. I understand this had actually been a menu item in some parts of the country but never here. But the crew would make it for themselves and then all their friends came in and wanted them.

"So, I decided to go ahead and sell it. It costs about 9¢ to make and I sold it for $1.40. It went like hotcakes. My supervisor even liked the idea because it made so much money. You could see the little dollar signs in his eyes when he first came into the store. And he said nothing. So we kept selling it.

"Then someone came from Oak Brook and they made us stop it.

"Just look how ridiculous that is. A slice of sausage is 60¢ as a regular menu item, and an English muffin is 45¢. So if you come in and ask for a sausage and an English muffin I can still sell them to you today for $1.05. But there's no way I can add the slice of cheese and put it in the box and get that $1.40.

"Basically, I can't be any more creative than a crew person. I can't take any more initiative than the person on the register."

"Speaking of cash registers and initiative," I said...and told him about Damita. I explained that she was honest, bright and had learned how to zero out at another store. "Do you let cashiers zero out?" I asked.

"I might let her in this case," Jon said. "The store she learned it at was probably a franchise and they were looser. But basically we don't need people like her. Thinking generally slows this operation down.

"When I first came to McDonald's, I said, 'How mechanical! These kids don't even know how to cook.' But the pace is so fast that if they didn't have all the systems, you couldn't handle it. It takes ninety seconds to cook a hamburger. In those seconds you have to toast the buns, dress it, sear it, turn it, take it off the grill and serve it. Meanwhile you've got maybe twenty-four burgers, plus your chicken, your fish. You haven't got time to pick up a rack of fillet and see if it's done. You have to press the timer, drop the fish and know, without looking, that when it buzzes it's done.

"It's the same thing with management. You have to record the money each night before you close and get it to the bank the next day by 11 A.M. So you have to trust the computer to do a lot of the job. These computers also calculate the payrolls, because they're hooked into the time clocks. My payroll is paid out of a bank in Chicago. The computers also tell you how many people you're going to need each hour. It's so fast that the manager hasn't got time to think about it. He has to follow the procedures like the crew. And if he follows the procedures everything is going to come out more or less as it's supposed to. So basically the computer manages the store."

Listening to Jon made me remember what Ray Kroc had written about his own job (head of the corporation) and computers:

> *We have a computer in Oak Brook that is designed to make real estate surveys. But those printouts are of no use to me. After we find a promising location, I drive around it in a car, go into the corner saloon and the neighborhood supermarket. I mingle with the people and observe their comings and goings. That tells me what I need to know about how a McDonald's store would do there.*

By combining twentieth-century computer technology with nineteenth-century time-and-motion studies, the McDonald's corporation has broken the jobs of griddleman, waitress, cashier and even manager down into small, simple steps. Historically these have been service jobs involving a lot of flexibility and personal flare. But the corporation has systematically extracted the decision-making elements from filling french fry boxes or scheduling staff. They've siphoned the know-how from the employees into the programs. They relentlessly weed out all variables that might make it necessary to make a decision at the store level, whether on pickles or on cleaning procedures.

It's interesting and understandable that Ray Kroc refused to work that way. The real estate computer may be as reliable as the fry vat probe. But as head of the company Kroc didn't have to surrender to it. He'd let the computer juggle all the demographic variables, but in the end Ray Kroc would decide, intuitively, where to put the next store.

Jon DeAngelo would like to work that way, too. So would Jason, June and Damita. If they had a chance to use some skill or intuition at their own levels, they'd not only feel more alive, they'd also be treated with more consideration. It's job organization, not malice, that allows (almost requires) McDonald's workers to be handled like paper plates. They feel disposable because they are.

I was beginning to wonder why Jon stayed on at McDonald's. He still yearned to open a restaurant. "The one thing I'd take from McDonald's to a French restaurant of my own is the fry vat computer. It really works." He seemed to have both the diligence and the style to run a personalized restaurant. Of course he may not have had the capital.

"So basically I would tell that girl [bringing me back to Damita] to find a different job. She's thinking too much and it slows things down. The way the system is set up, I don't need that in a register person, and they don't need it in me."

"Jon," I said, trying to be tactful, "I don't exactly know why you stay at McDonald's."

"As a matter of fact, I have already turned in my resignation."

"You mean you're not a McDonald's manager any more?" I was dismayed.

"I quit once before and they asked me to stay."

"I have had such a hard time getting a full-fledged manager to talk to me and now I don't know whether you count."

"They haven't actually accepted my resignation yet. You know I heard of this guy in another region who said he was going to leave and they didn't believe him. They just wouldn't accept his resignation. And you know what he did? One day, at noon, he just emptied the store, walked out, and locked the door behind him."

For a second Jon seemed to drift away on that beautiful image. It was like the kids telling me about Jason, the crewman who just walked out the back door.

"You know what that means to close a McDonald's at noon, to do a zero hour at lunch?"

"Jon," I said. "This has been fantastic. You are fantastic. I don't think anyone could explain the computers to me the way you do. But I want to talk to someone who's happy and moving up in the McDonald's system. Do you think you could introduce me to a manager who..."

"You won't be able to."

"How come?"

"First of all, there's the media hotline. If any press comes around or anyone is writing a book I'm supposed to call the regional office immediately and they will provide someone to talk to you. So you can't speak to a real corporation person except by arrangement with the corporation.

"Second, you can't talk to a happy McDonald's manager because 98 percent are miserable.

"Third of all, there is no such thing as a McDonald's manager. The computer manages the store."

❖ ❖ ❖

Dynamics

1. Garson's interviewees often focus on the McDonald's corporation's demand for "productivity." Locate some passages which mention "productivity" and determine what this concept means for the corporation. Then, in each passage, discuss how the meaning of productivity might change if it were defined from the worker's perspective. Where do the values of each group differ?

2. As you re-read Garson's essay, describe some of the relationships the essay suggests might exist between knowledge and action. How are these relationships different for each of the parties in the essay (the workers, management, the corporation, Garson herself)? Speculate about what these differences might mean.

Critical Tools

1. Garson's essay is a combination of interviews, research, and analysis. Looking at another essay that includes interviews with informants, try to figure out how each writer uses interviews to support, complicate, and/or extend her or his own analysis. How do their methods of "quoting" compare with those that you find in one of your own essays? How can you account for the differences you see?

2. What makes the exploitation of McDonald's workers possible? After listing the reasons that the essay and your own experience suggest, select a critical tool from another text that helps you to say more about the sources and implications of this exploitation.

Draft One/Draft Two

Draft One: Of all the jobs you have held, which one have you enjoyed the most (or disliked the least)? Which one was least enjoyable? After reading Garson's essay and reflecting on your own experience, list and comment on the factors that contribute to what you might call "job satisfaction."

Draft Two: For your second draft, think about another text from *Literacies* that focuses on work. Write an essay in which you consider how the questions of race and/or gender that this new essay raises might help to complicate the responses you offered in your first draft.

❖ ❖ ❖

Before Reading David Gilmore. . .

1. Describe what it means in your cultural tradition to be "a man" or "manly." If you are male, where and how did you learn to "be" a man? If you are female, where does your knowledge about masculinity come from? Explain whether you see a difference between being "male" and being "manly." How do you account for your response?

2. How would you expect the idea of "masculinity" to fit into a discussion of "community"? Where do you think "community" might fit into discussions of "masculinity"? Consider how your responses are shaped by your own cultural background. Write down some reflections on these questions and keep them in mind as you read Gilmore's essay.

Performative Excellence:
Circum-Mediterranean

David Gilmore

In Glendiot idiom, there is less focus on "being a good man" than on "being good at being a man"—a stance that stresses performative excellence, *the ability to foreground manhood by means of deeds that strikingly "speak for themselves."*

—Michael Herzfeld, *The Poetics of Manhood*

The lands of the Mediterranean Basin have for centuries been in close contact through trade, intermarriage, intellectual and cultural exchange, mutual colonization, and the pursuit of common regional interests (Braudel 1972; Peristiany 1965; Davis 1977). The use of terms such as *Mediterranean* or *Circum-Mediterranean* (Pitt-Rivers 1963; Giovannini 1987) to categorize these lands is not meant to imply a "culture area" as that term has been used in American ecological anthropology—for Mediterranean societies are as diverse and varied as anywhere else in the world— but rather to serve as a concept of heuristic convenience in ethnographic analysis and comparison (Pitt-Rivers 1977:viii). Although not representing a unity in the sense of cultural homogeneity (Herzfeld 1980), many Mediterranean societies place importance on "certain institutions" (Pitt-Rivers 1977:ix) that invite comparison. Aside from obvious resemblances in ecology, settlement patterns, and economic adaptations, what seems to provide a basis of comparison more than anything else is, in fact, a shared image of manhood. In his magisterial survey, *People of the Mediterranean*, John Davis (1977:22) writes,

> *Many observers assert the unity of the Mediterranean on various grounds, some of them more plausible than others. At a straightforward, noncausal level, anthropologists, tourists, even Mediterranean people themselves notice some common cultural features: attitudes, elements of culture that are recognizably*

*similar in a large proportion of Mediterranean societies, and that are readily
intelligible to other Mediterranean people. "I also have a moustache," is the phrase
happily recorded by J. G. Peristiany....In an emblematic way, it serves to denote not
only manliness, which is so common a concern around the Mediterranean, but also a
style of anthropological argument.*

This invocation of the mustache, of course, is shorthand for saying I am a man,
too, the equal of any, so afford me the respect of the hirsute sex. By appealing to this
common denominator, the statement is both a warning and an evocation of the
fiercely egalitarian (and competitive) values shared by many otherwise diverse
peoples of the region.

In the Mediterranean area, most men are deeply committed to an image of
manliness because it is part of their personal honor or reputation. But this image
not only brings respect to the bearer; it also brings security to his family, lineage, or
village, as these groups, sharing a collective identity, reflect the man's reputation
and are protected by it. Because of its competitive, sexually aggressive aspects,
Mediterranean male imagery has been perceived, at least in some of the Latin
countries, as self-serving, disruptive, and isolating, a matter of "personal vice" and·a
"social evil" (Pitt-Rivers 1961:118). This is part of a distancing stereotype shared by
many northern visitors who for their own reasons assume the south to be "different"
(Herzfeld 1987). But this overlooks the very important and often constructive group
implications of the male image as it exists in many Mediterranean societies and
which, as we shall see later, is not so different in effect from masculine imagery
elsewhere. I want to explore the implications of these male ideals in this chapter as
the first step in our quest for the meaning of manhood.

We begin our discussion of masculine imagery in the Mediterranean societies
by taking a negative example. This is the man who is not "good at being a man," in
Michael Herzfeld's felicitous phrase above. What does he lack? Let me start by
describing such a case from my own fieldwork in the Andalusian pueblo of
Fuenmayor (a pseudonym). Although the following discussion is geared to southern
Spain and to other areas in the northern littoral of the Mediterranean, much of
what I say here relates to parts of the Islamic Middle East as well.

Lorenzo

Like many other men in the Mediterranean area with whom they share the
common sensibilities alluded to by Davis, the Andalusians of Spain's deep south are
dedicated to proving their manliness publicly. Even more than other Iberians, they
are fervent followers of what the Spanish critic Enrique Tierno Galván (1961:74-76)
has called a quasi-religious Hispanic "faith in manhood." If you measure up in this
regard, you are "very much a man" (*muy hombre*), "very virile" (*muy macho*), or "lots
of man" (*mucho hombre*). If not, you are *flojo*, a weak and pathetic impostor. The
polysemous term *flojo* literally means empty, lazy, or flaccid; it is used also to

describe a dead battery, a flat tire, or some other hopeless tool that does not work. It connotes flabby inadequacy, uselessness, or inefficiency.

Our example, Lorenzo, was a callow fellow in his late twenties, a perennial student and bachelor. A gentle character of outstanding native intelligence, Lorenzo was the only person from Fuenmayor ever to have attended graduate school to pursue a doctorate, in this case in classic Castilian literature. But he was unable for various reasons ever to complete his dissertation, so he remained in a kind of occupational limbo, unable to find suitable work, indecisive and feckless. Because of his erudition, unusual in such backwater towns, Lorenzo was generally acknowledged as a sort of locally grown genius. Many people had high hopes for him. But the more traditionally minded people in town were not among his admirers. They found him reprehensible for their own curmudgeonly reasons, for in the important matter of gender appropriateness, Lorenzo was considered highly eccentric, even deviant. "A grave case," one townsman put it.

People pointed first to his living arrangements. Oddly, even perversely, Lorenzo stayed indoors with his widowed mother, studying, reading books, contemplating things, rarely leaving his cramped scholar's cloister. He had no discernible job, and as he earned no money, he contributed nothing concrete to his family's impoverished larder, a fact that made him appear parasitic to many. He lived off his uncomplaining old mother, herself hardworking but poor. Withdrawn and secretive, Lorenzo made no visible efforts to change this state of affairs; nor did he often, as other men are wont to do, enter the masculine world of the bars to drink with cronies, palaver, debate, or engage in the usual convivial banter. When he did, he drank little. Rarely did he enter into the aggressively competitive card games or the drunken bluster that men enjoy and expect from their fellows.

Perhaps most bizarre, Lorenzo avoided young women, claiming not to have time for romance. Along with his other faults, Lorenzo was actually intensely shy with girls. This is a very unusual dereliction indeed, one that is always greeted with real dismay by both men and women in Spain. Sexual shyness is more than a casual flaw in an Andalusian youth; it is a serious, even tragic inadequacy. The entire village bemoans shyness as a personal calamity and collective disgrace. People said that Lorenzo was afraid of girls, afraid to try his luck, afraid to gamble in the game of love. They believe that a real man must break down the wall of female resistance that separates the sexes; otherwise, God forbid, he will never marry and will sire no heirs. If that happens, everyone suffers, for children are God's gift to family, village, and nation.

Being a sensitive soul, Lorenzo was quite aware of the demands made upon him by importuning kith and kin. He felt the pressure to go out and run after women. He knew he was supposed to target a likely wife, get a paying job, and start a family. A cultural rebel by default or disinclination, he felt himself to be a man of modern, "European" sensibilities. Above all, he wanted to remain beyond that "stupid rigmarole" of traditional southern expectations, as he called it. He was clearly an agnostic in regards to Tierno Galván's Spanish faith in manhood.

One evening, after we had spent a pleasant hour talking about such things as the place of Cervantes in world literature, he looked up at me with his great, sad brown eyes, and confessed his cultural transgressions. He began by confiding his anxieties about the aggressive courting that is a man's presumed function. "I know you have to throw yourself violently at women," he said glumly, "but I prefer not to," adding, "It's just not me." Taking up his book, he shook his head and cast his mournful eyes to the ground with a shrug, awaiting a comforting word from a sympathetic and, he believed, enlightened foreigner. It was obvious he was pathologically afraid of rejection.

Because he was a decent and honest man, Lorenzo had his small circle of friends in the town. Like Lorenzo, they were all educated people. Given to introspective brooding, he was the subject of much concern among them. They feared he would never marry, bachelorhood being accounted the most lamentable fate outside of blatant homosexuality, which is truly disgusting to them. With the best intentions in mind, these people often took me aside to ask me if I did not think it was sad that Lorenzo was so withdrawn, and what should be done about him? Finally, one perceptive friend, discussing Lorenzo's case at length as we often did, summed up the problem in an unforgettable phrase that caused me to ponder. He expressed admiration for Lorenzo's brains, but he noted his friend's debilitating unhappiness, his social estrangement; he told me in all seriousness and as a matter obviously much considered that Lorenzo's problem was his failure "as a man." I asked him what he meant by this, and he explained that, although Lorenzo had pursued knowledge with a modicum of success, he had "forgotten" how to be a man, and his forgetting was the cause of his troubles. This friend laid the blame for Lorenzo's alienation squarely on a characterological defect of role-playing, a kind of stage fright. Shaking his head sadly, he uttered an aphoristic diagnosis: "Como hombre, no sirve" (literally, as a man he just doesn't serve, or work). He added, "Pobrecito, no sirve pa' na' " (poor guy, he's totally useless).

Spoken by a concerned friend in a tone of commiseration rather than reproach, this phrase, "no sirve," has much meaning. Loosely translated, it means that as a man Lorenzo fails muster in some practical way, the Spanish verb *servir* meaning to get things done, to work in the sense of proficiency or serviceability. There is a sense of the measurable quantity here—visible results. But what are these practical accomplishments of Andalusian manliness? Let me digress briefly in order to place Lorenzo and his apostasy from Tierno's "faith" in the broader context of the Circum-Mediterranean area by offering some comparisons from across the sea.

Manly Services

Lorenzo's friends made a connection between manhood and some code of effective or "serviceable" behavior. This echoes Chandos's (1984:346) description of the British public-school elite, the English locution connoting utility being both etymologically and conceptually cognate to the Spanish *sirve*. But more than simply serving, this behavior in Lorenzo's community had to be public, on the community stage, as it were. A man's effectiveness is measured as others see him in action, where they can evaluate his performance. This conflation of masculinity and efficaciousness into a theatrical image of performing finds powerful echoes in other Mediterranean lands. Let us take, for example, Greece. Luckily we have excellent data for that country, thanks to the untiring efforts of Michael Herzfeld. There, too, the manly man is one who performs, as Herzfeld has it, center stage. His role-playing is manifested in "foregrounded" deeds, in actions that are seen by everyone and therefore have the potential to be judged collectively. As Herzfeld says of the Greeks he studied, the excellent man, the admired man, is not necessarily a "good" man in some abstract moral sense. Rather he is good at being a man. This means not only adequate performance within set patterns (the male script); it also means publicity, being on view and having the courage to expose oneself to risk. In addition, it means decisive action that works or serves a purpose, action that meets tests and solves real problems consensually perceived as important.

A subtle and perceptive fieldworker, Herzfeld (1985a) describes for the village of Glendi in Crete—an island of Mediterranean cultural synthesis—the archetype of social acceptance that is most relevant to the present case. To be a man in Crete and Andalusia means a pragmatic, agential modality, an involvement in the public arena of acts and deeds and visible, concrete accomplishments. This showy modality has nothing to do with the security or domestic pleasures of the home or with introspection. These things are associated with self-doubt, hesitancy, withdrawal into the wings, that is, with passivity. It is here that Lorenzo, back in Spain, has been deficient. He is, above all else, a recessive man, staying demurely at home, avoiding life's challenges and opportunities. Manhood at both ends of the sea seems to imply a nexus of gregarious engagement, a male praxis endlessly conjoined on the stage of community life.

If we go back in time we find some intriguing echoes. The ancient Greeks also admired an outgoing, risk-taking manliness of effective action. They also judged a man not for being good but for whether or not he was useful in the role he played on the communal stage—an "efficient or defective working part of the communal mechanism" (Dover 1978:108). Their agonistic view of life is the ethos that informs the restless heroism of the Homeric sagas with a call to dramatic, even grandiose, gestures (Gouldner 1965). But this image is also associated with ideals of manly virtue that the ancient Greeks, like some of their modern descendants, held and still hold dear in its vulgar manifestation as *filotimo*, masculine pride or self-esteem (Herzfeld 1980:342-45). The Spaniards or Italians might call this right to pride by some cognate of "honor," *honra* or *onore*, or perhaps respect. It conveys a self-image deeply involved with the endless search for worldly success and fame, for approbation and admiration in the judgmental eyes of others. This emphasis on the dramatic gesture appears early in Greek culture. It shows up in Homer, in the *Iliad* most visibly: in Achilles' willingness to trade a long, uneventful life for a brief one filled with honor and glory, and in Agamemnon's willingness to trade several months of his life for an honorable death on the battlefield at Troy (Slater 1968:35).

This quest for fame and for the glorious deed as a measure of masculine virtue took on a life of its own in the ancient eastern Mediterranean world. Indeed, in the flourishing Athens of the fifth century B.C., male life seems to have been an unremitting struggle for personal aggrandizement—for "fame and honor, or for such goals as could lead to these (wealth, power, and so forth)" (ibid.:38). Despite the Greek emphasis on moderation that we cherish today, this obsessive glory-seeking grew more and more a part of Greek masculine ideals, to the point where the chronicler Thucydides was motivated to chastise his countrymen: "Reckless audacity came to be considered the courage of a loyal ally; prudent hesitation specious cowardice; moderation was held to be a cloak for unmanliness" (1951, iii:82). One mythological model of this manly man covered in glory, the embodiment of this Greek ideal, is the intrepid and wily traveller Odysseus.

The *Odyssey* is a parable of this kind of dramatized manliness uniting practical effect and moral vision. Its hero sets forth, engaging in countless struggles, surviving through physical strength and clever stratagems fair and foul. After innumerable encounters with the dangers and monsters of the world, he returns triumphantly in the final act to succor wife and kin, the ultimate heroic Greek male. Odysseus is no saint; he is portrayed as a trickster and manipulator. But his tricks "work." They have the desired end: the rescue of the endangered wife left at home, Penelope, and the restoration of the family's honor, threatened by the opportunistic suitors. The Homeric epic captures in legend the thrust of this peripatetic, pragmatic, and serviceable Mediterranean manhood.

From a psychological point of view, it is clear that this ancient morality of man-acting has something to do with the cultural encoding of impulse sublimation. An inspirational model of right action, it directs energies away from self-absorption and introspection toward a strategy of practical problem-solving and worldly concerns. The manly image in ancient Greece as well as in modern Andalusia is an inducement toward ceaseless enterprise judged by measurable ends. In an important sense, it is more than simply the sublimation of libido and aggression into culturally-approved channels of practical achievement; it is also the encouragement to resist their opposites: indolence, self-doubt, squeamishness, hesitancy, the impulse to withdraw or surrender, the "sleepiness" of quietude (symbolized in Greek legend by death by drowning—a universal metaphor for returning to the womb). As well as a commitment to commanding action in an agonistic context, an aggressive stance in service to proximate goals—what Gouldner has called the Greek contest system—manliness in much of the Mediterranean world can be called a social agoraphilia, a love for the sunlit public places, for crowds, for the proscenium of life. Such open contexts are associated not only with exposure and sociability but also with risk and opportunity, with the possibility or the grand exploit and the conspicuous deed. We can thus describe Lorenzo's first failure as a man as a refusal to sally forth into the fray.

Sex and Marriage

It is, of course, a commonplace version of this kind of mighty inner struggle against self-withdrawal that Lorenzo had become embroiled in and that he seemed to be losing in Spain. But there is more at stake here than a show of self-mastery and competitive fitness. There is also sex; or rather, an aggressive role in courtship. Lorenzo's friends bemoaned his failure to go out and capture a wife. "As a man he does not serve" refers explicitly to wife-capture and phallic predation.

In some Muslim areas, for example, rural Turkey (Bates 1974) and the southern Balkans (Lockwood 1974), this predation often takes the form of actual bride theft or prenuptial rape, often involving kidnapping or violence. Such things used to occur also in parts of southern Italy, where some men first raped and then married reluctant brides. Wife-by-capture is still common in parts of rural Greece (Herzfeld 1985b). This assertive courting, minus the violence, is an important, even essential requirement of manhood in Spain as well. It is a recurrent aspect of the male image in many parts of southern Europe, whereas it seems less critical in the northern countries.

Most of what we know about Mediterranean ideas of manhood, in fact, concerns their more expressive components—more precisely, their sexual assertiveness (Pitt-Rivers 1977): the *machismo* of Spain and the *maschio* of Sicily (Giovannini 1987) are examples. There is also the *rajula* (virility) complex of Morocco (Geertz 1979:364), which has been likened specifically to Hispanic *machismo* by a female anthropologist (Mernissi 1975:4-5). There are parallels in the Balkans, which anthropological observers Simic (1969, 1983) and Denich (1974), male and female scholars respectively, independently identify with the *machismo* of Hispanic culture. A real man in these countries is forceful in courtship as well as a fearless man of action. Both sex and economic enterprise are competitive and risky, because they place a man against his fellows in the quest for the most prized resource of all—women. Defeat and humiliation are always possible.

In Sicily, for instance, masculine honor is always bound up with aggression and potency. A real man in Sicily is "a man with big testicles" (Blok 1981:432-33); his potency is firmly established. Among the Sarakatsani of Greece, also, an adult male must be "well endowed with testicles" (J.K. Campbell 1964:269), quick to arousal, insatiable in the act. Such beliefs also hold true for much of Spain, especially the south (Pitt-Rivers 1965, 1977; Brandes 1980, 1981; Mitchell 1988), where a real man is said to have much *cojones*, or balls. Such big-balled men, naturally, tower over and dominate their less well-endowed and more phlegmatic fellows.

Yet there is more to this than competitive lechery (which, incidentally, is not as highly regarded in the Muslim countries, for in Islam unbridled lust is held to be socially disruptive and immoral for both sexes [Bates and Rassam 1983:215]). This extra dimension is important for a deeper understanding of the social matrix of Circum-Mediterranean ideas of manhood that I mentioned above. Even in those parts of southern Europe where the Don Juan model of sexual assertiveness is highly valued, a man's assigned task is not just to make endless conquests but to spread his seed. Beyond mere promiscuity, the ultimate test is that of competence in reproduction, that is, impregnating one's wife. For example, in Italy, "only a wife's pregnancy could sustain her husband's masculinity" (Bell 1979:105). Most importantly, therefore, the Mediterranean emphasis on manliness means results; it means procreating offspring (preferably boys). At the level of community endorsement, it is legitimate reproductive success, more than simply erotic acrobatics—a critical fact often overlooked by experts on Mediterranean honor who stress its disruptive or competitive elements (Pitt-Rivers 1977:11). Simply stated, it means creating a large and vigorous family. Promiscuous adventurism represents a prior (youthful) testing ground to a more serious (adult) purpose. Sexuality and economic self-sufficiency work in parallel ways.

In southern Spain, for example, people will heap scorn upon a married man without children, no matter how sexually active he may have been prior to marriage. What counts is results, not the preliminaries. Although both husband and wife suffer in prestige, the blame of barrenness is placed squarely on him, not his wife, for it is always the man who is expected to initiate (and accomplish) things. "Is he a man?" the people sneer. Scurrilous gossip circulates about his physiological defects. He is said to be incompetent, a sexual bungler, a clown. His mother-in-law becomes outraged. His loins are useless, she says, "no sirven," they don't work. Solutions are sought in both medical and magical means. People say that he has failed in his husbandly duty. In being sexually ineffectual, he has failed at being a man.

Beyond Sex: Provisioning

Aside from potency, men must seek to provision dependents by contributing mightily to the family patrimony. This, too, is measured by the efficiency quotient, by results (Davis 1977:77). What counts, again, is performance in the work role, measured in sacrifice or service to family needs. What has to be emphasized here is the sense of social sacrifice that this masculine work-duty entails. The worker in the fields often despises manual labor of any sort, because it rarely benefits him personally. For example, the rural Andalusians say that work is a "curse" (D. Gilmore 1980:55), because it can never make a man rich. For the poor man, working means contracting under humiliating conditions for a day-wage, battling with his fellows for fleeting opportunities in the work place, and laboring in the fields picking cotton and weeding sunflowers from dawn to dusk. Synonymous with suffering, work is something that most men will freely admit they hate and would avoid if they could.

Yet for the worker, the peasant, or any man who must earn his bread, work is also a responsibility—never questioned—of feeding dependents. And here, as in matters of sex and fatherly duty, the worker's reputation as a citizen and a man is closely bound up with clearly defined service to family. A man who shirks these obligations renounces his claim to both respectability and manhood; he becomes a despised less-than-man, a wastrel, a *gamberro*. The latter term means an irresponsible reprobate who acts like a carefree child or who lives parasitically off women.

Although it is true that women in Andalusia are often wage-earners too, the husband, to be a real man, must contribute the lion's share of income to support wife and family like a pillar and to keep the feminine machine of domestic production running smoothly. A man works hard, sometimes desperately, because, as they say, *se obliga*, you are bound to your family, not because you like it. In this sense, Spanish men are, as Brandes notes (1980:210), like men everywhere, actively pursuing the breadwinning role as a measure of their manhood. The only difference is that they rarely get pleasure or personal satisfaction from the miserable work available to them.

In southern Italy, much the same attitude is found. John Davis (1973:94-95) writes of the town of Pisticci: "Work is also justified in terms of the family of the man who works: 'If it were not for my family, I'd not be wearing myself out' (*non mi sacrifico*). The ability of a husband to support his wife and children is as important a component of his honour as his control of his wife's sexuality. Independence of others, in this context, thus implies both his economic and sexual honour.... Work, then, is not regarded as having any intrinsic rewards. Men work to produce food and some cash for their families."

This sacrifice in the service of family, this contribution to household and kin, is, in fact, what Mediterranean notions of honor are all about. Honor is about being good at *being a man*, which means building up and buttressing the family or kindred—the basic building blocks of society—no matter what the personal cost: "[Mediterranean] honor as ideology helps shore up the identity of a group (a family or a lineage) and commit to it the loyalties of otherwise doubtful members. Honor defines the group's social boundaries, contributing to its defense against the claims of equivalent competing groups" (Schneider 1971:17).

The emphasis on male honor as a domestic duty is widespread in the Mediterranean. In his seminal survey of the literature, John Davis, like Jane Schneider in the quote above, finds confirmation for his view of masculine honor as deriving from work and economic industry as much as from sexual success: "It should be said at the outset that honour is not primarily to do with sexual intercourse...but with performance of roles and is related to economic resources because feeding a family, looking after women, maintaining a following, can be done more easily when the family is not poor" (1977:77).

Sometimes this kind of economic service can be quantified in terms of money or other objects of value, or it can be expressed in material accumulations that are passed on to women and children, such as dowries. For example, Ernestine Friedl (1962), writing about a Greek peasant village in contemporary Boeotia, describes the honor of fathers as grounded in their ability to provide large dowries in cash and valuables to their daughters. This success assures them of the best in-laws, contributes to family prestige, and consequently enhances their image as provider. Manhood is measured at least partly in money, a man's only direct way of nourishing children. Manhood, then, as call to action, can be interpreted as a kind of moral compunction to provision kith and kin.

Man-the-Protector

After impregnating and provisioning comes bravery. Being a man in Andalusia, for example, is also based on what the people call *hombría*. Technically this simply means manliness, but it differs from the expressly virile or economic performances described above. Rather, hombría is physical and moral courage. Having no specific behavioral correlatives, it forms an intransitive component: it means standing up for yourself as an independent and proud actor, holding your own when challenged. Spaniards also call this *dignidad* (dignity). It is not based on threatening people or on violence, for Andalusians despise bullies and deplore physical roughness, which to them is mere buffoonery. Generalized as to context, hombría means a courageous and stoic demeanor in the face of any threat; most important, it means defending one's honor and that of one's family. It shows not aggressiveness in a physical sense but an unshakable loyalty to social group that signals the ultimate deterrent to challenge. The restraint on violence is always based on the capacity for violence, so that reputation is vital here.

As a form of masculine self-control and courage, hombría is shown multitudinously. For example, in Fuenmayor, a group of young men may wander down to the municipal cemetery late at night after a few drinks to display their disdain for ghosts. They take with them a hammer and a nail or spike. Posturing drunkenly together, they pound the nail into the cemetery's stucco wall. Challenging all manner of goblins and ghouls, they recite in unison the following formula to the rhythm of the hammer blows:

> Aquí hinco clavo
> del tio monero
> venga quién venga,
> aquí lo espero!

> I here drive a spike
> before goblin or sprite
> and whatever appear,
> I remain without fear!

The last man to run away wins the laurels as the bravest, the most manly. Sometimes adolescents will challenge each other to spend a night in the cemetery in a manner of competitive testing, but otherwise hombría is nonconfrontational, as the defiance is displaced onto a supernatural (nonsocial) adversary. Nevertheless, as the above example shows, it is competitive and, like virility and economic performance, needs proof in visible symbols and accomplishments. Hombría judges a man's fitness to defend his family. Pitt-Rivers (1961:89) has depicted it best: "The quintessence of manliness is fearlessness, readiness to defend one's own pride and that of one's family." Beyond this, hombría also has a specifically political connotation that enlarges its role in Spain.

For the past century, Spain, and Andalusia in particular, has been a land of political struggle. Class consciousness is strong as a result of deep antagonism between landowners and laborers (Martinez-Alier 1971). Hombría among the embattled workers and peasants has taken on a strongly political coloration from this class opposition: loyalty to social class. Among peasants and workers, manliness is expressed not only by loyalty to kindred but also by loyalty to the laboring class and by an active participation in the struggle for workers' rights. For example, workers are very manly who uphold laborers' rights by refusing to back down in labor disputes. This was an especially courageous act under the Franco dictatorship but is still admired today among the committed. Charismatic labor leaders—especially those jailed and beaten by the Franco police, as was Marcelino Camacho, the head of the underground Workers' Commissions—are highly admired as being very virile. In their group they are men with "lots of balls," envied by men, attractive to women. In the eyes of their political enemies they may be hated, but they are also respected and feared.

A concrete example: there was in Fuenmayor the famous case of the militant agitator nicknamed "Robustiano" (the Robust One), so called for his athletic build and his formidable courage. After the Civil War, when his left-leaning family was decimated by the Nationalists in the postwar persecutions, he had openly defied the Franco police by continuing his revolutionary activities. Beatings, threats, and blackballing had no effect. After each return from jail he took up the struggle anew, winning admiration from all sides, including his jailers. Despite torture, he never betrayed his comrades, always taking police abuse stoically as a matter of course. Robustiano developed a huge and loyal following; today he is remembered as one of the martyrs who kept up the workers' spirits during the dark days of the dictatorship. Beyond this, people remember Robustiano as a real man, an apotheosis of the Andalusian ideal of manhood.

Apart from politics, this call to dramatic action in defense of one's comrades finds echoes throughout the Mediterranean region where social class is less important than other primordial ties, as among patrilineal peoples of the African littoral. For example, among the Kabyles of Algeria, according to Bourdieu (1965, 1979a), the main attribute of the real man is that he stands up to other men and fiercely defends his agnates. "All informants give as the essential characteristic of the man of honour the fact that he *faces* others," Bourdieu remarks (1979a:128). A real man suffers no slights to self or, more importantly, to family or lineage. Nearby, in eastern Morocco, true men are those who stand ever ready to defend their families against outside threats; they "unite in defense of their livelihoods and collective identity" (Marcus 1987:50).

Likewise, among the Sarakatsani shepherds of modern-day Greece (J.K. Campbell 1964:269-70), the true man is described as *varvatos*, clearly cognate to the Italian *barbato*, bearded or hairy. Aside from indicating strength and virility (the facial hair again), this also "describes a certain ruthless ability in any form of endeavour" in defense of his kindred. Virile Sarakatsani shepherds are those who meet the demands of pastoral life in which " 'reputation' is impossible without strength" (ibid.:317). In this way the Sarakatsani man gains the respect of competitors and fends off threats to his domain. Thus he maintains his kindred's delicate position in a tough environment. "The reputation for manliness of the men of the family is a deterrent against external outrage" (ibid.:271). Campbell sees this stress on manliness in essentially functional terms. "Here again," he writes (ibid.:270), "we see the *'efficient'* aspect of manliness" (emphasis added).

Man-the-protector is everywhere encountered in the Mediterranean area. Throughout, bureaucratic protections are weakly developed, states are unstable, feuding is endemic, and political alignments, like patronage, are shifting and unreliable. Because of the capriciousness of fortunes and the scarcity of resources, a man ekes out a living and sustains his family through toughness and maneuvering. For example, in Sicily, *"un vero uomo"* (a real man) is defined by "strength, power, and cunning necessary to protect his women" (Giovannini 1987:68). At the same time, of course, the successfully protective man in Sicily or Andalusia garners praise through courageous feats and gains renown for himself as an individual. This inseparable functional linkage of personal and group benefit is one of the most ancient moral notions found in the Mediterranean civilizations. One finds it already in ancient seafaring Greece in the voyager Odysseus. His very name, from *odyne* (the ability to cause pain and the readiness to do so), implies a willingness to expose oneself to conflict, risk, and trouble and to strive against overwhelming odds in order to achieve great exploits. "To be Odysseus, then, is to adopt the attitude of the hunter of dangerous game: to deliberately expose one's self, but thereafter to take every advantage that the exposed position admits; the immediate purpose is injury, but the ultimate purpose is recognition and the sense of a great exploit" (Dimrock 1967:57).

But Odysseus's ultimate goal is not simply one vainglorious exploit after another. All his wayfaring heroism is directed at a higher purpose: to rescue wife and child and to disperse the sinister suitors who threaten them both. The real man gains renown by standing between his family and destruction, absorbing the blows of fate with equanimity. Mediterranean manhood is the reward given to the man who is an efficient protector of the web of primordial ties, the guardian of his society's moral and material integuments.

Autonomous Wayfarers

The ideals of manliness found in these places in the Mediterranean seem to have three moral imperatives: first, impregnating one's wife; second, provisioning dependents; third, protecting the family. These criteria demand assertiveness and resolve. All must be performed relentlessly in the loyal service of the "collective identities" of the self.

One other element needs mention. The above depend upon something deeper: a mobility of action, a personal autonomy. A man can do nothing if his hands are tied. If he is going to hunt dangerous game and, like Odysseus, save his family, he needs absolute freedom of movement. Equally important as sex and economic resourcefulness is the underlying appeal to independent action as the starting point of manly self-identity. To enter upon the road to manhood, a man must travel light and be free to improvise and to respond, unencumbered, to challenge. He must have a moral captaincy. In southern Spain, as reported by Brandes (1980:210), dependency for an Andalusian peasant is not just shameful; it is also a negation of his manly image. Personal autonomy is the goal for each and every man; without it, his defensive posture collapses. His strategic mobility is lost, exposing his family to ruin. This theme, too, has political implications in Spain.

An example comes from George Collier's account of the Spanish Civil War in an Andalusian village. Collier (1987:90) points out the role played by masculine pride in the labor movements of workers and peasants in western Andalusia. He describes the critical political connotations of what he calls the "cultural terms in which Andalusians relate autonomy to masculine honor" and the virtues attached to asserting this masculinity (ibid.:96). Collier's discussion of the violent conflicts between landowners and laborers during the Second Republic (1931-36) in the pueblo of Los Olivos (Huelva Province) shows that a driving force behind their confrontations was this issue of personal autonomy. The peasants and workers were defending not only their political rights but also their self-image as men from the domineering tactics of the rich and powerful. Autonomy permitted them to defend their family's honor. Encumbered or dependent, they could not perform their manly heroics. Their revolutionism, as Collier brilliantly shows, was as much a product of a manhood image as their political and economic demands. This was particularly true of southern Spain, but Collier sees this mixture of political ideology and masculine self-image as something more widely Mediterranean:

> Villagers in Los Olivos held to the ideal of masculine autonomy characteristic of property relations and the system of honor in the agrarian societies of the Mediterranean....The prepotent male discouraged challenges by continually reasserting this masculinity and potential for physical aggression while he guarded against assaults on the virtue of his women and stood up to others to protect his family's honor....The ideal of masculine autonomy thus charged employer-employee relations with special tension. In having to accept someone else's orders, the employee implicitly acknowledged his lack of full autonomy and his vulnerability to potential dishonor. (Ibid.:96-97)

To be dependent upon another man is bad enough, but to acknowledge dependence upon a woman is worse. The reason, of course, is that this inverts the normal order of family ties, which in turn destroys the formal basis for manhood. For instance, in Morocco, as reported by Hildred Geertz (1979:369), the major values of *rajula*, or manly pride, are "personal autonomy and force," which imply dominating and provisioning rather than being dominated and provisioned by women. There is indeed no greater fear among men than the loss of this personal autonomy to a dominant woman.

In Morocco there is in fact a recurrent anxiety that a man will fall under the magical spell of a powerful woman, a demonic seductress who will entrap him forever, as Venus entrapped Tannhaüser, or as Circe attempted to enslave Odysseus, causing him to forget his masculine role (Dwyer 1978). The psychological anthropologist Vincent Crapanzano has written an entire book about a Moroccan man who lived in terror of such a demonic female *jinn*. He tells us that this anxiety is widespread: "This theme of enslavement by a woman—the inverse of the articulated standards of male-female relations, of sex and marriage—pervades Moroccan folklore" (1980:102). There, as in Spain, a man must gain full and total independence from women as a necessary criterion of manhood. How can he provide for dependents and protect them when he himself is dependent like a child? This inversion of sex roles, because it turns wife into mother, subverts both the man and the family unit, sending both down to corruption and defeat.

Sexual Segregation

Many of these themes—activity versus passivity, extroversion versus introversion, autonomy versus dependence—are expressed in the physical context of Mediterranean rural community life. The requirement that the male separate conclusively from women could be no more clearly expressed than in the prohibitions against domesticity that pervade the ethnographic literature. In many Mediterranean societies (D. Gilmore 1982:194-96), the worlds of men and women are strictly demarcated. Male and female realms are, as Duvignaud says of Tunisia, "two separate worlds that pass without touching" (1977:16). Men are forced by this moral convention of spatial segregation to leave home during the day and to venture forth into the risky world outside. Like Lorenzo, a man hiding in the shadows of home during the daytime is immediately suspect. His masculinity is out of place and thus questionable. A real man must be out-of-doors among men, facing others, staring them down. In Cyprus, for example, a man who lingers at home with wife and children will have his manhood questioned: "What sort of man is he? He prefers hanging about the house with women" (Loizos 1975:92). And among the Algerian Kabyle described by Bourdieu (1979b:141), his fellows will malign a homebody for much the same reason: "A man who spends too much time at home in the daytime is suspect or ridiculous: he is 'a house man,' who 'broods at home like a hen at roost.' A self-respecting man must offer himself to be seen, constantly put himself in the gaze of others, confront them, face up to them (*qabel*). He is a man among men." So we can see the manly image working to catapult men out of the refuge of the house into the cockpit of enterprise.

Another Eccentric

To conclude, I will describe another negative case from Andalusia that illustrates these last points. There was a man in Fuenmayor who was a notorious homebody and whose family suffered the consequences. Alfredo was a rubicund little merchant with the non-Castilian surname Tissot (his ancestors had emigrated from Catalonia generations earlier). A sedentary man of middle age, he operated a small grocery establishment from out of his home—nothing unusual for men with small retail businesses. But Alfredo was unusual in that he rarely ventured out from his home, where he lived with his wife and two pretty grown daughters.

In Andalusia, as in Cyprus or Algeria, a man is expected to spend his free time outdoors, backslapping and glad-handing. This world is the street, the bar, the fields—public places where a man is seen. He must not give the impression of being under the spell of the home, a clinger to wife or mother. While out, men are also expected to become involved in standard masculine rivalries: games of cards and dominoes, competitive drinking and spending, and contests of braggadocio and song. Although aware of such expectations, Alfredo resisted them, because, as he confided to me one day, such socializing was a waste of time and money—you have to spend money in the bars; you have to buy rounds of drinks for the company of fellows, and you have to tipple and make merry. You have to boast and puff yourself up before your cronies. All this conviviality was expensive and boring, so the chubby grocer stayed at home with his family. He read books and watched television at night or went over his accounts.

Like all other townsmen, Alfredo was under the scrutiny of public opinion and was accountable as a man. Although grudgingly admitting his modest business acumen (said however to be based on his wife's capital), the townspeople did not accept his lame excuses for inappropriate comportment. As a descendant of distrusted ethnic outsiders (Catalans are known as a race of workaholics and misers), he was expected to display strange attitudes, but his refusal to enter the public world of men in favor of home was greeted with outrage and indignation. Especially vilified was his stinginess with both time and money, which was felt as an insult to the other men of the pueblo, a calculated withdrawal from the male role, which demands not just familiar provisioning but a certain degree of generosity in the wider society. A man of means is expected to spend freely and thus to support his community. People say such a man owes something to the town. Alfredo's withdrawal damaged both his own prestige and that of his family, which suffered equally in the public spotlight.

One hot afternoon, as I was walking past the Tissot house with a group of friends, my companions made passing comments on Alfredo's strangeness. "What kind of man is he," they muttered, pointing at his sealed and cloistered house, "spending his time at home?" Glowering ominously, they likened him to a mother hen. They offered colorful explanations for his contemptible secretiveness, alluding to certain despicable character traits such as cheapness and egoism. But beyond these picayune moral defects, my informants found something truly repulsive in the merchant's domesticity, furtiveness, and sedentariness. They suggested a basic failure at a deeper level in the most important thing of all: man-acting. Carrying this character assassination further, my informants left the realm of observable fact and ventured into gossipy speculation, which is common in such matters of serious deviance. Unequivocal explanations are deemed necessary when deeply-felt customs are violated.

The men then told me their suspicions about Alfredo. In the telling I could feel a palpable relaxation of their anxiety about him, for they had reduced the deviance to root causes that they could scapegoat and consensually reject in a way that corroborated their own self-image. It all boiled down to Alfredo's failure as a man. This was shown incontrovertibly, as in the case of Lorenzo, by his shadowy introversion. As a consequence of his withdrawn uxoriousness, in the minds of his fellows, the Tissot household, bereft of sexual respectability, was held necessarily to be abnormal in terms of sexual functioning. Its very existence was, therefore, by local standards, attributable to aberrant practices. Since Alfredo was not a real man, as his community had decided, then his daughters, by logical extension, could not be the product of his own seed. The explanation that tied all together (since the eccentric Catalan was also known as a moderately wealthy man) was that he was a panderer and a pimp for his wife, and his daughters and his wealth were the result of her secret whoring. The villagers had thus conceptually, if inaccurately, reversed provider and dependent roles in this ugly and ridiculous slander. The associated success of insemination was stolen by a hostile act of imagination. Poor Alfredo was utterly incapable of combatting this malicious attack because he had cut himself off from male communication, so he and his family suffered from the slights and contempt reserved for deviants.

Hypothetically classified as unnatural, then, Alfredo's inexplicable character traits fell into a kind of preordained order of the man-who-is-no-man. For example, there was the matter of his cooking. He was known to help wife and daughters in the kitchen, cutting, chopping, and so on, performing tasks absolutely unnatural to the male physiology and musculature. Andalusians recognize that there are professional chefs, but they are men who have learned a trade to earn a living, and so they retain their claim to manhood. At home, even chefs do not cook; their wives do. But Alfredo was said to help eagerly out of his own perverted volition. "Is he a man?" people scoffed, "cooking, hanging about in the kitchen like that?" The Andalusians believe fervidly that male and female anatomy provide for different, complementary skills. It was true that Alfredo helped in the kitchen. Since he invited me into his home (in itself an act of unusual, even deviant hospitality), I saw him. He never hid this indictable bit of information from me. I came to know him fairly well on these occasions. Being a didactic and helpful sort of man in a fussy way, he instructed my wife and myself in the proper preparation of certain specialties of Spanish cuisine, providing precise, often compulsive directions for grinding ingredients to make a tasty gazpacho. I learned how to whip up a savory, if smelly, garlic soup in the gleaming Tissot kitchen. He always watched that everything was done in the proper order. For example, the bread always went in the pot after you added the vinegar: no improvising here. Beaming maternally, the homebody took pride in his knowledge of local recipes and in my vocal appreciation of his culinary skills.

But his fellows in the streets laughed at him, scorning his hurried excuses, grimacing disgustedly when I spoke of him, holding both him and his superfluous wife in contempt. The placid pleasure Alfredo took in his own odd domesticity hastened his withdrawal from manly assemblages and activities. The introverted grocer failed to make it as a man by local standards. This failure in turn robbed his family of respectability, plunging them all into disrepute, so that, for example, his two daughters had to find fiancés in other towns. Alfredo's fatal flaw was that he failed even to present himself for the test of manhood. He failed, most decisively, to separate: his public identity was blurred by the proximity of women. He had withdrawn into a sheltered cocoon of domesticity, self-indulgently satisfied with good food and easeful luxury, unwilling or afraid to enter the risky ring of manhood. This withdrawal made the other men uncomfortable, so they conceptually emasculated him and stole his family's honor, placing them all beyond the pale and obviating the threat they represented.

And yet, Alfredo was for other men a subject of endless discussion and debate. Perhaps, despite their protestations, there was something about him that, though also repellent, attracted these tough, virile men? Or possibly he represented to them some contumacious principle—living well without visibly working, perhaps—that caused ambivalent feelings that had to be expunged through projection and denial? To explore this issue further, let us pull up stakes and move on to another place and another culture.

❖ ❖ ❖

Dynamics

1. In "Performative Excellence," Gilmore tries to represent the attitudes and thinking styles of his subjects as carefully as possible. How can you tell the difference between *his* opinions about Mediterranean gender roles and his descriptions of his subjects' own attitudes? Mark passages that fit each category and explain how you are able to tell the difference between them. Why might this be an important task?

2. Gilmore refers at one point to "the male script." Find as many examples of "scripted" behavior as you can in the essay. What relationship do you see between such "scripted" behavior and what Gilmore calls "foregrounded" deeds?

3. For the Spanish men in Gilmore's essay, work is both a "curse" and an honorable obligation. Looking back through the text, find other states or ideas that are valued in simultaneously positive and negative ways. What do these complicated dualisms tell you about the role of men in Mediterranean culture?

Critical Tools

1. Gilmore writes about a "moral convention of spatial segregation" for men and women in Mediterranean cultures. According to your understanding of Gilmore's research, what is the purpose of this "spatial segregation" and how does "morality" figure into it? Use your analysis of such segregation in Gilmore's text to re-think some kind of separation between social groups in another essay you have read. What is the significance of your findings?

2. Gilmore quotes another anthropologist, Jane Schneider, who writes of "honor as ideology." Using material from Gilmore's essay, explain what "ideology" might mean in this context. Looking back at the essays you have read, consider some other "ideologies" that affect people's experiences of gender. Which one(s) might fruitfully complicate Gilmore's readings of Mediterranean masculinity?

Draft One/Draft Two

Draft One: Think about the ideas and images of manhood that are prevalent in your own cultural tradition. Explain some ways in which you find these images confusing or contradictory. Then think about some ways in which such images might be misunderstood by observers from other cultures or classes. What arguments would you use in order to help an outsider understand your culture's notions of masculinity? To what extent would you find those arguments convincing yourself?

Draft Two: Extend the terms of your discussion in draft one by considering an essay that deals with "appropriate" gender roles for women. What sorts of experiences and feelings might men and women have in common as they go through the process of "learning" their gender identities? Explain how you have arrived at your conclusions.

❖ ❖ ❖

Before Reading David Halperin. . .

1. What, in your view, defines a person as gay or straight? Which general theories have you found to be persuasive as explanations of gay identity?

2. In your view, why do we need to define a person as either gay or straight? What purposes are served by such definitions?

"Homosexuality": A Cultural Construct
An Exchange with Richard Schneider

David M. Halperin

Schneider. A conference at Brown University, "Homosexuality in History and Culture, and the University Curriculum," held on 20-21 February 1987, highlighted an ongoing debate between you, John J. Winkler, and others, on the one hand, and John Boswell, on the other, concerning the genesis and cultural articulation of homosexuality. While Boswell argues that "homo-" and "heterosexual" are categories that many (or all) societies implicitly recognize, you contend that this dualism is actually a cultural construction of the last century or two in the West. I wonder if you could clarify this debate.

Halperin. The debate to which you refer reflects a longstanding (and, some would argue, sterile) ideological dispute within social science between "essentialists" and "constructionists." As that controversy applies to sexual categories, it divides those who believe that terms like "gay" and "straight" refer to positive, objective, culturally invariant properties of persons (in the same way as do the terms for different blood-types or genetic traits)* from those who believe that the experiences named by those terms are artefacts of specific, unique, and non-repeatable cultural and social processes. "Essentialists" typically consider sexual preference to be determined by such things as biological forces or hormonal levels, and treat sexual identities as "cognitive realizations of genuine, underlying differences" (to quote

---

*I owe these examples to Edward Stein, who points out to me that genetics may provide the best model for essentialist claims about sexuality, because a specific genetic potentiality may be realized or actuated differently in different environments without itself undergoing any change (the appeal to this genetic model, however, should not be taken to commit essentialists necessarily to the proposition that sexual orientations are "caused" by genetic factors—although some essentialists *may* coincidentally happen to believe that the genetic model merely provides an illustration of the way that an essentialist argument might work).

David M. Halperin, "Homosexuality: A Cultural Construct" from *One Hundred Years of Homosexuality*. Routledge, New York & London, 1990, pages 41-53.

Steven Epstein, who devoted an essay in a recent issue of the *Socialist Review* to an exploration and critique of this controversy), whereas "constructionists assume that sexual desires are learned and that sexual identities come to be fashioned through an individual's interaction with others. The debate between essentialists and constructionists largely recapitulates the old "nature/nurture" controversy over the relative influences on the individual of heredity and environment—or, as Boswell prefers, it may represent merely the most recent instance of a long-lived scholastic quarrel between "realists" and "nominalists" over the existence of universals. In any case, it is easy to understand why essentialists are inclined to regard sexual categories as relatively unchanging over time, despite the various social or cultural forms sexual expression may take, whereas constructionists believe that different times and places produce different "sexualities."

My own position is close to that of the constructionists. Anthropological and historical studies have shown to my satisfaction that patterns of sexual preference and configurations of desire vary enormously from one culture to the next. I know of no way to explain why human beings in different cultures grow up, *en masse*, with distinctly different sorts of sexual dispositions, temperaments, or tastes, which they themselves consider normal and natural, unless I am willing to grant a determining role in the constitution of individual desire to social or cultural factors. But even if I am wrong about the *causes* of variation among patterns of human sexual preference, the *extent* of such variation still remains to be gauged, and that can be done only if we do not insist on defining it in advance of actual research, allowing our current presuppositions to fix the contours of what has yet to be discovered. Constructionism may not turn out to be right in all of its preliminary claims, but in the meantime it encourages us to put some distance between ourselves and what we think we "know" about sex. And so, by bracketing in effect our "instinctive" and "natural" assumptions, it makes it easier for us to highlight different historical configurations of desire and to distinguish various means—both formal and informal—of institutionalizing them.

The very least that can be said on behalf of the constructionist hypothesis, in other words, is that it is immensely valuable as a guide for future research. It directs the scholar's attention to the salient particularities of sexual life in a given society, particularities that might have gone unnoticed—or, if noticed, unexamined—in the absence of a research program that called for scrutinizing them. It also helps the interpreter resist the temptation to integrate alien or exotic phenomena into a plausible discourse of the known, into a picture whose appeal derives largely from its familiarity to its viewers. Whether or not the accounts constructionists give of their own methods and aims are cogent, whether or not the conclusions they reach are well-founded, they have certainly turned up enough interesting material to demonstrate the heuristic value of their theories. When they have finished charting the various social and historical constructions of sexual meaning, we shall be in a better position to judge the validity of the constructionist hypothesis and to determine what, if anything, can be said on behalf of its essentializing competitors. In the meantime, it's too soon to close off debate on the theoretical issues: there's too much work to be done.

Now, with respect to the question you raise, constructionists have demonstrated, I believe, that the distinction between homosexuality and heterosexuality, far from being a fixed and immutable feature of some universal syntax of sexual desire, can be understood as a particular conceptual turn in thinking about sex and deviance that occurred in certain sectors of northern and northwestern European society in the eighteenth and nineteenth centuries. The new conceptualization, moreover, seems to coincide with the emergence, in the same period (or in the centuries immediately preceding it), of some new sexual types—namely, the homosexual and the heterosexual, defined not as persons who perform certain acts, or who adhere to one sexrole or another, or who are characterized by strong or weak desires, or who violate or observe gender-boundaries, but as persons who possess two distinct kinds of subjectivity, who are inwardly oriented in a specific direction, and who therefore belong to separate and determinate human *species*. From what I have been able to tell, these new sexual types, the homosexual and the heterosexual, do not represent merely new ways of classifying persons—that is, innovations in moral or judicial language—but new types of desire, new kinds of desiring human beings.

To say that homosexuality and heterosexuality are culturally constructed, however, is not to say that they are unreal, that they are mere figments of the imagination of certain sexual actors. (Constructionists sometimes *sound* as if they are saying something like that, and so there is some justification for Epstein's ascription of such a belief to them, but that is not—or, at least, it ought not to be—the constructionist claim.) Homosexuality and heterosexuality are not fictions inasmuch as there really are, nowadays, homosexual and heterosexual people, individuals whose own desires are organized or structured according to the pattern named by those opposed and contrasting terms. No one, save someone determined to uphold a theory at all costs, would say that homosexuals or heterosexuals are simply imagining things, that they are deluded in supposing that they are attracted to one sex rather than another: they really do desire what they do, and that is a *fact* about them. But if homo- and heterosexuality—within some sectors of our culture, anyway—are not fictions, neither are they pure *facts of life* (as such things used to be called), positive and changeless features of the natural world. Rather, they are among the cultural codes which, in any society, give human beings access to themselves as meaningful subjects of their experiences and which are thereby objectivated—that is, realized in actuality. Hence, we need, as Epstein as written, "a better understanding of the 'collectivization of subjectivity.' We must be able to speak of sexually based group identities without assuming *either* that the group has some mystical or biological unity, *or* that the 'group' doesn't exist and that its 'members' are indulging in a dangerous mystification."

Schneider. Many gay people are predisposed to take up with Boswell's argument, feeling their own homosexuality to be deeply rooted in childhood and thus unconditioned by cultural categories or norms. Your argument seems to contradict what many people claim to "know" intuitively about themselves—does it not?

Halperin. I don't think so. The more we become aware of the contingency of all forms of erotic life, the more we are disinclined to believe in such a thing as a "natural" sexuality, something we are simply born into. Now gay sub-cultures provide abundant evidence for the vast plurality of possible sexual styles. Many gay people must know, therefore, that "sexuality" is not the sort of thing that comes in only two kinds (i.e., "hetero-" and "homo-"). "Nature" is not exhausted by these two possibilities of sexual object-choice. The better we get to know ourselves and our friends, the more we realize—at least, I do—how idiosyncratic and various, how unsystematic sexuality is: is a gay woman into S/M more like a gay woman who is not or a straight woman who is? And to the extent that we define "gayness" as a kind of lifestyle or outlook or set of values rather than as the performance of certain sexual acts, to that extent we acknowledge that it is something more than a sexual reflex.

But perhaps I am dodging your question. Perhaps there is a sense in which the constructionist thesis is not only counter-intuitive but is *necessarily* so. The cultural construction of our sexuality is almost surely bound to be beyond the reach of intuitive recall. For our intuitions about the world and about ourselves are no doubt constituted at the same time as our sexuality itself: both are part of the process whereby we gain access to ourselves as self-conscious beings through language and culture. If we *could* recover the steps by which we were acculturated, we would not have been very securely acculturated in the first place, inasmuch as acculturation consists precisely in learning to accept as natural, normal, and inevitable what is in fact conventional and arbitrary. The arbitrary character of sexual acculturation is perhaps clearest in the case of heterosexuality: the production of a population of human males who are (supposedly) incapable of being sexually excited by a person of their own sex *under any circumstances* is itself a cultural event without, so far as I know, either precedent or parallel, and cries out for an explanation. No inquiry into the origins of homosexuality can therefore be divorced from an inquiry into the origins of heterosexuality. Although the explicit *conceptualization* of homosexuality precedes that of heterosexuality—which was a late and rather hasty appendix to it—the cultural construction of homosexuality is probably a mere reflex of the social processes that produced the (comparatively speaking) strange and distinctively bourgeois formation represented by exclusive heterosexuality.

In other words, I think the cultural production of "the homosexual" is an incidental result of the social changes responsible for the formation of "the heterosexual": in the course of constructing "the heterosexual," of producing sexual subjects constituted according to an exclusive (cross-sex) sexual object-choice, western European societies also created, as a kind of by-product of that imperfect process, other sexual subjects defined by a similarly exclusive, but same-sex, sexual object-choice. Homosexuals are, in this sense, casualties of the cultural construction of exclusive heterosexuality. For that reason, I don't think it makes any sense to ask what "causes" homosexuality while ignoring heterosexuality, and any account that purports to "explain" homosexuality in isolation from heterosexuality is bound to be inadequate and should arouse immediate suspicion on political grounds—as a maneuver designed to reassert the "normativity" of heterosexuality. Homosexuality and heterosexuality are part of the same system; they are equally problematic, and each stands in just as much need of analysis and understanding as the other.

Schneider. In arguing that "homo-" and "heterosexual" are role categories peculiar to modern Western society, are you saying that homosexuality itself does not exist in other societies?

Halperin. My claim is considerably more radical than that. I am claiming that there is no such thing as "homosexuality itself" or "heterosexuality itself." Those words do not name independent modes of sexual being, leading some sort of ideal existence apart from particular human societies, outside of history or culture. Homosexuality and heterosexuality are not the atomic constituents of erotic desire, the basic building-blocks out of which every person's sexual nature is constructed. They just represent one of the many patterns according to which human living-groups, in the course of reproducing themselves and their social structures, have drawn the boundaries that define the scope of what can qualify—and to whom—as sexually attractive. Because they happen to be the dominant organizing principles of sexual pleasure and sexual desire in our culture, homosexuality and heterosexuality also represent those categories of sexual psychology and behavior that we find most obvious and compelling, and so we interpret in terms of them the sexual phenomena that we encounter on our ethnographic excursions through other cultures. Because we do not tend to see our own sexual categories as arbitrary or conventional and because we regard them accordingly as empty of ideological content, we consider "homosexual" and "heterosexual" to be purely descriptive, trans-cultural, and trans-historical, terms, equally applicable to every culture and period. Now there is nothing necessarily wrong in granting those terms a wide application, so long as we recognize that they are not *native* to the pre-modern and non-Western societies to which we apply them, and that if we *do* insist on applying them to those societies we must be careful not to mistake the "data" produced by our research for something we have discovered, rather than something we have put there ourselves.

The dangers of taking our sexual categories for granted are well illustrated by the work of Boswell who, arguing correctly that many societies have contained individuals capable of deriving sexual pleasure from contact with members of their own sex, claims on that basis that homosexuality is universal. To be sure, even Boswell does not regard homosexuality as a *thing*, an item in a cultural inventory whose presence or absence can be simply and positively checked off; he contents himself with the more modest claim that homosexuality takes different forms in different contexts, changing its character according to its cultural environment. But redescribing same-sex sexual contact as homosexuality is not as innocent as it may appear: indeed, it effectively obliterates the many different ways of organizing sexual contacts and articulating sexual roles that are indigenous to human societies—as if one were to claim that, because feudal peasants work with their hands and factory laborers work with their hands, feudal peasantry was the form that proletarianism took before the rise of industrial capitalism! Does the "paederast," the classical Greek adult, married male who periodically enjoys sexually penetrating a male adolescent share *the same sexuality* with the "berdache," the Native American (Indian) adult male who from childhood has taken on many aspects of a woman and is regularly penetrated by the adult male to whom he has been married in a public and socially sanctioned ceremony? Does the latter share *the same sexuality* with the New Guinea tribesman and warrior who from the ages of eight to fifteen has been orally inseminated on a daily basis by older youths and who, after years of orally inseminating his juniors, will be married to an adult woman and have children of his own? Does any one of these three persons share *the same sexuality* with the modern homosexual? It would be more prudent to acknowledge that although there are persons who seek sexual contact with other persons of the same sex in many different societies, only recently and only in some sectors of our own society have such persons—or some portion of them—been homosexuals.

Schneider. As a classicist, you have argued that the touted approval of homosexuality in ancient Greece has been misunderstood, that what was being sanctioned was not homosexual love as such, but some other kind of erotic expression. Could you explain your thinking on this question?

Halperin. What was approved, and (in certain contexts) even celebrated, by free classical Athenian males was not homosexuality *per se,* but a certain hierarchical relation of structured inequality between a free adult male and an adolescent youth of citizen status—or a foreigner or slave (the latter combinations being considerably less glamorous). Let me unpack this formulation.

First, the relation had to be hierarchical: for a sexual contact between males to be deemed respectable the persons involved could not stand in a reciprocal or socially symmetrical relation to one another but had to be differentiated from one another in terms of their relative degrees of power or status; every male couple had to include one social superior and one social inferior. Second, the sexual acts performed by a male couple had to be congruent with the power-differential according to which the relation was structured: the superior partner took sexual precedence— he alone, that is, might initiate a sexual act, penetrate the body of his partner, and obtain sexual pleasure; thus, the lack of social reciprocity in the relation was mirrored by a lack of sexual reciprocity (the goods and services exchanged between male lovers were both unlike and unequal in value). So long as a mature male took as his sexual partner a statutory minor, maintained an "active" sexual role vis-à-vis that person, and did not consume his own estate in the process or give any other indication that he was "enslaved" to the sexual pleasure he obtained from contact with his partner, no reproach attached itself to his conduct. That, in brief, is what "the approval of homosexuality in ancient Greece" came down to.

The description I have just offered is, to be sure, highly schematic, and in any case it refers to *the moral conventions* governing sexual relations between males; it is not intended to define the limits of what could actually go on. In fact, there seems to have been a kind of twilight zone between youth and manhood where sexual relations between males of roughly the same age do seem to have occurred and were apparently tolerated.* Even in that context however, one youth seems to have been called upon to play an "active," the other a "passive" part, and I know of no evidence suggesting that such lovers took turns or switched roles. It was possible for a youth on the border between adolescence and adulthood to alternate between being "active" and "passive" but only insofar as he was involved in separate relationships with different people; he could not be both "active" and "passive" at once in relation to the same person.

Schneider. It is an axiom of gay liberation that "the 10 percent" is a roughly constant feature of societies worldwide. This claim, if valid, implies that a homosexual identity emerges regardless of the availability of role categories—or forces every society to create such categories to accommodate the variant minority. Do you have a sense of the anthropological evidence that leads you to reject the "universal" argument? Is our existence as a self-conscious social category truly singular in the annals of history?

Halperin. John J. Winkler has observed that "almost any imaginable configuration of pleasure can be institutionalized as conventional and perceived by its participants as natural." The notion that there is no such thing as a purely natural sexuality may be comforting to gay people today, since the label "unnatural," which has packed such a hefty moral wallop since the early modern period (though not, as Winkler has shown, in the ancient world), has so often been applied to gays. But to that comforting thought there corresponds the further disquieting possibility that the subjectivities generated by human cultures may vary; some societies may produce sexualities that exclude homosexual desire altogether: a claim to this effect has in fact been made quite recently in the case of an Amazonian people by Thomas Gregor (all such ethnographic reports should be taken with a grain of salt, however, and Gregor's own account raises not a few suspicions). Of course, many if not all societies produce people who are, according to the indigenous standards, sexual deviants. Such people, however, tend to constitute themselves sexually in opposition to the prevailing local norms rather than in terms approximating to the homosexual/heterosexual polarity familiar to us. Even when these deviants qualify as deviants by virtue of certain homosexual behaviors or practices, in other words, they do so in the course of reversing the conventional definitions of who they "should" be in their

*Numerous courting scenes on Greek vases, for example, depict youths of roughly similar age.

societies, and so they simply mirror, in inverted form, the norms of their own culture (just as homosexuals today reverse the cultural definition of heterosexuality). In the classical world, the *kinaidos* or *mollis*, the man who desires to be used "as a woman" by other men, may have been one of these "casualties" of sexual acculturation, expressing in his own person the social potential for "error," the tendency of societies to create inadvertently, as it were, life-forms exactly opposite to the ones they valorize. But, in any case, I have argued that *kinaidoi*, even if they actually existed, represented a type quite distinct from what is specified by the modern category of the homosexual.

I personally do not find the possibility that the proportion of homosexuals in the general population of a society may vary any more disturbing than that the proportion of liberals and conservatives in American society may vary. It may well be the case, as some anti-gay polemicists claim, that the number of homosexuals in our society has increased during the past century, but it does not follow that the number has increased simply as a result of "permissiveness," nor does it follow that a moral crack-down would eliminate the "problem." Changes in patterns of sexuality do not result from comparatively superficial fluctuations in the moral climate; they are signs of deep, seismic shifts in the structure of underlying social relations, and no society has come close to learning how to control the forces by which it is constituted. I suspect that the tendency to insist on a fixed percentage of homosexuals throughout societies worldwide is a defensive response on the part of gay people to the stigma of "unnaturalness," and I hope we are all now beyond that. I see nothing wrong with being truly singular in the annals of history: after all, if ever we achieve a society in which the relations between men and women cease to be structured hierarchically, that would be also something of a singular achievement, and a good one.

Schneider. What would happen to your argument if, as seems possible, sexual orientation turns out to have a biological or genetic basis?

Halperin. If it turns out that there actually is a gene, say, for homosexuality, my notions about the cultural determination of sexual object-choice will—obviously enough—prove to have been wrong. Even in that hypothetical case, however, the scientists and their allies will still have a fair amount of fast talking to do. Take, for example, the instance of the New Guinea tribesman mentioned earlier. According to our hypothesis, science will now be able to reveal definitively whether he is or is not gay. Neither alternative, though, is going to be very satisfactory. For, according to one possibility, the tribesman isn't *really* gay—he just spends half his life having oral sex with other males (which makes him start to sound like a character out of Jean Genet); according to the only other possibility, the tribesman really *is* gay, but then how shall we explain why he shows no erotic interest in males outside of initiatory contexts or why he does not hesitate to marry and does not experience any sexual difficulty in his adult relations with women? Far from solving the interpretative problems raised by the ethnographic evidence, in other words, the hypothetical scientific (genetic) solution simply compounds them.

But I don't think it's likely in any case that a scientific "solution" will be forthcoming, and the trend now seems to be in the opposite direction (the hormonal hypothesis, for example, has recently been disposed of by Ron Langevin and his co-workers). Any argument for the biological or genetic determination of sexual object-choice that I can envision seems destined to be reductionist, and thus to be vulnerable to the well-known "levels of description" objection—viz., that human meanings are not reducible to physical descriptions (hence, to specify the wave-length of green light is not to provide an exhaustive definition of the concept or the experience of green). Moreover, the search for a "scientific" aetiology of sexual orientation is itself a homophobic project, and it needs to be seen more clearly as such. Just as scientific attempts to describe in genetic terms the capacities of the various human races have now been generally abandoned—not because of their inherent scientific absurdity (*some* visible racial differentiae obviously have a genetic cause) but rather because of their long and odious history of complicity with racism—and just as scientific inquiries into biological and neurological differences between males and females are starting to fall into disrepute for similar reasons, so, too, will the effort to discover a genetic or hormonal basis for sexual preference eventually come to nothing, not so much for lack of scientific progress (which has never stopped research if other motives for it remained) as for lack of social credibility. All scientific inquiries into the aetiology of sexual orientation, after all, spring from a more or less implicit theory of sexual races, from the notion that there exist broad general divisions between types of human beings corresponding, respectively, to those who make a homosexual and those who make a heterosexual sexual object-choice. When the sexual racism underlying such inquiries is more plainly exposed, their rationale will suffer proportionately—or so one may hope.

In the meantime, it helps in evaluating current scientific work to have a good nose for smelling out a research plan that is designed to confirm current categories of analysis rather than to call those very categories into question. Let's take as an example the neurohormonal hypothesis, which may be the most fashionable aetiological theory of sexual orientation around at the moment. This rearguard defense of the dominant sexual ideology proceeds by a particularly ingenious and cunning route. Since adult homosexuals have finally been shown, despite many earlier "scientific" predictions to the contrary and decades of supposedly conclusive research, to be hormonally indistinguishable from adult heterosexuals, the most recent biological attempts to reify contemporary sexual categories have had to alter traditional explanatory strategies, looking now to pre-natal neurohormonal influences on the embryonic development of those who, many years later, turn out to be homosexuals or heterosexuals. (According to one expert, increased stress on pregnant German women during the Second World War and its neurohormonal consequences account for why "a higher proportion of homosexual men were born [*sic*] in Germany during World War II than before or after the war.") The hypothesized prenatal neurohormonal influences are admittedly transient—they leave no clear trace, conveniently enough, in the bodies of the adult homosexuals who might be tested for them—whereas the fetuses or infants in whom they are supposed to operate have little occasion to make either homo- or heterosexual sexual object-choices (especially in the absence of another fetus), and so do not manifest their sexuality.

The first thing to notice about the theory, in other words, is that it is so hypothetical that it's difficult to falsify. Nor are there any experiments currently underway, so far as I know, that would test this hypothesis as it ought to be tested—namely, by monitoring the neurohormonal influences on a random sample of fetuses from the moment of conception until the completion of their psychosexual development (such an experiment would, of course, be fiendishly difficult to devise, and no scientist wants to have to wait thirty-five years before being able to publish the results of his or her research). The most that can be established on the basis of current scientific work is that individuals with certain rare genetic defects whose hormonal functioning is thereby impaired are on average more likely to become homosexuals—but such deductions are no more informative about the human population at large than were earlier inferences about the criminality of sexual deviants drawn from the observation of inmates in prisons or insane asylums. And experiments performed on laboratory animals in support of the neurohormonal hypothesis are often remarkable for the extent of their unexamined assumptions about the relation between sex, sex-role, gender, and sexual identity, as well as for their criteria for what counts as "homosexuality" in a rat.

These are exactly the sorts of experiments that might have been performed in Victorian Britain to prove the once-fashionable hypothesis that the so-called lower orders of society were throw-backs to an earlier stage of evolutionary development—inherently less civilized or morally advanced than the professional and ruling classes—if only nineteenth-century science had possessed a sophisticated genetics or endocrinology. Present-day scientific research into sexual orientation is technically refined, but the ideology informing it remains as crude and unreflective as its Victorian predecessor. Just as one might, even without undertaking a scientific study, be justifiably skeptical of an experiment designed to determine the genetic or hormonal "cause" of the underclass in American society—because one might not believe that sociological phenomena have biological causes or because one might be morally repulsed by the idea of treating social inequities as reflections of natural, essential, and unalterable biological differences among groups of one's fellow-citizens—so one is entitled to remain skeptical, I think, about "scientific" experiments which provide a biological warrant for sexual racism and which are so plainly inscribed, despite the good intentions of many individual scientists, in prevailing strategies of homophobia.

Schneider. The idea that homosexuality was as deeply rooted as one's gender or race has been a cornerstone of the hope for increased social tolerance and eventual "liberation." Your argument seems to constitute a challenge to that hope, doesn't it?

Halperin. No, I don't think so. Just because my sexuality is an artefact of cultural processes doesn't mean I'm not stuck with it. Particular cultures are contingent, but the personal identities and forms of erotic life that take shape within the horizons of those cultures are not. To say that sexuality is learned is not to say that it can be unlearned—any more than to say that culture changes is to say that it is malleable. I'm not personally responsible for my sexuality any more than I am personally responsible for certain basic values that were part and parcel of my middle-class upbringing: yet both are constitutive of my character. I don't mean that I can't inquire into, criticize, or try to understand how I came to be what I am, but no amount of conscious reflection will enable me simply to walk away from my socialization and acquire a new cultural (or sexual) identity.

But I'm not sure in any case how politically useful it is to claim that sexuality is as essential and unalterable as gender or race. After all, something like that was tried by nineteenth-century German advocates for homosexual rights in an effort to persuade their contemporaries that homosexuality was not a sin or moral failing or acquired perversity for which homosexuals themselves were to blame but was rather a natural condition; indeed, these militants succeeded so well in convincing the early sexologists of their view that standard nineteenth-century accounts of "sexual inversion" often relied for their data on the self-representations of gay polemicists—with the result that instead of being sent to jail for a fixed term homosexuals were now shut up for life in insane asylums. Fighting entrenched social agencies and practices with nothing but ideology is not a game you can win (as feminists have discovered), because culturally dominant forces can always reconfigure whatever interpretation of yourself you may put forward to suit their own interests: no account is so positive as to be proof against hostile appropriation and transformation (thus, every positive image of women that feminists attempt to promote gets turned into an offensive stereotype). I don't think the possibilities for social tolerance depend upon, much less ought to dictate, our own self-representations.

There is, however, one kind of hope for liberation that my argument does in effect deny. I offer no comfort to those who aspire to liberate us from our current pleasures in favor of some more free-wheeling, polymorphous sexuality. The assumption underlying that liberationist position has to do with the possibility of recovering a "natural sexuality" which an artificial and repressive civilization has denatured. But there is no such thing as a natural sexuality, if that refers to a sexuality unformed by a cultural discourse that defines the boundaries of the sexual and the non-sexual, of the attractive and the unattractive. Any system in which our desires were entirely unstructured by such a discourse, in which we would be somehow free to choose at every step what we found sexually attractive or gratifying, would not be a system of *sexuality* at all—and I readily confess that I find the idea of living under such a system as unthinkable as I find the idea of being an ancient Greek or a disembodied spirit. Moreover, the project of freeing us to embrace a "natural sexuality" seems to be a coercive one, and in our immediate situation it can only serve the cause of repression by fortifying the ideological division between "good" and "bad" sexuality. If sexuality, by definition, is codified and scripted in certain respects, that does not mean it should in every case be liberated. We must remember that sexual boundaries do not merely *constrict* possibilities; they also *create* possibilities: they describe zones of freedom, pleasure, and erotic excitement.

Schneider. But isn't there a contradiction here? If homosexuality is a cultural construct, and if such constructs operate at the level of individual subjectivities to determine personal identity, how can any of us—indeed, how can you—accept in any genuine sense the position that you are arguing for, a position that would seem to place whoever occupies it outside the cultural and sexual systems into which we were all born?

Halperin. That's a very canny question, but I'm not ashamed of the awkward spot it puts me in. I would be very untrue to the position I've been arguing for if I didn't acknowledge squarely and forthrightly the cognitive dissonance it involves. I don't think there's any way that I, or anyone else who grew up in bourgeois America when I did, could ever believe in what I've been saying with the same degree of conviction with which I believe, despite everything I've said, in the categories of heterosexuality and homosexuality. Those categories aren't merely categories of thought, at least in my case; they're also categories of erotic response, and they therefore have a claim on my belief that's stronger than intellectual allegiance. That, after all, is what it means to be acculturated into a sexual system: the conventions of the system acquire the self-confirming inner truth of "nature." If one could simply think oneself out of one's acculturation, it wouldn't be acculturation in the first place. And I can't imagine de-acculturating myself any more than I can imagine de-sexualizing myself, as I said earlier. Nor, once again, does it seem necessarily desirable to do so: every intellectual perspective on the world is a perspective from a particular vantage point, after all. So I freely admit that, in a sense, I don't, and couldn't possibly, *believe* in what I've been saying—not, at least, at the same deep level of conviction as the level at which my own desires are structured. But—predisposed, perhaps, by a long-held sense that my own experience of the world, such as it is, is not representative—I can affirm what I've been saying with a solid intellectual conviction. There's just no other equally sensible way to interpret the evidence I'm familiar with or to understand the gap between the recorded experiences of persons living in ancient and in modern societies.

❖ ❖ ❖

Dynamics

1. Isolate passages in Halperin's essay where he contests or challenges prevailing definitions of sexuality. What assumptions has he made in order to do this? What kind of work has he had to do in order to assume the perspective he assumes?

2. How does Schneider, the interviewer, challenge, confirm, or provide a context for Halperin's ideas? Identify moments in this interview when you might have conducted the questioning differently and elaborate, both about how you might have framed your questions and how the general frame of this discussion might be altered. What is the significance of your findings?

Critical Tools

1. Halperin relates his discussion to "a long-lived scholastic quarrel between 'realists' and 'nominalists' over the existence of universals." In which category would you place your present ideas on this issue, and which ideas in Halperin's essay influence your conclusion? Use your ideas from this exercise to complete your response to the Before Reading questions.

2. Halperin offers several pairs of oppositional terms in order to advance and illustrate his ideas; isolate one or two of these pairs and show how they can help explain another essay in *Literacies*.

Draft One/Draft Two

Draft One: How do Halperin's terms, "essentialist" and "constructionist," help to clarify the discussion you began in your Before Reading exercise? In which specific ways has Halperin's discussion of homosexuality complicated the discussion?

Draft Two: Toward the conclusion of this interview, Halperin claims that:

> *I don't think there's any way that I, or anyone else who grew up in bourgeois America when I did, could ever believe in what I've been saying with the same degree of conviction with which I believe, despite everything I've said, in the categories of heterosexuality and homosexuality.*

What is the relationship of this statement to other passages from his argument that you find important? How does this remark affect your understanding of the essay as a whole? Explain with careful references to the text.

❖   ❖   ❖

Before Reading Paul Harrison. . .

1. Think about a time when you consciously imitated someone else. What prompted you to do so? How did you feel about imitation then? If your feelings about this imitation have changed, try to explain how and why.

2. Based on what you know, under what circumstances are people most likely to trade their own cultural customs for those of other cultures? Write about the possible benefits and disadvantages for people who adopt the customs of other groups.

The Westernization of the World

Paul Harrison

The bourgeoisie has, through its exploitation of the world market, given a cosmopolitan character to production and consumption in every country.

—Karl Marx

In Singapore, Peking opera still lives, in the back streets. On Boat Quay, where great barges moor to unload rice from Thailand, raw rubber from Malaysia, or timber from Sumatra, I watched a troupe of traveling actors throw up a canvas-and-wood booth stage, paint on their white faces and lozenge eyes, and don their resplendent vermilion, ultramarine, and gold robes. Then, to raptured audiences of bent old women and little children with perfect circle faces, they enacted tales of feudal princes and magic birds and wars and tragic love affairs, sweeping their sleeves and singing in strange metallic voices.

The performance had been paid for by a local cultural society as part of a religious festival. A purple cloth temple had been erected on the quayside, painted papier-mâché sculptures were burning down like giant joss sticks, and middle-aged men were sharing out gifts to be distributed among members' families: red buckets, roast ducks, candies, and moon cakes. The son of the organizer, a fashionable young man in Italian shirt and gold-rimmed glasses, was looking on with amused benevolence. I asked him why old people and children were watching the show.

"Young people don't like these operas," he said. "They are too old fashioned. We would prefer to see a high-quality Western variety show, something like that."

He spoke for a whole generation. Go to almost any village in the Third World and you will find youths who scorn traditional dress and sport denims and T-shirts. Go into any bank and the tellers will be dressed as would their European counterparts; at night the manager will climb into his car and go home to watch TV in a home that would not stick out on a European or North American estate. Every capital city in the world is getting to look like every other; it is Marshall McLuhan's global village, but the style is exclusively Western. And not just in consumer fashions: the mimicry extends to architecture, industrial technology, approaches to health care, education, and housing.

To the ethnocentric Westerner or the Westernized local, that may seem the most natural thing in the world. That is modern life, they might think. That is the way it will all be one day. That is what development and economic growth are all about.

Yet the dispassionate observer can only be puzzled by this growing world uniformity. Surely one should expect more diversity, more indigenous styles and models of development. Why is almost everyone following virtually the same European road? The Third World's obsession with the Western way of life has perverted development and is rapidly destroying good and bad in traditional cultures, flinging the baby out with the bathwater. It is the most totally pervasive example of what historians call cultural diffusion in the history of mankind.

Its origins, of course, lie in the colonial experience. European rule was something quite different from the general run of conquests. Previous invaders more often than not settled down in their new territories, interbred, and assimilated a good deal of local culture. Not so the Europeans. Some, like the Iberians or the Dutch, were not averse to cohabitation with native women; unlike the British, they seemed free of purely racial prejudice. But all the Europeans suffered from the same cultural arrogance. Perhaps it is the peculiar self-righteousness of Pauline Christianity that accounts for this trait. Whatever the cause, never a doubt entered their minds that native cultures could be in any way, materially, morally, or spiritually, superior to their own, and that the supposedly benighted inhabitants of the darker continents needed enlightening.

And so there grew up, alongside political and economic imperialism, that more insidious form of control—cultural imperialism. It conquered not just the bodies, but the souls of its victims, turning them into willing accomplices.

Cultural imperialism began its conquest of the Third World with the indoctrination of an elite of local collaborators. The missionary schools sought to produce converts to Christianity who would go out and proselytize among their own people, helping to eradicate traditional culture. Later the government schools aimed to turn out a class of junior bureaucrats and lower military officers who would help to exploit and repress their own people. The British were subtle about this, since they wanted the natives, even the Anglicized among them, to keep their distance. The French, and the Portuguese in Africa, explicitly aimed at the "assimilation" of gifted natives, by which was meant their metamorphosis into model Frenchmen and Lusitanians, distinguishable only by the tint of their skin.

The second channel of transmission was more indirect and voluntary. It worked by what sociologists call reference-group behavior, found when someone copies the habits and lifestyle of a social group he wishes to belong to, or to be classed with, and abandons those of his own group. This happened in the West when the new rich of early commerce and industry aped the nobility they secretly aspired to join. Not surprisingly the social climbers in the colonies started to mimic their conquerors. The returned slaves who carried the first wave of Westernization in West Africa wore black woolen suits and starched collars in the heat of the dry season. The new officer corps of India were molded into what the Indian writer Nirad Chaudhuri has called "imitation, polo-playing English subalterns," complete with waxed mustaches and peacock chests. The elite of Indians, adding their own caste-consciousness to the class-consciousness of their rulers, became more British than the British (and still are).

There was another psychological motive for adopting Western ways, deriving from the arrogance and haughtiness of the colonialists. As the Martiniquan political philosopher, Frantz Fanon, remarked, colonial rule was an experience in racial humiliation. Practically every leader of the newly independent state could recall some experience such as being turned out of a club or manhandled on the street by whites, often of low status. The local elite were made to feel ashamed of their color and of their culture. "I began to suffer from not being a white man," Fanon wrote, "to the degree that the white man imposes discrimination on me, makes me a colonized native, robs me of all worth, all individuality.... Then I will quite simply try to make myself white: that is, I will compel the white man to acknowledge that I am human." To this complex Fanon attributes the colonized natives' constant preoccupation with attracting the attention of the white man, becoming powerful like the white man, proving at all costs that blacks too can be civilized. Given the racism and culturism of the whites, this could only be done by succeeding in their terms, and by adopting their ways.

This desire to prove equality surely helps to explain why Ghana's Nkrumah built the huge stadium and triumphal arch of Black Star Square in Accra. Why the tiny native village of Ivory Coast president Houphouët-Boigny has been graced with a four-lane motorway starting and ending nowhere, a five-star hotel and ultramodern conference center. Why Sukarno transformed Indonesia's capital, Jakarta, into an exercise in gigantism, scarred with six-lane highways and neofascist monuments in the most hideous taste. The aim was not only to show the old imperialists, but to impress other Third World leaders in the only way everyone would recognize: the Western way.

The influence of Western lifestyles spread even to those few nations who escaped the colonial yoke. By the end of the nineteenth century, the elites of the entire non-Western world were taking Europe as their reference group. The progress of the virus can be followed visibly in a room of Topkapi, the Ottoman palace in Istanbul, where a sequence of showcases display the costumes worn by each successive sultan. They begin with kaftans and turbans. Slowly elements of Western military uniform creep in, until the last sultans are decked out in brocade, epaulettes, and cocked hats.

The root of the problem with nations that were never colonized, like Turkey, China, and Japan, was probably their consciousness of Western military superiority. The beating of these three powerful nations at the hands of the West was a humiliating, traumatic experience. For China and Japan, the encounter with the advanced military technology of the industrialized nations was as terrifying as an invasion of extraterrestrials. Europe's earlier discovery of the rest of the world had delivered a mild culture shock to her ethnocentric attitudes. The Orient's contact with Europe shook nations to the foundations, calling into question the roots of their civilizations and all the assumptions and institutions on which their lives were based.

In all three nations, groups of Young Turks grew up, believing that their countries could successfully take on the West only if they adopted Western culture, institutions, and even clothing, for all these ingredients were somehow involved in the production of Western technology. As early as the 1840s, Chinese intellectuals were beginning to modify the ancient view that China was in all respects the greatest civilization in the world. The administrator Wei Yüan urged his countrymen to "learn the superior technology of the barbarians in order to control them." But the required changes could not be confined to the technical realm. Effectiveness in technology is the outcome of an entire social system. "Since we were knocked out by cannon balls," wrote M. Chiang, "naturally we became interested in them, thinking that by learning to make them we could strike back. From studying cannon balls we came to mechanical inventions which in turn lead to political reforms, which lead us again to the political philosophies of the West." The republican revolution of 1911 attempted to modernize China, but her subjection to the West continued until another Young Turk, Mao Tse-tung, applied that alternative brand of Westernization: communism, though in a unique adaptation.

The Japanese were forced to open their border to Western goods in 1853, after a couple of centuries of total isolation. They had to rethink fast in order to survive. From 1867, the Meiji rulers Westernized Japan with astonishing speed, adopting Western science, technology, and even manners: short haircuts became the rule, ballroom dancing caught on, and *moningku* with *haikara* (morning coats and high collars) were worn. The transformation was so successful that by the 1970s the Japanese were trouncing the West at its own game. But they had won their economic independence at the cost of losing their cultural autonomy.

Turkey, defeated in the First World War, her immense empire in fragments, set about transforming herself under that compulsive and ruthless Westernizer, Kemal Atatürk. The Arabic script was abolished and replaced with the Roman alphabet. Kemal's strange exploits as a hatter will probably stand as the symbol of Westernization carried to absurd lengths. His biographer, Lord Kinross, relates that while traveling in the West as a young man, the future president had smarted under Western insults and condescension about the Turkish national hat, the fez. Later, he made the wearing of the fez a criminal offense. "The people of the Turkish republic," he said in a speech launching the new policy, "must prove that they are civilized and advanced persons in their outward respect also.... A civilized, international dress is worthy and appropriate for our nation and we will wear it. Boots or shoes on our feet, trousers on our legs, shirt and tie, jacket and waistcoat—and, of course, to complete these, a cover with a brim on our heads. I want to make this clear. This head covering is called a hat."

❖   ❖   ❖

Dynamics

1. Harrison writes that Western cultural imperialism "conquered not just the bodies, but the souls of its victims, turning them into willing accomplices." Look for words in Harrison's essay that suggest how he thinks this "conquest" worked. Based on the words you have identified, try to figure out how (or whether), in Harrison's terms, non-Western people might have resisted the forces of cultural imperialism.

2. According to Harrison, the "dispassionate observer can only be puzzled by this growing world uniformity." Identify passages where you see Harrison playing the role of the "dispassionate" critic, then find ones where he seems to be more "passionate" than detached. How do you account for the tension between passion and detachment in his essay?

Critical Tools

1. Use Harrison's examples of Westernization to decide what attitudes and desires are involved in the phenomenon he calls "reference-group behavior." Apply this concept to another essay you have read this semester. How does the "reference-group behavior" you have identified in the second essay compare to the kind that Harrison describes? Talk or write about any differences you notice.

2. Harrison's critique of Westernization comes out of his own Western perspective. Where might his analysis of Westernization be further complicated by including the perspectives of a non-Westerner? Use another essay from *Literacies* to re-read some of Harrison's examples.

Draft One/Draft Two

Draft One: Write about a concrete change in your daily life that occurred as a result of a change in your "reference-group behavior." You may wish to build on your response to the first pre-reading question. How do Harrison's terms and examples help you to talk about the meaning of the evolution you describe? Where, in your opinion, do they need to be revised to fit the new context you have created?

Draft Two: Bringing another text into the conversation you began in draft one, write an essay in which you discuss some of the relationships that might exist between "reference-group behavior" and "resistance."

❖ ❖ ❖

Before Reading Shirley Brice Heath. . .

1. Think of someone you know who uses his or her literacy skills very differently than you use yours. Describe the ways each of you uses your literacy, and then speculate on the significance of those differences.

2. What contexts give urgency and meaning to reading, in your experience? When have you read something very carefully, and why?

Literate Traditions

Shirley Brice Heath

In Trackton

Concepts of print

Newspapers, car brochures, advertisements, church materials, and homework and official information from school come into Trackton every day. In addition, there are numerous other rather more permanent reading materials in the community: boxes and cans of food products, house numbers, car names and license numbers, calendars and telephone dials, written messages on television, and name brands which are part of refrigerators, stoves, bicycles, and tools. There are few magazines, except those borrowed from the church, no books except school books, the Bible, and Sunday School lesson books, and a photograph album. Just as Trackton parents do not buy special toys for their young children, they do not buy books for them either; adults do not create reading and writing tasks for the young, nor do they consciously model or demonstrate reading and writing behaviors for them. In the home, on the plaza, and in the neighborhood, children are left to find their own reading and writing tasks: distinguishing one television channel from another, knowing the name brands of cars, motorcycles and bicycles, choosing one or another can of soup or cereal, reading price tags at Mr. Dogan's store to be sure they do not pay more than they would at the supermarket. The receipt of mail in Trackton is a big event, and since several houses are residences for transients the postman does not know, the children sometimes take the mail and give it to the appropriate person. Reading names and addresses and return addresses becomes a game-like challenge among all the children, as the school-age try to show the preschoolers how they know "what dat says."

Preschool and school-age children alike frequently ask what something "says," or how it "goes," and adults respond to their queries, making their instructions fit the requirements of the tasks. Sometimes they help with especially hard or unexpected items, and they always correct errors of fact if they hear them. When Lem, Teegie, and other children in Trackton were about two years of age, I initiated the game of reading traffic signs when we were out in the car. Lillie Mae seemed to pay little attention to this game, until one of the children made an error. If Lem termed a "Yield" sign "Stop," she corrected him, saying, "Dat ain't no stop, dat say yield; you have to give the other fellow the right of way." Often the children would read names of fastfood chains as we drove by. Once when one had changed name, and Teegie read the old name, Tony corrected him: "It ain't Chicken Delight no more; it Famous Recipe now." When the children were preparing to go to school, they chose book bags, tee shirts, and stickers for their notebooks which carried messages. Almost all the older boys and girls in the community wore tee shirts with writings scrawled across the front, and the children talked about what these said and vied to have the most original and sometimes the most suggestive.

Reading was a public group affair for almost all members of Trackton from the youngest to the oldest. Miss Lula sometimes read her Bible alone, and Annie Mae would sometimes quietly read magazines she brought home, but to read alone was frowned upon, and individuals who did so were accused of being antisocial. Aunt Berta had a son who as a child used to slip away from the cotton field and read under a tree. He is now a grown man with children, and he has obtained a college degree, but the community still tells tales about his peculiar boyhood habits of wanting to go off and read alone. In general, reading alone, unless one is very old and religious, marks an individual as someone who cannot make it socially.

Jointly or in group affairs, the children of Trackton *read to learn* before they go to school to *learn to read*. The modification of old or broken toys and their incorporation with other items to create a new toy is a common event. One mastermind, usually Tony, announces the idea, and all the children help collect items and contribute ideas. On some of these occasions, such as when one of the boys wants to modify his bicycle for a unique effect, he has to read selectively portions of brochures on bicycles and instructions for tool sets. Reading is almost always set within a context of immediate action: one needs to read a letter's address to prove to the mailman that one should be given the envelope; one must read the price of a bag of coal at Mr. Dogan's store to make the decision to purchase or not. Trackton children are sent to the store almost as soon as they can walk, and since they are told to "watch out for Mr. Dogan's prices," they must learn to read price changes there from week to week for commonly purchased items and remember them for comparisons with prices in the supermarket. As early as age four, Teegie, Lem, Gary, and Gary B. could scan the price tag, which might contain several separate pieces of information, on familiar items and pick out the price. The decimal point and the predictability of the number of numerals which would be included in the price were clues which helped the children search each tag for only those portions meaningful to their decision-making.

Children remember and reassociate the contexts of print. When they see a brand name, particular sets of numbers, or a particular logo, they often recall when and with whom they first saw it, or they call attention to how the occasion for this new appearance is not like the previous one. Slight shifts in print styles, and decorations of mascots used to advertise products, or alterations of written slogans are noticed by Trackton children. Once they have been in a supermarket to buy a loaf of bread, they remember on subsequent trips the location of the bread section and the placement of the kind of "light bread" their family eats. They seem to remember the scene and staging of print, so that upon recalling print they visualize the physical context in which it occurred and the reasons for reading it: that is, what it was they wanted to learn from reading a certain item or series of items. They are not tutored in these skills by adults of the community, but they are given numerous graded tasks from a very early age and are provided with older children who have learned to read to perform the tasks their daily life requires. Young children watch others read and write for a variety of purposes, and they have numerous opportunities for practice under the indirect supervision of older children, so that they come to use print independently and to be able to model appropriate behaviors for younger children coming up behind them.

The dependence on a strong sense of visual imagery often prevented efficient transfer of skills learned in one context to another. All of the toddlers knew the name brands and names of cereals as they appeared on the boxes or in advertisements. Kellogg's was always written in script—the name of the cereal (raisin bran, etc.) in all capital letters. On Nabisco products, Nabisco was written in small capitals and the cereal name in capital letters as well. I was curious to know whether or not the children "read" the names or whether they recognized the shapes of the boxes and the artwork on the boxes when they correctly identified the cereals. I cut out the name brands and cereal names and put them on plain cardboard of different sizes, and asked the children to read the names. After an initial period of hesitation, most of the children could read the newly placed names. All of the children could do so by age three. When they were between three and four, I cut out the printed letters from the cereal names to spell Kellogg's in small capitals and otherwise arranged the information on the plain cardboard as it appeared on the cereal boxes. The children volunteered the name of the cereal, but did not immediately read Kellogg's now that it was no longer in the familiar script. When I asked them to read it, they looked puzzled, said it looked "funny," and they were not sure what it was. When I pointed out to them that the print small-capital K was another way of writing the script K, they watched with interest as I did the same for the rest of the letters. They were dubious about the script e and the print E being "the same," but they became willing to accept that what configured on the box also configured on the paper, though in some different ways.

Gradually we developed a game of "rewriting" the words they could read, shifting from script to all capitals, and from all capitals to initial capitals and subsequent small letters for individual words. It was always necessary to do this by moving from the known mental picture and "reading" of the terms (i.e. the script Kellogg's) to the unknown or unfamiliar (rendering of Kellogg's in small print capitals). Once shown they already "knew" the item, they accepted that they could "know" these items in new contexts and shapes. We continued this type of game with many of the items from their daily life they already knew how to read. When I first wrote house numbers just as they appeared on the house on a piece of notebook paper, the three- and four-year-olds said they could not read it; if I varied slightly the shape of the numerals on the notebook paper, they also did not read the numbers. Once comparisons and differences were pointed out, they recognized that they already "knew" how to read what had seemed like strange information to them on the notebook paper. Using the "real" print and my re-created print in a metaphorical way provided a bridge from the known to the unknown which allowed the children to use their familiar rules for recognition of print. They transferred their own daily operations as successful readers in an interactive way to pencil-and-paper tasks which were not immediately relevant in the community context.

Their strong tendency to visualize how print looked in its surrounding context was revealed when I asked the three- and four-year-old children to "draw" house doors, newspapers, soup cans, and a letter they would write to someone. Figure 6.1 illustrates how Gary's representation of a newspaper shows that he knew the letters of headlines were bigger than what came below, and that what was below was organized in straight lines. Moreover, the "headline" near the bottom of the page is smaller than that at the top. Mel writes a "letter" which includes the date, salutation, body, closing, and signature. His "letter" is somewhat atypical, but, since Mel's mother, a transient, wrote frequently to her family up-North, he had numerous opportunities to see letters. None of the other preschoolers provided any of the components of a letter other than body and signature. Mel, however, not only indicates several parts, but also scatters some alphabet letters through the body, and signs his name. Mel also "drew" a soup can, making its name brand biggest, and schematically representing the product information and even what I take to be the vertical pricing and inventory information for computerized checking at the bottom of the can. When asked to "read" what they had written, some giggled, others asked older brothers and sisters to do it and some "read" their writing, explaining its context. Mel's reading of his letter was prefaced by "Now I send you dis letter." Then he read "Dear Miz Hea, bring me a truck we go to Hardee's, Mel." Everyone giggled with Mel who enjoyed the joke of having written what he so often said orally to me. His rendering contained only the primary message, not the date or his letter's closing. It is doubtful that Mel knew what went in these slots, since when I asked him if he had read those parts to me, he shrugged his shoulders and said "I dunno." Trackton children had learned before school that they could read to learn, and they had developed expectancies of print. The graphic and everyday-life contexts of writing were often critical to their interpretation of the meaning of print, for print to them was not isolated bits and pieces of lines and circles, but messages with varying internal structures, purposes, and uses. For most of these, oral communication surrounded the print.

"Talk is the thing"

In almost every situation in Trackton in which a piece of writing is integral to the nature of the participants' interactions and their interpretations of meaning, talk is a necessary component. Knowing which box of cereal is Kellogg's raisin bran does little good without announcing that choice to older brothers and sisters helping pour the cereal. Knowing the kind of bicycle tire and tube on one's old bike is translated into action only at Mr. Green's bicycle shop or with a friend who has an old bike he is not using. Certain types of talk describe, repeat, reinforce, frame, expand, and even contradict written materials, and children in Trackton learn not only how to read print, but also when and how to surround the print in their lives with appropriate talk. For them there are far more occasions in the community which call for appropriate knowledge of forms and uses of talk around or about writing, than there are actual occasions for reading and writing extended connected discourse.

For Trackton adults, reading is a social activity; when something is read in Trackton, it almost always provokes narratives, jokes, sidetracking talk, and active negotiation of the meaning of written texts among the listeners. Authority in the written word does not rest in the words themselves, but in the meanings which are negotiated through the experiences of the group. The evening newspaper is read on the front porch for most months of the year. The obituaries on the back page are usually read first, followed by employment listings, advertisements for grocery and department store sales, and captions beneath pictures and headlines. An obituary is read for some trace of acquaintance with either the deceased, his relatives, place of birth, church, or school; active discussion follows about who the individual was and who he might have known. Circulars or letters to individuals regarding the neighborhood center and its recreational or medical services are read aloud and their meanings jointly negotiated by those who have had experience with such activities or know about the forms to be filled out to be eligible for such services. Neighbors share stories of what they did or what happened to them in similar circumstances. One day when Lillie Mae had received a letter about a daycare program, several neighbors were sitting on porches, working on cars nearby, or sweeping their front yards. Lillie Mae came out on her front porch, read the first paragraph of a letter, and announced:

Trackton Text X

Lillie Mae: You hear this, it says Lem [then two years old] might can get into Ridgeway [a local neighborhood center daycare program], but I hafta have the papers ready and apply by next Friday.

Visiting friend: You ever been to Kent to get his birth certificate? [friend is mother of three children already in school]

Mattie Crawford: But what hours that program gonna be? You may not can get him there.

Lillie Mae: They want the birth certificate? I got his vaccination papers.

Annie Mae: Sometimes they take that, 'cause they can 'bout tell the age from those early shots.

Visiting
friend: But you better get it, 'cause you gotta have it when he go to school anyway.

Lillie Mae: But it says here they don't know what hours yet. How am I gonna get over to Kent? How much does it cost? Lemme see if the program costs anything. (She reads aloud part of the letter.)

Conversation on various parts of the letter continued for nearly an hour, while neighbors and Lillie Mae pooled their knowledge of the pros and cons of such programs. They discussed ways of getting rides to Kent, the county seat thirty miles away, to which all mothers had to go to get their children's birth certificates to prove their age at school entrance. The question "What does this mean?" was answered not only from the information in print, but from the group's joint bringing of experience to the text. Lillie Mae, reading aloud, decoded the written text, but her friends and neighbors interpreted the text's meaning through their own experiences. The experience of any one individual had to become common to the group, however, and that was done through the recounting of members' experiences. Such recounting re-created scenes, embellished the truth, illustrated the character of the individuals involved, and to the greatest extent possible brought the audience into the experience itself. Beyond these recountings of episodes (such as one mother's efforts to get her doctor to give her "papers" to verify her son's age), there was a reintegration of these now commonly shared experiences with the text itself. After the reading episode, Lillie Mae had to relate the text's meaning to the experiences she had heard shared, and she checked out this final synthesis of meaning for her with some of the group. Some members did not care about this final synthesis and had wandered off, satisfied to have told their stories, but others commented that they thought her chosen course of action the right one, and her understanding of the letter to fit their interpretations.

About the only material not delivered for group negotiation is that which involves private finances or information which members feel might somehow give them an opportunity their neighbors do not have. A postcard from a local mill announcing days on which the mill will be accepting new employment applications will not be shared aloud, but kept secret because of the competition for jobs. On the other hand, a newspaper story about the expansion of the mill will be read aloud, and all will pool information in general terms.

Tables 6.1 and 6.2 show that the uses of writing and reading in the community are multiple, though there are few occasions for reading of extended connected discourse and almost no occasions for writing such material, except by those school children who diligently try to complete their homework assignments. Foremost among the types of uses of reading and writing are those which are *instrumental*. Adults and children read what they have to read to solve practical problems of daily life: price tags, traffic signs, house numbers, bills, checks. Other uses are perhaps not as critical to problem-solving, but *social-interactional* uses give information relevant to social relations and contacts with persons not in Trackton's primary group. Some write letters; many send greeting cards; almost all read bumper stickers, newspaper obituaries and features, and church news bulletins. Other types of reading and writing are *news-related*. From the local newspaper, political flyers, memos from the city offices, and circulars from the neighborhood center, Trackton residents learn information about local and distant events. They rarely read much more than headlines about distant events, since the evening news programs on television give them the same national or metropolitan news. Stories about the local towns are, however, read, because there is often no other source of information on happenings there. Some individuals in Trackton read for *confirmation*—to seek support for beliefs or ideas they already hold. Miss Lula reads the Bible. When the mayor maintains that one kind of car gets better mileage than another, and others disagree, he has to produce a brochure from a car dealer to prove his point. Children who become involved in boasts often called on written proof to confirm their lofty accounts of themselves or others. Every home has some permanent records—loan notes, tax forms, birth certificates—which families keep, but can rarely find when they are needed. However, if they can be found and are read, they can confirm an oral statement.

Table 6.1 Types of uses of reading in Trackton

Instrumental:	Reading to accomplish practical goals of daily life (price tags, checks, bills, telephone dials, clocks, street signs, house numbers).
Social-Interactional/Recreational	Reading to maintain social relationships, make plans, and introduce topics for discussion and story-telling (greeting cards, cartoons, letters, newspaper features, political flyers, announcements of community meetings).
News-Related:	Reading to learn about third parties or distant events (local news items, circulars from the community center or school).
Confirmational:	Reading to gain support for attitudes or beliefs already held (Bible, brochures on cars, loan notes, bills).

Note. Listed in relative order of frequency of occasions when time on these types of tasks exceeded five minutes per day.

The most frequent occasions for writing are those when Trackton family members say they cannot trust their memory (*memory-supportive*), or they have to write to *substitute for an oral message*. Beside the telephone, women write frequently called numbers and addresses; they tack calendars on the kitchen wall and add notes reminding them of dates for their children's vaccinations and the school holidays, etc. Some few women in the community write letters. Lillie Mae often writes relatives up-North to invite them to come home and to thank them for bringing presents. Women sometimes have to write notes to school about children's absences or tardiness or to request a local merchant to extend credit a few weeks longer. Men almost never write except to sign their paychecks, public forms, and to collect information for income tax preparation. One exception in Trackton is the mayor who meets once a month with a group of other church members to prepare Sunday church bulletins as well as to handle business related to the building fund or to plan for revival meetings. These written materials are negotiated cooperatively at the meetings; no individual takes sole responsibility.

Community literacy activities are public and social. Written information almost never stands alone in Trackton. It is reshaped and reworded into an oral mode by adults and children who incorporate chunks of the written text in their talk. They

---

Table 6.2 Types of uses of writing in Trackton

Memory Aids: (primarily used by women)	Writing to serve as a reminder for the writer and, only occasionally, others (telephone numbers, notes on calendars).
Substitutes for Oral Messages: (primarily used by women)	Writing used when direct direct oral communication was not possible or would prove embarrassing (notes for tardiness or absence from school, greeting cards, letters).
Financial:	Writing to record numerals and to write out amounts and accompanying notes (signatures on checks and public forms, figures and notes for income tax preparation).
Public Records: (church only)	Writing to announce the order of the church services and forthcoming events and to record financial and policy decisions (church bulletins, reports of the church building fund committee).

Note. Listed in relative order of frequency of occasions when time on these types of tasks exceeded five minutes per day.

often reflect their own awareness that print imposes a different kind of organization on written materials than talk does. Literacy events in Trackton which bring the written word into a central focus in interactions and interpretations have their rules of occurrence and appropriateness, just as talking junk, fussing, or performing a playsong do. The group activities of reading the newspaper across porches, debating the power of a new car, or discussing the city's plans to bring in earthmoving equipment to clear lots behind the community, produce more speaking than reading, more group than individual effort. There are repeated metaphors, comparisons, and fast-paced, overlapping language as Trackton residents move from print to what it means in their lives. On some occasions, they attend to the text itself; on others, they use it only as a starting point for wide-ranging talk. On all occasions, they bring in knowledge related to the text and interpret beyond the text for their own context; in so doing, they achieve a new synthesis of information from the text and the joint experiences of community members.

❖ ❖ ❖

Dynamics

1. Summarize the differences Heath notes between the reading and writing practices of young and old people and of men and women in Trackton. What is the significance of these differences?

2. Heath mentions a number of things throughout the essay that the residents of Trackton do not do, or rarely do, in the area of reading and writing. Catalog these, and explore their significance.

3. Is the training provided to children in Trackton appropriate for the uses of literacy that they may take up as adults there? Is that training appropriate if these children should move into another social context? Explain your answers.

Critical Tools

1. Heath describes a social process of "talk around writing" that includes "negotiation" and "reintegration." Explain how this process works, and discuss how it can help explain some element of another text you have read in *Literacies*.

2. What evidence can you find in the essay that there are some links between interpretation, literacy practices, and social class? Summarize your findings and test them on another *Literacies* text.

Draft One/Draft Two

Draft One: Use terms from Heath's essay and from her charts to translate your answers to the "Before Reading" questions into an essay. What do her terms help you explore in your own literate practices? How does Heath help you explain the strengths and weaknesses of your own practices?

Draft Two: Extend draft one by adding another set of terms from a *Literacies* text that addresses the process of interpretation, such as the essay by Scholes or another you have read. What do these new terms help you say about your literate practices? What has happened to your understanding as you have examined it from these different perspectives?

❖ ❖ ❖

Before Reading Liliana Heker. . .

1. In this short story Liliana Heker writes about a series of encounters between a wealthy mother and daughter and their maid and her daughter. Do you expect any particular complications when people of different social classes spend time together? If so, what causes these complications and what can be done about them? If not, then what does happen when people of different social classes spend time together?

The Stolen Party

Liliana Heker

As soon as she arrived she went straight to the kitchen to see if the monkey was there. It was: what a relief! She wouldn't have liked to admit that her mother had been right. *Monkeys at a birthday?* her mother had sneered. *Get away with you, believing any nonsense you're told*! She was cross, but not because of the monkey, the girl thought; it's just because of the party.

"I don't like you going," she told her. "It's a rich people's party."

"Rich people go to Heaven too," said the girl, who studied religion at school.

"Get away with Heaven," said the mother. "The problem with you, young lady, is that you like to fart higher than your ass."

The girl didn't approve of the way her mother spoke. She was barely nine, and one of the best in her class.

"I'm going because I've been invited," she said. "And I've been invited because Luciana is my friend. So there."

"Ah yes, your friend," her mother grumbled. She paused. "Listen, Rosaura," she said at last. "That one's not your friend. You know what you are to them? The maid's daughter, that's what."

Rosaura blinked hard: she wasn't going to cry. Then she yelled: "Shut up! You know nothing about being friends!"

Every afternoon she used to go to Luciana's house and they would both finish their homework while Rosaura's mother did the cleaning. They had their tea in the kitchen and they told each other secrets. Rosaura loved everything in the big house, and she also loved the people who lived there.

"I'm going because it will be the most lovely party in the whole world, Luciana told me it would. There will be a magician, and he will bring a monkey and everything."

The mother swung around to take a good look at her child, and pompously put her hands on her hips.

"Monkeys at a birthday?" she said. "Get away with you, believing any nonsense you're told!"

Rosaura was deeply offended. She thought it unfair of her mother to accuse other people of being liars simply because they were rich. Rosaura too wanted to be rich, of course. If one day she managed to live in a beautiful palace, would her mother stop loving her? She felt very sad. She wanted to go to that party more than anything else in the world.

"I'll die if I don't go," she whispered, almost without moving her lips.

And she wasn't sure whether she had been heard, but on the morning of the party she discovered that her mother had starched her Christmas dress. And in the afternoon, after washing her hair, her mother rinsed it in apple vinegar so that it would be all nice and shiny. Before going out, Rosaura admired herself in the mirror, with her white dress and glossy hair, and thought she looked terribly pretty.

Señora Ines also seemed to notice. As soon as she saw her, she said:

"How lovely you look today, Rosaura."

Rosaura gave her starched skirt a slight toss with her hands and walked into the party with a firm step. She said hello to Luciana and asked about the monkey. Luciana put on a secretive look and whispered into Rosaura's ear: "He's in the kitchen. But don't tell anyone, because it's a surprise."

Rosaura wanted to make sure. Carefully she entered the kitchen and there she saw it: deep in thought, inside its cage. It looked so funny that the girl stood there for a while, watching it, and later, every so often, she would slip out of the party unseen and go and admire it. Rosaura was the only one allowed into the kitchen. Señora Ines had said: "You yes, but not the others, they're much too boisterous, they might break something." Rosaura had never broken anything. She even managed the jug of orange juice, carrying it from the kitchen into the dining-room. She held it carefully and didn't spill a single drop. And Señora Ines had said: "Are you sure you can manage a jug as big as that?" Of course she could manage. She wasn't a butter-fingers, like the others. Like that blonde girl with the bow in her hair. As soon as she saw Rosaura, the girl with the bow had said:

"And you? Who are you?"

"I'm a friend of Luciana," said Rosaura.

"No," said the girl with the bow, "you are not a friend of Luciana because I'm her cousin and I know all her friends. And I don't know you."

"So what," said Rosaura. "I come here every afternoon with my mother and we do our homework together."

"You and your mother do your homework together?" asked the girl, laughing.

"I and Luciana do our homework together," said Rosaura, very seriously.

The girl with the bow shrugged her shoulders.

"That's not being friends," she said. "Do you go to school together?"

"No."

"So where do you know her from?" said the girl, getting impatient.

Rosaura remembered her mother's words perfectly. She took a deep breath.

"I'm the daughter of the employee," she said.

Her mother had said very clearly: "If someone asks, you say you're the daughter of the employee; that's all." She also told her to add: "And proud of it." But Rosaura thought that never in her life would she dare say something of the sort.

"What employee?" said the girl with the bow. "Employee in a shop?"

"No," said Rosaura angrily. "My mother doesn't sell anything in any shop, so there."

"So how come she's an employee?" said the girl with the bow.

Just then Señora Ines arrived saying *shh shh*, and asked Rosaura if she wouldn't mind helping serve out the hot-dogs, as she knew the house so much better than the others.

"See?" said Rosaura to the girl with the bow, and when no one was looking she kicked her in the shin.

Apart from the girl with the bow, all the others were delightful. The one she liked best was Luciana, with her golden birthday crown; and then the boys. Rosaura won the sack race, and nobody managed to catch her when they played tag. When they split into two teams to play charades, all the boys wanted her for their side. Rosaura felt she had never been so happy in all her life.

But the best was still to come. The best came after Luciana blew out the candles. First the cake. Señora Ines had asked her to help pass the cake around, and Rosaura had enjoyed the task immensely, because everyone called out to her, shouting "Me, me!" Rosaura remembered a story in which there was a queen who had the power of life or death over her subjects. She had always loved that, having the power of life or death. To Luciana and the boys she gave the largest pieces, and to the girl with the bow she gave a slice so thin one could see through it.

After the cake came the magician, tall and bony, with a fine red cape. A true magician: he could untie handkerchiefs by blowing on them and make a chain with links that had no openings. He could guess what cards were pulled out from a pack, and the monkey was his assistant. He called the monkey "partner." "Let's see here, partner," he would say, "Turn over a card." And, "Don't run away, partner: time to work now."

The final trick was wonderful. One of the children had to hold the monkey in his arms and the magician said he would make him disappear.

"What, the boy?" they all shouted.

"No, the monkey!" shouted back the magician.

Rosaura thought that this was truly the most amusing party in the whole world.

The magician asked a small fat boy to come and help, but the small fat boy got frightened almost at once and dropped the monkey on the floor. The magician picked him up carefully, whispered something in his ear, and the monkey nodded almost as if he understood.

"You mustn't be so unmanly, my friend," the magician said to the fat boy.

"What's unmanly?" said the fat boy.

The magician turned around as if to look for spies.

"A sissy," said the magician. "Go sit down."

Then he stared at all the faces, one by one. Rosaura felt her heart tremble.

"You, with the Spanish eyes," said the magician. And everyone saw that he was pointing at her.

She wasn't afraid. Neither holding the monkey, nor when the magician made him vanish; not even when, at the end, the magician flung his red cape over Rosaura's head and uttered a few magic words...and the monkey reappeared, chattering happily, in her arms. The children clapped furiously. And before Rosaura returned to her seat, the magician said:

"Thank you very much, my little countess."

She was so pleased with the compliment that a while later, when her mother came to fetch her, that was the first thing she told her.

"I helped the magician and he said to me, 'Thank you very much, my little countess.' "

It was strange because up to then Rosaura had thought that she was angry with her mother. All along Rosaura had imagined that she would say to her: "See that the monkey wasn't a lie?" But instead she was so thrilled that she told her mother all about the wonderful magician.

Her mother tapped her on the head and said: "So now we're a countess!"

But one could see that she was beaming.

And now they both stood in the entrance, because a moment ago Señora Ines, smiling, had said: "Please wait here a second."

Her mother suddenly seemed worried.

"What is it?" she asked Rosaura.

"What is what?" said Rosaura. "It's nothing; she just wants to get the presents for those who are leaving, see?"

She pointed at the fat boy and at a girl with pigtails who were also waiting there, next to their mothers. And she explained about the presents. She knew, because she had been watching those who left before her. When one of the girls was about to leave, Señora Ines would give her a bracelet. When a boy left, Señora Ines gave him a yo-yo. Rosaura preferred the yo-yo because it sparkled, but she didn't mention that to her mother. Her mother might have said: "So why don't you ask for one, you blockhead?" That's what her mother was like. Rosaura didn't feel like explaining that she'd be horribly ashamed to be the odd one out. Instead she said: "I was the best-behaved at the party."

And she said no more because Señora Ines came out into the hall with two bags, one pink and one blue.

First she went up to the fat boy, gave him a yo-yo out of the blue bag, and the fat boy left with his mother. Then she went up to the girl and gave her a bracelet out of the pink bag, and the girl with the pigtails left as well.

Finally she came up to Rosaura and her mother. She had a big smile on her face and Rosaura liked that. Señora Ines looked down at her, then looked up at her mother, and then said something that made Rosaura proud:

"What a marvellous daughter you have, Herminia."

For an instant, Rosaura thought that she'd give her two presents: the bracelet and the yo-yo. Señora Ines bent down as if about to look for something. Rosaura also leaned forward, stretching out her arm. But she never completed the movement.

Señora Ines didn't look in the pink bag. Nor did she look in the blue bag. Instead she rummaged in her purse. In her hand appeared two bills.

"You really and truly earned this," she said handing them over. "Thank you for all your help, my pet."

Rosaura felt her arms stiffen, stick close to her body, and then she noticed her mother's hand on her shoulder. Instinctively she pressed herself against her mother's body. That was all. Except her eyes. Rosaura's eyes had a cold, clear look that fixed itself on Señora Ines's face.

Señora Ines, motionless, stood there with her hand outstretched. As if she didn't dare draw it back. As if the slightest change might shatter an infinitely delicate balance.

Translated by Alberto Manguel

❖ ❖ ❖

Dynamics

1. Several times during the story the narrator describes Rosaura's values or opinions, including sometimes even the source of her values. Locate several passages of this kind and write informally about what each passage helps you explain about her actions during this story. How thoroughly can we explain each of the things she does along the way? What is the significance of your findings?

2. After Señora Ines hands over the two bills, nothing more is spoken for the remainder of the story. Why not? What do the physical actions of the last few paragraphs "say" that the characters themselves do not say? After you have clarified what is unspoken in the story's conclusion, retrace the story's earlier events and locate passages where something is unspoken. What is your theory about the role of unspoken understandings in situations like these?

Critical Tools

1. Look up "class" in a good dictionary and note two or three definitions that apply to the events of this story. Write about two things: the aspects of the story the dictionary definitions help explain, and the aspects of the story that the dictionary definitions don't adequately address. Compose and explain a fuller definition of class, based on this story and your analysis of the dictionary terms.

2. Choose a term or idea from one of your earlier readings, and use it to explain the actions of Señora Ines, one by one, as they occur during the course of the party. Are these adequate explanations? How can you tell? Can you extend or complicate the term or idea from the earlier reading?

Draft One/Draft Two

Draft One: Prepare a "fuller definition of class," as described above in the first Critical Tools question, and then test that definition by applying it to some of the events in another text you have read this semester. How does this other reading help you extend or qualify the concept of class you have generated?

Draft Two: Try your revised concept of class as a way of analyzing a narrative of race or ethnicity, such as the essay by James Baldwin or the story by Maxine Hong

❖ ❖ ❖

Before Reading bell hooks and Cornel West. . .

1. Name the various kinds of "partnerships" that exist between men and women in American culture right now. Then think about the specific challenges that you see making partnership difficult. What are some of the social institutions or forces that have an effect on gender relations? How have *you* been affected by these forces?

2. Describe what you think of as your "community." Who belongs to it? Who has the power to define its boundaries, and where do those boundaries lie? What purposes does your community serve? If, according to your definition, you belong to more than one community, how are their memberships, boundaries, and purposes different?

Black Women And Men: partnership in the 1990s

*a dialogue between bell hooks and Cornel West presented at Yale
University's African American Cultural Center*

Give gifts to those who should know love.

> —Ntozake Shange
> *Sassafrass, Cypress, and Indigo*

*The history of the period has been written and will continue to be written without us.
The imperative is clear: Either we will make history or remain the victims of it.*

> —Michele Wallace

bh I requested that Charles sing "Precious Lord" because the conditions that
led Thomas Dorsey to write this song always make me think about gender issues,
issues of Black masculinity. Mr. Dorsey wrote this song after his wife died in childbirth. That experience caused him to have a crisis of faith. He did not think he
would be able to go on living without her. That sense of unbearable crisis truly
expresses the contemporary dilemma of faith. Mr. Dorsey talked about the way he
tried to cope with this "crisis of faith." He prayed and prayed for a healing and
received the words to this song. This song has helped so many folk when they are
feeling low, feeling as if they can't go on. It was my grandmother's favorite song. I
remember how we sang it at her funeral. She died when she was almost ninety. And
I am moved now as I was then by the knowledge that we can take our pain, work
with it, recycle it, and transform it so that it becomes a source of power.

Let me introduce to you my "brother," my comrade Cornel West.

CW First I need to just acknowledge the fact that we as Black people have
come together to reflect on our past, present, and future. That, in and of itself, is a

sign of hope. I'd like to thank the Yale African American Cultural Center for bringing us together. bell and I thought it would be best to present in dialogical form a series of reflections on the crisis of Black males and females. There is a state of siege raging now in Black communities across this nation linked not only to drug addiction but also to consolidation of corporate power as we know it, and redistribution of wealth from the bottom to the top, coupled with the ways with which a culture and society centered on the market, preoccupied with consumption, erode structures of feeling, community, tradition. Reclaiming our heritage and sense of history are prerequisites to any serious talk about Black freedom and Black liberation in the 21st century. We want to try to create that kind of community here today, a community that we hope will be a place to promote understanding. Critical understanding is a prerequisite for any serious talk about coming together, sharing, participating, creating bonds of solidarity so that Black people and other progressive people can continue to hold up the blood-stained banners that were raised when that song was sung in the civil rights movement. It was one of Dr. Martin Luther King's favorite songs, reaffirming his own struggle and that of many others who have tried to link some sense of faith, religious faith, political faith, to the struggle for freedom. We thought it would be best to have a dialogue to put forth analysis and provide a sense of what form a praxis would take. That praxis will be necessary for us to talk seriously about Black power, Black liberation in the 21st century.

bh Let us say a little bit about ourselves. Both Cornel and I come to you as individuals who believe in God. That belief informs our message.

CW One of the reasons we believe in God is due to the long tradition of religious faith in the Black community. I think, that as a people who have had to deal with the absurdity of being Black in America, for many of us it is a question of God and sanity, or God and suicide. And, if you are serious about Black struggle, you know that in many instances you will be stepping out on nothing, hoping to land on something. That is the history of Black folks in the past and present, and it continually concerns those of us who are willing to speak out with boldness and a sense of the importance of history and struggle. You speak, knowing that you won't be able to do that for too long because America is such a violent culture. Given those conditions, you have to ask yourself what links to a tradition will sustain you, given the absurdity and insanity we are bombarded with daily. And so the belief in God itself ·is not to be understood in a noncontextual manner. It is understood in relation to a particular context, to specific circumstances.

bh We also come to you as two progressive Black people on the Left.

CW Very much so.

bh I will read a few paragraphs to provide a critical framework for our discussion of Black power, just in case some of you may not know what Black power means. We are gathered to speak with one another about Black power in the 21st century. In James Boggs's essay, "Black Power: A Scientific Concept Whose Time Has Come," first published in 1968, he called attention to the radical political significance of the Black power movement, asserting: "Today the concept of Black power expresses the revolutionary social force which must not only struggle against the capitalist but against the workers and all who benefit by and support the system which has oppressed us." We speak of Black power in this very different context to remember, reclaim, re-vision, and renew. We remember first that the historical struggle for Black liberation was forged by Black women and men who were concerned about the collective welfare of Black people. Renewing our commitment to this collective struggle should provide a grounding for new direction in contemporary political practice. We speak today of political partnership between Black men and women. The late James Baldwin wrote in his autobiographical preface to *Notes of a Native Son*: "I think that the past is all that makes the present coherent and further that the past will remain horrible for as long as we refuse to accept it honestly." Accepting the challenge of this prophetic statement as we look at our contemporary past as Black people, the space between the sixties and the nineties, we see a weakening of political solidarity between Black men and women. It is crucial for the future of Black liberation struggle that we remain ever mindful that ours is a shared struggle, that we are each other's fate.

CW I think we can even begin by talking about the kind of existentialist chaos that exists in our own lives and our inability to overcome the sense of alienation and frustration we experience when we try to create bonds of intimacy and solidarity with one another. Now part of this frustration is to be understood again in relation to structures and institutions. In the way in which our culture of consumption has promoted an addiction to stimulation—one that puts a premium on packaged and commodified stimulation. The market does this in order to convince us that our consumption keeps oiling the economy in order for it to reproduce itself. But the effect of this addiction to stimulation is an undermining, a waning of our ability for qualitatively rich relationships. It's no accident that crack is the postmodern drug, that it is the highest form of addiction known to humankind, that it provides a feeling ten times more pleasurable than orgasm.

bh Addiction is not about relatedness, about relationships. So it comes as no surprise that, as addiction becomes more pervasive in Black life, it undermines our capacity to experience community. Just recently, I was telling someone that I would like to buy a little house next door to my parents' house. This house used to be Mr. Johnson's house but he recently passed away. And they could not understand why I would want to live near my parents. My explanation that my parents were aging did not satisfy. Their inability to understand or appreciate the value of sharing family life intergenerationally was a sign to me of the crisis facing our communities. It's as though as Black people we have lost our understanding of the importance of mutual interdependency, of communal living. That we no longer recognize as valuable the notion that we collectively shape the terms of our survival is a sign of crisis.

CW And when there is crisis in those communities and institutions that have played a fundamental role in transmitting to younger generations our values and sensibility, our ways of life and our ways of struggle, we find ourselves distanced, not simply from our predecessors but from the critical project of Black liberation.

And so, more and more, we seem to have young Black people who are very difficult to understand, because it seems as though they live in two very different worlds. We don't really understand their music. Black adults may not be listening to NWA (Niggers With Attitude) straight out of Compton, California. They may not understand why they are doing what Stetsasonic is doing, what Public Enemy is all about, because most young Black people have been fundamentally shaped by the brutal side of American society. Their sense of reality is shaped on the one hand by a sense of coldness and callousness, and on the other hand by a sense of passion for justice, contradictory impulses which surface simultaneously. Mothers may find it difficult to understand their children. Grandparents may find it difficult to understand us—and it's this slow breakage that has to be restored.

bh That sense of breakage, or rupture, is often tragically expressed in gender relations. When I told folks that Cornel West and I were talking about partnership between Black women and men, they thought I meant romantic relationships. I replied that it was important for us to examine the multi-relationships between Black women and men, how we deal with fathers, with brothers, with sons. We are talking about all our relationships across gender because it is not just the heterosexual love relationships between Black women and men that are in trouble. Many of us can't communicate with parents, siblings, etc. I've talked with many of you and asked, "What is it you feel should be addressed?" And many of you responded that you wanted us to talk about Black men and how they need to "get it together."

Let's talk about why we see the struggle to assert agency—that is, the ability to act in one's best interest—as a male thing. I mean, Black men are not the only ones among us who need to "get it together." And if Black men collectively refuse to educate themselves for critical consciousness, to acquire the means to be self-determined, should our communities suffer, or should we not recognize that both Black women and men must struggle for selfactualization, must learn to "get it together"? Since the culture we live in continues to equate Blackness with maleness, Black awareness of the extent to which our survival depends on mutual partnership between Black women and men is undermined. In renewed Black liberation struggle, we recognize the position of Black men and women, the tremendous role Black women played in every freedom struggle.

Certainly, Septima Clark's book *Ready from Within* is necessary reading for those of us who want to understand the historical development of sexual politics in Black liberation struggle. Clark describes her father's insistence that she not fully engage herself in civil rights struggle because of her gender. Later, she found the source of her defiance in religion. It was the belief in spiritual community, that no difference must be made between the role of women and that of men, that enabled her to be "ready within." To Septima Clark, the call to participate in Black liberation struggle was a call from God. Remembering and recovering the stories of how Black women learned to assert historical agency in the struggle for self-determination in the context of community and collectivity is important for those of us who struggle to promote Black liberation, a movement that has at its core a commitment to free our communities of sexist domination, exploitation, and oppression. We need to develop a political terminology that will enable Black folks to talk deeply about what we mean when we urge Black women and men to "get it together."

CW I think again that we have to keep in mind the larger context of American society, which has historically expressed contempt for Black men and Black women. The very notion that Black people are human beings is a new notion in Western Civilization and is still not widely accepted in practice. And one of the consequences of this pernicious idea is that it is very difficult for Black men and women to remain attuned to each other's humanity, so when bell talks about Black women's agency and some of the problems Black men have when asked to acknowledge Black women's humanity, it must be remembered that this refusal to acknowledge one another's humanity is a reflection of the way we are seen and treated in the larger society. And it's certainly not true that White folks have a monopoly on human relationships. When we talk about a crisis in Western Civilization, Black people are a part of that civilization, even though we have been beneath it, our backs serving as a foundation for the building of that civilization, and we have to understand how it affects us so that we may remain attuned to each other's humanity, so that the partnership that bell talks about can take on real substance and content. I think partnerships between Black men and Black women can be made when we learn how to be supportive and think in terms of critical affirmation.

bh Certainly, Black people have not talked enough about the importance of constructing patterns of interaction that strengthen our capacity to be affirming.

CW We need to affirm one another, support one another, help, enable, equip, and empower one another to deal with the present crisis, but it can't be uncritical, because if it's uncritical, then we are again refusing to acknowledge other people's humanity. If we are serious about acknowledging and affirming other people's humanity, then we are committed to trusting and believing that they are forever in process. Growth, development, maturation happens in stages. People grow, develop, and mature along the lines in which they are taught. Disenabling critique and contemptuous feedback hinders.

bh We need to examine the function of critique in traditional Black communities. Often it does not serve as a constructive force. Like we have that popular slang word "dissin'," and we know that "dissin' " refers to a kind of disenabling contempt—when we "read" each other in ways that are so painful, so cruel, that the person can't get up from where you have knocked them down. Other destructive forces in our lives are envy and jealousy. These undermine our efforts to work for a collective good. Let me give a minor example. When I came in this morning I saw Cornel's latest book on the table. I immediately wondered why my book was not there and caught myself worrying about whether he was receiving some gesture of respect or recognition denied me. When he heard me say, "Where's my book?" he pointed to another table.

Often when people are suffering a legacy of deprivation, there is a sense that there are never enough goodies to go around, so that we must viciously compete with one another. Again this spirit of competition creates conflict and divisiveness. In a larger social context, competition between Black women and men has surfaced around the issue of whether Black female writers are receiving more attention than Black male writers. Rarely does anyone point to the reality that only a small minority of Black women writers are receiving public accolades. Yet the myth that Black women who succeed are taking something away from Black men continues to permeate Black psyches and inform how we as Black women and men respond to one another. Since capitalism is rooted in unequal distribution of resources, it is not surprising that we as Black women and men find ourselves in situations of competition and conflict.

CW I think part of the problem is deep down in our psyche we recognize that we live in such a conservative society, a society disproportionately shaped by business elites, a society in which corporate power influences are assuring that a certain group of people do get up higher.

bh Right, including some of you in this room.

CW And this is true not only between male and female relations but also Black and Brown relations, and Black and Red, and Black and Asian relations. We are struggling over crumbs because we know that the bigger part has been received by elites in corporate America. One half of one percent of America owns twenty-two percent of the wealth, one percent owns thirty-two percent, and the bottom forty-five percent of the population has two percent of the wealth. So, you end up with this kind of crabs-in-the-barrel mentality. When you see someone moving up, you immediately think they'll get a bigger cut in big-loaf corporate America, and you think that's something real because we're still shaped by the corporate ideology of the larger context.

bh Here at Yale, many of us are getting a slice of that mini-loaf and yet are despairing. It was discouraging when I came here to teach and found in many Black people a quality of despair which is not unlike what we know is felt in "crack neighborhoods." I wanted to understand the connection between underclass Black despair and that of Black people here who have immediate and/or potential access to so much material privilege. This despair mirrors the spiritual crisis that is happening in our culture as a whole. Nihilism is everywhere. Some of this despair is rooted in a deep sense of loss. Many Black folks who have made it or are making it undergo an identity crisis. This is especially true for individual Black people working to assimilate into the "mainstream." Suddenly, they may feel panicked, alarmed by the knowledge that they do not understand their history, that life is without purpose and meaning. These feelings of alienation and estrangement create suffering. The suffering many Black people experience today is linked to the suffering of the past, to "historical memory." Attempts by Black people to understand that suffering, to come to terms with it, are the conditions which enable a work like Toni Morrison's *Beloved* to receive so much attention. To look back, not just to describe slavery but to try and reconstruct a psycho-social history of its impact has only recently been fully understood as a necessary stage in the process of collective Black self-recovery.

CW The spiritual crisis that has happened, especially among the well-to-do Blacks, has taken the form of the quest for therapeutic release. So that you can get very thin, flat, and one-dimensional forms of spirituality that are simply an attempt to sustain the well-to-do Black folks as they engage in their consumerism and privatism. The kind of spirituality we're talking about is not the kind that serves as an opium to help you justify and rationalize your own cynicism vis-à-vis the disadvantaged folk in our community. We could talk about churches and their present role in the crisis of America, religious faith as the American way of life, the gospel of health and wealth, helping the bruised psyches of the Black middle class make it through America. That's not the form of spirituality that we're talking about. We're talking about something deeper—you used to call it conversion—so that notions of service and risk and sacrifice once again become fundamental. It's very important, for example, that those of you who remember the days in which Black colleges were hegemonic among the Black elite remember them critically but also acknowledge that there was something positive going on there. What was going on was that you were told every Sunday, in chapel, that you had to give service to the race. Now it may have been a petty bourgeois form, but it created a moment of accountability, and with the erosion of the service ethic the very possibility of putting the needs of others alongside of one's own diminishes. In this syndrome, me-ness, selfishness, and egocentricity become more and more prominent, creating a spiritual crisis where you need more psychic opium to get you over.

bh We have experienced such a change in that communal ethic of service that was so necessary for survival in traditional Black communities. That ethic of service has been altered by shifting class relations. And even those Black folks who have little or no class mobility may buy into a bourgeois class sensibility; TV shows like *Dallas* and *Dynasty* teach ruling class ways of thinking and being to underclass poor people. A certain kind of bourgeois individualism of the mind prevails. It does not correspond to actual class reality or circumstances of deprivation. We need to remember the many economic structures and class politics that have led to a shift of priorities for "privileged" Blacks. Many privileged Black folks obsessed with living out a bourgeois dream of liberal individualistic success no longer feel as though they have any accountability in relation to the Black poor and underclass.

CW We're not talking about the narrow sense of guilt privileged Black people can feel, because guilt usually paralyzes action. What we're talking about is how one uses one's time and energy. We're talking about the ways in which the Black middle class, which is relatively privileged vis-à-vis the Black working class, working poor, and underclass, needs to acknowledge that along with that privilege goes responsibility. Somewhere I read that for those to whom much is given, much is required. And the question becomes, "How do we exercise that responsibility, given our privilege?" I don't think it's a credible notion to believe the Black middle class will give up on its material toys. No, the Black middle class will act like any other middle class in human history; it will attempt to maintain its privilege. There is something seductive about comfort and convenience. The Black middle class will not return to the ghetto, especially given the territorial struggles going on with gangs and so forth. Yet, how can we use what power we do have to be sure more resources are available to those who are disadvantaged? So the question becomes "How do we use our responsibility and privilege?" Because, after all, Black privilege is a result of Black struggle.

I think the point to make here is that there is a new day in Black America. It is the best of times and the worst of times in Black America. Political consciousness is escalating in Black America, among Black students, among Black workers, organized Black workers and trade unions. Increasingly we are seeing Black local leaders with vision. The Black church is on the move, Black popular music, political themes and motifs are on the move. So don't think in our critique we somehow ask you to succumb to a paralyzing pessimism. There are grounds for hope and when that corner is turned—and we don't know what particular catalytic event will serve as the take-off for it (just like we didn't know December 1955 would be the take-off)—but when it occurs we have got to be ready. The privileged Black folks can play a rather crucial role if we have a service ethic, if we want to get on board, if we want to be part of the progressive, prophetic bandwagon. And that is the question we will have to ask ourselves and each other.

bh We also need to remember that there is a joy in struggle. Recently, I was speaking on a panel at a conference with another Black woman from a privileged background. She mocked the notion of struggle. When she expressed, "I'm just tired of hearing about the importance of struggle; it doesn't interest me," the audience clapped. She saw struggle solely in negative terms, a perspective which led me to question whether she had ever taken part in any organized resistance movement. For if you have, you know that there is joy in struggle. Those of us who are old enough to remember segregated schools, the kind of political effort and sacrifice folks were making to ensure we would have full access to educational opportunities, surely remember the sense of fulfillment when goals that we struggled for were achieved. When we sang together "We shall overcome," there was a sense of victory, a sense of power that comes when we strive to be self-determining. When Malcolm X spoke about his journey to Mecca, the awareness he achieved, he gives expression to that joy that comes from struggling to grow. When Martin Luther King talked about having been to the mountain top, he was sharing with us that he arrived at a peak of critical awareness, and it gave him great joy. In our liberatory pedagogy, we must teach young Black folks to understand that struggle is process, that one moves from circumstances of difficulty and pain to awareness, joy, fulfillment. That the struggle to be critically conscious can be that movement which takes you to another level, that lifts you up, that makes you feel better. You feel good, you feel your life has meaning and purpose.

CW A rich life is fundamentally a life of serving others, a life of trying to leave the world a little better than you found it. That rich life comes into being in human relationships. This is true at the personal level. Those of you who have been in love know what I am talking about. It is also true at the organizational and communal level. It's difficult to find joy by yourself even if you have all the right toys. It's difficult. Just ask somebody who has got a lot of material possessions but doesn't have anybody to share them with. Now that's at the personal level. There is a political version of this. It has to do with what you see when you get up in the morning and look in the mirror and ask yourself whether you are simply wasting time on the planet or spending time in an enriching manner. We are talking fundamentally about the meaning of life and the place of struggle. bell talks about the significance of struggle and service. For those of us who are Christians there are certain theological foundations on which our commitment to serve is based. Christian life is understood to be a life of service. Even so, Christians have no monopoly on the joys that come from service and those of you who are part of secular culture can also enjoy this sense of enrichment. Islamic brothers and sisters share in a religious practice which also places emphasis on the importance of service. When we speak of commitment to a life of service we must also talk about the fact that such a commitment goes against the grain, especially the foundations of our society. To talk this way about service and struggle, we must also talk about strategies that will enable us to sustain this sensibility, this commitment.

bh When we talk about that which will sustain and nurture our spiritual growth as a people, we must once again talk about the importance of community. For one of the most vital ways we sustain ourselves is by building communities of resistance, places where we know we are not alone. In *Prophetic Fragments*, Cornel began his essay on Martin Luther King by quoting the lines of the spiritual, "He promised never to leave me, never to leave me alone." In Black spiritual tradition, the promise that we will not be alone cannot be heard as an affirmation of passivity. It does not mean we can sit around and wait for God to take care of business. We are not alone when we build community together. Certainly, there is a great feeling of community in this room today. And yet when I was here at Yale I felt that my labor was not appreciated. It was not clear that my work was having meaningful impact. Yet I feel that impact today. When I walked into the room a Black woman sister let me know how much my teaching and writing had helped her. There's more of the critical affirmation Cornel spoke of. That critical affirmation says, "Sister, what you're doing is uplifting me in some way." Often folk think that those folks who are spreading the message are so "together" that we do not need affirmation, critical dialogue about the impact of all that we teach and write about and how we live in the world.

CW It is important to note the degree to which Black people in particular, and progressive people in general, are alienated and estranged from communities that would sustain and support us. We are often homeless. Our struggles against a sense of nothingness and attempts to reduce us to nothing are ongoing. We confront regularly the question: "Where can I find a sense of home?" That sense of home can only be found in our construction of those communities of resistance bell talks about and the solidarity we can experience within them. Renewal comes through participating in community. That is the reason so many folks continue to go to church. In religious experience they find a sense of renewal, a sense of home. In community one can feel that we are moving forward, that struggle can be sustained. As we go forward as Black progressives, we must remember that community is not about homogeneity. Homogeneity is dogmatic imposition, pushing your way of life, your way of doing things onto somebody else. That is not what we mean by community. Dogmatic insistence that everybody think and act alike causes rifts among us, destroying the possibility of community. That sense of home that we are talking about and searching for is a place where we can find compassion, recognition of difference, of the importance of diversity, of our individual uniqueness.

   bh When we evoke a sense of home as a place where we can renew ourselves, where we can know love and the sweet communion of shared spirit, I think it's important for us to remember that this location of well-being cannot exist in a context of sexist domination, in a setting where children are the objects of parental domination and abuse. On a fundamental level, when we talk about home, we must speak about the need to transform the African American home, so that there, in that domestic space, we can experience the renewal of political commitment to the Black liberation struggle. So that there in that domestic space we learn to serve and honor one another. If we look again at the civil rights movement, at the Black power movement, folks organized so much in homes. They were the places where folks got together to educate themselves for critical consciousness. That sense of community, cultivated and developed in the home, extended outward into a larger, more public context. As we talk about Black power in the 21st century, about political partnership between Black women and men, we must talk about transforming our notions of how and why we bond. In *Beloved*, Toni Morrison offers a paradigm for relationships between Black men and women. Sixo describes his love for Thirty-Mile Woman, declaring, "She is a friend of mind. She gather me, man. The pieces I am, she gather them and give them back to me in all the right order. It's good, you know, when you got a woman who is a friend of your mind." In this passage, Morrison evokes a notion of bonding that may be rooted in passion, desire, even romantic love, but the point of connection between Black women and men is that space of recognition and understanding, where we know one another so well, our histories, that we can take the bits and pieces, the fragments of who we are, and put them back together, re-member them. It is this joy of intellectual bonding, of working together to create liberatory theory and analysis that Black women and men can give one another, that Cornel and I give to each other. We are friends of one another's mind. We find a home with one another. It is that joy in community we celebrate and share with you this morning.

❖ ❖ ❖

Dynamics

1. How are the writers' arguments shaped by what they call "context"? In each passage where hooks or West mention "context," try to figure out what is to be gained by thinking in terms of context or recontextualization.

2. hooks argues that "we must teach young Black folks to understand that struggle is process, that one moves from circumstances of difficulty and pain to awareness, joy, fulfillment." Trace the notion of "struggle" as it appears throughout the essay. In what ways do hooks's and West's uses of this idea reflect hooks's claim that "struggle is process"?

3. hooks and West talk at several points in their dialogue about the importance of "remembering." Examine the individual contexts in which this idea appears. Then try to determine what, for hooks and West, is involved in "remembering." How is their definition different from those you might be familiar with?

Critical Tools

1. This text is labeled a "dialogue"; it is a record of two people speaking to each other before a large audience. Re-read the text, looking for evidence of what West calls "dialogical" thinking. Find words or phrases from the essay that you think might connect to the idea of dialogue. Who, besides hooks, West, and their immediate audience, is included in the "dialogue" they are creating? How do some examples of "dialogism" in other essays you have read compare to those in this one?

2. West suggests that members of Black communities need to practice "critical affirmation." Find some passages in the text that help you to define this idea. How might "critical affirmation" offer a useful approach to analyzing what is (or isn't) occurring in another essay you have read this semester?

Draft One/Draft Two

Draft One: hooks uses the word "multi-relationships" to stress that she is describing "all our relationships across gender" and not simply heterosexual romantic relationships. How would you characterize your own "multi-relationships"? Describe how their rules differ, the possibilities that each one offers for personal growth, the obstacles each one encounters and why. What could each of these relationships "teach" the others?

Draft Two: In what senses do healthy "multi-relationships" contribute to the creation of "communities of resistance"? Apply some of hooks's and West's ideas both to your own draft one and to another essay in which people are trying to build a "community of resistance." What is the significance of your findings?

❖ ❖ ❖

Before Reading Maxine Hong Kingston. . .

1. Identify a relative or family acquaintance who has been the topic of your own
    family's discussions at one time or another. Discuss what it is that draws such
    attention to this particular person, what this close attention suggests about your
    family's attitudes, and which aspects of this person's story seem incomplete in
    your family's version of it.

No Name Woman

Maxine Hong Kingston

"You must not tell anyone," my mother said, "what I am about to tell you. In China your father had a sister who killed herself. She jumped into the family well. We say that your father has all brothers because it is as if she had never been born.

"In 1924 just a few days after our village celebrated seventeen hurry-up weddings—to make sure that every young man who went 'out on the road' would responsibly come home—your father and his brothers and your grandfather and his brothers and your aunt's new husband sailed for America, the Gold Mountain. It was your grandfather's last trip. Those lucky enough to get contracts waved goodbye from the decks. They fed and guarded the stowaways and helped them off in Cuba, New York, Bali, Hawaii. 'We'll meet in California next year,' they said. All of them sent money home.

"I remember looking at your aunt one day when she and I were dressing; I had not noticed before that she had such a protruding melon of a stomach. But I did not think, 'She's pregnant,' until she began to look like other pregnant women, her shirt pulling and the white tops of her black pants showing. She could not have been pregnant, you see, because her husband had been gone for years. No one said anything. We did not discuss it. In early summer she was ready to have the child, long after the time when it could have been possible.

"The village had also been counting. On the night the baby was to be born the villagers raided our house. Some were crying. Like a great saw, teeth strung with lights, files of people walked zigzig across our land, tearing the rice. Their lanterns doubled in the disturbed black water, which drained away through the broken bunds. As the villagers closed in, we could see that some of them, probably men and women we knew well, wore white masks. The people with long hair hung it over their faces. Women with short hair made it stand up on end. Some had tied white bands around their foreheads, arms, and legs.

"At first they threw mud and rocks at the house. Then they threw eggs and began slaughtering our stock. We could hear the animals scream their deaths—the roosters, the pigs, a last great roar from the ox. Familiar wild heads flared in our night windows; the villagers encircled us. Some of the faces stopped to peer at us, their eyes rushing like searchlights. The hands flattened against the panes, framed heads, and left red prints.

"The villagers broke in the front and the back doors at the same time, even though we had not locked the doors against them. Their knives dripped with the blood of our animals. They smeared blood on the doors and walls. One woman swung a chicken, whose throat she had slit, splattering blood in red arcs about her. We stood together in the middle of our house, in the family hall with the pictures and tables of the ancestors around us, and looked straight ahead.

"At that time the house had only two wings. When the men came back, we would build two more to enclose our courtyard and a third one to begin a second courtyard. The villagers rushed through both wings, even your grandparents' rooms, to find your aunt's, which was also mine until the men returned. From this room a new wing for one of the younger families would grow. They ripped up her clothes and shoes and broke her combs, grinding them underfoot. They tore her work from the loom. They scattered the cooking fire and rolled the new weaving in it. We could hear them in the kitchen breaking our bowls and banging the pots. They overturned the great waisthigh earthenware jugs; duck eggs, pickled fruits, vegetables burst out and mixed in acrid torrents. The old woman from the next field swept a broom through the air and loosed the spirits-of-the-broom over our heads. 'Pig.' 'Ghost.' 'Pig,' they sobbed and scolded while they ruined our house.

"When they left, they took sugar and oranges to bless themselves. They cut pieces from the dead animals. Some of them took bowls that were not broken and clothes that were not torn. Afterward we swept up the rice and sewed it back up into sacks. But the smells from the spilled preserves lasted. Your aunt gave birth in the pigsty that night. The next morning when I went for the water, I found her and the baby plugging up the family well.

"Don't let your father know that I told you. He denies her. Now that you have started to menstruate, what happened to her could happen to you. Don't humiliate us. You wouldn't like to be forgotten as if you had never been born. The villagers are watchful."

Whenever she had to warn us about life, my mother told stories that ran like this one, a story to grow up on. She tested our strength to establish realities. Those in the emigrant generations who could not reassert brute survival died young and far from home. Those of us in the first American generations have had to figure out how the invisible world the emigrants built around our childhoods fit in solid America.

The emigrants confused the gods by diverting their curses, misleading them with crooked streets and false names. They must try to confuse their offspring as well, who, I suppose, threaten them in similar ways—always trying to get things straight, always trying to name the unspeakable. The Chinese I know hide their names; sojourners take new names when their lives change and guard their real names with silence.

Chinese-Americans, when you try to understand what things in you are Chinese, how do you separate what is peculiar to childhood, to poverty, insanities, one family, your mother who marked your growing with stories, from what is Chinese? What is Chinese tradition and what is the movies?

If I want to learn what clothes my aunt wore, whether flashy or ordinary, I would have to begin, "Remember Father's drowned-in-the-well sister?" I cannot ask that. My mother has told me once and for all the useful parts. She will add nothing unless powered by Necessity, a riverbank that guides her life. She plants vegetable gardens rather than lawns; she carries the odd-shaped tomatoes home from the fields and eats food left for the gods.

Whenever we did frivolous things, we used up energy; we flew high kites. We children came up off the ground over the melting cones our parents brought home from work and the American movie on New Year's Day—*Oh, You Beautiful Doll* with Betty Grable one year, and *She Wore a Yellow Ribbon* with John Wayne another year. After the one carnival ride each, we paid in guilt; our tired father counted his change on the dark walk home.

Adultery is extravagance. Could people who hatch their own chicks and eat the embryos and the heads for delicacies and boil the feet in vinegar for party food, leaving only the gravel, eating even the gizzard lining—could such people engender a prodigal aunt? To be a woman, to have a daughter in starvation time was a waste enough. My aunt could not have been the lone romantic who gave up everything for sex. Women in the old China did not choose. Some man had commanded her to lie with him and be his secret evil. I wonder whether he masked himself when he joined the raid on her family.

Perhaps she encountered him in the fields or on the mountain where the daughters-in-law collected fuel. Or perhaps he first noticed her in the marketplace. He was not a stranger because the village housed no strangers. She had to have dealings with him other than sex. Perhaps he worked an adjoining field, or he sold her the cloth for the dress she sewed and wore. His demand must have surprised, then terrified her. She obeyed him; she always did as she was told.

When the family found a young man in the next village to be her husband, she stood tractably beside the best rooster, his proxy, and promised before they met that she would be his forever. She was lucky that he was her age and she would be the first wife, an advantage secure now. The night she first saw him, he had sex with her. Then he left for America. She had almost forgotten what he looked like. When she tried to envision him, she only saw the black and white face in the group photograph the men had taken before leaving.

The other man was not, after all, much different from her husband. They both gave orders: she followed. "If you tell your family, I'll beat you. I'll kill you. Be here again next week." No one talked sex, ever. And she might have separated the rapes from the rest of living if only she did not have to buy her oil from him or gather wood in the same forest. I want her fear to have lasted just as long as rape lasted so that the fear could have been contained. No drawn-out fear. But women at sex hazarded birth and hence lifetimes. The fear did not stop but permeated everywhere. She told the man, "I think I'm pregnant." He organized the raid against her.

On nights when my mother and father talked about their life back home, sometimes they mentioned an "outcast table" whose business they still seemed to be settling, their voices tight. In a commensal tradition, where food is precious, the powerful older people made wrongdoers eat alone. Instead of letting them start separate new lives like the Japanese, who could become samurais and geishas, the Chinese family, faces averted but eyes glowering sideways, hung on to the offenders and fed them leftovers. My aunt must have lived in the same house as my parents and eaten at an outcast table. My mother spoke about the raid as if she had seen it, when she and my aunt, a daughter-in-law to a different household, should not have been living together at all. Daughters-in-law lived with their husbands' parents, not their own; a synonym for marriage in Chinese is "taking a daughter-in-law." Her husband's parents could have sold her, mortgaged her, stoned her. But they had sent her back to her own mother and father, a mysterious act hinting at disgraces not told me. Perhaps they had thrown her out to deflect the avengers.

She was the only daughter; her four brothers went with her father, husband, and uncles "out on the road" and for some years became western men. When the goods were divided among the family, three of the brothers took land, and the youngest, my father, chose an education. After my grandparents gave their daughter away to her husband's family, they had dispensed all the adventure and all the property. They expected her alone to keep the traditional ways, which her brothers, now among the barbarians, could fumble without detection. The heavy, deep-rooted women were to maintain the past against the flood, safe for returning. But the rare urge west had fixed upon our family, and so my aunt crossed boundaries not delineated in space.

The work of preservation demands that the feelings playing about in one's guts not be turned into action. Just watch their passing like cherry blossoms. But perhaps my aunt, my forerunner, caught in a slow life, let dreams grow and fade and after some months or years went toward what persisted. Fear at the enormities of the forbidden kept her desires delicate, wire and bone. She looked at a man because she liked the way the hair was tucked behind his ears, or she liked the question-mark line of a long torso curving at the shoulder and straight at the hip. For warm eyes or a soft voice or a slow walk—that's all—a few hairs, a line, a brightness, a sound, a pace, she gave up family. She offered us up for a charm that vanished with tiredness, a pigtail that didn't toss when the wind died. Why, the wrong lighting could erase the dearest thing about him.

It could very well have been, however, that my aunt did not take subtle enjoyment of her friend, but, a wild woman, kept rollicking company. Imagining her free with sex doesn't fit, though. I don't know any women like that, or men either. Unless I see her life branching into mine, she gives me no ancestral help.

To sustain her being in love, she often worked at herself in the mirror, guessing at the colors and shapes that would interest him, changing them frequently in order to hit on the right combination. She wanted him to look back.

On a farm near the sea, a woman who tended her appearance reaped a reputation for eccentricity. All the married women blunt-cut their hair in flaps about their ears or pulled it back in tight buns. No nonsense. Neither style blew easily into heart-catching tangles. And at their weddings they displayed themselves in their long hair for the last time. "It brushed the backs of my knees," my mother tells me. "It was braided, and even so, it brushed the backs of my knees."

At the mirror my aunt combed individuality into her bob. A bun could have been contrived to escape into black streamers blowing in the wind or in quiet wisps about her face, but only the older women in our picture album wear buns. She brushed her hair back from her forehead, tucking the flaps behind her ears. She looped a piece of thread, knotted into a circle between her index fingers and thumbs, and ran the double strand across her forehead. When she closed her fingers as if she were making a pair of shadow geese bite, the string twisted together catching the little hairs. Then she pulled the thread away from her skin, ripping the hairs out neatly, her eyes watering from the needles of pain. Opening her fingers, she cleaned the thread, then rolled it along her hairline and the tops of her eyebrows. My mother did the same to me and my sisters and herself. I used to believe that the expression "caught by the short hairs" meant a captive held with a depilatory string. It especially hurt at the temples, but my mother said we were lucky we didn't have to have our feet bound when we were seven. Sisters used to sit on their beds and cry together, she said, as their mothers or their slave removed the bandages for a few minutes each night and let the blood gush back into their veins. I hope that the man my aunt loved appreciated a smooth brow, that he wasn't just a tits-and-ass man.

Once my aunt found a freckle on her chin, at a spot that the almanac said predestined her for unhappiness. She dug it out with a hot needle and washed the wound with peroxide.

More attention to her looks than these pullings of hairs and pickings at spots would have caused gossip among the villagers. They owned work clothes and good clothes, and they wore good clothes for feasting the new seasons. But since a woman combing her hair hexes beginnings, my aunt rarely found an occasion to look her best. Women looked like great sea snails—the corded wood, babies, and laundry they carried were the whorls on their backs. The Chinese did not admire a bent back; goddesses and warriors stood straight. Still there must have been a marvelous freeing of beauty when a worker laid down her burden and stretched and arched.

Such commonplace loveliness, however, was not enough for my aunt. She dreamed of a lover for the fifteen days of New Year's, the time for families to exchange visits, money, and food. She plied her secret comb. And sure enough she cursed the year, the family, the village, and herself.

Even as her hair lured her imminent lover, many other men looked at her. Uncles, cousins, nephews, brothers would have looked, too, had they been home between journeys. Perhaps they had already been restraining their curiosity, and they left, fearful that their glances, like a field of nesting birds, might be startled and caught. Poverty hurt, and that was their first reason for leaving. But another, final reason for leaving the crowded house was the never-said.

She may have been unusually beloved, the precious only daughter, spoiled and mirror gazing because of the affection the family lavished on her. When her husband left, they welcomed the chance to take her back from the in-laws; she could live like the little daughter for just a while longer. There are stories that my grandfather was different from other people, "crazy ever since the little Jap bayoneted him in the head." He used to put his naked penis on the dinner table, laughing. And one day he brought home a baby girl, wrapped up inside his brown western-style greatcoat. He had traded one of his sons, probably my father, the youngest, for her. My grandmother made him trade back. When he finally got a daughter of his own, he doted on her. They must have all loved her, except perhaps my father, the only brother who never went back to China, having once been traded for a girl.

Brothers and sisters, newly men and women, had to efface their sexual color and present plain miens. Disturbing hair and eyes, a smile like no other, threatened the ideal of five generations living under one roof. To focus blurs, people shouted face to face and yelled from room to room. The immigrants I know have loud voices, unmodulated to American tones even after years away from the village where they called their friendships out across the fields. I have not been able to stop my mother's screams in public libraries or over telephones. Walking erect (knees straight, toes pointed forward, not pigeon-toed, which is Chinese-feminine) and speaking in an inaudible voice, I have tried to turn myself American-feminine. Chinese communication was loud, public. Only sick people had to whisper. But at the dinner table, where the family members came nearest one another, no one could talk, not the outcasts nor any eaters. Every word that falls from the mouth is a coin lost. Silently they gave and accepted food with both hands. A preoccupied child who took his bowl with one hand got a sideways glare. A complete moment of total attention is due everyone alike. Children and lovers have no singularity here, but my aunt used a secret voice, a separate attentiveness.

She kept the man's name to herself throughout her labor and dying; she did not accuse him that he be punished with her. To save her inseminator's name she gave silent birth.

He may have been somebody in her own household, but intercourse with a man outside the family would have been no less abhorrent. All the village were kinsmen, and the titles shouted in loud country voices never let kinship be forgotten. Any man within visiting distance would have been neutralized as a lover—"brother," "younger brother," "older brother"—one hundred and fifteen relationship titles. Parents researched birth charts probably not so much to assure good fortune as to circumvent incest in a population that has but one hundred surnames. Everybody has eight million relatives. How useless then sexual mannerisms, how dangerous.

As if it came from an atavism deeper than fear, I used to add "brother" silently to boys' names. It hexed the boys, who would or would not ask me to dance; and made them less scary and as familiar and deserving of benevolence as girls.

But, of course, I hexed myself also—no dates. I should have stood up, both arms waving, and shouted out across libraries, "Hey, you! Love me back." I had no idea, though, how to make attraction selective, how to control its direction and magnitude. If I made myself American-pretty so that the five or six Chinese boys in the class fell in love with me, everyone else—the Caucasian, Negro, and Japanese boys—would too. Sisterliness, dignified and honorable, made much more sense.

Attraction eludes control so stubbornly that whole societies designed to organize relationships among people cannot keep order, not even when they bind people to one another from childhood and raise them together. Among the very poor and the wealthy, brothers married their adopted sisters, like doves. Our family allowed some romance, paying adult brides' prices and providing dowries so that their sons and daughters could marry strangers. Marriage promises to turn strangers into friendly relatives—a nation of siblings.

In the village structure, spirits shimmered among the live creatures, balanced and held in equilibrium by time and land. But one human being flaring up into violence could open up a black hole, a maelstrom that pulled in the sky. The frightened villagers, who depended on one another to maintain the real, went to my aunt to show her a personal, physical representation of the break she had made in the "roundness." Misallying couples snapped off the future, which was to be embodied in true offspring. The villagers punished her for acting as if she could have a private life, secret and apart from them.

If my aunt had betrayed the family at a time of large grain yields and peace, when many boys were born, and wings were being built on many houses, perhaps she might have escaped such severe punishment. But the men—hungry, greedy, tired of planting in dry soil, cuckolded—had had to leave the village in order to send food-money home. There were ghost plagues, bandit plagues, wars with the Japanese, floods. My Chinese brother and sister had died of an unknown sickness. Adultery, perhaps only a mistake during good times, became a crime when the village needed food.

The round moon cakes and round doorways, the round tables of graduated size that fit one roundness inside another, round windows and rice bowls—these talismans had lost their power to warn this family of the law: a family must be whole, faithfully keeping the descent line by having sons to feed the old and the dead, who in turn look after the family. The villagers came to show my aunt and her lover-in-hiding a broken house. The villagers were speeding up the circling of events because she was too shortsighted to see that her infidelity had already harmed the village, that waves of consequences would return unpredictably, sometimes in disguise, as now, to hurt her. This roundness had to be made coin-sized so that she would see its circumference: punish her at the birth of her baby. Awaken her to the inexorable. People who refused fatalism because they could invent small resources insisted on culpability. Deny accidents and wrest fault from the stars.

After the villagers left, their lanterns now scattering in various directions toward home, the family broke their silence and cursed her. "Aiaa, we're going to die. Death is coming. Death is coming. Look what you've done. You've killed us. Ghost! Dead ghost! Ghost! You've never been born." She ran out into the fields, far enough from the house so that she could no longer hear their voices, and pressed herself against the earth, her own land no more. When she felt the birth coming, she thought that she had been hurt. Her body seized together. "They've hurt me too much," she thought. "This is gall, and it will kill me." With forehead and knees against the earth, her body convulsed and then relaxed. She turned on her back, lay on the ground. The black well of sky and stars went out and out and out forever; her body and her complexity seemed to disappear, without home, without a companion, in eternal cold and silence. An agoraphobia rose in her, speeding higher and higher, bigger and bigger; she would not be able to contain it; there would be no end to fear.

Flayed, unprotected against space, she felt pain return, focusing her body. This pain chilled her—a cold, steady kind of surface pain. Inside, spasmodically, the other pain, the pain of the child, heated her. For hours she lay on the ground, alternately body and space. Sometimes a vision of normal comfort obliterated reality: she saw the family in the evening gambling at the dinner table, the young people massaging their elders' backs. She saw them congratulating one another, high joy on the mornings the rice shoots came up. When these pictures burst, the stars drew yet further apart. Black space opened.

She got to her feet to fight better and remembered that old-fashioned women gave birth in their pigsties to fool the jealous, pain-dealing gods, who do not snatch piglets. Before the next spasms could stop her, she ran to the pigsty, each step a rushing out into emptiness. She climbed over the fence and knelt in the dirt. It was good to have a fence enclosing her, a tribal person alone.

Laboring, this woman who had carried her child as a foreign growth that sickened her every day, expelled it at last. She reached down to touch the hot, wet, moving mass, surely smaller than anything human, and could feel that it was human after all—fingers, toes, nails, nose. She pulled it up on to her belly, and it lay curled there, butt in the air, feet precisely tucked one under the other. She opened her loose shirt and buttoned the child inside. After resting, it squirmed and thrashed and she pushed it up to her breast. It turned its head this way and that until it found her nipple. There, it made little snuffling noises. She clenched her teeth at its preciousness, lovely as a young calf, a piglet, a little dog.

She may have gone to the pigsty as a last act of responsibility: she would protect this child as she had protected its father. It would look after her soul, leaving supplies on her grave. But how would this tiny child without family find her grave when there would be no marker for her anywhere, neither in the earth nor the family hall? No one would give her a family hall name. She had taken the child with her into the wastes. At its birth the two of them had felt the same raw pain of separation, a wound that only the family pressing tight could close. A child with no descent line would not soften her life but only trail after her, ghost-like, begging her to give it purpose. At dawn the villagers on their way to the fields would stand around the fence and look.

Full of milk, the little ghost slept. When it awoke, she hardened her breasts against the milk that crying loosens. Toward morning she picked up the baby and walked to the well.

Carrying the baby to the well shows loving. Otherwise abandon it. Turn its face into the mud. Mothers who love their children take them along. It was probably a girl; there is some hope of forgiveness for boys.

"Don't tell anyone you had an aunt. Your father does not want to hear her name. She has never been born." I have believed that sex was unspeakable and words so strong and fathers so frail that "aunt" would do my father mysterious harm. I have thought that my family, having settled among immigrants who had also been their neighbors in the ancestral land, needed to clean their name, and a wrong word would incite the kinspeople even here. But there is more to this silence: they want me to participate in her punishment. And I have.

In the twenty years since I heard this story I have not asked for details nor said my aunt's name; I do not know it. People who can comfort the dead can also chase after them to hurt them further—a reverse ancestor worship. The real punishment was not the raid swiftly inflicted by the villagers, but the family's deliberately forgetting her. Her betrayal so maddened them, they saw to it that she would suffer forever, even after death. Always hungry, always needing, she would have to beg food from other ghosts, snatch and steal it from those whose living descendants give them gifts. She would have to fight the ghosts massed at crossroads for the buns a few thoughtful citizens leave to decoy her away from village and home so that the ancestral spirits could feast unharassed. At peace, they could act like gods, not ghosts, their descent lines providing them with paper suits and dresses, spirit money, paper houses, paper automobiles, chicken, meat, and rice into eternity—essences delivered up in smoke and flames, steam and incense rising from each rice bowl. In an attempt to make the Chinese care for people outside the family, Chairman Mao encourages us now to give our paper replicas to the spirits of outstanding soldiers and workers, no matter whose ancestors they may be. My aunt remains forever hungry. Goods are not distributed evenly among the dead.

My aunt haunts me—her ghost drawn to me because now, after fifty years of neglect, I alone devote pages of paper to her, though not origamied into houses and clothes. I do not think she always means me well. I am telling on her, and she was a spite suicide, drowning herself in the drinking water. The Chinese are always very frightened of the drowned one, whose weeping ghost, wet hair hanging and skin bloated, waits silently by the water to pull down a substitute.

❖ ❖ ❖

Dynamics

1. How does Kingston interpret Chinese "thrift" in her various discussions of it, and in what ways does she find this thrift connected to the story of her aunt? Locate some passages where you see the idea of thrift affecting the way Kingston tells her story.

2. Isolate moments in Kingston's essay when she moves from the "facts" of her aunt's story to "fiction" or fantasy about it. What feelings in the story seem to signal or precede these shifts? Explain what you see happening to these emotions once Kingston moves into a more "fictional" style.

Critical Tools

1. Use passages from Kingston's text to define what she might mean by "the invisible world." In what senses does "the invisible world" relate to Kingston's understanding of kinship? Adapt her notion of "the invisible world" to some context described by another writer in *Literacies*.

2. Locate some points in the text where Kingston suggests that the desire for "individuality" might have been a problem for her aunt. According to your reading of her text, what are some of the factors that determine the way a culture views individuality? How does another writer's perspective on individuality compare to Kingston's? Explain how you might account for the differences you see.

Draft One/Draft Two

Draft One: Explain what you think Kingston means when she says that her mother "tested [Kingston's] strength to establish realities." Where in her essay do you see Kingston "establish[ing] realities" that are different from those approved by her Chinese and American cultures? What does that process have to do with writing? Use some of your own experiences as a college writer to explore what Kingston means by "establish[ing] realities."

Draft Two: Working with insights from your first draft, discuss the strategies that another writer in *Literacies* uses to establish his or her own "realities." Consider some of the obstacles that each writer—you, Kingston, and the new writer—faces in his or her attempts to present a perspective that seems faithful to personal experience. Try to differentiate between obstacles that come from "inside" and "outside" the writer.

❖   ❖   ❖

Before Reading Jonathan Kozol. . .

1. Kozol's essay includes the testimony of a homeless family about their experiences in shelters and welfare "hotels." In your experience, how do most people's attitudes about homelessness develop? Write informally about the factors that contribute to the way a person understands homelessness. Where have your opinions about homelessness come from?

2. What groups of people would you expect to have useful information and theories about homelessness? What kinds of information do you think you might approach with skepticism or even distrust? Why?

3. How do you expect the idea of "family" to fit into a discussion of homelessness? Explain how other readings in *Literacies* have shaped your thinking about the meaning of "family."

Rachel and Her Children

Jonathan Kozol

Mr. Allesandro is too shaken to attempt to hide his frailties from me. He tells me: "When you're running scared you do some things you'd rather not..." He does not regard himself as saint or martyr. There are virtues, feelings and commitments he has forfeited during this long ordeal. Love is not one of them. His desperation for his son and daughters and his adoration of his mother are as solid and authentic as the marble pillars of the Martinique Hotel. The authenticity of love deserves some mention in discussion of the homeless.

Houses can be built without a number of ingredients that other ages viewed as indispensable. Acrylics, plastics and aluminum may substitute for every substance known to nature. Parental love cannot be synthesized. Even the most earnest and methodical foster care demonstrates the limits of synthetic tenderness and surrogate emotion. So it seems of keen importance to consider any ways, and *every* way, by which a family, splintered, jolted and imperiled though it be by loss of home and subsequent detention in a building like the Martinique, may nonetheless be given every possible incentive to remain together.

The inclination to judge harshly the behavior of a parent under formidable stress seems to be much stronger than the willingness to castigate the policies that undermine the competence and ingenuity of many of these people in the first place.

"Men can be unequal in their needs, in their honor, in their possessions," writes historian Michael Ignatieff, "but also in their rights to judge others." The king's ultimate inequality, he says, "is that he is never judged." An entire industry of scholarship and public policy exists to judge the failing or defective parent; if we listen to some of these parents carefully we may be no less concerned by their impaired abilities, but we may be less judgmental or, if we remain compelled to judge, we may redirect our energies in more appropriate directions.

New Year's Eve.

She stalks into the room. Her eyes are reddened and her clothes in disarray. She wears a wrinkled and translucent nightgown. On her feet: red woolen stockings.

At her throat: a crucifix. Over her shoulders is a dark and heavy robe. Nothing I have learned in the past week prepares me for this apparition.

She cries. She weeps. She paces left and right and back and forth. Pivoting and turning suddenly to face me. Glaring straight into my eyes. A sudden halt. She looks up toward the cracked and yellowish ceiling of the room. Her children stand around her in a circle. Two little girls. A frightened boy. They stare at her, as I do, as her arms reach out—for what? They snap like snakes and coil back. Her hair is gray—a stiff and brushlike Afro.

Angelina is twelve years old, Stephen is eleven, Erica is nine. The youngest child, eleven months, is sitting on the floor. A neighbor's child, six years old, sits in my lap and leans her head against my chest; she holds her arms around my neck. Her name or nickname (I do not know which) is Raisin. When she likes she puts her fingers on my mouth and interrupts the conversation with a tremolo of rapid words. There are two rooms. Rachel disappears into the second room, then returns and stands, uneasy, by the door.

Angie: "Ever since August we been livin' here. The room is either very hot or freezin' cold. When it be hot outside it's hot in here. When it be cold outside we have no heat. We used to live with my aunt but then it got too crowded there so we moved out. We went to welfare and they sent us to the shelter. Then they shipped us to Manhattan. I'm scared of the elevators. 'Fraid they be stuck. I take the stairs."

Raisin: "Elevator might fall down and you would die."

Rachel: "It's unfair for them to be here in this room. They be yellin'. Lots of times I'm goin' to walk out. Walk out on the street and give it up. No, I don't do it. BCW (Bureau of Child Welfare) come to take the children. So I make them stay inside. Once they walk outside that door they are in danger."

Angie: "I had a friend Yoki. They was tryin' to beat her. I said: 'Leave her.' They began to chase me. We was runnin' to the door. So we was runnin'. I get to the door. The door was stuck. I hit my eye and it began to bleed. So I came home and washed the blood. Me and my friends sat up all night and prayed. Prayin' for me. 'Dear Lord, can you please help me with my eye? If you do I promise to behave.' I was askin' God why did this happen. I wish someone in New York could help us. Put all of the money that we have together and we buy a building. Two or three rooms for every family. Everybody have a kitchen. Way it is, you frightened all the time. I think this world is coming to the end."

Stephen: "This city is rich."

Angie: "Surely is!"

Erica: "City and welfare, they got something goin'. Pay $3,000 every month to stay in these here rooms..."

Rachel: "I believe the City Hall got something goin' here. Gettin' a cut. They got to be. My children, they be treated like chess pieces. Send all of that money off to Africa? You hear that song? They're not thinking about people starvin' here in the United States. I was thinkin': Get my kids and all the other children here to sing, 'We are the world. We live here too.' How come do you care so much for people you can't see? Ain't we the world? Ain't we a piece of it? We are so close they be afraid to see. Give us a shot at something. We are something! Ain't we *something*? I'm depressed. But we are *something*! People in America don't want to see."

Angie: "Christmas is sad for everyone. We have our toys. That's not the reason why. They givin' you toys and that do help. I would rather that we have a place to be."

Erica: "I wrote a letter to Santa Claus. Santa say that he don't have the change."

Raisin: "I saw Santa on the street. Then I saw Santa on another street. I pulled his beard and he said something nasty."

Angie: "There's one thing I ask: a home to be in with my mother. That was my only wish for Christmas. But it could not be."

Raisin: "I saw Mr. Water Bug under my mother's bed. Mr. Rat be livin' with us too."

Angie: "It's so cold right now you got to use the hot plate. Plug it in so you be warm. You need to have a hot plate. Are you goin' to live on cold bologna all your life?"

Raisin: "Mr. Rat came in my baby sister's crib and bit her. Nobody felt sorry for my sister. Then I couldn't go to sleep. I started crying. All of a sudden I pray and went to sleep and then I woke up in the mornin', make my bed, and took a bath, and ate, and went to school. So I came back and did my homework. And all of a sudden there was something *irritatin'* at my hand. I looked out the window and the moon was goin' up. And then—I had a dream. I went to sleep and I was dreamin' and I dreamed about a witch that bit me. I felt *dead*. When I woke back up I had a headache."

Angie: "School is bad for me. I feel ashamed. They know we're not the same. My teacher do not treat us all the same. They know which children live in the hotel."

Erica: "My teacher isn't like that. She treats all of us the same. We all get smacked. We all get punished the same way."

Stephen: "I'm in sixth grade. When I am a grown-up I be a computer."

Erica: "You're in the fifth. You lie."

Raisin: "When I grow up I want to be multiplication and subtraction and division."

Angie: "Last week a drug addict tried to stab me. With an ice pick. Tried to stab my mother too. Older girls was botherin' us. They try to make us fight. We don't fight. We don't start fires. They just pickin' on us. We ran home and got our mother. They ran home and got their mother."

Raisin: "Those girls upstairs on the ninth floor, they be bad. They sellin' crack."

Erica: "Upstairs, ninth floor, nine-o-five, they sellin' crack."

Raisin: "A man was selling something on the street. He had some reefers on him and the po-lice caught him and they took him to the jail. You know where the junkies put the crack? Put the crack inside the pipe. Smoke it like that. They take a torch and burn the pipe and put it in their mouth. They go like this." [Puffs.]

I ask: "Why do they do it?"

Erica: "Feel good! Hey! Make you feel fine!"

Angie: "This girl I know lives in a room where they sell drugs. One day she asks us do we want a puff. So we said: 'No. My mother doesn't let us do it.' One day I was walkin' in the hall. This man asked me do I want some stuff. He said: 'Do you want some?' I said no and I ran home."

Raisin: "One day my brother found these two big plastic bags inside his teddy bear. Po-lice came up to my room and took that teddy bear." She's interrupted. "I ain't finished! And they took it. One day we was by my uncle's car and this man came and he said: 'Do you want some?' We said no. We told my uncle and he went and found the man and he ran to the bar and went into the women's bathroom in the bar. And so we left."

Angie: "I think this world is ending. Yes. Ending. Everybody in this city killin' on each other. Countries killin' on each other. Why can't people learn to stick together? It's no use to fightin'. Fightin' over nothin'. What they fightin' for? A flag! I don't know what we are fightin' for. President Reagan wants to put the rockets on the moon. What's he doin' messin' with the moon? If God wanted man and woman on the moon He would of put us there. They should send a camera to the moon and feed the people here on earth. Don't go messin' there with human beings. Use that money to build houses. Grow food! Buy seeds! Weave cloth! Give it to the people in America!"

Erica: "When we hungry and don't have no food we borrow from each other. Her mother [Raisin's] give us food. Or else we go to Crisis. In the mornin' when we wake up we have a banana or a cookie. If the bus ain't late we have our breakfast in the school. What I say to President Reagan: Give someone a chance! I believe he be a selfish man. Can't imagine how long he been president."

Raisin: "Be too long."

Angie: "Teacher tell us this be a democracy. I don't know. I doubt it. Rich people, couldn't they at least give us a refund?"

Raisin: "This man say his son be gettin' on his nerves. He beat his little son 'bout two years old. A wooden bat. He beat him half to death. They took him to the hospital and at five-thirty he was dead. A little boy. [Interrupted.] Let me talk!"

Erica: "The little boy. He locked himself into the bathroom. He was scared. After he died police came and his father went to jail. His mother, she went to the store."

Raisin, in a tiny voice: "People fight in here and I don't like it. Why do they do it? 'Cause they're sad. They fight over the world. I ain't finished!"

Erica: "One time they was two cops in the hall. One cop pulled his gun and he was goin' shoot me. He said did I live there? I said no. So I came home."

Raisin: "I was in this lady room. She be cryin' because her baby died. He had [mispronounced] pneumonia. He was unconscious and he died." Soft voice: "Tomorrow is my birthday."

The children are tended by a friend. In the other bedroom, Rachel, who is quieter now, paces about and finally sits down.

"Do you know why there's no carpet in the hall? If there was a carpet it would be on fire. Desperate people don't have no control. You have to sleep with one eye open. Tell the truth, I do not sleep at night.

"Before we lived here we were at the Forbell shelter [barracks shelter on Forbell Street in Brooklyn]. People sleep together in one room. You sleep across. You have to dress in front of everybody. Men and women. When you wake, some man lookin' at you puttin' on your clothes. Lookin' at your children too. Angelina, she be only twelve years old...

"There's one thing. My children still are pure. They have a concept of life. Respect for life. But if you don't get 'em out of here they won't have anything for long. If you get 'em out right now. But if you don't...My girls are innocent still. They are unspoiled. Will they be that way for long? Try to keep 'em in the room. But you can't lock 'em up for long.

"When we moved here I was forced to sign a paper. Everybody has to do it. It's a promise that you will not cook inside your room. So we lived on cold bologna. Can you feed a child on that? God forgive me but nobody shouldn't have to live like this. I can't even go downstairs and get back on the elevator. Half the time it doesn't work. Since I came into this place my kids begun to get away from me."

There's a crucifix on the wall. I ask her: "Do you pray?"

"I don't pray! Pray for what? I been prayin' all my life and I'm still here. When I came to this hotel I still believed in God. I said: 'Maybe God can help us to survive.' I lost my faith. My hopes. And everything. Ain't nobody—no God, no Jesus—gonna help us in no way.

"God forgive me. I'm emotional. I'm black. I'm in a blackness. Blackness is around me. In the night I'm scared to sleep. In the mornin' I'm worn out. I don't eat no breakfast. I don't drink no coffee. If I eat, I eat one meal a day. My stomach won't allow me. I have ulcers. I stay in this room. I hide. This room is safe to me. I am afraid to go outside.

"If I go out, what do I do? People drink. Why do they drink? A person gets worn out. They usin' drugs. Why they use drugs? They say: 'Well, I won't think about it now.' Why not? You ain't got nothin' else to do, no place to go. 'Where I'm gonna be tomorrow or the next day?' They don't know. All they know is that they don't have nothin'. So they drink. And some of them would rather not wake up. Rather be dead. That's right.

"Most of us are black. Some Puerto Rican. Some be white. They suffer too. Can you get the government to know that we exist? I know that my children have potential. They're intelligent. They're smart. They need a chance. There's nothin' wrong with them for now. But not for long. My daughter watches junkies usin' needles. People smokin' crack in front a them. Screwin' in front a them. They see it all. They see it everywhere. What is a man and woman gonna do when they are all in the same room?

"I met a girl the other day. She's twelve years old. Lives on the fourteenth floor. She got a baby the same age as mine. Her mother got five children of her own. I don't want my daughter havin' any baby. She's a child. Innocent. Innocent. No violence. She isn't bitter. But she's scared. You understand? This is America. These children growin' up too fast. We have no hope. And you know why? Because we all feel just the same way deep down in our hearts. Nowhere to go...I'm not a killer. My kids ain't no killers. But if they don't learn to kill they know they're goin' to die.

"They didn't go to school last week. They didn't have clean clothes. Why? Because the welfare messed my check. It's supposed to come a week ago. It didn't come. I get my check today. I want my kids to go to school. They shouldn't miss a day. How they gonna go to school if they don't got some clothes? I couldn't wash. I didn't have the money to buy food.

"Twice the welfare closed my case. When they do it you are s'posed to go for a fair hearing. Take some papers, birth certificates. So I went out there in the snow. Welfare worker wasn't there. They told me to come back. Mister, it ain't easy to be beggin'. I went to the Crisis. And I asked her, I said, 'Give me somethin' for the kids to eat. Give me *somethin*'! Don't turn me away when I am sittin' here in front of you and askin' for your help!' She said she had nothin'. So my kids went out into the street. That's right! Whole night long they was in Herald Square panhandlin'. Made five dollars. So we bought bologna. My kids is good to me. We had bread and bologna.

"Welfare, they are not polite. They're personal. 'Did you do this? Did you do that? Where your husband at?' Understand me? 'Cause they sittin' on the other side of this here desk, they think we're stupid and we do not understand when we're insulted. 'Oh, you had another baby?' Yeah! I had another baby! What about it? Are you goin' to kill that baby? I don't say it, but that's what I feel like sayin'. You learn to be humble.

"I'm here five miserable months. So I wonder: Where I'm goin'? Can't the mayor give us a house? A part-time job? I am capable of doin' *somethin*'.

"You go in the store with food stamps. You need Pampers. You're not s'posed to use the stamps for Pampers. Stores will accept them. They don't care about the law. What they do is make you pay a little extra. They know you don't have no choice. So they let you buy the Pampers for two dollars extra.

"Plenty of children livin' here on nothin' but bread and bologna. Peanut butter. Jelly. Drinkin' water. You buy milk. I bought one gallon yesterday. Got *this* much left. They drink it fast. Orange juice, they drink it fast. End up drinkin' Kool Aid.

"Children that are poor are used like cattle. Cattle or horses. They are owned by welfare. They know they are bein' used—for what? Don't use them! Give 'em somethin'!

"In this bedroom I'm not sleepin' on a bed. They won't give me one. You can see I'm sleepin' on a box spring. I said to the manager: 'I need a bed instead of sleepin' on a spring.' Maid give me some blankets. Try to make it softer."

The Bible by her bed is opened to the Twenty-third Psalm.

"I do believe. God forgive me. I believe He's there. But when He sees us like this, I am wonderin' where is He? I am askin': Where the hell He gone?

"Before they shipped us here we lived for five years in a basement. Five years in a basement with no bathroom. One small room. You had to go upstairs two floors to use the toilet. No kitchen. It was fifteen people in five rooms. Sewer kept backing up into the place we slept. Every time it flooded I would have to pay one hundred dollars just to get the thing unstuck. There were all my children sleepin' in the sewage. So you try to get them out and try to get them somethin' better. But it didn't get no better. I came from one bad place into another. But the difference is this is a place where I cannot get out.

"If I can't get out of here I'll give them up. I have asked them: 'Do you want to go away?' I love my kids and, if I did that, they would feel betrayed. They love me. They don't want to go. If I did it, I would only do it to protect them. They'll live anywhere with me. They're innocent. Their minds are clean. They ain't corrupt. They have a heart. All my kids love people. They love life. If they got a dime, a piece of bread, they'll share it. Letting them panhandle made me cry. I had been to welfare, told the lady that my baby ain't got Pampers, ain't got nothin' left to eat. I got rude and noisy and it's not my style to do that but you learn that patience and politeness get you nowhere.

"When they went out on the street I cried. I said: 'I'm scared. What's gonna happen to them?' But if they're hungry they are goin' to do *something*. They are gonna find their food from somewhere. Where I came from I was fightin' for my children. In this place here I am fightin' for my children. I am tired of fightin'. I don't want to fight. I want my kids to live in peace.

"I was thinkin' about this. If there was a place where you could sell part of your body, where they buy an arm or somethin' for a thousand dollars, I would do it. I would do it for my children. I would give my life if I could get a thousand dollars. What would I lose? I lived my life. I want to see my children grow up to live theirs.

"A lot of women do not want to sell their bodies. This is something that good women do not want to do. I will sell mine. I *will*. I will solicit. I will prostitute if it will feed them."

I ask: "Would you do it?"

"Ain't no 'would I?' I would do it." Long pause..."Yes. I *did*.

"I had to do it when the check ain't come. Wasn't no one gonna buy my arm for any thousand dollars. But they's plenty gonna pay me twenty dollars for my body. What was my choice? Leave them out there on the street, a child like Angelina, to panhandle? I would take my life if someone found her dead somewhere. I would go crazy. After she did it that one time I was ashamed. I cried that night. All night I cried and cried. So I decided I had one thing left. In the mornin' I got up out of this bed. I told them I was goin' out. Out in the street. Stand by the curb. It was a cold day. Freezin'! And my chest is bad. I'm thirty-eight years old. Cop come by. He see me there. I'm standin' out there cryin'. Tells me I should go inside. Gives me three dollars. 'It's too cold to be outside.' Ain't many cops like that. Not many people either...

"After he's gone a man come by. Get in his car. Go with him where he want. Takin' a chance he crazy and he kill me. Wishin' somehow that he would.

"So he stop his car. And I get in. I say a price. That's it. Go to a room. It's some hotel. He had a lot of money so he rented a deluxe. Asked me would I stay with him all night. I tell him no I can't 'cause I have kids. So, after he done...whatever he did...I told him that I had to leave. Took out a knife at me and held it at my face. He made me stay. When I woke up next day I was depressed. Feel so guilty what I did. I feel real scared. I can understand why prostitutes shoot drugs. They take the drugs so they don't be afraid.

"When he put that knife up to my throat, I'm thinkin' this: What is there left to lose? I'm not goin' to do any better in this life. If I be dead at least my kids won't ever have to say that I betrayed them. I don't like to think like that. But when things pile up on you, you do. 'I'm better if I'm dead.'

"So I got me twenty dollars and I go and buy the Pampers for the baby and three dollars of bologna and a loaf of bread and everyone is fed.

"That cross of Jesus on the wall I had for seven years. I don't know if I believe or not. Bible say that Jesus was God's son. He died for us to live here on this earth. See, I believe—Jesus was innocent. But, when He died, what was it for? He died for nothin'. Died in vain. He should a let us die like we be doin'—we be dyin' all the time. We dyin' every day.

"God forgive me. I don't mean the things I say. God had one son and He gave His son. He gave him up. I couldn't do it. I got four. I could not give any one of them. I couldn't do it. God could do it. Is it wrong to say it? I don't know if Jesus died in vain."

She holds the Bible in her hands. Crying softly. Sitting on the box spring in her tangled robe.

"They laid him in a manger. Right? Listen to me. I didn't say that God forsaken us. I am confused about religion. I'm just sayin' evil overrules the good. So many bad things goin' on. Lot of bad things right here in this buildin'. It's not easy to believe. I don't read the Bible no more 'cause I don't find no more hope in it. I don't believe. But yet and still...I know these words." She reads aloud: " 'Lie down in green pastures...leadeth me beside still waters...restores my soul...I shall not want.'

"All that I want is somethin' that's my own. I got four kids. I need four plates, four glasses, and four spoons. Is that a lot? I know I'm poor. Don't have no bank account, no money, or no job. Don't have no nothin'. No foundation. Then and yet my children have a shot in life. They're innocent. They're pure. They have a chance." She reads: " 'I shall not fear...' I fear! A long, long time ago I didn't fear. Didn't fear for nothin'. I said God's protectin' me and would protect my children. Did He do it?

"Yeah. I'm walkin'. I am walkin' in the wilderness. That's what it is. I'm walkin'. Did I tell you that I am an ex-drug addict? Yeah. My children know it. They know and they understand. I'm walkin'. Yeah!"

The room is like a chilled cathedral in which people who do not believe in God ask God's forgiveness. "How I picture God is like an old man who speaks different languages. His beard is white and He has angels and the instruments they play are white and everything around is white and there is no more sickness, no more hunger for nobody. No panhandlin'. No prostitutes. No drugs. I had a dream like that.

"There's no beauty in my life except two things. My children and"—she hesitates—"I write these poems. How come, when I write it down, it don't come out my pencil like I feel? I don't know. I got no dictionary. Every time I read it over I am finding these mistakes.

Deep down in my heart
I do not mean these things I said.
Forgive me. Try to understand me.
I love all of you the same.
Help me to be a better mother.

"When I cry I let 'em know. I tell 'em I was a drug addict. They know and they try to help me to hold on. They helpin' me. My children is what's holdin' me together. I'm not makin' it. I'm reachin'. And they see me reachin' out. Angelina take my hand. They come around. They ask me what is wrong. I do let them know when I am scared. But certain things I keep inside. I try to solve it. If it's my department, I don't want them to be sad. If it be too bad, if I be scared of gettin' back on drugs, I'll go to the clinic. They have sessions every other night.

"Hardest time for me is night. Nightmares. Somethin's grabbin' at me. Like a hand. Some spirit's after me. It's somethin' that I don't forget. I wake up in a sweat. I'm wonderin' why I dream these dreams. So I get up, turn on the light. I don't go back to sleep until the day is breakin'. I look up an' I be sayin': 'Sun is up. Now I can go to sleep.'

"After the kids are up and they are dressed and go to school, then I lay down. I go to sleep. But I can't sleep at night. After the sun go down makes me depressed. I want to turn the light on, move around.

"Know that song—'Those Monday Blues'? I had that album once."

I say the title: " 'Monday Blues'?"

"I got 'em every day. Lots of times, when I'm in pain, I think I'm goin' to die. That's why I take a drink sometimes. I'm 'fraid to die. I'm wonderin': Am I dying?"

❖ ❖ ❖

Dynamics

1. At the beginning of his essay, Kozol quotes the historian Michael Ignatieff, who writes that people can be unequal "in their possessions...but also in their rights to judge others." As you re-read "Rachel and Her Children," trace the way that judgment works in Kozol's text. What kinds of judgments seem to carry particular weight in the essay, and for whom? Locate some moments in the text where the idea of judgment becomes especially important or problematic. How are your judgments complicated by those which are made by the people Kozol quotes?

2. In their conversations with Kozol, Rachel and her children show how their experiences of homelessness have shaped their perceptions of the world. As you look back through the essay, be alert to the relationship between "experience" and "belief" for each of these people. At what points does this relationship seem confusing, either to them or to you? What can you conclude about the meaning of this "confusion"?

Critical Tools

1. Before he introduces Rachel, Kozol refers to "policies that undermine the competence and ingenuity" of people like her. Looking closely at what Rachel and her children say about their experiences of homelessness, find some passages that help you to explain what it means to be "undermined." Discuss another text in which you sense that a process of undermining is occurring. How might you use the idea of being undermined to re-frame your interpretation of the second essay?

2. Consider how Kozol use voices—his own, Rachel's, and the children's—as a tool that helps him to build his arguments. Working with one or more readings from *Literacies* in which "voice" (either in Kozol's sense or in some other that you define) seems important to the author's meanings, develop your own theory of voice as a critical tool. Pay close attention to differences between writers' uses of voice in their texts, and speculate about the significance of these differences.

Draft One/Draft Two

Draft One: In one of their conversations together, Rachel tells Jonathan Kozol that her children are treated like "cattle" who are "owned by welfare." Write an essay in which you use some of Rachel's comments about her family's relationship to institutional power in order to evaluate your own relationship to some social institution (school, the health care system, and the military are a few examples). How might her statements need to be revised or challenged in order to make sense in your own context?

Draft Two: Pick another reading from *Literacies* and write an essay in which you use both "Rachel and Her Children" and the conclusions you reached in your first draft as the starting point for a re-consideration of the relationship between individuals and institutional power. In each of these texts—Kozol's, your own, and the new reading that you have chosen—try to determine the conditions that make the exercise of institutional power possible. Then, based on what you have read, discuss the conditions that make (or could make) resistance possible.

❖ ❖ ❖

Before Reading Bernard Lewis. . .

1. What is your understanding of the conflict between the Islamic countries of the Middle East and Western countries like the United States?

2. What are the implications of living in a secular society as opposed to a religious society, as far as you can tell?

The Roots of Muslim Rage

Bernard Lewis

In one of his letters Thomas Jefferson remarked that in matters of religion "the maxim of civil government" should be reversed and we should rather say, "Divided we stand, united, we fall." In this remark Jefferson was setting forth with classic terseness an idea that has come to be regarded as essentially American: the separation of Church and State. This idea was not entirely new; it had some precedents in the writings of Spinoza, Locke, and the philosophers of the European Enlightenment. It was in the United States, however, that the principle was first given the force of law and gradually, in the course of two centuries, became a reality.

If the idea that religion and politics should be separated is relatively new, dating back a mere three hundred years, the idea that they are distinct dates back almost to the beginnings of Christianity. Christians are enjoined in their Scriptures to "render...unto Caesar the things which are Caesar's and unto God the things which are God's." While opinions have differed as to the real meaning of this phrase, it has generally been interpreted as legitimizing a situation in which two institutions exist side by side, each with its own laws and chain of authority—one concerned with religion, called the Church, the other concerned with politics, called the State. And since they are two, they may be joined or separated, subordinate or independent, and conflicts may arise between them over questions of demarcation and jurisdiction.

This formulation of the problems posed by the relations between religion and politics, and the possible solutions to those problems, arise from Christian, not universal, principles and experience. There are other religious traditions in which religion and politics are differently perceived, and in which, therefore, the problems and the possible solutions are radically different from those we know in the West. Most of these traditions, despite their often very high level of sophistication and achievement, remained or became local—limited to one region or one culture or one people. There is one, however, that in its worldwide distribution, its continuing vitality, its universalist aspirations, can be compared to Christianity, and that is Islam.

Islam is one of the world's great religions. Let me be explicit about what I, as a historian of Islam who is not a Muslim, mean by that. Islam has brought comfort and peace of mind to countless millions of men and women. It has given dignity and meaning to drab and impoverished lives. It has taught people of different races to live in brotherhood and people of different creeds to live side by side in reasonable tolerance. It inspired a great civilization in which others besides Muslims lived creative and useful lives and which, by its achievement, enriched the whole world. But Islam, like other religions, has also known periods when it inspired in some of its followers a mood of hatred and violence. It is our misfortune that part, though by no means all or even most, of the Muslim world is now going through such a period, and that much, though again not all, of that hatred is directed against us.

We should not exaggerate the dimensions of the problem. The Muslim world is far from unanimous in its rejection of the West, nor have the Muslim regions of the Third World been the most passionate and the most extreme in their hostility. There are still significant numbers, in some quarters perhaps a majority, of Muslims with whom we share certain basic cultural and moral, social and political, beliefs and aspirations; there is still an imposing Western presence—cultural, economic, diplomatic—in Muslim lands, some of which are Western allies. Certainly nowhere in the Muslim world, in the Middle East or elsewhere, has American policy suffered disasters or encountered problems comparable to those in Southeast Asia or Central America. There is no Cuba, no Vietnam, in the Muslim world, and no place where American forces are involved as combatants or even as "advisers." But there is a Libya, an Iran, and a Lebanon, and a surge of hatred that distresses, alarms, and above all baffles Americans.

At times this hatred goes beyond hostility to specific interests or actions or policies or even countries and becomes a rejection of Western civilization as such, not only what it does but what it is, and the principles and values that it practices and professes. These are indeed seen as innately evil, and those who promote or accept them as the "enemies of God."

This phrase, which recurs so frequently in the language of the Iranian leadership, in both their judicial proceedings and their political pronouncements, must seem very strange to the modern outsider, whether religious or secular. The idea that God has enemies, and needs human help in order to identify and dispose of them, is a little difficult to assimilate. It is not, however, all that alien. The concept of the enemies of God is familiar in preclassical and classical antiquity, and in both the Old and New Testaments, as well as in the Koran. A particularly relevant version of the idea occurs in the dualist religions of ancient Iran, whose cosmogony assumed not one but two supreme powers. The Zoroastrian devil, unlike the Christian or Muslim or Jewish devil, is not one of God's creatures performing some of God's more mysterious tasks but an independent power, a supreme force of evil engaged in a cosmic struggle against God. This belief influenced a number of Christian, Muslim, and Jewish sects, through Manichaeism and other routes. The almost forgotten religion of the Manichees has given its name to the perception of problems as a stark and simple conflict between matching forces of pure good and pure evil.

The Koran is of course strictly monotheistic, and recognizes one God, one universal power only. There is a struggle in human hearts between good and evil, between God's commandments and the tempter, but this is seen as a struggle ordained by God, with its outcome preordained by God, serving as a test of mankind, and not, as in some of the old dualist religions, a struggle in which mankind has a crucial part to play in bringing about the victory of good over evil. Despite this monotheism, Islam, like Judaism and Christianity, was at various stages influenced, especially in Iran, by the dualist idea of a cosmic clash of good and evil, light and darkness, order and chaos, truth and falsehood, God and the Adversary, variously known as devil, Iblis, Satan, and by other names.

The Rise of the House of Unbelief

In Islam the struggle of good and evil very soon acquired political and even military dimensions. Muhammad, it will be recalled, was not only a prophet and a teacher, like the founders of other religions; he was also the head of a polity and of a community, a ruler and a soldier. Hence his struggle involved a state and its armed forces. If the fighters in the war for Islam, the holy war "in the path of God," are fighting for God, it follows that their opponents are fighting against God. And since God is in principle the sovereign, the supreme head of the Islamic state—and the Prophet and, after the Prophet, the caliphs are his vicegerents—then God as sovereign commands the army. The army is God's army and the enemy is God's enemy. The duty of God's soldiers is to dispatch God's enemies as quickly as possible to the place where God will chastise them—that is to say, the afterlife.

Clearly related to this is the basic division of mankind as perceived in Islam. Most, probably all, human societies have a way of distinguishing between themselves and others: insider and outsider, in-group and out-group, kinsman or neighbor and foreigner. These definitions not only define the outsider but also, and perhaps more particularly, help to define and illustrate our perception of ourselves.

In the classical Islamic view, to which many Muslims are beginning to return, the world and all mankind are divided into two: the House of Islam, where the Muslim law and faith prevail, and the rest, known as the House of Unbelief or the House of War, which it is the duty of Muslims ultimately to bring to Islam. But the greater part of the world is still outside Islam, and even inside the Islamic lands, according to the view of the Muslim radicals, the faith of Islam has been undermined and the law of Islam has been abrogated. The obligation of holy war therefore begins at home and continues abroad, against the same infidel enemy.

Like every other civilization known to human history, the Muslim world in its heyday saw itself as the center of truth and enlightenment, surrounded by infidel barbarians whom it would in due course enlighten and civilize. But between the different groups of barbarians there was a crucial difference. The barbarians to the east and the south were polytheists and idolaters, offering no serious threat and no competition at all to Islam. In the north and west, in contrast, Muslims from an early date recognized a genuine rival—a competing world religion, a distinctive civilization inspired by that religion, and an empire that, though much smaller than theirs, was no less ambitious in its claims and aspirations. This was the entity known to itself and others as Christendom, a term that was long almost identical with Europe.

The struggle between these rival systems has now lasted for some fourteen centuries. It began with the advent of Islam, in the seventh century, and has continued virtually to the present day. It has consisted of a long series of attacks and counterattacks, jihads and crusades, conquests and reconquests. For the first thousand years Islam was advancing, Christendom in retreat and under threat. The new faith conquered the old Christian lands of the Levant and North Africa, and invaded Europe, ruling for a while in Sicily, Spain, Portugal, and even parts of France. The attempt by the Crusaders to recover the lost lands of Christendom in the east was held and thrown back, and even the Muslims' loss of southwestern Europe to the Reconquista was amply compensated by the Islamic advance into southeastern Europe, which twice reached as far as Vienna. For the past three hundred years, since the failure of the second Turkish siege of Vienna in 1683 and the rise of the European colonial empires in Asia and Africa, Islam has been on the defensive, and the Christian and post-Christian civilization of Europe and her daughters has brought the whole world, including Islam, within its orbit.

For a long time now there has been a rising tide of rebellion against this Western paramountcy, and a desire to reassert Muslim values and restore Muslim greatness. The Muslim has suffered successive stages of defeat. The first was his loss of domination in the world, to the advancing power of Russia and the West. The second was the undermining of his authority in his own country, through an invasion of foreign ideas and laws and ways of life and sometimes even foreign rulers or settlers, and the enfranchisement of native non-Muslim elements. The third—the last straw—was the challenge to his mastery in his own house, from emancipated women and rebellious children. It was too much to endure, and the outbreak of rage against these alien, infidel, and incomprehensible forces that had subverted his dominance, disrupted his society, and finally violated the sanctuary of his home was inevitable. It was also natural that this rage should be directed primarily against the millennial enemy and should draw its strength from ancient beliefs and loyalties.

Europe and her daughters? The phrase may seem odd to Americans, whose national myths, since the beginning of their nationhood and even earlier, have usually defined their very identity in opposition to Europe, as something new and radically different from the old European ways. This is not, however, the way that others have seen it; not often in Europe, and hardly ever elsewhere.

Though people of other races and cultures participated, for the most part involuntarily, in the discovery and creation of the Americas, this was, and in the eyes of the rest of the world long remained, a European enterprise, in which Europeans predominated and dominated and to which Europeans gave their languages, their religions, and much of their way of life.

For a very long time voluntary immigration to America was almost exclusively European. There were indeed some who came from the Muslim lands in the Middle East and North Africa, but few were Muslims; most were members of the Christian and to a lesser extent the Jewish minorities in those countries. Their departure for America, and their subsequent presence in America, must have strengthened rather than lessened the European image of America in Muslim eyes.

In the lands of Islam remarkably little was known about America. At first the voyages of discovery aroused some interest; the only surviving copy of Columbus's own map of America is a Turkish translation and adaptation, still preserved in the Topkapi Palace Museum, in Istanbul. A sixteenth-century Turkish geographer's account of the discovery of the New World, titled *The History of Western India*, was one of the first books printed in Turkey. But thereafter interest seems to have waned, and not much is said about America in Turkish, Arabic, or other Muslim languages until a relatively late date. A Moroccan ambassador who was in Spain at the time wrote what must surely be the first Arabic account of the American Revolution. The Sultan of Morocco signed a treaty of peace and friendship with the United States in 1787, and thereafter the new republic had a number of dealings, some friendly, some hostile, most commercial, with other Muslim states. These seem to have had little impact on either side. The American Revolution and the American republic to which it gave birth long remained unnoticed and unknown. Even the small but growing American presence in Muslim lands in the nineteenth century— merchants, consuls, missionaries, and teachers—aroused little or no curiosity, and is almost unmentioned in the Muslim literature and newspapers of the time.

The Second World War, the oil industry, and postwar developments brought many Americans to the Islamic lands; increasing numbers of Muslims also came to America, first as students, then as teachers or businessmen or other visitors, and eventually as immigrants. Cinema and later television brought the American way of life, or at any rate a certain version of it, before countless millions to whom the very name of America had previously been meaningless or unknown. A wide range of American products, particularly in the immediate postwar years, when European competition was virtually eliminated and Japanese competition had not yet arisen, reached into the remotest markets of the Muslim world, winning new customers and, perhaps more important, creating new tastes and ambitions. For some, America represented freedom and justice and opportunity. For many more, it represented wealth and power and success, at a time when these qualities were not regarded as sins or crimes.

And then came the great change, when the leaders of a widespread and widening religious revival sought out and identified their enemies as the enemies of God, and gave them "a local habitation and a name" in the Western Hemisphere. Suddenly, or so it seemed, America had become the archenemy, the incarnation of evil, the diabolic opponent of all that is good, and specifically, for Muslims, of Islam. Why?

Some Familiar Accusations

Among the components in the mood of anti-Westernism, and more especially of anti-Americanism, were certain intellectual influences coming from Europe. One of these was from Germany, where a negative view of America formed part of a school of thought by no means limited to the Nazis but including writers as diverse as Rainer Maria Rilke, Ernst Jünger, and Martin Heidegger. In this perception, America was the ultimate example of civilization without culture: rich and comfortable, materially advanced but soulless and artificial; assembled or at best constructed, not grown; mechanical, not organic; technologically complex but lacking the spirituality and vitality of the rooted, human, national cultures of the Germans and other "authentic" peoples. German philosophy, and particularly the philosophy of education, enjoyed a considerable vogue among Arab and some other Muslim intellectuals in the thirties and early forties, and this philosophic anti-Americanism was part of the message.

After the collapse of the Third Reich and the temporary ending of German influence, another philosophy, even more anti-American, took its place—the Soviet version of Marxism, with a denunciation of Western capitalism and of America as its most advanced and dangerous embodiment. And when Soviet influence began to fade, there was yet another to take its place, or at least to supplement its working—the new mystique of Third Worldism, emanating from Western Europe, particularly France, and later also from the United States, and drawing at times on both these earlier philosophies. This mystique was helped by the universal human tendency to invent a golden age in the past, and the specifically European propensity to locate it elsewhere. A new variant of the old golden-age myth placed it in the Third World, where the innocence of the non-Western Adam and Eve was ruined by the Western serpent. This view took as axiomatic the goodness and purity of the East and the wickedness of the West, expanding in an exponential curve of evil from Western Europe to the United States. These ideas, too, fell on fertile ground, and won widespread support.

But though these imported philosophies helped to provide intellectual expression for anti-Westernism and anti-Americanism, they did not cause it, and certainly they do not explain the widespread anti-Westernism that made so many in the Middle East and elsewhere in the Islamic world receptive to such ideas.

It must surely be clear that what won support for such totally diverse doctrines was not Nazi race theory, which can have had little appeal for Arabs, or Soviet atheistic communism, which can have had little appeal for Muslims, but rather their common anti-Westernism. Nazism and communism were the main forces opposed to the West, both as a way of life and as a power in the world, and as such they could count on at least the sympathy if not the support of those who saw in the West their principal enemy.

But why the hostility in the first place? If we turn from the general to the specific, there is no lack of individual policies and actions, pursued and taken by individual Western governments, that have aroused the passionate anger of Middle

Eastern and other Islamic peoples. Yet all too often, when these policies are abandoned and the problems resolved, there is only a local and temporary alleviation. The French have left Algeria, the British have left Egypt, the Western oil companies have left their oil wells, the westernizing Shah has left Iran—yet the generalized resentment of the fundamentalists and other extremists against the West and its friends remains and grows and is not appeased.

The cause most frequently adduced for anti-American feeling among Muslims today is American support for Israel. This support is certainly a factor of importance, increasing with nearness and involvement. But here again there are some oddities, difficult to explain in terms of a single, simple cause. In the early days of the foundation of Israel, while the United States maintained a certain distance, the Soviet Union granted immediate *de jure* recognition and support, and arms sent from a Soviet satellite, Czechoslovakia, saved the infant state of Israel from defeat and death in its first weeks of life. Yet there seems to have been no great ill will toward the Soviets for these policies, and no corresponding good will toward the United States. In 1956 it was the United States that intervened, forcefully and decisively, to secure the withdrawal of Israeli, British, and French forces from Egypt—yet in the late fifties and sixties it was to the Soviets, not America, that the rulers of Egypt, Syria, Iraq, and other states turned for arms; it was with the Soviet bloc that they formed bonds of solidarity at the United Nations and in the world generally. More recently, the rulers of the Islamic Republic of Iran have offered the most principled and uncompromising denunciation of Israel and Zionism. Yet even these leaders, before as well as after the death of Ayatollah Ruhollah Khomeini, when they decided for reasons of their own to enter into a dialogue of sorts, found it easier to talk to Jerusalem than to Washington. At the same time, Western hostages in Lebanon, many of them devoted to Arab causes and some of them converts to Islam, are seen and treated by their captors as limbs of the Great Satan.

Another explanation, more often heard from Muslim dissidents, attributes anti-American feeling to American support for hated regimes, seen as reactionary by radicals, as impious by conservatives, as corrupt and tyrannical by both. This accusation has some plausibility, and could help to explain why an essentially inner-directed, often anti-nationalist movement should turn against a foreign power. But it does not suffice, especially since support for such regimes has been limited both in extent and—as the Shah discovered—in effectiveness.

Clearly, something deeper is involved than these specific grievances, numerous and important as they may be—something deeper that turns every disagreement into a problem and makes every problem insoluble.

This revulsion against America, more generally against the West, is by no means limited to the Muslim world; nor have Muslims, with the exception of the Iranian mullahs and their disciples elsewhere, experienced and exhibited the more virulent forms of this feeling. The mood of disillusionment and hostility has affected many other parts of the world, and has even reached some elements in the United

States. It is from these last, speaking for themselves and claiming to speak for the oppressed peoples of the Third World, that the most widely publicized explanations—and justifications—of this rejection of Western civilization and its values have of late been heard.

The accusations are familiar. We of the West are accused of sexism, racism, and imperialism, institutionalized in patriarchy and slavery, tyranny and exploitation. To these charges, and to others as heinous, we have no option but to plead guilty—not as Americans, nor yet as Westerners, but simply as human beings, as members of the human race. In none of these sins are we the only sinners, and in some of them we are very far from being the worst. The treatment of women in the Western world, and more generally in Christendom, has always been unequal and often oppressive, but even at its worst it was rather better than the rule of polygamy and concubinage that has otherwise been the almost universal lot of womankind on this planet.

Is racism, then, the main grievance? Certainly the word figures prominently in publicity addressed to Western, Eastern European, and some Third World audiences. It figures less prominently in what is written and published for home consumption, and has become a generalized and meaningless term of abuse—rather like "fascism," which is nowadays imputed to opponents even by spokesmen for one-party, nationalist dictatorships of various complexions and shirt colors.

Slavery is today universally denounced as an offense against humanity, but within living memory it has been practiced and even defended as a necessary institution, established and regulated by divine law. The peculiarity of the peculiar institution, as Americans once called it, lay not in its existence but in its abolition. Westerners were the first to break the consensus of acceptance and to outlaw slavery, first at home, then in the other territories they controlled, and finally wherever in the world they were able to exercise power or influence—in a word, by means of imperialism.

Is imperialism, then, the grievance? Some Western powers, and in a sense Western civilization as a whole, have certainly been guilty of imperialism, but are we really to believe that in the expansion of Western Europe there was a quality of moral delinquency lacking in such earlier, relatively innocent expansions as those of the Arabs or the Mongols or the Ottomans, or in more recent expansions such as that which brought the rulers of Muscovy to the Baltic, the Black Sea, the Caspian, the Hindu Kush, and the Pacific Ocean? In having practiced sexism, racism, and imperialism, the West was merely following the common practice of mankind through the millennia of recorded history. Where it is distinct from all other civilizations is in having recognized, named, and tried, not entirely without success, to remedy these historic diseases. And that is surely a matter for congratulation, not condemnation. We do not hold Western medical science in general, or Dr. Parkinson and Dr. Alzheimer in particular, responsible for the diseases they diagnosed and to which they gave their names.

Of all these offenses the one that is most widely, frequently, and vehemently denounced is undoubtedly imperialism—sometimes just Western, sometimes Eastern (that is, Soviet) and Western alike. But the way this term is used in the literature of Islamic fundamentalists often suggests that it may not carry quite the same meaning for them as for its Western critics. In many of these writings the term "imperialist" is given a distinctly religious significance, being used in association, and sometimes interchangeably, with "missionary," and denoting a form of attack that includes the Crusades as well as the modern colonial empires. One also sometimes gets the impression that the offense of imperialism is not—as for Western critics—the domination by one people over another but rather the allocation of roles in this relationship. What is truly evil and unacceptable is the domination of infidels over true believers. For true believers to rule misbelievers is proper and natural, since this provides for the maintenance of the holy law, and gives the misbelievers both the opportunity and the incentive to embrace the true faith. But for misbelievers to rule over true believers is blasphemous and unnatural, since it leads to the corruption of religion and morality in society, and to the flouting or even the abrogation of God's law. This may help us to understand the current troubles in such diverse places as Ethiopian Eritrea, Indian Kashmir, Chinese Sinkiang, and Yugoslav Kossovo, in all of which Muslim populations are ruled by non-Muslim governments. It may also explain why spokesmen for the new Muslim minorities in Western Europe demand for Islam a degree of legal protection which those countries no longer give to Christianity and have never given to Judaism. Nor, of course, did the governments of the countries of origin of these Muslim spokesmen ever accord such protection to religions other than their own. In their perception, there is no contradiction in these attitudes. The true faith, based on God's final revelation, must be protected from insult and abuse; other faiths, being either false or incomplete, have no right to any such protection.

There are other difficulties in the way of accepting imperialism as an explanation of Muslim hostility, even if we define imperialism narrowly and specifically, as the invasion and domination of Muslim countries by non-Muslims. If the hostility is directed against imperialism in that sense, why has it been so much stronger against Western Europe, which has relinquished all its Muslim possessions and dependencies, than against Russia, which still rules, with no light hand, over many millions of reluctant Muslim subjects and over ancient Muslim cities and countries? And why should it include the United States, which, apart from a brief interlude in the Muslim-minority area of the Philippines, has never ruled any Muslim population? The last surviving European empire with Muslim subjects, that of the Soviet Union, far from being the target of criticism and attack, has been almost exempt. Even the most recent repressions of Muslim revolts in the southern and central Asian republics of the USSR incurred no more than relatively mild words of expostulation, coupled with a disclaimer of any desire to interfere in what are quaintly called the "internal affairs" of the USSR and a request for the preservation of order and tranquillity on the frontier.

One reason for this somewhat surprising restraint is to be found in the nature of events in Soviet Azerbaijan. Islam is obviously an important and potentially a growing element in the Azerbaijani sense of identity, but it is not at present a dominant element, and the Azerbaijani movement has more in common with the liberal patriotism of Europe than with Islamic fundamentalism. Such a movement would not arouse the sympathy of the rulers of the Islamic Republic. It might even alarm them, since a genuinely democratic national state run by the people of Soviet Azerbaijan would exercise a powerful attraction on their kinsmen immediately to the south, in Iranian Azerbaijan.

Another reason for this relative lack of concern for the 50 million or more Muslims under Soviet rule may be a calculation of risk and advantage. The Soviet Union is near, along the northern frontiers of Turkey, Iran, and Afghanistan; America and even Western Europe are far away. More to the point, it has not hitherto been the practice of the Soviets to quell disturbances with water cannon and rubber bullets, with TV cameras in attendance, or to release arrested persons on bail and allow them access to domestic and foreign media. The Soviets do not interview their harshest critics on prime time, or tempt them with teaching, lecturing, and writing engagements. On the contrary, their ways of indicating displeasure with criticism can often be quite disagreeable.

But fear of reprisals, though no doubt important, is not the only or perhaps even the principal reason for the relatively minor place assigned to the Soviet Union, as compared with the West, in the demonology of fundamentalism. After all, the great social and intellectual and economic changes that have transformed most of the Islamic world, and given rise to such commonly denounced Western evils as consumerism and secularism, emerged from the West, not from the Soviet Union. No one could accuse the Soviets of consumerism; their materialism is philosophic—to be precise, dialectical—and has little or nothing to do in practice with providing the good things of life. Such provision represents another kind of materialism, often designated by its opponents as crass. It is associated with the capitalist West and not with the communist East, which has practiced, or at least imposed on its subjects, a degree of austerity that would impress a Sufi saint.

Nor were the Soviets, until very recently, vulnerable to charges of secularism, the other great fundamentalist accusation against the West. Though atheist, they were not godless, and had in fact created an elaborate state apparatus to impose the worship of their gods—an apparatus with its own orthodoxy, a hierarchy to define and enforce it, and an armed inquisition to detect and extirpate heresy. The separation of religion from the state does not mean the establishment of irreligion by the state, still less the forcible imposition of an anti-religious philosophy. Soviet secularism, like Soviet consumerism, holds no temptation for the Muslim masses, and is losing what appeal it had for Muslim intellectuals. More than ever before it is Western capitalism and democracy that provide an authentic and attractive alternative to traditional ways of thought and life. Fundamentalist leaders are not mistaken in seeing in Western civilization the greatest challenge to the way of life that they wish to retain or restore for their people.

A Clash of Civilizations

The origins of secularism in the west may be found in two circumstances—in early Christian teachings and, still more, experience, which created two institutions, Church and State; and in later Christian conflicts, which drove the two apart. Muslims, too, had their religious disagreements, but there was nothing remotely approaching the ferocity of the Christian struggles between Protestants and Catholics, which devastated Christian Europe in the sixteenth and seventeenth centuries and finally drove Christians in desperation to evolve a doctrine of the separation of religion from the state. Only by depriving religious institutions of coercive power, it seemed, could Christendom restrain the murderous intolerance and persecution that Christians had visited on followers of other religions and, most of all, on those who professed other forms of their own.

Muslims experienced no such need and evolved no such doctrine. There was no need for secularism in Islam, and even its pluralism was very different from that of the pagan Roman Empire, so vividly described by Edward Gibbon when he remarked that "the various modes of worship, which prevailed in the Roman world, were all considered by the people, as equally true; by the philosopher, as equally false; and by the magistrate, as equally useful." Islam was never prepared, either in theory or in practice, to accord full equality to those who held other beliefs and practiced other forms of worship. It did, however, accord to the holders of partial truth a degree of practical as well as theoretical tolerance rarely paralleled in the Christian world until the West adopted a measure of secularism in the late-seventeenth and eighteenth centuries.

At first the Muslim response to Western civilization was one of admiration and emulation—an immense respect for the achievements of the West, and a desire to imitate and adopt them. This desire arose from a keen and growing awareness of the weakness, poverty, and backwardness of the Islamic world as compared with the advancing West. The disparity first became apparent on the battlefield but soon spread to other areas of human activity. Muslim writers observed and described the wealth and power of the West, its science and technology, its manufactures, and its forms of government. For a time the secret of Western success was seen to lie in two achievements: economic advancement and especially industry; political institutions and especially freedom. Several generations of reformers and modernizers tried to adapt these and introduce them to their own countries, in the hope that they would thereby be able to achieve equality with the West and perhaps restore their lost superiority.

In our own time this mood of admiration and emulation has, among many Muslims, given way to one of hostility and rejection. In part this mood is surely due to a feeling of humiliation—a growing awareness, among the heirs of an old, proud, and long dominant civilization, of having been overtaken, overborne, and over-whelmed by those whom they regarded as their inferiors. In part this mood is due to events in the Western world itself. One factor of major importance was certainly the impact of two great suicidal wars, in which Western civilization tore itself apart, bringing untold destruction to its own and other peoples, and in which the belligerents conducted an immense propaganda effort, in the Islamic world and elsewhere, to discredit and undermine each other. The message they brought found many listeners, who were all the more ready to respond in that their own experience of Western ways was not happy. The introduction of Western commercial, financial, and industrial methods did indeed bring great wealth, but it accrued to transplanted Westerners and members of Westernized minorities, and to only a few among the mainstream Muslim population. In time these few became more numerous, but they remained isolated from the masses, differing from them even in their dress and style of life. Inevitably they were seen as agents of and collaborators with what was once again regarded as a hostile world. Even the political institutions that had come from the West were discredited, being judged not by their Western originals but by their local imitations, installed by enthusiastic Muslim reformers. These, operating in a situation beyond their control, using imported and inappropriate methods that they did not fully understand, were unable to cope with the rapidly developing crises and were one by one overthrown. For vast numbers of Middle Easterners, Western-style economic methods brought poverty, Western-style political institutions brought tyranny, even Western-style warfare brought defeat. It is hardly surprising that so many were willing to listen to voices telling them that the old Islamic ways were best and that their only salvation was to throw aside the pagan innovations of the reformers and return to the True Path that God had prescribed for his people.

Ultimately, the struggle of the fundamentalists is against two enemies, secularism and modernism. The war against secularism is conscious and explicit, and there is by now a whole literature denouncing secularism as an evil neo-pagan force in the modern world and attributing it variously to the Jews, the West, and the United States. The war against modernity is for the most part neither conscious nor explicit, and is directed against the whole process of change that has taken place in the Islamic world in the past century or more and has transformed the political, economic, social, and even cultural structures of Muslim countries. Islamic fundamentalism has given an aim and a form to the otherwise aimless and formless resentment and anger of the Muslim masses at the forces that have devalued their traditional values and loyalties and, in the final analysis, robbed them of their beliefs, their aspirations, their dignity, and to an increasing extent even their livelihood.

There is something in the religious culture of Islam which inspired, in even the humblest peasant or peddler, a dignity and a courtesy toward others never exceeded and rarely equalled in other civilizations. And yet, in moments of upheaval and disruption, when the deeper passions are stirred, this dignity and courtesy toward others can give way to an explosive mixture of rage and hatred which impels even the government of an ancient and civilized country—even the spokesman of a great spiritual and ethical religion—to espouse kidnapping and assassination, and try to find, in the life of their Prophet, approval and indeed precedent for such actions.

The instinct of the masses is not false in locating the ultimate source of these cataclysmic changes in the West and in attributing the disruption of their old way of life to the impact of Western domination, Western influence, or Western precept and example. And since the United States is the legitimate heir of European civilization and the recognized and unchallenged leader of the West, the United States has inherited the resulting grievances and become the focus for the pent-up hate and anger. Two examples may suffice. In November of 1979 an angry mob attacked and burned the U.S. Embassy in Islamabad, Pakistan. The stated cause of the crowd's anger was the seizure of the Great Mosque in Mecca by a group of Muslim dissidents—an event in which there was no American involvement whatsoever. Almost ten years later, in February of 1989, again in Islamabad, the USIS center was attacked by angry crowds, this time to protest the publication of Salman Rushdie's *Satanic Verses*. Rushdie is a British citizen of Indian birth, and his book had been published five months previously in England. But what provoked the mob's anger, and also the Ayatollah Khomeini's subsequent pronouncement of a death sentence on the author, was the publication of the book in the United States.

It should by now be clear that we are facing a mood and a movement far transcending the level of issues and policies and the governments that pursue them. This is no less than a clash of civilizations—the perhaps irrational but surely historic reaction of an ancient rival against our Judeo-Christian heritage, our secular present, and the worldwide expansion of both. It is crucially important that we on our side should not be provoked into an equally historic but also equally irrational reaction against that rival.

Not all the ideas imported from the West by Western intruders or native Westernizers have been rejected. Some have been accepted by even the most radical Islamic fundamentalists, usually without acknowledgment of source, and suffering a sea of change into something rarely rich but often strange. One such was political freedom, with the associated notions and practices of representation, election, and constitutional government. Even the Islamic Republic of Iran has a written constitution and an elected assembly, as well as a kind of episcopate, for none of which is there any prescription in Islamic teaching or any precedent in the Islamic past. All these institutions are clearly adapted from Western models. Muslim states have also retained many of the cultural and social customs of the West and the symbols that express them, such as the form and style of male (and to a much lesser extent female) clothing, notably in the military. The use of Western-invented guns and tanks and planes is a military necessity, but the continued use of fitted tunics and peaked caps is a cultural choice. From constitutions to Coca-Cola, from tanks and television to T-shirts, the symbols and artifacts, and through them the ideas, of the West have retained—even strengthened—their appeal.

The movement nowadays called fundamentalism is not the only Islamic tradition. There are others, more tolerant, more open, that helped to inspire the great achievements of Islamic civilization in the past, and we may hope that these other traditions will in time prevail. But before this issue is decided there will be a hard struggle, in which we of the West can do little or nothing. Even the attempt might do harm, for these are issues that Muslims must decide among themselves. And in the meantime we must take great care on all sides to avoid the danger of a new era of religious wars, arising from the exacerbation of differences and the revival of ancient prejudices.

To this end we must strive to achieve a better appreciation of other religious and political cultures, through the study of their history, their literature, and their achievements. At the same time, we may hope that they will try to achieve a better understanding of ours, and especially that they will understand and respect, even if they do not choose to adopt for themselves, our Western perception of the proper relationship between religion and politics.

To describe this perception I shall end as I began, with a quotation from an American President, this time not the justly celebrated Thomas Jefferson but the somewhat unjustly neglected John Tyler, who, in a letter dated July 10, 1843, gave eloquent and indeed prophetic expression to the principle of religious freedom:

> *The United States have adventured upon a great and noble experiment, which is believed to have been hazarded in the absence of all previous precedent—that of total separation of Church and State. No religious establishment by law exists among us. The conscience is left free from all restraint and each is permitted to worship his Maker after his own judgement. The offices of the Government are open alike to all. No tithes are levied to support an established Hierarchy, nor is the fallible judgement of man set up as the sure and infallible creed of faith. The Mahommedan, if he will to come among us would have the privilege guaranteed to him by the constitution to worship according to the Koran; and the East Indian might erect a shrine to Brahma if it so pleased him. Such is the spirit of toleration inculcated by our political Institutions.... The Hebrew persecuted and downtrodden in other regions takes up his abode among us with none to make him afraid.... and the Aegis of the Government is over him to defend and protect him. Such is the great experiment which we have tried, and such are the happy fruits which have resulted from it; our system of free government would be imperfect without it.*
>
> *The body may be oppressed and manacled and yet survive; but if the mind of man be fettered, its energies and faculties perish, and what remains is of the earth, earthly. Mind should be free as the light or as the air.*

❖ ❖ ❖

Dynamics

1. Lewis organizes his essay in part on a succession of possible or partial explanations. Review several of these partial explanations and describe the effect this organizing strategy has on his argument.

2. What, finally, are the important similarities and differences that Lewis notes between these two cultures? How do you situate yourself in the debate between cultures that he describes?

Critical Tools

1. Lewis argues that "our ways of distinguishing between [ourselves] and others....not only define the outsider but also, and perhaps more particularly, help to define and illustrate our perception of ourselves." Locate an example or two in his essay and explain how this process works, and then apply your understanding to a cultural encounter represented in another *Literacies* text.

2. Try out the organizing technique you studied in Dynamics Question 1 by choosing about three *Literacies* texts that each offer a critical tool or perspective, then using them in succession as Lewis does to examine a problem described in another text. Comment on the results of this procedure in your essay and in Lewis's.

Draft One/Draft Two

Draft One: Catalog the concepts and definitions of America, both critical and otherwise, that Lewis mentions, and test them against the your experience. What is the significance of your findings?

Draft Two: Extend your first draft by considering the American experience described in another *Literacies* text. How do the various perspectives illuminate or complicate each other? What aspects of American life do you find highlighted by this study, and why?

❖ ❖ ❖

Before Reading Audre Lorde. . .

1. Examine experiences of anger, both your own and that of others. In which instances has anger been an instructive or constructive force? What similarities unite these instances?

2. How, in your view, might the dynamics of a speech or talk be different from those of written expression? Explain your answer with a detailed hypothetical example or two.

The Uses of Anger:
Women Responding to Racism

Audre Lorde

Racism. The belief in the inherent superiority of one race over all others and thereby the right to dominance, manifest and implied.

Women respond to racism. My response to racism is anger. I have lived with that anger, ignoring it, feeding upon it, learning to use it before it laid my visions to waste, for most of my life. Once I did it in silence, afraid of the weight. My fear of anger taught me nothing. Your fear of that anger will teach you nothing, also.

Women responding to racism means women responding to anger; the anger of exclusion, of unquestioned privilege, of racial distortions, of silence, ill-use, stereotyping, defensiveness, misnaming, betrayal, and co-optation.

My anger is a response to racist attitudes and to the actions and presumptions that arise out of those attitudes. If your dealings with other women reflect those attitudes, then my anger and your attendant fears are spotlights that can be used for growth in the same way I have used learning to express anger for my growth. But for corrective surgery, not guilt. Guilt and defensiveness are bricks in a wall against which we all flounder; they serve none of our futures.

Because I do not want this to become a theoretical discussion, I am going to give a few examples of interchanges between women that illustrate these points. In the interest of time, I am going to cut them short. I want you to know there were many more. For example:

- I speak out of direct and particular anger at an academic conference, and a white woman says, "Tell me how you feel but don't say it too harshly or I cannot hear you." But is it my manner that keeps her from hearing, or the threat of a message that her life may change?
- The Women's Studies Program of a southern university invites a Black woman to read following a week-long forum on Black and white women. "What has this week given to you?" I ask. The most vocal white woman says, "I think I've

gotten a lot. I feel Black women really understand me a lot better now; they have a better idea of where I'm coming from." As if understanding her lay at the core of the racist problem.

■ After fifteen years of a women's movement which professes to address the life concerns and possible futures of all women, I still hear, on campus after campus, "How can we address the issues of racism? No women of Color attended." Or, the other side of that statement, "We have no one in our department equipped to teach their work." In other words, racism is a Black women's problem, a problem of women of Color, and only we can discuss it.

■ After I read from my work entitled "Poems for Women in Rage,"[1] a white woman asks me: "Are you going to do anything with how we can deal directly with *our* anger? I feel it's so important." I ask, "How do you use *your* rage?" And then I have to turn away from the blank look in her eyes, before she can invite me to participate in her own annihilation. I do not exist to feel her anger for her.

■ White women are beginning to examine their relationships to Black women, yet often I hear them wanting only to deal with little colored children across the roads of childhood, the beloved nursemaid, the occasional second-grade classmate—those tender memories of what was once mysterious and intriguing or neutral. You avoid the childhood assumptions formed by the raucous laughter at Rastus and Alfalfa, the acute message of your mommy's handkerchief spread upon the park bench because I had just been sitting there, the indelible and dehumanizing portraits of Amos 'n' Andy and your daddy's humorous bedtime stories.

■ I wheel my two-year-old daughter in a shopping cart through a supermarket in Eastchester in 1967, and a little white girl riding past in her mother's cart calls out excitedly, "Oh look, Mommy, a baby maid!" And your mother shushes you, but she does not correct you. And so fifteen years later, at a conference on racism, you can still find that story humorous. But I hear your laughter is full of terror and dis-ease.

■ A white academic welcomes the appearance of a collection by non-Black women of Color.[2] "It allows me to deal with racism without dealing with the harshness of Black women," she says to me.

■ At an international cultural gathering of women, a well-known white American woman poet interrupts the reading of the work of women of Color to read her own poem, and then dashes off to an "important panel."

If women in the academy truly want a dialogue about racism, it will require recognizing the needs and the living contexts of other women. When an academic woman says, "I can't afford it," she may mean she is making a choice about how to spend her available money. But when a woman on welfare says, "I can't afford it," she means she is surviving on an amount of money that was barely subsistence in

1972, and she often does not have enough to eat. Yet the National Women's Studies Association here in 1981 holds a conference in which it commits itself to responding to racism, yet refuses to waive the registration fee for poor women and women of Color who wished to be present and conduct workshops. This has made it impossible for many women of Color—for instance, Wilmette Brown, of Black Women for Wages for Housework—to participate in this conference. Is this to be merely another case of the academy discussing life within the closed circuits of the academy?

To the white women present who recognize these attitudes as familiar, but most of all, to all my sisters of Color who live and survive thousands of such encounters—to my sisters of Color who like me still tremble their rage under harness, or who sometimes question the expression of our rage as useless and disruptive (the two most popular accusations)—I want to speak about anger, my anger, and what I have learned from my travels through its dominions.

Everything can be used / except what is wasteful / (you will need / to remember this when you are accused of destruction.)[3]

Every woman has a well-stocked arsenal of anger potentially useful against those oppressions, personal and institutional, which brought that anger into being. Focused with precision it can become a powerful source of energy serving progress and change. And when I speak of change, I do not mean a simple switch of position or a temporary lessening of tensions, nor the ability to smile or feel good. I am speaking of a basic and radical alteration in those assumptions underlining our lives.

I have seen situations where white women hear a racist remark, resent what has been said, become filled with fury, and remain silent because they are afraid. That unexpressed anger lies within them like an undetonated device, usually to be hurled at the first woman of Color who talks about racism.

But anger expressed and translated into action in the service of our vision and our future is a liberating and strengthening act of clarification, for it is in the painful process of this translation that we identify who are our allies with whom we have grave differences, and who are our genuine enemies.

Anger is loaded with information and energy. When I speak of women of Color, I do not only mean Black women. The woman of Color who is not Black and who charges me with rendering her invisible by assuming that her struggles with racism are identical with my own has something to tell me that I had better learn from, lest we both waste ourselves fighting the truths between us. If I participate, knowingly or otherwise, in my sister's oppression and she calls me on it, to answer her anger with my own only blankets the substance of our exchange with reaction. It wastes energy. And yes, it is very difficult to stand still and to listen to another woman's voice delineate an agony I do not share, or one to which I myself have contributed.

In this place we speak removed from the more blatant reminders of our embattlement as women. This need not blind us to the size and complexities of the forces mounting against us and all that is most human within our environment. We are not here as women examining racism in a political and social vacuum. We operate in the teeth of a system for which racism and sexism are primary, established, and necessary props of profit. Women responding to racism is a topic so dangerous that when the local media attempt to discredit this conference they choose to focus upon the provision of lesbian housing as a diversionary device—as if the Hartford *Courant* dare not mention the topic chosen for discussion here, racism, lest it become apparent that women are in fact attempting to examine and to alter all the repressive conditions of our lives.

Mainstream communication does not want women, particularly white women, responding to racism. It wants racism to be accepted as an immutable given in the fabric of your existence, like eveningtime or the common cold.

So we are working in a context of opposition and threat, the cause of which is certainly not the angers which lie between us, but rather that virulent hatred leveled against all women, people of Color, lesbians and gay men, poor people—against all of us who are seeking to examine the particulars of our lives as we resist our oppressions, moving toward coalition and effective action.

Any discussion among women about racism must include the recognition and the use of anger. This discussion must be direct and creative because it is crucial. We cannot allow our fear of anger to deflect us nor seduce us into settling for anything less than the hard work of excavating honesty; we must be quite serious about the choice of this topic and the angers entwined within it because, rest assured, our opponents are quite serious about their hatred of us and of what we are trying to do here.

And while we scrutinize the often painful face of each other's anger, please remember that it is not our anger which makes me caution you to lock your doors at night and not to wander the streets of Hartford alone. It is the hatred which lurks in those streets, that urge to destroy us all if we truly work for change rather than merely indulge in academic rhetoric.

This hatred and our anger are very different. Hatred is the fury of those who do not share our goals, and its object is death and destruction. Anger is a grief of distortions between peers, and its object is change. But our time is getting shorter. We have been raised to view any difference other than sex as a reason for destruction, and for Black women and white women to face each other's angers without denial or immobility or silence or guilt is in itself a heretical and generative idea. It implies peers meeting upon a common basis to examine difference, and to alter those distortions which history has created around our difference. For it is those distortions which separate us. And we must ask ourselves: Who profits from all this?

Women of Color in america have grown up within a symphony of anger, at being silenced, at being unchosen, at knowing that when we survive, it is in spite of a world that takes for granted our lack of humanness, and which hates our very existence outside of its service. And I say *symphony* rather than *cacophony* because we have had to learn to orchestrate those furies so that they do not tear us apart. We have had to learn to move through them and use them for strength and force and insight within our daily lives. Those of us who did not learn this difficult lesson did not survive. And part of my anger is always libation for my fallen sisters.

Anger is an appropriate reaction to racist attitudes, as is fury when the actions arising from those attitudes do not change. To those women here who fear the anger of women of Color more than their own unscrutinized racist attitudes, I ask: Is the anger of women of Color more threatening than the woman-hatred that tinges all aspects of our lives?

It is not the anger of other women that will destroy us but our refusals to stand still, to listen to its rhythms, to learn within it, to move beyond the manner of presentation to the substance, to tap that anger as an important source of empowerment.

I cannot hide my anger to spare you guilt, nor hurt feelings, nor answering anger; for to do so insults and trivializes all our efforts. Guilt is not a response to anger; it is a response to one's own actions or lack of action. If it leads to change then it can be useful, since it is then no longer guilt but the beginning of knowledge. Yet all too often, guilt is just another name for impotence, for defensiveness destructive of communication; it becomes a device to protect ignorance and the continuation of things the way they are, the ultimate protection for changelessness.

Most women have not developed tools for facing anger constructively. CR groups in the past, largely white, dealt with how to express anger, usually at the world of men. And these groups were made up of white women who shared the terms of their oppressions. There was usually little attempt to articulate the genuine differences between women, such as those of race, color, age, class, and sexual identity. There was no apparent need at that time to examine the contradictions of self, woman as oppressor. There was work on expressing anger, but very little on anger directed against each other. No tools were developed to deal with other women's anger except to avoid it, deflect it, or flee from it under a blanket of guilt.

I have no creative use for guilt, yours or my own. Guilt is only another way of avoiding informed action, of buying time out of the pressing need to make clear choices, out of the approaching storm that can feed the earth as well as bend the trees. If I speak to you in anger, at least I have spoken to you: I have not put a gun to your head and shot you down in the street; I have not looked at your bleeding sister's body and asked, "What did she do to deserve it?" This was the reaction of two white women to Mary Church Terrell's telling of the lynching of a pregnant Black woman whose baby was then torn from her body. That was in 1921, and Alice Paul had just refused to publicly endorse the enforcement of the Nineteenth Amendment for all women—by refusing to endorse the inclusion of women of Color, although we had worked to help bring about that amendment.

The angers between women will not kill us if we can articulate them with precision, if we listen to the content of what is said with at least as much intensity as we defend ourselves against the manner of saying. When we turn from anger we turn from insight, saying we will accept only the designs already known, deadly and safely familiar. I have tried to learn my anger's usefulness to me, as well as its limitations.

For women raised to fear, too often anger threatens annihilation. In the male construct of brute force, we were taught that our lives depended upon the good will of patriarchal power. The anger of others was to be avoided at all costs because there was nothing to be learned from it but pain, a judgment that we had been bad girls, come up lacking, not done what we were supposed to do. And if we accept our powerlessness, then of course any anger can destroy us.

But the strength of women lies in recognizing differences between us as creative, and in standing to those distortions which we inherited without blame, but which are now ours to alter. The angers of women can transform difference through insight into power. For anger between peers births change, not destruction, and the discomfort and sense of loss it often causes is not fatal, but a sign of growth.

My response to racism is anger. That anger has eaten clefts into my living only when it remained unspoken, useless to anyone. It has also served me in classrooms without light or learning, where the work and history of Black women was less than a vapor. It has served me as fire in the ice zone of uncomprehending eyes of white women who see in my experience and the experience of my people only new reasons for fear or guilt. And my anger is no excuse for not dealing with your blindness, no reason to withdraw from the results of your own actions.

When women of Color speak out of the anger that laces so many of our contacts with white women, we are often told that we are "creating a mood of hopelessness," "preventing white women from getting past guilt," or "standing in the way of trusting communication and action." All these quotes come directly from letters to me from members of this organization within the last two years. One woman wrote, "Because you are Black and Lesbian, you seem to speak with the moral authority of suffering." Yes, I am Black and Lesbian, and what you hear in my voice is fury, not suffering. Anger, not moral authority. There is a difference.

To turn aside from the anger of Black women with excuses or the pretexts of intimidation is to award no one power—it is merely another way of preserving racial blindness, the power of unaddressed privilege, unbreached, intact. Guilt is only another form of objectification. Oppressed peoples are always being asked to stretch a little more, to bridge the gap between blindness and humanity. Black women are expected to use our anger only in the service of other people's salvation or learning. But that time is over. My anger has meant pain to me but it has also meant survival, and before I give it up I'm going to be sure that there is something at least as powerful to replace it on the road to clarity.

What woman here is so enamoured of her own oppression that she cannot see her heelprint upon another woman's face? What woman's terms of oppression have become precious and necessary to her as a ticket into the fold of the righteous, away from the cold winds of self-scrutiny?

I am a lesbian woman of Color whose children eat regularly because I work in a university. If their full bellies make me fail to recognize my commonality with a woman of Color whose children do not eat because she cannot find work, or who has no children because her insides are rotted from home abortions and sterilization; if I fail to recognize the lesbian who chooses not to have children, the woman who remains closeted because her homophobic community is her only life support, the woman who chooses silence instead of another death, the woman who is terrified lest my anger trigger the explosion of hers; if I fail to recognize them as other faces of myself, then I am contributing not only to each of their oppressions but also to my own, and the anger which stands between us then must be used for clarity and mutual empowerment, not for evasion by guilt or for further separation. I am not free while any woman is unfree, even when her shackles are very different from my own. And I am not free as long as one person of Color remains chained. Nor is any one of you.

I speak here as a woman of Color who is bent not upon destruction but upon survival. No woman is responsible for altering the psyche of her oppressor, even when that psyche is embodied in another woman. I have suckled the wolf's lip of anger and I have used it for illumination, laughter, protection, fire in places where there was no light, no food, no sisters, no quarter. We are not goddesses or matriarchs or edifices of divine forgiveness; we are not fiery fingers of judgment or instruments of flagellation; we are women forced back always upon our woman's power. We have learned to use anger as we have learned to use the dead flesh of animals, and bruised, battered, and changing, we have survived and grown and, in Angela Wilson's words, we *are* moving on. With or without uncolored women. We use whatever strengths we have fought for, including anger, to help define and fashion a world where all our sisters can grow, where our children can love, and where the power of touching and meeting another woman's difference and wonder will eventually transcend the need for destruction.

For it is not the anger of Black women which is dripping down over this globe like a diseased liquid. It is not my anger that launches rockets, spends over sixty thousand dollars a second on missiles and other agents of war and death, slaughters children in cities, stockpiles nerve gas and chemical bombs, sodomizes our daughters and our earth. It is not the anger of Black women which corrodes into blind, dehumanizing power, bent upon the annihilation of us all unless we meet it with what we have, our power to examine and to redefine the terms upon which we will live and work; our power to envision and to reconstruct, anger by painful anger, stone upon heavy stone, a future of pollinating difference and the earth to support our choices.

We welcome all women who can meet us, face to face, beyond objectification and beyond guilt.

NOTES

1. One poem from this series is included in *Chosen Poems: Old and New* (W.W. Norton and Company, New York, 1978), pp. 105-108.

2. *This Bridge Called My Back: Writings by Radical Women of Color,* edited by Cherríe Moraga and Gloria Anzaldua (Kitchen Table: Women of Color Press, New York, 1984), first published in 1981.

3. From "For Each of You," first published in *From a Land Where Other People Live* (Broadside Press, Detroit, 1973), and collected in *Chosen Poems:Old and New* (W.W. Norton and Company, New York, 1982), p.42.

❖ ❖ ❖

Dynamics

1. Isolate a few passages in which Lorde directs her discussion to white feminist women. What do these moments reveal about Lorde's understanding of feminist goals in their present form? What specific alterations or complications does Lorde offer and why?

2. Isolate a few moments in Lorde's essay when she states or implies that anger may be misused. Explain in your own words the principles that guide her to this conclusion, and evaluate those principles in light of your own experience. In what ways would you revise Lorde's ideas about the misuse of anger?

Critical Tools

1. Lorde discusses the uses and misuses of various emotions in her essay. Isolate an emotion other than anger that she evaluates in her essay and test her evaluation by locating the same emotion in another text in *Literacies*. How does the other text help you extend or complicate Lorde's ideas about that emotion?

Draft One/Draft Two

Draft One: Locate the moments in Lorde's essay when it becomes clear that she is addressing a very specific listener. To what degree is anger a feature of these moments? Describe in some detail how those moments of direct address work in her essay, including especially the role of emotion.

Draft Two: Discuss the similarities and differences you see between the way Lorde addresses specific listeners and her own ideas about the role of emotions in political life. Use her ideas and practices to explain as well as challenge each other.

❖   ❖   ❖

Before Reading Alistair MacLeod. . .

1. Discuss some of the reasons why young adults choose either to leave or to remain in their families' homes. To what extent are these decisions influenced by class, gender, geography, or other social categories?

2. Explain how your view of your grandparents (or other older relatives) contributes to the way you look at your own parents. What are some of the important continuities you see between your grandparents' and parents' lives? Between their lives and your own?

The Vastness of the Dark

Alistair MacLeod

On the twenty-eighth day of June, 1960, which is the planned day of my deliverance, I awake at exactly six A.M. to find myself on my eighteenth birthday, listening to the ringing of the bells from the Catholic church which I now attend only reluctantly on Sundays. "Well," I say to the bells and to myself, "at least tomorrow I will be free of you." And yet I do not move but lie quietly for a while looking up and through the window at the green poplar leaves rustling softly and easily in the Nova Scotian dawn.

The reason that I do not arise immediately on such a momentous day is partially due, at least, to a second sound that is very unlike the regular, majestic booming of the bells. It is the irregular and moistly rattling-rasping sound of my father's snoring which comes from the adjoining room. And although I can only hear him I can see very vividly in my mind how he must be: lying there on his back with his thinning iron-grey hair tousled upon the pillow and with his hollow cheeks and even his jetblack eyebrows rising and falling slightly with the erratic pattern of his breathing. His mouth is slightly open and there are little bubbles of saliva forming and breaking at its corners, and his left arm and perhaps even his left leg are hanging over the bed's edge and resting upon the floor. It seems, with his arm and leg like that, as if he were prepared within his sleeping consciousness for any kind of unexpected emergency that might arise; so that if and when it does he will only have to roll slightly to his left and straighten and be immediately standing. Half of his body already touches the floor in readiness.

In our home no one gets up before he does; but in a little while, I think, that too will happen. He will sort of gasp in a strangled way and the snoring will cease. Then there will be a few stealthy movements and the ill-fitting door will open and close and he will come walking through my room carrying his shoes in his left hand while at the same time trying to support his trousers and also to button and buckle

From *The Lost Salt Gift of Blood* by Alistair MacLeod. Used by permission of the Canadian Publishers, McClelland & Stewart, Toronto.

them with his right. As long as I can remember he has finished dressing while walking but he does not handle buttons nor buckles so well since the dynamite stick at the little mine where he used to work ripped the first two fingers from his scarred right hand. Now the remaining fingers try to do what is expected of them: to hold, to button, to buckle, to adjust, but they do so with what seems a sort of groping uncertainty bordering on despair. As if they realized that there is now just too much for them to do even though they try as best they can.

When he comes through this room he will be walking softly so as not to awaken me and I will close my eyes and do my imitation of sleep so that he will think himself successful. After he has gone downstairs to start the fire there will be a pause and perhaps a few exploratory coughs exchanged between my mother and me in an unworded attempt to decide who is going to make the next move. If I cough it will indicate that I am awake and usually that means I will get up next and follow the route of my father downstairs. If, on the other hand, I make no sound, in a few minutes my mother also will come walking through my room. As she passes I will close my eyes a second time but I have always the feeling that it does not work for her; that unlike my father she can tell the difference between sleep which is real and that which is feigned. And I feel always dishonest about my deception. But today, I think, it will be the last time, and I want both of them down the stairs before I myself descend. For today I have private things to do which can only be done in the brief interval between the descent of my parents and the rising of my seven younger brothers and sisters.

Those brothers and sisters are now sleeping in a very different world across the hallway in two large rooms called generally "the girls' room" and "the boys' room." In the former there are my sisters and their names and ages are: Mary, 15, Judy, 14, Catherine, 12, and Bernadette, 3. In the other there are Daniel, 9, Harvey, 7, and David, 5. They live there, across the hall, in an alien but sociable world of half-suppressed giggles, impromptu pantomimes and muffled-silent pillow fights and fall to sleep in beds filled with oft-exchanged comic books and the crumbs of smuggled cookies. On "our" side of the hall it is very different. There is only one door for the two rooms and my parents, as I have said, have always to walk through my room to get to theirs. It is not a very good arrangement and at one time my father intended to cut another door from the hallway into their room and to close off the inadequate connecting door between their room and mine. But at one time he also probably planned to seal and cover the wooden beams and ribs that support the roof in all our rooms and he has not done that either. On the very coldest winter mornings you can look up and see the frost on the icy heads of the silver nails and see your breath in the coldly crystal air.

Sleeping over here on this side of the hall I have always felt very adult and separated from my younger brothers and sisters and their muffled worlds of laughter. I suppose it has something to do with the fact that I am the oldest by three years and circumstances have made me more alone. At one time each of us has slept in a crib in my parents' room and as I was the first I was not moved very far—only into the next room. Perhaps they kept me close because they were more nervous about me, and for a longer time, as they had not had much experience at that time with babies or younger children. So I have been here in this bed all by myself for as long as I can remember. The next three in our family are girls and I am separated from Daniel, the nearest boy, by an unbridgeable abyss of nine years. And by that time it seems my parents felt there was no point in either moving him in with me or me across the hall with him, as if they had somehow gotten used to hearing me breathing in the room so close to theirs and knew that I knew a great deal about them and about their habits and had been kind of backed into trusting me as if I were, perhaps, a younger brother or perhaps more intimately a friend. It is a strange and lonely thing to lie awake at night and listen to your parents making love in the next room and to be able even to count the strokes. And to know that they really do not know how much you know, but to know that they do know that you know; and not to know when the knowledge of your knowing came to them any more than they know when it came to you. And during these last four or five years lying here while the waves of embarrassed horniness roll over me, I have developed, apart from the problems of my own tumescent flesh, a sort of sympathy for the problem that must be theirs and for the awful violation of privacy that all of us represent. For it must be a very difficult thing for two people to try to have a sex life together when they know that the first product of that life is lying listening to them only a few feet away. Also, I know something else that I do not think they know I know.

I was told it by my paternal grandfather seven years ago when I was ten and he was eighty, on a spring day when, warmed by the sun, he had gone downtown and sat in a tavern most of the afternoon, drinking beer and spitting on the floor and slapping the table and his knee with the palm of his hand, his head wreathed in the pipe smoke of the mine-mutilated old men who were his friends. And as I passed the tavern's open door with my bag of papers he had hailed me as if I were some miniature taxi-cab and had said that he wished to go home. And so we had wended our way through the side streets and the back alleys, a small slightly embarrassed boy and a staggering but surprisingly erect old man who wanted me beside him but not to physically support him as that would hurt his pride.

"I am perfectly capable of walking home by myself, James," he said, looking down at me off the tip of his nose and over his walrus moustache, "no one is taking me home, I only want company. So you stay over on your side and I will stay on mine and we will just be friends going for a walk as indeed we are."

But then we had turned into an alley where he had placed his left arm against a building's brick wall and leaned, half-resting, his forehead against it while his right hand fumbled at his fly. And standing there with his head against the wall and with his shoes two feet from its base he had seemed like some strange, speaking hypotenuse from the geometry books at school and standing in the steam of his urine he had mumbled into the wall that he loved me, although he didn't often say so, and that he had loved me even before I was born.

"You know," he said, "when I learned that your mother was knocked up I was so happy I was just ashamed. And my wife was in a rage and your mother's parents were weeping and wringing their silly hands and whenever I was near them I would walk around looking at my shoes. But I think that, God forgive me, I may have even prayed for something like that and when I heard it I said, 'Well he will have to stay now and marry her because that's the kind of man he is, and he will work in my place now just as I've always wanted.'"

Then his forehead seemed to slide off his resting arm and he lurched unsteadily, almost bumping into me and seeming to see me for the first time. "Oh God," he said with a startled, frightened expression, "what a selfish old fool! What have I done now? Forget everything I said!" And he had squeezed my shoulder too tightly at first but then relaxed his grip and let his gigantic hand lie there limply all the way to his home. As soon as he entered his door, he flopped into the nearest chair and said almost on the verge of tears, "I think I told him. I think I told him." And my grandmother who was ten years younger turned on him in alarm but only asked, "What?" and he, raising both hands off his lap and letting them fall back in a sort of helpless gesture of despair said, "Oh you know, you know," as if he were very much afraid.

"Go on home James," she said to me evenly and kindly although I knew she was very angry, "and pay no attention to this old fool. He has never in all his life known when to open and close his pants or his mouth." As I turned to leave, I noticed for the first time that he had not redone his trousers after urinating in the alley and that his underwear was awry.

No one has ever mentioned it since but because one of my grandparents was so frightened and the other so angry I know that it is true because they do not react that strongly to anything that is not real. And knowing so I have never checked it further. And it is strange too with this added knowledge to lie in bed at night and to hear the actual beginnings of your brother and sisters, to almost share in it in an odd way and to know that you did not begin really in that same way or at least not in that bed. And I have imagined the back seats of the old cars I've seen in pictures, or the grassy hills behind the now torndown dance halls or the beaches of sand beside the sea. I like to think somehow that it had been different for them at my conception and that there had been joy instead of grim release. But I suppose we, all of us, like to think of ourselves as children of love rather than of necessity. That we have come about because there was a feeling of peace and well-being before the erection rather than its being the other way around. But of course I may be as wrong about that as I am about many things and perhaps I do not know what they feel now anymore than what they might have felt then.

But after today, I will probably not have to think about it anymore. For today I leave behind this grimy Cape Breton coal-mining town whose prisoner I have been for all of my life. And I have decided that almost any place must be better than this one with its worn-out mines and smoke-black houses; and the feeling has been building within me for the last few years. It seems to have come almost with the first waves of sexual desire and with it to have grown stronger and stronger with the passing months and years. For I must not become as my father whom I now hear banging the stove-lids below me as if there were some desperate rush about it all and some place that he must be in a very short time. Only to go nowhere. And I must not be as my grandfather who is now an almost senile old man, nearing ninety, who sits by the window all day saying his prayers and who in his moments of clarity remembers mostly his conquests over coal, and recounts tales of how straight were the timbers he and my father erected in the now caved-in underground drifts of twenty-five years ago when he was sixty-two and my father twenty-five and I not yet conceived.

It is a long, long time since my grandfather has worked and all the big mines he worked in and which he so romanticizes now are closed. And my father has not worked since early March, and his presence in a house where he does not want to be breeds a tension in us all that is heightened now since school is closed and we are all home and forced in upon ourselves. And as he moves about on this morning, banging stove-lids, pretending it is important that he does so, that he is wanted somewhere soon and therefore must make this noisy rush, I feel myself separated from him by a wide and variegated gulf and very far away from the man, who, shortly after he became my father, would take me for rides upon his shoulders to buy ice-cream at the drugstore, to see the baseball games I did not understand, or into the open fields to pat the pit-horses and be placed upon their broad and gentle backs. As we would approach the horses he would speak softly to them so that they might know where we were and be unafraid when he finally placed his hand upon them, for all of them were blind. They had been so long in the darkness of the mine that their eyes did not know the light, and the darkness of their labour had become that of their lives.

But now my father does not do such things with his younger children even as he no longer works. And he is older and greyer and apart from the missing fingers on his right hand, there is a scar from a broken bit that begins at his hairline and runs like violent lightning down the right side of his face and at night I can hear him coughing and wheezing from the rock dust on his lungs. And perhaps that coughing means that because he has worked in bad mines with bad air these last few years he will not live so very much longer. And perhaps my brothers and sisters across the hall will never hear him, when they are eighteen, rattling the stove-lids as I do now.

And as I lie here now on my back for the last time, I think of when I lay on my stomach in the underground for the first time with him there beside me in the small bootleg mine which ran beneath the sea and in which he had been working since the previous January. I had joined him at the end of the school year for a few short weeks before the little mine finally closed and I had been rather surprisingly proud to work there and my grandfather in one of his clearer moments said, "Once you start it takes a hold of you, once you drink underground water, you will always come back to drink some more. The water gets in your blood. It is in all of our blood. We have been working in the mines here since 1873."

The little mine paid very low wages and was poorly equipped and ventilated and since it was itself illegal there were no safety regulations. And I had thought, that first day, that I might die as we lay on our stomachs on the broken shale and on the lumps of coal while the water seeped around us and into us and chilled us with unflagging constancy whenever we ceased our mole-like movements. It was a very narrow little seam that we attacked, first with our drilling steels and bits, and then with our dynamite, and finally with our picks and shovels. And there was scarcely thirty-six inches of headroom where we sprawled, my father shovelling over his shoulders like the machine he had almost become while I tried to do what I was told and to be unafraid of the roof coming in or of the rats that brushed my face, or of the water that numbed my legs, my stomach and my testicles or of the fact that at times I could not breathe because the powder-heavy air was so foul and had been breathed before.

And I was aware once of the whistling wind of movement beside me and over me and saw by the light of my lamp the gigantic pipe-wrench of my father describing an arc over me and landing with a squealing crunch an arm's length before me; and then I saw the rat, lying on its back and inches from my eyes. Its head was splattered on the coal and on the wrench and it was still squeaking while a dying stream of yellow urine trickled down between its convulsively jerking legs. And then my father released the wrench and seizing the not quite dead rat by the tail hurled it savagely back over his shoulder so that the thud of its body could be heard behind us as it bounced off the wall and then splashed into the water. "You dirty son of a bitch," he said between clenched teeth and wiped the back of the wrench against the rocky wall. And we lay there then for a while without moving, chilled together in the dampness and the dark.

And now, strangely enough, I do not know if that is what I hate and so must leave, or if it is the fact that now there is not even that mine, awful as it was, to go to, and perhaps it is better to have a place to go to that you hate than to have no place at all. And it is the latter which makes my father now increasingly tense and nervous because he has always used his body as if it were a car with its accelerator always to the floor and now as it becomes more scarred and wasted, he can only use it for sex or taut too-rapid walks along the seashore or back into the hills; and when everything else fails he will try to numb himself with rum and his friends will bring him home in the evenings and dump him with his legs buckling beneath him, inside his kitchen door. And my mother and I will half carry and half drag him through the dining room to the base of the stairs and up the fourteen steps, counting them to ourselves, one by one. We do not always get that far; once he drove his left fist through the glass of the dining room window and I wrestled with him back and forth across the floor while the wildly swinging and still-clenched fist flashed and flecked its scarlet blood upon the floor and the wallpaper and the curtains and the dishes and the foolish sad dolls and coloring books and *Great Expectations* which lay upon the table. And when he was subdued and the fist became a hand we had to ask him politely to clench it again so that the wounds would reopen while the screaming iodine was poured over and into them and the tweezers probed for the flashing slivers of glass. And we had prayed then, he included, that no tendons were damaged and that no infection would set in because it was the only good hand that he had and all of us rode upon it as perilous passengers on an unpredictably violent sea.

Sometimes when he drinks so heavily my mother and I cannot always get him to his bed and leave him instead on mine, trying to undress him as best we can, amidst his flailing arms and legs and shouted obscenities, hoping at least to get his shoes, and loosen his collar and belt and trousers. And during the nights that follow such days I lie rigid beside him, trying to overcome the nausea caused by the sticky, sweet stench of the rum and listening to the sleep-talker's mumbled, incoherent words, his uneven snoring, and the frightening catches in his breathing caused by the phlegm within his throat. Sometimes he will swing out unexpectedly with either hand and once his forearm landed across my nose with such force that the blood and tears welled to the surface simultaneously and I had to stuff the bedclothes into my mouth to stifle the cry that rose upon my lips.

But yet it seems that all storms subside first into gusts and then into calm and perhaps without storms and gusts we might never have any calm, or perhaps having it we would not recognize it for what it is; and so when he awakens at one or two A.M. and lies there quietly in the dark it is the most peaceful of all times, like the quiet of the sea, and it is only then that I catch glimpses of the man who took me for the rides upon his shoulders. And I arise and go down the stairs as silently as I can, through the sleeping house, and fetch the milk which soothes the thickness of his tongue and the parched and fevered dryness of his throat and he says "Thank you," and that he is sorry, and I say that it is all right and that there is really nothing to be sorry for. And he says that he is sorry that he has acted the way he has and that he is sorry he has been able to give me so little but if he cannot give he will try very hard not to take. And that I am free and owe my parents nothing. That in itself is perhaps quite a lot to give, for many people like myself go to work very young here or did when there was work to go to and not everyone gets into high school or out of it. And perhaps even the completion of high school is the gift that he has given me along with that of life.

But that is also now ended, I think, the life here and the high school and the thought jolts me into the realization that I have somehow been half-dozing, for although I think I clearly remember everything, my mother has obviously already passed through this room for now I hear her moving about downstairs preparing breakfast. I am rather grateful that at least I have not had to pretend to be asleep on this the last of all these days.

Moving now as quickly as I can, I remove from beneath the mattress the battered old packsack that was my father's in earlier, younger days. "Would it be all right if I use that old packsack sometime?" I had asked as casually as possible some months before, trying to make my plans for it sound like some weary camping expedition. "Sure," he had said in an even non-committal fashion.

Now I pack it quietly, checking with my ball-point pen the items that I have listed on the back of the envelope kept beneath my pillow. Four pairs of underwear, five pairs of socks, two pairs of pants, four shirts, one towel, some handkerchiefs, a gabardine jacket, a plastic raincoat and a shaving set. The latter is the only item that is new and unused and is the cheapest that Gillette manufactures. Up until this time I have always used my father's razor which is battered and verdigris green from years of use. I have used it for some years now—more often, at times, than my questionable beard demanded.

As I move down the stairs there is still no movement from the two larger rooms across the hall and for this I am most grateful. I do not really know how to say good-bye as I have never before said it to anyone and because I am uncertain I wish to say it now to as few as possible. Who knows, though, perhaps I may even be rather good at it. I lay the packsack down on the second stair from the bottom where it is not awfully visible and walk into the kitchen. My mother is busy at her stove and my father is standing with his back to the room looking through the window over a view of slate-grey slag heaps and ruined skeletal mine tipples and out toward the rolling sea. They are not greatly surprised to see me as it is often like this, just the three of us in the quiet early morning. But today I cannot afford to be casual and I must say what must be said in the short space of time occupied by only the three of us. "I think I'll go away today," I say, trying to sound as offhand as possible. Only a slight change in the rhythm of my mother's poking at the stove indicates that she has heard me, and my father still stands looking through the window out to sea. "I think I'll go right now," I add, my voice sort of trailing off, "before the others get up it will be easier that way."

My mother moves the kettle, which has started to boil, toward the back of the stove, as if stalling for time, then she turns and says, "Where will you go? To Blind River?"

Her response is so little like that which I anticipated that I feel strangely numb. For I had somehow expected her to be greatly surprised, astounded, astonished, and she is none of these. And her mention of Blind River, the centre of Northern Ontario's uranium mines, is something and someplace that I had never even thought of. It is as if my mother had not only known that I was to leave but had even planned my route and final destination. I am reminded of my reading in school of the way Charles Dickens felt about the blacking factory and his mother's being so fully in favour of it. In favour of a life for him which he considered so terrible and so far beneath his imagined destiny.

My father turns from the window and says, "You are only eighteen today, perhaps you could wait awhile. Something might turn up." But within his eyes I see no strong commitment to his words and I know he feels that waiting is at best weary and at worst hopeless. This also makes me somehow rather disappointed and angry as I had thought somehow my parents would cling to me in a kind of desperate fashion and I would have to be very firm and strong.

"What is there to wait for?" I say, asking a question that is useless and to which I know the all too obvious answer. "Why do you want me to stay here?"

"You misunderstand," says my father, "you are free to go if you want to. We are not forcing you or asking you to do anything. I am only saying that you do not *have* to go now.

But suddenly it becomes very important that I *do* go now, because it seems things cannot help but get worse. So I say, "Good-bye. I will write but it will not be from Blind River." I add the last as an almost unconscious little gibe at my mother.

I go and retrieve my packsack and then pass back through the house, out the door and even through the little gate. My parents follow me to the gate. My mother says, "I was planning a cake for today . . . " and then stops uncertainly, her sentence left hanging in the early morning air. She is trying to make amends for her earlier statement and rather desperately gropes her way back to the fact of my birthday. My father says, "Perhaps you should go over home. They may not be there if and when you come again."

It is but a half block to "over home," the house of my father's parents, who have always been there as long as I can remember and who have always provided a sort of haven for all of us through all our little storms and my father's statement that they will not be there forever is an intimation of something that I have never really considered before. So now I move with a sort of apprehension over the ashes and cinder-filled pot-holes of the tired street toward the old house blackened with the coal dust of generations. It is as yet hardly seven A.M. and it is as if I am some early morning milkman moving from one house to another to leave good-byes instead of bottles beside such quiet doors.

Inside my grandparents' house, my grandfather sits puffing his pipe by the window, while passing the beads of his rosary through fingers which are gnarled and have been broken more times than he can remember. He has been going deaf for some time and he does not turn his head when the door closes behind me. I decide that I will not start with him because it will mean shouting and repetition and I am not sure I will be able to handle that. My grandmother, like my mother, is busy at her stove. She is tall and white-haired and although approaching eighty she is still physically imposing. She has powerful, almost masculine hands and has always been a big-boned person without ever having been heavy or ever having any difficulty with her legs. She still moves swiftly and easily and her eyesight and hearing are perfect.

"I am going away today," I say as simply as I can.

She pokes with renewed energy at her stove and then answers: "It is just as well. There is nothing for one to do here anyway. There was never anything for one to do here."

She has always spoken with the Gaelic inflection of her youth and in that detached third-person form which I had long ago suggested that she modernize.

"Come here James," she says and takes me into her pantry, where with surprising agility she climbs up on a chair and takes from the cupboard's top shelf a huge cracked and ancient sugar bowl. Within it there are dusty picture postcards, some faded yellow payslips which seem ready to disintegrate at the touch, and two yellowed letters tied together with a shoelace. The locations on the payslips and on the postcards leap at me across a gulf of dust and years: Springhill, Scranton, Wilkes-Barre, Yellowknife, Britannia Beach, Butte, Virginia City, Escanaba, Sudbury, Whitehorse, Drumheller, Harlan, Ky., Elkins, W. Va., Fernie, B.C., Trinidad, Colo.—coal and gold, copper and lead, gold and iron, nickel and gold and coal. East and West and North and South. Mementoes and messages from places that I so young and my grandmother so old have never seen.

"Your father was under the ground in all those places," she says half-angrily, "the same way he was under the ground here before he left and under it after he came back. It seems we will be underground long enough when we are dead without seeking it out while we are still alive."

"But still," she says after a quiet pause and in a sober tone, "it was what he was good at and wanted to do. It was just not what I wanted him to do, or at least I did not want him to do it here."

She unties the shoelace and shows me the two letters. The first is dated March 12, 1938, and addressed General Delivery, Kellogg, Idaho: "I am getting old now and I would like very much if you would come back and take my working place at the mine. The seam is good for years yet. No one has been killed for some time now. It is getting better. The weather is mild and we are all fine. Don't bother writing. Just come. We will be waiting for you. Your fond father."

The second bears the same date and is also addressed General Delivery, Kellogg, Idaho: "Don't listen to him. If you return here you will never get out and this is no place to lead one's life. They say the seam will be finished in another few years. Love, Mother."

I have never seen my grandfather's handwriting before and for some reason, although I knew he read, I had always thought him unable to write. Perhaps, I think now, it is because his hands have been so broken and misshapen; and with increasing age, hard to control for such a fine task as writing.

The letters are written with the same broad-nibbed pen in an ink which is of a blackness that I have never seen and somehow these letters now seem like a strangely old and incompatible married couple, each cancelling out the other's desires while bound together by a single worn and dusty lace.

I go out of the pantry and to the window where my grandfather sits. "I am going away today," I shout, leaning over him.

"Oh yes," he says in a neutral tone of voice, while continuing to look out the window and finger his rosary. He does not move and the pipe smoke curls upward from his pipe which is clenched between his worn and strongly stained teeth. Lately he has taken to saying, "Oh yes," to almost everything as a means of concealing his deafness and now I do not know if he has really heard me or is merely giving what seems a standard and safe response to all of the things he hears but partially if at all. I do not feel that I can say it again without my voice breaking and so I turn away. At the door I find that he has shuffled behind me.

"Don't forget to come back James," he says, "it's the only way you'll be content. Once you drink underground water it becomes a part of you like the blood a man puts into a woman. It changes her forever and never goes away. There's always a part of him running there deep inside her. It's what will wake you up at night and never ever leave you alone."

Because he knows how much my grandmother is opposed to what he says he has tried to whisper to me. But he is so deaf that he can hardly hear his own voice and he has almost shouted in the way deaf people do; his voice seems to echo and bounce off the walls of his house and to escape out into the sunshot morning air. I offer him my hand to shake and find it almost crushed in the crooked broken force of his. I can feel the awful power of his oddly misshapen fingers, his splayed and flattened too broad thumb, the ridges of the toughened, blackened scars and the abnormally large knobs that are his twisted misplaced knuckles. And I have a feeling for a terrible moment that I may never ever get away or be again released. But he finally relaxes and I feel that I am free.

Even pot-holed streets are lonely ones when you think you may not see them again for a very long time or perhaps forever. And I travel now mostly the back streets because I am conspicuous with my packsack and I do not want any more conversations or attempted and failed and futile explanations. At the outskirts of the town a coal truck stops for me and we travel for twenty-five miles along the shore-line of the sea. The truck makes so much noise and rides so roughly that conversation with the driver is impossible and I am very grateful for the noisy silence in which we are encased.

By noon after a succession of short rides in a series of oddly assorted vehicles I am finally across the Strait of Canso, off Cape Breton Island and at last upon my way. It is only when I have left the Island that I can feel free to assume my new identity which I don like carefully preserved new clothes taken from within their pristine wrappings. It assumes that I am from Vancouver which is as far away as I can imagine.

I have been somehow apprehensive about even getting off Cape Breton Island, as if at the last moment it might extend gigantic tentacles, or huge monstrous hands like my grandfather's to seize and hold me back. Now as I finally set foot on the mainland I look across at the heightened mount that is Cape Breton now, rising mistily out of the greenness and the white-capped blueness of the sea.

My first ride on the mainland is offered by three Negroes in a battered blue Dodge pickup truck that bears the information "Rayfield Clyke, Lincolnville, N.S., Light Trucking" on its side. They say they are going the approximately eighty miles to New Glasgow and will take me if I wish. They will not go very fast, they say, because their truck is old and I might get a better ride if I choose to wait. On the other hand, the driver says, I will at least be moving and I will get there sooner or later. Anytime I am sick of it and want to stop I can bang on the roof of the cab. They would take me in the cab but it is illegal to have four men in the cab of a commercial vehicle and they do not want any trouble with the police. I climb into the back and sit on the worn spare tire and the truck moves on. By now the sun is fairly high and when I remove the packsack from my shoulders I can feel although I cannot see the two broad bands of perspiration traced and crossing upon my back. I realize now that I am very hungry and have eaten nothing since last evening's supper.

In New Glasgow I am let off at a small gas station and my Negro benefactors point out the shortest route to the western outskirts of the town. It leads through cluttered back streets where the scent of the greasy hamburgers reeks out of the doors of the little lunch-counters with their overloud juke-boxes; simultaneously pushing Elvis Presley and the rancid odours of the badly cooked food through the half open doors. I would like to stop but somehow there is a desperate sense of urgency now as if each of the cars on the one-way street is bound for a magical destination and I feel that should I stop for even a moment's hamburger I might miss the one ride that is worthwhile. The sweat is running down my forehead now and stings my eyes and I know the two dark patches of perspiration upon my back and beneath the straps are very wide.

The sun seems at its highest when the heavy red car pulls over to the highway's gravelled shoulder and its driver leans over to unlock the door on the passenger side. He is a very heavy man of about fifty with a red perspiring face and a brown cowlick of hair plastered down upon his damply glistening forehead. His coat is thrown across the back of the seat and his shirt pocket contains one of those plastic shields bristling with pens and pencils. The collar of the shirt is open and his tie is loosened and awry; his belt is also undone, as is the button at the waistband of his trousers. His pants are grey and although stretched tautly over his enormous thighs they still appear as damply wrinkled. Through his white shirt the sweat is showing darkly under his armpits and also in large blotches on his back which are visible when he leans forward. His hands seem very white and disproportionately small.

As we move off down the shimmering highway with its mesmerizing white line, he takes a soiled handkerchief that has been lying on the seat beside him and wipes the wet palms of his hands and also the glistening wet blackness of the steering wheel.

"Boy, it sure is hot," he says, "hotter'n a whore in hell."

"Yes," I say, "it sure is. It really is."

"Dirty little town back there," he says, "you can spend a week there just driving through."

"Yes, it isn't much."

"Just travelling through?"

"Yes, I'm going back to Vancouver."

"You got a whole lot of road ahead of you boy, a whole lot of road. I never been to Vancouver, never west of Toronto. Been trying to get my company to send me west for a long while now but they always send me down here. Three or four times a year. Weather's always miserable. Hotter'n hell like this here or in the winter cold enough to freeze the balls off a brass monkey." He beats out a salvo of hornblasts at a teenage girl who is standing uncertainly by the roadside.

Although the windows of the car are open, it is very hot and the redness of the car seems to intensify the feeling and sense of heat. All afternoon the road curves and winds ahead of us like a bucking, shimmering snake with a dirty white streak running down its back. We seem to ride its dips and bends like captive passengers on a roller-coaster, leaning our bodies into the curves, and bracing our feet against the tension of the floorboards. My stomach vanishes as we hurtle into the sudden unexpected troughs and returns as quickly as we emerge to continue our twists and turns. Insects ping and splatter against the windshield and are transformed into yellow splotches. The tires hiss on the superheated asphalt and seem almost to leave tracks. I can feel my clothes sticking to me, to my legs and thighs and back. On my companion's shirt the blotches of sweat are larger and more plentiful. Leaning his neck and shoulders back against the seat he lifts his heavy body from the sweat-stained upholstery and thrusts his right hand through his opened trousers and deep into his crotch. "Let a little air in there," he says, as he manoeuvres his genitals, "must be an Indian made this underwear, it keeps creeping up on me."

All afternoon as we travel we talk or rather he talks and I listen which I really do not mind. I have never really met anyone like him before. The talk is of his business (so much salary, so much commission plus other 'deals' on the side), of his boss (a dumb bastard who is lucky he has good men on the road), of his family (a wife, one son and one daughter, one of each is enough), of sex (he can't get enough of it and will be after it until he dies), of Toronto (it is getting bigger every day and it is not like it used to be), of taxes (they keep getting higher and it doesn't pay a man to keep up his property, also too many Federal giveaways). He goes on and on. I have never listened to anyone like him before. He seems so confident and sure of everything. It is as if he knows that he knows everything and is on top of everything and he seems never to have to hesitate nor stop nor run down nor even to think; as if he were a juke-box fed from some mysterious source by an inexhaustible supply of nickels, dimes and quarters.

The towns and villages and train stations speed by. Fast and hot; Truro, Glenholme and Wentworth and Oxford. We are almost out of Nova Scotia with scarcely thirty miles of it ahead according to my companion. We are almost at the New Brunswick border. I am again in a stage of something like exhausted relief as I approach yet another boundary over which I can escape and leave so much behind. It is the feeling I originally had on leaving Cape Breton only now it has been heavied and dulled by the journey of the day. For it has been long and hot and exhausting.

Suddenly the road veers to the left and no longer hooks and curves but extends up and away from us into a long, long hill, the top of which we can see almost a half mile away. Houses appear on either side as we begin the climb and then there are more and more of them strung out loosely along the road.

My companion blasts out a rhythm of hornblasts at a young girl and her mother who are stretching up on their tiptoes to hang some washing on a clothes-line. There is a basket of newly washed clothes on the ground between them and their hands are busy on the line. They have some clothespins in their teeth so they will not have to bend to reach them and lose their handhold on the line.

"If I had my way, they'd have something better'n that in their mouths," he says, "wouldn't mind resting my balls on the young one's chin for the second round."

He has been looking at them quite closely and the car's tires rattle in the roadside gravel before he pulls it back to the quiet of the pavement.

The houses are closer together now and more blackened and the yards are filled with children and bicycles and dogs. As we move toward what seems to be the main intersection I am aware of the hurrying women in their kerchiefs, and the boys with their bags of papers and baseball gloves and the men sitting or squatting on their heels in tight little compact knots. There are other men who neither sit nor squat but lean against the buildings or rest upon canes or crutches or stand awkwardly on artificial limbs. They are the old and the crippled. The faces of all of them are gaunt and sallow as if they had been allowed to see the sun only recently, when it was already too late for it to do them any good.

"Springhill is a hell of a place," says the man beside me, "unless you want to get laid. It's one of the best there is for that. Lots of mine accidents here and the men killed off. Women used to getting it all the time. Mining towns are always like this. Look at all the kids. This here little province of Nova Scotia leads the country in illegitimacy. They don't give a damn."

The mention of the name Springhill and the realization that this is where I have come is more of a shock than I would ever have imagined. As if in spite of signposts and geography and knowing it was "there," I have never thought of it as ever being "here."

And I remember November 1956: the old cars, mudsplattered by the land and rusted by the moisture of the sea, parked outside our house with their motors running. Waiting for the all-night journey to Springhill which seemed to me then, in my fourteenth year, so very far away and more a name than even a place. Waiting for the lunches my mother packed in wax paper and in newspaper and the thermos bottles of coffee and tea, and waiting for my father and the same packsack which now on this sweating day accompanies me. Only then it was filled with the miners' clothes he would need for the rescue that they hoped they might perform. The permanently blackened underwear, the heavy woollen socks, the boots with the steel-reinforced toes, the blackened, sweat-stained miner's belt which sagged on the side that carried his lamp, the crescent wrench, the dried and dustied water-bag, trousers and gloves and the hard hat chipped and dented and broken by the years of falling rock.

And all of that night my grandfather with his best ear held to the tiny radio for news of the buried men and of their rescuers. And at school the teachers taking up collections in all of the class-rooms and writing in large letters on the blackboard, "Springhill Miners' Relief Fund, Springhill, N.S." which was where we were sending the money, and I remember also my sisters' reluctance at giving up their hoarded nickels, dimes and quarters because noble causes and death do not mean very much when you are eleven, ten and eight and it is difficult to comprehend how children you have never known may never see their fathers any more, not walking through the door nor perhaps even being carried through the door in the heavy coffins for the last and final look. Other people's buried fathers are very strange and far away but licorice and movie matinees are very close and real.

"Yeah," says the voice beside me, "I was in here six months ago and got this little, round woman. Really giving it to her, pumping away and all of a sudden she starts kind of crying and calling me by this guy's name I never heard of. Must have been her dead husband or something. Kind of scared the hell out of me. Felt like a goddamn ghost or something. Almost lost my rod. Might have too but I was almost ready to shoot it into her."

We are downtown now and it is late afternoon in the period before the coming of the evening. The sun is no longer as fierce as it was earlier and it slants off the blackened buildings, many of which are shells bleak and fire-gutted and austere. A Negro woman with two light-skinned little boys crosses the street before us. She is carrying a bag of groceries and the little boys have each an opened sixteen-ounce bottle of Pepsi-Cola. They put their hands over the bottles' mouths and shake them vigorously to make the contents fizz.

"Lots of people around here marry niggers," says the voice. "Guess they're so black underground they can't tell the difference in the light. All the same in the dark as the fellow says. Had an explosion here a few years ago and some guys trapped down there, I dunno how long. Eaten the lunches of the dead guys and the bark off the timbers and drinking one another's piss. Some guy in Georgia offered the ones they got out a trip down there but there was a nigger in the bunch so he said he couldn't take him. Then the rest wouldn't go. Damned if I'd lose a trip to Georgia because of a single nigger that worked for the same company. Like I say, I'm old enough to be your father or even your grandfather and I haven't even been to Vancouver."

It is 1958 that he is talking about now and it is much clearer in my mind than 1956 which is perhaps the difference between being fourteen and sixteen when something happens in your life. A series of facts or near facts that I did not even realize I possessed flash now in succession upon my mind: the explosion in 1958 occurred on a Thursday as did the one in 1956; Cumberland No. 2 at the time of the explosion was the deepest coal mine in North America; in 1891, 125 men were killed in that same mine; that 174 men went down to work that 1958 evening; that most were feared lost; that 18 were found alive after being buried beneath 1,000 tons of rock for more than a week; that Cumberland No. 2 once employed 900 men and now employs none.

And I remember again the cars before our house with their motors running, and the lunches and the equipment and the waiting of the week: the school collections, my grandfather with his radio, this time the added reality of a T.V. at a neighbour's house; and the quietness of our muted lives, our footsteps without sound. And then the return of my father and the haunted greyness of his face and after the younger children were in bed the quiet and hushed conversations of seep-ing gas and lack of oxygen and the wild and belching smoke and flames of the subterranean fires nourished there by the everlasting seams of the dark and dia-mond coal. And also of the finding of the remains of men flattened and crushed if they had died beneath the downrushing roofs of rock or if they had been blown apart by the explosion itself, transformed into forever lost and irredeemable pieces of themselves; hands and feet and blown-away faces and reproductive organs and severed ropes of intestines festooning the twisted pipes and spikes like grotesque Christmas-tree loops and chunks of hair-clinging flesh. Men transformed into grisly jig-saw puzzles that could never more be solved.

"I don't know what the people do around here now," says the voice at my side. "They should get out and work like the rest of us. The Government tries to resettle them but they won't stay in a place like Toronto. They always come back to their graveyards like dogs around a bitch in heat. They have no guts."

The red car has stopped now before what I am sure is this small town's only drugstore. "Maybe we'll stop here for a while," he says. "I've just about had it and need something else. All work and no play, you know. I'm going in here for a minute first to try my luck. As the fellow says, an ounce of prevention beats a pound of cure."

As he closes the door he says, "Maybe later you'd like to come along. There's always some left over."

The reality of where I am and of what I think he is going to do seems now to press down upon me as if it were the pressure of the caving-in roof which was so recently within my thoughts. Although it is still hot I roll up the windows of the car. The people on the street regard me casually in this car of too bright red which bears Ontario licence plates. And I recognize now upon their faces a look that I have seen upon my grandfather's face and on the faces of hundreds of the people from my past and even on my own when seeing it reflected from the mirrors and windows of such a car as this. For it is as if I am not part of their lives at all but am only here in a sort of movable red and glass showcase, that has come for a while to their private anguish-ridden streets and will soon roll on and leave them the same as before my coming; part of a movement that passes through their lives but does not really touch them. Like flotsam on yet another uninteresting river which flows through their permanent banks and is bound for some invisible destination around a bend where they have never been and cannot go. Their glances have summed me up and dis-missed me as casually as that. "What can he know of our near deaths and pain and who lies buried in our graves?"

And I am overwhelmed now by the awfulness of oversimplification. For I realize that not only have I been guilty of it through this long and burning day but also through most of my yet young life and it is only now that I am doubly its victim that I begin vaguely to understand. For I had somehow thought that "going away" was but a physical thing. And that it had only to do with movement and with labels like the silly "Vancouver" that I had glibly rolled from off my tongue; or with the crossing of bodies of water or with the boundaries of borders. And because my father had told me I was "free" I had foolishly felt that it was really so. Just like that. And I realize now that the older people of my past are more complicated than perhaps I had ever thought. And that there are distinctions between my sentimental, romantic grandfather and his love for coal, and my stern and practical grandmother and her hatred of it; and my quietly strong but passive mother and the soaring extremes of my father's passionate violence and the quiet power of his love. They are all so different. But yet they have somehow endured and given me the only life I know for all these eighteen years. Their lives flowing into mine and mine from out of theirs. Different but somehow more similar than I had ever thought. Perhaps it is possible I think now to be both and yet to see only the one. For the man in whose glassed-in car I now sit sees only similarity. For him the people of this multi-scarred little town are reduced to but a few phrases and the act of sexual intercourse. They are only so many identical goldfish leading identical, incomprehensible lives within the glass prison of their bowl. And the people on the street view me behind my own glass in much the same way and it is the way that I have looked at others in their "foreign licence" cars and it is the kind of judgement that I myself have made. And yet it seems that neither these people nor this man are in any way unkind and not to understand does not necessarily mean that one is cruel. But one should at least be honest. And perhaps I have tried too hard to be someone else without realizing at first what I presently am. I do not know. I am not sure. But I do know that I cannot follow this man into a house that is so much like the one I have left this morning and go down into the sexual embrace of a woman who might well be my mother. And I do not know what she, my mother, may be like in the years to come when she is deprived of the lightning movement of my father's body and the hammered pounding of his heart. For I do not know when he may die. And I do not know in what darkness she may then cry out his name nor to whom. I do not know very much of anything, it seems, except that I have been wrong and dishonest with others and myself. And perhaps this man has left footprints on a soul I did not even know that I possessed.

It is dark now on the outskirts of Springhill when the car's headlights pick me up in their advancing beams. It pulls over to the side and I get into its back seat. I have trouble closing the door behind me because there is no handle so I pull on the crank that is used for the window. I am afraid that even it may come off in my hand. There are two men in the front seat and I can see only the outlines of the backs of their heads and I cannot tell very much about them. The man in the back seat beside me is not awfully visible either. He is tall and lean but from what I see of his face it is difficult to tell whether he is thirty or fifty. There are two sacks of miner's gear on the floor at his feet and I put my sack there too because there isn't any other place.

"Where are you from?" he asks as the car moves forward. "From Cape Breton," I say and tell him the name of my home.

"We are too," he says, "but we're from the Island's other side. I guess the mines are pretty well finished where you're from. They're the old ones. They're playing out where we're from too. Where are you going now?"

"I don't know," I say, "I don't know.."

"We're going to Blind River," he says. "If it doesn't work there we hear they've found uranium in Colorado and are getting ready to start sinking shafts. We might try that, but this is an old car and we don't think it'll make it to Colorado. You're welcome to come along with us though if you want. We'll carry you for a while."

"I don't know," I say, "I don't know. I'll have to think about it. I'll have to make up my mind."

The car moves forward into the night. Its headlights seek out and follow the beckoning white line which seems to lift and draw us forward, upward and inward, forever into the vastness of the dark.

"I guess your people have been on the coal over there for a long time?" asks the voice beside me.

"Yes," I say, "since 1873."

"Son of a bitch," he says, after a pause, "it seems to bust your balls and it's bound to break your heart."

❖ ❖ ❖

Dynamics

1. James's mother asks whether he will look for work in the uranium mines at Blind River. What relationship(s) do you see between "blindness" and "rivers" in this story? Trace these images as they appear in the text and speculate about their significance.

2. Near the beginning of MacLeod's story, James decides that "we...like to think of ourselves as children of love rather than of necessity." Find passages from the story that support his desire to see himself as a child of "love," and passages that point to the role of "necessity" in his identity. How does MacLeod manage the tension between "love" and "necessity" in this text? Why might this be an important question?

3. Using your response to the last question as a model, find some other tensions or oppositions in MacLeod's text and analyze them in the same way. How does MacLeod's use of such oppositions contribute to the meanings you find in his story?

Critical Tools

1. After listening to the driver's insensitive comments about the Nova Scotian miners and their families, James ponders the "awful" "over-simplifications" that have marked his decision to leave home. Looking back through his story, locate some of the over-simplifications that James does not include in his list. How does James's new understanding of "over-simplification" and "complication" help you talk about the ways these issues work in another text you have read this semester?

2. Early in the story, James remembers how the blood from his father's cut fist spattered onto a copy of Charles Dickens' novel *Great Expectations*. Use your interpretation of this episode to talk about the roles of expectation, anticipation, and waiting in MacLeod's story. Discuss the extent to which James's and the other characters' experiences of expectation can be symbolized by the image of blood on *Great Expectations*. Where and how does this image become insufficient for your analysis?

Draft One/Draft Two

Draft One: James notes that his unemployed father is "increasingly tense and nervous because he has always used his body as if it were a car with its accelerator always to the floor." Use MacLeod's story and your own memories of your father or another male relative to explore the specific pressures experienced by men in North American culture. How do James's observations about his father, his grandfather, and himself compare with your own understanding of men's experience and identity?

Draft Two: Choose a reading from *Literacies* that allows you to re-frame the theories about masculinity you introduced in draft one. In particular, explain how considerations of ethnicity, social class, sexuality, or some other social category might complicate your earlier draft.

❖   ❖   ❖

Before Reading Czeslaw Milosz. . .

1. Describe some of the things you accept as "natural." Try to include both day-to-
    day activities and significant once-in-a-lifetime events. What aspects of these
    things make them seem "natural"? How would you respond to the knowledge
    that some of these things might not be accepted as natural by everyone?

2. Think of a few instances in which you had to adjust relatively quickly to new
    circumstances. In what ways did the adjustments you made change aspects of
    yourself, your behaviors, or your beliefs? Consider why you might have been
    willing to adjust some of your ideas and actions but not others.

American Ignorance of War

Czeslaw Milosz

"Are Americans *really* stupid?" I was asked in Warsaw. In the voice of the man who posed the question, there was despair, as well as the hope that I would contradict him. This question reveals the attitude of the average person in the people's democracies toward the West: it is despair mixed with a residue of hope.

During the last few years, the West has given these people a number of reasons to despair politically. In the case of the intellectual, other, more complicated reasons come into play. Before the countries of Central and Eastern Europe entered the sphere of the Imperium,[1] they lived through the Second World War. That war was much more devastating there than in the countries of Western Europe. It destroyed not only their economies, but also a great many values which had seemed till then unshakable.

Man tends to regard the order he lives in as *natural*. The houses he passes on his way to work seem more like rocks rising out of the earth than like products of human hands. He considers the work he does in his office or factory as essential to the harmonious functioning of the world. The clothes he wears are exactly what they should be, and he laughs at the idea that he might equally well be wearing a Roman toga or medieval armor. He respects and envies a minister of state or a bank director, and regards the possession of a considerable amount of money as the main guarantee of peace and security. He cannot believe that one day a rider may appear on a street he knows well, where cats sleep and children play, and start catching passersby with his lasso. He is accustomed to satisfying those of his physiological needs which are considered private as discreetly as possible, without realizing that such a pattern of behavior is not common to all human societies. In a word, he behaves a little like Charlie Chaplin in *The Gold Rush*, bustling about in a shack poised precariously on the edge of a cliff.

His first stroll along a street littered with glass from bomb-shattered windows shakes his faith in the "naturalness" of his world. The wind scatters papers from hastily evacuated offices, papers labeled "Confidential" or "Top Secret" that evoke visions of safes, keys, conferences, couriers, and secretaries. Now the wind blows them through the street for anyone to read; yet no one does, for each man is more urgently concerned with finding a loaf of bread. Strangely enough, the world goes on even though the offices and secret files have lost all meaning. Farther down the street, he stops before a house split in half by a bomb, the privacy of people's homes—the family smells, the warmth of the beehive life, the furniture preserving the memory of loves and hatreds—cut open to public view. The house itself, no longer a rock, but a scaffolding of plaster, concrete, and brick; and on the third floor, a solitary white bathtub, rain-rinsed of all recollection of those who once bathed in it. Its formerly influential and respected owners, now destitute, walk the fields in search of stray potatoes. Thus overnight money loses its value and becomes a meaningless mass of printed paper. His walk takes him past a little boy poking a stick into a heap of smoking ruins and whistling a song about the great leader who will preserve the nation against all enemies. The song remains, but the leader of yesterday is already part of an extinct past.

He finds he acquires new habits quickly. Once, had he stumbled upon a corpse on the street, he would have called the police. A crowd would have gathered, and much talk and comment would have ensued. Now he knows he must avoid the dark body lying in the gutter, and refrain from asking unnecessary questions. The man who fired the gun must have had his reasons; he might well have been executing an Underground sentence.

Nor is the average European accustomed to thinking of his native city as divided into segregated living areas, but a single decree can force him to this new pattern of life and thought. Quarter A may suddenly be designated for one race; B, for a second; C, for a third. As the resettlement deadline approaches, the streets become filled with long lines of wagons, carts, wheelbarrows, and people carrying bundles, beds, chests, caldrons, and bird cages. When all the moves are effected, 2,000 people may find themselves in a building that once housed 200, but each man is at last in the proper area. Then high walls are erected around quarter C, and daily a given lot of men, women, and children are loaded into wagons that take them off to specially constructed factories where they are scientifically slaughtered and their bodies burned.

And even the rider with the lasso appears, in the form of a military van waiting at the corner of a street. A man passing that corner meets a leveled rifle, raises his hands, is pushed into the van, and from that moment is lost to his family and friends. He may be sent to a concentration camp, or he may face a firing squad, his lips sealed with plaster lest he cry out against the state; but, in any case, he serves as a warning to his fellow men. Perhaps one might escape such a fate by remaining at home. But the father of a family must go out in order to provide bread and soup for his wife and children; and every night they worry about whether or not he will return. Since these conditions last for years, everyone gradually comes to look upon the city as a jungle, and upon the fate of twentieth-century man as identical with that of a caveman living in the midst of powerful monsters.

It was once thought obvious that a man bears the same name and surname throughout his entire life; now it proves wiser for many reasons to change them and to memorize a new and fabricated biography. As a result, the records of the civilian state become completely confused. Everyone ceases to care about formalities, so that marriage, for example, comes to mean little more than living together.

Respectable citizens used to regard banditry as a crime. Today, bank robbers are heroes because the money they steal is destined for the Underground. Usually they are young boys, mothers' boys, but their appearance is deceiving. The killing of a man presents no great moral problem to them.

The nearness of death destroys shame. Men and women change as soon as they know that the date of their execution has been fixed by a fat little man with shiny boots and a riding crop. They copulate in public, on the small bit of ground surrounded by barbed wire—their last home on earth. Boys and girls in their teens, about to go off to the barricades to fight against tanks with pistols and bottles of gasoline, want to enjoy their youth and lose their respect for standards of decency.

Which world is "natural"? That which existed before, or the world of war? Both are natural, if both are within the realm of one's experience. All the concepts men live by are a product of the historic formation in which they find themselves. Fluidity and constant change are the characteristics of phenomena. And man is so plastic a being that one can even conceive of the day when a thoroughly self-respecting citizen will crawl on all fours, sporting a tail of brightly colored feathers as a sign of conformity to the order he lives in.

The man of the East cannot take Americans seriously because they have never undergone the experiences that teach men how relative their judgments and thinking habits are. Their resultant lack of imagination is appalling. Because they were born and raised in a given social order and in a given system of values, they believe that any other order must be "unnatural," and that it cannot last because it is incompatible with human nature. But even they may one day know fire, hunger, and the sword. In all probability this is what will occur, for it is hard to believe that when one half of the world is living through terrible disasters, the other half can continue a nineteenth-century mode of life, learning about the distress of its distant fellow men only from movies and newspapers. Recent examples teach us that this cannot be. An inhabitant of Warsaw or Budapest once looked at newsreels of bombed Spain or burning Shanghai, but in the end he learned how these and many other catastrophes appear in actuality. He read gloomy tales of the NKVD[2] until one day he found he himself had to deal with it. *If something exists in one place, it will exist everywhere.* This is the conclusion he draws from his observations, and so he has no particular faith in the momentary prosperity of America. He suspects that the years 1933-1945 in Europe[3] prefigure what will occur elsewhere. A hard school, where ignorance was punished not by bad marks but by death, has taught him to think sociologically and historically. But it has not freed him from irrational feelings. He is apt to believe in theories that foresee violent changes in the countries of the West, for he finds it unjust that they should escape the hardships he had to undergo.

NOTES
1. Empire; that is, the Soviet Union.—ED.
2. The Soviet secret police, 1935-1945.—ED.
3. Hitler's takeover of Germany through World War II.—ED.

Dynamics

1. What relationship(s) do you see between "naturalness" and "ignorance" in Milosz's essay? Work with specific uses of these concepts in the essay to examine the meanings they take on when referring to the "east" and "west." How might your analysis of these terms complicate your response to Milosz's arguments?

2. What function does the idea of "experience" play in Milosz's argument? Consider how his treatment of one kind of experience matches up with his treatment of other kinds. How does his treatment of different kinds of experience shape your responses to his essay?

Critical Tools

1. Near the end of his essay, Milosz states the idea that "if something exists in one place, it will exist everywhere." How does Milosz's response to this idea relate to his arguments throughout the essay? As you explore this relationship, work with another essay that challenges our understanding of the "natural." How do the ideas from the second essay help you respond to Milosz's handling of this statement?

2. Milosz writes that "all the concepts men live by are a product of the historic formation in which they find themselves." Consider another reading in which you see elements of the "historic formation" that helped to shape the text. Examine the relationships you find between these historic formations and the arguments of the essay. How might this discussion help you understand the influences of Milosz's own historic formations on his arguments?

Draft One / Draft Two

1. *Draft One:* According to Milosz, "boys and girls in their teens" who face extreme stress and hardship "want to enjoy their youth and lose their respect for standards of decency." Examine your response to Milosz's claim by considering a personal experience of extreme stress. How did this experience affect your views about "standards of decency" or any other code of expected/acceptable behavior?

    Draft Two: Use your new insights about your own experience to evaluate the choices made by someone who faced particular hardship in another reading. Within the context of that reading, which elements of those choices seem "natural"? Why?

2. *Draft One:* What is your response to Milosz's use of the question, "Are Americans *really* stupid?" Consider some of the ways his arguments might suggest his indirect answer to this question.

    Draft Two: Choose another reading that seems to focus on or challenge traditionally "western" views. How might your response in your first draft contribute to the way you understand the second writer's management of western views?

❖ ❖ ❖

Before reading Pratibha Parmar...

1. As a student, you share an "identity" with other students, and therefore might group yourself with them for certain purposes. What are some of the other social groups that come to mind when you consider aspects of your own "identity"? What benefits do you gain by associating yourself with each of these groups?

2. How do the various groups that you describe in question one relate to one another? Explain how your participation or membership in each group complicates your identity within the others.

Unity for What?
Black Feminism and Identity Politics

Pratibha Parmar

Identity Politics

In these postmodernist times the question of identity has taken on colossal weight
particularly for those of us who are post-colonial migrants inhabiting histories of
diaspora. Being cast into the role of the Other, marginalised, discriminated against
and too often invisible, not only within everyday discourses of affirmation but also
within the 'grand narratives' of European thought, black women in particular have
fought to assert privately and publicly our sense of self: a self that is rooted in
particular histories, cultures and languages. Black feminism has provided a space
and a framework for the articulation of our diverse identities as black women from
different ethnicities, classes and sexualities, even though at times that space had to
be fought for and negotiated.

To assert an individual and collective identity as black women has been a
necessary historical process which was both empowering and strengthening. To
organise self-consciously as black women was and continues to be important; that
form of organisation is not arbitrary, but is based on a political analysis of our
common economic, social and cultural oppressions. It is also based on an assumption
of shared subjectivities, of the ways in which our experiences of the world 'out there'
are shaped by common objective factors such as racism and sexual exploitation.

However, these assumptions have led to a political practice which employs a
language of 'authentic subjective experience'. The implications of such a practice are
multifold. It has given rise to a self-righteous assertion that if one inhabits a certain
identity this gives one the legitimate and moral right to guilt-trip others into particular ways of behaving. The women's movement in general has become dominated
by such tendencies. There has been an emphasis on accumulating a collection of
oppressed identities which in turn have given rise to a hierarchy of oppression. Such

From *Identity: Community, Culture, Difference* edited by Jonathan Rutherford. © 1990 Lawrence & Wishart.
Reprinted by permission of the publisher.

scaling has not only been destructive, but divisive and immobilising. Unwilling to work across all our differences, many women have retreated into ghettoised 'lifestyle politics' and find themselves unable to move beyond personal and individual experience.

Identity politics or a political practice which takes as its starting point only the personal and experiential modes of being has led to a closure which is both retrogressive and sometimes spine-chilling. Take for instance, the example of an article that appeared in *Spare Rib* entitled 'Ten Points for White Women to Feel Guilty About'. The title alone made some of us cringe in despair and consternation. There is an inherent essentialism in such articulations which has become pervasive within the women's movement in general and has led to political fragmentation. Lynne Segal has convincingly critiqued the biologistic and essentialist thinking which has begun to dominate much feminist analysis and practice in the 1980s and I would agree with the conclusion that 'Whereas the problem for women's liberation was once how to assert personal issues as political, the problem has now reversed to one where feminists need to argue that the political does not reduce to the personal'.[1]

Racial Identities

Another problem that has been more specific to black women and the black communities is that of shifting definitions of black identity. While I do want to point to some of the problems and consequences of identity politics I would not want to conclude that any analysis of the political and cultural articulations around identity should be abandoned. Rather, as Stuart Hall has argued:

> It seems to me that it is possible to think about the nature of new political identities, which isn't founded on the notion of some absolute, integral self and which clearly can't arise from some fully closed narrative of the self. A politics which accepts the 'no necessary or essential correspondence' of anything with anything, and there has to be *a politics of articulation*—politics as a hegemonic project.[2]

In trying to find my way towards such a politics I myself have turned to the writings of June Jordan, a black American poet and essayist[3] whose work has clarified many of my doubts and confusions and helped to clear the cobwebs of depair and anger. Val Amos and I found her book *Civil Wars* invaluable when we taught an adult education class on 'Women and Racism' at London University in 1984. At a time when many contemporary movements need to reassess the method and basis of their organising, June Jordan's moral and political vision offers an inspiration. Her commitment to internationalism and her ability to articulate the complex links and contradictions between the deeply personal and the deeply political in a clear and passionate way is rare. Her writings are a timely reminder that identity politics 'may be enough to get started on but not enough to get anything finished.' She visited Britain for the first time in September 1987 when I talked to her about some of the problems I have outlined above. Below are extracts from this interview by way of a conclusion.[4]

Pratibha: One of the most interesting and challenging things I have found in your writings is the way in which your radicalism refuses to suppress the complexity of our identities as women and as black people. In Britain there has been a tendency in the women's movement, both black and white, to organise around the assumptions of our shared identities but in the process of political organising many of these assumptions have fallen apart. Can you talk about some of the issues raised around identity politics and what you think it means to define oneself as a political person.

June Jordan: We have been organising on the basis of identity, around immutable attributes of gender, race and class for a long time and it doesn't seem to have worked. There are obvious reasons for getting together with other people because someone else is black or she is a woman but I think we have to try to develop habits of evaluation in whatever we attempt politically. People get set into certain ways of doing things and they don't evaluate whether it's working or not. Or if they do evaluate then it's to say it's not working but it's not our fault, there couldn't possibly be anything wrong with our thinking on this subject or the issue. The problem invariably is that the enemy is simply inflexible or impregnable. This is a doomed *modus operandi*. We have to find out what works and some things may work to a certain extent and not beyond that.

I don't think that gender politics or that race politics *per se* are isolated from other ways of organising for change, whether reformist change or revolutionary change. I don't think that they will take us where we want to go. I think that's abundantly clear if we look at our history as black people. We as black people have enormous problems everywhere in the world and we women have colossal problems everywhere in the world. I think there is something deficient in the thinking on the part of anybody who proposes either gender identity politics or race identity politics as sufficient, because every single one of us is more than whatever race we represent or embody and more than whatever gender category we fall into. We have other kinds of allegiances, other kinds of dreams that have nothing to do with whether we are white or not white.

A lot of awareness of ourselves as women, as black people and Third World people really comes out of our involuntary forced relationships with people who despise us on the basis of what we are rather than what we do. In other words our political awareness of ourselves derives more often than not from a necessity to find out why it is that this particular kind of persecution continues either for my people, or myself or my kind. Once you try to answer that question you find yourself in the territory of people who despise you, people who are responsible for the invention of the term racism or sexism. I think it's important to understand that each one of us is more than what cannot be changed about us. That seems self-evident and accordingly our politics should reflect that understanding.

This is not at all to disparage or dismiss the necessity for what I would call issue-oriented unity among different kinds of people, women, black people, or black women. I am not dismissing it but just saying that it's probably not enough. It may be enough to get started on something but I doubt very much whether it's enough to get anything finished.

Pratibha: So you are saying that in order to move forward, a crucial part of the political process is to go beyond the personal and experiential ways of organising. You have written, 'It occurs to me that much organisational grief could be avoided if people understood that partnership in misery does not necessarily provide for partnership for change: *when we get the monsters off our backs all of us may want to run in very different directions.*'

June Jordan: Yes, for example, I think that for any woman who has ever been raped, the existence of feminist or all-female rape counseling centres is absolutely necessary, the recourse to a refuge where a woman can retire to repair herself without fear. But the problem is more than an individual problem. She didn't rape herself. In order to eliminate the possibility of rape or even the likelihood of rape for women generally we have to go beyond ourselves. We have to sit down with and/or stand up to and finally in some way impact upon men. I don't think it's ever enough on your own. And I would say the same thing about race identity politics. I didn't, nor did my people or my parents, invent the problems that we as black people have to solve. We black people, the victims of racism are not the ones that have to learn new ways of thinking about things so that we can stop racist habits of thought. Neither do we have the power to be placed in appropriate situations to abolish the social and economic arrangements that have assured the continuity of racism in our lives. That's for white people. What we really need to do is pass the taking of succour from each other, so to speak, and build on our collective confidence and pride. Some people who I have met since I have been in London have been saying, it's terrible because nothing is going on politically. But that's not the point. I don't mean to knock that at all, but okay, now you know and I know that something is terrible, what are you going to do about it. Let's not sit inside our sorrows, let's not describe things to death. My orientation is activism. Other than that it's like a kind of vanity or a decadence. I will tell you how I suffer and you tell me how you suffer ... it's bad enough to suffer but to talk about it endlessly ... I say to them stop it ... stop it ...

Pratibha: Many movements such as the women's movement, the black movement and black women's groups have been organising for a number of years around their shared oppressions. But it seems to me that many of these movements are stagnating because there is a refusal to acknowledge the need to move away from modes of being, that is accumulating all the 'isms' of race, sex, class, disability etc, to modes of doing. What do you think are the dangers of this? How do you think we can move forward from this paralysis.

June Jordan: I am sure there is a danger. The first part of the political process is to recognise that there is a political problem and then to find people who agree with you. But the last part of the political process which is to get rid of it is necessary and something too many of us forget. I am not interested in struggle, I am interested in victory. Let's get rid of the problems, let's not just sit around and talk about it and hold each other's hands. That's where you make the evaluation: is it getting us there? If it's not, then let's have other kinds of meetings with other kinds of people. I think people can get stuck absolutely. What is the purpose of your identity? That is the question. 'So what?' is the way I would put it in my abrupt American way. What do you want to do on the basis of that? You just think that if you fill a room by putting out flyers, with 50 women of the same colour as you, somehow you have accomplished everything you set out to accomplish. I don't think so. Not at all, why are you meeting?

Almost every year black students at Stony Brook where I teach, come around to say to me that they want to hold a meeting and I say yes, and I ask what's it about. They say unity and I say unity for what? I am already black and you are black so we unify okay but I don't need to meet with you about that. When we get together, what's the purpose of that, what do you want to do? I don't need to sit in a room with other people who are black to know that I am black—that's not unity. Unity has to have some purpose to it otherwise we are not talking politics. I don't know what we are talking, maybe a mode of social life. That's okay, but beyond that people have to begin to understand that just because somebody is a woman or somebody is black does not mean that he or she and I should have the same politics. I don't think that's necessarily the case.

We should try to measure each other on the basis of what we do for each other rather than on the basis of who we are.

Pratibha: There has been a strong tendency in the women's movement to create hierarchies of oppression. What is your experience of this?

June: I have a tremendous instinctive aversion to the idea of ranking oppression. In other words for nobody to try and corner misery. I think it's dangerous. It seems to me to be an immoral way of going about things. The difficulty here is the sloppiness of language. We call everything an oppression, going to the dentist is an oppression, then the word does not mean anything. Revisions in our language might help and it might also steer us clear from saying something as useless as, but mine is this and yours is that. If I, a black woman poet and writer, a professor of English at State University, if I am oppressed then we need another word to describe a woman in a refugee camp in Palestine or the mother of six in a rural village in Nicaragua or any counterpart inside South Africa.

Pratibha: In the last few years there has been much talk about the need for coalitions and alliances between different groups of women not only nationally but internationally. What is your assessment of this form of political organising?

June: I would say about coalitions what I said about unity, which is what for? The issue should determine the social configuration of politics. I am not going to sit in a room with other people just to demonstrate black unity, we have got to have some reason for unity. Why should I coalesce with you and why do you coalesce with me? There has to be a reason why we need each other. It seems to me that an awareness of the necessity for international coalition should not be hard to come by in many spheres of feminist discourse because so many of our problems, apparently have universal currency. I think that never having been to London, for example, I can still be quite sure that most women here, whatever class or colour, are going to feel shy about walking out at night just as I do. I just assume that. That's about safety in the street. There is a universal experience for women, which is that physical mobility is circumscribed by our gender and by the enemies of our gender. This is one of the ways they seek to make us know their hatred and respect it. This holds throughout the world for women and literally we are not to move about in the world freely. If we do then we have to understand that we may have to pay for it with our bodies. That is the threat. They don't ask you what you are doing in the street, they rape you and mutilate you bodily to let you remember your place. You have no rightful place in public.

Everywhere in the world we have the least amount of income, everywhere in the world the intensity of the bond between women is seen to be subversive and it seems to me there would be good reasons to attempt international work against some of these common conditions. We cannot eliminate the problems unless we see them in their global dimensions. We should not fear the enlargement of our deliberate connections in this way. We should understand that this is a source of strength. It also makes it more difficult for anyone to destroy our movement. Okay, they can do whatever they want to in London, but there is Bangladesh, it's hydra-headed, it's happening everywhere, you can't destroy it. That's not to negate the necessity or obviate the need to work where you live but this is only part of a greater environment. I am talking against shortsightedness

I also think it's a good idea not to have any fixed notions in one's head. I don't want any one to tell me where I should put my attention first. If down the line we can try to respect each other according to the principle of self-determination then we can begin to move forward. There are enough of us to go around and you don't have to do what I do and vice versa. I do this and you do that, there is plenty of room.

Notes

1 Lynne Segal, *op.cit.*, p243.

2 Stuart Hall, 'Minimal Selves', in *ICA Documents*, London 1987, No.6, p45.

3 June Jordan was born in Harlem and raised in Brooklyn. She is the author of several award-winning books which include six volumes of poetry and two collections of political essays. Her poems and reviews have appeared in *The New York Times, The Nation, Essence* magazine and elsewhere. Two collections of her work, *Lyrical Campaigns: Selected Poems* and *Moving Towards Home: Selected Essays* have been published in 1989 by Virago.

4 Pratibha Parmar, 'Other Kinds of Dreams: an Interview with June Jordan', in *Spare Rib*, October 1987.

❖ ❖ ❖

Dynamics

1. Isolate a few passages in which Parmar or Jordan agree that "identity politics" can be valuable. How does their understanding of these values compare to your own? Explain how your experience or understanding of identity politics affects your response to this essay.

2. Parmar asks us to think of her interview with June Jordan as a "conclusion" to her own comments. Which of Jordan's statements seem to follow through on ideas raised by Parmar, and how do they do it? Which of Jordan's statements seem to be departures from Parmar's lines of thought? Explain what you see as the relationship between Parmar's comments and the interview with Jordan.

Critical Tools

1. Jordan writes that "partnership in misery does not necessarily provide for partnership for change." Locate passages in the essay and interview that help you to explain why this might be true for Jordan and Parmar. Then choose another text which, in your view, makes a similar argument. What do the two readings together tell you about the limitations of partnerships based on oppression? Where do the second reading's ideas challenge your interpretation of Jordan and Parmar?

2. According to Jordan, "Unity has to have some purpose to it otherwise we are not talking politics." Use Jordan's statement to evaluate expressions of "unity" in another essay you have read this semester. How and at what points does "unity" become "politics" in this second reading? Where do the expressions of unity that you find fall short of appearing "political" to you?

Draft One/Draft Two

Draft One: At one point in her interview with Parmar, June Jordan claims that she is "not interested in struggle, [she] is interested in victory." Compare Jordan's notions of "struggle" and "victory" with those you find in another essay in *Literacies*. What relationships do you find between these concepts in the second reading? How does this new reading help you to re-frame Jordan's comments?

Draft Two: Using the conclusions you reached in your first draft and your own experiences as a participant in or observer of political activism, explain your theory of the relationship between political struggle and victory. How has your reading of the other essays complicated your ideas about these relationships?

❖ ❖ ❖

Before Reading Clara Piriz. . .

1. Piriz writes about her changing conception of the man's and woman's roles in her marriage. Write informally about some of the ways you have seen marriage roles change. Are these changes caused by economic conditions, new social values, interpersonal dynamics, or other reasons? Explain what you think is happening to marriage. Do any other pieces you have read this semester help you talk about these questions?

2. Piriz also writes about the difficulties of living in exile, where she is assigned to a "marginal" place in a country far from her homeland. As far as you know, what are the biggest challenges to a person living "on the margin" of a society? What resources does a person on the margin have to work with?

Marriage by Pros and Cons

Clara Piriz

Abcoude, Holland,
May 12, 1984

Dear Kiddo,

I'm writing this letter with no margins, without counting lines, or pages, without measuring my words a damn bit. Our first communication uncensored and uncut.[1]

The big question is if I will manage to write without self-censorship...internalized censorship. Fear. My fear of causing you pain, of showing myself as I am, of confusing you in my confusion...My fear of losing what I've gained and gaining what I've lost...

A while ago I wrote you that it would be good for you to try to get out with a passport that would allow you to come and go. Let me explain why. At bottom it just has to do with another fear: the fear of ruining your life...even more.

Living in exile is a bitch. "Sure," you say, "it can't be worse than prison." True, prison is much worse. But, there is one fundamental difference: In prison you have to use all your energy to survive in a situation that doesn't depend on you and that you can't change. To survive in exile you have to use all your energy to change a situation of terrible inertia and, if it changes, it will be only because of your personal effort.

You arrive here with nothing, no friends, no job, no house, no family. You don't understand the system in which you've somehow got to function. The place assigned to you is marginal, socially, economically, politically, culturally, emotionally. No one gives a damn about you. You have no history. Or rather, the history you have, no one cares about. Although suddenly it occurs to some reporter to use you as material for an article. A monkey in the zoo. And you accept, of course, because it's part of the political work: call attention to Uruguay, get political pressure. But if you achieve anything, no one cares. There are too many people. Most of all there are too many

From Alicia Partnoy, ed., *You Can't Drown the Fire: Latin American Women Writing in Exile.* Cleis Press 1988. Reprinted by permission of the publisher.

foreigners. Discrimination exists, and it is rough. It sucks to feel looked down on, it sucks to have to do twice as much to get credit for half. It sucks when you say something and they look at you: *"and where did you crawl out..."* Not to mention worse things, like insults and violence.

But not all of it comes from outside of us; a lot we bring on ourselves. Most of the exiles resist adapting. They don't want to be here; they didn't choose to come to this country; everything is going wrong for them. The Dutch "smell bad"; *"you know how they are."* The exiles don't want to learn this fucking language, they refuse to give two and be counted for one. *"What for, anyway, if I'm going to leave..."* Result: Many of them have ended up completely screwed. Ten years of doing nothing of any worth, always running around, drinking beer and Geneva gin. Some of them read a lot, they remind me of your brother, a vagabond with books under his arm. Others have made a way for themselves, working like mules. Some have had the advantage of having studied, others of being stubborn workers with the "nasty habit of earning their living." This small group has one other problem: We are isolated because there's not enough time and energy to work, learn the language, etc...and still maintain friendships scattered all around the country.

A while ago I was talking with two Chileans and an Argentine woman I see regularly (a recently found remedy for the isolation). They said that even though they work, speak Dutch and have Dutch friends, communication with them had a limit they couldn't cross. I've heard that from other people. I must confess that is not the case with me. I have good friends who are Dutch, with whom my communication is excellent.

Well, as you see I'm not painting you a very pleasant picture. I can imagine that after twelve years in jail all this seems banal, but experience shows that once you are here the twelve years of jail don't help you think, *"What a terrific time I'm having."* On the contrary, those years are one more problem.

In your case, there might be some points in your favor. Supposing our relationship works out (another subject altogether), I have made a way that can make your adjustment easier.

You might ask yourself if I am telling you this to try to discourage you. No. What it means is that I know what you'll have to face if you come here. And I don't want to have it on my conscience that I lured you with a siren song.

Our situation is not very encouraging either: two years of living together in very abnormal conditions. Twelve years without seeing each other: you in jail, which has certainly changed you. Neither one of us knows what problems are going to crop up from that. Certainly, within normal limits, you've changed a great deal. But it's also logical to expect less normal changes. There is no superman who can come unscathed out of one of those places. I don't believe those people—and there are some—who come out saying, *"Prison? A great experience, it's nothing."* I also have lived through very hard experiences; I also am very much marked.

Besides, as a couple we're going to face a very strange situation. I have matured in this country, I have carried out a whole process of learning, of critical integration, of getting situated here, which you, one way or another, will have to carry out. This puts you in a position of dependence on me, which does not contribute to a healthy adult emotional relationship.

I'm finishing this letter today, June 24. Happy birthday! After yesterday's phone conversation I have such anxiety to see you, to talk to you, to touch you, that I can't imagine how I'm going to live from now until we see each other.

Yet there's so much we will have to discuss and go through!

And don't get all romantic on me and tell me that love, or the will to love, can overcome everything. No. It can overcome a lot, it is an essential condition, but not enough. I've seen so many who could not withstand the pressures of the change.

From a very young age, I have been bothered by rules without reasons, by *just because* or *because I said so* or *because that's the way it has to be*. It has bothered me as much in my social as in my private life. And systematically I have created a new set of rules based on my own experiences, on their analysis and synthesis and also on the reading and studies of the ideas of other (wiser) people. This attitude toward life is not new for me. Just think, if not, Carolina would not exist. Carolina was not an impulse, a mistake, a trangression. For me she was a conscious moral act which I have never regretted.

It was not always so easy: For years I struggled inside myself. Because sincerity is one of my values, at times I had to choose between the risk of destroying you or lying in the gentle way, by keeping quiet. Sometimes I kept quiet, sometimes I didn't. Finally I arrived at a formula: I'd try to let you know as best as possible how I felt about a lot of things and avoid the details that could be painful for you.

But my evolution is not only in that area. Most important to me is my maturity and my independence. That's why I made that comment on the phone yesterday: "You are going to have a hard time with me." I don't like to be ordered around, or told what to do. I reaffirm my right to my own decisions, your right to your own decisions, our right to be and think differently.

When I stayed alone with the girls I had to perform all of the roles; I was their mother and their father and their pet dog, too. I got used to it and from there I chose what I liked best to do, and that's not necessarily the womanly duties. Therefore (referring to a fantasy you wrote me about that frightened me): If you want home-made ravioli, make them yourself. I'll help you eat them. And I'll drink the wine. As a housekeeper I am consciously a disaster. My work is much more important to me, and my personal and professional development more than anything. For years my possibilities were limited by the urgency of moment to moment life, and by the girls' ages. Nevertheless, I got started with a brave effort. Now they are grown, they have their own independence, they're not attached to me, and I have found a phenomenal job. You can imagine that I'm grabbing onto that with all my strength. At my age it's my last chance and I can't and don't want to miss it.

We don't know what each of us means by a "primary relationship." You said it very blithely, as if there was a universally accepted formula. But I am certain that it's not that way. When I was twenty years old, I believed it, but not now, and that is not disillusionment, not at all, it's wisdom.

For instance, you asked me if I had a boyfriend. You didn't know how to deal with my answer. You said that could surely be the biggest stumbling block, and I answer you that the stumbling block is not that he exists...but the fact that *I* am capable of having a boyfriend.

I hold that I have been relentlessly faithful. Perhaps not in the way that you mean, but I'd bet if we talked about it, you'd see my way is much better.

Why do I want to see you? Because I do. Because I also allow myself the right to be (every once in a while) compulsive. I'm doing fine, I have a good job, a good social life, a serene and comforting relationship, the girls are growing up with no problems. Then why create problems for myself? Why not leave things as they are? Because I want to see you. Because I would feel terribly frustrated not to see you, because it would be a lack of respect for you, for me, for what we were, for what we are, and perhaps for what we might become...Because I want a second chance. Because only you and I can decide if it'll work or not. That decision is not for time, or distance, much less for the military to take. It's ours.

On the phone I found it hard to say I love you, for fear you misunderstood what I felt. So, I'll say: In my own way I love you. We'll have to see if my way and yours will meet—and grow.

Bye,
Clara

Translated by Regina M. Kreger

NOTE
1. This letter is Piriz's "first uncensored communication with her husband, who had been a political prisoner in Uruguay for twelve years."

Dynamics

1. Locate several places in Piriz's letter where she suggests a contrast between someone's expectations about life in Holland and her own experience there as a woman in exile. For each of these passages describe the goals or values of the outsider's expectations as well as the contrasting goals or values of Piriz. Review your findings and discuss the pattern or patterns you see there.

2. Consider several places in her letter where Piriz challenges a traditional notion of a woman's role in marriage. Look closely at the language she uses in each of those passages, and use the words and phrases you find there to help you describe her values and the values she is resisting. What kind of evidence does she find persuasive as she argues for a new role in marriage? Do you find the same evidence persuasive? Why or why not?

3. What relations do you see between Piriz's understanding of exile and her understanding of marriage, especially as you have traced them both in your answers to questions 1 and 2, above?

Critical Tools

1. Piriz is concerned that she find a way to communicate without "self-censorship" or "internalized censorship." Locate one or two passages that help you explain what she means by this and why this goal is so important to her. How does this goal relate to two or three of the important decisions she describes later in the letter?

2. In the section of the letter about the exile's life on the margin of society, Piriz talks about being "marked." Find some passages that allow you to define that term, or the process that must go along with it. How does this idea of being marked apply to another text you have read this semester?

3. Piriz says that she has always resisted "rules without reasons," and she goes on to describe a systematic program for resisting them. Test that program on the events she describes in her letter or on the events in another text you have read this semester. How does it work?

Draft One/Draft Two

Draft One: Think about the ways her experiences in exile and in marriage have helped her define her goals and values. Use passages from both parts of her letter to explain, as much as you can, what for Piriz is "the good life." How do you situate yourself in relation to these values, and why?

Draft Two: Test the answer you have sketched in draft one against the goals and values of a person from another text you have read this semester. As you examine the experiences of someone like Rosaura (from "The Stolen Party") or James Baldwin or Maya Angelou, how do the goals and values and sense of "the good life" belonging to Piriz and to you work in this other context? What complications arise? How do you resolve them?

❖ ❖ ❖

Before Reading Adrienne Rich. . .

1. In your experience, under what circumstances do people tend to lie? When would you pardon a lie and why?

2. How would you define a "white lie"? How are "white lies" different from other kinds of lies?

Women and Honor: Some Notes on Lying

Adrienne Rich

These notes were first read at the Hartwick Women Writers' Workshop, founded and directed by Beverly Tanenhaus, at Hartwick College, Oneonta, New York, in June 1975. They were published as a pamphlet by Motheroot Press in Pittsburgh, 1977; in *Heresies: A Feminist Magazine of Art and Politics*, vol. 1, no. 1; and in a French translation by the Québecois feminist press, Les Editions du Remue-Ménage, 1979.

It is clear that among women we need a new ethics; as women, a new morality. The problem of speech, of language, continues to be primary. For if in our speaking we are breaking silences long established, "liberating ourselves from our secrets" in the words of Beverly Tanenhaus, this is in itself a first kind of action. I wrote *Women and Honor* in an effort to make myself more honest, and to understand the terrible negative power of the lie in relationships between women. Since it was published, other women have spoken and written of things I did not include: Michelle Cliff's "Notes on Speechlessness" in *Sinister Wisdom* no. 5 led Catherine Nicolson (in the same issue) to write of the power of "deafness," the frustration of our speech by those who do not want to hear what we have to say. Nelle Morton has written of the act of "hearing each other into speech."* How do we listen? How do we make it possible for another to break her silence? These are some of the questions which follow on the ones I have raised here.

(These notes are concerned with relationships between and among women. When "personal relationship" is referred to, I mean a relationship between two women. It will be clear in what follows when I am talking about women's relationships with men.)

*Nelle Morton, "Beloved Image!", paper delivered at the National Conference of the American Academy of Religion, San Francisco, California, December 28, 1977.

The old, male idea of honor. A man's "word" sufficed—to other men—without guarantee.

"Our Land Free, Our Men Honest, Our Women Fruitful"—a popular colonial toast in America.

Male honor also having something to do with killing: *I could not love thee, Dear, so much/Lov'd I not Honour more* ("To Lucasta, On Going to the Wars"). Male honor as something needing to be avenged: hence, the duel.

Women's honor, something altogether else: virginity, chastity, fidelity to a husband. Honesty in women has not been considered important. We have been depicted as generically whimsical, deceitful, subtle, vacillating. And we have been rewarded for lying.

Men have been expected to tell the truth about facts, not about feelings. They have not been expected to talk about feelings at all.

Yet even about facts they have continually lied.

We assume that politicians are without honor. We read their statements trying to crack the code. The scandals of their politics: not that men in high places lie, only that they do so with such indifference, so endlessly, still expecting to be believed. We are accustomed to the contempt inherent in the political lie.

• • •

To discover that one has been lied to in a personal relationship, however, leads one to feel a little crazy.

• • •

Lying is done with words, and also with silence.

The woman who tells lies in her personal relationships may or may not plan or invent her lying. She may not even think of what she is doing in a calculated way.

A subject is raised which the liar wishes buried. She has to go downstairs, her parking meter will have run out. Or, there is a telephone call she ought to have made an hour ago.

She is asked, point-blank, a question which may lead into painful talk: "How do you feel about what is happening between us?" Instead of trying to describe her feelings in their ambiguity and confusion, she asks, "How do *you* feel?" The other, because she is trying to establish a ground of openness and trust, begins describing her own feelings. Thus the liar learns more than she tells.

And she may also tell herself a lie: that she is concerned with the other's feelings, not with her own.

But the liar is concerned with her own feelings.

The liar lives in fear of losing control. She cannot even desire a relationship without manipulation, since to be vulnerable to another person means for her the loss of control.

The liar has many friends, and leads an existence of great loneliness.

• • •

The liar often suffers from amnesia. Amnesia is the silence of the unconscious.

To lie habitually, as a way of life, is to lose contact with the unconscious. It is like taking sleeping pills, which confer sleep but blot out dreaming. The unconscious wants truth. It ceases to speak to those who want something else more than truth.

In speaking of lies, we come inevitably to the subject of truth. There is nothing simple or easy about this idea. There is no "the truth," "a truth"—truth is not one thing, or even a system. It is an increasing complexity. The pattern of the carpet is a surface. When we look closely, or when we become weavers, we learn of the tiny multiple threads unseen in the overall pattern, the knots on the underside of the carpet.

This is why the effort to speak honestly is so important. Lies are usually attempts to make everything simpler—for the liar—than it really is, or ought to be.

In lying to others we end up lying to ourselves. We deny the importance of an event, or a person, and thus deprive ourselves of a part of our lives. Or we use one piece of the past or present to screen out another. Thus we lose faith even with our own lives.

The unconscious wants truth, as the body does. The complexity and fecundity of dreams come from the complexity and fecundity of the unconscious struggling to fulfill that desire. The complexity and fecundity of poetry come from the same struggle.

• • •

An honorable human relationship—that is, one in which two people have the right to use the word "love"—is a process, delicate, violent, often terrifying to both persons involved, a process of refining the truths they can tell each other.

It is important to do this because it breaks down human self-delusion and isolation.

It is important to do this because in so doing we do justice to our own complexity.

It is important to do this because we can count on so few people to go that hard way with us.

• • •

I come back to the questions of women's honor. Truthfulness has not been considered important for women, as long as we have remained physically faithful to a man, or chaste.

We have been expected to lie with our bodies: to bleach, redden, unkink or curl our hair, pluck eyebrows, shave armpits, wear padding in various places or lace ourselves, take little steps, glaze finger and toe nails, wear clothes that emphasized our helplessness.

We have been required to tell different lies at different times depending on what the men of the time needed to hear. The Victorian wife or the white southern lady, who were expected to have no sensuality, to "lie still"; the twentieth-century "free" woman who is expected to fake orgasms.

We have had the truth of our bodies withheld from us or distorted; we have been kept in ignorance of our most intimate places. Our instincts have been punished: clitoridectomies for "lustful" nuns or for "difficult" wives. It has been difficult, too, to know the lies of our complicity from the lies we believed.

The lie of the "happy marriage," of domesticity—we have been complicit, have acted out the fiction of a well-lived life, until the day we testify in court of rapes, beatings, psychic cruelties, public and private humiliations.

Patriarchal lying has manipulated women both through falsehood and through silence. Facts we needed have been withheld from us. False witness has been borne against us.

And so we must take seriously the question of truthfulness between women, truthfulness among women. As we cease to lie with our bodies, as we cease to take on faith what men have said about us, is a truly womanly idea of honor in the making?

· · ·

Women have been forced to lie, for survival, to men. How to unlearn this among other women?

"Women have always lied to each other."

"Women have always whispered the truth to each other."

Both of these axioms are true.

"Women have always been divided against each other."

"Women have always been in secret collusion."

Both of these axioms are true.

In the struggle for survival we tell lies. To bosses, to prison guards, the police, men who have power over us, who legally own us and our children, lovers who need us as proof of their manhood.

There is a danger run by all powerless people: that we forget we are lying, or that lying becomes a weapon we carry over into relationships with people who do not have power over us.

· · ·

I want to reiterate that when we talk about women and honor, or women and lying, we speak within the context of male lying, the lies of the powerful, the lie as false source of power.

Women have to think whether we want, in our relationships with each other, the kind of power that can be obtained through lying.

Women have been driven mad, "gaslighted," for centuries by the refutation of our experience and our instincts in a culture which validates only male experience. The truth of our bodies and our minds has been mystified to us. We therefore have a primary obligation to each other: not to undermine each others' sense of reality for the sake of expediency; not to gaslight each other.

Women have often felt insane when cleaving to the truth of our experience. Our future depends on the sanity of each of us, and we have a profound stake, beyond the personal, in the project of describing our reality as candidly and fully as we can to each other.

• • •

There are phrases which help us not to admit we are lying: "my privacy," "nobody's business but my own." The choices that underlie these phrases may indeed be justified; but we ought to think about the full meaning and consequences of such language.

Women's love for women has been represented almost entirely through silence and lies. The institution of heterosexuality has forced the lesbian to dissemble, or be labeled a pervert, a criminal, a sick or dangerous woman, etc., etc. The lesbian, then, has often been forced to lie, like the prostitute or the married women.

Does a life "in the closet"—lying, perhaps of necessity, about ourselves to bosses, landlords, clients, colleagues, family, because the law and public opinion are founded on a lie—does this, can it, spread into private life, so that lying (described as *discretion*) becomes an easy way to avoid conflict or complication? Can it become a strategy so ingrained that it is used even with close friends and lovers?

Heterosexuality as an institution has also drowned in silence the erotic feelings between women. I myself lived half a lifetime in the lie of that denial. That silence makes us all, to some degree, into liars.

When a woman tells the truth she is creating the possibility for more truth around her.

• • •

The liar leads an existence of unutterable loneliness.

The liar is afraid.

But we are all afraid: without fear we become manic, hubristic, self-destructive. What is this particular fear that possesses the liar?

She is afraid that her own truths are not good enough.

She is afraid, not so much of prison guards or bosses, but of something unnamed within her.

The liar fears the void.

The void is not something created by patriarchy, or racism, or capitalism. It will not fade away with any of them. It is part of every woman.

"The dark core," Virginia Woolf named it, writing of her mother. The dark core. It is beyond personality; beyond who loves us or hates us.

We begin out of the void, out of darkness and emptiness. It is part of the cycle understood by the old pagan religions, that materialism denies. Out of death, re-birth; out of nothing, something.

The void is the creatrix, the matrix. It is not mere hollowness and anarchy. But in women it has been identified with lovelessness, barrenness, sterility. We have been urged to fill our "emptiness" with children. We are not supposed to go down into the darkness of the core.

Yet, if we can risk it, the something born of that nothing is the beginning of our truth.

The liar in her terror wants to fill up the void, with anything. Her lies are a denial of her fear; a way of maintaining control.

• • •

Why do we feel slightly crazy when we realize we have been lied to in a relationship?

We take so much of the universe on trust. You tell me: "In 1950 I lived on the north side of Beacon Street in Somerville." You tell me: "She and I were lovers, but for months now we have only been good friends." You tell me: "It is seventy degrees outside and the sun is shining." Because I love you, because there is not even a question of lying between us, I take these accounts of the universe on trust: your address twenty-five years ago, your relationship with someone I know only by sight, this morning's weather. I fling unconscious tendrils of belief, like slender green threads, across statements such as these, statements made so unequivocally, which have no tone or shadow of tentativeness. I build them into the mosaic of my world. I allow my universe to change in minute, significant ways, on the basis of things you have said to me, of my trust in you.

I also have faith that you are telling me things it is important I should know; that you do not conceal facts from me in an effort to spare me, or yourself, pain.

Or, at the very least, that you will say, "There are things I am not telling you."

When we discover that someone we trusted can be trusted no longer, it forces us to reexamine the universe, to question the whole instinct and concept of trust. For awhile, we are thrust back onto some bleak, jutting ledge, in a dark pierced by sheets of fire, swept by sheets of rain, in a world, before kinship, or naming, or tenderness exist; we are brought close to formlessness.

• • •

The liar may resist confrontation, denying that she lied. Or she may use other language: forgetfulness, privacy, the protection of someone else. Or, she may bravely declare herself a coward. This allows her to go on lying, since that is what cowards do. She does not say, *I was afraid*, since this would open the question of other ways of handling her fear. It would open the question of what is actually feared.

She may say, *I didn't want to cause pain*. What she really did not want is to have to deal with the other's pain. The lie is a short-cut through another's personality.

• • •

Truthfulness, honor, is not something which springs ablaze of itself; it has to be created between people.

This is true in political situations. The quality and depth of the politics evolving from a group depends in very large part on their understanding of honor.

Much of what is narrowly termed "politics" seems to rest on a longing for certainty even at the cost of honesty, for an analysis which, once given, need not be reexamined. Such is the deadendedness—for women—of Marxism in our time.

Truthfulness anywhere means a heightened complexity. But it is a movement into evolution. Women are only beginning to uncover our own truths; many of us would be grateful for some rest in that struggle, would be glad just to lie down with the sherds we have painfully unearthed, and be satisfied with those. Often I feel this like an exhaustion in my own body.

The politics worth having, the relationships worth having, demand that we delve still deeper.

• • •

The possibilities that exist between two people, or among a group of people, are a kind of alchemy. They are the most interesting thing in life. The liar is someone who keeps losing sight of these possibilities.

When relationships are determined by manipulation, by the need for control, they may possess a dreary, bickering kind of drama, but they cease to be interesting. They are repetitious; the shock of human possibilities has ceased to reverberate through them.

When someone tells me a piece of the truth which has been withheld from me, and which I needed in order to see my life more clearly, it may bring acute pain, but it can also flood me with a cold, sea-sharp wash of relief. Often such truths come by accident, or from strangers.

It isn't that to have an honorable relationship with you, I have to understand everything, or tell you everything at once, or that I can know, beforehand, everything I need to tell you.

It means that most of the time I am eager, longing for the possibility of telling you. That these possibilities may seem frightening, but not destructive, to me. That I feel strong enough to hear your tentative and groping words. That we both know we are trying, all the time, to extend the possibilities of truth between us.

The possibility of life between us.

❖ ❖ ❖

Dynamics

1. What relation do you see between the style (or form) of Rich's essay and the issues she explores in her writing? Find some passages where this relationship seems significant and explain why you think it is important.

2. How is Rich's definition of "truth" complicated by the examples of lying that she offers?

3. Rich writes, at one point, that "the liar fears the void." Later she states that, when we realize that someone is lying to us, "we are brought close to formlessness." Using passages from her essay, try to figure out the connection between "the void" and what Rich calls "formlessness." Why, according to your reading of her essay, might this relationship be important to understand?

Critical Tools

1. Rich writes that "it has been difficult...to know the lies of our complicity from the lies we believed." Which passages in her essay help you to determine what "complicity" means for Rich? Once you have a working definition of this term, apply it to another text you have read this semester. How does your definition need to change when you place it within a different context?

2. Near the end of her essay, Rich argues that honor "has to be created between people." Use Rich's theories of honor in order to evaluate another essay in which honor seems to be an important issue. What, so far as you can tell, are the factors that contribute to a group's understanding of honor? How would Rich respond to these other notions of honor?

Draft One/Draft Two

Draft One: To what extent does your own experience of the relationship between truthfulness and gender reflect the cultural patterns that Rich maps out in her text? Write an essay in which you show where and how you learned what it meant for a woman or for a man to be "truthful." How have these lessons about gender and honor helped to shape your current relationships with other people (both male and female)?

Draft Two: Re-read your own experiences with honor and gender in terms of another text you have read this semester. Consider how class, ethnicity, or some other social category complicates a person's understanding of sexual honor.

❖ ❖ ❖

Before Reading Richard Rodriguez. . .

1. In which ways do race or ethnic origin shape what a person will attain in life? Discuss the various--even conflicting--ideas that arise for you in connection with this question.

2. In general terms, how would you define the attribute called "power"? Offer examples of traits that indicate power, in your estimation, and explain why they do. List as many traits and examples as you can think of.

Complexion

Richard Rodriguez

Visiting the East Coast or the gray capitals of Europe during the long months of winter, I often meet people at deluxe hotels who comment on my complexion. (In such hotels it appears nowadays a mark of leisure and wealth to have a complexion like mine.) Have I been skiing? In the Swiss Alps? Have I just returned from a Caribbean vacation? No. I say no softly but in a firm voice that intends to explain: My complexion is dark. (My skin is brown. More exactly, terra-cotta in sunlight, tawny in shade. I do not redden in sunlight. Instead, my skin becomes progressively dark; the sun singes the flesh.)

When I was a boy the white summer sun of Sacramento would darken me so, my T-shirt would seem bleached against my slender dark arms. My mother would see me come up the front steps. She'd wait for the screen door to slam at my back. 'You look like a *negrito*,' she'd say, angry, sorry to be angry, frustrated almost to laughing, scorn. 'You know how important looks are in this country. With *los gringos* looks are all that they judge on. But you! Look at you! You're so careless!' Then she'd start in all over again. 'You won't be satisfied till you end up looking like *los pobres* who work in the fields, *los braceros*.'

(*Los braceros:* Those men who work with their *brazos*, their arms; Mexican nationals who were licensed to work for American farmers in the 1950s. They worked very hard for very little money, my father would tell me. And what money they earned they sent back to Mexico to support their families, my mother would add. *Los pobres*—the poor, the pitiful, the powerless ones. But paradoxically also powerful men. They were the men with brown-muscled arms I stared at in awe on Saturday mornings when they showed up downtown like gypsies to shop at Woolworth's or Penney's. On Monday nights they would gather hours early on the steps of the Memorial Auditorium for the wrestling matches. Passing by on my bicycle in summer, I would spy them there, clustered in small groups, talking—frightening and fascinating men—some wearing Texas *sombreros* and T-shirts which shone fluorescent in the twilight. I would sit forward in the back seat of our family's '48 Chevy to see them, working alongside Valley highways: dark men on an even horizon, loading a truck amid rows of straight green. Powerful, powerless men. Their fascinating darkness—like mine—to be feared.)

'You'll end up looking just like them.'

1

Regarding my family, I see faces that do not closely resemble my own. Like some other Mexican families, my family suggests Mexico's confused colonial past. Gathered around a table, we appear to be from separate continents. My father's face recalls faces I have seen in France. His complexion is white—he does not tan; he does not burn. Over the years, his dark wavy hair has grayed handsomely. But with time his face has sagged to a perpetual sigh. My mother, whose surname is inexplicably Irish—Moran—has an olive complexion. People have frequently wondered if, perhaps, she is Italian or Portuguese. And, in fact, she looks as though she could be from southern Europe. My mother's face has not aged as quickly as the rest of her body; it remains smooth and glowing—a cool tan—which her gray hair cleanly accentuates. My older brother has inherited her good looks. When he was a boy people would tell him that he looked like Mario Lanza, and hearing it he would smile with dimpled assurance. He would come home from high school with girl friends who seemed to me glamorous (because they were) blonds. And during those years I envied him his skin that burned red and peeled like the skin of the *gringos*. His complexion never darkened like mine. My youngest sister is exotically pale, almost ashen. She is delicately featured, Near Eastern, people have said. Only my older sister has a complexion as dark as mine, though her facial features are much less harshly defined than my own. To many people meeting her, she seems (they say) Polynesian. I am the only one in the family whose face is severely cut to the line of ancient Indian ancestors. My face is mournfully long, in the classical Indian manner; my profile suggests one of those beak-nosed Mayan sculptures—the eaglelike face upturned, open-mouthed, against the deserted, primitive sky.

'We are Mexicans,' my mother and father would say, and taught their four children to say whenever we (often) were asked about our ancestry. My mother and father scorned those 'white' Mexican-Americans who tried to pass themselves off as Spanish. My parents would never have thought of denying their ancestry. I never denied it: My ancestry is Mexican, I told strangers mechanically. But I never forgot that only my older sister's complexion was as dark as mine.

My older sister never spoke to me about her complexion when she was a girl. But I guessed that she found her dark skin a burden. I knew that she suffered for being a 'nigger.' As she came home from grammar school, little boys came up behind her and pushed her down to the sidewalk. In high school, she struggled in the adolescent competition for boyfriends in a world of football games and proms, a world where her looks were plainly uncommon. In college, she was afraid and scornful when dark-skinned foreign students from countries like Turkey and India

found her attractive. She revealed her fear of dark skin to me only in adulthood
when, regarding her own three children, she quietly admitted relief that they were
all light.

That is the kind of remark women in my family have often made before. As a
boy, I'd stay in the kitchen (never seeming to attract any notice), listening while my
aunts spoke of their pleasure at having light children. (The men, some of whom
were dark-skinned from years of working out of doors, would be in another part of
the house.) It was the woman's spoken concern: the fear of having a dark-skinned
son or daughter. Remedies were exchanged. One aunt prescribed to her sisters the
elixir of large doses of castor oil during the last weeks of pregnancy. (The remedy
risked an abortion.) Children born dark grew up to have their faces treated regularly with a mixture of egg white and lemon juice concentrate. (In my case, the solution never would take.) One Mexican-American friend of my mother's, who regarded
it a special blessing that she had a measure of English blood, spoke disparagingly of
her husband, a construction worker, for being so dark. 'He doesn't take care of
himself,' she complained. But the remark, I noticed, annoyed my mother, who sat
tracing an invisible design with her finger on the tablecloth.

There was affection too and a kind of humor about these matters. With daring
tenderness, one of my uncles would refer to his wife as *mi negra*. An aunt regularly
called her dark child *mi feito* (my little ugly one), her smile only partially hidden as
she bent down to dig her mouth under his ticklish chin. And at times relatives spoke
scornfully of pale, white skin. A *gringo*'s skin resembled *masa*—baker's dough—
someone remarked. Everyone laughed. Voices chuckled over the fact that the *gringos* spent so many hours in summer sunning themselves. ('They need to get sun
because they look like *los muertos.*')

I heard the laughing but remembered what the women had said, with unsmil-
ing voices, concerning dark skin. Nothing I heard outside the house, regarding my
skin, was so impressive to me.

In public I occasionally heard racial slurs. Complete strangers would yell out at
me. A teenager drove past, shouting, 'Hey, Greaser! Hey, Pancho!' Over his shoulder
I saw the giggling face of his girl friend. A boy pedaled by and announced matter-of-
factly, 'I pee on dirty Mexicans.' Such remarks would be said so casually that I
wouldn't quickly realize that they were being addressed to me. When I did, I would
be paralyzed with embarrassment, unable to return the insult. (Those times I
happened to be with white grammar school friends, *they* shouted back. Imbued with
the mysterious kindness of children, my friends would never ask later why I hadn't
yelled out in my own defense.)

In all, there could not have been more than a dozen incidents of name-calling.
That there were so few suggests that I was not a primary victim of racial abuse. But
that, even today, I can clearly remember particular incidents is proof of their impact. Because of such incidents, I listened when my parents remarked that Mexicans
were often mistreated in California border towns. And in Texas. I listened carefully
when I heard that two of my cousins had been refused admittance to an 'all-white'

swimming pool. And that an uncle had been told by some man to go back to Africa. I followed the progress of the southern black civil rights movement, which was gaining prominent notice in Sacramento's afternoon newspaper. But what most intrigued me was the connection between dark skin and poverty. Because I heard my mother speak so often about the relegation of dark people to menial labor, I considered the great victims of racism to be those who were poor and forced to do menial work. People like the farm workers whose skin was dark from the sun.

After meeting a black grammar school friend of my sister's, I remember thinking that she wasn't really 'black.' What interested me was the fact that she wasn't poor. (Her well-dressed parents would come by after work to pick her up in a shiny green Oldsmobile.) By contrast, the garbage men who appeared every Friday morning seemed to me unmistakably black. (I didn't bother to ask my parents why Sacramento garbage men always were black. I thought I knew.) One morning I was in the backyard when a man opened the gate. He was an ugly, square-faced black man with popping red eyes, a pail slung over his shoulder. As he approached, I stood up. And in a voice that seemed to me very weak, I piped, 'Hi.' But the man paid me no heed. He strode past to the can by the garage. In a single broad movement, he overturned its contents into his larger pail. Our can came crashing down as he turned and left me watching, in awe.

'*Pobres negros,*' my mother remarked when she'd notice a headline in the paper about a civil rights demonstration in the South. 'How the *gringos* mistreat them.' In the same tone of voice she'd tell me about the mistreatment her brother endured years before. (After my grandfather's death, my grandmother had come to America with her son and five daughters.) 'My sisters, we were still all just teenagers. And since *mi pápa* was dead, my brother had to be the head of the family. He had to support us, to find work. But what skills did he have! Twenty years old. *Pobre.* He was tall, like your grandfather. And strong. He did construction work. "Construction!" The *gringos* kept him digging all day, doing the dirtiest jobs. And they would pay him next to nothing. Sometimes they promised him one salary and paid him less when he finished. But what could he do? Report them? We weren't citizens then. He didn't even know English. And he was dark. What chances could he have? As soon as we sisters got older, he went right back to Mexico. He hated this country. He looked so tired when he left. Already with a hunchback. Still in his twenties. But old-looking. No life for him here. *Pobre.*'

Dark skin was for my mother the most important symbol of a life of oppressive labor and poverty. But both my parents recognized other symbols as well.

My father noticed the feel of every hand he shook. (He'd smile sometimes— marvel more than scorn—remembering a man he'd met who had soft, uncalloused hands.)

My mother would grab a towel in the kitchen and rub my oily face sore when I came in from playing outside. 'Clean the *graza* off of your face!' (*Greaser!*)

Symbols: When my older sister, then in high school, asked my mother if she could do light housework in the afternoons for a rich lady we knew, my mother was frightened by the idea. For several weeks she troubled over it before granting conditional permission: 'Just remember, you're not a maid. I don't want you wearing a uniform.' My father echoed the same warning. Walking with him past a hotel, I watched as he stared at a doorman dressed like a Beefeater. 'How can anyone let himself be dressed up like that? Like a clown. Don't you ever get a job where you have to put on a uniform.' In summertime neighbors would ask me if I wanted to earn extra money by mowing their lawns. Again and again my mother worried: 'Why did they ask *you*? Can't you find anything better?' Inevitably, she'd relent. She knew I needed the money. But I was instructed to work after dinner. ('When the sun's not so hot.') Even then, I'd have to wear a hat. *Un sombrero de* baseball.

(*Sombrero*. Watching gray cowboy movies, I'd brood over the meaning of the broad-rimmed hat—that troubling symbol—which comically distinguished a Mexican cowboy from real cowboys.)

From my father came no warnings concerning the sun. His fear was of dark factory jobs. He remembered too well his first jobs when he came to this country, not intending to stay, just to earn money enough to sail on to Australia. (In Mexico he had heard too many stories of discrimination in *los Estados Unidos*. So it was Australia, that distant island-continent, that loomed in his imagination as his 'America.') The work my father found in San Francisco was work for the unskilled. A factory job. Then a cannery job. (He'd remember the noise and the heat.) Then a job at a warehouse. (He'd remember the dark stench of old urine.) At one place there were fistfights; at another a supervisor who hated Chinese and Mexicans. Nowhere a union.

His memory of himself in those years is held by those jobs. Never making money enough for passage to Australia; slowly giving up the plan of returning to school to resume his third-grade education—to become an engineer. My memory of him in those years, however, is lifted from photographs in the family album which show him on his honeymoon with my mother—the woman who had convinced him to stay in America. I have studied their photographs often, seeking to find in those figures some clear resemblance to the man and the woman I've known as my parents. But the youthful faces in the photos remain, behind dark glasses, shadowy figures anticipating my mother and father.

They are pictured on the grounds of the Coronado Hotel near San Diego, standing in the pale light of a winter afternoon. She is wearing slacks. Her hair falls seductively over one side of her face. He appears wearing a double-breasted suit, an unneeded raincoat draped over his arm. Another shows them standing together, solemnly staring ahead. Their shoulders barely are touching. There is to their pose an aristocratic formality, an elegant Latin hauteur.

The man in those pictures is the same man who was fascinated by Italian grand opera. I have never known just what my father saw in the spectacle, but he has told me that he would take my mother to the Opera House every Friday night— if he had money enough for orchestra seats. ('Why go to sit in the balcony?') On Sundays he'd don Italian silk scarves and a camel's hair coat to take his new wife to the polo matches in Golden Gate Park. But one weekend my father stopped going to the opera and polo matches. He would blame the change in his life on one job—a warehouse job, working for a large corporation which today advertises its products with the smiling faces of children. 'They made me an old man before my time,' he'd say to me many years later. Afterward, jobs got easier and cleaner. Eventually, in middle age, he got a job making false teeth. But his youth was spent at the warehouse. 'Everything changed,' his wife remembers. The dapper young man in the old photographs yielded to the man I saw after dinner: haggard, asleep on the sofa. During 'The Ed Sullivan Show' on Sunday nights, when Roberta Peters or Licia Albanese would appear on the tiny blue screen, his head would jerk up alert. He'd sit forward while the notes of Puccini sounded before him. ('Un bel dí.')

By the time they had a family, my parents no longer dressed in very fine clothes. Those symbols of great wealth and the reality of their lives too noisily clashed. No longer did they try to fit themselves, like paper-doll figures, behind trappings so foreign to their actual lives. My father no longer wore silk scarves or expensive wool suits. He sold his tuxedo to a secondhand store for five dollars. My mother sold her rabbit fur coat to the wife of a Spanish radio station disc jockey. ('It looks better on you than it does on me,' she kept telling the lady until the sale was completed.) I was six years old at the time, but I recall watching the transaction with complete understanding. The woman I knew as my mother was already physically unlike the woman in her honeymoon photos. My mother's hair was short. Her shoulders were thick from carrying children. Her fingers were swollen red, toughened by housecleaning. Already my mother would admit to foreseeing herself in her own mother, a woman grown old, bald and bowlegged, after a hard lifetime of working.

In their manner, both my parents continued to respect the symbols of what they considered to be upper-class life. Very early, they taught me the *propria* way of eating *como los ricos*. And I was carefully taught elaborate formulas of polite greeting and parting. The dark little boy would be invited by classmates to the rich houses on Forty-fourth and Forty-fifth streets. 'How do you do?' or 'I am very pleased to meet you,' I would say, bowing slightly to the amused mothers of classmates. 'Thank you very much for the dinner; it was very delicious.'

I made an impression. I intended to make an impression, to be invited back. (I soon realized that the trick was to get the mother or father to notice me.) From those early days began my association with rich people, my fascination with their secret. My mother worried. She warned me not to come home expecting to have the things my friends possessed. But she needn't have said anything. When I went to the big houses, I remembered that I was, at best, a visitor to the world I saw there. For that reason, I was an especially watchful guest. I was my parents' child. Things most middle-class children wouldn't trouble to notice, I studied. Remembered to see: the starched black and white uniform worn by the maid who opened the door; the Mexican gardeners—their complexions as dark as my own. (One gardener's face, glassed by sweat, looked up to see me going inside.)

'Take Richard upstairs and show him your electric train,' the mother said. But it was really the vast polished dining room table I'd come to appraise. Those nights when I was invited to stay for dinner, I'd notice that my friend's mother rang a small silver bell to tell the black woman when to bring in the food. The father, at his end of the table, ate while wearing his tie. When I was not required to speak, I'd skate the icy cut of crystal with my eye; my gaze would follow the golden threads etched onto the rim of china. With my mother's eyes I'd see my hostess's manicured nails and judge them to be marks of her leisure. Later, when my schoolmate's father would bid me goodnight, I would feel his soft fingers and palm when we shook hands. And turning to leave, I'd see my dark self, lit by chandelier light, in a tall hallway mirror.

2

Complexion. My first conscious experience of sexual excitement concerns my complexion. One summer weekend, when I was around seven years old, I was at a public swimming pool with the whole family. I remember sitting on the damp pavement next to the pool and seeing my mother, in the spectators' bleachers, holding my younger sister on her lap. My mother, I noticed, was watching my father as he stood on a diving board, waving to her. I watched her wave back. Then saw her radiant, bashful, astonishing smile. In that second I sensed that my mother and father had a relationship I knew nothing about. A nervous excitement encircled my stomach as I saw my mother's eyes follow my father's figure curving into the water. A second or two later, he emerged. I heard him call out. Smiling, his voice sounded, buoyant, calling me to swim to him. But turning to see him, I caught my mother's eye. I heard her shout over to me. In Spanish she called through the crowd: 'Put a towel on over your shoulders.' In public, she didn't want to say why. I knew.

That incident anticipates the shame and sexual inferiority I was to feel in later years because of my dark complexion. I was to grow up an ugly child. Or one who thought himself ugly. (*Feo*.) One night when I was eleven or twelve years old, I locked myself in the bathroom and carefully regarded my reflection in the mirror over the sink. Without any pleasure I studied my skin. I turned on the faucet. (In my mind I heard the swirling voices of aunts, and even my mother's voice, whispering, whispering incessantly about lemon juice solutions and dark, *feo* children.) With a bar of soap, I fashioned a thick ball of lather. I began soaping my arms. I took my father's straight razor out of the medicine cabinet. Slowly, with steady deliberateness, I put the blade against my flesh, pressed it as close as I could without cutting, and moved it up and down across my skin to see if I could get out, somehow lessen, the dark. All I succeeded in doing, however, was in shaving my arms bare of their hair. For as I noted with disappointment, the dark would not come out. It remained. Trapped. Deep in the cells of my skin.

Throughout adolescence, I felt myself mysteriously marked. Nothing else about my appearance would concern me so much as the fact that my complexion was dark. My mother would say how sorry she was that there was not money enough to get braces to straighten my teeth. But I never bothered about my teeth. In three-way mirrors at department stores, I'd see my profile dramatically defined by a long nose, but it was really only the color of my skin that caught my attention.

I wasn't afraid that I would become a menial laborer because of my skin. Nor did my complexion make me feel especially vulnerable to racial abuse. (I didn't really consider my dark skin to be a racial characteristic. I would have been only too happy to look as Mexican as my light-skinned older brother.) Simply, I judged myself ugly. And, since the women in my family had been the ones who discussed it in such worried tones, I felt my dark skin made me unattractive to women.

Thirteen years old. Fourteen. In a grammar school art class, when the assignment was to draw a self-portrait, I tried and I tried but could not bring myself to shade in the face on the paper to anything like my actual tone. With disgust then I would come face to face with myself in mirrors. With disappointment I located myself in class photographs—my dark face undefined by the camera which had clearly described the white faces of classmates. Or I'd see my dark wrist against my long-sleeved white shirt.

I grew divorced from my body. Insecure, overweight, listless. On hot summer days when my rubber-soled shoes soaked up the heat from the sidewalk, I kept my head down. Or walked in the shade. My mother didn't need anymore to tell me to watch out for the sun. I denied myself a sensational life. The normal, extraordinary, animal excitement of feeling my body alive—riding shirtless on a bicycle in the warm wind created by furious self-propelled motion—the sensations that first had excited in me a sense of my maleness, I denied. I was too ashamed of my body. I wanted to forget that I had a body because I had a brown body. I was grateful that none of my classmates ever mentioned the fact.

I continued to see the *braceros*, those men I resembled in one way and, in another way, didn't resemble at all. On the watery horizon of a Valley afternoon, I'd see them. And though I feared looking like them, it was with silent envy that I regarded them still. I envied them their physical lives, their freedom to violate the taboo of the sun. Closer to home I would notice the shirtless construction workers, the roofers, the sweating men tarring the street in front of the house. And I'd see the Mexican gardeners. I was unwilling to admit the attraction of their lives. I tried to deny it by looking away. But what was denied became strongly desired.

In high school physical education classes, I withdrew, in the regular company of five or six classmates, to a distant corner of a football field where we smoked and talked. Our company was composed of bodies too short or too tall, all graceless and all—except mine—pale. Our conversation was usually witty. (In fact we were intelligent.) If we referred to the athletic contests around us, it was with sarcasm. With savage scorn I'd refer to the 'animals' playing football or baseball. It would have been important for me to have joined them. Or for me to have taken off my shirt, to have let the sun burn dark on my skin, and to have run barefoot on the warm wet grass. It would have been very important. Too important. It would have been too telling a gesture—to admit the desire for sensation, the body, my body.

Fifteen, sixteen. I was a teenager shy in the presence of girls. Never dated. Barely could talk to a girl without stammering. In high school I went to several dances, but I never managed to ask a girl to dance. So I stopped going. I cannot remember high school years now with the parade of typical images: bright drive-ins or gliding blue shadows of a Junior Prom. At home most weekend nights, I would pass evenings reading. Like those hidden, precocious adolescents who have no real-life sexual experiences, I read a great deal of romantic fiction. 'You won't find it in your books,' my brother would playfully taunt me as he prepared to go to a party by freezing the crest of the wave in his hair with sticky pomade. Through my reading, however, I developed a fabulous and sophisticated sexual imagination. At seventeen, I may not have known how to engage a girl in small talk, but I had read *Lady Chatterley's Lover*.

It annoyed me to hear my father's teasing: that I would never know what 'real work' is; that my hands were so soft. I think I knew it was his way of admitting pleasure and pride in my academic success. But I didn't smile. My mother said she was glad her children were getting their educations and would not be pushed around like *los pobres*. I heard the remark ironically as a reminder of my separation from *los braceros*. At such times I suspected that education was making me effeminate. The odd thing, however, was that I did not judge my classmates so harshly. Nor did I consider my male teachers in high school effeminate. It was only myself I judged against some shadowy, mythical Mexican laborer—dark like me, yet very different.

Language was crucial. I knew that I had violated the ideal of the *macho* by becoming such a dedicated student of language and literature. *Machismo* was a word never exactly defined by the persons who used it. (It was best described in the 'proper' behavior of men.) Women at home, nevertheless, would repeat the old Mexican dictum that a man should be *feo, fuerte, y formal*. 'The three *F*'s,' my mother called them, smiling slyly. *Feo* I took to mean not literally ugly so much as ruggedly handsome. (When my mother and her sisters spent a loud, laughing afternoon determining ideal male good looks, they finally settled on the actor Gilbert Roland, who was neither too pretty nor ugly but had looks 'like a man.') *Fuerte*, 'strong,' seemed to mean not physical strength as much as inner strength, character. A dependable man is *fuerte*. *Fuerte* for that reason was a characteristic subsumed by the last of the three qualities, and the one I most often considered—*formal*. To be *formal* is to be steady. A man of responsibility, a good provider. Someone *formal* is also constant. A person to be relied upon in adversity. A sober man, a man of high seriousness.

I learned a great deal about being *formal* just by listening to the way my father and other male relatives of his generation spoke. A man was not silent necessarily. Nor was he limited in the tones he could sound. For example, he could tell a long, involved, humorous story and laugh at his own humor with high-pitched giggling. But a man was not talkative the way a woman could be. It was permitted a woman to be gossipy and chatty. (When one heard many voices in a room, it was usually women who were talking.) Men spoke much less rapidly. And often men spoke in monologues. (When one voice sounded in a crowded room, it was most often a man's voice one heard.) More important than any of this was the fact that a man never verbally revealed his emotions. Men did not speak about their unease in moments of crisis or danger. It was the woman who worried aloud when her husband got laid off from work. At times of illness or death in the family, a man was usually quiet, even silent. Women spoke up to voice prayers. In distress, women always sounded quick ejaculations to God or the Virgin; women prayed in clearly audible voices at a wake held in a funeral parlor. And on the subject of love, a woman was verbally expansive. She spoke of her yearning and delight. A married man, if he spoke publicly about love, usually did so with playful, mischievous irony. Younger, unmarried men more often were quiet. (The *macho* is a silent suitor. *Formal.*)

At home I was quiet, so perhaps I seemed *formal* to my relations and other Spanish-speaking visitors to the house. But outside the house—my God!—I talked. Particularly in class or alone with my teachers, I chattered. (Talking seemed to make teachers think I was bright.) I often was proud of my way with words. Though, on other occasions, for example, when I would hear my mother busily speaking to women, it would occur to me that my attachment to words made me like her. Her son. Not *formal* like my father. At such times I even suspected that my nostalgia for sounds—the noisy, intimate Spanish sounds of my past—was nothing more than effeminate yearning.

High school English teachers encouraged me to describe very personal feelings in words. Poems and short stories I wrote, expressing sorrow and loneliness, were awarded high grades.

In my bedroom were books by poets and novelists—books that I loved—in which male writers published feelings the men in my family never revealed or acknowledged in words. And it seemed to me that there was something unmanly about my attachment to literature. Even today, when so much about the myth of the *macho* no longer concerns me, I cannot altogether evade such notions. Writing these pages, admitting my embarrassment or my guilt, admitting my sexual anxieties and my physical insecurity, I have not been able to forget that I am not being *formal.*

So be it.

3

I went to college at Stanford, attracted partly by its academic reputation, partly because it was the school rich people went to. I found myself on a campus with golden children of western America's upper middle class. Many were students both ambitious for academic success *and* accustomed to leisured life in the sun. In the afternoon, they lay spread out, sunbathing in front of the library, reading Swift or Engels or Beckett. Others went by in convertibles, off to play tennis or ride horses or sail. Beach boys dressed in tank-tops and shorts were my classmates in undergraduate seminars. Tall tan girls wearing white strapless dresses sat directly in front of me in lecture rooms. I'd study them, their physical confidence. I was still recognizably kin to the boy I had been. Less tortured perhaps. But still kin. At Stanford, it's true, I began to have something like a conventional sexual life. I don't think, however, that I really believed that the women I knew found me physically appealing. I continued to stay out of the sun. I didn't linger in mirrors. And I was the student at Stanford who remembered to notice the Mexican-American janitors and gardeners working on campus.

It was at Stanford, one day near the end of my senior year, that a friend told me about a summer construction job he knew was available. I was quickly alert. Desire uncoiled within me. My friend said that he knew I had been looking for summer employment. He knew I needed some money. Almost apologetically he explained: It was something I probably wouldn't be interested in, but a friend of his, a contractor, needed someone for the summer to do menial jobs. There would be lots of shoveling and raking and sweeping. Nothing too hard. But nothing more interesting either. Still, the pay would be good. Did I want it? Or did I know someone who did?

I did. Yes, I said, surprised to hear myself say it.

In the weeks following, friends cautioned that I had no idea how hard physical labor really is. ('You only *think* you know what it is like to shovel for eight hours straight.') Their objections seemed to me challenges. They resolved the issue. I became happy with my plan. I decided, however, not to tell my parents. I wouldn't tell my mother because I could guess her worried reaction. I would tell my father only after the summer was over, when I could announce that, after all, I did know what 'real work' is like.

The day I met the contractor (a Princeton graduate, it turned out), he asked me whether I had done any physical labor before. 'In high school, during the summer,' I lied. And although he seemed to regard me with skepticism, he decided to give me a try. Several days later, expectant, I arrived at my first construction site. I would take off my shirt to the sun. And at last grasp desired sensation. No longer afraid. At last become like a *bracero*. 'We need those tree stumps out of here by tomorrow,' the contractor said. I started to work.

I labored with excitement that first morning—and all the days after. The work was harder than I could have expected. But it was never as tedious as my friends had warned me it would be. There was too much physical pleasure in the labor. Especially early in the day, I would be most alert to the sensations of movement and straining. Beginning around seven each morning (when the air was still damp but the scent of weeds and dry earth anticipated the heat of the sun), I would feel my body resist the first thrusts of the shovel. My arms, tightened by sleep, would gradually loosen; after only several minutes, sweat would gather in beads on my forehead and then—a short while later—I would feel my chest silky with sweat in the breeze. I would return to my work. A nervous spark of pain would fly up my arm and settle to burn like an ember in the thick of my shoulder. An hour, two passed.

Three. My whole body would assume regular movements; my shoveling would be described by identical, even movements. Even later in the day, my enthusiasm for primitive sensation would survive the heat and the dust and the insects pricking my back. I would strain wildly for sensation as the day came to a close. At three-thirty, quitting time, I would stand upright and slowly let my head fall back, luxuriating in the feeling of tightness relieved.

Some of the men working nearby would watch me and laugh. Two or three of the older men took the trouble to teach me the right way to use a pick, the correct way to shovel. 'You're doing it wrong, too fucking hard,' one man scolded. Then proceeded to show me—what persons who work with their bodies all their lives quickly learn—the most economical way to use one's body in labor.

'Don't make your back do so much work,' he instructed. I stood impatiently listening, half listening, vaguely watching, then noticed his work-thickened fingers clutching the shovel. I was annoyed. I wanted to tell him that I enjoyed shoveling the wrong way. And I didn't want to learn the right way. I wasn't afraid of back pain. I liked the way my body felt sore at the end of the day.

I was about to, but, as it turned out, I didn't say a thing. Rather it was at that moment I realized that I was fooling myself if I expected a few weeks of labor to gain me admission to the world of the laborer. I would not learn in three months what my father had meant by 'real work.' I was not bound to this job; I could imagine its rapid conclusion. For me the sensations of exertion and fatigue could be savored. For my father or uncle, working at comparable jobs when they were my age, such sensations were to be feared. Fatigue took a different toll on their bodies—and minds.

It was, I know, a simple insight. But it was with this realization that I took my first step that summer toward realizing something even more important about the 'worker.' In the company of carpenters, electricians, plumbers, and painters at lunch, I would often sit quietly, observant. I was not shy in such company. I felt easy, pleased by the knowledge that I was casually accepted, my presence taken for granted by men (exotics) who worked with their hands. Some days the younger men would talk and talk about sex, and they would howl at women who drove by in cars. Other days the talk at lunchtime was subdued; men gathered in separate groups. It depended on who was around. There were rough, good-natured workers. Others were quiet. The more I remember that summer, the more I realize that there was no single *type* of worker. I am embarrassed to say I had not expected such diversity. I certainly had not expected to meet, for example, a plumber who was an abstract painter in his off hours and admired the work of Mark Rothko. Nor did I expect to meet so many workers with college diplomas. (They were the ones who were not surprised that I intended to enter graduate school in the fall.) I suppose what I really want to say here is painfully obvious, but I must say it nevertheless: The men of that summer were middle-class Americans. They certainly didn't constitute an oppressed society. Carefully completing their work sheets; talking about the fortunes of local football teams; planning Las Vegas vacations; comparing the gas mileage of various makes of campers—they were not *los pobres* my mother had spoken about.

On two occasions, the contractor hired a group of Mexican aliens. They were employed to cut down some trees and haul off debris. In all, there were six men of varying age. The youngest in his late twenties; the oldest (his father?) perhaps sixty years old. They came and they left in a single old truck. Anonymous men. They were never introduced to the other men at the site. Immediately upon their arrival, they would follow the contractor's directions, start working—rarely resting—seemingly driven by a fatalistic sense that work which had to be done was best done as quickly as possible.

I watched them sometimes. Perhaps they watched me. The only time I saw them pay me much notice was one day at lunchtime when I was laughing with the other men. The Mexicans sat apart when they ate, just as they worked by themselves. Quiet. I rarely heard them say much to each other. All I could hear were their voices calling out sharply to one another, giving directions. Otherwise, when they stood briefly resting, they talked among themselves in voices too hard to overhear.

The contractor knew enough Spanish, and the Mexicans—or at least the oldest of them, their spokesman—seemed to know enough English to communicate. But because I was around, the contractor decided one day to make me his translator. (He assumed I could speak Spanish.) I did what I was told. Shyly I went over to tell the Mexicans that the *patrón* wanted them to do something else before they left for the day. As I started to speak, I was afraid with my old fear that I would be unable to pronounce the Spanish words. But it was a simple instruction I had to convey. I could say it in phrases.

The dark sweating faces turned toward me as I spoke. They stopped their work to hear me. Each nodded in response. I stood there. I wanted to say something more. But what could I say in Spanish, even if I could have pronounced the words right? Perhaps I just wanted to engage them in small talk, to be assured of their confidence, our familiarity. I thought for a moment to ask them where in Mexico they were from. Something like that. And maybe I wanted to tell them (a lie, if need be) that my parents were from the same part of Mexico.

I stood there.

Their faces watched me. The eyes of the man directly in front of me moved slowly over my shoulder, and I turned to follow his glance toward *el patrón* some distance away. For a moment I felt swept up by that glance into the Mexicans' company. But then I heard one of them returning to work. And then the others went back to work. I left them without saying anything more.

When they had finished, the contractor went over to pay them in cash. (He later told me that he paid them collectively—'for the job,' though he wouldn't tell me their wages. He said something quickly about the good rate of exchange 'in their own country.') I can still hear the loudly confident voice he used with the Mexicans. It was the sound of the *gringo* I had heard as a very young boy. And I can still hear the quiet, indistinct sounds of the Mexican, the oldest, who replied. At hearing that voice I was sad for the Mexicans. Depressed by their vulnerability. Angry at myself. The adventure of the summer seemed suddenly ludicrous. I would not shorten the distance I felt from *los pobres* with a few weeks of physical labor. I would not become like them. They were different from me.

After that summer, a great deal—and not very much really—changed in my life. The curse of physical shame was broken by the sun; I was no longer ashamed of my body. No longer would I deny myself the pleasing sensations of my maleness. During those years when middle-class black Americans began to assert with pride, 'Black is beautiful,' I was able to regard my complexion without shame. I am today darker than I ever was as a boy. I have taken up the middle-class sport of long-distance running. Nearly every day now I run ten or fifteen miles, barely clothed, my skin exposed to the California winter rain and wind or the summer sun of late afternoon. The torso, the soccer player's calves and thighs, the arms of the twenty-year-old I never was, I possess now in my thirties. I study the youthful parody shape in the mirror: the stomach lipped tight by muscle; the shoulders rounded by chin-ups; the arms veined strong. This man. A man. I meet him. He laughs to see me, what I have become.

The dandy. I wear double-breasted Italian suits and custom-made English shoes. I resemble no one so much as my father—the man pictured in those honeymoon photos. At that point in life when he abandoned the dandy's posture, I assume it. At the point when my parents would not consider going on vacation, I register at the Hotel Carlyle in New York and the Plaza Athenée in Paris. I am as taken by the symbols of leisure and wealth as they were. For my parents, however, those symbols became taunts, reminders of all they could not achieve in one lifetime. For me those same symbols are reassuring reminders of public success. I tempt vulgarity to be reassured. I am filled with the gaudy delight, the monstrous grace of the nouveau riche.

In recent years I have had occasion to lecture in ghetto high schools. There I see students of remarkable style and physical grace. (One can see more dandies in such schools than one ever will find in middle-class high schools.) There is not the look of casual assurance I saw students at Stanford display. Ghetto girls mimic high-fashion models. Their dresses are of bold, forceful color; their figures elegant, long; the stance theatrical. Boys wear shirts that grip at their overdeveloped muscular bodies. (Against a powerless future, they engage images of strength.) Bad nutrition does not yet tell. Great disappointment, fatal to youth, awaits them still. For the moment, movements in school hallways are dancelike, a procession of postures in a sexual masque. Watching them, I feel a kind of envy. I wonder how different my adolescence would have been had I been free.... But no, it is my parents I see—their optimism during those years when they were entertained by Italian grand opera.

The registration clerk in London wonders if I have just been to Switzerland. And the man who carries my luggage in New York guesses the Caribbean. My complexion becomes a mark of my leisure. Yet no one would regard my complexion the same way if I entered such hotels through the service entrance. That is only to say that my complexion assumes its significance from the context of my life. My skin, in itself, means nothing. I stress the point because I know there are people who would label me 'disadvantaged' because of my color. They make the same mistake I made as a boy, when I thought a disadvantaged life was circumscribed by particular occupations. That summer I worked in the sun may have made me physically indistinguishable from the Mexicans working nearby. (My skin was actually darker because, unlike them, I worked without wearing a shirt. By late August my hands were probably as tough as theirs.) But I was not one of *los pobres*. What made me different from them was an attitude of *mind*, my imagination of myself.

I do not blame my mother for warning me away from the sun when I was young. In a world where her brother had become an old man in his twenties because he was dark, my complexion was something to worry about. 'Don't run in the sun,' she warns me today. I run. In the end, my father was right—though perhaps he did not know how right or why—to say that I would never know what real work is. I will never know what he felt at his last factory job. If tomorrow I worked at some kind of factory, it would go differently for me. My long education would favor me. I could act as a public person—able to defend my interests, to unionize, to petition, to speak up—to challenge and demand. (I will never know what real work is.) I will never know what the Mexicans knew, gathering their shovels and ladders and saws.

Their silence stays with me now. The wages those Mexicans received for their labor were only a measure of their disadvantaged condition. Their silence is more telling. They lack a public identity. They remain profoundly alien. Persons apart. People lacking a union obviously, people without grounds. They depend upon the relative good will or fairness of their employers each day. For such people, lacking a better alternative, it is not such an unreasonable risk.

Their silence stays with me. I have taken these many words to describe its impact. Only: the quiet. Something uncanny about it. Its compliance. Vulnerability. Pathos. As I heard their truck rumbling away, I shuddered, my face mirrored with sweat. I had finally come face to face with *los pobres*.

❖ ❖ ❖

Dynamics

1. Locate several passages in which Rodriguez discusses *los pobres* and explain the attitudes he reveals toward them in each passage. What is the significance of your findings?

2. Trace Rodriguez's use of the terms *feo*, *formal*, and *fuerte*. Consider how he redefines the terms, and explain how he uses these terms to shape himself or his understanding of himself.

Critical Tools

1. Rodriguez decides that what distinguishes him from *los pobres* was his "attitude of mind, [his] imagination of [him]self." Isolate some of Rodriguez's thoughts about, or interactions with, *los pobres* in order to frame a discussion about the nature of these alternate "attitudes of mind." How do you evaluate his theory?

2. In his essay Rodriguez emphatically distinguishes his personal experience from the experience of his cultural or ethnic group. Choose another writer in *Literacies* who does the same thing, and compare the ways the two authors relate to their cultural or ethnic group. Consider also the procedures by which they distinguish themselves from the group. How do you evaluate these two writers' efforts at cultural differentiation?

Draft One/Draft Two

Draft One: Consider Rodriguez's response to the "powerful, powerless" working men he viewed as a child. Which aspects of these men's lives seem not to have occurred to Rodriguez and how do these aspects challenge or complicate Rodriguez's arguments?

Draft Two: Choose another text from *Literacies* that addresses issues of power. How do the ideas, implications, and examples of power from these two texts reflect on each other? How, in turn, does this new perspective allow you to revise your understanding of the "powerful, powerless" working men in draft one?

❖   ❖   ❖

Before Reading Renato Rosaldo. . .

1. Write briefly about an experience you have had with the death of a family member or friend. In what specific ways was your reaction to his or her death distinct from that of someone with a different relation to that person? How do you explain the difference?

2. Think about some issue between yourself and a friend which you have trouble resolving because of some social difference (race, age, gender, class, religious background, etc.). What kinds of arguments do each of you tend to use in order to explain your position to the other? If you have had success in working through this issue, what would you say made that understanding possible (besides your desire to maintain the relationship)?

Grief and a Headhunter's Rage

Renato Rosaldo

If you ask an older Ilongot man of northern Luzon, Philippines, why he cuts off human heads, his answer is brief, and one on which no anthropologist can readily elaborate: He says that rage, born of grief, impels him to kill his fellow human beings. He claims that he needs a place "to carry his anger." The act of severing and tossing away the victim's head enables him, he says, to vent and, he hopes, throw away the anger of his bereavement. Although the anthropologist's job is to make other cultures intelligible, more questions fail to reveal any further explanation of this man's pithy statement. To him, grief, rage, and headhunting go together in a self-evident manner. Either you understand it or you don't. And, in fact, for the longest time I simply did not.

In what follows, I want to talk about how to talk about the cultural force of emotions. The *emotional force* of a death, for example, derives less from an abstract brute fact than from a particular intimate relation's permanent rupture. It refers to the kinds of feelings one experiences on learning, for example, that the child just run over by a car is one's own and not a stranger's. Rather than speaking of death in general, one must consider the subject's position within a field of social relations in order to grasp one's emotional experience.

My effort to show the force of a simple statement taken literally goes against anthropology's classic norms, which prefer to explicate culture through the gradual thickening of symbolic webs of meaning. By and large, cultural analysts use not *force* but such terms as *thick description, multivocality, polysemy, richness,* and *texture.* The notion of force, among other things, opens to question the common anthropological assumption that the greatest human import resides in the densest forest of symbols and that analytical detail, or "cultural depth," equals enhanced explanation of a culture, or "cultural elaboration." Do people always in fact describe most thickly what matters most to them?

The Rage in Ilongot Grief

Let me pause a moment to introduce the Ilongots, among whom my wife, Michelle Rosaldo, and I lived and conducted field research for thirty months (1967-69, 1974). They number about 3,500 and reside in an upland area some 90 miles northeast of Manila, Philippines. They subsist by hunting deer and wild pig and by cultivating rain-fed gardens (swiddens) with rice, sweet potatoes, manioc, and vegetables. Their (bilateral) kin relations are reckoned through men and women. After marriage, parents and their married daughters live in the same or adjacent households. The largest unit within the society, a largely territorial descent group called the *bertan*, becomes manifest primarily in the context of feuding. For themselves, their neighbors, and their ethnographers, head-hunting stands out as the Ilongots' most salient cultural practice.

When Ilongots told me, as they often did, how the rage in bereavement could impel men to headhunt, I brushed aside their one-line accounts as too simple, thin, opaque, implausible, stereotypical, or otherwise unsatisfying. Probably I naively equated grief with sadness. Certainly no personal experience allowed me to imagine the powerful rage Ilongots claimed to find in bereavement. My own inability to conceive the force of anger in grief led me to seek out another level of analysis that could provide a deeper explanation for older men's desire to headhunt.

Not until some fourteen years after first recording the terse Ilongot statement about grief and a headhunter's rage did I begin to grasp its overwhelming force. For years I thought that more verbal elaboration (which was not forthcoming) or another analytical level (which remained elusive) could better explain older men's motives for headhunting. Only after being repositioned through a devastating loss of my own could I better grasp that Ilongot older men mean precisely what they say when they describe the anger in bereavement as the source of their desire to cut off human heads. Taken at face value and granted its full weight, their statement reveals much about what compels these older men to headhunt.

In my efforts to find a "deeper" explanation for headhunting, I explored exchange theory, perhaps because it had informed so many classic ethnographies. One day in 1974, I explained the anthropologist's exchange model to an older Ilongot man named Insan. What did he think, I asked, of the idea that headhunting resulted from the way that one death (the beheaded victim's) canceled another (the next of kin). He looked puzzled, so I went on to say that the victim of a beheading was exchanged for the death of one's own kin, thereby balancing the books, so to speak. Insan reflected a moment and replied that he imagined somebody could think such a thing (a safe bet, since I just had), but that he and other Ilongots did not think any such thing. Nor was there any indirect evidence for my exchange theory in ritual, boast, song, or casual conversation.

In retrospect, then, these efforts to impose exchange theory on one aspect of Ilongot behavior appear feeble. Suppose I had discovered what I sought? Although the notion of balancing the ledger does have a certain elegant coherence, one wonders how such bookish dogma could inspire any man to take another man's life at the risk of his own.

My life experience had not as yet provided the means to imagine the rage that can come with devastating loss. Nor could I, therefore, fully appreciate the acute problem of meaning that Ilongots faced in 1974. Shortly after Ferdinand Marcos declared martial law in 1972, rumors that firing squads had become the new punishment for headhunting reached the Ilongot hills. The men therefore decided to call a moratorium on taking heads. In past epochs, when headhunting had become impossible, Ilongots had allowed their rage to dissipate, as best it could, in the course of everyday life. In 1974, they had another option; they began to consider conversion to evangelical Christianity as a means of coping with their grief. Accepting the new religion, people said, implied abandoning their old ways, including headhunting. It also made coping with bereavement less agonizing because they could believe that the deceased had departed for a better world. No longer did they have to confront the awful finality of death.

The force of the dilemma faced by the Ilongots eluded me at the time. Even when I correctly recorded their statements about grieving and the need to throw away their anger, I simply did not grasp the weight of their words. In 1974, for example, while Michelle Rosaldo and I were living among the Ilongots, a six-month-old baby died, probably of pneumonia. That afternoon we visited the father and found him terribly stricken. "He was sobbing and staring through glazed and blood-shot eyes at the cotton blanket covering his baby." The man suffered intensely, for this was the seventh child he had lost. Just a few years before, three of his children had died, one after the other, in a matter of days. At the time, the situation was murky as people present talked both about evangelical Christianity (the possible renunciation of taking heads) and their grudges against lowlanders (the contemplation of headhunting forays into the surrounding valleys).

Through subsequent days and weeks, the man's grief moved him in a way I had not anticipated. Shortly after the baby's death, the father converted to evangelical Christianity. Altogether too quick on the inference, I immediately concluded that the man believed that the new religion could somehow prevent further deaths in his family. When I spoke my mind to an Ilongot friend, he snapped at me, saying that "I had missed the point: what the man in fact sought in the new religion was not the denial of our inevitable deaths but a means of coping with his grief. With the advent of martial law, headhunting was out of the question as a means of venting his wrath and thereby lessening his grief. Were he to remain in his Ilongot way of life, the pain of his sorrow would simply be too much to bear." My description from 1980 now seems so apt that I wonder how I could have written the words and nonetheless failed to appreciate the force of the grieving man's desire to vent his rage.

Another representative anecdote makes my failure to imagine the rage possible in Ilongot bereavement all the more remarkable. On this occasion, Michelle Rosaldo and I were urged by Ilongot friends to play the tape of a headhunting celebration we had witnessed some five years before. No sooner had we turned on the tape and heard the boast of a man who had died in the intervening years than did people abruptly tell us to shut off the recorder. Michelle Rosaldo reported on the tense conversation that ensued:

As Insan braced himself to speak, the room again became almost uncannily electric. Backs straightened and my anger turned to nervousness and something more like fear as I saw that Insan's eyes were red. Tukbaw, Renato's Ilongot "brother," then broke into what was a brittle silence, saying he could make things clear. He told us that it hurt to listen to a headhunting celebration when people knew that there would never be another. As he put it: "The song pulls at us, drags our hearts, it makes us think of our dead uncle." And again: "It would be better if I had accepted God, but I still am an Ilongot at heart; and when I hear the song, my heart aches as it does when I must look upon unfinished bachelors whom I know that I will never lead to take a head." Then Wagat, Tukbaw's wife, said with her eyes that all my questions gave her pain, and told me: "Leave off now, isn't that enough? Even I, a woman, cannot stand the way it feels inside my heart."

From my present position, it is evident that the tape recording of the dead man's boast evoked powerful feelings of bereavement, particularly rage and the impulse to headhunt. At the time I could only feel apprehensive and diffusely sense the force of the emotions experienced by Insan, Tukbaw, Wagat, and the others present.

The dilemma for the Ilongots grew out of a set of cultural practices that, when blocked, were agonizing to live with. The cessation of headhunting called for painful adjustments to other modes of coping with the rage they found in bereavement. One could compare their dilemma with the notion that the failure to perform rituals can create anxiety. In the Ilongot case, the cultural notion that throwing away a human head also casts away the anger creates a problem of meaning when the headhunting ritual cannot be performed. Indeed, Max Weber's classic problem of meaning in *The Protestant Ethic and the Spirit of Capitalism* is precisely of this kind. On a logical plane, the Calvinist doctrine of predestination seems flawless: God has chosen the elect, but his decision can never be known by mortals. Among those whose ultimate concern is salvation, the doctrine of predestination is as easy to grasp conceptually as it is impossible to endure in everyday life (unless one happens to be a "religious virtuoso"). For Calvinists and Ilongots alike, the problem of meaning resides in practice, not theory. The dilemma for both groups involves the practical matter of how to live with one's beliefs, rather than the logical puzzlement produced by abstruse doctrine.

How I Found the Rage in Grief

One burden of this introduction concerns the claim that it took some fourteen years for me to grasp what Ilongots had told me about grief, rage, and headhunting. During all those years I was not yet in a position to comprehend the force of anger possible in bereavement, and now I am. Introducing myself into this account requires a certain hesitation both because of the discipline's taboo and because of its increasingly frequent violation by essays laced with trendy amalgams of continental philosophy and autobiographical snippets. If classic ethnography's vice was the slippage from the ideal of detachment to actual indifference, that of present-day reflexivity is the tendency for the self-absorbed Self to lose sight altogether of the culturally different Other. Despite the risks involved, as the ethnographer I must enter the discussion at this point to elucidate certain issues of method.

The key concept in what follows is that of the positioned (and repositioned) subject. In routine interpretive procedure, according to the methodology of hermeneutics, one can say that ethnographers reposition themselves as they go about understanding other cultures. Ethnographers begin research with a set of questions, revise them throughout the course of inquiry, and in the end emerge with different questions than they started with. One's surprise at the answer to a question, in other words, requires one to revise the question until lessening surprises or diminishing returns indicate a stopping point. This interpretive approach has been most influentially articulated within anthropology by Clifford Geertz.

Interpretive method usually rests on the axiom that gifted ethnographers learn their trade by preparing themselves as broadly as possible. To follow the meandering course of ethnographic inquiry, field-workers require wide-ranging theoretical capacities and finely tuned sensibilities. After all, one cannot predict beforehand what one will encounter in the field. One influential anthropologist, Clyde Kluckhohn, even went so far as to recommend a double initiation: first, the ordeal of psychoanalysis, and then that of fieldwork. All too often, however, this view is extended until certain prerequisites of field research appear to guarantee an authoritative ethnography. Eclectic book knowledge and a range of life experiences, along with edifying reading and self-awareness, supposedly vanquish the twin vices of ignorance and insensitivity.

Although the doctrine of preparation, knowledge, and sensibility contains much to admire, one should work to undermine the false comfort that it can convey. At what point can people say that they have completed their learning or their life experience? The problem with taking this mode of preparing the ethnographer too much to heart is that it can lend a false air of security, an authoritative claim to certitude and finality that our analyses cannot have. All interpretations are provisional; they are made by positioned subjects who are prepared to know certain things and not others. Even when knowledgeable, sensitive, fluent in the language, and able to move easily in an alien cultural world, good ethnographers still have their limits, and their analyses always are incomplete. Thus, I began to fathom the force of what Ilongots had been telling me about their losses through my own loss, and not through any systematic preparation for field research.

My preparation for understanding serious loss began in 1970 with the death of my brother, shortly after his twenty-seventh birthday. By experiencing this ordeal with my mother and father, I gained a measure of insight into the trauma of a parent's losing a child. This insight informed my account, partially described earlier, of an Ilongot man's reactions to the death of his seventh child. At the same time, my bereavement was so much less than that of my parents that I could not then imagine the overwhelming force of rage possible in such grief. My former position is probably similar to that of many in the discipline. One should recognize that ethnographic knowledge tends to have the strengths and limitations given by the relative youth of field-workers who, for the most part, have not suffered serious losses and could have, for example, no personal knowledge of how devastating the loss of a long-term partner can be for the survivor.

In 1981 Michelle Rosaldo and I began field research among the Ifugaos of northern Luzon, Philippines. On October 11 of that year, she was walking along a trail with two Ifugao companions when she lost her footing and fell to her death some 65 feet down a sheer precipice into a swollen river below. Immediately on finding her body I became enraged. How could she abandon me? How could she have been so stupid as to fall? I tried to cry. I sobbed, but rage blocked the tears. Less than a month later I described this moment in my journal: "I felt like in a nightmare, the whole world around me expanding and contracting, visually and viscerally heaving. Going down I find a group of men, maybe seven or eight, standing still, silent, and I heave and sob, but no tears." An earlier experience, on the fourth anniversary of my brother's death, had taught me to recognize heaving sobs without tears as a form of anger. This anger, in a number of forms, has swept over me on many occasions since then, lasting hours and even days at a time. Such feelings can be aroused by rituals, but more often they emerge from unexpected reminders (not unlike the Ilongots' unnerving encounter with their dead uncle's voice on the tape recorder).

Lest there be any misunderstanding, bereavement should not be reduced to anger, neither for myself nor for anyone else. Powerful visceral emotional states swept over me, at times separately and at other times together. I experienced the deep cutting pain of sorrow almost beyond endurance, the cadaverous cold of realizing the finality of death, the trembling beginning in my abdomen and spreading through my body, the mournful keening that started without my willing, and frequent tearful sobbing. My present purpose of revising earlier understandings of Ilongot headhunting, and not a general view of bereavement, thus focuses on anger rather than on other emotions in grief.

Writings in English especially need to emphasize the rage in grief. Although grief therapists routinely encourage awareness of anger among the bereaved, upper-middle-class Anglo-American culture tends to ignore the rage devastating losses can bring. Paradoxically, this culture's conventional wisdom usually denies the anger in grief at the same time that therapists encourage members of the invisible community of the bereaved to talk in detail about how angry their losses make them feel. My brother's death in combination with what I learned about anger from Ilongots (for them, an emotional state more publicly celebrated than denied) allowed me immediately to recognize the experience of rage.

Ilongot anger and my own overlap, rather like two circles, partially overlaid and partially separate. They are not identical. Alongside striking similarities, significant differences in tone, cultural form, and human consequences distinguish the "anger" animating our respective ways of grieving. My vivid fantasies, for example, about a life insurance agent who refused to recognize Michelle's death as job-related did not lead me to kill him, cut off his head, and celebrate afterward. In so speaking, I am illustrating the discipline's methodological caution against the reckless attribution of one's own categories and experiences to members of another culture. Such warnings against facile notions of universal human nature can, however, be carried too far and harden into the equally pernicious doctrine that, my own group aside, everything human is alien to me. One hopes to achieve a balance between recognizing wide-ranging human differences and the modest truism that any two human groups must have certain things in common.

Only a week before completing the initial draft of an earlier version of this introduction, I rediscovered my journal entry, written some six weeks after Michelle's death, in which I made a vow to myself about how I would return to writing anthropology, if I ever did so, "by writing Grief and a Headhunter's Rage..." My journal went on to reflect more broadly on death, rage, and headhunting by speaking of my "wish for the Ilongot solution; they are much more in touch with reality than Christians. So, I need a place to carry my anger—and can we say a solution of the imagination is better than theirs? And can we condemn them when we napalm villages? Is our rationale so much sounder than theirs?" All this was written in despair and rage.

Not until some fifteen months after Michelle's death was I again able to begin writing anthropology. Writing the initial version of "Grief and a Headhunter's Rage" was in fact cathartic, though perhaps not in the way one would imagine. Rather than following after the completed composition, the catharsis occurred beforehand. When the initial version of this introduction was most acutely on my mind, during the month before actually beginning to write, I felt diffusely depressed and ill with a fever. Then one day an almost literal fog lifted and words began to flow. It seemed less as if I were doing the writing than that the words were writing themselves through me.

My use of personal experience serves as a vehicle for making the quality and intensity of the rage in Ilongot grief more readily accessible to readers than certain more detached modes of composition. At the same time, by invoking personal experience as an analytical category one risks easy dismissal. Unsympathetic readers could reduce this introduction to an act of mourning or a mere report on my discovery of the anger possible in bereavement. Frankly, this introduction is both and more. An act of mourning, a personal report, *and* a critical analysis of anthropological method, it simultaneously encompasses a number of distinguishable processes, no one of which cancels out the others. Similarly, I argue in what follows that ritual in general and Ilongot headhunting in particular form the intersection of multiple coexisting social processes. Aside from revising the ethnographic record, the paramount claim made here concerns how my own mourning and consequent reflection on Ilongot bereavement, rage, and headhunting raise methodological issues of general concern in anthropology and the human sciences.

Death in Anthropology

Anthropology favors interpretations that equate analytical "depth" with cultural "elaboration." Many studies focus on visibly bounded arenas where one can observe formal and repetitive events, such as ceremonies, rituals, and games. Similarly, studies of word play are more likely to focus on jokes as programmed monologues than on the less scripted, more free-wheeling improvised interchanges of witty banter. Most ethnographers prefer to study events that have definite locations in space with marked centers and outer edges. Temporally, they have middles and endings. Historically, they appear to repeat identical structures by seemingly doing things today as they were done yesterday. Their qualities of fixed definition liberate such events from the untidiness of everyday life so that they can be "read" like articles, books, or, as we now say, *texts*.

Guided by their emphasis on self-contained entities, ethnographies written in accord with classic norms consider death under the rubric of ritual rather than bereavement. Indeed, the subtitles of even recent ethnographies on death make the emphasis on ritual explicit. William Douglass's *Death in Murelaga* is subtitled *Funerary Ritual in a Spanish Basque Village*; Richard Huntington and Peter Metcalf's *Celebrations of Death* is subtitled *The Anthropology of Mortuary Ritual*; Peter Metcalf's *A Borneo Journey into Death* is subtitled *Berawan Eschatology from Its Rituals*. Ritual itself is defined by its formality and routine; under such descriptions, it more nearly resembles a recipe, a fixed program, or a book of etiquette than an open-ended human process.

Ethnographies that in this manner eliminate intense emotions not only distort their descriptions but also remove potentially key variables from their explanations. When anthropologist William Douglass, for example, announces his project in *Death in Murelaga*, he explains that his objective is to use death and funerary ritual "as a heuristic device with which to approach the study of rural Basque society." In other words, the primary object of study is social structure, not death, and certainly not bereavement. The author begins his analysis by saying, "Death is not always fortuitous or unpredictable." He goes on to describe how an old woman, ailing with the infirmities of her age, welcomed her death. The description largely ignores the perspective of the most bereaved survivors, and instead vacillates between those of the old woman and a detached observer.

Undeniably, certain people do live a full life and suffer so greatly in their decrepitude that they embrace the relief death can bring. Yet the problem with making an ethnography's major case study focus on "a very easy death" (I use Simone de Beauvoir's title with irony, as she did) is not only its lack of representativeness but also that it makes death in general appear as routine for the survivors as this particular one apparently was for the deceased. Were the old woman's sons and daughters untouched by her death? The case study shows less about how people cope with death than about how death can be made to appear routine, thereby fitting neatly into the author's view of funerary ritual as a mechanical programmed unfolding of prescribed acts. "To the Basque," says Douglass, "ritual is order and order is ritual."

Douglass captures only one extreme in the range of possible deaths. Putting the accent on the routine aspects of ritual conveniently conceals the agony of such unexpected early deaths as parents losing a grown child or a mother dying in childbirth. Concealed in such descriptions are the agonies of the survivors who muddle through shifting, powerful emotional states. Although Douglass acknowledges the distinction between the bereaved members of the deceased's domestic group and the more public ritualistic group, he writes his account primarily from the viewpoint of the latter. He masks the emotional force of bereavement by reducing funerary ritual to orderly routine.

Surely, human beings mourn both in ritual settings *and* in the informal settings of everyday life. Consider the evidence that willy-nilly spills over the edges in Godfrey Wilson's classic anthropological account of "conventions of burial" among the Nyakyusa of South Africa:

> That some at least of those who attend a Nyakyusa burial are moved by grief it is easy to establish. I have heard people talking regretfully in ordinary conversation of a man's death; I have seen a man whose sister had just died walk over alone towards her grave and weep quietly by himself without any parade of grief; and I have heard of a man killing himself because of his grief for a dead son.

Note that all the instances Wilson witnesses or hears about happen outside the circumscribed sphere of formal ritual. People converse among themselves, walk alone and silently weep, or more impulsively commit suicide. The work of grieving, probably universally, occurs both within obligatory ritual acts and in more everyday settings where people find themselves alone or with close kin.

In Nyakyusa burial ceremonies, powerful emotional states also become present in the ritual itself, which is more than a series of obligatory acts. Men say they dance the passions of their bereavement, which includes a complex mix of anger, fear, and grief:

> "This war dance (ukukina)," said an old man, "is mourning, we are mourning the dead man. We dance because there is war in our hearts. A passion of grief and fear exasperates us (ilyyojo likutusila)." ...Elyojo means a passion or grief, anger or fear; ukusila means to annoy or exasperate beyond endurance. In explaining ukusila one man put it like this: "If a man continually insults me then he exasperates me (ukusila) so that I want to fight him." Death is a fearful and grievous event that exasperates those men nearly concerned and makes them want to fight.

Descriptions of the dance and subsequent quarrels, even killings, provide ample evidence of the emotional intensity involved. The articulate testimony by Wilson's informants makes it obvious that even the most intense sentiments can be studied by ethnographers.

Despite such exceptions as Wilson, the general rule seems to be that one should tidy things up as much as possible by wiping away the tears and ignoring the tantrums. Most anthropological studies of death eliminate emotions by assuming the position of the most detached observer. Such studies usually conflate the ritual process with the process of mourning, equate ritual with the obligatory, and ignore the relation between ritual and everyday life. The bias that favors formal ritual risks assuming the answers to questions that most need to be asked. Do rituals, for example, always reveal cultural depth?

Most analysts who equate death with funerary ritual assume that rituals store encapsulated wisdom as if it were a microcosm of its encompassing cultural macrocosm. One recent study of death and mourning, for example, confidently begins by affirming that rituals embody "the collective wisdom of many cultures." Yet this generalization surely requires case-by-case investigation against a broader range of alternative hypotheses.

At the polar extremes, rituals either display cultural depth or brim over with platitudes. In the former case, rituals indeed encapsulate a culture's wisdom; in the latter instance they act as catalysts that precipitate processes whose unfolding occurs over subsequent months or even years. Many rituals, of course, do both by combining a measure of wisdom with a comparable dose of platitudes.

My own experience of bereavement and ritual fits the platitudes and catalyst model better than that of microcosmic deep culture. Even a careful analysis of the language and symbolic action during the two funerals for which I was a chief mourner would reveal precious little about the experience of bereavement. This statement, of course, should not lead anyone to derive a universal from somebody else's personal knowledge. Instead, it should encourage ethnographers to ask whether a ritual's wisdom is deep or conventional, and whether its process is immediately transformative or but a single step in a lengthy series of ritual and everyday events.

In attempting to grasp the cultural force of rage and other powerful emotional states, both formal ritual and the informal practices of everyday life provide crucial insight. Thus, cultural descriptions should seek out force as well as thickness, and they should extend from well-defined rituals to myriad less circumscribed practices.

Grief, Rage, and Ilongot Headhunting

When applied to Ilongot headhunting, the view of ritual as a storehouse of collective wisdom aligns headhunting with expiatory sacrifice. The raiders call the spirits of the potential victims, bid their ritual farewells, and seek favorable omens along the trail. Ilongot men vividly recall the hunger and deprivation they endure over the days and even weeks it takes to move cautiously toward the place where they set up an ambush and await the first person who happens along. Once the raiders kill their victim, they toss away the head rather than keep it as a trophy. In tossing away the head, they claim by analogy to cast away their life burdens, including the rage in their grief.

Before a raid, men describe their state of being by saying that the burdens of life have made them heavy and entangled, like a tree with vines clinging to it. They say that a successfully completed raid makes them feel light of step and ruddy in complexion. The collective energy of the celebration with its song, music, and dance reportedly gives the participants a sense of well-being. The expiatory ritual process involves cleansing and catharsis.

The analysis just sketched regards ritual as a timeless, self-contained process. Without denying the insight in this approach, its limits must also be considered. Imagine, for example, exorcism rituals described as if they were complete in themselves, rather than being linked with larger processes unfolding before and after the ritual period. Through what processes does the afflicted person recover or continue to be afflicted after the ritual? What are the social consequences of recovery or its absence? Failure to consider such questions diminishes the force of such afflictions and therapies for which the formal ritual is but a phase. Still other questions apply to differently positioned subjects, including the person afflicted, the healer, and the audience. In all cases, the problem involves the delineation of processes that occur before and after, as well as during, the ritual moment.

Let us call the notion of a self-contained sphere of deep cultural activity the *microcosmic view*, and an alternative view *ritual as a busy intersection*. In the latter case, ritual appears as a place where a number of distinct social processes intersect. The crossroads simply provides a space for distinct trajectories to traverse, rather than containing them in complete encapsulated form. From this perspective, Ilongot headhunting stands at the confluence of three analytically separable processes.

The first process concerns whether or not it is an opportune time to raid. Historical conditions determine the possibilities of raiding, which range from frequent to likely to unlikely to impossible. These conditions include American colonial efforts at pacification, the Great Depression, World War II, revolutionary movements in the surrounding lowlands, feuding among Ilongot groups, and the declaration of martial law in 1972. Ilongots use the analogy of hunting to speak of such historical vicissitudes. Much as Ilongot huntsmen say they cannot know when game will cross their path or whether their arrows will strike the target, so certain historical forces that condition their existence remain beyond their control. My book *Ilongot Headhunting, 1883-1974* explores the impact of historical factors on Ilongot headhunting.

Second, young men coming of age undergo a protracted period of personal turmoil during which they desire nothing so much as to take a head. During this troubled period, they seek a life partner and contemplate the traumatic dislocation of leaving their families of origin and entering their new wife's household as a stranger. Young men weep, sing, and burst out in anger because of their fierce desire to take a head and wear the coveted red hornbill earrings that adorn the ears of men who already have, as Ilongots say, arrived (*tabi*). Volatile, envious, passionate (at least according to their own cultural stereotype of the young unmarried man [*buintaw*]), they constantly lust to take a head. Michelle and I began fieldwork among the Ilongots only a year after abandoning our unmarried youths; hence our ready empathy with youthful turbulence. Her book on Ilongot notions of self explores the passionate anger of young men as they come of age.

Third, older men are differently positioned than their younger counterparts. Because they have already beheaded somebody, they can wear the red hornbill earrings so coveted by youths. Their desire to headhunt grows less from chronic adolescent turmoil than from more intermittent acute agonies of loss. After the death of somebody to whom they are closely attached, older men often inflict on themselves vows of abstinence, not to be lifted until the day they participate in a successful headhunting raid. These deaths can cover a range of instances from literal death, whether through natural causes or beheading, to social death where, for example, a man's wife runs off with another man. In all cases, the rage born of devastating loss animates the older men's desire to raid. This anger at abandonment is irreducible in that nothing at a deeper level explains it. Although certain analysts argue against the dreaded last analysis, the linkage of grief, rage, and headhunting has no other known explanation.

My earlier understandings of Ilongot headhunting missed the fuller significance of how older men experience loss and rage. Older men prove critical in this context because they, not the youths, set the processes of headhunting in motion. Their rage is intermittent, whereas that of youths is continuous. In the equation of headhunting, older men are the variable and younger men are the constant. Culturally speaking, older men are endowed with knowledge and stamina that their juniors have not yet attained, hence they care for (*saysay*) and lead (*bukur*) the younger men when they raid.

In a preliminary survey of the literature on headhunting, I found that the lifting of mourning prohibitions frequently occurs after taking a head. The notion that youthful anger and older men's rage lead them to take heads is more plausible than such commonly reported "explanations" of headhunting as the need to acquire mystical "soul stuff" or personal names. Because the discipline correctly rejects stereotypes of the "bloodthirsty savage," it must investigate how headhunters create an intense desire to decapitate their fellow humans. The human sciences must explore the cultural force of emotions with a view to delineating the passions that animate certain forms of human conduct.

Summary

The ethnographer, as a positioned subject, grasps certain human phenomena better than others. He or she occupies a position or structural location and observes with a particular angle of vision. Consider, for example, how age, gender, being an outsider, and association with a neocolonial regime influence what the ethnographer learns. The notion of position also refers to how life experiences both enable and inhibit particular kinds of insight. In the case at hand, nothing in my own experience equipped me even to imagine the anger possible in bereavement until after Michelle Rosaldo's death in 1981. Only then was I in a position to grasp the force of what Ilongots had repeatedly told me about grief, rage, and headhunting. By the same token, so-called natives are also positioned subjects who have a distinctive mix of insight and blindness. Consider the structural positions of older versus younger Ilongot men, or the differing positions of chief mourners versus those less involved during a funeral. My discussion of anthropological writings on death often achieved its effects simply by shifting from the position of those least involved to that of the chief mourners.

Cultural depth does not always equal cultural elaboration. Think simply of the speaker who is filibustering. The language used can sound elaborate as it heaps word on word, but surely it is not deep. Depth should be separated from the presence or absence of elaboration. By the same token, one-line explanations can be vacuous or pithy. The concept of force calls attention to an enduring intensity in human conduct that can occur with or without the dense elaboration conventionally associated with cultural depth. Although relatively without elaboration in speech, song, or ritual, the rage of older Ilongot men who have suffered devastating losses proves enormously consequential in that, foremost among other things, it leads them to behead their fellow humans. Thus, the notion of force involves both affective intensity and significant consequences that unfold over a long period of time.

Similarly, rituals do not always encapsulate deep cultural wisdom. At times they instead contain the wisdom of Polonius. Although certain rituals both reflect and create ultimate values, others simply bring people together and deliver a set of platitudes that enable them to go on with their lives. Rituals serve as vehicles for processes that occur both before and after the period of their performance. Funeral rituals, for example, do not "contain" all the complex processes of bereavement. Ritual and bereavement should not be collapsed into one another because they neither fully encapsulate nor fully explain one another. Instead, rituals are often but points along a number of longer processual trajectories; hence, my image of ritual as a crossroads where distinct life processes intersect.

The notion of ritual as a busy intersection anticipates the critical assessment of the concept of culture developed in the following chapters. In contrast with the classic view, which posits culture as a self-contained whole made up of coherent patterns, culture can arguably be conceived as a more porous array of intersections where distinct processes crisscross from within and beyond its borders. Such heterogeneous processes often derive from differences of age, gender, class, race, and sexual orientation.

This book argues that a sea change in cultural studies has eroded once-dominant conceptions of truth and objectivity. The truth of objectivism—absolute, universal, and timeless—has lost its monopoly status. It now competes, on more nearly equal terms, with the truths of case studies that are embedded in local contexts, shaped by local interests, and colored by local perceptions. The agenda for social analysis has shifted to include not only eternal verities and lawlike generalizations but also political processes, social changes, and human differences. Such terms as *objectivity, neutrality,* and *impartiality* refer to subject positions once endowed with great institutional authority, but they are arguably neither more nor less valid than those of more engaged, yet equally perceptive, knowledgeable social actors. Social analysis must now grapple with the realization that its objects of analysis are also analyzing subjects who critically interrogate ethnographers—their writings, their ethics, and their politics.

❖ ❖ ❖

Dynamics

1. In your opinion, is Rosaldo's lack of experience with mourning the only way to explain his earlier inability to comprehend the Ilongots' statements regarding grief and headhunting? What other partial explanations does his essay offer? Show how these partial explanations might complicate his emphasis on mourning.

2. Study passages in the essay where Rosaldo is engaged in acts of interpretation, either in the context of a face-to-face conversation or in his readings of written texts. How would you describe his ways of "positioning" himself in these passages? Describe how his acts of interpretation fit in with or challenge the theories he offers about interpretation.

Critical Tools

1. Look closely at those places in Rosaldo's essay where he uses quotations from his own earlier writings. How and why does Rosaldo choose to "quote" himself? Consider what his use of these quotations tells you about his process of re-reading and revision. In what ways are his own and your revision practices similar?

2. Pick another essay from *Literacies* that, in your opinion, uses emotion in an illuminating way. How do Rosaldo's theories about "the cultural force of emotions" help you to think freshly about this new essay? How is your understanding of Rosaldo complicated by the other writer's use of emotion?

Draft One/Draft Two

1. *Draft One:* Rosaldo describes the "practical" dilemma of "how to live with one's beliefs." The Ilongots are faced with this "dilemma" when they can no longer get rid of their anger by headhunting. Using your own experience, describe some aspect of your life that conflicts uncomfortably with some belief that you share with your culture. How does this conflict become a "problem of meaning" in your life?

   Draft Two: Using another text from *Literacies*, expand the discussion you began in your first draft by considering the perspectives of the new writer and his or her subjects. Taking your own and these other positions into account, what can you conclude about the problem of "living with one's beliefs"?

2. *Draft One:* At the end of "Grief and a Headhunter's Rage," Rosaldo writes that

   Social analysis must now grapple with the realization that its objects of analysis are also analyzing subjects who critically interrogate ethnographers-- their writings, their ethics, and their politics.

   This writing assignment is an exercise in understanding a writer's terms from the context in which they appear. Without relying on a dictionary, use Rosaldo's essay to explain what the words "subject," "object," "subjective," and "objective" might mean for him. Suggest why these terms might be important for the kind of work Rosaldo's essay is doing.

   Draft Two: Using observations and conclusions from your first draft, write an essay in which you describe first how Rosaldo approaches subject/object relation- ships in his work (as he is representing that work to the reader), and then how another writer in *Literacies* does the same thing. What is the significance of the similarities and differences you observe?

❖ ❖ ❖

Before Reading Nawal el-Saadawi. . .

1. Discuss a story or TV program that, in your view, misrepresents a social group to which you belong. Which cultural characteristics of your group have become distorted? What, in your experience, are some concrete social effects of this distortion?

Love and Sex in the Life of the Arab

Nawal el-Saadawi

A famous work of art, *A Thousand and One Nights*, has been used by many Western researchers and authors, who describe themselves as 'orientalists', as a source of material and information for studying the life of the Arab. They consider that these stories, especially those dealing with love and sexual intrigues, afford an insight into the understanding of the Arab character, seeing them as keys with which to open the doors to the 'Arab Soul', and as valuable means towards penetrating the depths, or rather the shallow waters, of the Arab mind and heart.

Yet anyone with the slightest knowledge of Arab literature knows that the stories related in *A Thousand and One Nights* are only a partial and one-sided reflection of a very narrow section of Arab society, as it lived and dreamed, loved and fornicated, intrigued and plundered, more than ten centuries ago. I do not know very much about the level reached by European civilization at the time, the state of human affairs in society there, in the sciences and in the arts, but I at least know enough to be able to say that Arab society had undoubtedly advanced much further. Many are the scholars, writers and researchers who have made comparisons between the West and the Arab World, only drawing their examples from a period in our history, now more than a thousand years old. One would have to have a very bad memory to forget, in one gigantic leap, what is in terms of time half the number of years which have elapsed since the birth of Christ. How can we depict the contrasts between the Arab character at the time when the people of *A Thousand and One Nights* flew on their magic carpets, and the Western mind of the Victorian era when purity floated like a thick veil over the corrupt and bloated features of a hypocritical society. How much more true and scientific would a comparative study have been of the lifestyles of Arab and European men from the same period, or at least from the Middles Ages when the clergy, who were the male intelligentsia of the time, were busy prompting women accused of sorcery to utter the most obscene sexual epithets, and, under insufferable torture, forcing them to admit to the very crimes which they had been taught to describe?

This picture of the sex-mad Arab fawning on an extensive harem is maintained with dubious insistence even today. Without exception the films, magazines and newspapers that roll out from the reels of Western producers and the dark-rooms of Western monopolies, depict Arab men as trotting behind the skirts of women, ogling the ample bosoms of seductive blondes, and squandering their money, or quenching their thirst for alcohol or sex. Arab women, in their turn, are depicted as twisting and turning in snake-like dances, flaunting their naked bellies and quivering hips, seducing men with the promise of dark passion, playful, secretive and intriguing, a picture drawn from the palaces of *A Thousand and One Nights* and the slave women of the Caliph, Haroun El Rachid.

Is it possible to believe that this distorted image of Arab men and women is representative of their true life and character in the Arab world of today? Personally, I am sure that it is not even representative of men and women living at the time of Haroun El Raschid. Perhaps it has some authenticity as a reflection of certain aspects of the life led by palace rulers and their concubines in those bygone days, but these were only an infinitesimal minority compared to the vast mass of Arabs, who led a harsh and difficult existence with no room for, nor possibility of ever experiencing, the silken cushions, soft flesh and fiery liquids of dissipation. The sexual life of kings and princely rulers, whether in the past or present, in the modern West or more archaic East, to the South of the Earth's equator or to the North, has maintained the same essential pattern, embroidered with a greater or lesser degree of sophistication or refinement, sadism or depravity.

Sweeping judgments, which depict the nature of Arabs in general, and the men of the Arab world in particular, as being obsessed with sex and more inclined to pursue the pleasures of the body than men from other regions or countries, are therefore unfounded and incorrect. Their aim is to contribute to and maintain a distorted image of the Arabs in the minds of people all over the world, to falsify the true colours of their struggle for independence, progress and control over their destinies, and to facilitate the task of conservative, reactionary and imperialist forces that continue to survive and prosper by such means.

I believe that freedom in all its forms, whether sexual, intellectual, social or economic, is a necessity for every man and woman, and for all societies. Nevertheless, I feel that the sexual freedom that has accompanied the evolution of modern capitalist society has been developed very much in a unilateral direction and has not been linked with, or been related to, a parallel development of social and economic freedoms. This sheds some doubt on the real motives behind the consistent and ever increasing campaign calling upon men and women to throw their sexual inhibitions and beliefs overboard. It also jeopardizes the chances of human progress and fulfilment, since a one-sided development that does not take into consideration the totality of life can only lead to new distortions and monstrosities.

This is why there is a growing realization that sexual freedom, as it is preached today in modern capitalist society, has no valid answers or solutions to many of the problems of personal life and human happiness, and that it is only another and perhaps more ingenuous way of making people pay the price of ever expanding consumption, of accumulating profits and of feeding the appetites of monopolistic giants. Another opium to be inhaled and imbibed so that mobilized energies may be dissipated rather than built up into a force of resistance and revolt against all forms of exploitation.

In this respect, Eastern and Arab societies have not differed from the West. Here again it is mainly economic necessity which governs the direction in which values, human morals and norms of sexual behaviour move. The economic imperatives of Arab society required a wide degree of sexual freedom to ensure the provision of large numbers of offspring. Polygamy, as against polyandry, tends to be more prolific as far as children are concerned. Arab society, still primitive and badly equipped to face the vicissitudes and harshness of desert life, suffered from a very high mortality rate, especially among infants and children, which had to be compensated for by correspondingly high birth rates. The economic and military strength of tribes and clans in a society which possessed neither modern tools or machines, nor modern weapons, depended very much on their numbers. In addition, the simple crude existence of desert life and the extreme poverty of nomadic tribes meant that, while the cost of maintaining a child was minimal, the child could play useful roles in meeting the productive needs of the time, being capable of running errands or looking after the camels and sheep.

Wars and battles were an integral part of tribal life and flared up at frequent intervals, and death took a heavy toll of the men. This was particularly the case after Islam started to establish itself and expand. It was natural that this new threat should meet with the resistance of the neighbouring rulers and the older religions entrenched in the surrounding regions, and that the Muslims should be obliged to fight numerous battles before they could succeed in establishing and stabilizing their new State. The result was heavy losses in men and a marked imbalance characterized by a much higher number of women, accentuated by the throngs of women slave prisoners brought back from victorious battles.

The easiest and most natural solution to such a situation was to allow men to marry more than one woman, and in addition to choose from among the women brought back from the wars, or sold in the markets, those whom they considered suitable to be wives, concubines or slaves in their households. Each man did so according to his means, and these means of course varied widely from one man to another. With a superfluity of women, a man would take pride in the number of women he could maintain, and the bigger this number, the more occasion for him to boast about the extensiveness of his female retinue, and about his powers over women, whether in marriage or in love. On the other hand, women would compete for the favours of men and excel in subtle allurements to attract men towards marriage, love and sex.

This was perhaps an additional factor which tended to make Arab women more forward and positive in love and sex, characteristics in clear contrast to the passive attitudes assumed by the vast majority of women living in our modern era. The other factors, mentioned previously, were the matriarchal vestiges which at the time were still strong in Arab society, and the naturalistic attitudes of Islamic teachings which prevented love and sex from being considered sinful as they were by Christianity. On the contrary, Islam described sexual pleasure as one of the attractions of life, one of the delights for those who go to Paradise after death. As a result, Arab women had no hesitation in being positive towards sex, in expressing their desire for men, in exercising their charms, and weaving their net around whoever might be the object of their attentions. Perhaps they were following in the footsteps of their mother, Eve, who had so ably enticed Adam to comply with her wishes and fall victim to *fitna*, with the result that he dropped from the high heavens in which he was confined and landed with his two feet on the solid, rough, but warm and living earth.

For the Arabs the word 'woman' invariably evokes the word *fitna*. Arab women combined the qualities of a positive personality and *fitna*, or seductiveness, to such an extent that they became an integral part of the Islamic ethos which has, as one of its cornerstones, the sexual powers of women, and which maintains that their seductiveness can lead to a *fitna* within society. Here the word is used in a related but different sense to mean an uprising, rebellion, conspiracy or anarchy which would upset the existing order of things established by Allah (and which, therefore, is not to be changed). From this arose the conception that life could only follow its normal steady and uninterrupted course, and society could only avoid any potential menace to its stability and structure, or any disruption of the social order, if men continued to satisfy the sexual needs of their women, kept them happy, and protected their honour. If this was not ensured a *fitna* could easily be let loose, since the honour of women would be in doubt, and as a result uneasiness and trouble could erupt at any moment. The virtue of women had to be ensured if peace was to reign among men, not an easy task in view of the *fitna* (seductiveness) of women.

Islam's contribution to the understanding of love, sex and the relations between the sexes has never to my knowledge been correctly assessed and given the consideration it deserves. However, the contradictory aspects inherent in Islamic society are reflected in another dramatically opposed tendency which runs through the body of Islamic teaching, and is a continuation of the rigid, reactionary and conservative reasoning that dominated the concepts and practices of Judaism and Christianity in matters related to sex.

Islam inherited the old image of Eve and of women that depicts them as the close followers and instruments of Satan, the body of women being his abode. A well-known Arab saying maintains that: 'Whenever a man and a woman meet together, their third is always Satan.' Mahomet the Prophet, despite his love for and understanding of women, warns that: 'After I have gone, there will be no greater danger menacing my nation and more liable to create anarchy and trouble than women.'

This attitude towards woman was prominent throughout Islamic thought and she always remained a source of danger to man and to society on account of her power of attraction or *fitna*. Man in the face of such seduction was portrayed as helpless, drained of all his capacities to be positive or to resist. Although this was not a new idea, it assumed big proportions in Islamic theology and was buttressed by many *Ahadith* (proverbs and sayings).

Woman was therefore considered by the Arabs as a menace to man and society, and the only way to avoid the harm she could do was to isolate her in the home, where she could have no contact with either one or the other. If for any reason she had to move outside the walls of her prison, all necessary precautions had to be taken so that no one could get a glimpse of her seductiveness. She was therefore enveloped in veils and flowing robes like explosive material which has to be well packed. In some Arab societies, this concern to conceal the body of women went so far that the split-second uncovering of a finger or a toe was considered a potential source of *fitna* in society which might therefore lead to anarchy, uprisings, rebellions and the total destruction of the established order!

Thus it is that Islam confronted its philosophers and theologians with two contradictory, and in terms of logic, mutually exclusive conceptions: 1) Sex is one of the pleasures and attractions of life; 2) To succumb to sex will lead to *fitna* in society—that is crisis, disruption and anarchy.

The only way out of this dilemma, the only path that could reconcile these two conflicting views, was to lay down a system or framework for sex which on the one hand had to avoid *fitna* while on the other would permit abundant reproduction and a good deal of pleasure within the limits of Allah's prescriptions.

The Imam, El Ghazali, explains how the will of Allah and his wisdom are manifested in the fact that he created sexual desire in both men and women. This is expressed in the words of his Prophet when he said: 'Marry and multiply.' 'Since Allah has revealed his secret to us, and has instructed us clearly what to do, refraining from marriage is like refusing to plough the earth, and wasting the seed. It means leaving the useful tools which Allah has created for us idle, and is a crime against the self-evident reasons and obvious aims of the phenomenon of creation, aims written on the sexual organs in Divine handwriting.'

For El Ghazali, apart from reproduction, marriage aims at immunity from the Devil, breaking the sharp point of desire, avoiding the dangers of passion, keeping our eyes away from what they should not see, safeguarding the female sexual organs, and following the directives of our Prophet when he said: 'He who marries has ensured for himself the fulfilment of half his religion. Let him therefore fear Allah for the other half.'

Islamic thought admits the strength and power of sexual desire in women, and in men also. Fayad Ibn Nageeh said that, 'if the sexual organ of the man rises up, a third of his religion is lost'. One of the rare explanations given to the Prophet's words by Ibn Abbas, Allah's blessing be upon both of them, is that 'he who enters into a woman is lost in a twilight' and that 'if the male organ rises up, it is an overwhelming catastrophe for once provoked it cannot be resisted by either reason or religion. For this organ is more powerful than all the instruments used by Satan against man.' That is why the Prophet, Allah's peace be upon him, said, 'I have not seen creatures lacking in mind and religion more capable of overcoming men of reason and wisdom than you [women].' He also warned men: 'Do not enter the house of those who have absent ones'—meaning those women whose husbands are away—

'for Satan will run out from one of you, like hot blood'. And we said, 'From you also, O Prophet!' He answered, 'And from me also, but Allah has given me his support and so Satan has been subdued.'

From the above, it is clear that the Arabs were accustomed to discuss freely with Mahomet and treated him as an ordinary human being like themselves. If he said that Satan ran in their blood, they would riposte that Satan also ran in his blood. Upon which, Mahomet admitted that he was no different from them except in the fact that Allah has come to his rescue and subdued Satan within him. The Arabic word which has been translated into 'subdued' is *aslam*, which means 'to become a Muslim' (to know peace, to be saved). The meaning of Mahomet's words, therefore, is that his Satan has become a Muslim. Mahomet emphasized the same point when he said: 'I have been preferred to Adam in two ways. His wife incited him to disobedience, whereas my wives have helped me to obey. His Satan was a heretic, whereas mine was a Muslim inviting me always to do good.'

Islam, therefore, inherited the attitude of Judaism towards Eve, the sinful woman who disobeyed God, and towards sex as related essentially to women, and to Satan. Man, on the other hand, though endowed with an overpowering sexual passion, does not commit sin except if incited to do so by the seductiveness and devilry of woman. He is therefore enjoined to marry and thereby is able to beat back the evils of Satan and the bewitching temptations of women.

Islam encourages men to marry. Mahomet the Prophet of the Muslims, says to them: 'Marriage is my law. He who loves my way of life, let him therefore follow my law.'

Despite the fact that Islam recognized the existence of sexual passion in both women and men, it placed all its constraints on women, thus forgetting that their sexual desire also was extremely strong. Islam never ignored the deep-seated sexual passion that lies in men, and therefore suggested the solutions that would ensure its satisfaction.

Islamic history, therefore, witnessed men who married hundreds of women. In this connection we may once more quote El Ghazali: 'And it was said of Hassan Ibn Ali that he was a great marrier of women, and that he had more than two hundred wives. Sometimes he would marry four at a time, or divorce four at a time and replace them by others. The Prophet Mahomet, Allah's blessings and Peace be upon him, said of Hassan Ibn Ali: 'You resemble me, and my creativity.' The Prophet had once said of himself that he had been given the power of forty men in sex.' Ghazali admits that sexual desire in men is very strong and that: 'Some natures are overwhelmed by passion and cannot be protected by only one woman. Such men should therefore preferably marry more than one woman and may go up to four.'

Some of the close followers of Mahomet (El Sahaba) who led an ascetic life would break their fast by having sexual intercourse before food. At other times they would share a woman's bed before the evening prayer, then do their ablutions and pray. This was in order to empty the heart of everything and so concentrate on the worship of Allah. Thus it was that the secretions of Satan were expelled from the body.

Ghazali carries his thoughts further and says: 'Since among Arabs passion is an overpowering aspect of their nature, they have been allowed to marry women slaves if at some time they should fear that this passion will become too heavy a burden for their belief and lead to its destruction. Though it is true that such a marriage could lead to the birth of a child that will be a slave, yet enslaving the child is a lighter offence than the destruction of religious belief.' Ghazali evidently believes that religion cannot be preserved from destruction unless men are allowed to marry as many women as they wish, even though in so doing they would be harming the interests of the children.

It is clear that Islam has been very lenient with men in so far as the satisfaction of their sexual desires is concerned. This was true even if it led to the enslavement of children and injustice to innocent creatures or if sought at the expense of a woman slave completely deprived of a wife's normal rights and whose children were destined never to enjoy the rights of a free child born of a free mother.

The inevitable question which arises in the face of these facts is: Why has religion been so lenient towards man? Why did it not demand that he control his sexual passions and limit himself to one wife, just as it demanded of the woman that she limit herself to one husband, even though it had recognized that women's sexual desire was just as powerful, if not more so, as that of men? Why is it that religion was so understanding and helpful where men were concerned, to the extent of sacrificing the interests of the family, the women and even the children, in order to satisfy their desires? Why, in contrast, was it so severe with woman that death could be her penalty if she so much as looked at a man other than her husband?

Islam made marriage the only institution within which sexual intercourse could be morally practised between men and women. Sexual relations, if practised outside this framework, were immediately transformed into an act of sin and corruption. A young man whom society had not endowed with the possibilities of getting married, or buying a woman slave from the market, or providing himself with a concubine, had no way of expending or releasing his pent-up sexual energies. Not even masturbation was permissible.

Ibn Abbas was once asked what he thought of masturbation? He exclaimed: 'Ouph, it is indeed bad. I spit on it. To marry a slave woman is better. And to marry a slave woman is preferable to committing adultery.' Thus it is that an unmarried youth is torn between three evils. The least of them is to marry a slave woman and have a slave child. The next is masturbation, and the most sinful of all is adultery.

Of these three evils, only the first two were considered permissible. However, the institution of marriage remained very different for men to what it was for women, and the rights accorded to husbands were distinct from those accorded to wives. In fact, it is probably not accurate to use the term 'rights of the woman' since a woman under the Islamic system of marriage has no human rights unless we consider that a slave has rights under a slave system. Marriage, in so far as women are concerned, is just like slavery to the slave, or the chains of serfdom to the serf. Ghazali expressed this fact clearly and succinctly when speaking of the rights enjoyed by a husband over his wife: 'Perhaps the real answer is that marriage is a form of serfdom. The woman is man's serf and her duty therefore is absolute obedience to the husband in all that he asks of her person.' Mahomet himself said: 'A woman, who at the moment of death enjoys the full approval of her husband, will find her place in Paradise.'

The right enjoyed by a wife in Islam is to receive the same treatment as her husband's other wives. Yet such 'justice' is impossible, as the Koran itself has stated: 'You will not be able to treat your women equally even if you exert much effort.' The Prophet himself preferred some of his wives to others. Some Muslim thinkers opposed polygamous marriage for this reason, and maintained that marriage to more than one woman in Islam was tied to a condition which itself was impossible to fulfil, namely to treat the different wives in exactly the same way and avoid any injustice to one or other of them. A man obviously desires his new wife more than the preceding one(s), otherwise he would not seek to marry her. Justice in this context should mean equality in love, or at least the absence of any tendency to like one wife more and so prefer her to the other(s).

Some Muslim thinkers interpret the two relevant verses of the Koran differently: 'Marry as many women as you like, two, three, or four. If you fear not to treat them equally, then marry only one' and 'You will not succeed in being just with your women, no matter how careful you are.' They consider that justice in this context simply implies providing the women with an equal share of material means for the satisfaction of their needs and that it does not refer to equality in the love and affection borne by the husband for his women.

The question, however, is: What is more important to a woman, or to any human being who respects her dignity and her human qualities, justice in the apportioning of a few piastres, or justice in true love and human treatment? Is marriage a mere commercial transaction by which a woman obtains some money from her husband, or is it a profound exchange of feelings and emotions between a man and a woman?

Even if we were to assume the impossible, and arrive at a situation where the man treats his wives equally, it would not be possible to call this a 'right,' since the first and foremost criterion of any right is that it should be enjoyed equally by all individuals without distinction or discrimination. If a man marries four wives, even if he treats them equally, it still means that each woman among them has only a quarter of a man, whereas the man has four women. The women here are only equal in the sense that they suffer an equal injustice, just as in bygone days all slaves were 'equal' in that sense under the system of slavery. This can in no way be considered equality or justice or rights for women.

The slave and feudal systems came into being in order to serve the interests of the slave and feudal landowners. In the same way, the system of marriage was created to serve the interests of the man against those of the woman and the children.

El Ghazali when speaking of the benefits of marriage for men expresses himself in these words:

Marriage relieves the mind and heart of the man from the burden of looking after the home, and of being occupied with cooking, sweeping, cleaning utensils and arranging for the necessities of life. If the human being did not possess a passion for living with a mate, he would find it very difficult to have a home to himself, since if obliged to undertake all the tasks of looking after the home, he would find most of his time wasted and would not be able to devote himself to work and to knowledge. A good woman, capable of setting things to rights in the home, is an invaluable aid to religious holiness. If however things go wrong in this area, the heart becomes the seat of anxieties and disturbances, and life is seized with things that chase away its calm. For these reasons Soleiman El Darani has said: "A good wife is not a creation of this world, for in fact she permits you to be occupied with the life of the hereafter, and this is so because she looks after the affairs of your home and in addition assuages your passions."

Thus it is that a man cannot devote himself to his religious life, or to knowledge, unless he has a wife who is completely preoccupied with the affairs of his home, with serving him, and feeding him, cleaning his clothes and looking after all his needs. But are we not justified in asking: What about the wife? How can she in turn devote herself to her religious life and the search for knowledge? It is clear that no one has ever thought of the problem from this angle, as if it were a foregone conclusion that women have nothing to do with either religion or knowledge. That their sole function in life is sweeping, cooking, washing clothes and cleaning utensils, and undertaking those tasks that Ghazali has described as a source of trouble and disturbance to the heart, and that chase away the calm of life.

How clear it is that the mind of women and their ambitions, whether in science or in culture, have been completely dropped from all consideration, so that man can consecrate himself completely to such fields of human activity. He furthermore imposes on woman the troubles and disturbances of the heart and mind that result from being occupied with such domestic tasks, after which she is accused of being stupid and lacking in religious conviction. Woman shoulders all these burdens without receiving any remuneration except the food, clothing and shelter required to keep her alive. Man not only exploits her mind for his own ends by abolishing it, or at least preventing it from developing any potential through science, culture and knowledge, not only does he plunge her whole life into working for him without reward, but he also uses her to satisfy his sexual desires to the extent required by him. It is considered one of her duties, and she must respond to his desires at any time. If she fails to do so, falls ill, refuses, or is prevented by her parents, it is his right to divorce her, and in addition deprive her of alimony.

Among the sacred duties of the wife is complete obedience to the husband. She is not allowed to differ with him, to ask questions, or even to argue certain points. The man on the other hand is not expected to obey his wife. On the contrary, it is considered unworthy of a man to do what his wife suggests or asks of him. Omar Ibn El Khattab once said: 'Differ with your women and do not do what they ask. Thus you will be blessed. For it is said: 'Consult them and then act differently.' The Prophet advises: 'Do not live a slave to your wife.' The Muslim religious leader, El Hassan, goes even further when he maintains that: 'Whenever a man has started to obey the desires and wishes of his woman, it has ended by Allah throwing him into the fires of Purgatory.'

One of the rights of a woman is to be paid a sum of money in the form of a dowry when she is married, and to receive another sum of money as alimony if her husband divorces her. In addition, he is supposed to feed and clothe her, to give her shelter in a home. However, the woman cannot specify any conditions as far as the home she is expected to live in is concerned. It might be a hut made of wood or mud, or a beautiful brick house, depending on the means of the husband. She cannot determine the size of the dowry, or the sum paid to her as alimony, or the food which she is supposed to eat and the clothes she will wear. All these things are decided by the husband according to his assessment of the financial means at his disposal, and how he should spend them.

According to Islamic rules, a woman can ask to be paid for breastfeeding her child. The husband is obliged to pay her for this from his earnings, if the child itself has not some financial resources laid aside for it. If these exist, the payment is made to the mother out of them. The mother is not forced to breastfeed the child if she does not want to, even if pay is offered to her. She can ask to be paid as long as there is no other woman who has voluntarily agreed to breastfeed the child, and to whom the father has no objection. However, if such a woman does exist, the wife no longer has the right to ask for any nursing payment.

Here again it is the husband's will that is crucial, since he can prevent the mother from being paid for nursing her child by finding another woman for this purpose, either on a voluntary basis or for a lower wage.

The mother is also eligible for payment for the rearing of her children, but here again it is the father's prerogative to choose another woman who can offer her services either on a voluntary basis or for less pay.

Such limited rights are almost insignificant, surrounded as they are by impossible conditions and cannot be considered of any real value. On the contrary, they afford the man a possibility of dispensing with the services of the children's mother immediately after she makes a request to be paid, thereby in fact obliging her to forego her right to payment for nursing or child-rearing. The vast majority of women, unable to be immune to the tendency for society and families to exaggerate and sanctify the functions of motherhood, cannot but sacrifice themselves for their children and give them everything, including their lives. To sacrifice some minor sum of money is therefore a matter of no consequence.

The exploitation to which a wife and a mother is exposed is evident from the fact that she carries out a number of vital functions without being paid. She is cook, sweeper, cleaner, washerwoman, domestic servant, nurse, governess and teacher to the children, in addition to being an instrument of sexual satisfaction and pleasure to her husband. All this she does free of charge, except for the expenses of her upkeep, in the form of food, clothing and shelter. She is therefore the lowest paid labourer in existence.

The exploitation of woman is built upon the fact that man pays her the lowest wage known for any category of human beasts of burden. It is he who decides what she is paid, be it in the form of a few piastres, some food, a dress, or simply a roof over her head. With this meagre compensation, he can justify the authority he exercises over her. Men exercise their tutelage over women because, as stated in the Koran, they provide them with the means of livelihood.

Man's lordship over woman is therefore enforced through the meagre piastres he pays her and also through imposing a single husband upon her to ensure that the piastres he owns are not inherited by the child of another man. Preserving this inheritance is the motive force behind the severe and rigid laws which seek to maintain a woman's loyalty to her husband so that no confusion can affect the line of descent. It is not love between husband and wife which is sought to be nurtured and cherished by these rules. If it were love between the couple that was the basis of this search for loyalty between husband and wife, such loyalty would be required equally from both the woman and the man. However, since loyalty is sought in the woman alone, by imposing monogamy on her, whereas the man is permitted to multiply and diversify his sexual relations, it becomes self-evident that conjugal devotion is not a human moral value, but one of the instruments of social oppression exercised against the woman to make sure that the succession and inheritance is kept intact. The line of descent which is sought to be preserved is, of course, that of the man. Thus adultery on the part of the woman, her betrayal of the nuptial vows sworn to on the day of marriage, means the immediate destruction of patrilineal descent and inheritance.

Money is therefore the foundation of morals, or at least of the morals prevalent where property, exploitation and inheritance are the essence of the economic system. Yet in religion it is assumed that true morals are dependent rather on human values. The Koran clearly says: 'Neither your wealth, nor your children can, even if you tread the path of humiliation, bring you close to me.' 'The highest esteem is given by Allah to those who are the purest.'

We have mentioned before that society realized early on the powerful biological and sexual nature of women, which power it compared to that of Satan. It was therefore inevitable that her loyalty and chastity could only be ensured by preventing her from having relations with any males apart from her husband and the men with whom she was forbidden to have sex such as the father, brother, and paternal or maternal uncles. This is the reason behind the segregation that arose between men and women, and the outlawing of free intermixing between them, a segregation put into effect by imprisoning the women within the four walls of the home. This confinement of women to the home permits the attainment of three inter-related aims: 1) It ensures the loyalty of the woman and prevents her from mixing with strange men; 2) It permits her to devote herself entirely to the care of her home, husband and children and the aged members of the family; and 3) It protects men from the dangers inherent in women and their powers of seduction, which are so potent that when faced by them 'men lose two-thirds of their reason and become incapable of thinking about Allah, science and knowledge.'

The Muslim philosophers who so oft proclaim such opinions borrow most of their ideas from the myth of Adam and Eve, seeing woman as a replica of Eve, endowed with powers that are dangerous and destructive to society, to man, and to religion. They believe that civilization has been gradually built up in the struggle against these 'female powers,' in an attempt to control and suppress them, so as to protect the men and to avoid their minds from being preoccupied with women to the detriment of their duties towards Allah and society.

In order to preserve society and religion from such evils, it was essential to segregate the sexes, and subjugate women by fire and steel when necessary for fire and steel alone can force slaves to submit to unjust laws and systems built on exploitation. Woman's status within marriage is even worse than that of the slave, for woman is exploited both economically and sexually. This apart from the moral, religious and social oppression exercised over her to ensure the maintenance of her double exploitation. Slaves, at least, are partially compensated for the efforts they make in the form of some material reward. But a woman is an unpaid servant to the husband, children and elderly people within the home. And a slave may be liberated by his master to become a free man, and thus enjoy the rights of free men, foremost amongst which is the recognition that he has a brain and religious conviction. But a woman, as long as she remains a woman, has no chance or hope of ever possessing the brain and religious conviction of a man. For women are 'lacking in their minds and in their religious faith.'

Since men possess more reason and wisdom than women it has become their right, and not that of women, to occupy the positions of ruler, legislator, governor etc. One of the primary conditions in Islam to become a religious or political leader (Imam) or governor (Wali) is to be a 'male.' Then follow piety, knowledge and competence.

The major ideas on which Islam has based itself in dealing with the question of women and sex can thus be listed as follows:

1) Men should exercise their tutelage over women because they provide for them economically. They are also superior to women as far as reason, wisdom, piety, knowledge and religious conviction are concerned. Authority is the right of men, and obedience the duty of women.

2) Men's energies should be expended in worship, religious activities and in the search for knowledge. This is to be attained by making women devote themselves to serving their men in the home, preparing food and drink, washing, cleaning and caring for the children and elderly.

3) The sexual desires of men should be duly satisfied so that they can concentrate with a clear mind and heart on religious activities, the worship of Allah, the search for knowledge, and the service of society. This also aims to ensure that religion is safeguarded and society preserved from being undermined, or even collapsing. Sexual desire is to be satisfied through marriage, the aims of which are reproduction and also experience of one of the pleasures promised in Paradise, so that men may

be motivated to do good and so be rewarded in the after-life. It is men's uncontested right to fully satisfy their sexual needs by marrying several women, or by taking unto themselves women slaves and concubines. Masturbation however is an evil, and adultery an even greater sin. 'Let those who cannot marry remain chaste so that Allah may bestow upon them of His riches. Let he who can marry a woman, who has matured without marriage, take her as a wife. If he cannot, then abstinence is the path.'

4) The seduction of women and their powers of temptation are a danger and a source of destruction. Men must be protected from their seductive powers and this is ensured by confining them to the home. Man is exposed to annihilation if he succumbs to the temptations of women. In the words of Ibrahim Ebn Adham, 'he who is accustomed to the thighs of women will never be a source of anything.'

5) Women are forbidden to leave the home and enter the outside world of men except if an urgent necessity to do this arises, as in illness or death. If a woman goes outside her home she must cover her body completely and not expose her attractions or anything that is liable to seduce a man. Her ornaments should be hidden and her external genital organs preserved intact.

Islam encouraged men to marry and went as far as considering it a religious duty. A familiar Arab saying goes as follows: 'Marriage is half of religion.' Men were not only asked to marry, but permitted to take several wives, and to have extramarital sexual relations almost at will, by living with concubines or women slaves. They were thus led to boast of the number of women they owned, and to speak with pride of their sexual powers.

The sexual powers of man became a part of the Arab ethos, and within this ethos, were related to manliness and virility. It became a matter for shame if a man was known to be impotent or sexually weak. Obviously, it could only be a woman who would be able to know, and therefore judge, if a man was sexually deficient, and in this resided another source of woman's hidden strength enhancing the dangers she represented. Men therefore had to be protected from her, and society did this by ensuring that her eyes were prevented from seeing anything outside the home—like an animal that becomes blind from being kept in the dark—by covering her face with the thickest of veils, and by obscuring her mind so she would become incapable of discerning the weak from the strong. This is the origin of the greater value attached to a virgin as compared with a woman, when the time comes for her to marry. The virgin knows little or nothing about men and sex, whereas a woman has experience drawn from her past relations with men and from her knowledge of the arts of sex. She can easily discern where lie the weaknesses of a man and where lies his strength. Hence the reduced value attached to a widow or a divorced woman.

Mahomet the Prophet, however, did not comply with these general rules of male conduct in Arab society. He was married fourteen times to women who had been divorced or widowed. The only virgin he married was Aisha. In this respect he was also much more progressive, and much more open-minded than most of the men of today, who still prefer to marry a virgin and look for the usual bloodstains on the nuptial sheet or cloth. That is why, especially in rural areas, the custom of defloration by the husband's or *daya's* finger is still widespread, and is meant to demonstrate the red evidence of virginity on a white cloth, symbolic of purity and an intact family honour.

As we have seen, the status of women and the attitudes towards them changed rapidly after the death of Mahomet. In the very essence of Islam, and in its teachings as practised in the life of the Prophet, women occupied a comparatively high position. But once they were segregated from men and made to live within the precincts of the home, the values of honour, self-respect and pride characteristic of Arab tribal society became closely and almost indissolubly linked to virginity, and to preventing the womenfolk of the family from moving into the outside world. A popular saying among the Palestinians, very common until the middle of the 20th century, goes: 'My woman never left our home until the day she was carried out.' I remember my mother describing my grandmother and saying that she had only ever moved through the streets on two occasions. The first was when she left her father's house and went to her husband after marriage. And the second when she was carried out of her husband's house to be buried. Both times no part of her body remained uncovered.

Segregation between the world of men and that of women was so strict that a woman who dared to go outside the door of her home was liable to be maltreated at the hands of men. They might limit themselves to a few rude and insolent glances, or resort to coarse sexual remarks and insults, but very often things would go even further. A man or a boy might stretch out his hand and seize her by the arm or the breast. Sometimes young boys would throw stones at her in the lanes and by-roads of cities and towns, and follow in her footsteps with jeering remarks or sexual insults, in which the organs of her body would be vilified in a chorus of loud voices. As a girl I used to be scared of going out into the streets in some of the districts of Cairo during my secondary school days (1943-48). I remember how boys sometimes threw stones at me, or shouted out crude insults as I passed by, such as 'Accursed be the cunt of your mother' or 'Daughter of the bitch fucked by men.' In some Arab countries women have been exposed to physical or moral aggression in the streets simply because their fingers were seen protruding from the sleeves of their dress.

This tendency among males to harm any woman caught crossing the boundaries of her home, and therefore the outer limits of the world prescribed for her by men, or who dares break into and walk through domains reserved for men, proves that they cannot consider her as merely weak and passive. On the contrary, they look upon her as a dangerous aggressor the moment she steps over the frontiers, an aggressor to be punished and made to return immediately to the restrictions of her abode. This attitude bears within itself the proof of woman's strength, a strength from which man seeks to protect himself by all possible means. Not only does he imprison woman within the house, but he also surrounds the male world with all sorts of barricades, stretches of barbed wire, fortifications and even heavy guns.

The female world, on the other hand, is looked upon by men as an area surrounded by, and peopled with, obscure and puzzling secrets, filled with all the dark mystery of sorcery, devilry and the works of Satan. It is a world that a man may only enter with the greatest caution, and a prayer for Allah's help, Allah who alone can give us strength and show us the way. Thus it is that the Arab man in the rural areas of Egypt mutters a string of Allah's names through pursed, fast moving lips, on entering a house in which there are women: 'Ya Hafez, ya Hafes, ya Lateef, ya Sattar, ya Rab, ya Satir, ya Karim.' ('O great preserver, almighty one, God the compassionate, who art alone shielder from all harm, protector from evil, bountiful and generous'). In some Arab societies the man might add *destour*, which is the same word used by peasants to chase away evil spirits or devils.

Here again we can observe the commonly held idea of a close link between women and devils or evil spirits. It goes back to the story of Eve, and the belief that she was positive and active where evil is concerned, an instrument of Satan's machinations. The development of a Sufi theology in Islam, characterized by renunciation of the world, and meditation and love for Allah—which became a cult of love in general—allowed women to rise to the level of saints. However, the number of women saints remained extremely small as compared with men. On the other hand, where it came to evil spirits 80% of them were popularly considered to be female.

The history of the Arabs shows that the women were undoubtedly much less afraid of the men than the men were of the women. The tragedy of Arab men however, or rather of most men all over the world, is that they fear woman and yet desire her. But I think it can be said that Arab men in some periods, especially in the pre-Islamic and early Islamic eras, were able to overcome their fear of women to a much greater degree than men in the West. Or perhaps, more precisely, the men's desire for their women was stronger than the inhibitions built from fear. This is due to the difference in the objective conditions prevailing in Arab societies as compared to the West, and to the fact, discussed earlier, that Islam (contrary to Christianity) recognized the validity and legitimacy of sexual desire.

As a result, sex and love occupied a much more important place in the life of the Arabs, and in their literature and arts. But parallel to this flowering in the passions which bind men and women together, there was an opposite and almost equally strong tendency in the teachings of philosophers and men of wisdom, and in the literary works of writers and poets, that warned against indulging in the pleasures of sex. Men were abjured not to become 'impassioned' with women or to fall victims to their seductions. One of the famous injunctions of the prominent Arab thinker, Ibn El Mokafa, says: 'Know well that one of the things that can cause the worst of disasters in religion, the greatest exhaustion to the body, the heaviest strain on the purse, the highest harm to the mind and reason, the deepest fall in man's chivalry, and the fastest dissipation of his majesty and poise, is a passion for women.'

Ibn Mokafa was no doubt directing his remarks exclusively to those men who possessed 'majesty', 'poise', and a well garnished purse, since only those who possessed these trappings could possibly lose them through love of women. Other men, those that constituted the vast majority among the people and who possessed neither majesty, nor poise, nor purse of any kind could not benefit from his advice, or even be in the least concerned with it. They were completely, or almost completely, stripped of all worldly possessions and therefore sometimes even of the means to have just one lawful wife, pay her dowry and keep her children. Such men could not be expected to strut back and forth on the scenes of love and passion.

In Arab society, as in all societies governed by a patriarchal class system where enormous differences exist between various social levels, sex and love, sexual freedom and license and a life of pleasure were only the lot of a very small minority. The vast majority of men and women were destined to toss and turn on a bed of nails, to be consumed by the flames of sacrifice and to be subjugated by a load of traditions, laws and codes which forbid sex to all except those who can pay its price.

The Arabs, exposed as they were to the shortages and harshness of desert life, to the difficulties and perils of obtaining the bare necessities in a backward and rather savage society, and to the burden of exploitation by their own and surrounding ruling classes, were known for their fortitude, patience, and capacity to stand all kinds of deprivation, whether from food, sex or even water. Yet they were capable, like people in all lands, and at all stages in human development, of finding compensation in other things. This might explain to us why the Arab people were so fond of listening to the stories of *A Thousand and One Nights*, pulsating as they were with the passions of beautiful women and the seductions of sex. This eagerness to listen to, and repeat, what had been told over a thousand nights, aroused a fiery imagination and substituted illusions for what life could not give them in fact. These stories, as Sadek El Azm describes them, 'have as their theme incidents and happenings that have been built around an intricate web of passion and love, which appeared all the more fascinating in that it did not conform with the moral codes and religious laws that held sway in the life of society, nor with the way in which good and evil, legitimate and illegitimate, permissible and impermissible were conceived of.' Thus it is that wives are made to betray their husbands with lovers and male slaves, virgins to meet with their handsome favourites in secret, and men to abandon their wives and seek out their mistresses in the rapture of soft summer nights. All those with whom these stories deal are engaged in the sole occupation of giving free rein to their voluptuous and hotly flowing desires, with all the means at their disposal, even if this should entail lying, deceiving, betraying people's confidence and running away from facing the consequences of one's acts. The predominance of these themes in the popular stories of this book echoes the yearnings that lie buried in the hidden depths of every man and woman condemned to live through the daily grind of a routine life, and dreaming of a chance to experience the throbbings of a violent passion. Yet where is the way out when everything around them stands like a vigilant sentinel intent on keeping their footsteps away from the exciting, sinuous and dangerous paths? The only door that remains open is that of tales and stories where people can live in imagination what is forbidden to them in fact by custom and tradition.

❖ ❖ ❖

Dynamics

1. How do you account for the shifts and turns in the way el-Saadawi presents her relationship to Islamic teaching in this essay? Find some passages that help you to explain why "authority" might be a problem for an Arab woman who wants to discuss the role of women in Arab culture.

2. El-Saadawi offers two main meanings for the Arabic word "fitna." Which passages from her essay could you use to show how the first kind of fitna—women's "seductiveness"—might be expected in Arab culture to lead to the second kind?

Critical Tools

1. Near the beginning of her text, el-Saadawi writes that "it is mainly economic necessity which governs the direction in which values, human morals and norms of sexual behaviour move." Identify the points in this essay which seem to support her claim. Then apply her statement to an essay from *Literacies* which examines gender relations in another culture. What relationship do you see between "economic necessity" and "sexual behavior" in this new context?

2. El-Saadawi might be described as a loving but stern judge of her own cultural tradition. Look for passages in her text that display some tension between impulses to praise and to criticize Islamic practice. Find a critical tool from another essay you have read this semester that helps you to talk about the dangers and benefits of el-Saadawi's brand of cultural critique.

Draft One/Draft Two

Draft One: Though she identifies herself as a faithful Muslim, el-Saadawi uses the tools of feminist analysis to re-think her relationship to her own tradition. For your first draft, consider some ways in which your loyalty to your own cultural tradition or social group has been (or could be) complicated by applying the perspectives of another group or a new analytical tool to your own experience.

Draft Two: The notion of "fitna" is central to el-Saadawi's exploration of gender relations in Arab culture. Write about some characteristic which, within your own cultural tradition, seems to threaten social order the way that "fitna" does for Arabs. Using some of the insights you developed in your first draft, try to explain how you have arrived at your own position on this issue. In what ways is your attitude that of an "insider"? How has your interpretation of this issue been shaped by "outsider" perspectives?

❖ ❖ ❖

Before Reading Carol de Saint Victor . . .

1. If you have ever visited a society that is very different from your own, what pleasures and complications did you experience? What do you make of them?

2. To what degree have you been able to understand and respect a particular spiritual tradition other than your own? Describe the process, including any limitations you might sense.

3. What complications do you expect to encounter in an essay about a woman travelling alone through a foreign country?

Go Slowly and You Arrive

Carol de Saint Victor

Old Delhi

MY FIRST MORNING IN INDIA. I wake up at dawn and take a motor rickshaw to Old Delhi: just any street in Old Delhi, I tell the driver. It is as if I walk through familiar photographs and movies: men wash themselves at pumps, brush their teeth with sticks, sleep on rope beds; women prepare tea on open fires, sweeping a little space in front of doors; children run about; the continuous movement of people around carts past cows between rickshaws, seemingly without beginning and without end, contained only by two- and three-storey buildings of ground-level shops, upper-level living quarters and storage areas. I emerge from the narrow street to one that accommodates two lanes of traffic, and a parade is approaching. In front are drummers and horn players, each of whom seems to play his own desultory tune, oblivious to the sounds around him. Behind the musicians are fifty or sixty men with black eyes, black hair, and brown naked bodies. I look around in search of someone who might tell me who these men are, what their march without clothes is intended to signify, but the people behind me appear to be more interested in me, a middle-aged American woman, fully clothed, than about this parade of undisguisedly mysterious men. I am in India, and I do not understand much of what I see: that is what this moment comes to mean to me, and it will recur to me like a refrain, like the private tune each musician plays.

Kouki

Jaisalmer, the oldest of the desert cities of Rajasthan, is my farthest point west into the Thar Desert, part of the expanse of sand that for centuries served as the highway between Africa and Asia. My first morning here I awake before dawn in order to be out in the hilltop village when light first appears. I climb a wall of the fort, the highest point of the village, and look out at the desert as the sun rises high and hot behind me. It is here that the hard sand gives way to rolling plains of loose sand, and the wind shapes dunes sometimes several kilometers long and sixty to eighty meters high. This is the *maroosthali*, the region of death, a large part of which was once submerged under the Indian Ocean. And now, where the annual rainfall averages about ten inches, and temperatures in May rise to 115°F, this great stretch of desert looks like a sea, as if this parched land were remembering it was once covered by tide.

I walk down a narrow cobblestone street that turns in labyrinthine fashion between rows of houses, some of which are five hundred years old, and they are built of stones that are the colors of the desert—yellow, gold, faint green. Their facades are ornamented with open web-like patterns in stone. Women are washing surfaces and clothes, men are washing themselves, white cows and black goats with large seemingly translucent white ears wander about, smelling for food, children are running about. I find a small restaurant on a square, or a triangle rather, where, outside, there is a table and three benches. The sunlight onto the terrace where I sit is broken by a large tree with the heart-shaped leaf of a linden. I order a pot of tea. A plate of tea? the waiter asks. Yes, I reply, not knowing what I will be served. On the other side of the tree I can see, stretching high into the sky, a gold-tinted sandstone house with a terrace mounted across the top storey. The light dances on the carved arches and balustrade of what might have been the home of a merchant who grew wealthy from trade and taxes levied on camel caravans plying the long lucrative route from the Sahara to Delhi and Agra. On one side of the merchant's house there is a newer, plainer house where a little boy, perhaps four years old, swings on a gate, and when a dirty, limping dog appears and settles in the gutter in front of it, the boy yells at the dog and pushes the gate against it. The dog pulls his aching body farther downhill and collapses under some steps. On the terrace of the house on the other side of the merchant's home, a woman in a yellow sari crouches, and holds at arm's length a short broom with which she draws a large arch, over and over again. The sounds: Indian music from a radio somewhere above the cafe; birds; a woman berating someone in the shop next door; footsteps of people and animals on the cobblestone roadway in front of me. The smells: urine and rot (I am sitting next to an open gutter). A little girl walks by carrying on her head a bowl filled with moist cow dung. Somewhere she will sit down and make round flat pies of it which she will spread in the sun to dry. Trishaws, their motors turned off, coast downhill. Two men sit on the bench farthest from me, drinking tea; one of the two men pours some of the tea from his cup into another cup for a third man who arrives and joins their conversation. One wears earrings, and another a turban of coiled red cotton. They all wear embroidered slippers with pointed upturned toes. A boy hangs rectangles of fabric from the second-floor terrace above the General Store. An old man walks by wearing a pink turban and a white *dhoti*. I take a photo of a camel pushing against the cart that is behind him, to prevent his descending the hill too fast; the driver smiles at me. A policeman in a white uniform and a tan cap walks by, yawning. A cow walks by, pauses to drop a pound of dung, moves on. A black dog with a henna tail follows. A plate of tea is a cup of tea on a metal tray.

A woman approaches the tables where I am sitting and asks if she may sit down. Her eyes are on the traffic and so I may look at her. She is perhaps thirty-five, falsely blond, with green eyes. Makeup does not conceal the fatigue around her eyes or the dirt on her neck. She wears large silver earrings, many bracelets, and her nose is pierced to hold a diamond. Her right hand is intricately painted, in black and red filigree. She has her feet on the bench, and she clutches her knees close to her face. She smokes Gold Flake cigarettes. A boy with a cherubic face arrives and sits by her, and they speak Hindi. She takes a cassette from her bag and gives it to him: *Chipmunk Adventure.* The cherub tells me that Kouki speaks Hindi but she is not Indian. He works for the store above the General Store. Am I interested in clothes, wall hangings? Do I want to see? His English is barely comprehensible to me. Kouki helps him out: "Looking is free," she translates for me, and teaches him the phrase. She has a fan which the cherub opens and closes as they talk. Kouki orders an onion omelette, dry toast and tea. A woman trudges uphill, her stomach hanging over her sari, like a goatskin of wine hanging over the edge of a table in a Spanish inn.

I tell Kouki I would guess she is either Greek or Italian.

Nearly. She was born in Paris (with the perfect exaggerated *s* of a European) but she soon moved to Spain with her mother. She is Spanish but carries a French passport. She studied art history for four years in Perpignan. She has come to India many times. She first came when she was twenty years old, to take photographs, and her camera was stolen. She has been robbed of seven or eight cameras. For five years she was so fed up she did not have a camera, but now she has one which she does not like. It is automatic. It makes noises she does not like and it does what it wants. A camera should do what Kouki tells it to do, not what it chooses to do.

The cherub is interested in my camera. Do I want to sell it? No but he may look at it. He takes a picture of Kouki and then of me. He wants to study photography, Kouki tells me. He touts for a camera shop too. He goes for photos of Rajasthan to show me: only a rupee for small ones, two rupees for big ones. He returns with a stack of photos, many of them studio shots with fake backgrounds. One is of a young woman in sari and jewels lying voluptuously against a perfectly etched dune. He disappears and returns wearing a jeweled vest from the fabric store. "Looking is free," he says, and points to the store.

Kouki looks through the stacks of photos for one of a man of Jaisalmer who had moustaches five meters long which coiled in tight rings on either cheek. He was a musician: he played a flute; he played ancient songs of Rajasthan. He was born in Jaisalmer, and he was killed in Jaisalmer. For many generations there had been a feud between his family and a family in what is now West Pakistan. Every twenty or thirty years someone of one family kills someone of the other family. Thirty years ago his father killed a man of the Pakistani family, and three years ago the son of that man came to Jaisalmer and murdered the man with the long moustaches in his own house, in front of his wife and children. The Pakistani cut off the gloriously mustachioed head of the Rajasthani, put it in a suitcase, took it across the desert in a jeep and then on a camel and into Pakistan. He took the head in a suitcase to Pakistan.

The dust is terrible, Kouki says. Sometimes there is a dust storm, and dust gets into everything. Into your eyes, your ears, your mouth. Her Japanese friend, who came to Jaisalmer to take photos for a travel book, was obliged to clean his camera five or six times a day. The cherub admires one of her necklaces, a gold chain with small colored stones spaced along it. She speaks in Hindi to him and then in English to me. The necklace is for her mother, who had one like it but with diamonds instead of cheap stones like this one. The necklace was in her mother's purse with other jewelry, and the purse was stolen from her in the street. For three nights she could not sleep, and she cried, she did not want to live. And then she said, It is crazy to care about such things. It is crazy to wake up to unhappiness. If I have things okay, if I don't okay too. I have my daughter who loves me, and it does not matter anything else.

I pay my bill, and tell Kouki I want to see the library at the Jain Temple before it closes at one pm. She says she will be at the cafe in the afternoon if I want to come back. She suggests I go to Pushgar. Agra, she says, is nothing. I should not waste my time going to see the Taj Mahal. I am to tell the guy who sells tickets to the Temple that I am Kouki's friend.

I walk up the hill to the Temple area where there are, my book tells me, 6666 images of the Jain gods. The Jains broke away from Hinduism in five hundred BC, and differed from most other sects in their creed of non-violence, in their belief that the Universe is infinite and eternal and therefore there is no Supreme Creator, and in their holding that to achieve the world of spirit one must learn to control one's senses. One branch of Jainism was especially contemptuous of women, considering them to be a curse of humanity. I do not know which branch of Jainism flourished in Rajasthan, this legendary region of violence, art and commerce.

I tell the ticket vendor that I am Kouki's friend. He sells me a ticket and tells me to go into the temple and he will find the key to the library. I look at a few of the 6666 images. The cupolas are as beautiful as the statues and bas-reliefs they protect, and it is cooler here than in the streets. The vendor at last appears. Am I a good friend of Kouki? I just met her at the cafe, I tell him. We walk down the narrow staircase to a door that is no more than five feet high. The library he shows me is a tiny room, four feet square, in which there are four palm-leaf manuscripts on display. The light is poor, and I do not stay long. At the top of the stairs he points to a temple I did not visit. I should see it, he says. I walk up the polished brown sandstone steps to another cupola and more reliefs of dancers, musicians, lovers. The Jains of Jaisalmer were not, it seems, of the more ascetic sect. Do I want to sit down? he asks; it is very hot. In Jaisalmer, he says, we have very good hash. Did you say hash? Yes hash; you want hash? No, I don't think so. Later? No, not later. I get up to continue my walk along the path to the world of spirit with dancers, more musicians, more lovers. He follows me and shows me something black the size of a half a dollar. Just a little bit for nothing, he offers. No, really no, I'm not interested. Just a little bit, he suggests. Very cheap, what you come for, he hazards. I walk on, then stop for a last photograph of a dancer, his feet and legs turn west, his head and torso east, he smiles at me.

I walked beyond the temples, away from Kouki's friend, along a street that follows close to the wall of the fort. A silversmith sits in a tiny shop about three feet above street level. The shop is at most three feet wide. More goats, cows, women beating clothes on a stone terrace beside a pump. Next to them, a calf sits beneath a wall on which cow dung is drying. A little girl, perhaps eight years old, touts. What is my name? Where am I from? Do I like India? Do I want to see her house? Do I want to take her picture? No thank you. *"Je suis belle?"* she asks, holding her skirt in a half circle. I take a picture of the calf beneath the medallions of dying dung and walk on.

Before I leave Jaisalmer I go to the cafe to say goodbye to Kouki, to tell the cherub I'll buy something from the shop above the General Store. Kouki is inside the cafe where, in darkness, she and two men are watching television. They watch a woman cry and a man try to comfort her. Kouki appears to be engrossed in the drama. I say goodbye and wonder if she hears me, and I walk out into the bright desert sunlight.

Jaipur street

I move in jerks along a street barely wider than the motor rickshaw I am riding in. It is night, and on either side of the street vendors sit in the shops that are raised several feet above the street. Vendors and their customers sit on white mattresses and cushions under fluorescent bulbs or beside kerosene lamps, a few beside candles. Vendors weigh their wares with brass balances: chappati, brightly colored powders, silver and jewels. We arrive at a work compound where, on the ground, women and children work by small dim lights. They sort stones by sifting them through round trays with perforations of different sizes. My guide tells me these things, but I see only grey shadows and hear shoosh, shoosh, shoosh.

Mr. Sanjee

It is too hard to trek into the desert, Mr. Sanjee tells me. But he will drive me to villages near Jaisalmer this evening, when the worst heat is over. He speaks in a language I do not understand to the young man standing behind him. Always there is a young man standing behind Mr. Sanjee, waiting for orders which are spoken in the same deep soft voice he uses with me. Mr. Sanjee wears white linen pants and a white shirt; he wears cloth slippers with pointed toes that turn up. He smokes Benson and Hedges.

We leave the old city where I am staying in one of Mr. Sanjee's villas. His brother runs Jaisalmer's only deluxe hotel, and I had intended to stay there, having earned myself a deluxe room after spending a night on a train, I told myself, but the rooms were unpleasantly dark, the furnishings gloomily heavy, the air thick with disinfectant. Next to the deluxe hotel, on the other side of a recently built wall, is Mr. Sanjee's simpler place, where I have a room with a ceiling fan, and windows that allow the night air to enter. I imagine the room was part of a very old building, perhaps quarters for workers, or storage rooms, and now its interior walls are whitewashed, and there is no telephone, no overstuffed chairs. Only a bed and a table with a mirror, and a bathroom with one tap, for cold water. Mr. Sanjee tells me to look back at Jaisalmer as we drive away. The view I have is what camel caravans centuries ago saw: the old part of the city has not changed, and the new part is hidden from our view. Twentieth-century wars and boundary disputes have changed the world Jaisalmer now inhabits. Now it is a tourist town, and people no longer care about the past. The old part of the city has not changed, but everything else has, Mr. Sanjee says.

Mr. Sanjee does not come out to the dunes very often, but this is the off-season, and so he can take time from his hotel. I am his only guest, and it is the hot season, but in July and August many French and Italians will arrive, the monsoons will have cooled the air, and his twelve rooms will be filled. He loves the desert but he visits it now with a heavy heart. Here, at Bada Bagh, we may walk through ceno-taphs with carved ceilings and equestrian statues of former rules, but I am to notice that stones are missing, statues are damaged: people come and take souvenirs. No one else is here now, and in the distance we can see camels grazing near a dump of trees that are not as tall as the camels. Further west we visit a Jain temple which has been rebuilt, and here one may see some of the loveliest geometrical patterns of carved stone in all of Rajasthan. Only here, Mr. Sanjee says, may one see designs like these: facades that grow wider as they rise, and give one the impression of bird wings opening. He points to abandoned houses on streets leading to the temple. Sand partially covers their facades. There was once a city here, but no longer. Now, there is only the rebuilt temple guarded by an old priest who accepts coins from visitors. On the road once again, we pass three hitchhikers; one is crippled and walks with a crutch. We do not stop.

On to Mool Sagar and Amar Sagar, dried and disintegrating remnants of formal gardens where once there were fountains and pools and enough water to keep trees green and lush with fruit. There is a wall filled with small niches where candles once were placed, and above, running just beneath the top of the wall, is a narrow slit through which water flowed, down and in front of the candles, to a pool beneath. Can I imagine the sight and the sound at night, of candles burning behind a veil of water? Now people come and take stones away, to use as paper weights and lamp bases. Every year there is less of old Rajasthan, and one day there will be nothing left to remind people of earlier times, of better times. A camel with strangely blotched, perhaps diseased, skin wanders about. A bougainvillea waits in a corner of a disintegrating wall. On the road we again pass the three hitchhikers.

It is dark when we return to Jaisalmer, and I have only a little time before my train leaves to take me back to Jodhpur. Mr. Sanjee invites me to have tea with him at a table in the courtyard outside my room. A younger man is with him who may be his son. Mr. Sanjee does not introduce us, but the young man speaks English as well as Mr. Sanjee.

I recognize the eucalyptus tree to one side of us, but what is the other tree, with yellow leaves? It is a *peepul*, a holy tree. This is its autumn, and so its leaves will soon fall, and women will come to worship it. Indians worship all things—the sun, the stars, snakes, all animals, trees—all things of the universe. To an Indian all things are part of God. I ask if it will be all right if I do not drink the glass of water put before me, as is customary, before we are served tea. Of course, he understands; he says something to the young man standing behind him, and the young man takes my glass, puts it on a tray, stumbles, looks quickly at Mr. Sanjee, who speaks to him in his usual soft voice.

Will I go to Varanasi? Then I will see the holy river, where, in spite of corpses and garbage and all other filth thrown into it, the water is pure. I could fill the jar with water from the Ganges and months later it would still be clear, unlike water from any other river. Yes, he would drink water from the Ganges at Varanasi and bathe in it. But people no longer go to Varanasi to die, as they once did. Little by little, the past is chipped away, and maybe someday people will not believe the Ganges is pure, and it will not be pure. Long ago there were a few people who were very wealthy and many who were moderately wealthy, and everybody had enough to eat. Life was good for all. Now no one in Jaisalmer is wealthy, and no one appreciates the culture of the past except as something to show tourists. There are no longer gardens where friends spend evenings listening to water fall over candlelight, watching dancers. Now we watch television and wait for tourists. Now taxes are very high. I should come back to Jaisalmer in October, when there are few tourists and it is cool. Then I could trek, for four days perhaps, and we would take tents, and we would get beyond telephone wires and hotels, and we could imagine how it was centuries ago.

Brahmin

"I am not a guide. I am a student. I study biology. I have examinations in two weeks. I came to the fort to borrow a book from my friend. My father is a teacher. He teaches English, Hindi, mathematics, history, biology. He teaches all subjects. We have a large house. My mother is a cook. She cooks for my father and my sister and me. Will you visit my house? It is a Brahmin house. We are Brahmins, the highest caste. Do you see the very large tree? My house is beside the very large tree. My house is very large. My mother and my younger sister will be so happy to meet you."

We take a shortcut to the village of blue houses we could see from the wall of the fort of Jodhpur. We walk over loose stones, scarcely a path, that trace the steep incline of the hill. The student asks me where I am from, if I like India, where is my husband, how many children I have, how old they are. The student's name is Mahesh, and he is the age of my son.

"This is the house of my cousin. She is my cousin and my friend. This is my house. Knock on the door. My mother and my sister will be so happy to meet you."

His sister is twelve and wears glasses and a Western-style dress. His mother wears a green sari and does not speak English. They are watching television in a tiny room where there is a bed and a table on which the television sits. The mother sits on the floor, the sister on the bed next to me, Mahesh on a stool he pulls out from beneath the table. The mother and sister continue to watch television: a woman is angry, another one is crying. Mahesh and his mother and sister speak in Hindi about what is happening on television. Mahesh offers to show me the house while his mother and sister continue to watch television drama. Adjoining the room we are sitting in are two other rooms, one for women and the other the kitchen. The room where the television is is for men. The family sleeps outside, either on the roof or in the courtyard.

When the program is over the sister and mother go to the kitchen to prepare tea. Mahesh says he wants to give me a special gift—a very old coin, a very old and valuable coin, which appears to be made of aluminum and is dated 1967. He also gives me a green rope necklace which he says is very valuable. I should not wear it outside because I will be robbed. Now he would like a gift from me. I give his sister two ballpoint pens and I give Mahesh my pocket knife. I have nothing else I can give except money, which I think I should not offer. I have cigarettes in my suitcase at the train station, I explain, when I see that my gifts to Mahesh and his sister are disappointing. Would his father like American cigarettes? Mahesh would prefer something he could keep to remind him of me, something that is very dear to me. Would I give him my watch? I cannot give him my watch: it was a gift to me, and also I need it. How many cigarettes do I have in my suitcase? He will meet me at 9:30 tonight, but not in the station. I am to meet him in the street beside the station. There will be policemen in the station. I tell him I will not meet him. I give him fifty rupees and leave.

Donald

Udaipur belies its desert location. It is, I have read, the Venice of the East. Surrounding it in the distance are the Aravalli Mountains and, close by, three lakes, on which palaces and gardens seem to float. I visit the City Palace and walk beneath eighteenth-century marble arches where Maharajahs and Mogul emperors were weighed in silver and gold which, once a year, was distributed to the citizens. Or so my book says. I walk the short distance between shops to the city's seventeenth-century Jagdish temple, where women sit on the floor and sing to the accompaniment of three male instrumentalists. A tout will not be discouraged. He is a student, he says, and he wants to practice his English. Also he wants me to visit the college where he and his fellow students are studying painting and sculpture under their guru. "Why are you so unfriendly?" he charges. "Do you not want to meet people? Why are you alone?" he hazards. "You ask too much," I say to myself, about myself.

My book tells me to go to Sunset Point for a quiet spot from which to gaze on the lake and hill beyond as night falls. To Sunset Point, I tell a rickshaw driver: how much? (I offer half, and we are off, but not before the student-artist finds me, goads me once more: "Oh God, why are you so arrogant?" he yells. I do not look back. I lift an arm to say goodbye.)

We drive through the new commercial area of Udaipur, which is not like Venice, or any city I have seen except in India. Where animals still walk about even as motorized vehicles spew black fumes at them and me. With every turn of the rickshaw wheels, pain stabs my body. The heat and noises are so intense, the sun so bright, the sights so sharply colored that I feel as if my sensory apparatus has been turned up high—as if my eyes are dilated and so everything I look at hurts me, as if my body is diseased and therefore inflamed by the slightest sensation. India imbues me.

As the driver stops to chat with another rickshaw driver, a young man jumps into our rickshaw, sits beside the driver, and turns around to me and smiles. What is my name? Where am I from? How long am I here? Do I like India?

I am tired. I cannot fight another battle. His friends call him Donald, his skin shines like the temple steps in Jaisalmer, and I do not try to get rid of him.

We arrive at Sunset Hill and Donald leads me to a cafe terrace. He leaves me for a moment to talk with the waiter. He returns.

"It is beautiful, is it not? I will teach you useful phrases: *Chola, chola*–go away. That is a useful phrase, but useful tomorrow, not today. Today we must be friends. If we are friends we will feel it from the heart. Do you want to see India? You do not know this country. You are a foreigner, you are a woman, you are alone. Everything is dangerous for a woman who is a foreigner and alone. Life is dangerous, that is true, and we do not get through it without great hurt."

The waiter brings us bottles of sweet red liquid. I ask Donald what the wall is that follows the crest of a hill on the horizon.

It is a wall that separates Moslems from Hindus. Many years ago. Today it is history, the wall. History is not important. What is important? I do not know. Life is not important. Death is not important. A palmist tells me I will die by accident. Seven months ago my father is killed in a bus. My father is a bus driver, and he accidents into a truck. No man is lucky. Now I am alone with my mother. I save all that I earn. My friends give me things. I have many friends all over the world. Sandra from San Francisco gives me the pants, the shirt, the shoes I now wear. I do not buy anything. I make twenty rupees a day at the studio. What I earn depends on the quality of my work and also the size. If I make a small miniature I earn little. Forget it if you cannot do it. Forget it. If I work hard I will have success. I want to be a talented artist. I speak Italian, German, French, and English. I was born just with my mother: no one was there, just my mother and baby Donald. Now I live alone. I am a flower beside the road, someone sees me, sometimes stops, sometimes not. We are alike, Donald and Carol from Iowa. No father for me, no husband for you.

"I do not live with my mother. Our paths are different. Her path is to Jaisalmer and my path is from Jaisalmer. I will not marry. I do not like marriage. Yes I am a Hindu. But I am all religious. There is only one god but with different names. Which one is real god I don't know. But everyone dies. Life may be two days or three days and then finish. Everyone must leave this. We look at the sunset today and then we die. You see, I tell you truth, Carol of Iowa. I never speak a lie in my life.

"I go to Nepal with a German girl. She pays for my ticket, and I am her guide. I am very happy in Nepal. I sit in the mountains at night with a candle burning and I have food to eat and beer to drink: I am very happy. Candles there are very many every night in the mountains. German girl say, "Donald, I want mineral water." I say, "Be quiet or I am angry." One night, she is asleep, and Donald goes away. And now German girl is at her home. Maybe she will write. If she does not write, I say okay. If she want to forget, I forget: who is this German girl? I forget her. If you want to forget Donald, okay. Then I say, "Who is this American woman"? I forget her. *"Shanta, Shanta"*: quiet, quiet. A useful phrase. I will not marry. Like candles, there are many women every night. I am in this business three years. I am enjoying of my life.

"Where do you go tomorrow? O you must not take bus tomorrow because I want you not to die. Go slowly and you arrive. I will tell you a story. Jenny from California is antique woman. Boys do not want to be in bed with antique. She likes to play. She wants boy like a puppet. My friend tells her, 'No I do not want to make romantic with you.' So Jenny from California find another boy, and she give her boy thousands of rupees. Then she get sick and for one month she is in hospital, and then she go home. And now her boy wear old clothes and he poor and he says he is sorry he make romantic with Jenny. People want to cheat with Donald, I say forget it. I have many experiences. I go with German girl to Nepal. Hotel manager in Nepal does not give me good respect. Hotel manager thinks I am poor Indian. I tell hotel manager I am from England. Hotel manager ask, which place? Birmingham, I say. I know many places—London, Chester, Bolton. I give address: 33 Bolton Road, Manchester. I want good respect. I want to be natural, not like Michael Jackson.

"I will go when I die and be with people. I don't like animals. Camel is love, horse is power, elephant is good luck. I like only elephant. My friend Sandra from San Francisco sends me twenty-five letters, and gives me this shirt and pants. I will visit her some day. You must not travel by bus. If I am your son and I die, then you do not want to live because I am your son. If you die, then your son does not want to live because you are his mother. You die, you bring very great hurt to your son.

"It is dark now. Many birds. They go to sleep now. I like to travel to meet people and see different things. Now we visit my school. Perhaps you buy souvenir to remember your friend Donald in Udaipur. If not, forget it. *Shanta, Shanta.*"

Hotel Manager

The hotel manager is a young man. He started his business three years ago. Friends say he has changed. Before, he was carefree, happy; now, he worries. He wants to create a nice atmosphere at the hotel, but he has little money. He wants to put a fountain in the little courtyard onto which the seven rooms of the hotel open. He does not want to think about the election. It is very divisive. No one is interested in the country, only themselves. With independence there were many fights, and still there are fights. India is a violent country. Businesses should be privatized. With 900 million people there is no shortage of manpower, but nothing is done, nothing happens, no one cares. Politicians talk, and people fight or do nothing. He advises me to watch people in the street if I want to learn about India. It happens in the streets. Watch people, try to understand them. This one is eating, that one is sleeping, this one is being shaved, that one is having a tooth pulled, that one waits— for what? for change, for violence, for nothing.

Jodhpur temple

In the temple of Jodhpur I deal with yet another tout. He is a student, he says, and he wants only to practice his English. At last he leaves. The temple carvings express meditation, my book says. The carvings I see are of couples touching one another. A row of horses and a row of elephants serve as borders to a series of couples. I sit against a marble column and listen to an old man with a white moustache sitting on the floor singing as he plays a harmonium. Occasionally the dozen or so women in yellow, saffron, mauve, violet, light green, red, royal blue and burgundy saris chant together. A toothless old woman approaches me and asks me something I do not understand. She looks at my notebook with puzzlement in her eyes. An old man enters the temple clapping his hands in time with the music. The women take turns pulling a cord from which hangs a cloth, a punkah, which cools a priest at the little altar in the center of the temple.

Soldiers

I am on a train to Jodhpur. The reservation sheet posted on the platform indicates that I will be the only person in this compartment. The reservation sheet indicates, after my name, my gender and my age. After the train begins to move and the conductor has punched my ticket, two soldiers or policemen—they wear tan uniforms and carry batons—enter the compartment. The younger one is remarkably handsome, is aware of it, smiles, touches his cap to me.

"Where are you from? Do you like India? This is dangerous territory. We must close windows and shades," the young man says as he closes them.

They sit on the bench opposite me, the young man still smiling, the older one not. The younger one rests his hands on his baton, which he has positioned on the floor, between his legs.

"You will sleep there," the younger man says to me, pointing to the top berth.

"My reservation is for this berth," I say, indicating the one I am sitting on.

"You will sleep there," the younger man repeats. "I will sleep here and my friend will sleep here." He points to the lower berths as theirs.

"Sorry. I sleep here. Number 16, as my ticket says."

"I order you to sleep there," the younger man says, and now he is not smiling.

I open the shutter and window on my side, and let the warm wind and dust in. "I will sleep here," I tell them, "and you may sleep wherever you like." Eventually the older soldier stretches out on the berth across from me, and the young soldier roams about, returning frequently, sitting either at the end of my berth or on the one where his friend is resting. They talk between themselves. The older man is sleepy, the younger one is enraged. All night the light is left on, and I sit on the berth next to the open window. From another compartment I hear the voice of a woman who does not stop talking. All night I sit, lulled by words I do not understand spoken by a woman I will never see.

Eklingji

I take a bus to Eklingji, an ancient town twenty-three kilometers north of Udaipur. There is no empty seat when I get on the bus, but the conductor finds a place for me in the front compartment, where the driver sits. People are carrying cloth bags filled with clothes and food. No one appears to be taking the bus for the reason I am, to see some of the remains of a time and culture that indulged aristocratic pleasures with artificial lakes, palaces, much decorated temples. Eklingji is a highway town—a series of small shops lining the road on either side—and an older village built against the side of a hill that rises to the east. The temple in the village will not be open for another hour, giving me time to see the Sas Bahu temples a kilometer away. A guide finds me when I step off the bus, a thin, handsome young man who may be eighteen, maybe twenty-five. He speaks and walks fast, and he does not smile. Yes we can see the temples beyond the village, he says, and off we take, up the steep cobblestone path that runs through the village. Is it far? I ask. Not far, I will see. He wears thongs and is smoking, but the climb and heat appear not to affect him. He stands at the top of the road waiting for me, his neatly pressed white shirt accentuating his dark skin. When I reach him I can see a lake in the distance and a small temple nearby. Are these the Sas Bahu temples? You want to see the Sas Bahu temples? And off we go, down the cobblestone path, back to the main road and across it to a cobblestone road covered with a canopy of large trees. This road lies beneath and along the highway the bus traveled, but I did not see—I could not have seen—this older road. It too follows an incline, but one less steep than the first one, and the shade makes the walk pleasant. Some young men bathing in a large stone reservoir call hello and exchange words with my guide.

We come to the end of the road and tree canopy, and to the edge of a lake, perhaps five acres large. I can see the hard-surfaced road that runs halfway around it, and, on the other side of the lake, beyond the flat green field my guide points to, are the temples. A cliff of bare red rock rises above the road, and along the lower part of it blanket-size pieces of cloth are drying in the morning sun. We walk around the lake. At the foot of wide stairs leading to it are bathers, and at the far end, where we walk, women are washing clothes, beating them on rocks with wooden paddles. The voices and paddles echo like bells and drums against the cliff as we walk along. Water buffalo rest in the water near the women. We circle the lake past the women and water buffalo, and through a grove of trees. A short way to the temples, my guide says. We come to a large open field, and in the middle of it, far from a road or shop or other people, are two temples of red stone built on a marble pavilion, and in front of the pavilion are two columns, which may have supported a lintel and served as entrance to the sacred area. Now, the columns support nothing.

"These temples built by mother-in-law and daughter-in-law for the king, in competition. Do you understand? Mother-in-law and daughter-in-law jealous for the king, and they built temples to make him happy. First we look at daughter-in-law temple. Here is Shiva, the Destroyer, and Brahma, the Creator, and Vishnu the Preserver. This is cobra, this is Shiva's snake. Cobra is respect. This is Parvati, wife of Ganesh. Shiva wants to be wife to Parvati, but Ganesh says no. And Shiva is very angry and cuts off head of Ganesh, and then sorry, and Shiva gives head of elephant to Ganesh. Elephant is good luck. Now Ganesh is god of good luck. This is Sati, wife of Shiva. Sati puts fire to self. This is Shakti, with skulls on her head, and this is Durga, who has ten hands and rides a tiger."

"Are there erotic statues here?" I ask.

"Erotic statues? Madame wants to see fuck statues?"

He leads me to the side of the temple and points to four rectangles of stone reliefs.

"Shiva temple is for everybody. This statue is for dance, for Krishna dance."

My guide sings and dances to help me understand the reliefs.

He sings and dances without smiling, seriously. On the pavilion, in the middle of an immense barren field, in front of statues for everybody, my guide sings and dances, his head bent toward the ground, his arms bent, his feet moving back and forth in short quick steps.

> "Come to my heart.
> I'm going to die.
> I know only Hari Krishna.
> Hari Hari Krishna.
> Hari Hari Krishna.
> Hari Hari Krishna
> Hari Krishna.

"This statue is for music. This one for religion, for meditation. And this for erotic. Temple is everybody. What you write? You happy this day? What is your nature? Some like dance, some like religion, meditation, and some like erotic. It is your nature. Have you been to Mt. Ebu? Much erotic at Mt. Ebu. You go there. It is your nature. Do you have a match?"

"No, I'm sorry."

"Why you sorry? *Eklengji* means *one body, respect.* Do you write *Eklengji*? You must have respect. I am clean, I am always clean. I have respect. My friends are jealous. My family kick me. My father kick me, my mother kick me. Do you understand? Kick me out, yes. I am no longer in my family, no longer in the house of my family. I have only myself."

"How did you learn English?"

"How did I learn English? What do you mean how do I learn English? I don't know. I just know. You talk to me and I know. You tell me erotic statue and now I know fuck statue is also erotic statue. I know nothing by myself. Everything happen is like accident. Accident I born. I live one day, one minute, and I die—accident. I don't care. I show you more erotic statue."

We walk to the mother-in-law temple, though my book does not identify either by the family relationships my guide has talked about. On the sun-filled side of the temple he climbs to a ledge to point out the small figures of lovers in various positions, performing actions that time has not made obscure.

"I have no fix nature. I am different. I like too much experience, many things. I want all experience. I will see the world someday. No I do not vote. I have no respect for politics. I go to politician, and he say he will help me, I will get visa to go to America. I see him next month. Who are you? he say. He talk with someone else. I have no family, I have only myself."

He jumps onto a railing of a porch sheltering the temple entrance. He embraces a column with one arm and stretches his other arm to a frieze of lovers.

"One day Moslems come to destroy Hindu temples. Here, Moslems destroy monkey-god Hanuman, and Krishna, who made romantic with many girls. Moslems break statues, and then they see erotic, and they look at them and they stop. In religion no erotic, Moslems say. This is no temple, Moslems say. They do not understand: Hindus make temple with erotic statues to protect it from Moslems."

As we walk back to the lake and then to the village my guide talks further about himself, but only in answer to direct questions I ask.

"I live on floor and little by little I go up. I do not want to live in sky. My father kick me when I am very young. I have no one, no mother, no father, no brother, no sister. I have only myself. Why is that? Life is accident. An accident we meet because I am born poor and you are born rich. I do not know if I have another life. I do not think so. I only know today, not tomorrow, and yesterday does not matter. I sleep everywhere. I sleep by the water, I sleep under a tree. When I have money I sleep in guest house. I have clean clothes. My friend keeps my clothes in his room. I go there, I put on clean clothes. I am not dirty. Do not give pen to that boy. It is nonsense. He does not go to school. See the temple on the hill? It is not just for religion. Indian couple go there. Madame, this is India. You must experience all things. You live long time, you have happiness ten minutes, and after all, sorrow. Do you understand? Life is like accident."

Watching

As I walk along a street of shops where people sit outside and watch the crowd go by, on a street that is less congested than most, I look ahead to see how soon I am noticed—how alert the people of this place are to my intrusions. They see me long before I reach them, perhaps half a city block or more before I pass them. Some say hello, or offer to sell me something, but most pretend not to see me, even as they notice me. I am their spectacle and they are mine. More than in any other country I am now allowed here to be only an observer. I am observed, or I am a participant for a little while in the lives of these people. I think I understand better the scenes in *A Passage to India* when Mrs. Moore and Adela experience assault, violation, involuntary engagement—and then I wonder: am I what I seem? There are times when I think I want to leave India early. I have presumed much in having come here. Let me walk around, I have said; let me observe you. Let our exchanges be brief, formal, seemingly immaterial. And then I will pay well for my observations. I expect to be shown respect, deference. You should understand what it means that I am from another country, that I come here alone, that I depend on your civility. I cannot control the desire that you acquiesce to my expectations. My dismay turns inward.

Night scene

Always I am early. The train is to leave at 11:30 pm. At 10:45 I am already in my compartment. No one else is in the compartment, no one else is in the car. There are no lights on in the train, not till 11:30, when the train will start. I sit next to the window and watch people on the platform. I sense I am well concealed in darkness. On the platform soldiers are unrolling bedpacks and preparing to go to sleep under the fluorescent lights that hang from the high roofs. A young man sitting on a bench combs his long black hair, twists it and wraps it around his head. He combs his beard. He puts on a red turban and checks his appearance in a small cosmetic mirror he has resting on his suitcase. A soldier who will not sleep but keep watch leans against a pile of chicken crates, holds his rifle between his legs, and smokes a cigarette. A family squats in a circle and shares food the woman takes from a cloth bag. And then I feel something touching my leg. When I look down toward the floor I see nothing but blackness and then, as my eyes adjust, a face—gaunt, immobile— takes form, barely discernible from the surrounding darkness. And then I see that his legs are twisted useless stumps, and I watch his hand reach onto my lap. For what seems a long time, before I can tell him to go away, I sit there, unable to free myself from the unexpected night visitor. Then he turns away, and drags his body out of the compartment into the corridor. I hear his body sweep to the end of the car. The realization comes to me again and again: I am always observed, I am always engaged, I always want to purge myself of part of myself.

Busride

I sit in the bus station of Jodhpur. I share a stone bench with a couple and their daughter. Behind us are buses that bear no indication of destination. In front of us, four queues in front of four windows. The one on the right is labeled *Inquiry Counter*. I stand there and inquire if I can get a ticket to Udaipur. I am told to go to the fourth window. I stand in line at Window Four waiting for the shade that has been drawn to hide the clerk to be lifted, which happens, periodically and for a few minutes at a time. My obsession with being early serves me now. I ask for a ticket to Udaipur. No tickets to Udaipur will be sold until 11:30; the bus leaves at 12:00. May I reserve a seat? Go to Window Three, *Reservations*. Again I wait for the shade to go up. No reservations for the Udaipur bus. Behind the clerks at the windows there are several other men. They talk, drink tea, and, at well-spaced intervals, sell tickets and sometimes answer questions.

An old woman approaches me. Her eyes are tearful, and her face is deeply lined. She is barefooted and wears silver bracelets around her ankles. Her body is covered in dark colorless fabric. She points to the man on the ground beside her. He has a rope tied around his neck, the end of which she holds in one hand. He crawls about, and his head jerks from side to side. Occasionally he moans, like a cow, but he obeys the commands of the woman who perhaps is his mother, who perhaps maimed him as an infant in order that he become a more effective beggar. His legs are twisted and withered from the knees down. He has a short greying beard and his hair is cut very short. The family next to me refuses to give her money though the old woman asks them several times. A young man walks up and gives the old woman a coin. The old woman walks away, her son crawling beside her.

At 11:30 I stand in line again, but I am told tickets will not be sold until later. The bus has not arrived. I keep my place in line. At 11:45 the woman in front of me gets a ticket. She turns to me and says, "Now ticket to Udaipur," but the vendor closes the window, and I continue my wait. At last the shade goes up. He gives me a ticket and I give him a hundred-rupee note. The ticket costs 65 rupees. Do I have change? He has no change. Stall Two, he says. I take my ticket and go to the bus. I take one of the last seats. On one side are seats for three people and on the other, seats for two. I sit on a seat for three, near the aisle. There is no place for my bags except in the aisle. As the driver starts the motor many people rush onto the bus. The aisle is filled with luggage and people.

We drive to the edge of Jodhpur where we stop while people get off the bus and buy tickets. Eventually we are out of the city and on our way south through flat dry land. Goats graze under groves of delicately leafed trees; they stand with their front legs against the tree trunks and try to reach the leaves. There are goats of many colors, but most are patterned in black and white; some have long hair, some short; some have large ears, some small. Shepherds carry long crooks and sit in the shade wrapped in loose cloth, their heads in turbans. Camels pull carts of wood and grain-filled gunny sacks. The bus is very noisy. The interior is made of rattling metal parts. Through a hole in the floor the size of an apple I see the road roll by under us.

The road looks smooth but the ride is very rough. We stop frequently, sometimes for several minutes when we may buy tea or fruit, sometimes ice cream and cold drinks. I am the only Westerner on the bus. People occasionally speak to me, but I do not understand them. The boy behind me gestures for some of my water. I say no, but he insists. I give him my bottle of mineral water and he turns the bottle up and pours water into his mouth without touching his lips.

Across the aisle from me sits a woman with an infant. At first I did not realize that she had a child, it was so concealed in her dark colorful loose attire. She has with her two sacks filled with clothes which she pushes against my feet. She keeps her face covered with a veil. I notice the infant first when the woman uncovers it to nurse it. It is a boy, the lower part of his body is naked. He has bangles on his ankles and wrists, and his face is painted with mascara and powder. He is very small, maybe 20 inches long and weighing 10 pounds. His eyes seem fixed. When he yawns I can see that he has four teeth. His mother offers him her breast often, but he does not seem to want to be nourished. All during the trip, which lasts thirteen hours, I do not think he makes a sound.

We cross many riverbeds, all of them are bone dry. By 5:00 we are in the halls. The ride is rougher now, and I put a motion-sickness patch behind my ear. The landscape reminds me of the south of France: there is much vegetation now, and land is divided into small fields by walls made of stones collected from the earth around. But there is something different about the landscape, which has been, perhaps, more recalcitrant to the human hand. Here the land seems poised, ready to fall back to its untended, its preferred state.

The only middle-class looking family on the bus is a couple with three young daughters. The father and two daughters sit toward the front, and the mother and one daughter sit in the seat in front of me, next to a man at the window who is smoking. The woman asks the man to open the window, and he does. She is polite to him, speaks something further to him, and he responds, apparently pleased that she engages him in conversation. The father notices what is going on and turns to his wife and says something. The wife and the man by the window say nothing more to one another. We stop again, as it is about to get dark.

We stop in a village where there are many stalls and stores. I buy a cup of tea and wander about. A tall older man dressed in a white shirt and *dhoti* approaches. He could be a Rajasthan warrior of the seventeenth century, I think. He offers me a cigarette, like the one hanging from the corner of his mouth. He speaks no English, but he speaks to me nonetheless, and he smiles. Two other men, his friends, joins us. They share the tall warrior's cigarette.

We take off once more, and a few minutes later the bus stops in response to the honking of a jeep behind us. The man who sat by the window earlier gets on the bus. He appears to be drunk. He struggles to a seat in the front of the bus, near the driver, on the command of the conductor.

It is dark as we pass many marble factories. During the long day I have sat next to two men who I presume are brothers. They are dressed in *longhis*, or loin cloths, and yellow turbans. One has a small face, and seems to depend on his brother, who gets off the bus when we stop and brings him some refreshment—a popsicle, a cup of tea. The small-faced man cannot find one of his slippers. People around laugh as the caretaker brother struggles in the darkness, with luggage and people's feet, looking for the slipper. At last he finds it, and he hands it to his brother who quickly puts it on.

We arrive at Udaipur at 1 am. The bus stops at a well-lit square, where there are many motor rickshaws and hotels. A driver says he will take me to the hotel I name, but he wants to show me another, a better and cheaper hotel first. A police-man drags a rickshaw driver to the street and beats him with his baton. The driver does not make a sound, does not resist in any way. People stand about and watch. I cannot tell whether they sympathize with the officer or the driver, or if they just enjoy the spectacle.

Exchange

As I pass a little girl carrying a pan of wet cow dung on her head she wipes her shit-filled hand on my arm. I cannot find water to wash it off. I try to clean myself with a tissue. My arm is quite red, and for days I imagine my skin where she touched me is burning.

Blessing

I am sitting on the pavilion of a temple in Agra. Three middle-aged men sit on the ground, each surrounded by six or eight women in saris of coral, yellow, green, red. The men appear to be performing rituals. They wear *dhotis* and are barefooted, as are the women. Most of the women are older, some are in their thirties. There is a small wood fire before one priest, and candles in front of the other two. The women come with trays of flowers and fruit and jars of water. The priests sway as they chant over the offerings. The women leave coins for the priests, who put them in purses inside their shirts. There is much talk among the women and the priests, each of whom has a thick layer of red powder caked to his forehead. A woman will occasionally add powder to what the priests are wearing. An old man in white shirt and pants, with long white hair and a beard, and a saffron turban sits across from me, apart from the priests and women. He gestures for me to take his picture, and then he asks for money. I give him two rupees. It is not enough. I give him two rupees more. A young man comes to sit next to me. His bare feet are very wide and thick as are his hands. He appears to be sleepy, perhaps drugged. He asks for my watch. I tell him no. He repeats his request between moments of apparent sleep. He wants my watch. He does not have a watch. He does not know the time. He wants my watch. He lights a cigarette. As a woman leaves her circle she sprinkles water on her friends, the old man, the young man and me.

Varanasi

I get up at 4 am in order to be at the Ganges when the sun rises. My hotel is far from the river. I wait in the darkness for the first taxi that comes along—a cycle rickshaw. The driver wears a scarf around his neck, and he is barefooted. For a while all I can see is the motion of his back as he peddles; he is lean rather than muscular, and very strong. We ride along the street that was overflowing with life eight hours ago. Now, there are few people, few vehicles. At the edge of the road people sleep on carts, on rope and plastic beds, on the ground, next to dogs and cows. A few people are beginning their day. They light fires, they prepare tea, they wash at a pump. I can see inside some rooms: small, with uncovered bulbs hanging from the ceiling or oil lamps on the floor, but no people are visible in those rooms. Most of the houses and shops are dark.

As we approach the river a procession begins to take shape. People are on their way to the Ganges. I pay the driver and join the pilgrims. I can walk faster now than he can drive. There is a crowd now, and as I walk down the steps of the *ghat* I pass a line of beggars: some are lepers, some are limbless, some are just old. The river is very wide, calm, and oil-smooth. On the far side, beneath the barely grey sky, there are a few trees and a sandbar or beach, I cannot tell which; there are no buildings there that I can see.

I walk down the steps and sit near the river, where bathers stand in the water and face the east. They lift water in their hands, and let it slip through their fingers, or they fill small brass pots with water and then pour it out slowly as they murmur prayers. They dip their heads in the water many times. Leaves carrying flowers and burning candles float down the river, toward the rising sun. At the *ghat* next to us there are stacks of wood and in the water in front of it, boats laden with wood. There is one fire I can see. It is there that the dead are cremated, and their ashes thrown into the Ganges to cross India and go to the sea. Hindus come to Varanasi in hopes of not being reborn to another life. They do not want to wake up to unhappiness again. The sacred river, the constantly changing river, promises them stasis. They may stop. No more births, no more lives, no more suffering, no more deaths: that is their prayer. Release their souls from the cycle of rebirth, O Mother: that is their prayer.

My eyes rest on one woman, standing waist-deep in the river. Her face is turned to the sun, to which she offers water held in her hands briefly, before it returns to the river. I have one life, I think, and she has had thousands. I am burdened with the need of experiencing life as fully as I can in the short time I have. She is in no hurry. She has lived fully, many, too many times over. She has come slowly and now she is ready to arrive. Older than I am able to calculate, she has no age, as I do. I cannot escape the noise that surrounds me. She hears only her prayer, listens only for a reply. I focus on the life about me, she on the sun. I sit on a stone step, and she stands in the eternal, ever-changing water that begins in the Himalayas and flows across India collecting the dead, purifying the living, and promising some they need not live again in this world. Answer her prayer, O Mother, and tell me what my prayer should be. Dogs run in the sand between the *ghats*, cows wander about, a priest stands over a corpse covered with a red cloth, and then two men lift the corpse and carry it to the fire as the sun rises over the river.

❖   ❖   ❖

Dynamics

1. Identify a couple of passages where de Saint Victor represents or summarizes the speech of another person without using quotation marks. Is the author's opinion implied in those sentences? How do those sentences differ from other passages where she describes events or her own thoughts? How should a reader deal with passages of "speech without quotation marks"? How do they influence your understanding of the essay?

2. At the beginning of her essay de Saint Victor says, "I do not understand much of what I see." Locate several incidents throughout the essay where you see her grappling with the problem of understanding what she sees. What exactly are the barriers to understanding in each of these incidents? What are her strategies for understanding? How good are the results of these strategies?

3. Locate passages where de Saint Victor considers history. What does local history mean to her in each of these cases, and what does it mean to the people she encounters? What roles does history play?

Critical Tools

1. Compare de Saint Victor's comments on the role of the observer (in the "Watching" section and elsewhere) with those of one or two other writers in *Literacies*, such as Nancy Scheper-Hughes, Ann Fienup-Riordan, or James Clifford. What understandings do they share, and how do their insights differ? What can these other writers help explain about de Saint Victor's experience?

2. In what ways does commerce ease or complicate the meeting of peoples from different cultures in this essay and in another *Literacies* text you have read? How does commerce work as a cultural force, based on these two texts?

Draft One/Draft Two

Draft One: Compare the understanding of spiritual life found in the section about Mr. Sanjee, the section about Varanasi, and in your own experience and observations. Based on your findings, what can you say about the roles of spirituality in people's lives?

Draft Two: Turn to one or two other texts in *Literacies* that address religious or spiritual experience, and use them to extend and complicate your discussion in draft one.

❖ ❖ ❖

Before Reading Scott Russell Sanders. . .

1. Select a male figure who has played a significant role in your life, and examine his role in a "personal" context. Consider his social status, power, and authority in relation to your own. What aspects of your interaction seem most relevant to you as you make your response? Think about some of your ideas of "masculinity" and the ways these ideas contribute to your responses.

2. Re-evaluate the same male figure in a broader, social context rather than a personal one. You might consider his role in his extended family, his place of work, his school, his community, etc. In what ways do his status, power, and authority in these contexts change from what they were in his relationship with you? How do you account for the differences or similarities you find in his personal and social contexts, his personal and social "masculinities"?

3. Like many other writers in *Literacies*, Sanders relies upon personal experiences and memories to make claims about larger social categories. What are some of the advantages and disadvantages of using one's own experiences to make arguments about gender, gender relationships, gendered identity? As you think about this question, you might consider some of the ways you have used your own experiences in discussions about gender with friends, family, or in response to something you've read.

The Men We Carry In Our Minds

Scott Russell Sanders

"This must be a hard time for women," I say to my friend Anneke. "They have so many paths to choose from, and so many voices calling them."

"I think it's a lot harder for men," she replies.

"How do you figure that?"

"The women I know feel excited, innocent, like crusaders in a just cause. The men I know are eaten up with guilt."

We are sitting at the kitchen table drinking sassafras tea, our hands wrapped around the mugs because this April morning is cool and drizzly. "Like a Dutch morning," Anneke told me earlier. She is Dutch herself, a writer and midwife and peacemaker, with the round face and sad eyes of a woman in a Vermeer painting who might be waiting for the rain to stop, for a door to open. She leans over to sniff a sprig of lilac, pale lavender, that rises from a vase of cobalt blue.

"Women feel such pressure to be everything, do everything," I say. "Career, kids, art, politics. Have their babies and get back to the office a week later. It's as if they're trying to overcome a million years' worth of evolution in one lifetime."

"But we help one another. We don't try to lumber on alone, like so many wounded grizzly bears, the way men do." Anneke sips her tea. I gave her the mug with owls on it, for wisdom. "And we have this deep-down sense that we're in the *right*—we've been held back, passed over, used—while men feel they're in the wrong. Men are the ones who've been discredited, who have to search their souls."

I search my soul. I discover guilty feelings aplenty—toward the poor, the Vietnamese, Native Americans, the whales, an endless list of debts—a guilt in each case that is as bright and unambiguous as a neon sign. But toward women I feel something more confused, a snarl of shame, envy, wary tenderness, and amazement. This muddle troubles me. To hide my unease I say, "You're right, it's tough being a man these days."

"Don't laugh." Anneke frowns at me, mournful-eyed, through the sassafras steam. "I wouldn't be a man for anything. It's much easier being the victim. All the victim has to do is break free. The persecutor has to live with his past."

How deep is that past? I find myself wondering after Anneke has left. How much of an inheritance do I have to throw off? Is it just the beliefs I breathed in as a child? Do I have to scour memory back through father and grandfather? Through St. Paul? Beyond Stonehenge and into the twilit caves? I'm convinced the past we must contend with is deeper even than speech. When I think back on my childhood, on how I learned to see men and women, I have a sense of ancient, dizzying depths. The back roads of Tennessee and Ohio where I grew up were probably closer, in their sexual patterns, to the campsites of Stone Age hunters than to the genderless cities of the future into which we are rushing.

The first men, besides my father, I remember seeing were black convicts and white guards, in the cottonfield across the road from our farm on the outskirts of Memphis. I must have been three or four. The prisoners wore dingy gray-and-black zebra suits, heavy as canvas, sodden with sweat. Hatless, stooped, they chopped weeds in the fierce heat, row after row, breathing the acrid dust of boll-weevil poison. The overseers wore dazzling white shirts and broad shadowy hats. The oiled barrels of their shotguns flashed in the sunlight. Their faces in memory are utterly blank. Of course those men, white and black, have become for me an emblem of racial hatred. But they have also come to stand for the twin poles of my early vision of manhood—the brute toiling animal and the boss.

When I was a boy, the men I knew labored with their bodies. They were marginal farmers, just scraping by, or welders, steelworkers, carpenters; they swept floors, dug ditches, mined coal, or drove trucks, their forearms ropy with muscle; they trained horses, stoked furnaces, built tires, stood on assembly lines wrestling parts onto cars and refrigerators. They got up before light, worked all day long whatever the weather, and when they came home at night they looked as though somebody had been whipping them. In the evenings and on weekends they worked on their own places, tilling gardens that were lumpy with clay, fixing broken-down cars, hammering on houses that were always too drafty, too leaky, too small.

The bodies of the men I knew were twisted and maimed in ways visible and invisible. The nails of their hands were black and split, the hands tattooed with scars. Some had lost fingers. Heavy lifting had given many of them finicky backs and guts weak from hernias. Racing against conveyor belts had given them ulcers. Their ankles and knees ached from years of standing on concrete. Anyone who had worked for long around machines was hard of hearing. They squinted, and the skin of their faces was creased like the leather of old work gloves. There were times, studying them, when I dreaded growing up. Most of them coughed, from dust or cigarettes, and most of them drank cheap wine or whiskey, so their eyes looked bloodshot and bruised. The fathers of my friends always seemed older than the mothers. Men wore out sooner. Only women lived into old age.

As a boy I also knew another sort of men, who did not sweat and break down like mules. They were soldiers, and so far as I could tell they scarcely worked at all. During my early school years we lived on a military base, an arsenal in Ohio, and every day I saw GIs in the guardshacks, on the stoops of barracks, at the wheels of olive drab Chevrolets. The chief fact of their lives was boredom. Long after I left the

Arsenal I came to recognize the sour smell the soldiers gave off as that of souls in limbo. They were all waiting—for wars, for transfers, for leaves, for promotions, for the end of their hitch—like so many braves waiting for the hunt to begin. Unlike the warriors of older tribes, however, they would have no say about when the battle would start or how it would be waged. Their waiting was broken only when they practiced for war. They fired guns at targets, drove tanks across the churned-up fields of the military reservation, set off bombs in the wrecks of old fighter planes. I knew this was all play. But I also felt certain that when the hour for killing arrived, they would kill. When the real shooting started, many of them would die. This was what soldiers were *for*, just as a hammer was for driving nails.

Warriors and toilers: those seemed, in my boyhood vision, to be the chief destinies for men. They weren't the only destinies, as I learned from having a few male teachers, from reading books, and from watching television. But the men on television—the politicians, the astronauts, the generals, the savvy lawyers, the philosophical doctors, the bosses who gave orders to both soldiers and laborers—seemed as remote and unreal to me as the figures in tapestries. I could no more imagine growing up to become one of these cool, potent creatures than I could imagine becoming a prince.

A nearer and more hopeful example was that of my father, who had escaped from a red-dirt farm to a tire factory, and from the assembly line to the front office. Eventually he dressed in a white shirt and tie. He carried himself as if he had been born to work with his mind. But his body, remembering the earlier years of slogging work, began to give out on him in his fifties, and it quit on him entirely before he turned sixty-five. Even such a partial escape from man's fate as he had accomplished did not seem possible for most of the boys I knew. They joined the Army, stood in line for jobs in the smoky plants, helped build highways. They were bound to work as their fathers had worked, killing themselves or preparing to kill others.

A scholarship enabled me not only to attend college, a rare enough feat in my circle, but even to study in a university meant for the children of the rich. Here I met for the first time young men who had assumed from birth that they would lead lives of comfort and power. And for the first time I met women who told me that men were guilty of having kept all the joys and privileges of the earth for themselves. I was baffled. What privileges? What joys? I thought about the maimed, dismal lives of most of the men back home. What had they stolen from their wives and daughters? The right to go five days a week, twelve months a year, for thirty or forty years to a steel mill or a coal mine? The right to drop bombs and die in war? The right to feel every leak in the roof, every gap in the fence, every cough in the engine, as a wound they must mend? The right to feel, when the lay-off comes or the plant shuts down, not only afraid but ashamed?

I was slow to understand the deep grievances of women. This was because, as a boy, I had envied them. Before college, the only people I had ever known who were interested in art or music or literature, the only ones who read books, the only ones who ever seemed to enjoy a sense of ease and grace were the mothers and daughters. Like the menfolk, they fretted about money, they scrimped and made-do. But, when the pay stopped coming in, they were not the ones who had failed. Nor did they have to go to war, and that seemed to me a blessed fact. By comparison with the narrow, ironclad days of fathers, there was an expansiveness, I thought, in the days of mothers. They went to see neighbors, to shop in town, to run errands at school, at the library, at church. No doubt, had I looked harder at their lives, I would have envied them less. It was not my fate to become a woman, so it was easier for me to see the graces. Few of them held jobs outside the home, and those who did filled thankless roles as clerks and waitresses. I didn't see, then, what a prison a house could be, since houses seemed to me brighter, handsomer places than any factory. I did not realize—because such things were never spoken of—how often women suffered from men's bullying. I did learn about the wretchedness of abandoned wives, single mothers, widows; but I also learned about the wretchedness of lone men. Even then I could see how exhausting it was for a mother to cater all day to the needs of young children. But if I had been asked, as a boy, to choose between tending a baby and tending a machine, I think I would have chosen the baby. (Having now tended both, I know I would choose the baby.)

So I was baffled when the women at college accused me and my sex of having cornered the world's pleasures. I think something like my bafflement has been felt by other boys (and by girls as well) who grew up in dirt-poor farm country, in mining country, in black ghettos, in Hispanic barrios, in the shadows of factories, in Third World nations—any place where the fate of men is as grim and bleak as the fate of women. Toilers and warriors. I realize now how ancient these identities are, how deep the tug they exert on men, the undertow of a thousand generations. The miseries I saw, as a boy, in the lives of nearly all men I continue to see in the lives of many—the body-breaking toil, the tedium, the call to be tough, the humiliating powerlessness, the battle for a living and for territory.

When the women I met at college thought about the joys and privileges of men, they did not carry in their minds the sort of men I had known in my childhood. They thought of their fathers, who were bankers, physicians, architects, stockbrokers, the big wheels of the big cities. These fathers rode the train to work or drove cars that cost more than any of my childhood houses. They were attended from morning to night by female helpers, wives and nurses and secretaries. They were never laid off, never short of cash at month's end, never lined up for welfare. These fathers made decisions that mattered. They ran the world.

The daughters of such men wanted to share in this power, this glory. So did I. They yearned for a say over their future, for jobs worthy of their abilities, for the right to live at peace, unmolested, whole. Yes, I thought, yes yes. The difference between me and these daughters was that they saw me, because of my sex, as destined from birth to become like their fathers, and therefore as an enemy to their desires. But I knew better. I wasn't an enemy, in fact or in feeling. I was an ally. If I had known, then, how to tell them so, would they have believed me? Would they now?

❖ ❖ ❖

Dynamics

1. Sanders investigates definitions of gender and experiences of masculinity from a number of different perspectives. Think about which perspectives he adopts, and how these perspectives might lead him to different conclusions. How does Sanders manage or juggle his several perspectives on gender and experience?

2. Sanders invokes several important concepts; "guilt," "persecution," "inheritance," and "shame" are just a few of the notions he raises and in some way returns to. Trace one or two important concepts through Sanders's argument. How do his initial understandings of these concepts relate to your own? How and why does he speak about them or respond to them differently as his argument develops?

Critical Tools

1. Much of Sanders's argument develops from his use of "class" as a lens through which he views and examines our different experiences of and thoughts about "gender." How could you build upon Sanders's analysis by using "class" as a lens through which you might examine a social category in a second essay? An interesting aspect of this exercise might be the way your new understandings of another category or categories leads you to discover new things not only about the second reading, but also about the role of class in Sanders's argument.

2. Think about the effect of Sanders's concluding paragraph and questions. Why might he have left these questions unanswered? Consider how his essay might imply answers to these questions without directly stating them. Work with a critical tool from another reading to help you evaluate your response to the strategy of Sanders's final paragraph. As you develop your ideas, consider why you chose the critical tool you're working with, how that tool worked in the reading you borrow it from, and what revisions to the tool you make in order to use it in the context of Sanders's essay.

Draft One/Draft Two

Draft One: Sanders notes the "ancient, dizzying depths" he comes to associate with his beliefs about gender. Where do his beliefs about gender come from, and what does he mean when he speaks of investigating "memory" as, perhaps, an important part of his coming to terms with his own experiences of gender? Relate a set of beliefs you were taught by family and friends to your actual experiences. How might your analysis complicate Sanders' ideas about history, memory, and gender?

Draft Two: Select a second reading in which the author uses her or his remembrances of childhood or an earlier phase in life. How do this second author's uses of the past help you discover something new about your own relationship to beliefs you held as a child—beliefs you may still hold now? How do they help you explore or challenge the "dizzying depths" of the origins of our beliefs as individuals, families, and communities?

❖ ❖ ❖

Before Reading Shelley Saywell. . .

1. Think about a time when someone tried to explain his or her reasons for doing something that you might have considered unethical or immoral. What kinds of arguments did that person use to persuade you that he or she was doing the "right" thing? What arguments did you resort to? How has your understanding of this situation changed with the passing of time?

2. The women Saywell interviews are both mothers and warriors. Write informally about the traits you associate with each of these identities. Where do they intersect? How do current events or trends contribute to your thinking about these subjects?

Another Reality
El Salvador, 1975-

Shelley Saywell

We had some problems with chauvinism in the beginning. The men didn't want us to join, or they wanted us to stay in subservient roles. But soon they realized the importance of having as many people fighting as possible, and they changed a bit. I think it actually helped make male-female relationships more equal.

—Ileana,
Urban guerrilla, El Salvador

I used to carry a huge bag with all this kids' stuff in it—talcum powder, diapers, baby bottles. I hid my gun and pamphlets underneath.... The soldiers never thought of checking in the baby's diapers.

—Maria,
Guerrilla, El Salvador

The two women who speak in this chapter were interviewed in Toronto, Canada, where there is a growing community of political refugees from Latin America. They have asked me to change their names to protect themselves and members of their families who are still in El Salvador. I will call them Ileana and Maria. At the time of this writing both women are twenty-five years old, both are mothers and both have spent the past decade fighting for the revolutionary forces in El Salvador.

The similarity does not end there. Both women have been arrested, tortured and imprisoned, and both were released because of internal and international pressure on their behalf from organizations including the Catholic church in El Salvador and Amnesty International. Each woman has lost her husband: one killed by a death squad, the other by official government forces. Finally, both Ileana and Maria were sent to Canada to recuperate.

Ileana has now returned to El Salvador to continue fighting. She was in Toronto for eighteen months, and during that time she worked for the Farabundo Marti Front for National Liberation (FMLN), seeking audiences with politicians and concerned citizens. Now she has left her infant daughter in the care of a Canadian family and returned home. Maria has arrived only recently and is still recovering from the scars of two and a half years at Ilopango Prison. She was unable to walk for six months after her release.

The women differ both physically and in character. Ileana is the more political. She gave up the religious beliefs that first got her involved in protest groups when they ceased to help her understand the tragedy of her country. Now she believes in socialist revolution. She is a small woman with large dark eyes and a soft voice. She wears no make-up, and nondescript clothes. It was difficult to get her to talk about herself. She still cannot talk about her husband's death because it is too painful. She softens considerably when she speaks of her young daughter, and when she finally agreed to tell me her own story she became very emotional.

Maria speaks no English and is still adjusting to being in Canada. She is still reeling from the blow of her husband's death and is deeply concerned about the welfare of her two small children, who have remained in El Salvador. Maria is more feminine in appearance than Ileana: she wears make-up and colourful clothes. She looks small and fragile; she is very thin and looks impossibly young to be a mother or to have such a long and bitter personal history. Still a devout Catholic, Maria believes that revolution in El Salvador has little to do with Marxism. "There are Marxists and socialists fighting," she concedes, "but there are also many of us who believe in democracy. We have united because revolution is the only way to end the tyranny."

It is important to keep in mind that these conversations are about things that are going on today and that these woman do not have the hindsight that is available to the other women interviewed for this book. They are still experiencing or preparing to experience again the situation they describe. The war is far from over, and they cannot be anything but partisan about it or their roles in it.

The war in El Salvador is a passionate subject, going back a hundred years to the 1880s, when the government decreed laws that recognized only private property, thereby effectively destroying the traditional communal landownership of the peasants. Illiterate peasants were never truly informed about the new laws, and the rich bought their land out from under them and turned it into coffee plantations, which produced wealth for the oligarchy but left the peasants with only seasonal labour at pitiful wages. Worse, coffee growing meant less land for growing food. The rich imported most of their food. The poor starved. Today the rich largely control the government and an economy that is described by experts as the most inegalitarian in that part of the world.

It is passionate, too, because it is a struggle that we cannot fully understand; some believe it is a Marxist-dominated revolution instigated abroad and a threat to Western security, while others believe it is the natural uprising of an oppressed people against a series of corrupt and brutal governments. The facts remain that El Salvador today is a country in which seventy-five percent of the population have no land, no education and not enough to eat. Obscene acts of violence and murder are daily perpetrated by the ruling government against nuns and priests, pregnant women and even children.

The women's actions, as always, speak for themselves. The women are hard because they have to be, because they have survived combat, rape, torture, imprisonment, fear and loss of loved ones. They are hard because there is no time or place to be soft, no time to indulge in the day-to-day life that people in peacetime perceive as reality. They do discuss issues like sexual discrimination, and see already that the fighting has given Latin American women new roles. But these are not issues that concern them greatly at the moment. They are interested in talking to me only because they want their stories told. They want people to know at least their side of the reality that is El Salvador at war.

Ten years ago Ileana was a fifteen-year-old high school student in San Salvador, a deeply religious Catholic, reared in a middle-class home, who liked rock and roll, boys and nice clothes. Today she is a committed revolutionary, living underground, rotating between the city and the countryside where she carries out organizational work and participates in armed actions against the government.

"I believe now that armed confrontation is the only way for El Salvador, even if it is the most painful way, because all the political expressions of the people have been suppressed, all the peaceful means of protest have been attacked and even our archbishop was killed for his views. What other way is there to change things? The only way left is to pick up our guns and fight for a better life."

After eighteen months of safety and rest in Canada, her choice to return was in many ways more difficult than her decision to become a revolutionary in the first place, because now she knows all too well what being there means. "It frightens me," she said before leaving, "because here I've grown used to being safe, and I've lost many of the instinctive defence habits I once had in El Salvador, the things that I used to do automatically to keep safe. Here you can walk down the street day or night, sit in a restaurant, talk about politics, and your life is not endangered. I feel that I need more preparation, that I'm no longer ready to face the confrontation. I have to find the strength to leave my daughter, knowing I might not return, and then both her parents will be dead."

She looks at me with wide eyes but speaks with the hardened resolve of a veteran revolutionary who has robbed banks, kidnapped men and killed. She has done these things because "I believe that only revolution can bring about the changes we need in our country."

The guerrilla war in El Salvador has veteran Vietnam correspondents shivering with *déjà vu* in the tropical jungle. American involvement continues to escalate in the region, and there is equal evidence of aid and military advisers from the Socialist bloc. Families are divided; sons and daughters fight each other. The television images are hardly distinguishable from the scenes the world watched not so long ago from Southeast Asia. But comparisons with Vietnam serve only to remind us that protracted civil wars become part of wider geopolitical cold war—and that millions of people die.

Ileana's father was a politician and businessman throughout his active life. His beliefs were to greatly influence the fate of his family and the choices made by his children. "He was involved in the struggle in his time," she says. "As a politician he saw too clearly the poverty and desperation of most of the people of El Salvador. He spoke up about it and was imprisoned and 'disappeared' several times. Finally he was exiled from the country. El Salvadorans have been opposing the regime for decades. In 1932 the peasants rebelled against their low wages and loss of employment. Thirty thousand were massacred by the military and landowners. Because of my father's activities in the 1950s, we went to live in Guatemala for a while. Ever since I was a child we have lived in fear of what was going to happen to us. After we returned from Guatemala my father decided not to get involved in politics anymore. He could not take imprisonment or torture at his age. When we kids became active he told us to be careful. He is scared for us, but he supports us."

Ileana's mother was never really involved: "She really didn't understand anything, even after all those years with my father. Now they are separated, but even when she was with him she didn't understand. Still, she is very good-hearted and always helps us when we need her."

There had always been revolutionary currents, predominantly stemming from the middle class. The seeds of the present state of civil war were sown in 1970 when university students and professors began to protest against the excesses and corruption of the government, including nepotism, electoral frauds, pay-offs by the rich for legislation of benefit to them, and suppression by threats, torture and murder of opposition politicians and clergy.

In a country where the vast majority of the population is Catholic, priests and nuns working among the lower class also became opponents of the regime. They began to organize Christian-based rural communities that were in effect communes where peasants could collectively manage such needs as medical services and education. It was through church groups that Ileana and Maria became involved in their war.

Ileana remembers: "I was religious then, at fifteen. I belonged to a Church group and did social work in the community. It was at that time that many of the priests began to preach that our rulers were not good. The Church became more and more involved in the problems of the people—not spiritually, but in day-to-day life—and then they began to talk about it."

It was 1975 when Maria, also fifteen, joined a Church group in the town of Aguilares. "My father was from the lower middle class," she says. "He works as the overseer of a manor, and so from childhood I lived on manors and saw how the peasants lived, the kind of work they were subjected to and the problems they had just to feed their large families. I started studying in the nearby town of Aguilares, and that is when I first came into contact with Father Rutilio Grande."

Grande, a Salvadoran Jesuit, had arrived in Aguilares in 1972. In the rich, sugar-growing regions outside the town the peasants were unable to get more than three or four months' labour each year, back-breaking work that helped provide the average annual income per family of seven hundred dollars. The rampant malnutrition of their children affected him deeply. He and three other priests began organizing rural communities and preached that "they must not live in conditions of such tremendous inequality that the very Fatherhood of God is denied." During the next four years Father Rutilio led peasants in several strikes and sit-ins at the haciendas in the vicinity.

Maria remembers the effect Grande had on the people: "He told us that in the Bible it says that people must not be exploited, people must not be oppressed. A hacienda in the area was an example of the way people lived. The peasants who worked there during harvest season were starving to death, and the rich widow who owned the estate would not allow most of it to be cultivated because she wanted it to be a memorial to her dead husband. The peasants had no running water, no electricity in their one-room huts. They had no education for their children, no medical care. Father Rutilio and three co-workers visited the widow and suggested an agreement for share-cropping in which the peasants would pay her for the use of her land. She refused, and so we organized a take-over of the hacienda. About two hundred peasants simply squatted on her land. We put up armed sentinels at different points, and we were prepared to confront the authorities." Maria was armed. Asked about weapons training, she said she had already been taught to shoot by her father, for recreation and hunting on the hacienda. Her parents believed her still a student who dutifully came home on weekends. But she had quit school and devoted all her time to the cause.

It was May 1975. The peasants remained on the estate for three months. They had begun to cultivate the land when the area was surrounded and attacked by the Security Forces in the middle of the night. "One of our sentinels had fallen asleep on guard," says Maria. "The troops were already inside the estate when our second sentry gave us the warning. We had prepared for this and had our escape routes planned. Each of us who was armed was responsible for leading out a small group of peasants—about fourteen or fifteen people. Others were assigned to cover our retreat. About fifteen minutes after we heard the warning, helicopters came and began dropping barrels of flaming gasoline on us. Our plastic, plywood shacks caught fire immediately. A lot of people were badly burned. We walked...ran, through the night. We had to cross a river. One of the women was in labour. She gave birth during the night." Maria led her group to a prearranged location where they met up with the others the next day. The peasants were told to disperse and remain silent about their involvement in the take-over.

Asked if they weren't expecting that kind of reaction to the illegal take-over of the hacienda, Maria said, "We were of course expecting the authorities to come and make us leave. What we didn't expect was that the army would attack us in the middle of the night with helicopters and flaming gasoline. I was very scared after that backlash, but my older brother, who was also involved, said to me, 'Sure you can stay home and Daddy will pay for your studies. You'll have something to eat. But what about the other people?' "

Father Rutilio Grande continued his work among the peasants. He organized literacy classes in which Maria and other young students helped teach the children. But the local landowners had by now had enough of the priests in Aguilares who, they said, "were instigating class warfare," and members of the Christian movement realized that there would be further violence.

"We were given training, told what to do if we were captured and questioned, how to respond, to make up a story quickly. They taught us how to deal with many problems. Throughout the rest of 1975 we led demonstrations in Aguilares. We went to the high schools and got more students involved."

In the capital, San Salvador, dissent was brewing in schools and universities. In July 1975 the army attacked a student demonstration protesting the government expenditure of three million dollars to host a Miss Universe Pageant. The army blocked off the streets to those trying to escape and opened fire on the crowds. Twelve students were killed, eighty wounded and twenty-four "disappeared." Ileana: "It was a peaceful demonstration, and they attacked us with tanks! People were screaming, in complete panic. It was terrifying. We joined together with other protest groups and decided on a joint action. Several days later we took over one of the cathedrals of San Salvador. We did it to denounce the army and what it had done at the demonstration. We asked the government to state who was responsible for the killing, and that the chief of police and the army be forced to resign.

"The one thing we did succeed in was getting attention, letting people know the truth. Because all the newspapers are controlled by the rich people, when things like that happened they would write a lot of lies. For example, if the army killed one hundred people, they would write that three people died in a cross-fire between guerrillas and the army.

"This joint action was important because it brought several groups together— peasants, students, teachers, labour unions and people from the ghettos. We discussed a revolution which would change the whole basis of society. We had learned that it was impossible to achieve reforms in the existing government. They would never change. By 1975 we were thinking of armed revolution. Several political groups formed armed sections and began taking armed actions against the government. They began in the cities, and then more and more grew in the countryside. I left the Church group. It was good, but I didn't think it was doing enough. That is when I joined the Revolutionary Popular Front."

By the end of that year there were many groups of opposition to the government, several with their own guerrilla armies. Eventually the left wing and liberals united and formed the Democratic Revolutionary Front (FDR) whose military arm was the Farabundo Marti Front for National Liberation (FMLN), named after the most famous communist leader of the 1932 peasant rebellion.

By 1976 guerrillas were conducting kidnappings and robberies to finance their weapons expenditures. Ileana: "We organized several kidnappings of rich people in

San Salvador. I know that in Canada, when you hear about kidnappings, it sounds very bad, but for us it is not so bad. These are very rich people who got rich by taking money from peasants for the last one hundred years. We felt we had the right to ask them for the money they had ripped off. Some of the kidnappings were to get our friends—political prisoners—released."

Ileana quit university to work full time for the front. "I was responsible for working with and developing the peasant organization. I had to move to the countryside, spend time with the peasants and gain their confidence. Then I would explain to them the necessity of becoming organized. I practically lived with them, only going to San Salvador periodically to get my things. I was living underground. My family knew I was involved, but they didn't know the details. I didn't want to endanger them."

Ileana's family were mostly involved or at least sympathetic, but many middle-class families have been torn apart by the war. Because the army has remained the most direct route to advancement socially and economically, many middle-class boys volunteered for it. Many families have children who are on different sides of the war. Ileana: "It has been the most difficult on the middle class. For the poor, it has been an easy choice—they know what the fighting is all about. But in the middle class the mothers are mostly housewives: they don't go out to work, they don't see what is going on. They read the newspapers and watch TV, and hear from the media that the guerrillas are wrong. When their children become involved it is very frightening for them."

Maria had not told her parents that she had quit school, nor did they have any idea that she was involved with Father Rutilio in Aguilares. Since she lived with her sister in Aguilares while at school, she let them believe she was still studying and reported home dutifully on weekends. Her older brothers and sisters all belonged to the front, and they had a tacit conspiracy to keep silent at home. In 1976, at sixteen years of age, Maria married one of the *compañeros* ("comrades-in-arms") with whom she had participated in several actions. She says she married so young because of the situation in her family home. "I had not been able to discuss anything with my parents. I couldn't tell them what I was doing, thinking or feeling. I was completely absorbed in the revolution and often endangered, and yet I went home on weekends and pretended to be a meek, obedient little school girl. Getting married was my freedom from this double life." She adds, "My husband was a few years older than me, and it was an intense relationship: we believed in the same things and took the same risks."

Shortly thereafter Maria had her first baby, a daughter. Asked if becoming a mother had led her to consider leaving the movement, to avoid the risks, she said no. "Having a child reinforced my commitment. As a mother I felt even more strongly about helping to create a new society for our children to grow up in." But only fifteen days after the baby was born, she and her husband were arrested in Aguilares. "We were caught spraying slogans on a wall. I was not mistreated, just interrogated. They asked me why I was doing this, who my family was. I told them my uncle was a colonel in the Security Forces and hoped that would carry some weight. After two weeks they released us.

"After we were released from jail we stayed in Aguilares for two more months. Then Father Rutilio told us we should relocate and begin living underground. The police had our number, they were watching us, so we moved to another district and went 'underground.' "

Ileana was also married that year, to a man she had met in the cathedral take-over in August 1975. He had subsequently joined the guerrillas. "For the first four months we lived separately. Then the organization authorized us to live together, but we were told to be careful because it would be dangerous for us to be identified together. That is because he was a known guerrilla, while I was still working in the open. I was only home one or two days a week. The rest of the time I was in the countryside. It was a difficult period. I felt as though I didn't have any home. I was always travelling from one place to another, sleeping here and there, and worrying about my husband while we were apart."

In a political climate where ten thousand people became *desaparecidos*, or "disappeared," each year, working underground in the city created enormous stress. Maria says: "It was very tense. We constantly had to change our names and identities. We were always on the move. Sometimes I would forget what name I had used with different people. I would run into someone and not know how to respond, desperately trying to remember what I had told them about myself. But the nature of our work gave me energy. I found it so rewarding. I got used to the pressure."

Maria's work was still with Christian groups. "We had contacts in different parishes with different priests and we would join them in their discussion groups. We worked in their parishes in the shanty towns or slums. We discussed ways of helping the poor. We related the Bible to the reality in which we were living. We helped the poor with their sick children, and even with their household chores." In 1977, she and her husband left this work and joined the People's Army. The move was a personal reaction to the assassination of Father Rutilio Grande on 12 March 1977. He was gunned down as he drove to Sunday mass.

That year the military government of Colonel Arturo Molina had launched an all-out campaign to terrorize and kill parish priests and nuns. Anonymous pamphlets dropped into the street blamed the war on "Marxist priests." The slogan ran, "Be a patriot! Kill a priest!" When Rutilio Grande was killed, the newly appointed Archbishop Romero, a man noted for his moderation, openly condemned the Molina government. Molina had come to power in 1972 in a particularly scandalous election. Though his opponent, Napolean Duarte, was ahead at the polls by two to one, Molina's well-placed supporters in the previous administration stopped all election broadcasts and finally pronounced the colonel president. The Christian Democrats were outraged by the flagrant fraud. Molina's answer was to have Duarte arrested, imprisoned and tortured, although he was released when international pressure was brought to bear.

A month before his death Grande had told a crowd, "Nowadays it is dangerous and practically illegal to be an authentic Christian in Latin America. I greatly fear that very soon the Bible and the Gospel will not be allowed within the confines of our country. Only the bindings will arrive, nothing else, because all the pages are subversive—they are against sin." Despite a government-declared state of siege, over a hundred thousand people risked their lives to attend Grande's funeral at a San Salvador cathedral. Eight bishops, Archbishop Romero and four hundred priests held mass for the slain father.

For Maria, who had known and loved the priest, it was a deep personal loss. It seemed that the last vestiges of humanity had been swept away, and in their place the war became uglier and uglier. That year when President Molina retired, his minister of defence, General Carlos Humberto Romero, was "elected" president in his place. The priest-killing campaign continued. Priests were found decapitated, disfigured by battery acid and otherwise mutilated. In Aguilares the army launched an attack in which several more Jesuits were murdered, and code-named it Operation Rutilio.

"Things really heated up," recalls Ileana. "Women in large numbers began to join the revolutionary movement. I think they found this final obscenity impossible to condone or ignore. Up until this time there had been a lot of groups in which the majority of members were women, but no women's organization per se. In 1977 the mothers of political prisoners and the disappeared formed an organization. Women from the markets also began to form groups. In 1978 the Association of Women in El Salvador [AMES] was formed in order to gather together all diverse groups so women could make more effective contributions and gain more power. It was set up to represent the needs and concerns of women."

Male chauvinism in Latin America has always burdened women there, especially in the lower classes, where it remained the only power left to unemployed, illiterate men, who dominated and made life even more miserable for their wives. In El Salvador the women have consistently been the labourers, working seasonally at harvest time. Often they have been abandoned with many children, their husbands leaving to spend time with other "wives"—sometimes for good, sometimes not. Without proper medical attention or adequate nutrition, one-tenth of all infants in El Salvador die either at birth or within the first year of life. It should come as no surprise that women, affected by social injustice in which their lot is inevitably worse than men's, have become a significant presence in the revolutionary forces.

Ileana: "We had some problems with chauvinism in the beginning. The men didn't want us to join, or they wanted us to stay in subservient roles. But soon they realized the importance of having as many people fighting as possible, and they changed a bit. I think it actually helped make male-female relationships more equal."

Maria adds, "I remember we talked about sexual discrimination in our meetings. It was decided that women should be allowed and encouraged to participate in all the activities—literature distribution, underground work, even fighting. Men were told they were equally capable of taking care of the children when their wives weren't there, and cooking and cleaning and washing. My husband did these things when we led a relatively normal existence. But usually we were far from being a regular family."

Ileana remained active in the "political" side of the front, but says there was not always a clearcut distinction between political and military. "We organized training practices in the countryside. I was taught self-defence, small arms, and how to make home-made explosives. I always carried a gun in the countryside because if the Security Forces came and searched the house I lived in and found my subversive literature, I would be killed. I had to be ready to defend myself."

Maria and her husband were asked to open a supermarket in San Salvador that would serve as a cover for shipping supplies to the guerrillas. "We lived over the store—my husband, our two daughters and two of my husband's sisters. Our house became a meeting place and the kids used to help camouflage it. When we were having a meeting one of us would go out and play with the kids on the street in front of the houses, making sure the coast was clear. We all carried guns for personal protection. We knew if we were searched by the authorities we would be killed. I used to carry a huge bag with all this kids' stuff in it—talcum powder, diapers, baby bottles. I hid my gun and pamphlets underneath. Sometimes I would even put my gun in my baby's diapers. The soldiers never thought of checking in the baby's diapers.

"The supermarket was a good front. We had a delivery van and I used to deliver goods to the groups in the countryside. I took them everything—shoes, beans and Kotex. Kotex was used for dressing wounds because if we took real bandages it would be too obvious.

"On one occasion when I drove to the place where I was supposed to meet our contacts, I was met by two members of the Civil Defence. I pushed the kids down on the floor of the van, jumped out and began running into the bushes. They opened fire and I fired back at them. I don't know if I killed them or wounded them, but the firing stopped. After a little while I returned to the van and there was no sight of them. My kids were still huddled on the floor where I'd left them."

Maria and her husband participated in several bank robberies in the capital. She described one that ended in tragedy. "We spent two weeks going over the plans down to the last detail—who would do this, who would do that; who would go in and give the order, who would stake out outside. It was perfectly worked out, but as the date got closer we got really nervous. The night before we did not even leave our home. We stayed in and drank lots of herbal tea to try to calm down. I took a couple of tranquillizers for my nerves.

"The next morning as we set out I was still really scared, but now it was a matter of self-discipline. We had to time everything, but when we drove up outside the bank things went wrong. Unexpectedly, the three policemen inside the bank were just being relieved and there was a patrol car waiting for them. One of our *compañeros* went in and demanded the money. He didn't realize there were now six cops in the vicinity of the bank, because he had come in from a different door. We couldn't get to him in time to warn him. I was staked outside, ready to cover the .

retreat. Suddenly I heard a lot of shooting and screaming. I rushed in and saw that three of my friends had been shot. Two were killed. The other, a woman, had been shot in the legs. I ran to her to help her get out. She said, 'Get out of here, Maria. It is better they kill three of us than all six.' She knew she would be killed anyhow, so she began screaming slogans. The police shot her to stop her from yelling out FMLN chants. I was running. I couldn't believe what was happening. It was so terrible to hear her screaming out and not to be able to help her....

"My husband and I were severely depressed for quite a long time afterwards. We tried to bolster each other's spirits. We told each other that death was a part of the process of revolution."

In July 1979 the Sandinista revolution in neighbouring Nicaragua succeeded in overthrowing dictator Anastasio Somoza. "When we saw them succeed," says Ileana, "it gave us hope. I really didn't believe they could succeed so quickly. We thought if they can do it, we can too. But on the other hand, the United States learned a lot from the Nicaraguan revolution. Now they are applying that knowledge to El Salvador, giving enormous aid to the government for the military. They began sending in military advisers."

In Washington the Carter administration was sore on the point of human rights abuses, perpetrated by the Romero regime in San Salvador, which were making it increasingly difficult to get military aid bills through Congress. Washington needed a more moderate government in El Salvador. On 15 October 1979 a military-civilian junta overthrew the ruling regime in a brief *coup d'etat*. The junta was comprised of younger, more moderate officers, and a number of representatives of opposition parties were appointed to the cabinet. The new government immediately began land reforms designed to restore land to the peasants. The reforms were ill-fated from the start. Army troops sent to redistribute parcels of land took over haciendas, helped themselves to the goods, then systematically murdered peasants who came to claim their new plots. Pay-offs and threats protected the estates of the richest families.

One by one the more moderate civilian politicians were forced out of office by the military leaders who controlled the army. One such politician, Hector Dada Hirezi, wrote in his letter of resignation: "The facts are indisputable proof of the conclusion. We have been unable to stop the repression, and those who commit acts of repression in defiance of the junta's authority remain unpunished; the promised dialogue with the popular organizations has not come about; the possibilities of generating reforms supported by the people have retreated beyond our grasp."

Six months after the new junta took power, the archbishop of San Salvador, Archbishop Oscar Amulfo Romero y Galdames, was assassinated as he gave mass. *Time* and *Newsweek* magazines recounted the carnage that followed when thousands of people attended his funeral and army troops opened fire into the crowds. Three weeks after the archbishop's assassination the United States government committed another $5.7 million in military aid to the ruling junta. By this time it was estimated that in the country of five million people, two thousand people a week were dying in the war.

Ileana was caught in 1980. She says, "I can't tell you everything, but I was at the house of one of our *compañeros* for a meeting. The army found out about us and came and surrounded the house. We heard the trucks and jeeps pull up, and out stormed dozens of soldiers with machine-guns. We considered holding them off and trying to escape, but when we realized we were surrounded we surrendered. They arrested everyone in the house.

"I was taken to the National Guard's secret jail, where they interrogate political prisoners, and kept there for one week. I was raped repeatedly and tortured with electric shocks. I was three months pregnant, but thank God it didn't show. I knew if they found out it would be worse. They would have tried to hurt the baby, to abort it or something. They would have asked me who the father was. They continually threatened to kill me and my family. Sometimes I had to answer them, but I would just tell them things that they already knew, like where I had studied. Other times I would make up stories. I always thought about what I was saying and tried not to endanger the others.

"They didn't treat me better because I was a woman. To them there was no difference. I think for women it was worse. They thought we were worthless, so they wanted to defile us. I was constantly pawed, threatened with rape or raped. They were pigs." She pauses, then adds, "I know this sounds hard to believe. I was very lucky because many, many people never get out of those clandestine jails. I tried to keep myself together by telling myself how many others were in the same situation I was in. It made me stronger. When I was being tortured I kept thinking of my friends who had gone through this, as an example to keep me brave. I kept thinking that they had held out in even worse situations. It wasn't faith in God that kept me going. By this time I had lost my religious faith.

"I think in the beginning, despite enquiries from outside, the National Guard denied they were holding us. But the organization knew where we were. They notified our parents and began to lobby and talk to foreign diplomats and journalists and to people in the government. The archbishop even mentioned our names in his mass—the Church still had some influence. When the pressure from publicity grew, the National Guard handed us over to the legal institutions for a trial and prison sentence.

"We were very lucky," she admits. "Today we have so many people who have disappeared in the clandestine jails, and been killed. Despite pressure on the government, in the Church, no one reacts much to it now. Even international pressure and Amnesty International no longer have much power.

"We were taken to court. They said a lot of things. They said we were guerrillas, that they had found guns and subversive literature in the house, and that they had all the evidence. We were guerrillas, but the funny thing is that our house had been clean. They had no evidence at all.

"My husband didn't know I had been arrested until I was sentenced and sent to the penal institution. Of course he couldn't come to see me. But it was a regular prison run by the Ministry of Justice, so I had visitors every Sunday. My family came and brought me some things—milk, because I was pregnant. I was kept there for four months."

On 5 March 1980 Napolean Duarte, the Christian Democrat who had run against Colonel Arturo Molina in 1972, been arrested and later exiled, agreed to head the eroding junta. Those who considered Duarte a moderate could not understand why he chose to become a part of the corrupt and brutal government, but those who knew him well have said that his tremendous ego eventually dictated his quest for leadership, even at the helm of a mutinous group of military leaders.

One of Duarte's first public statements was that "the Security Forces had been trained for fifty years to do things 'the other way.'" He said it would take "time to change things." He refused to negotiate with the FMLN despite the fact that Mexico, several European governments and many Salvadoran clergy recommended that he do so. Instead, he declared the country in a state of siege.

By 1980 the revolutionary forces had greatly expanded and were said to have gained widespread public support. They claimed in that year that forty percent of their leadership were women, and women were increasingly adopting military roles in the war. A women's military school was opened, offering a twenty-day training course to all women between sixteen and twenty-two years of age. At least two all-women battalions were formed, and Maria fought with one of them for a few months in the guerrilla-controlled zones of the countryside.

"In October 1980 I was sent to the liberated zone to prepare for the general insurrection we had planned. I needed more military training." The guerrilla camps were located as close as twenty miles from San Salvador. Most of them were hidden in the hills and jungles but could be reached on foot from the government offices in the city. When Maria arrived she noted a community atmosphere. Peasant women cooked and tended livestock that wandered around outside the assortment of mud and thatched-roof huts. Outside in the sun teenagers as young as thirteen and fourteen were taking apart their guns to clean them while they listened to rock music. At the camp Maria was taught to make explosives and to operate a G-3, German-made automatic rifle. Her husband had by now been in charge of several armed actions.

Against the army's superior fire-power, deployed in daytime search-and-destroy missions supported by A-37 Dragonfly jets and Huey helicopters, the FMLN pitted classic guerrilla tactics. The guerrillas continually launched lightning attacks and ambushes on the army patrols that passed through the region. At night they attacked army bases, throwing explosives into the barracks and shooting the soldiers as they tried to escape. They moved into small towns, only to vacate them again as soon as army forces appeared, operating on classic "everywhere and nowhere" guerrilla war tactics. Local peasants who support them, called *las masas*, passed on food and intelligence.

Maria participated in two main military actions during her stay with the guerrillas. "We planned to ambush an army patrol," she remembers. "We had to hide alongside the road and wait for the patrol to come by. I was terrified. I was clutching my G-3 and my hands were sweating, making it slippery. I felt like vomiting. As soon as I heard the first sounds of their armoured cars I sprang up and started to run away. I was thinking, 'I have two children, I'm going to get killed....' One of the others grabbed my arm and said, 'You have to stay here. If you start running they will see you and start shooting. If you run, you are dead.' " Maria stayed and opened fire. "A bullet grazed my hand. Maybe that brought me back to reality. I wasn't frightened anymore."

Maria and her husband had left their two small daughters with friends in the city during this period. The couple spent time at several guerrilla camps, and finally Maria was sent to train for one month at an all-women camp of the women's Anti-Yankee Battalion. The battalion, consisting of about 250 women, operated in the San Cuentes area. Most of the women combatants were extremely young. "To be thirty in any of the guerrilla units was considered old," she smiles.

The women taught Maria many new manoeuvres. "For example, how to cross a river using ropes. We would throw the ropes like lassos, and swing ourselves across the river holding the rope with one arm and our grenades and weapons with the other. We covered each other as we made our way. We left these ropes on the trees and periodically went to check to make sure they were not rotting and the knots were still secure. Work was the same as in the mixed guerrilla groups," she says. "But when the enemy was killed or ambushed by the women's battalions they found it more demoralizing. They consider women worthless.

"We used this to our advantage. Whenever we successfully killed a number of army troops we always put out communiqués saying that we were responsible. We wanted to rub it in.

"I found that the all-women battalion was even more disciplined than the mixed units. For example, if we were given an order not to smoke all day because we were staked out somewhere, we wouldn't. If it had been men, someone would have found a way to sneak a cigarette. Women were more punctual about meeting times and places, too."

Maria says that despite their youth most of the women combatants had children, who were left in care of their families or friends. "Women still did most things during their pregnancies," she says. "It was just for a short time after the baby was born that they couldn't do all the things they normally did." She shows an easy acceptance of motherhood, at any age or in any circumstances, that "is prevalent in El Salvador. It just doesn't seem onerous to us to have babies. We don't wait for the right time and place." Despite the availability of birth control, both Maria and Ileana said that most women wanted to become pregnant because it was psychologically uplifting to give birth when so much death was going on around them.

Ileana had been released from jail and had given birth to a daughter. Six months later her husband was killed. "They came at five in the morning to murder him," she says. "That is when the death squads operate. Dawn is the most terrifying time for all of us. We would lie awake and half expect to hear the loud knocks and yells at the door. I hid myself and the baby while he went to hold them off. They took him away and shot him. Members of the organization came for me and took me to a safe place. I stayed in El Salvador for seven more months before they got me out to Canada."

The FMLN planned to instigate a general offensive in January 1981 for which Maria and her husband had been training in the countryside's "liberated zones." They were told to return to the city in December 1980 to help co-ordinate the uprising there. On the first of December four American Catholic nuns were assassinated by members of the government forces. American President Jimmy Carter condemned the murders and ordered all military and economic aid to the junta suspended. Five weeks later, on 3 January 1981, two American economic aid consultants with the American Institute for Free Labor Development (AIRFLD) were shot to death in a hotel coffee shop, presumably by government enforcers of the agrarian "reform" program: the Americans had been privy to information that exposed corruption within the program. Washington leaders were outraged at the excesses, which were causing an uproar at home and making it increasingly difficult to get public support for American aid to the regime.

On 10 January Maria and her husband waited at home for their final orders. The next day guerrillas overran a classical music radio station and broadcast an appeal to the people of the country to rise up in a general insurrection.

A number of guerrilla units operating in the capital launched hit-and-run attacks against police and military targets. Maria was assigned to a unit attacking the air force base. "The base is located a little way from the centre of the city. We were to go in and plant the explosives, liquidate the guards and get as many of their munitions as we could. I was in charge of distributing arms to different groups after we got hold of them.

"The offensive began at seven o'clock in the evening, when there would be a minimum of patrol cars, and the majority of people would be at home. That way there would be fewer civilian casualties. We managed to attack the air base and get the weapons. But we were identified. They saw our car and the licence plate number. We returned home and hid the armaments in the back room."

The general insurrection had failed. The army had mobilized within the capital and imposed martial law and a dusk-to-dawn curfew. The FMLN had poorly co-ordinated their own forces and had counted, unrealistically it seemed, on the majority of the people in the city to rise up. In the countryside guerrilla gains were substantial, but in the cities the uprising was a failure.

The following morning the army surrounded Maria's home. "We heard their tanks and trucks and patrol cars surrounding the house. The trucks were full of soldiers. There were six adults and six children there, and we were all captured.

"I was taken to a cell where I was raped and beaten. For a few days they kept me inside a gas drum, and when they took me out for interrogation I would be tied hands and feet on metal bars, suspended horizontally with bags of sand on my stomach and then beaten. They used psychological torture as well. They would bring in my children, point pistols at their heads and ask me to talk.... I would make up things to trick them for a while.

"I was being kept at the National Police headquarters. In the beginning they said that they had documents to back up all their accusations. They told me they had spoken to my parents and that my parents had told them to kill me, had said bitter things about me, that I was a terrorist and should be killed.

"I was given electrical shocks, attached to all parts of my body. I was raped many times. I had tried to prepare psychologically for this. I had answers ready for them, a lot of garbage that they already knew or that was fabricated."

After two and a half months at the National Guard headquarters she was removed to Ilopango Prison for women political prisoners. Her children were allowed into the custody of relatives, her husband imprisoned elsewhere. The cell at Ilopango was her world for the next two years, during which time she participated in three hunger strikes that badly affected her health. The electric shocks had caused partial paralysis in her legs, which she is only now recovering from.

"Our capture was broadcast on the Liberation Radio, a station run by the FMLN. The archbishop, the Red Cross and Amnesty International began to lobby for our release. Because of the six children who had been taken at the same time there was a lot of across-the-board pressure on the government not to let us "disappear"— not to kill us. That is the only reason I am still alive. In April 1983 I was released from prison. My husband was already dead—he was killed at some point during those two years. I left my children with my relatives and came to Canada. I was sent here by the FMLN to recuperate, basically. This is a recovery period."

Since Maria has been in Canada, the civil war has escalated in El Salvador. The Reagan administration continues to pour large amounts of military aid into the country despite continued pressure and documentation, by human rights organizations, of the junta's atrocities. The killings continue, indiscriminately; labourers, priests and nuns, students, suspected leftists and even foreign journalists are targets. The majority of the killing is attributed to the right-wing death squads operating for Napolean Duarte's government. He has ruled continuously since 1980 and was "elected" to office in June 1984 when he ran against an ultra-rightist candidate without any challenge from FMLN candidates. As one foreign journalist wrote: "The government's stand—and Duarte's—is that the guerrillas must lay down their guns and join an electoral process set up by the government. For the guerrilla movement, the problem with this stance is that it may mean both literal and figurative suicide. Literal because leftists could not campaign in El Salvador without getting murdered.... The left could never afford to lose an election, and the U.S. government would never allow it to win."

The FMLN has moved noticeably further to the left and undoubtedly receives financial support from the Socialist bloc. One American journalist who travelled deep into guerrilla zones recently was asked by local villagers if he was the guerrillas' Russian adviser. It is apparent that despite the many political beliefs that united to form the FMLN, it has now turned for help to those who are sympathetic— typically the Socialist countries. Once again a civil war fought only because of brutal internal oppression has become a battleground for the superpowers. Still, women like Ileana and Maria remain convinced that the only way to effect change in their country is to fight.

"It is such a strange state of consciousness to leave that reality and come to this one," says Maria. "I don't think I have really adapted at all. There are always reminders. I am never without the presence of El Salvador. If I am eating a good meal, I think about those who don't have enough to eat there, people so poor that they eat roots and weeds. I think of my children every minute. It has not been a tranquil time here, either.

"So little is brought out in the press here about that reality. The reasons for the war, the things that moved people like myself to fight. There are a lot of places where the children only eat once a day, or don't eat at all some days. These are terrible facts that aren't being discussed. If people think that the war in El Salvador is a Moscow- or Cuba-directed Marxist revolution, they should come down and spend some time in our shanty towns, with our peasants or in our prisons. Maybe then they would understand why we fight. We take help where we find it. If the Americans had decided to help the people overthrow fifty years of military rule, no one would call this a Marxist revolution. But instead, they support a government responsible for the disappearance of ten thousand people each year. They forced us to turn elsewhere for help....

"I'm ready to go back. That is not a difficult decision. My first concern is to get my children out of there and bring them safely to Canada. Then I will find a sympathetic family to take care of them, and I will return. I know it will be difficult to prepare to go back, but I will go. I couldn't remain living here, knowing what is going on there. I would hate myself for not continuing to fight for the things I believe are necessary."

"It is an area of strategic importance to the United States," Ileana told me before she returned, "so they continue to support the government and ignore the human rights abuses. I think the war will continue for a long time. Mothers are fighting, kids are fighting, priests and nuns are fighting or helping us to fight. We won't give up. We have tried to negotiate, but it never works. It is not to their advantage to come to an agreement with us. They have all the power and all the wealth, so why should they? They just go on suppressing the movement and increasing their military strength."

In late 1984 Napolean Duarte arranged the first meeting to discuss future negotiations between his government and leaders of the FMLN. The meeting was positive, if only in bringing the two sides together, and all agreed to meet again.

Meanwhile war and rumours of war escalate throughout the region. The Sandinista government of Nicaragua fears an attack from the United States, whose government has accused them of disrupting the balance of power in Central America and arming the revolutionaries in El Salvador.

Maria: "We are willing to die to change the basis of our society, to feed and educate our children, to end the murders, the terror and the oppression. You might not understand that, here. But there, it is another reality."

❖ ❖ ❖

Dynamics

1. Saywell writes that Ileana and Maria "cannot be anything but partisan about...their roles" in the Salvadoran revolutionary effort. Look for evidence of what Saywell calls "partisanship" in passages where Saywell herself relates or comments on the two women's experiences. Where do you see changes in her attitude toward "partisanship"? How do you account for these changes?

2. Ileana and Maria describe their world as a place made up of several different contexts or "realities." Select a couple of these "realities" and trace the meanings of concepts like "patriotism," "family," "duty," and "terrorism" (try to find others in Saywell's text) within each "reality" as the women's contexts change. How does this "slippage" in meaning affect the way you understand Maria's and Ileana's values?

Critical Tools

1. Think about the feelings you had as you first encountered some of the violent images in Saywell's text. Write briefly about some of the ways in which your response to the essay was informed by the emotions you were experiencing. Apply these insights to another essay that contains violent or shocking images. What can you conclude about the place of violence in your own process of interpretation?

2. Maria tells Saywell that "when the enemy was killed or ambushed by the women's battalions they found it more demoralizing" than when they were attacked by men's or mixed-sex units. How does a critical tool from another reading help you to make sense of the gender roles and acts of gendered violence that Maria and Ileana describe?

Draft One/Draft Two

Draft One: Though "Another Reality: El Salvador, 1975-" is most noticeably a story about political oppression and revolution, it is also a story about the movement of two women from adolescence to adulthood. These women have a strong awareness of the relationship between their own development and changes in their political or social environment. For your first draft, consider some of the local, national, or world events that have influenced the development of your priorities as you approach(ed) adulthood. How does the relationship you trace in your own experience compare to the relationship you see in the stories of Maria and Ileana?

Draft Two: Using your draft one as a foundation, offer some hypotheses to account for the relationship between "external" events and the development of personal or "internal" values. Apply these hypotheses to one or two readings which also deal with the transition from youth to maturity. In what ways do your theories need to be revised in order to fit the new context(s) you have created?

❖ ❖ ❖

Before Reading Nancy Scheper-Hughes. . .

1. What do you believe or imagine are the primary challenges to an anthropologist as she prepares a written description of a society's ways?

2. Discuss some of the barriers you see between specialists of whatever field and the people they study, and speculate about the ways those barriers can be crossed.

3. Describe an incident of social criticism that you know of, and discuss its effect on those involved. What, in your view, is the role of social criticism?

The Anthropological Looking Glass

Nancy Scheper-Hughes

Preface to the Second Edition

> *Description is revelation. It is neither*
> *The thing described, nor false facsimile.*
> *It is an artificial thing that exists,*
> *In its own seeming, plainly visible,*
>
> *Yet not too closely the double of our lives*
> *Intenser than any actual life could be.*
>
> —Wallace Stevens

One source of ethnographic data frequently absent in anthropological analysis is the response of the people studied to the ethnographer's description and interpretation of the meaning of their lives.[1] For the most part anthropologists (as well as the communities studied) have been shielded from any local repercussions and aftershocks resulting from publication because we have traditionally worked in what were until recently "exotic" cultures and among preliterate peoples. In most cases the "natives" never knew what had been said about them, their patterns of kinship and marriage, their sexual practices, their beliefs and values or—God help us!— their basic personality structures. The anthropologist might, as a professional courtesy, send a village headman or a mestizo *mayordomo* a copy of the published ethnography which was often proudly displayed in the village. Its contents, however, normally remained as mysterious as the private life of the "masked" white man, that professional lone stranger, who would periodically reappear (sometimes bearing gifts) and then just as inexplicably vanish (not infrequently at the start of the rainy season). Within this traditional fieldwork paradigm our once colonized subjects remain disempowered and mute.

Such local invisibility (and hence invulnerability) has not been the fate of those who have studied "modern" cultures, and in particular that most literate and self-reflexive people, the rural Irish. Irish reaction to, analysis of, and commentary on anthropological writing generally has been swift, frequently harsh, and (at least for the ethnographer) most unsettling.[2] Although, for example, Conrad Arensberg's *The Irish Countryman* (1937) was well received in the Republic as a sympathetic portrait of rural lives, the Irish did *not* like the image of themselves as an appropriate subject for anthropological inquiry. Hence, it was not too long before an enormously popular book appeared by the Anglo-Irish novelist Honor Tracy (*The Straight and Narrow Path*, 1956) which parodied the anthropologist protagonist in an Irish village as a naive, bumbling and pompous fool of uncertain moral principles, given to inept interpretations of local custom, and prone to the perpetration of malicious gossip. Fair enough: the anthropological looking glass reflected back on ourselves. And very reminiscent of the rather blunt warning offered by one resident of "Ballybran": "Ye'll only know how it feels to have your whole family history spilled out for the whole world to see when it's been done to yourselves."

At an early stage in the writing of this book I was tempted to entitle it *The Confessional Conscience*, so struck was I by the rigorously self-critical mode of the Irish villager. I trust that a touch of that same reflexivity and introspection has rubbed off on myself as, over the past three years, I have had ample time and opportunities to observe the impact of publication on the lives of those who "so kindly took us in" as total strangers on that stormy day in 1974 and who, during the ensuing months, entrusted to my keeping a few of the "darkest secrets" of their souls.

The ethical dilemma that has gradually emerged through an exchange of letters, a series of review articles and replies in the Irish press,[3] and through a brief return to Ballybran, was most succinctly stated by the village schoolmaster:

> *It's not your science [i.e., your accuracy] I'm questioning, but this: don't we have the right to lead unexamined lives, the right* not *to be analyzed? Don't we have a right to hold on to an image of ourselves as 'different' to be sure, but as innocent and unblemished all the same?*

If our anthropological code of ethics can be said, minimally, to reflect the medical profession's proscription to "do no harm," then it would be fitting on this occasion of a second edition to reflect on the fundamental question raised by Sir Raymond Firth[4]—*Cui Bonum?* To whose advantage or for whose good do we cast what is so often a critical gaze on the contradictions and paradoxes implicit in the character of human relations, institutions and organizations?

What have they lost, what have they gained in "Ballybran" as a result of the publication of *Saints, Scholars and Schizophrenics*, a book that clearly departs from the traditional anthropological stance of cultural relativism in order to examine the social and cultural contributions to psychological suffering? I will relay here what I have learned by a moving and often painful return to "Ballybran" during the spring of 1981, our first visit since 1976.

They have lost a hitherto unchallenged native interpretation of the meaning of their lives as ones based on the implicitly cherished values of familistic loyalty, obedience and sacrifice. I was told that one village lass has not been the same since identifying herself in the following pages. Until that time she herself (and the parish at large) viewed her decision to give up a disapproved "love match" in order to stay at home and care for her widowed father and unmarried brothers as the good, moral, "Christian" thing to do. As was said: "her father and brothers 'had right' to claim her." But now there is an alternative view, and a hint of pity has been introduced: "Oh, what a shame, the poor creature." Worse, a suggestion of something subliminal: "Could she be overly attached to them?"

I intruded into their "commonsense world" with an alternative and sometimes shattering vision—that provided by psychological anthropology. And they are angry at me, not so much for exposing their lives to the larger world outside, but rather for exposing their hurt and pain to each other. So, I was scolded: "Why couldn't you have left it a dusty dissertation on a library shelf that no one would read, or a scholarly book that only the 'experts' would read? Why did you have to write it in a way that *we* could read it and understand exactly what you were saying?"

There is an irony here and a "double-bind." The irony is that my colleagues in the Society for Applied Anthropology honored me in 1981 with the Margaret Mead Award in recognition of a work that "interprets anthropological data and principles in ways that make them meaningful to a broadly concerned public." Probably the most immediately concerned part of that "public," the villagers of Ballybran, rather wish I had kept my mouth shut or else had said what I did in a jargon so confounding that *they* would not have had to deal with it. Committed as I am, however, to writing for "the public" rather than for a scientific elite, the mandate from "the people," so to speak, to render myself inaccessible and unintelligible posed a real paradox.

While it would be implausible to expect that the members of a community would wholeheartedly agree with the outsider's perspective, with his or her rendition of their social, cultural and psychological situation, that same rendition should not be *so* foreign or removed from their commonsense interpretation of the meaning of their lives as to do violence to it. Any ethnography ultimately stands or falls on the basis of whether or not it *resonates*: it should ring true, strike a familiar (even if occasionally painful) chord. It should not leave the "native" reader cold and confused. Angry and hurt, perhaps, but not confused or perplexed.

When I protested in Ballybran during my return visit that there should have been no surprises in the book, that I revealed no "personal" secrets, but only commonly known and widely shared "community" secrets (such as the questionable status of the community as an Irish-speaking or *Gaeltacht* parish, the depressions and drinking associated with the lonely winter months, the difficulty of keeping an heir on the land, and the distance and alienation between the sexes), I was told pointedly:

There is quite a difference between whispering something beside a fire or across a counter and seeing it printed for the world to see. It becomes a public shame.

There were other objections and responses to what I had written, among them:

She should be shot.

There's a lot of truth in what she said, you can't deny that. But did she have the right to say it, so?

'Bad 'Cess to anyone from here who throws good Irish pounds after a copy of that Yankee work.

To be accurate there was also the quite predictable praise from the young emigrés of Ballybran, reporting back from their new homes in America or from University College in Cork or Dublin. As one young scholar wrote to his distraught mother, already fearful for the loss of his soul at University College, Dublin:

...and you can tell Da that 'that book' is the first one to speak the truth about this secret Ireland of ours.

And there was also the silence—the traditional Irish cut-off—from many of those closest to us and, hence, most stunned by my candor.

I never did learn exactly how many villagers had "thrown away good Irish pounds" after the book since one of the best kept secrets in Ballybran today is just *who* owns a copy, and after that, who has actually read it. Most deny both. *Irish Times* correspondent Michael Viney reported after his investigations in Ballybran that "two or three copies of the book have been passing from house to house, [with] hurt and anger flaring up like a gunpowder trail" (*Irish Times*, 9/24/80). My village friends, however, tell me that there are a good forty or fifty copies in private circulation through the parish:

Everyone is curious, of course, to see if they are in it, and everyone is ashamed to look curious by borrowing it. So most have their own copy. It is difficult to say what the 'public consensus' is because 'it' is never discussed openly and in public, but only privately and among kin.

"How do they get '*it*'?" I asked, falling into the local term of reference.

Oh, they're cute, mind you. They won't go walking into a Tralee [in County Kerry] bookseller and ask for it. They'll get it through contacts going to Cork or Dublin. Or they'll have relatives send it from America the same way we did.

When I argued, somewhat lamely, that it would be pointless for individuals to try to identify themselves since I carefully constructed *composite* characters that would defy any attempts at labeling or identification, I was silenced:

> *Nonsense! You know us far better than that. You think we didn't, each of us, sit down poring over every page until we had recognized the bits and pieces of ourselves strewn about here and there. You turned us into amputees with hooks for fingers and some other blackguard's heart beating inside our own chest. How do you think I felt reading my words come out of some Tom-O or Pat-O or some publican's mouth? Recognize ourselves, indeed! I've gone on to memorize some of my best lines.*

Sensing a possible wedge, I asked my friends whether they could not at least see through to my affection for them and for their way of life. I was brought up short with the answer:

> *Affection, appreciation, we could see that all right. But wasn't it a case of 'Look, I can love you warts and all'? Isn't love more generous than that? Couldn't you have overlooked the warts?*

Cui Bonum? For whose good? What, if anything, has been gained? The "problem of the aged," discussed in the following pages, is being actively debated and a local village association has been formed to look after the solitary elderly to prevent their premature hospitalization. One villager confided that for the first time in their years of friendship she and another wife and mother have been able to discuss family and marital problems they share in common:

> *A kind of great burden has been lifted. There's no need to hide it and worry over it alone—it's part of the public record, now, anyway.*

My suggestion that the *Gaeltacht* status of the community is debatable wounded deeply, and has been met by an even fiercer attempt to revive and restore Irish usage. The new curate, who takes a rather dim view of the Irish revival and who has refused to celebrate the Mass in Irish, has been firmly ignored by the once docile parishioners who have weekly attempted to shout down his English liturgy with their bold Irish responses and Séan O'Riada hymns. "Now, make sure you record *that* next time," I was told. And so I have.

Finally, a new (I will not say better) insight into themselves has been gained. "We are less naive now," said a village teacher,

> *We can see more clearly what our problems are, and how deep the roots of them go. Your book made me very sad. After all, it isn't a very pretty picture. But I have said to myself, 'Let's stop grieving over it, and let's get on with what has to be done.' Quod scriptum est, scriptum est. There are old lives that need caring for, and new ones still in formation. And I was wondering what might be done for some of our young bachelors, before it's too late. A small, informal marriage information bureau, do you think that might work?*

Quod scriptum est, scriptum est. Therefore, as advised, I leave the original work intact, although the impulse to cut and paste, to excise this phrase or that section, to erase those few words now known by me to have caused pain to one individual or another in Ballybran, is strong. I had already in the original Prologue asked villagers' forgiveness for "exposing the darker and weaker side of their venerable culture." I now understand that this forgiveness is not forthcoming. And while I can never ask my fellow travelers in Ballybran to "bless the work" in the characteristically Kerryman fashion, I can pass on to them what I was told upon leaving Ballybran by a "village elder" when I asked whether it would be at all right for me to accept the Mead award in Scotland for a book that had caused so much local controversy. He thought long and hard about it.

> *'Take it,' he said finally, 'but take it for Ballybran, and for what you have learned from us. For better or for worse our lives are inextricably linked.'*

And he cited the Celtic proverb: *Ar scath a chéile a mhaireas na daoine*—In the shadows of each other we must build our lives.

Chapel Hill, 1982

NOTES

Some portions of this text were originally presented as the Margaret Mead Award Address at the 41st Annual Meeting of the Society for Applied Anthropology, Edinburgh, Scotland, and later appeared as *"Cui Bonum*—For Whose Good? A Dialogue With Sir Raymond Firth" in *Human Organization* 1981 40(4): 371-372.

1. One notable exception is the volume recently edited by Jay Ruby, *A Crack in the Mirror: Reflexive Perspectives in Anthropology* (Philadelphia: University of Pennsylvania Press, 1982). See especially Eric Michael's contribution to the above volume, "How To Look at Us Looking at the Yanomami": pp. 133-148.

2. See, for example, John Messenger's biting reply to his Irish critics in his paper "When the 'Natives' Can Read and Respond: A New Projective Test," *American Anthrolopogical Association Meetings*, Los Angeles 12/5/81.

3. In chronological order: David Nowland, "Death by Suppression," *Irish Times* 8/4/79; Eileen Kane, "Is Rural Ireland Blighted?," *The Irish Press* 12/13/79: 1; Michael Viney, "Geared For a Gale," *Viney's Irish Journey, The Irish Times* 9/24/80: 12; Nancy Scheper-Hughes, "Reply to Ballybran," *The Irish Times* (*Weekend* supplement) 2/21/81: 9-10.

4. Sir Raymond Firth, 1981, "Engagement and Detachment: Reflections on Applying Social Anthropology to Public Affairs," *Human Organization* 40(3): 193-201. Originally presented as the Malinowski Award Address at the 41st Annual Meeting of the Society for Applied Anthropology, Edinburgh, Scotland.

Introduction to the First Edition
Mental Illness and Irish Culture

> *Things fall apart;*
> *The center cannot hold;*
> *Mere anarchy is loosed upon the world.*

—*W.B. Yeats,* Collected Poems

Each time I have been asked to give a lecture to a university audience on my research, I have approached it with some amount of trepidation. Usually I begin by asking the group (often a lecture hall of two hundred to four hundred people) how many of them are at least partly of Irish descent. Depending on geographical region, from one-quarter to one-third will normally raise their hands. My next response is some version of the theme *"You're* the reason why western Ireland is underpopulated and in distress!" If there is a certain amount of discomfort engendered in the process of addressing an audience about problematic themes from their own cultural background, there is also some satisfaction in demonstrating that anthropologists can bring the exotic home to roost. In learning about the plight of a small Irish village, trapped by circumstances into a state of cultural decline and widespread anomie, we can learn something about ourselves. For it was from such isolated little communities of the western coast that has come a succession of our statesmen and leaders, our local police and our teachers, our clergy and our bartenders—in short, many of those who have guided public and private morality.

The high morale and stunning accomplishments of the Irish abroad are, ironically and sadly, often contrasted to the demoralization of the Irish at home (see Brody 1973; Healy 1968; R. Kennedy 1973; Lynn 1968). There is little doubt from available statistics (*WHO Statistics Reports*, 1961: 221-245; 1968: 529-551) that the Republic of Ireland has the highest hospitalization treatment rate for mental illness in the world. A recent census of the Irish psychiatric hospital population (O'Hare and Walsh 1974) indicates that schizophrenia is the core problem—more than half of the patients are so diagnosed.

The association between Irish ethnicity and mental illness has perplexed the Irish medical profession (see Walsh and Walsh 1968) and social scientists at large (Lynn 1971; Malzberg and Lee 1956; H. B. M. Murphy 1975) for nearly half a century, and they remain divided on the basic issue of etiology: genetic, biochemical, or environmental. In this book, based on a year of fieldwork in a representatively small, isolated rural community of the Kerry Gaeltacht* I attempt a broad *cultural* diagnosis of those pathogenic stresses that surround the coming of age in rural Ireland today. I explore the particularly high vulnerability of young and middle-aged bachelor farmers to schizophrenic episodes in light of such social and cultural problems as the current disintegration of village social life and institutions; the remarkable separation and alienation of the sexes; a guilt- and shame-oriented socialization process that guarantees the loyalty of at least one male child to parents, home, and village through the systematic scapegoating of this (usually the youngest) son; and, finally, cultural attitudes toward the resolution of stress *outside* of family life and through patterns of dependency upon "total" institutions.

This work can be placed within the tradition of earlier "culture and personality" studies (e.g., Benedict 1928,1934; Erikson 1950; M. Mead 1928, 1935; Powdermaker 1953), which attempted to delineate the cultural parameters of personality development and adult behavior. In addition, it falls into that relatively newer field called transcultural (or ethno-) psychiatry, which explores the interplay of culture and social structure upon the form, frequency, severity, diagnosis, and

---

*One of several small enclaves within the Republic where Irish is still the spoken language in many homes.

treatment of mental disorders (e.g., Aberle 1952; Benedict 1935; Boyer 1964; DeVos 1965; Hallowell 1934; H. B. M. Murphy 1965; Opler 1959).

My orientation is both psychological and social structural, insofar as I shall examine the interplay of historical circumstance and economic determinants with the largely symbolic spheres of beliefs, values, and behavior. Throughout the book I shall emphasize the importance of the antithetical social spheres of the sexes to the quality of the emotional life, as well as the oppositional role of older to younger siblings—both grounded in the basic economic strategy of rural farm families. It is a major hypothesis that these preordained age and sex statuses are pivotal in defining parental expectations for their children, and result in entirely different socialization and later life experiences—weighted in favor of the mental health of girls and earlier-born sons, and against the chances for healthy ego-integration of later-born male children.

I share with other recent ethnographers, among them Hugh Brody (1973) and Robert Cresswell (1969), the belief that rural Ireland is dying and its people are consequently infused with a spirit of anomie and despair. This anomie is expressed most markedly in the decline of the traditional agricultural, sheep grazing, and fishing industries and in the virtual dependence of the small communities of the west upon welfare schemes and the ubiquitous "dole"—this despite marketing improvements through membership in the Common Market and government inducements to production through cattle, dairy, and wool subsidies. The flight of young people—especially women—from the desolate parishes of the western coast, drinking patterns among the stay-at-home class of bachelor farmers, and the general disinterest of the local populace in sexuality, marriage, and procreation are further signs of cultural stagnation. Finally, the relative ease with which a growing proportion of the young, single, male farmers are able to accept voluntary incarceration in the mental hospital as a panacea for their troubles is a final indication that western Ireland, one of the oldest and most continually settled human communities in Europe, is in a virtual state of psychocultural decline.

In chapter one I set the parish of Ballybran (which like all personal names used is a pseudonym) in space and in time, examining vignettes of its history from the oral tradition of legend, myth, and folktale. This section is, more properly speaking, an ethnohistory insofar as I allow the villagers to select and order the significant events of their past as they themselves perceived and remember them. In this way I introduce the reader not so much to an objectively accurate history of the locality, which can be gotten elsewhere, but to the ways in which villagers attempt to validate themselves in terms of a "corrected" and "rewritten" past. Chapter two looks at the present situation of Ballybran: its demographic and economic patterns, the failure of the initially enthusiastically embraced language-revival movement, and its perhaps irreversible decline as a viable and self-sustaining community.

In chapter three I focus on the most visible effect of cultural disorganization and demoralization as I sketch an epidemiological profile of mental illness in the rural west. I suggest that the high psychiatric hospitalization rates must be discussed within the context of what has been called "labeling theory" (see Scheff 1966)—that is, through an examination of community definitions of normal and abnormal behavior, variations in diagnostic usage, and cultural attitudes toward treatment and institutionalization.

Chapter four discusses the relationship between celibacy and mental illness through an ethnographic description of relations between the sexes both within and outside the institution of marriage. I attempt to answer the oft-raised question concerning the source of the Irish antipathy to sex and marriage, and I offer an explanation grounded as much in current social and economic determinants (e.g., the refusal of women to marry into the small farms of Kerry) as in psychological predispositions (including a regressed adult sexuality seemingly fixated on early brother-sister incestual longings).

In addition to participant observation in the lifestyle of Ballybran, two groups of villagers were singled out for particular study—mothers and children. Twenty-eight village parents representing twenty nuclear or extended households were interviewed and observed on the norms of child rearing, following a modified version of the interview schedule outlined in John Whiting *et al., Field Guide for a Study of Socialization* (1966: 78-82). Like the anthropologists involved in the seminal "six cultures" study of child rearing (see B. Whiting 1963), I was primarily interested in the values and beliefs of the society as revealed through socialization techniques. But beyond that, I was problem oriented, attempting to determine if certain rural Irish child-rearing practices might be contributing factors in the etiology of mental illness.

The "children" interviewed ranged in age from newborns to middle-aged bachelors and spinsters still living under the roof and under the thumb of the "old people." The parents interviewed, consequently, spanned three generations and gave me the opportunity to add a historical dimension and note some dramatic changes in child rearing over the past forty or fifty years. In addition I examined, with the help of Professor Sean O'Sullivan, relevant material on child rearing collected in the form of proverbs, folktales, and "old piseogas" (i.e., superstitions) by the Irish Folklore Commission in Dublin. Likewise, I read with care and with relish all the autobiographical literature to have come from the recently defunct culture of the Blasket Islands—once just a short canoe trip from the little market town of Dingle. From the bitter-sweet and poetic recollections of Peig Sayers (1962), Tomás O'Crohan (1951), and Maurice O'Sullivan (1957), I gleaned a picture of Irish attitudes toward children and the principles of child tending "uncorrupted" by sustained contact with outsiders and prior to the decline of Gaelic culture.

Chapters five and six examine current socialization practice and raise this question: Is there something in the nature of parent-child interactions in Ballybran which might be defined as psychogenic, or more exactly, as schizophrenogenic? A qualified yes is suggested by the data, and in chapter five I discuss the cultural pattern of minimal handling and isolation of the infant, and the absence for the very young of what some psychologists call necessary attachment or maternal bonding behavior (see Bowlby 1969, 1973). The casual aloofness and seeming emotional inadequacy of mothers toward infants observed in some rural homes seem to be related to the austere and puritanical cast of Irish Catholicism with its many restrictions on physical expression, and to the, at times, excessive reliance on corporal punishment both in the home and in the classroom. For the more psychologically fragile, the end product of such a socialization experience, I suggest, may be a tendency for the individual to withdraw from painful interactions into the characteristic delusional state of schizophrenia.

In chapter six I attempt to distinguish the "vulnerable" children from the "less vulnerable" in terms of the differential treatment of daughters and sons and of later-to earlier-born siblings. The pattern of fixed statuses—pets, leftovers, whiteheaded boys, and black sheep—attendant to sex and birth order is discussed in terms of the economic requirements of farm succession and its ultimate effect on the emotional and mental health of the chosen heir.

As the research progressed, I became directly involved with the rural young adults themselves and with the succession of conflicts, stresses, and ultimate decisions which resulted in emigration, in stoical resignation, or in cyclical maladjustment expressed in mental illness and alcoholism. In order to probe largely repressed attitudes of late adolescents toward marriage, sexuality, achievement, and generativity, I administered a variety of projective tests—among them the Thematic Apperception and Draw-a-Person Tests, and the Values Hierarchy Scale—to a sizable portion of young adults in the parish. In addition I assigned essays and compositions on a number of relevant topics to the students at the parish secondary school. These essays covered a myriad of topics, such as "Why Does a Good God Allow Suffering and Sickness?" "Is Violence and Aggression Natural to Man?" "How Does the Idealized Image of Marriage Presented in Films Differ from a Realistic Approach to Marriage?"

Most fruitful of the instruments, and to be discussed in greatest detail, was the Thematic Apperception Test (TAT), which was initially administered to thirty-six average village youths between the ages of fifteen and eighteen (twenty-two young women and fourteen young men). Each was tested individually while I transcribed their responses by hand. Whenever possible, the youths were interviewed following the test, on general topics of life history: schooling, family relations, vocational and other goal orientations. Nine of the fourteen boys tested (ages fifteen to eighteen) were potential, if reluctant, farm heirs, while the remaining five had serious designs for higher education or emigration. By contrast, all but three of the twenty-two girls tested expected to leave the village within the next few years in order to pursue a nursing or teaching career or to work abroad. These differences were not selected for, but were a natural reflection of, demographic patterns in the area.

Finally, one day each week for a period of three months I observed, interviewed, and tested young patients of the district mental hospital in Killarney and at the psychiatric clinic in Dingle. Through intensive interviewing of these young adults, already demonstrating early signs of a basic inability to cope, I hoped to identify the major stresses surrounding the coming of age in rural Kerry today. A total of twenty-two patients—eleven of each sex—were tested and interviewed on their life histories. These patients were selected at the discretion of the clinic and hospital directors. My only stipulations were that the patients be young, come from a rural Kerry background, and volunteer for the testing. The latter stipulation (in order to comply with federal regulations for the protection of human subjects) necessarily resulted in a "natural selection" of the most sociable, outgoing, cooperative, and least disturbed patients. The average length of hospitalization for these patients was short—just under one month—and for most it was their first admission to a psychiatric institution. Ten of the twenty-two were diagnosed as schizophrenic, or paranoid.

There was a decided advantage to using written and verbal projective testing among the rural Irish. Forced to generalize, one could say that Irish villagers are extremely reserved and unused to, as well as uncomfortable with, the task of discussing feelings and attitudes relating to personal relationships. If asked directly, for example, how he got along with mother or father, the rural Kerryman will invariably answer with a stylized "Yerra, nothing to complain about," or will reverse the question into a question of his own: "And why would ye be wanting to know that, may I ask?" Needless to say, direct questioning often resulted in stalemate. However, the Kerryman is particularly adept at innuendo, ambiguity, and metaphor. All but two of the fifty-eight respondents *thoroughly* enjoyed the testing, which gave them an opportunity to express, indirectly, their feelings on topics such as family relations and religious beliefs, which would have been socially taboo were they brought up in a direct manner.

The fifty-eight youths told a total of 835 Thematic Apperception Test stories, which were later coded according to the ten basic motivational concerns suggested by George DeVos (1973: 20-21). Five of the dimensions are instrumental (goal-oriented) and five are expressive (directly related to feeling).

Instrumental Concerns

Achievement-Anomie
Competence-Inadequacy
Responsibility-Negligence
Control (Dominance-Submission)
Mutuality (Competitive-Cooperative)

Expressive Concerns

Harmony-Discord
Affiliation-Isolation
Nurturance-Deprivation
Appreciation-Disdain
Pleasure-Suffering

Each story is characterized by one dominant theme, but often contains from two to five additional subthemes, depending on length and complexity of the tale. In coding the stories I avoided themes that were implied and relied only on material that was expressly stated. In addition to thematic coding, I noted the sequences and outcomes of the stories and paid particular attention to the roles played by family figures. The results of the test are used illustratively throughout the book, and in detail in Appendix D (tables D-1 to D-6).*

In general the Irish records reveal large areas of feeling and motivation locked into conflict. Ambivalence is a dominant psychological mode for all the youth, as village lads vacillate between achievement orientation and anomie, and as village girls and boys debate their responsibility to home and parents versus their own personal drive for escape from home and village. A sense of shame and incompetence blocks male strivings for achievement, and an oppressive guilt often interferes with their need to excel *or* escape. A certain superficiality in interpersonal relations is expressed in the desire of village and hospitalized males to be affably sociable without the pressures of intimacy. And throughout all the records runs a strong current of sexual repression and personal asceticism—one that interferes not only with intimacy between the sexes, but with the nurturant and generative aspects of personality as well. With the exception of the schizophrenic patients, whose stories are readily distinguished on the basis of their more idiosyncratic themes, the greatest statistical differences were found between the sexes, rather than between the "average" and hospitalized villagers. Given the separate social realities occupied by males and females in County Kerry (see chapter four), it is the culture of sex rather than the culture of mental illness that is most recognizable in the TAT records. Most poignantly, the tests illustrate the differential stresses experienced by girls, often forced into premature emigration, and by village boys, frequently the casualties of this same female exodus.

The research team was the family—myself, my husband, and our three children: Jenny, aged five, Sarah, aged two, and Nathanael, five months at the start of fieldwork. We could hardly avoid being *participant* observers in the community as we shared with the hardy villagers day in and out their lifestyle, their celebrations, their ennui and depressions during the seemingly endless winter, their fear of the truly awesome wind storms that rocked the peninsula, and their joy at the coming of spring—the flowing of cow's milk and the birth of the calves and lambs. We worshipped with them on Sundays and holy days; we confessed our sins to the same curate; we visited their old and sick, and mourned with them their dead. My elder daughter attended the local primary school, where she learned bilingual reading, math, her prayers, sewing, Irish dancing and music, and how to duck the bamboo rod. She admired her strict Scottish-highlander-trained teacher and enjoyed her peers. Although for the first few weeks Jenny was able to relate fascinating tidbits of information to me about school and yard activities, before very long she was socialized by her friends to the extent that she adopted their world view and joined the

*All tables have been deleted.— *The Editors*

conspiracy of silence that separates Irish children and their parents. From that time on I lost her as a prime "informant." All the children, however, served as "rites of entry" into the normally closed lives of villagers, and remarks and criticisms of the way in which we handled our children, as well as comments on their behavior vis-à-vis their own children's, were an invaluable source of information with regard to socialization.

My husband was the second member of the team to withdraw somewhat from the research, particularly after he was given the highly sanctioned role of second-ary-school teacher. His identification with the school and the Church and his shared perception with some of the villagers that there was something a little sacrilegious about the way I took notes at wakes and enquired about personal and intimate aspects of religious belief, sexual practice, and emotional life made him a rather reluctant co-worker and informant—particularly when it concerned sharing with me the jokes, stories, and opinions exchanged with village men at the pub. As Jenny was socialized into the children's world, Michael joined the circle of "round"-drinking and tale-swapping bachelor farmers. And my presence at the pub, silent though it was (with the exception of singing an occasional ballad), put his companions ill at ease. So, after a few months, I resignedly left the pub mates in peace. I had in any case learned by then all that I wanted to know (and then some) about the "culture" of Guinness stout. Nonetheless, my husband with the cooperation of the schoolmistress gave me free access to his secondary school classes and agreed to assign the essays and compositions on topics which I suggested. He accompanied me on the long trip each week to the county mental hospital, where he assisted in interviewing and testing mental patients. Finally, and most importantly, Michael's natural sensitivity and kindred spirit with the reserved rural Irish served as a foil and a censor, correcting me when I delved too far or pushed too hard or too quickly, and constantly reminding me that my primary obligation was not to "science" or to the academic community at large, but to the community—protecting the villagers' dignity, reserve, and sensitivities, and guarding them from embarrassment or emotional injury of any kind. And for these gentle reminders I am grateful to him beyond words.

There was, at first, some confusion over the nature of my research. When one village publican learned that I was in Ballybran to conduct an "anthropological survey," he informed me that this had already been done some twenty years before, and to come right to the point, he did not want to have his nose and lips and skull measured again! While at first I explained to villagers in the broadest of terms that I was a social anthropologist interested in the culture and way of life of the parish, I was soon pressed by some of the village schoolteachers to give the *exact* nature of the research and to inform them in advance the title of the book I would write and its contents. To this just enough demand, I would reply as honestly as I could at the time: "Interpersonal Relations in a Rural Irish Community." Like most anthropolo-gists, I began my research with the broad areas of interest mapped out, a "sense of problem," and a rather flexible methodology, which would allow for that fortuitous creative process·which some call "serendipity" to take over at will. As it became increasingly apparent that I was concentrating on mothers, children, and adolescents, the village seemed to relax somewhat.

However, there were a few very tense incidents with regard to the research—both occurring in a pub during the summertime, and both taking place under the encouragement of outsiders—specifically Irish tourists from Dublin. In one rather trying experience, a local shepherd made belligerent by alcohol and losses at the local sheep market announced to all and sundry that he had been told by some Dubliners that "the anthropologist" was only interested in the villagers' sex practices and that I would write a book which would convert "people into numbers," and that I would ultimately degrade the Irish way of life. When my attempts at reversing the accusation into jovial banter failed, I promised Brian the shepherd a copy of Arensberg's *The Irish Countryman* (1939), which I thought might be to his liking, and told him that part of my aim in coming to Ballybran was to "modernize" the Yankee's image of Ireland because there had been such vast changes since Arensberg's time. Brian read at least parts of Arensberg, asked to keep the book, and offered magnanimously, "There's lots of truth in that book; the man didn't lie." From that day on, Brian and I were on a first name basis, and the shepherd even offered to recite some political verses and songs into my tape recorder.

The second incident occurred some weeks later when a Dublin tourist himself offered to "introduce" me to my drinking mates of some time by explaining at a pub session the basic thesis of Irish Catholic sexual repression presented in John Messenger's recent ethnography of the Aran Islands, *Inis Beag* (1969)—a book which incurred the wrath of several Irish social scientists and which received a bad press in Dublin papers as well as censorship at libraries in the west. Luckily for me, the villagers were embarrassed by the flamboyant personality of the Dubliner and, as confirmed celibates, could not relate at all to the outsider's brash charges that "anthropologists are 'peeping Toms' who write that the Irish take only the 'missionary position.' "

The perhaps apocryphal days of yesteryear, when the anthropologist was accepted and adopted as "hero" into the local kinship of an innocent and guileless people, are over—for the best, I am certain—as once isolated villages and small communities throughout the world become more enlightened as to the uses and abuses of anthropology. Today each anthropologist must confront the awesome task of slowly proving himself or herself blameless and worthy of acceptance and confidence, despite the increasingly "bad press" accorded the profession. Hence, I became keenly aware of the sensibilities of the people in Ballybran, who were not only suspicious of social science research, but who were still angered over the "stage Irishman" impression given by the films *Playboy of the Western World* and, more recently, *Ryan's Daughter*—both of which were filmed in part on the Dingle Peninsula. I worried about their reaction to a book dealing with the death of the countryside, anomie, and mental illness, topics which were not designed before the research had begun, but which grew naturally out of immersion within the depressed community.

After a particularly revelatory and intimate conversation with a village mother for whom I had a great deal of affection, I returned home one evening in Ballybran to fall into a fitful sleep during which I dreamed that a villager invited me in for tea and insisted upon giving me a suit of armor that had belonged to their family for generations, since the time of the Norman Conquest. I reluctantly accepted the unwieldy present, but as I was walking home through the bog with it, a group of strangers appeared and began to chase me, yelling that I had "stolen" the armor of the village. The dream brought to consciousness my still lingering anxiety over whether it is defensible behavior to befriend and ultimately "disarm" a people and "steal," as it were, their guarded secrets. While I never asked intimate questions of villagers until I felt that they had extended to me the role of "confessor," knowing that what passed their lips to my ears would be considered a sacred trust and used with discretion, yet often even the closest of friends would laugh at the impertinence of a particular enquiry: "What?" demanded the tailor of Ballybran with false gruffness, after I had asked him why he had never chosen to marry, "What, my girleen? Will you even have the darkest secrets of my soul?"

One could hardly discuss data gathering among villagers without mentioning the Irish love of *blas*—skill with words—and the recreational arts of blarney (flattery) and codding (teasing). What about the reliability of my data given that peculiarly Irish form of banter that says one thing and means another? Wouldn't the naive anthropologist, notebook in hand and indiscreet question on the tip of the tongue, be a sitting duck for the tall tale and other useful evasions of the Irish? Without a doubt, communicating with the Irish is tricky for the plodding, literal-minded Saxon, and in many an initial encounter I would think myself to be following a linear path of conversation, only to find myself lost on a forked road, waylaid by shortcuts and switchbacks, and invariably led up a blind alley or cul-de-sac. In short, I was being *had*, Irish style. Well, no matter. Reputation of the Irish aside, I'd also been had in the past by Mexican and Brazilian peasants (and more than once found myself on the wrong bus en route to nowhere), and I had eventually learned to crack *their* code. Yes, the Irish lie, and lie they do with admirable touches of wit and ingenuity. Add to the normal defensiveness of the peasant, a folk Catholic moral code that is quite "soft" on lying, and a lack of tolerance for *overt* acts of aggression, and you have a very strong propensity to "cod" (sometimes rather cruelly) the outsider. Beyond cross-checking information, the only safeguard the fieldworker has against "converting the lies of peasants into scientific data" (as one critic of the participant-observation method commented) is simply getting to know the villagers well enough to read the nonverbal cues that signal evasiveness or lying. Unfortunately, those villagers who are most eager to talk to the outsider from the onset are often the most mischievous informants. Weeding out the "unreliables" from the initially small coterie of "gifted informants" can be a painful procedure. An important point, however, and one that statistically oriented social scientists often miss, is that lies *are* data, and very essential data at that. Once I am able to figure out to what extent villagers lie, when and to whom they are most likely to lie, and who in the community have the dubious reputations of being the greatest liars, I go about systematically analyzing the values of villagers as demonstrated by what they want to believe about themselves; what they want me to believe about them; and what they think I want to believe about them. I compare these findings against my own observations and perceptions of what actually does go on in the village—the way people behave "as if" things were, even though they may define the situation quite differently.

No anthropologist likes to depart from his time-honored conventional stance of "cultural relativity" in order to ask the kinds of questions that come more easily to the clinical psychologist, the medical doctor, and the social worker, such as, What has gone wrong with this organism (or this society)? or, What is so pathogenic about the quality of interpersonal relations in this family (or in this village)? The anthropologist is the product of a historical tradition and a moral commitment dedicated to seeing the "good" in every culture. Few colleagues today would defend a traditional "functionalist" view of human societies, such that whatever exists in the culture is there by virtue of its necessity to the operation of the whole, and hence if it exists it is by definition "good." Yet there is still some calling into question the objectivity of those social scientists, like Oscar Lewis (1951), Edward Banfield (1958), and George Foster (1967), who noted dysfunction as well as function and who, in particular, describe peasant social life as often characterized by suspiciousness, greed, envy, uncooperativeness, and interactions as charged with hostility and aggressiveness.

Even more difficult is it to embark on an ethnographic study of a subject as delicate and normally shielded from the gaze of outsiders as mental illness. In raising such questions as whether there is something in the nature of rural Irish socialization practices which might be diagnosed as schizophrenogenic, some may wonder whether I am looking to assign blame on parents, teachers, priests, and social institutions. They may ask whether I am engaged in a perverse, cultural witch-hunt. It might be wise, therefore, for me to begin with a few caveats regarding my orientation and choice of subject matter. My interest in Irish madness is an outgrowth of an earlier research interest in rituals of racial and sexual pollution (Scheper-Hughes 1973). The following pages should be taken not so much as a thesis on mental illness as a book about rural Irish society seen in part through the eyes of its indigenous outsiders. By this I mean that I am not so much interested in the phenomenon of schizophrenia, the disease, as I am in schizophrenics, the social outcasts or social critics (as the case may be), and in the rituals of definition, inclusion, and exclusion that surround them.

In this regard, I am heir to the insights of Michel Foucault, who has suggested that madness be seen as a projection of cultural themes. In his brilliant work *Madness and Civilization* (1967), Foucault documents Western society's search for a scapegoat—the leper, the criminal, or the madman—whose existence emphasizes, by contrast conception, the "normalcy" of others. Madness, like racial and caste categories, is one of the ways of drawing margins around the psychological reality of a social group. But even as a society refuses to recognize itself in the suffering individuals it rejects or locks up, it gives eloquent testimony to the repressed fears, longings, and insecurities of the group. And that particular configuration of Irish schizophrenia, as revealed through the life histories of young mental patients, expresses the continuing dialogue between the repressed and unfulfilled wishes of childhood, and the miseries of adult life in devitalized rural Ireland.

The "madhouse" of Killarney is not altogether dissimilar from the menstrual hut of Lesu or the "Blacks Only" entrance at the back of the dentist's office in Selma, Alabama. And, just as Black sharecroppers from Gees Bend taught me more about rural economics than the county extension agent (Scheper and Hunt 1970), I thought that I would learn as much or even more about Irish society from the patients of the district mental hospital than I might from the village curate or schoolmaster. Every culture has its own "normality threshold," and a society reveals itself perhaps most clearly in the phenomena it rejects, excludes, and confines.

Others may question to what degree fieldwork observation and analysis are influenced by the personality of the researcher. Ralph Piddington observed in this regard that "a critic once remarked that the Trobriand Islanders are very much like Malinowski and the Tikopia very like Professor Raymond Firth" (1957: 546). Similarly, when Reo Fortune published his *Sorcerers of Dobu* (1963), in which he described a tribal people torn asunder by seemingly paranoid witchcraft fear accusations and counter-accusations, and when Oscar Lewis published his contradictory restudy (1951) of Robert Redfield's original ethnography of Tepotzlan (1930), critics were quick to make reference to the large subjective element in the interpretation of behavior. Redfield defended his original description of an almost idyllic social life in Tepotzlan (1955) by offering that where he was concerned with villagers' enjoyment of life, Lewis was concerned primarily with their woes and sorrows. By implication, Redfield was a romantic optimist and Lewis was an unremitting pessimist in search of the evil and tragedy of human existence. However, the question of subjectivity based on the personality dispositions of researchers should not be so simply dismissed. Social scientists, despite their biases and temperaments, should be able to describe with some amount of objectivity the actual nature of social relations in any given community.

Certainly, psychologically oriented anthropologists tend to look with a more studied eye on the unconscious content of interpersonal relations, child rearing, religious institutions, and so forth, and thereby introduce different sets of data than does a social structuralist looking at the same community. My own biases— grounded in the experiences of growing up in a New York City slum, community organizing among sugarcane cutters of Northeast Brazil, and civil rights work in rural Alabama—can be summarized in the belief that nowhere is the human condition very good for the great number, nor free from pain, either physical or psychological. Yet, I maintain a faith in the possibility for positive change and social healing so long as individuals can be alerted to and moved by the needs of their fellow human beings. To romanticize, ignore, or whitewash the darker side of the life of the peoples we study contributes to the perpetuation of social ills.

Finally, there is the question of the degree to which the remote little parish of Ballybran is representative of the Irish, or even of the rural or western Irish—terms I use interchangeably with the more restrictive terms parishioners and villagers. Are not anthropologists notorious romantics, drawn to the exceptional and exotic in human societies? How peculiar, then, to the rest of Ireland are the Seans and Paddys and Peigs written about here? While not wishing to overextend my expertise on the Irish, my observations, psychological testing, and interviewing went beyond the parish of Ballybran. Through the weekly visits to the mental hospital and psychiatric clinic, I had in-depth exposure to the lives of individuals and their families from villages throughout rural Kerry. In addition, I shared my perceptions on "the rural Irish" with psychiatrists who worked with patients throughout the western counties. In a culture area as small and homogeneous as western Ireland, I feel relatively confident in generalizing, within limits, from the village I know best. Unfortunately, Ballybran is not an exception—there are hundreds of Ballybrans just like it up and down the rugged coast of western Ireland.

In the final analysis, I am less concerned with what my anthropological colleagues and critics will think and say than I am about what my friends in Ballybran will *feel* about what is written here. I trust they realize that although I stress some of the more dismal aspects of their life—the death of the countryside, the seemingly irreversible desertion by young people, the alienation between the sexes, the high rates of anxiety and depression—that they will accept the large measure of my concern for their physical, emotional, and spiritual well-being, and my appreciation of their warmth and double-edged humor. Their children were beautiful—their scrubbed ruddy faces and perpetually muddy Wellington boots, their quixotic smiles and shocks of hair that refused to stay in place, their bread and jam sandwiches— and are engraved permanently in my memory. I only lament that in another decade there will be so many the less of these beautiful children born into Ballybran—a loss not so much for this little community as for the world at large, which has been, for generations, the recipient of some of the best of these lads and lasses as they reached adulthood.

❖ ❖ ❖

Dynamics

1. Identify some of the terms that Scheper-Hughes uses in her "Introduction to the First Edition" to explain her methods and findings. Then locate terms the villagers use in the "Preface" as they respond to her book. Finally, identify terms Scheper-Hughes uses in the "Preface" to explain her understanding of their response. What values do each of these sets of terms imply? What is the significance of your findings?

2. In her closing paragraph Scheper-Hughes distinguishes between what her professional colleagues "think" and what the villagers of Ballybran "feel" about her findings. By setting these two terms in opposition to each other, what does Scheper-Hughes highlight in the work of anthropologists and the actions of the villagers? What does she obscure?

Critical Tools

1. Draw up a set of guidelines for anthropologists, based on your understanding of Scheper-Hughes's experience. Test those guidelines on another anthropological text in this book, or on another text in which an author describes the social customs of a people. What is the significance of your findings?

2. Use some of the terms from your answer to the first Dynamics question to discuss a second reading in *Literacies*. What do the three perspectives you addressed in that question help you say about the society described in the other text?

Draft One/Draft Two

Draft One: Describe the risks that villagers and anthropologists take in encountering one another. Recall an incident you have participated in where members of two different social groups risked an encounter with each other. Tell the story of that encounter, and discuss the ways that it resembles and differs from the encounter described in Scheper-Hughes's text.

Draft Two: Turn to another essay in *Literacies* where an author describes what you see as the risk of encounter between two social groups. Discuss the ways this new text complicates your findings from draft one, as well as the ways your findings in that draft help explain the new text.

❖ ❖ ❖

Before Reading Robert Scholes. . .

1. Think about some movies, TV shows, books, or stories that you enjoy. What aspects of these things appeal to you? Explore the relationship between the parts of these "texts" that you like most. How, in your opinion, do people learn how to enjoy texts?

2. What role(s) do you believe the media should play in society? Evaluate two or three media forms (for instance, something on TV, or a particular magazine) with which you are familiar. What seem to be the goals of these media? Relate them to your own thoughts about the role of the media.

3. What kinds of knowledge and skills do you believe are important for life in contemporary society? Explore some of the ways you gain this information.

On Reading a Video Text

Robert Scholes

The moments of surrender proposed to us by video texts come in many forms, but all involve a complex dynamic of power and pleasure. We are, for instance, offered a kind of power through the enhancement of our vision. Close-ups position us where we could never stand. Slow motion allows us an extraordinary penetration into the mechanics of movement, and, combined with music, lends a balletic grace to ordinary forms of locomotion. Filters and other devices cause us to see the world through jaundiced or rose-colored optics, coloring events with emotion more effectively than verbal pathetic fallacy and less obtrusively. These derangements of normal visual processing can be seen as either constraints or extensions of visual power—that is, as power over the viewer or as extensions of the viewer's own optical power, or both. Either way they offer us what is perhaps the greatest single virtue of art: change from the normal, a defense against the ever-present threat of boredom. Video texts, like all except the most utilitarian forms of textuality, are constructed upon a base of boredom, from which they promise us relief.

Visual fascination—and I have mentioned only a few of its obvious forms—is just one of the matrices of power and pleasure that are organized by video texts. Others include narrativity and what I should like to call, at least tentatively, cultural reinforcement. By narrativity, of course, I mean the pleasures and powers associated with the reception of stories presented in video texts. By cultural reinforcement, I mean the process through which video texts confirm viewers in their ideological positions and reassure them as to their membership in a collective cultural body. This function, which operates in the ethical-political realm, is an extremely important element of video textuality and, indeed, an extremely important dimension of all the mass media. This is a function performed throughout much of human history by literature and the other arts, but now, as the arts have become more estranged from their own culture and even opposed to it, the mass media have come to perform this role. What the epic poem did for ancient cultures, the romance for feudalism, and the novel for bourgeois society, the media—and especially television—now do for the commodified, bureaucratized world that is our present environment.

It is time, now, to look at these processes as they operate in some specific texts. Let us begin with a well-known Budweiser commercial, which tells—most frequently in a format of twenty-eight seconds, though a longer version also exists—the life story of a black man pursuing a career as a baseball umpire. In this brief period of time, we are given enough information to construct an entire life story—provided we have the cultural knowledge upon which this construction depends. The story we construct is that of a young man from the provinces, who gets his "big break," his chance to make it in the big city, to rise to the top of his profession. We see him working hard in the small-time, small-town atmosphere of the minor leagues, where the pace of events is slower and more relaxed than it is "at the top." He gets his chance for success—the voice-over narrator says, "In the minors you got to make all the calls, and then one day you *get* the call"—after which we see him face his first real test. He must call an important and "close" play correctly and then withstand the pressure of dispute, neither giving ground by changing his mind (which would be fatal) nor reacting too vigorously to the challenge of his call by an offended manager. His passing of this test and being accepted is presented through a later scene in a bar, in which the manager who had staged the protest "toasts" the umpire with a bottle of Budweiser beer, with a chorus in the background singing, "You keep America working. This Bud's for you." From this scene we conclude that the ump has now "made it" and will live happily ever after. From a few scenes, then, aided by the voice-over narration and a music track, we construct an entire life. How do we do this? We draw upon a storehouse of cultural information that extends from fairy tales and other basic narrative structures to knowledge about the game and business of baseball.

In processing a narrative text we actually construct the story, bringing a vast repertory of cultural knowledge to bear upon the text that we are contemplating. Our pleasure in the narrative is to some extent a constructive pleasure, based upon the sense of accomplishment we achieve by successfully completing this task. By "getting" the story, we prove our competence and demonstrate our membership in a cultural community. And what is the story that we "get"? It is the myth of America itself, of the racial melting pot, of upward mobility, of justice done without fear or favor. The corporate structure of baseball, with minor leagues offering a path for the talented to the celebrity and financial rewards of the majors, embodies values that we all possess, we Americans, as one of the deepest parts of our cultural heritage or ideology. It is, of course, on the playing field that talent triumphs most easily over racial or social barriers. Every year in baseball new faces arrive. Young men, having proved themselves in the minors, get their chance to perform at the highest level. Yale graduates and high-school dropouts who speak little or no English are judged equally by how well they hit, run, throw, and react to game situations. If baseball is still the national pastime, it is because in it our cherished myths materialize—or appear to materialize.

The commercial we are considering is especially interesting because it shows us a black man competing not with his body but with his mind, his judgment and his emotions, in a cruelly testing public arena. Americans who attend to sports are aware that black athletes are just beginning to find acceptance at certain "leadership" positions, such as quarterback in professional football, and that there is still an active scandal over the slender representation of blacks at baseball's managerial and corporate levels. The case of the black umpire reminds viewers of these problems, even as it suggests that here, too, talent will finally prevail. The system works, America works. We can take pride in this. The narrative reduces its story to the absolutely bare essentials, making a career turn, or seem to turn, on a single decision. The ump must make a close call, which will be fiercely contested by a manager who is deliberately testing him. This is a story of initiation, in that respect, an ordeal that the ump must meet successfully. The text ensures that we know this is a test, by showing us the manager plotting in his dugout, and it gives us a manager with one of those baseball faces (Irish? German?) that have the history of the game written on them. This is not just partisan versus impartial judge, it is old man against youth, and white against black. We root for the umpire because we want the system to work—not just baseball but the whole thing: America. For the story to work, of course, the ump must make the right call, and we must know it to be right. Here, the close-up and slow motion come into play—just as they would in a real instant replay—to let us see both how close the call is and that the umpire has indeed made the right call. The runner is out. The manager's charge from the dugout is classic baseball protest, and the ump's self-control and slow walk away from the angry manager are gestures in a ritual we all know. That's right, we think, that's the way it's done. We know these moves the way the contemporaries of Aeschylus and Sophocles knew the myths upon which the Greek tragedies were based. Baseball is already a ritual, and a ritual we partake of mostly through the medium of television. The commercial has only to organize these images in a certain way to create a powerful narrative.

At the bar after the game, we are off stage, outside that ritual of baseball, but we are still in the world of myth. The manager salutes the ump with his tilted bottle of beer; the old man acknowledges that youth has passed its test. The sword on the shoulder of knighthood, the laying on of hands, the tilted Bud—all these are ritual gestures in the same narrative structure of initiation. To the extent that we have wanted this to happen we are gratified by this closing scene of the narrative text, and many things, as I have suggested, conspire to make us want this ending. We are dealing with an archetypal narrative that has been adjusted for maximum effect within a particular political and social context, and all this has been deployed with a technical skill in casting, directing, acting, photographing, and editing that is of a high order. It is very hard to resist the pleasure of this text, and we cannot accept the pleasure without, for the bewildering minute at least, also accepting the ideology that is so richly and closely entangled with the story that we construct from the video text. To accept the pleasure of this text is to believe that America works; and this is a comforting belief, itself a pleasure of an even higher order—for as long as we can maintain it. Does the text also sell Budweiser? This is something only market research (if you believe it) can tell. But it surely sells the American way first and then seeks to sell its brand of beer by establishing a metonymic connection between the product and the nation: a national beer for the national pastime.

An audience that can understand this commercial, successfully constructing the ump's story from the scenes represented in the text and the comments of the narrative voice, is an audience that understands narrative structure and has a significant amount of cultural knowledge as well, including both data (how baseball leagues are organized, for instance, and how the game is played) and myth (what constitutes success, for example, and what initiation is). At a time when critics such as William Bennett and E. D. Hirsch are bewailing our ignorance of culture, it is important to realize that many Americans are not without culture; they simply have a different culture from that of Bennett and Hirsch. What they really lack, for the most part, is any way of analyzing and criticizing the power of a text like the Budweiser commercial—not its power to sell beer, which is easily resisted, especially once you have tasted better beer—but its power to sell America. For the sort of analysis that I am suggesting, it is necessary to recover (as Eliot says) from the surrender to this text, and it is also necessary to have the tools of ideological criticism. Recovery, in fact, may depend upon critical analysis, which is why the analysis of video texts needs to be taught in all our schools.

Before moving on to the consideration of a more complex textual economy, we would do well to pause and consider the necessity of ideological criticism. One dimension of the conservative agenda for this country has been conspicuously anticritical. The proposals of William Bennett and E. D. Hirsch, for instance, different as they are in certain respects, are both recipes for the indoctrination of young people in certain cultural myths. The great books of past ages, in the eyes of Bennett, Hirsch, and Allan Bloom, are to be mythologized, turned into frozen monuments of Greatness in which our "cultural heritage" is embodied. This is precisely what Bloom does to Plato, for instance, turning the dialectical search for truth into a fixed recipe for "greatness of soul." The irony of this is that Plato can only die in this process. Plato's work can better be kept alive in our time by such irreverent critiques as that of Jacques Derrida, who takes Plato seriously as an opponent, which is to say, takes him dialectically. In this age of massive manipulation and disinformation, criticism is the only way we have of taking something seriously. The greatest patriots in our time will be those who explore our ideology critically, with particular attention to the gaps between mythology and practice. Above all, we must start with our most beloved icons, not the ones we profess allegiance to, but those that really have the power to move and shake us. I propose to conclude this discussion by examining such an icon, as it existed for my own generation, across the media of film, radio, phonograph, and television. More current icons I shall prudently leave to more current investigators. Each generation has its own work to do.

❖ ❖ ❖

Dynamics

1. How does Scholes use the concept of "America" in his essay? Examine several passages in which Scholes refers to "America." What relationship do you see between these references and the development of Scholes's argument?

2. Scholes raises positive and negative aspects of "cultural reinforcement." How does the relationship between "mythology and practice" in his essay affect your response to his ideas about cultural reinforcement?

matrix — the base from which it forms.

Mentorroming —

Critical Tools

1. What do you think Scholes means by "the dialectical search for truth"? Explore some important moments in his essay in order to develop your understanding of what it means to approach something dialectically. Experiment with your ideas about dialectical criticism by using them to analyze a second essay.

2. What are some of the ways a writer might achieve some of the effects Scholes claims for video texts in his opening paragraph? Investigate one or two moments in another essay where you see the author "filtering" or otherwise influencing how you get to view an event, argument, or idea. How do these moments operate as "constraints" and "extensions" of your power as a critical reader?

3. What does Scholes mean by "ritual"? What kinds of knowledge does he produce by viewing events such as baseball as rituals? Examine your response to his use of "ritual" by analyzing an important element of another reading as a "ritual."

Draft One/Draft Two

1. *Draft One:* What do you think is at stake in the way Scholes talks about patriotism? Consider your own ideas about patriotism in relation to those suggested by Scholes. How might his juxtaposition of patriotism and "ideological criticism" complicate your understanding of patriotism?

    Draft Two: Extend your ideas from draft one by relating them to your response to the first Dynamics question. How do Scholes's views of patriotism and America affect each other? Use your insights to explore something in American culture that Scholes, in his final paragraph, might call a "beloved icon."

2. *Draft One:* Scholes discusses the way "we draw upon a storehouse of cultural information" in order to make our interpretations. Locate some important points in his argument and examine how your own "storehouse of cultural information" contributes to your understanding of, and response to, his claims.

    Draft Two: Select a reading that you feel challenges your ability to interpret because it draws upon information, assumptions, or narrative forms that lie outside your cultural knowledge. On what bases were you able to construct your interpretations? Consider some of the implications of your experience for the arguments that Scholes makes in his essay.

❖ ❖ ❖

Before Reading Victor Seidler. . .

1. "Language and Masculinity" is a text written by a British philosopher. What ways of talking and thinking do you associate with philosophers in Western culture? Make a list of verbs and adjectives describing the actions and attitudes of a "typical" (or stereotypical) philosopher. Where do your impressions come from?

2. Where does "male" identity or "female" identity come from? Think about the ways in which you learned how to "be" a woman or a man. Which people had the most influence over your development as a gendered person? What forms did that influence take? Keeping these questions in mind, write briefly about a time when you began to "know" your gender identity.

3. What connections might you expect to find between "language" and "masculinity"? When you hear or participate in discussions of these issues, what kinds of statements do you often hear? Describe your role in such discussions, and your reactions to them.

Language and Masculinity

Victor Seidler

Because rationality is taken to be a universal quality, it becomes difficult to realize how rationality becomes an important basis for male superiority in social life. One of the women's movement's more powerful insights has been the identification of the ways that power relationships can be consolidated and sustained through men's assumption of a stance of overview of a situation, creating a relationship of communication in which what women have to say is branded with the status of the particular, whilst men offer what they see as an encompassing and objectively-grounded account. To see this is to see that men and women do not have the same relationship to language. In the light of it, it is important to explore men's relationships to language, sensitive to the possibility that men can learn to use language to distance and hold in check their experience. This is an investigation which structuralism leaves little space for, convinced as it is that experience is itself constituted through language. The effect of displacing experience in this way is to close off questions about people's different relationships to language and expression; experience is assimilated into language so that qualitative differences in experience cannot be recognized, let alone grasped in their full significance. Language remains at some level autonomous of experience.

It is a strength of Wittgenstein's later work to challenge a Cartesian rationalism that has underpinned the identification of masculinity with reason that has been so crucial in a post-Enlightenment culture. Wittgenstein is undercutting the claim to superiority we grow up to assume as men over our feelings and emotions. I want to show that rationalist conceptions of language fail to illuminate, how, as men, we can learn to use language instrumentally to conceal ourselves and in so doing form and shape the kind of personal and sexual relationships we can have with others.

Language and Male Identity

Within a liberal moral culture, the very notion of personal identity has been made problematic. As individuals we take ourselves to be the embodiment of univer-

Victor Seidler, "Language" from *Rediscovering Masculinity.* Routledge, New York & London, 1989, pages 123-142.

sal qualities though we acknowledge that some people have more of these qualities than others. Some people are more intelligent than others and some can run faster. This is deeply rooted in the rationalist tradition. We witness it in that aspect of Kant's ethical theory that would argue that we are each deserving of respect since we are equally moral beings, or at least have an equal capacity for morality. But Kant was also careful to identify this capacity with our individual powers to reason. This was a possession which was historically since the Enlightenment more closely identified with masculinity. Our very sense of masculinity was consolidated as an experience of superiority over our wants, desires, emotions and feelings. To prove our masculinity, we had to keep our 'inclinations' in check. We had to learn to dominate our inner natures. But this also meant that our masculinity could be upset or challenged. It was not anything we could take for granted, but had to be constantly proved. We still live in the shadow of this conception. We can experience it for ourselves as men in our constant tendency to push ourselves to the edge of exhaustion as if this is the way we can prove ourselves individually and sustain our self-control.

But reason is essentially impersonal. The more our sense of self is identified with reason, the more we are in a process as men of impersonalizing ourselves. At the same time, we have to recognize that historically this was important for the emancipation of classes and ethnic groups who would otherwise have been discriminated against, excluded and humiliated. But at another level this is emancipation at a price, since it is also a pact with the devil as it makes for instance, your blackness, Jewishness or gayness, essentially *incidental* aspects of yourself. We learn to give up these aspects of our history and culture to be treated as equals by others. It is as if we have to pay the price of the painful and difficult work of deconstructing our identities to be treated fairly and equally with others. This means we have to learn to redefine our interests so that we can articulate them in universal terms. In capitalist society this means we want to be richer and more successful than the next person. Our class and ethnic identity become private matters but no part of the 'official identity' we can assume in the larger society.

In this way we become *estranged* from important aspects of our history and culture. We lose an important source of our own power as we are left divided. It should be hardly surprising if those suffering from class, ethnic or gender oppression find it hard to define themselves clearly in the larger society. I have learnt how subtle but powerful is the way that, in discounting my Jewishness, I have discounted an important source of my power and identity. But people often feel uneasy and embarrassed if you bring these 'emotional considerations' into serious intellectual discussion. Rather we are encouraged within a liberal moral culture to think of our class and ethnicity as 'emotional attachments' we will eventually outgrow. It is clear that emotionality has culturally to do with infancy.

This is an integral part of assuming our masculinity in the larger society. I remember feeling that being a 'real man' meant being taller than I was, stronger than I was. Very far from being a residual category, masculinity was something we had to give our lives aspiring towards, never sure that we would ever really make it. It is no accident that the idea of a 'Jewish man' was experienced by me as a kind of contradiction in terms. Jewishness was related to the emotional, and so with the feminine. Growing up, we had to work hard to reassert a notion of Jewish maleness, often forcing ourselves to react against weakness and vulnerability more harshly. This was a potent source of shame.

I am concerned to understand how our inherited conceptions of masculinity connect to processes through which we learn to *displace* important aspects of ourselves. This seems to weaken and impoverish our individuality, but it also makes it harder for Jewish men to define themselves in their own terms, as they are constantly anxious to compete or prove themselves to others. In some way this can make Jewish men adaptable and understanding in their relationships, though at another level leaving them rigid and unforgiving. I know how subtly I work to get my own way, doing well at concealing my tracks. This can mean taking out particular tensions and frustrations on those closest to us, assuming they understand a predicament we have often never explained to them, since we rarely have the language to explain it ourselves. It is of the essence of the situation that we can never make ourselves acceptable to others, since we are constantly on edge that they might discover a different side of ourselves. This is a no-win situation. What is more, we lose our strength in the process.

We betray our cultural integrity as Jewish men, and in a real sense we emasculate ourselves as we are constantly doing our best to prove ourselves in the eyes of others. They inevitably withhold their final approval, since with this they lose their power over us. It is an exhausting and painful process, though one rendered largely invisible through the success and achievement we may have individually achieved. I have had to fight it through myself. I am left haunted by a sense of weakness, since this is no way to discover my own historical and ethnic grounding. But it is a powerful way of sustaining those who have institutional power in the larger society, since the cost of a particularistic identification seems to be minimal, especially if we no longer have a language in which to illuminate the bargain we have struck. Since they set the terms, they are made invulnerable to criticism. This is an important aspect of the centrality notions of equality of opportunity have assumed in legitimating relations of power and subordination in late capitalist society.

Even though this is a predicament that could illuminate the situation of working-class people, women and ethnic minorities, it also reveals something central about contemporary masculinity: the identification of masculinity with rationality undermines the identity of men. The impersonal character of reason makes it hard for us to appropriate a history and culture of masculinity, especially one in opposition to the dominant culture. What is more, it weakens any sense that this could be important to us individually as men. We learn to ground ourselves in our ideas, in our heads. This is the way we protect ourselves. We do our best to capture the claim to be rational and reasonable, which seems to move our own behaviour and experience beyond criticism. It is always others—usually women—who are emotional, if not hysterical. It is always us who have to wait patiently for them to calm down, before we can add the weight of our arguments to the situation. We learn not to lose our self-control, since this is often the basis for our feeling of superiority in the situation. We hold tight.

As men, we are brought up to identify with our 'rationality' as the very core of our masculinity. We learn to appropriate rationality as if it were an exclusively male quality and we deny it to others, especially women. We also deny it to animals and children. The very possession of reason amounts to a claim to superiority, though this can be difficult to realize, since it is also taken to be a universal quality shared by all human beings. This is one of the sources of ambiguity in the liberal tradition of equality. So it becomes difficult to realize how rationality becomes an important basis for male superiority in social life.

Since we identify 'rationality' with knowledge, we systematically deny knowledge to women and children, who are more closely identified with emotions and feelings. Emotions and feelings are systematically denied as genuine sources of knowledge, though they may illuminate how individuals have responded to situations; but often they are indications of weakness and a lack of self-control. They are antithetical to our very sense of masculinity. Even feelings like anger become indications of a lack of control, which men learn to be wary of. This has powerfully influenced the shape and tone of our language and the relationship men grow up to have with language. Even though we are powerfully influenced by traditions, such as romanticism, which show language to be expressive, helping to articulate and form the nature of the self, these visions have been continually marginalized within a scientific culture which, at least since the seventeenth century, has powerfully identified masculinity with dominant forms of scientific knowledge.

The dominant view of language has been a correspondence theory which has seen our words as existing in a one-to-one relationship with objects in the world. For our sentences to have meaning, they have had to correspond to an existing state of affairs in the empirical world. This view found a powerful form in the twentieth century in the writings of the Vienna Circle and the early Wittgenstein, but it articulates a vision that has its source in the scientific revolutions of the seventeenth century. This was the historical period in which our common-sense notions of objectivity and impartiality were formed. From the beginning this was closely tied to a reformulation of masculinity. Lukács helps illuminate some of the key antinomies of this period, within *History and Class Consciousness.*

Foucault's early work, entitled *Madness and Civilization,* is also crucial in showing how our notions of reason and objectivity were historically formulated in the sixteenth and seventeenth centuries. He shows the crucial importance of a distinction between reason and unreason in isolating certain forms of behaviour as threatening. We could no longer learn from the insights of madness or treat it as an occasion in otherwise normal lives. This was also the period of the witch trials and the violent and brutal assertion of a new form of masculinity identified with the new sciences. These historical processes have been rendered invisible and their brutality legitimized as we have learnt to think of this as 'The Age of Reason'. This has become an integral part of the identification of reason, science and progress. To question science in this new period was to stand in the way of progress. This legitimized some of the worst forms of oppression and suffering.

Often the tensions in our modern experience have their source in this period. Both capitalist and socialist societies have sought to legitimize themselves in this conception of science. We cannot understand their development unless we are prepared to place them within the historical framework of the Enlightenment. This was something the Frankfurt School only partially managed to achieve in their pioneering study *The Dialectic of Enlightenment*. They tended to assume the identification of progress with the domination of nature, but at least this opened the way for a more ecological critique of Marx and the tradition of Marxism. It was with the new self-identified masculinist sciences of the seventeenth century that the split between reason and emotions, feelings and desires was most clearly institutionalized. This inevitably fragmented our experience as we found our emotions, feelings, dreams and visions denigrated as forms of 'unreason'. This was systematically to negate the experience of women and destroy the sources of any forms of instinctual knowledge. We were to learn systematically to separate the workings of our intellectual reason from our felt experience and embodied natures.

Even though analytical philosophy has done important work in questioning the appropriateness of Cartesian dualism for our understanding of our experience, we continue to live our lives in its hidden grip. We still believe in the autonomy and independence of reason. We deny our bodies as genuine sources of knowledge, and we tend to see them as machines which do the work of carrying our minds around. We marginalize what we could otherwise learn from the knowledge of our hearts, as we continue to think in the dualistic terms of mind and body. This is one reason that Reich has been so despised and misunderstood. He threatens not simply the conceptual terms in which we constitute our identities, but the very organization of our everyday experience as he calls us into a different relationship with ourselves. We find it almost impossible to think clearly of ways we are more open or closed to our experience, even though we can be dimly aware that nothing in our experience seems to touch us.

Reich understood this in terms of the over-bounded character of people who have developed a rigid armouring, but he did not connect this enough to the learning of our masculinity or to the historical identification of reason with masculinity. This helps to estrange us from a deeper understanding of self, as we somehow take up a position beyond our own experience. We lose any sense of *grounding* ourselves in our own embodied experience as we identify our sense of masculinity with being objective and impartial. This involves our discounting our own experience and so denying one of the deepest sources of our identity and knowledge.

Descartes saw the human body as a machine organized according to mechanical laws. The body was to be made a part of the natural world to be investigated using the methods of the new sciences. The person was to be identified with the mind, which was seen as essentially impersonal to the extent that people acted rationally. In its own way this was to give secular expression to a Christian tradition which had often denigrated the body as a source of spiritual knowledge. Our bodies held us to the animal world that we should learn to control and dominate. Our sense of ourselves as 'civilized' depended upon us claiming a superiority to the natural world of animal wants and desires. It was as if we were continually trying to free ourselves from the demands of the body, which would inherently undermine our freedom and autonomy as it determined our behaviour externally. Women were taken to be 'unfree', to the extent that they allowed themselves to be moved by their emotions and feelings. This was the way Rousseau and Kant argued that women could only be free if they agreed to subordinate themselves to men; but men could only guarantee their own freedom if they insisted upon identifying themselves with their rational powers. We had to learn to disdain our emotions, feelings, dependence and desires, lest they were to fundamentally compromise our masculinity.

Not only were men to learn to identify themselves with rationality, but this was to be fundamentally separated from any sense of embodied experience. Even our bodies are no part of our identities as men. We had to investigate them as matter, as part of the empirical world. In a very real sense, as men, we are fundamentally estranged from this world which we can only observe from a distance. It is no accident that issues of perception became central to modern philosophy. We become historically obsessed with the truthfulness of our perceptions of a world that is estranged and distant. We are systematically estranged from a world we can only 'observe'. We conceive of the mind, in Richard Rorty's phrase, as the mirror of the world.

This conception of mind has been crucially significant, not only for the form of modern philosophy, but also for the gender experience of masculinity which is so closely identified with this form of rationality. This reveals a much deeper connection between masculinity and the forms of philosophical thought in which they have implicitly found expression. Within the rationalist tradition, men learn automatically to relate to themselves and their social relations in an instrumental way. Of course this is not specific to men, since women come under this pervasive influence within a masculinist culture. This means they are also constantly encouraged to turn their experience into a test in which they have to prove themselves, even if this is not so closely identified with a sense of women's identity.

For men, our very identification with our reason gives us a vantage point of superiority in relation to women outside and beyond our own lived experience, which we can only appropriate in the most abstract of terms. We are trapped as observers, not only of the natural and social worlds, but also of ourselves. We are left as observers, rather than as participants, in our own lives. This is part of the pervasive distinction between subjective and objective understandings of the social world within which social theory has so long been trapped. Marx attempts to reinstate a sense of ourselves as sensuous beings who are practically involved in activities and relationships. But unfortunately he does not systematically develop the hints left in the 'Theses on Feuerbach'. These ideas have found echoes in the continual renewals of Marxist theory which have recognized the enduring significance of Hegel for Marx. Richard Rorty has looked in *Philosophy and the Mirror of Nature* for similar breaks with a Cartesian inheritance in the dominant tradition to be found in the writings of Dewey, Heidegger and Wittgenstein.

The abiding strength in the rationalist tradition was to reinstate the active importance of the mind in organizing our experience. The categories of the mind through which we organize our sense of the empirical world was Kant's direct challenge to the empiricist tradition of Hume. Empiricism tended to see the mind as a passive receptor of impressions and ideas coming from the world. But within the empiricist tradition we can also discover a powerful democratic strain which recognizes that each person could test for himself or herself the results of scientific knowledge. People were no longer expected to accept things on faith. People learnt to challenge traditional forms of religious authority as they learnt only to accept the authority of their own sense-experience. This was part of a democratic impulse of the new sciences of the seventeenth century, even if it eventually gave way to a new basis of hierarchical authority built upon the possession of knowledge. More particularly, it has been within a British empiricist tradition that the emphasis upon perception has been most developed.

Analytical philosophy was partly initiated as a challenge to theories of sense perception and sense-experience in the period after 1945. This tradition has had its influence upon empiricist traditions of social science in fragmenting our conception of social knowledge into discrete pieces of data that can be collected. But the rationalist tradition has had a deeper grip upon the development of social theory. Both Weber and Durkheim remained deeply influenced by the Kantian tradition, and most of the phenomenology which has developed within sociology has remained trapped within this intellectualist framework. But both traditions, as Lukács realized in his *History and Class Consciousness*, leave people as observers of an external social reality which they cannot change. Our understanding is not something we can develop in our active involvement in relationships and activities. This is an insight that connects Marx to the later Wittgenstein. In their different ways they are both contesting the influence of Descartes. In Wittgenstein this is clearest in one of his latest works, *On Certainty*.

The identification of masculinity with reason has left a strong impulse for men to become observers of their own experience. We struggle for a certain form of impartiality and objectivity in assessing a situation fairly. Consequently the difficulties we often have as men to say what we personally feel and experience in a situation has deep cultural and historical roots. As men we often become more adept at assessing the different interests involved in a situation than saying what we want individually and negotiating with others on this basis. Rather the forms of moral rationalism we inherit tend to make us feel uneasy about asserting our own individual wants and desires. Often we think of this as a form of 'selfishness'.

This also has deep roots in our upbringing in a culture in which we learn automatically to discount our individual emotions and feelings as having no part in our 'true rational self'. This is a process which psychoanalytic theory can sometimes illuminate. As boys we often learn to identify emotions and feelings with our mothers, and with the feminine. This is something we are forced to separate from to prove ourselves as men. We also have to separate from what we identify as the feminine within ourselves. Masculinity is such an uneasy inheritance. We have to be prepared to defend it at any moment, even if this means striking down parts of ourselves.

We would need to investigate these processes in a way that is specific to class and historical moment. It has only been with the development of a more egalitarian ethos between the sexes that a man's word has been questioned as law within the home. Since domestic life has often been automatically organized around men's needs, little has had to be said: men had to talk very little. D.H. Lawrence illuminates this in *Sons and Lovers*, when he shares his growing up in a mining community. John Cleese has talked about the lower middle class of Weston Super Mare, 'where emotions were kept as hidden as possible. Making scenes wasn't allowed. Anger wasn't shown. It was wrong for anyone to assert themselves. You had to work out what everyone else wanted. All change was dangerous. "You haven't changed a bit" was a tremendous compliment' (The *Guardian*, Monday 2 January, 1984).

Class differences are very significant, as are the forms of control men can exert in relationships. But within a supposedly more egalitarian period, issues of control are still central if we are not to experience our masculinity as threatened. Often we use our reason to define 'what would be best in the situation', and so get others to agree. In this way we often assume to take the interests of others into account without really giving others a chance to identify and *define their own interests*. It is in the name of reason that we often, as middle-class men, silence others at the same time as giving them no chance of getting back at us. Often this remains a potent source of power, as we can in all honesty present ourselves as working out the most 'rational' way of doing things. Our rationality is often a hidden weapon, since it allows us to assimilate and control the interests of others. It also puts us beyond reproach.

It is within the context of an instrumental notion of masculinity that we learn our language. Often this is a practical language of action, where we are setting out to prove ourselves to others. Since it is what we think that makes us what we are as men, we find ourselves without any natural connection to our emotions and feelings. These are not experienced as integral aspects of our individuality. Our individuality is defined in relation to our thoughts, and often our emotions and feelings have to be turned into thoughts so that we can deal with them in familiar ways. At best we can learn to talk about emotions and feelings.

In the middle class, men have often grown up to be reticent, even scared, of sharing emotions and feelings, lest they threaten the control which sustains our very sense of masculinity. We can feel apologetic and embarrassed if we are emotional with others. We fear that others will see us as weak and unmasculine. We often prefer to withdraw into a sullen silence, unaware of how controlling this silence can be. Our emotions automatically seem to signal a lack of control. We find it almost impossible to identify our anger, resentment or sadness as a rational response to a situation. Only *in extremis* can we allow ourselves these feelings. Rationality has to do with coolness and control. It seems to have no place in our consideration of our emotional and somatic lives.

Language and Experience

Men have often assumed a control of language. Since we automatically assume that language has to do with reason, logic and rationality, we easily treat it as our own. Certainly men have often had power in the larger society to define the reality of others, but we have to be careful not to assume universally that language itself is 'man made', in the sense Dale Spender developed in *Man Made Language*. Women have not simply had to conform to a reality men have created, as long as they have remained within the private and domestic sphere. It has been in the public realm that men have most clearly created the terms on which women could gain access. But we should not forget, as Gramsci was struggling to show in his *Prison Notebooks*, that even here, language is essentially contested.

Gramsci was developing a tradition in which language is embodied in ongoing social relationships in which people are constantly clarifying and redefining a sense of their individual needs, wants and desires. Language does not constitute individuality in the way structuralism has assumed. Gramsci also realized the tension between what we say and what we do, especially where relationships of power and subordination are involved. Oppressed people are constantly trying to make language their own, as they attempt to discover and redefine their experience. This is an ongoing historical process, in which women are not to be conceived as completely passive. Our common sense remains inherently contradictory as it brings together different elements in men's and women's experience.

Again, we are questioning the pervasiveness of a Kantian inheritance which sees language as a set of categories, or a framework, that we place over the social world to make sense of it. At one level, as language users we are already involved in such a system of meaning, but at another level it supposedly remains a more or less arbitrary construction. This is part of the linguistic relativism which exists in both structuralist and phenomeno-logical traditions. This is why it is so important to understand the historical appeal of this form of relativism. This has to do with the same tradition of rationalism and its internal connection to masculinity. This kind of theory promises an overview of a culture or society, in terms of the categories or classifications people invoke to order their experience. So it promises a superiority over others, who in their ignorance do not realize the contingent nature of the social world they have 'constructed' or 'negotiated' for themselves.

But the different forms of the rationalist tradition give no way of situating individual experience socially and historically. The very notion of experience was abandoned as irrevocably tied to an empiricist tradition. Even though phenomenology, in particular, has aspired towards some notion of reflexivity, apart from the early work of Gouldner which was more influenced by the insights of the New Left, this has been an intellectualist exercise. The current was flowing too quickly in other directions to allow this form of personal and intellectual self-consciousness to develop outside the context of feminism and sexual politics. This was politically too threatening, but also too threatening to the impersonal character of masculinity. As Lukács realized, people were left in a fundamentally contemplative position towards a social world from which they were estranged. Certainly people had learnt within the rationalism of structuralism to change the world through giving different interpretations of it, but this was different from the historical transformations of Marx and Gramsci.

As long as we continue to see language as a screen or net to be placed against the social world, we remain trapped by the picture Wittgenstein articulated in the *Tractatus*. Unfortunately this is the conception of language informing Spender's work, which otherwise illuminates central issues of the relationship of language to relations of power and subordination. The view Wittgenstein was developing in his later writings is less aware of relations of power, but has a keen awareness of how we learn to talk in the context of learning social activities.

Language is no longer conceived as a single system, though it remains important to acknowledge our capacities to use language. Wittgenstein remarks that 'Children do not learn that there are books, that there are armchairs, etc., etc., but they learn to fetch books, sit in armchairs, etc.' (*On Certainty*, p.476). We learn language as an integral aspect of learning to do these things. In some crucial sense our language grows out of and extends these activities.

Norman Malcolm in his article, 'Wittgenstein: the relation of language to instinctive behaviour' (*Philosophical Investigations* Vol. 5 No. I) argues that

> *the child who retaliates against the one who crashes into him does not do this because he 'knows' or 'believes' that this caused his fall. He simply does it. It is an instant reaction, like brushing away an insect that is tickling one's skin (p.6).*

He goes on to question an empiricist reading

> *that the child affirms in his mind the proposition that the other one certainly knocked him down, or that the child has a perception or intuitive awareness of the causal connection between his being crashed into and his falling down. No. Wittgenstein means that the hitting back at the other child is instinctive....The 'certainty' he is talking about is a certainty in behaviour, not a certainty in propositional thought (p.6).*

As Wittgenstein himself says:

> *The primitive form of the language-game is certainty, not uncertainty. For uncertainty could never lead to action. The basic form of the game must be one in which we act.*

Wittgenstein was concerned fundamentally to shift our relationship to language and challenge our inherited rationalism, when he remarked in *On Certainty* that 'Language did not emerge from reasoning' (p.475). As a child learns words and sentences, this marks a transition from say, non-linguistic to linguistic expressions of pain. In learning linguistic expressions of pain the child learns 'new pain-behaviour' (*Philosophical Investigations*, p.244). As Malcolm reminds us, Wittgenstein calls these 'first person utterances, Ausserungen, to indicate that they are *immediate expressions* of pain, fear, surprise, desire and so on, and are not the result of thought' (p.3). In this way Wittgenstein is undercutting and subverting our common sense rationalism which has built itself upon a fragmentation in our experience between what is 'natural' or 'instinctive' and what is 'cultural' and 'linguistic'. This is a dualism that finds powerful expression in Descartes and Kant. Against this conception is the vision that our language grows out of our pre-linguistic behaviour and can only be grasped if we ground it in these early experiences. So we can see how deeply was Wittgenstein's challenge to our inherited traditions when he says in *Culture and Value*:

> The origin and the primitive form of language-game is a reaction; only from this can the more complicated forms grow. Language—I want to say—is a refinement; 'in the beginning was the deed' (p.31).

So we can see how deeply misguided it has been to interpret Wittgenstein's notion of a 'language game' as if it were a linguistic phenomenon, so putting his work at the service of a tradition he was seeking to subvert and challenge. It is only in the context of our deeds that we can begin to grasp the meaning of our utterances. As soon as we separate language as a system of meanings, we have lost its vital interconnection with the ongoing practices of everyday life. It is as a critique of theories of language as an independent and autonomous system through which we make sense of or organize our social world, that we can possibly think of Wittgenstein as developing a form of 'linguistic materialism'.

Wittgenstein is tacitly subverting the basis upon which we identify masculinity with reason. He is unwittingly and unknowingly undercutting the claim to superiority we grow up to assume as men over our feelings and emotions. Rather he can help us understand how we have hurt ourselves through misunderstanding and misconstruing the place of reason in our lives. We have set up a duality where none should exist. We have failed to realize how our thoughts are nurtured from the same ground of actions and deeds as are our emotions and feelings. To the extent that Kant has encouraged us to identify our morality exclusively with our reason, he has limited and injured our sense of ourselves as moral beings and the nature of our relationships with others.

Rationalism has continually undercut our sense of connection with others, forcing us morally to justify whatever care and help one individual might give another. This is related to our inherited notion of masculinity as independence and self-sufficiency. As soon as we act from feelings, we are accused of being 'soft', as if our masculinity is affirmed in our insistence on finding reasons for each of our actions. There is no way to acknowledge our need to be dependent and vulnerable in our relations with others if we are to give these relations depth and substance. As men, we fear this vulnerability which threatens our very sense of masculinity.

Malcolm realizes how Wittgenstein places our relations with others on a different basis, though he resists drawing the implications for our sense of morality and politics. I think it important to quote this part of his article in full since it helpfully shows how rationalist notions are questioned:

> This conception of certain linguistic expressions as replacements for unlearned reactions, was seen by Wittgenstein to extend to some of the sentences that we use to refer to other persons. Not only 'I'm in pain' but also 'He's in pain', can take the place of instinctive behaviour. In Zettel Wittgenstein observes that 'it is a primitive reaction to tend, to treat, the part that hurts when someone else is in pain, and not merely when oneself is' (Z 540).... Wittgenstein asks himself what he means by saying that these reactions are 'primitive'; and he answers:

> 'Surely that this way of behaving is prelinguistic: that a language-game is based on it, that it is the prototype of a way of thinking and not the result of thinking.' (Z 541)

> Wittgenstein is disagreeing with a 'rationalistic' explanation of this behaviour—for example, the explanation that we have a sympathetic reaction to an injured person 'because by analogy with our own case we believe that he too is experiencing pain' (Z 542). The actions of comforting or trying to help, that go with the words 'He's in pain', are no more a product of reasoning from analogy than is the similar behaviour in deer or birds. Wittgenstein goes on to say that

> 'Being sure that someone is in pain, doubting whether he is, and so on, are so many natural, instinctive, kinds of relationship towards other human beings, and our language is merely an auxiliary to, and further extension of, this behaviour. Our language-game is an extension of primitive behaviour. (For our language-game is behaviour). (Instinct) (Z 545).'

So through our words we find another way of comforting those in grief. We could just as well put our arm on their shoulder. This questions any attempt to privilege our language. But it also challenges crude versions of historical materialism which would seek to relate language as an aspect of ideology to an underlying level of material relationships. When Wittgenstein says that language can replace pre-linguistic behaviour, it is to be understood that it serves as an extension, refinement or elaboration of that behaviour. This is the ground we have to place it back into if we are to recover a sense of its meaning and significance in our lives.

Philosophers have mistakenly interpreted the idea that the meaning of an expression is in its use as meaning words and sentences have to be placed in a larger linguistic context of use. This mistake is common in the appropriation of Wittgenstein's writings in conversational analysis in sociology. This places his writings firmly back in the very 'rationalistic' tradition he was struggling to break with. But it is only when we learn how much of our experience has been shaped within this tradition that we can begin to grasp the difficulties of breaking with it. This also involves breaking with an inherited conception of masculinity.

We limit our understanding of the nature of moral relations in assuming we always need to give reasons to explain why one person should care for another, especially if the person is not a close relation or friend. This assumes egoism is to be identified with self-interest and universally treated as the natural character of our relations with others rather than as encouraged by the social relations of a particular society. Morality begins when we give reasons to extend a sense of fair and equal treatment beyond those for whom we have feelings. It is within an assumed framework of liberal individualism that the moral discussion between egoism and altruism takes place. But Wittgenstein questions the basis upon which this distinction is often drawn. In doing this, not only does he question the priority we give to reason in our moral relations, but he opens up a way for the recognition of our emotions and feelings in the 'natural, instinctive, kinds of relationships towards other human beings'. It is not that our language constitutes our individuality and defines these moral relations, but, as Wittgenstein says, 'our language is merely an auxiliary to, and further extension of, this behaviour'.

This marks a profound challenge to the assumptions of liberal individualism. It is not simply that some people will feel this way towards others and others will not. Rather, what is presented as the 'normal' situation of egoistic self-interest becomes something we need to explain, even if we acknowledge the enormous differences that exist between individuals. Possibly it is at this point that we require a clearer distinction between ends individuals choose for themselves, so indicating the different ways individuals find their happiness, and some sense of shared human needs.

Liberal theory often resists any such distinction, wanting to treat needs as if they are simply an extension of the ends people individually choose for themselves. This reticence may grow out of a healthy suspicion that, before we know it, some people will be claiming to decide the human needs of others. But this only makes it crucially important for people to identify and recognize their needs for themselves. Nor can we ever be sure of the road individuals are going to take. This is an arrogance that has sometimes been shared, in their different ways, by both revolutionaries and psychotherapists.

But what Wittgenstein helps us reinstate is a sense of the core nature of our needs for others. We misconstrue the place of morality in our lives and we misunderstand ourselves if we think we can exist as totally independent and self-sufficient people. It is this very masculine ideal which can damage and hurt men's lives. This is not a matter of placing before ourselves ideals which are unworthy, but of recognizing the harm we do ourselves through attempting to form ourselves in their image. This is not something we can begin to grasp unless we already question the identification of masculinity with reason.

This helps us realize that this is not simply a matter of replacing one ideal of masculinity by another. If we already assume that our emotional, somatic and spiritual lives can have no bearing upon the nature of our moral lives, all this talk of 'hurt' and 'damage' carries little weight. It is simply that we learn tacitly to accept to live up to the ideal of self-sufficiency that we have automatically grown up to accept. As men we grow up to feel good if we do not need anything from others. As I have argued, it is a sign of our strength that we can be supportive for others without needing any support for ourselves. We prove our masculinity through showing we do not need anything from others.

Wittgenstein suggests that if we deny our needs to respond directly towards others we are denying something important in ourselves. This is no longer a contingent issue. This is a direct challenge to Kant's idea that we should gradually weaken our instinctive responses towards others, since not only are they unreliable, but they take away from the moral worth of an action performed purely out of a sense of duty. It is Kant who helps sustain traditional notions of masculinity as he warns us of the help others might offer us since this will lessen the moral worth of our own individual efforts. Even though Kant was centrally concerned to illuminate the nature of human beings as moral beings, his implicit identification of reason, morality and masculinity, especially in his earlier more systematic writings, minimized the importance people can have for each other. Our moral lives are essentially individualistic; we are constantly proving our moral worth as individuals. At some level others are distractions taking us away from our moral tasks, or else occasions to show our moral goodness. Our relationships with others are essentially secondary to our sense of moral identity, even our sexual and personal relationships.

Within a 'rationalist' culture, men learn to use language as a way of asserting themselves individually. We learn to hide our vulnerability since we know it will be interpreted as weakness. Language itself comes to exist as an independent and autonomous system that has been separated from any ongoing sense of our somatic and emotional selves. In this way language is less likely to betray our masculinity as it shows us to be vulnerable and feeling human beings. In bringing us into a different relationship to our language Wittgenstein is also bringing us back to ourselves. But he is also implicitly questioning the way our male identities are constructed out of our achievements, as if the accumulation of wealth and property necessarily reflects back on the quality of self.

As we learn to discount our needs for others, we also learn to grow up as men to discount our history and culture of masculinity. We are more than our reasons and thoughts. We injure ourselves as men, as our culture leaves us with a distorted sense of the importance of reason in our lives. What is more, it even weakens the quality of our thought, as reason constantly becomes formal and abstract as it is systematically separated from emotions and feelings. But we also impoverish ourselves as we learn to deny our history and culture to become equal citizens in civil society. As Mill realized, we become so anxious to prove we are 'normal' like everyone else, that we develop a real fear of anything that would make us different from others. Mill realized in *On Liberty* that even though people heralded individualism within the moral culture of liberalism, the social relations worked to impoverish people's sense of their own individuality.

When we learn to use language as boys, we very quickly learn how to conceal ourselves through language. We learn to 'master' language so that we can control the world around us. We use language as an instrument that will help show us as independent, strong, self-sufficient and masculine. But as we learn to deny and estrange our individual and collective needs and wants so that we can live up to these ideals of ourselves we form and shape the kind of personal and sexual relationships we can have with others. Even though we learn to blame others for our unhappiness and misery in relationships we also know at some unspoken level how our masculinity has been limited and injured as we touch the hurt and pain of realizing how little we seem to feel about anything, even our friends and close relationships. Often we feel trapped and lost since the culture continually tells us we have the world to inherit. We do not know that the price is often knowledge of and relationship to ourselves.

❖ ❖ ❖

Dynamics

1. Much of Seidler's argument is concerned with the way our culture determines what "counts" as knowledge for men and for women. Go back through his essay and trace the connections Seidler makes between "the body" and "knowledge." Which of these connections seem familiar to you in your own experience? Which ones seem relatively alien? Do you see a pattern? If so, how can you account for it?

2. Seidler writes that boys in Western culture "learn automatically to discount our individual emotions and feelings as having no part in our 'true rational self.'" Why does Seidler place the phrase "true rational self" in quotation marks? In your re-reading, locate what might be some competing definitions of the "true self." What values are associated with each of these definitions? Which of these definitions, if any, seem persuasive to you?

Critical Tools

1. Seidler frequently refers to the notion of "instrumental" language use. Which passages in the essay help you to define "instrumentalism"? Apply "instrumentalism" as a critical tool to another reading from *Literacies*. How do the implications of using this tool change when the context is no longer "language and masculinity" but, say, language and women's experience or language and ethnic identity?

2. Near the middle of his essay, Seidler writes that "oppressed people are constantly trying to make language their own, as they attempt to discover and redefine their experience." Pick two essays that you have read so far this semester, and use passages from them to evaluate the implications of Seidler's statement. Where, exactly, do you see the other writers "redefin[ing] their experience" by "mak[ing] language their own"? How do the examples you have identified encourage you to revise or build upon Seidler's insights?

Draft One/Draft Two

Draft One: Seidler tells men that

> we lose any sense of *grounding* ourselves in our own embodied experience as we
> identify our sense of masculinity with being objective and impartial. This involves
> our discounting our own experience and so denying one of the deepest sources of our
> identity and knowledge.

Using one or two of your own experiences as material, describe how you (whether
you are male or female) have handled the tension between cultural demands for
"objectivity" and the desire to make personal experience a part of your analytical
processes. At some point in your essay, examine the concrete ways in which this
tension affects the writing you do as a college student.

Draft Two: Working with your own, Seidler's, and another writer's text, explore
Seidler's argument that the use of personal experience as an analytic category
makes new forms of social and intellectual understanding possible.

❖ ❖ ❖

Before Reading Susan Sontag...

1. What is your understanding of metaphor? Identify a subject you and your friends or family speak about euphemistically or metaphorically. How does this way of speaking affect your thoughts about the subject?

2. How have your thoughts about AIDS changed since you were first aware of it? Explore some of the different kinds of knowledge about AIDS you have gained from different sources (friends, pamphlets, TV, etc.). How do your thoughts about AIDS relate to your thoughts about other serious illnesses?

AIDS and Its Metaphors

Susan Sontag

Rereading *Illness as Metaphor* now, I thought:

1

By metaphor I meant nothing more or less than the earliest and most succinct definition I know, which is Aristotle's, in his *Poetics* (1457b). "Metaphor," Aristotle wrote, "consists in giving the thing a name that belongs to something else." Saying a thing is or is like something-it-is-not is a mental operation as old as philosophy and poetry, and the spawning ground of most kinds of understanding, including scientific understanding, and expressiveness. (To acknowledge which I prefaced the polemic against metaphors of illness I wrote ten years ago with a brief, hectic flourish of metaphor, in mock exorcism of the seductiveness of metaphorical thinking.) Of course, one cannot think without metaphors. But that does not mean there aren't some metaphors we might well abstain from or try to retire. As, of course, all thinking is interpretation. But that does not mean it isn't sometimes correct to be "against" interpretation.

Take, for instance, a tenacious metaphor that has shaped (and obscured the understanding of) so much of the political life of this century, the one that distributes, and polarizes, attitudes and social movements according to their relation to a "left" and a "right." The terms are usually traced back to the French Revolution, to the seating arrangements of the National Assembly in 1789, when republicans and radicals sat to the presiding officer's left and monarchists and conservatives sat to the right. But historical memory alone can't account for the startling longevity of this metaphor. It seems more likely that its persistence in discourse about politics to this day comes from a felt aptness to the modern, secular imagination of metaphors drawn from the body's orientation in space—left and right, top and bottom, forward and backward—for describing social conflict, a metaphoric practice that did add something new to the perennial description of society as a kind of body, a well-disciplined body ruled by a "head." This has been the dominant metaphor for the polity since Plato and Aristotle, perhaps because of its usefulness in justifying repression. Even more than comparing society to a family, comparing it to a body makes an authoritarian ordering of society seem inevitable, immutable.

Rudolf Virchow, the founder of cellular pathology, furnishes one of the rare scientifically significant examples of the reverse procedure, using political metaphors to talk about the body. In the biological controversies of the 1850s, it was the metaphor of the liberal state that Virchow found useful in advancing his theory of the cell as the fundamental unit of life. However complex their structures, organisms are, first of all, simply "multicellular"—multicitizened, as it were; the body is a "republic" or "unified commonwealth." Among scientist-rhetoricians Virchow was a maverick, not least because of the politics of his metaphors, which, by mid-nineteenth-century standards, are antiauthoritarian. But likening the body to a society, liberal or not, is less common than comparisons to other complex, integrated systems, such as a machine or an economic enterprise.

At the beginning of Western medicine, in Greece, important metaphors for the unity of the body were adapted from the arts. One such metaphor, harmony, was singled out for scorn several centuries later by Lucretius, who argued that it could not do justice to the fact that the body consists of essential and unessential organs, or even to the body's materiality: that is, to death. Here are the closing lines of Lucretius' dismissal of the musical metaphor—the earliest attack I know on metaphoric thinking about illness and health:

> *Not all the organs, you must realize,*
> *Are equally important nor does health*
> *Depend on all alike, but there are some—*
> *The seeds of breathing, warm vitality—*
> *Whereby we are kept alive; when these are gone*
> *Life leaves our dying members. So, since mind*
> *And spirit are by nature part of man,*
> *Let the musicians keep that term brought down*
> *To them from lofty Helicon—or maybe*
> *They found it somewhere else, made it apply*
> *To something hitherto nameless in their craft—*
> *I speak of* harmony. *Whatever it is,*
> *Give it back to the musicians.*
>
> —*De Rerum Natura,* III, 124-35
> trans. Rolfe Humphries

A history of metaphoric thinking about the body on this potent level of generality would include many images drawn from other arts and technology, notably architecture. Some metaphors are anti-explanatory, like the sermonizing, and poetic, notion enunciated by Saint Paul of the body as a temple. Some have considerable scientific resonance, such as the notion of the body as a factory, an image of the body's functioning under the sign of health, and of the body as a fortress, an image of the body that features catastrophe.

The fortress image has a long prescientific genealogy, with illness itself a metaphor for mortality, for human frailty and vulnerability. John Donne in his great cycle of prose arias on illness, *Devotions upon Emergent Occasions* (1627), written when he thought he was dying, describes illness as an enemy that invades, that lays siege to the body-fortress:

> *We study Health, and we deliberate upon our meats, and drink, and ayre, and exercises, and we hew and wee polish every stone, that goes to that building; and so our Health is a long and a regular work; But in a minute a Canon batters all, overthrowes all, demolishes all; a Sicknes unprevented for all our diligence, unsuspected for all our curiositie....*

Some parts are more fragile than others: Donne speaks of the brain and the liver being able to endure the siege of an "unnatural" or "rebellious" fever that "will blow up the heart, like a mine, in a minute." In Donne's images, it is the illness that invades. Modern medical thinking could be said to begin when the gross military metaphor becomes specific, which can only happen with the advent of a new kind of scrutiny, represented in Virchow's cellular pathology, and a more precise understanding that illnesses were caused by specific, identifiable, visible (with the aid of a microscope) organisms. It was when the invader was seen not as the illness but as the microorganism that causes the illness that medicine really began to be effective, and the military metaphors took on new credibility and precision. Since then, military metaphors have more and more come to infuse all aspects of the description of the medical situation. Disease is seen as an invasion of alien organisms, to which the body responds by its own military operations, such as the mobilizing of immunological "defenses," and medicine is "aggressive," as in the language of most chemotherapies.

The grosser metaphor survives in public health education, where disease is regularly described as invading the society, and efforts to reduce mortality from a given disease are called a fight, a struggle, a war. Military metaphors became prominent early in the century, in campaigns mounted during World War I to educate people about syphilis, and after the war about tuberculosis. One example, from the campaign against tuberculosis conducted in Italy in the 1920s, is a poster called "*Guerre alle Mosche*" (War against Flies), which illustrates the lethal effects of fly-borne diseases. The flies themselves are shown as enemy aircraft dropping bombs of death on an innocent population. The bombs have inscriptions. One says "*Microbi,*" microbes. Another says "*Germi della tisi,*" the germs of tuberculosis. Another simply says "*Malattia,*" illness. A skeleton clad in a hooded black cloak rides the foremost fly as passenger or pilot. In another poster, "With These Weapons We Will Conquer Tuberculosis," the figure of death is shown pinned to the wall by drawn swords, each of which bears an inscription that names a measure for combating tuberculosis. "Cleanliness" is written on one blade. "Sun" on another. "Air." "Rest." "Proper food." "Hygiene." (Of course, none of these weapons was of any significance. What conquers—that is, cures—tuberculosis is antibiotics, which were not discovered until some twenty years later, in the 1940s.)

Where once it was the physician who waged *bellum contra morbum*, the war against disease, now it's the whole society. Indeed, the transformation of war-making into an occasion for mass ideological mobilization has made the notion of war useful as a metaphor for all sorts of ameliorative campaigns whose goals are cast as the defeat of an "enemy." We have had wars against poverty, now replaced by "the war on drugs," as well as wars against specific diseases, such as cancer. Abuse of the military metaphor may be inevitable in a capitalist society, a society that increasingly restricts the scope and credibility of appeals to ethical principle, in which it is thought foolish not to subject one's actions to the calculus of self-interest and profitability. War-making is one of the few activities that people are not sup-posed to view "realistically"; that is, with an eye to expense and practical outcome. In all-out war, expenditure is all-out, unprudent—war being defined as an emer-gency in which no sacrifice is excessive. But the wars against diseases are not just calls for more zeal, and more money to be spent on research. The metaphor imple-ments the way particularly dreaded diseases are envisaged as an alien "other," as enemies are in modern war; and the move from the demonization of the illness to the attribution of fault to the patient is an inevitable one, no matter if patients are thought of as victims. Victims suggest innocence. And innocence, by the inexorable logic that governs all relational terms, suggests guilt.

●

Military metaphors contribute to the stigmatizing of certain illnesses and, by extension, of those who are ill. It was the discovery of the stigmatization of people who have cancer that led me to write *Illness as Metaphor*.

Twelve years ago, when I became a cancer patient, what particularly enraged me—and distracted me from my own terror and despair at my doctors' gloomy prognosis—was seeing how much the very reputation of this illness added to the suffering of those who have it. Many fellow patients with whom I talked during my initial hospitalizations, like others I was to meet during the subsequent two and a half years that I received chemotherapy as an outpatient in several hospitals here and in France, evinced disgust at their disease and a kind of shame. They seemed to be in the grip of fantasies about their illness by which I was quite unseduced. And it occurred to me that some of these notions were the converse of now thoroughly discredited beliefs about tuberculosis. As tuberculosis had been often regarded sentimentally, as an enhancement of identity, cancer was regarded with irrational revulsion, as a diminution of the self. There were also similar fictions of responsibil-ity and of a characterological predisposition to the illness: cancer is regarded as a disease to which the psychically defeated, the inexpressive, the repressed—espe-cially those who have repressed anger or sexual feelings—are particularly prone, as tuberculosis was regarded throughout the nineteenth and early twentieth centuries (indeed, until it was discovered how to cure it) as a disease apt to strike the hypersensitive, the talented, the passionate.

These parallels—between myths about tuberculosis to which we can all feel superior now, and superstitions about cancer still given credence by many cancer patients and their families—gave me the main strategy of a little book I decided to write about the mystifications surrounding cancer. I didn't think it would be useful—and I wanted to be useful—to tell yet one more story in the first person of how someone learned that she or he had cancer, wept, struggled, was comforted, suffered, took courage...though mine was also that story. A narrative, it seemed to me, would be less useful than an idea. For narrative pleasure I would appeal to other writers; and although more examples from literature immediately came to mind for the glamorous disease, tuberculosis, I found the diagnosis of cancer as a disease of those who have not really lived in such books as Tolstoy's "The Death of Ivan Ilyich," Arnold Bennett's *Riceyman Steps*, and Bernanos's *The Diary of a Country Priest*.

And so I wrote my book, wrote it very quickly, spurred by evangelical zeal as well as anxiety about how much time I had left to do any living or writing in. My aim was to alleviate unnecessary suffering—exactly as Nietzsche formulated it, in a passage in *Daybreak* that I came across recently:

> Thinking about illness!—*To calm the imagination of the invalid, so that at least he should not, as hitherto, have to suffer more from thinking about his illness than from the illness itself—that, I think, would be something! It would be a great deal!*

The purpose of my book was to calm the imagination, not to incite it. Not to confer meaning, which is the traditional purpose of literary endeavor, but to deprive something of meaning: to apply that quixotic, highly polemical strategy, "against interpretation," to the real world this time. To the body. My purpose was, above all, practical. For it was my doleful observation, repeated again and again, that the metaphoric trappings that deform the experience of having cancer have very real consequences: they inhibit people from seeking treatment early enough, or from making a greater effort to get competent treatment. The metaphors and myths, I was convinced, kill. (For instance, they make people irrationally fearful of effective measures such as chemotherapy, and foster credence in thoroughly useless remedies such as diets and psychotherapy.) I wanted to offer other people who were ill and those who care for them an instrument to dissolve these metaphors, these inhibitions. I hoped to persuade terrified people who were ill to consult doctors, or to change their incompetent doctors for competent ones, who would give them proper care. To regard cancer as if it were just a disease—a very serious one, but just a disease. Not a curse, not a punishment, not an embarrassment. Without "meaning." And not necessarily a death sentence (one of the mystifications is that cancer = death). *Illness as Metaphor* is not just a polemic, it is an exhortation. I was saying: Get the doctors to tell you the truth; be an informed, active patient; find yourself good treatment, because good treatment does exist (amid the widespread ineptitude). Although *the* remedy does not exist, more than half of all cases can be cured by existing methods of treatment.

In the decade since I wrote *Illness as Metaphor*—and was cured of my own cancer, confounding my doctors' pessimism—attitudes about cancer have evolved. Getting cancer is not quite as much of a stigma, a creator of "spoiled identity" (to use Erving Goffman's expression). The word cancer is uttered more freely, and people are not often described anymore in obituaries as dying of a "very long illness." Although European and Japanese doctors still regularly impart a cancer diagnosis first to the family, and often counsel concealing it from the patient, American doctors have virtually abandoned this policy; indeed, a brutal announcement to the patient is now common. The new candor about cancer is part of the same obligatory candor (or lack of decorum) that brings us diagrams of the rectal-colon or genito-urinary tract ailments of our national leaders on television and on the front pages of newspapers—more and more it is precisely a virtue in our society to speak of what is supposed *not* to be named. The change can also be explained by the doctors' fear of lawsuits in a litigious society. And not least among the reasons that cancer is now treated less phobically, certainly with less secrecy, than a decade ago is that it is no longer the most feared disease. In recent years some of the onus of cancer has been lifted by the emergence of a disease whose charge of stigmatization, whose capacity to create spoiled identity, is far greater. It seems that societies need to have one illness which becomes identified with evil, and attaches blame to its "victims," but it is hard to be obsessed with more than one.

2

Just as one might predict for a disease that is not yet fully understood as well as extremely recalcitrant to treatment, the advent of this terrifying new disease, new at least in its epidemic form, has provided a large-scale occasion for the metaphorizing of illness.

Strictly speaking, AIDS—acquired immune deficiency syndrome—is not the name of an illness at all. It is the name of a medical condition, whose consequences are a spectrum of illnesses. In contrast to syphilis and cancer, which provide proto-types for most of the images and metaphors attached to AIDS, the very definition of AIDS requires the presence of other illnesses, so-called opportunistic infections and malignancies. But though not in *that* sense a single disease, AIDS lends itself to being regarded as one—in part because, unlike cancer and like syphilis, it is thought to have a single cause.

AIDS has a dual metaphoric genealogy. As a microprocess, it is described as cancer is: an invasion. When the focus is transmission of the disease, an older metaphor, reminiscent of syphilis, is invoked: pollution. (One gets it from the blood or sexual fluids of infected people or from contaminated blood products.) But the military metaphors used to describe AIDS have a somewhat different focus from those used in describing cancer. With cancer, the metaphor scants the issue of causality (still a murky topic in cancer research) and picks up at the point at which rogue cells inside the body mutate, eventually moving out from an original site or organ to overrun other organs or systems—a domestic subversion. In the description of AIDS the enemy is what causes the disease, an infectious agent that comes from the outside:

> *The invader is tiny, about one sixteen-thousandth the size of the head of a pin....*
> *Scouts of the body's immune system, large cells called macrophages, sense the*
> *presence of the diminutive foreigner and promptly alert the immune system. It begins*
> *to mobilize an array of cells that, among other things, produce antibodies to deal*
> *with the threat. Single-mindedly, the AIDS virus ignores many of the blood cells in*
> *its path, evades the rapidly advancing defenders and homes in on the master*
> *coordinator of the immune system, a helper T cell....*

This is the language of political paranoia, with its characteristic distrust of a pluralistic world. A defense system consisting of cells "that, among other things, produce antibodies to deal with the threat" is, predictably, no match for an invader who advances "single-mindedly." And the science-fiction flavor, already present in cancer talk, is even more pungent in accounts of AIDS—this one comes from *Time* magazine in late 1986—with infection described like the high-tech warfare for which we are being prepared (and inured) by the fantasies of our leaders and by video entertainments. In the era of Star Wars and Space Invaders, AIDS has proved an ideally comprehensible illness:

> *On the surface of that cell, it finds a receptor into which one of its envelope proteins*
> *fits perfectly, like a key into a lock. Docking with the cell, the virus penetrates the*
> *cell membrane and is stripped of its protective shell in the process....*

Next the invader takes up permanent residence, by a form of alien takeover familiar in science-fiction narratives. The body's own cells *become* the invader. With the help of an enzyme the virus carries with it,

> *the naked AIDS virus converts its RNA into...DNA, the master molecule of life. The*
> *molecule then penetrates the cell nucleus, inserts itself into a chromosome and takes*
> *over part of the cellular machinery, directing it to produce more AIDS viruses.*
> *Eventually, overcome by its alien product, the cell swells and dies, releasing a flood*
> *of new viruses to attack other cells....*

As viruses attack other cells, runs the metaphor, so "a host of opportunistic diseases, normally warded off by a healthy immune system, attacks the body," whose integrity and vigor have been sapped by the sheer replication of "alien product" that follows the collapse of its immunological defenses. "Gradually weakened by the onslaught, the AIDS victim dies, sometimes in months, but almost always within a few years of the first symptoms." Those who have not already succumbed are described as "under assault, showing the telltale symptoms of the disease," while millions of others "harbor the virus, vulnerable at any time to a final, all-out attack."

Cancer makes cells proliferate; in AIDS, cells die. Even as this original model of AIDS (the mirror image of leukemia) has been altered, descriptions of how the virus does its work continue to echo the way the illness is perceived as infiltrating the society. "AIDS Virus Found to Hide in Cells, Eluding Detection by Normal Tests" was the headline of a recent front-page story in *The New York Times* announcing the discovery that the virus can "lurk" for years in the macrophages—disrupting their disease-fighting function without killing them, "even when the macrophages are filled almost to bursting with virus," and without producing antibodies, the chemicals the body makes in response to "invading agents" and whose presence has been regarded as an infallible marker of the syndrome.* That the virus isn't lethal for *all* the cells where it takes up residence, as is now thought, only increases the illness-foe's reputation for wiliness and invincibility.

What makes the viral assault so terrifying is that contamination, and therefore vulnerability, is understood as permanent. Even if someone infected were never to develop any symptoms—that is, the infection remained, or could by medical intervention be rendered, inactive—the viral enemy would be forever within. In fact, so it is believed, it is just a matter of time before something awakens ("triggers") it, before the appearance of "the telltale symptoms." Like syphilis, known to generations of doctors as "the great masquerader," AIDS is a clinical construction, an inference. It takes its identity from the presence of *some* among a long, and lengthening, roster of symptoms (no one has everything that AIDS could be), symptoms which "mean" that what the patient has is this illness. The construction of the illness rests on the invention not only of AIDS as a clinical entity but of a kind of junior AIDS, called AIDS-related complex (ARC), to which people are assigned if they show "early" and often intermittent symptoms of immunological deficit such as fevers, weight loss, fungal infections, and swollen lymph glands. AIDS is progressive, a disease of time. Once a certain density of symptoms is attained, the course of the illness can be swift, and brings atrocious suffering. Besides the commonest "presenting" illnesses (some hitherto unusual, at least in a fatal form, such as a rare skin cancer and a rare form of pneumonia), a plethora of disabling, disfiguring, and humiliating symptoms make the AIDS patient steadily more infirm, helpless, and unable to control or take care of basic functions and needs.

---

*The larger role assigned to the macrophages—"to serve as a reservoir for the AIDS virus because the virus multiplies in them but does not kill them, as it kills T-4 cells"—is said to explain the not uncommon difficulty of finding infected T-4 lymphocytes in patients who have antibodies to the virus and symptoms of AIDS. (It is still assumed that antibodies will develop once the virus spreads to these "key target" cells.) Evidence of presently infected populations of cells has been as puzzlingly limited or uneven as the evidence of infection in the populations of human societies—puzzling, because of the conviction that the disease is everywhere, and must spread. "Doctors have estimated that as few as one in a million T-4 cells are infected, which led some to ask where the virus hides...." Another resonant speculation, reported in the same article (*The New York Times,* June 7, 1988): "Infected macro-phages can transmit the virus to other cells, possibly by touching the cells."

The sense in which AIDS is a slow disease makes it more like syphilis, which is characterized in terms of "stages," than like cancer. Thinking in terms of "stages" is essential to discourse about AIDS. Syphilis in its most dreaded form is "tertiary syphilis," syphilis in its third stage. What is called AIDS is generally understood as the last of three stages—the first of which is infection with a human immunodeficiency virus (HIV) and early evidence of inroads on the immune system—with a long latency period between infection and the onset of the "telltale" symptoms. (Apparently not as long as syphilis, in which the latency period between secondary and tertiary illness might be decades. But it is worth noting that when syphilis first appeared in epidemic form in Europe at the end of the fifteenth century, it was a rapid disease, of an unexplained virulence that is unknown today, in which death often occurred in the second stage, sometimes within months or a few years.) Cancer *grows* slowly: it is not thought to be, for a long time, latent. (A convincing account of a process in terms of "stages" seems invariably to include the notion of a normative delay or halt in the process, such as is supplied by the notion of latency.) True, a cancer is "staged." This is a principal tool of diagnosis, which means classifying it according to its gravity, determining how "advanced" it is. But it is mostly a spatial notion: that the cancer advances through the body, traveling or migrating along predictable routes. Cancer is first of all a disease of the body's geography, in contrast to syphilis and AIDS, whose definition depends on constructing a temporal sequence of stages.

Syphilis is an affliction that didn't have to run its ghastly full course, to paresis (as it did for Baudelaire and Maupassant and Jules de Goncourt), and could and often did remain at the stage of nuisance, indignity (as it did for Flaubert). The scourge was also a cliché, as Flaubert himself observed. "SYPHILIS. Everybody has it, more or less" reads one entry in the *Dictionary of Accepted Opinions*, his treasury of mid-nineteenth-century platitudes. And syphilis did manage to acquire a darkly positive association in late-nineteenth- and early-twentieth-century Europe, when a link was made between syphilis and heightened ("feverish") mental activity that parallels the connection made since the era of the Romantic writers between pulmonary tuberculosis and heightened emotional activity. As if in honor of all the notable writers and artists who ended their lives in syphilitic witlessness, it came to be believed that the brain lesions of neurosyphilis might actually inspire original thought or art. Thomas Mann, whose fiction is a storehouse of early-twentieth-century disease myths, makes this notion of syphilis as muse central to his *Doctor Faustus*, with its protagonist a great composer whose voluntarily contracted syphilis—the Devil guarantees that the infection will be limited to the central nervous system—confers on him twenty-four years of incandescent creativity. E. M. Cioran recalls how, in Romania in the late 1920s, syphilis-envy figured in his adolescent expectations of literary glory: he would discover that he had contracted syphilis, be rewarded with several hyperproductive years of genius, then collapse into madness. This romanticizing of the dementia characteristic of neurosyphilis was the forerunner of the much more persistent fantasy in this century about mental illness as a source of artistic creativity or spiritual originality. But with AIDS—though dementia is also a common, late symptom—no compensatory mythology has arisen, or seems likely to arise. AIDS, like cancer, does not allow romanticizing or sentimentalizing, perhaps because its association with death is too powerful. In Krzysztof Zanussi's film *Spiral* (1978), the most truthful account I know of anger at dying, the protagonist's illness is never specified; therefore, it *has* to be cancer. For several generations now, the generic idea of death has been a death from cancer, and a cancer death is experienced as a generic defeat. Now the generic rebuke to life and to hope is AIDS.

❖ ❖ ❖

Dynamics

1. What does "meaning" mean at different points in Sontag's essay? Work with several passages in which Sontag seems to make an argument "for" or "against" meaning. How do these stances on meaning complicate her argument?

2. Sontag evaluates the tension between "innocence" and "guilt." How does this tension inform her arguments throughout her essay? Examine how connotations of "innocence" or "guilt" affect your response to her ideas.

Critical Tools

1. How does Sontag analyze some of the uses to which metaphors have been put? Work with those of her methods which seem most productive to you. Use them to discuss the metaphorical language in a second reading. What new insights do you gain about that reading?

2. Evaluate some of your own experiences of illness in terms of Sontag's arguments. How do your experiences condition your response to her ideas? Consider how some of her arguments might complicate your understanding of your experience.

Draft One/Draft Two

Draft One: According to Sontag, many serious illnesses have been assigned a number of "roles" in society. Why do you think society responds to serious illnesses in these ways? You might consider why different illnesses carry different connotations or associations. How does your discussion complicate your own perspectives about AIDS?

Draft Two: Locate a second reading that you believe identifies some aspect of experience which, like "illness" in Sontag's essay, seems to perform some "role" in society. Use your ideas from draft one to examine how that aspect of experience functions. What implications does this analysis have for your response to Sontag's discussion of illness?

❖ ❖ ❖

Before Reading Wole Soyinka. . .

1. Would you describe yourself as a "believer"? Write a paragraph or so about the meaning(s) this word carries for you within the context of your own cultural tradition or traditions. Consider how your beliefs are different from your parents' or your grandparents'. How can you account for these differences?

2. Think about a story you were told as a child about an older family member. What does that story tell you about the history and values of your family? Why did that story get re-told? Why would you choose to tell it (or not to tell it) to your younger family members? What other essays in *Literacies* might help you to think about the function of such "family stories" in your cultural tradition?

AKÉ
The Years of Childhood

Wole Soyinka

An evil thing has happened to Aké parsonage. The land is eroded, the lawns are bared and mystery driven from its once secretive combs. Once, each new day opened up an unseen closure, a pocket of rocks, a clump of bush and a colony of snails. The motor-hulk has not moved from its staging-point where children clambered into it for journeys to fabled places; now it is only a derelict, its eyes rusted sockets, its dragon face collapsed with a progressive loss of teeth. The abandoned incinerator with its lush weeds and glistening snakes is marked by a mound of mud. The surviving houses, houses which formed the battlements of Aké parsonage are now packing cases on a depleted landscape, full of creaks, exposed and nerveless.

And the moods are gone. Even the open lawns and broad paths, bordered with whitewashed stones, lilies and lemon grass clumps, changed nature from season to season, from weekday to Sunday and between noon and nightfall. And the echoes off the walls in lower Parsonage acquired new tonalities with the seasons, changed with the emptying of the lawns as the schools dispersed for holidays.

If I lay across the lawn before our house, face upwards to the sky, my head towards BishopsCourt, each spread-out leg would point to the inner compounds of Lower Parsonage. Half of the Anglican Girls' School occupied one of these lower spaces, the other half had taken over BishopsCourt. The lower area contained the school's junior classrooms, a dormitory, a small fruit-garden of pawpaws, guava, some bamboo and wild undergrowth. There were always snails to be found in the rainy season. In the other lower compound was the mission bookseller, a shrivelled man with a serene wife on whose ample back we all, at one time or the other slept, or reviewed the world. His compound became a short cut to the road that led to Ibarà, Lafenwá or Igbèin and its Grammar School over which Ransome-Kuti presided and lived with his family. The bookseller's compound contained the only well in the parsonage; in the dry season, his place was never empty. And his soil appeared to produce the only coconut trees.

BishopsCourt, of Upper Parsonage, is no more. Bishop Ajayi Crowther would sometimes emerge from the cluster of hydrangea and bougainvillea, a gnomic face with popping eyes whose formal photograph had first stared at us from the frontispiece of his life history. He had lived, the teacher said, in BishopsCourt and from that moment, he peered out from among the creeping plants whenever I passed by the house on an errand to our Great Aunt, Mrs Lijadu. BishopsCourt had become a boarding house for the girls' school and an extra playground for us during the holidays. The Bishop sat, silently, on the bench beneath the wooden porch over the entrance, his robes twined through and through with the lengthening tendrils of the bougainvillea. I moved closer when his eyes turned to sockets. My mind wandered then to another photograph in which he wore a clerical suit with waistcoat and I wondered what he really kept at the end of the silver chain that vanished into the pocket. He grinned and said, Come nearer, I'll show you. As I moved towards the porch he drew on the chain until he had lifted out a wholly round pocket-watch that gleamed of solid silver. He pressed a button and the lid opened, revealing, not the glass and the face-dial but a deep cloud-filled space. Then he winked one eye, and it fell from his face into the bowl of the watch. He winked the other and this joined its partner in the watch. He snapped back the lid, nodded again and his head went bald, his teeth disappeared and the skin pulled backward till the whitened cheek-bones were exposed. Then he stood up and, tucking the watch back into the waist-coat pocket, moved a step towards me. I fled homewards.

BishopsCourt appeared sometimes to want to rival the Canon's house. It looked a house-boat despite its guard of whitewashed stones and luxuriant flowers, its wooden fretwork frontage almost wholly immersed in bougainvillea. And it was shadowed also by those omnipresent rocks from whose clefts tall, stout-boled trees miraculously grew. Clouds gathered and the rocks merged into their accustomed grey turbulence, then the trees were carried to and fro until they stayed suspended over BishopsCourt. This happened only in heavy storms. BishopsCourt, unlike the Canon's house, did not actually border the rocks or the woods. The girls' playing fields separated them and we knew that this buffer had always been there. Obviously bishops were not inclined to challenge the spirits. Only the vicars could. That Bishop Ajayi Crowther frightened me out of that compound by his strange transformations only confirmed that the Bishops, once they were dead, joined the world of spirits and ghosts. I could not see the Canon decaying like that in front of my eyes, nor the Rev J.J. who had once occupied that house, many years before, when my mother was still like us. J.J. Ransome-Kuti had actually ordered back several ghommids in his life-time; my mother confirmed it. She was his grand niece and, before she came to live at our house, she had lived in the Rev J.J.'s household. Her brother Sanya also lived there and he was acknowledged by all to be an òrò,* which made him at home in the woods, even at night. On one occasion however, he must have gone too far.

*A kind of tree daemon.

'They had visited us before,' she said, 'to complain. Mind you, they wouldn't actually come into the compound, they stood far off at the edge, where the woods ended. Their leader, the one who spoke, emitted wild sparks from a head that seemed to be an entire ball of embers—no, I'm mixing up two occasions—that was the second time when he chased us home. The first time, they had merely sent an emissary. He was quite dark, short and swarthy. He came right to the backyard and stood there while he ordered us to call the Reverend.

'It was as if Uncle had been expecting the visit. He came out of the house and asked him what he wanted. We all huddled in the kitchen, peeping out.'

'What was his voice like? Did he speak like an *egúngún*?'

'I'm coming to it. This man, well, I suppose one should call him a man. He wasn't quite human, we could see that. Much too large a head, and he kept his eyes on the ground. So, he said he had come to report us. They didn't mind our coming to the woods, even at night, but we were to stay off any area beyond the rocks and that clump of bamboo by the stream.'

'Well, what did Uncle say? And you haven't said what his voice was like.'

Tinu turned her elder sister's eye on me. 'Let Mama finish the story.'

'You want to know everything. All right, he spoke just like your father. Are you satisfied?'

I did not believe that but I let it pass. 'Go on. What did Grand Uncle do?'

'He called everyone together and warned us to keep away from the place.'

'And yet you went back!'

'Well, you know your Uncle Sanya. He was angry. For one thing the best snails are on the other side of that stream. So he continued to complain that those *òrò* were just being selfish, and he was going to show them who he was. Well, he did. About a week later he led us back. And he was right you know. We gathered a full basket and a half of the biggest snails you ever saw. Well, by this time we had all forgotten about the warning, there was plenty of moonlight and anyway, I've told you Sanya is an *òrò* himself....'

'But why? He looks normal like you and us.'

'You won't understand yet. Anyway, he is *òrò*. So with him we felt quite safe. Until suddenly this sort of light, like a ball of fire began to glow in the distance. Even while it was still far we kept hearing voices, as if a lot of people around us were grumbling the same words together. They were saying something like, "You stubborn, stiff-necked children, we've warned you and warned you but you just won't listen...." '

Wild Christian looked above our heads, frowning to recollect the better. 'One can't even say, "they." It was only this figure of fire that I saw and he was still very distant. Yet I heard him distinctly, as if he had many mouths which were pressed against my ears. Every moment, the fireball loomed larger and larger.'

'What did Uncle Sanya do? Did he fight him?'

'Sanya wo ni yen? He was the first to break and run. Bo o ló o ya mi, o di kítìpa kítìpa!* No one remembered all those fat snails. That *iwin*** followed us all the way to the house. Our screams had arrived long before us and the whole household was—well, you can imagine the turmoil. Uncle had already dashed down the stairs and was in the backyard. We ran past him while he went out to meet the creature. This time that *iwin* actually passed the line of the woods, he continued as if he meant to chase us right into the house, you know, he wasn't running, just pursuing us steadily.' We waited. This was it! Wild Christian mused while we remained in suspense. Then she breathed deeply and shook her head with a strange sadness.

'The period of faith is gone. There was faith among our early christians, real faith, not just church-going and hymn-singing. Faith. *Igbàgbó*. And it is out of that faith that real power comes. Uncle stood there like a rock, he held out his Bible and ordered, "Go back! Go back to that forest which is your home. Back I said, in the name of God." Hm. And that was it. The creature simply turned and fled, those sparks falling off faster and faster until there was just a faint glow receding into the woods.' She sighed. 'Of course, after prayers that evening, there was the price to be paid. Six of the best on every one's back. Sanya got twelve. And we all cut grass every day for the next week.'

I could not help feeling that the fright should have sufficed as punishment. Her eyes gazing in the direction of the square house, Wild Christian nonetheless appeared to sense what was going on in my mind. She added, 'Faith and—Discipline. That is what made those early believers. Psheeaw! God doesn't make them like that any more. When I think of that one who now occupies that house...'

Then she appeared to recall herself to our presence. 'What are you both still sitting here for? Isn't it time for your evening bath? Lawanle!' 'Auntie' Lawanle replied 'Ma' from a distant part of the house. Before she appeared I reminded Wild Christian, 'But you haven't told us why Uncle Sanya is *òrò*.'

She shrugged, 'He is. I saw it with my own eyes.'

We both clamoured. 'When? When?'

She smiled. 'You won't understand. But I'll tell you about it some other time. Or let him tell you himself next time he is here.'

'You mean you saw him turn into an *òrò*?'

Lawanle came in just then and she prepared to hand us over, 'Isn't it time for these children's bath?'

I pleaded, 'No, wait Auntie Lawanle', knowing it was a waste of time. She had already gripped us both, one arm each. I shouted back, 'Was Bishop Crowther an *òrò*?'

Wild Christian laughed. 'What next are you going to ask? Oh I see. They have taught you about him in Sunday school have they?'

'I saw him.' I pulled back at the door, forcing Lawanle to stop. 'I see him all the time. He comes and sits under the porch of the Girls School. I've seen him when crossing the compound to Auntie Mrs Lijadu.'

---

*If you aren't moving, get out of my way!
**A 'ghommid'; a wood sprite which is also believed to live in the ground.

'All right,' sighed Wild Christian. 'Go and have your bath.'

'He hides among the bougainvillea....' Lawanle dragged me out of hearing.

Later that evening, she told us the rest of the story. On that occasion, Rev J.J. was away on one of his many mission tours. He travelled a lot, on foot and on bicycle, keeping in touch with all the branches of his diocese and spreading the Word of God. There was frequent opposition but nothing deterred him. One frightening experience occurred in one of the villages in Ijebu. He had been warned not to preach on a particular day, which was the day for an *egúngún* outing, but he persisted and held a service. The *egúngún* procession passed while the service was in progress and, using his ancestral voice, called on the preacher to stop at once, disperse his people and come out to pay obeisance. Rev J.J. ignored him. The *egúngún* then left, taking his followers with him but, on passing the main door, he tapped on it with his wand, three times. Hardly had the last member of his procession left the church premises than the building collapsed. The walls simply fell down and the roof disintegrated. Miraculously however, the walls fell outwards while the roof supports fell among the aisles or flew outwards—anywhere but on the congregation itself. Rev J.J. calmed the worshippers, paused in his preaching to render a thanksgiving prayer, then continued his sermon.

Perhaps this was what Wild Christian meant by Faith. And this tended to confuse things because, after all, the *egúngún* did make the church building collapse. Wild Christian made no attempt to explain how that happened, so that feat tended to be of the same order of Faith which moved mountains or enabled Wild Christian to pour ground-nut oil from a broad-rimmed bowl into an empty bottle without spilling a drop. She had the strange habit of sighing with a kind of rapture, crediting her steadiness of hand to Faith and thanking God. If however the basin slipped and she lost a drop or two, she murmured that her sins had become heavy and that she needed to pray more.

If Rev J.J. had Faith however, he also appeared to have Stubbornness in common with our Uncle Sanya. Stubbornness was one of the earliest sins we easily recognized, and no matter how much Wild Christian tried to explain the Rev J.J. preaching on the *egúngún*'s outing day, despite warnings, it sounded much like stubbornness. As for Uncle Sanya there was no doubt about his own case; hardly did the Rev J.J. pedal out of sight on his pastoral duties than he was off into the woods on one pretext or the other, and making for the very areas which the *òrò* had declared out of bounds. Mushrooms and snails were the real goals, with the gathering of firewood used as the dutiful excuse.

Even Sanya had however stopped venturing into the woods at night, accepting the fact that it was far too risky; daytime and early dusk carried little danger as most wood spirits only came out at night. Mother told us that on this occasion she and Sanya had been picking mushrooms, separated by only a few clumps of bushes. She could hear his movements quite clearly, indeed, they took the precaution of staying very close together.

Suddenly, she said, she heard Sanya's voice talking animatedly with someone. After listening for some time she called out his name but he did not respond. There was no voice apart from his, yet he appeared to be chatting in friendly, excited tones with some other person. So she peeped through the bushes and there was Uncle Sanya seated on the ground chattering away to no one that she could see. She tried to penetrate the surrounding bushes with her gaze but the woods remained empty except for the two of them. And then her eyes came to rest on his basket.

It was something she had observed before, she said. It was the same, no matter how many of the children in the household went to gather snails, berries or whatever, Sanya would spend most of the time playing and climbing rocks and trees. He would wander off by himself, leaving his basket anywhere. And yet, whenever they prepared to return home, his basket was always fuller than the others'. This time was no different. She came closer, startling our Uncle who snapped off his chatter and pretended to be hunting snails in the undergrowth.

Mother said that she was frightened. The basket was filled to the brim, impossibly bursting. She was also discouraged, so she picked up her near empty basket and insisted that they return home at once. She led the way but after some distance, when she looked back, Sanya appeared to be trying to follow her but was being prevented, as if he was being pulled back by invisible hands. From time to time he would snatch forward his arm and snap, 'Leave me alone. Can't you see I have to go home? I said I have to go.'

She broke into a run and Sanya did the same. They ran all the way home.

That evening, Sanya took ill. He broke into a sweat, tossed on his mat all night and muttered to himself. By the following day the household was thoroughly frightened. His forehead was burning to the touch and no one could get a coherent word out of him. Finally, an elderly woman, one of J.J.'s converts, turned up at the house on a routine visit. When she learnt of Sanya's condition, she nodded wisely and acted like one who knew exactly what to do. Having first found out what things he last did before his illness, she summoned my mother and questioned her. She told her everything while the old woman kept on nodding with understanding. Then she gave instructions:

'I want a basket of *àgìdi*, containing 50 wraps. Then prepare some *èkuru* in a large bowl. Make sure the *èkuru* stew is prepared with plenty of locust bean and crayfish. It must smell as appetizing as possible.'

The children were dispersed in various directions, some to the market to obtain the *àgìdi*, others to begin grinding the beans for the amount of *èkuru* which was needed to accompany 50 wraps of *àgìdi*. The children's mouths watered, assuming at once that this was to be an appeasement feast, a *sàarà** for some offended spirits.

When all was prepared however, the old woman took everything to Sanya's sick-room, plus a pot of cold water and cups, locked the door on him and ordered everybody away.

'Just go about your normal business and don't go anywhere near the room. If you want your brother to recover, do as I say. Don't attempt to speak to him and don't peep through the keyhole.'

---

*An offering, food shared out as offering.

She locked the windows too and went herself to a distant end of the courtyard where she could monitor the movements of the children. She dozed off soon after however, so that mother and the other children were able to glue their ears to the door and windows even if they could not see the invalid himself. Uncle Sanya sounded as if he was no longer alone. They heard him saying things like:

'Behave yourself, there is enough for everybody. All right you take this, have an extra wrap...Open your mouth...here...you don't have to fight over that bit, here's another piece of crayfish... behave, I said...'

And they would hear what sounded like the slapping of wrists, a scrape of dishes on the ground or water slopping into a cup.

When the woman judged it was time, which was well after dusk, nearly six hours after Sanya was first locked up, she went and opened the door. There was Sanya fast asleep but, this time, very peacefully. She touched his forehead and appeared to be satisfied by the change. The household who had crowded in with her had no interest in Sanya however. All they could see, with astonished faces, were the scattered leaves of 50 wraps of *àgìdi*, with the contents gone, a large empty dish which was earlier filled with *èkuru*, and a water-pot nearly empty.

No, there was no question about it, our Uncle Sanya was an *òrò*; Wild Christian had seen and heard proofs of it many times over. His companions were obviously the more benevolent type or he would have come to serious harm on more than one occasion, J.J.'s protecting Faith notwithstanding. Uncle Sanya was very rarely with us at this time, so we could not ask him any of the questions which Wild Christian refused to answer. When he next visited us at the parsonage, I noticed his strange eyes which hardly ever seemed to blink but looked straight over our heads even when he talked to us. But he seemed far too active to be an *òrò*; indeed for a long time I confused him with a local scoutmaster who was nicknamed Activity. So I began to watch the Wolf Cubs who seemed nearest to the kind of secret company which our Uncle Sanya may have kept as a child. As their tight little faces formed circles on the lawns of Aké, building little fires, exchanging secret signs with hands and twigs, with stones specially placed against one another during their jamboree, I felt I had detected the hidden companions who crept in unseen through chinks in the door and even from the ground, right under the aggrieved noses of Wild Christian and the other children in J.J.'s household, and feasted on 50 wraps of *àgìdi* and a huge bowl of *èkuru*.

❖ ❖ ❖

Dynamics

1. Locate passages that point to different kinds of "belief" or "faith" in Soyinka's story. How would you describe the relationship between these various kinds of "faith"? Talk or write about some places in the text where seemingly inconsistent forms of belief meet. What do these "meeting places" tell you about Nigerian culture at the time of Soyinka's childhood?

2. Soyinka writes that "stubbornness was one of the earliest sins we easily recognized." What kinds of "stubbornness" do you see in this text? Explain why stubbornness might be a "sin" within each of the belief systems you see represented in Soyinka's text. How does your own cultural perspective on "stubbornness" compare to those you encounter in this story? Try to explain the differences you see.

Critical Tools

1. This story includes a number of words in Ibo, a language spoken in Nigeria. Think about the ways that you deal with unfamiliar language when you are reading. What definitions did you develop for words like *òrò* and *egúngún*? Point to the passages that helped you to understand Soyinka's meanings. How does the method you used here compare to strategies you have used for understanding other difficult texts?

2. "AKE" tells the story of a family living between and among African and Western cultures. Find a critical tool from another reading that helps you to think freshly about the intersections you see between Ibo and Christian religious practices, or between traditional Ibo living customs and English/colonial styles. Why does the critical tool you have chosen seem appropriate to you?

Draft One/Draft Two

Draft One: The narrator of Soyinka's text sometimes seems sensitive to his status as an "outsider" within his own culture; there are stories and customs that he wants to know and events that he wishes to share with his family. Write an essay in which you compare Soyinka's experiences of "initiation" to one or more of your own. In the formal or informal rites of initiation you are discussing, explain how cultural authority gets used, transferred, and/or strengthened.

Draft Two: Using your first draft as a "jumping-off" point, pick another essay and use it to explore some ways that you see cultural authority being transmitted from one generation to another. In each of the texts under discussion—Soyinka's, your own, and the new essay—try to pinpoint what's at stake in this transfer of power. How do issues like race, sexuality, or class figure into this process?

❖ ❖ ❖

Before Reading Amy Tan. . .

1. Think about some of the characteristics (both positive and negative) either you or society in general associates with two or three different cultural backgrounds. Where did your familiarity with these characteristics come from? In what ways might these ideas shape your expectations about people from those backgrounds?

2. Consider an experience or two in which you tried to get an idea across to someone who continually claimed to understand what you were saying, but whose words, tone, or gestures alerted you that their way of comprehending the idea remained fundamentally different from your own. How would you account for these sometimes frustrating barriers to communication? What strategies did you adopt in an effort to overcome these barriers?

The Language of Discretion

Amy Tan

At a recent family dinner in San Francisco, my mother whispered to me: "Sau-sau [Brother's Wife] pretends too hard to be polite! Why bother? In the end, she always takes everything."

My mother thinks like a *waixiao*, an expatriate, temporarily away from China since 1949, no longer patient with ritual courtesies. As if to prove her point, she reached across the table to offer my elderly aunt from Beijing the last scallop from the Happy Family seafood dish.

Sau-sau scowled. *"B'yao, zhen b'yao!"* (I don't want it, really I don't!) she cried, patting her plump stomach.

"Take it! Take it!" scolded my mother in Chinese.

"Full, I'm already full," Sau-sau protested weakly, eyeing the beloved scallop.

"Ai!" exclaimed my mother, completely exasperated. "Nobody else wants it. If you don't take it, it will only rot!"

At this point, Sau-sau sighed, acting as if she were doing my mother a big favor by taking the wretched scrap off her hands.

My mother turned to her brother, a high-ranking communist official who was visiting her in California for the first time: "In America a Chinese person could starve to death. If you say you don't want it, they won't ask you again forever."

My uncle nodded and said he understood fully: Americans take things quickly because they have no time to be polite.

I thought about this misunderstanding again—of social contexts failing in translation—when a friend sent me an article from the *New York Times Magazine* (24 April 1988). The article, on changes in New York's Chinatown, made passing reference to the inherent ambivalence of the Chinese language.

Chinese people are so "discreet and modest," the article stated, there aren't even words for "yes" and "no."

That's not true, I thought, although I can see why an outsider might think that. I continued reading.

If one is Chinese, the article went on to say, "One compromises, one doesn't hazard a loss of face by an overemphatic response."

My throat seized. Why do people keep saying these things? As if we truly were those little dolls sold in Chinatown tourist shops, heads bobbing up and down in complacent agreement to anything said!

I worry about the effect of one-dimensional statements on the unwary and guileless. When they read about this so-called vocabulary deficit, do they also conclude that Chinese people evolved into a mild-mannered lot because the language only allowed them to hobble forth with minced words?

Something enormous is always lost in translation. Something insidious seeps into the gaps, especially when amateur linguists continue to compare, one-for-one, language differences and then put forth notions wide open to misinterpretation: that Chinese people have no direct linguistic means to make decisions, assert or deny, affirm or negate, just say no to drug dealers, or behave properly on the witness stand when told, "Please answer yes or no."

Yet one can argue, with the help of renowned linguists, that the Chinese are indeed up a creek without "yes" and "no." Take any number of variations on the old language-and-reality theory stated years ago by Edward Sapir: "Human beings...are very much at the mercy of the particular language which has become the medium for their society.... The fact of the matter is that the 'real world' is to a large extent built up on the language habits of the group."[1]

This notion was further bolstered by the famous Sapir-Whorf hypothesis, which roughly states that one's perception of the world and how one functions in it depends a great deal on the language used. As Sapir, Whorf, and new carriers of the banner would have us believe, language shapes our thinking, channels us along certain patterns embedded in words, syntactic structures, and intonation patterns. Language has become the peg and the shelf that enables us to sort out and categorize the world. In English, we see "cats" and "dogs"; what if the language had also specified *glatz*, meaning "animals that leave fur on the sofa," and *glotz*, meaning "animals that leave fur and drool on the sofa"? How would language, the enabler, have changed our perceptions with slight vocabulary variations?

And if this were the case—of language being the master of destined thought—think of the opportunities lost from failure to evolve two little words, *yes* and *no*, the simplest of opposites! Ghenghis Khan could have been sent back to Mongolia. Opium wars might have been averted. The Cultural Revolution could have been side-stepped.

There are still many, from serious linguists to pop psychology cultists, who view language and reality as inextricably tied, one being the consequence of the other. We have traversed the range from the Sapir-Whorf hypothesis to est and neurolinguistic programming, which tell us "you are what you say."

I too have been intrigued by the theories. I can summarize, albeit badly, ages-old empirical evidence: of Eskimos and their infinite ways to say "snow," their ability to see the differences in snowflake configurations, thanks to the richness of their vocabulary, while non-Eskimo speakers like myself founder in "snow," "more snow," and "lots more where that came from."

I too have experienced dramatic cognitive awakenings via the word. Once I added "mauve" to my vocabulary I began to see it everywhere. When I learned how to pronounce *prix fixe*, I ate French food at prices better than the easier-to-say *à la carte* choices.

But just how seriously are we supposed to take this?

Sapir said something else about language and reality. It is the part that often gets left behind in the dot-dot-dots of quotes: "...No two languages are ever sufficiently similar to be considered as representing the same social reality. The worlds in which different societies live are distinct worlds, not merely the same world with different labels attached."

When I first read this, I thought, Here at last is validity for the dilemmas I felt growing up in a bicultural, bilingual family! As any child of immigrant parents knows, there's a special kind of double bind attached to knowing two languages. My parents, for example, spoke to me in both Chinese and English; I spoke back to them in English.

"Amy-ah!" they'd call to me.

"What?" I'd mumble back.

"Do not question us when we call," they scolded me in Chinese. "It is not respectful."

"What do you mean?"

"Ai! Didn't we just tell you not to question?"

To this day, I wonder which parts of my behavior were shaped by Chinese, which by English. I am tempted to think, for example, that if I am of two minds on some matter it is due to the richness of my linguistic experiences, not to any personal tendencies toward wishy-washiness. But which mind says what?

Was it perhaps patience—developed through years of deciphering my mother's fractured English—that had me listening politely while a woman announced over the phone that I had won one of five valuable prizes? Was it respect—pounded in by the Chinese imperative to accept convoluted explanations—that had me agreeing that I might find it worthwhile to drive seventy-five miles to view a time-share resort? Could I have been at a loss for words when asked, "Wouldn't you like to win a Hawaiian cruise or perhaps a fabulous Star of India designed exclusively by Carter and Van Arpels?"

And when this same woman called back a week later, this time complaining that I had missed my appointment, obviously it was my type A language that kicked into gear and interrupted her. Certainly, my blunt denial—"Frankly I'm not interested"—was as American as apple pie. And when she said, "But it's in Morgan Hill," and I shouted, "Read my lips. I don't care if it's Timbuktu," you can be sure I said it with the precise intonation expressing both cynicism and disgust.

It's dangerous business, this sorting out of language and behavior. Which one is English? Which is Chinese? The categories manifest themselves: passive and aggressive, tentative and assertive, indirect and direct. And I realize they are just variations of the same theme: that Chinese people are discreet and modest.

Reject them all!

If my reaction is overly strident, it is because I cannot come across as too emphatic. I grew up listening to the same lines over and over again, like so many rote expressions repeated in an English phrasebook. And I too almost came to believe them.

Yet if I consider my upbringing more carefully, I find there was nothing discreet about the Chinese language I grew up with. My parents made everything abundantly clear. Nothing wishy-washy in their demands, no compromises accepted: "Of course you will become a famous neurosurgeon," they told me. "And yes, a concert pianist on the side."

In fact, now that I remember, it seems that the more emphatic outbursts always spilled over into Chinese: "Not that way! You must wash rice so not a single grain spills out."

I do not believe that my parents—both immigrants from mainland China—are an exception to the modest-and-discreet rule. I have only to look at the number of Chinese engineering students skewing minority ratios at Berkeley, MIT, and Yale. Certainly they were not raised by passive mothers and fathers who said, "It is up to you, my daughter. Writer, welfare recipient, masseuse, or molecular engineer—you decide."

And my American mind says, See, those engineering students weren't able to say no to their parents' demands. But then my Chinese mind remembers: Ah, but those parents all wanted their sons and daughters to be *pre-med*.

Having listened to both Chinese and English, I also tend to be suspicious of any comparisons between the two languages. Typically, one language—that of the person doing the comparing—is often used as the standard, the benchmark for a logical form of expression. And so the language being compared is always in danger of being judged deficient or superfluous, simplistic or unnecessarily complex, melodious or cacophonous. English speakers point out that Chinese is extremely difficult because it relies on variations in tone barely discernible to the human ear. By the same token, Chinese speakers tell me English is extremely difficult because it is inconsistent, a language of too many broken rules, of Mickey Mice and Donald Ducks.

Even more dangerous to my mind is the temptation to compare both language and behavior *in translation*. To listen to my mother speak English, one might think she has no concept of past or future tense, that she doesn't see the difference between singular and plural, that she is gender blind because she calls my husband "she." If one were not careful, one might also generalize that, based on the way my mother talks, all Chinese people take a circumlocutory route to get to the point. It is, in fact, my mother's idiosyncratic behavior to ramble a bit.

Sapir was right about differences between two languages and their realities. I can illustrate why word-for-word translation is not enough to translate meaning and intent. I once received a letter from China which I read to non-Chinese speaking friends. The letter, originally written in Chinese, had been translated by my brother-in law in Beijing. One portion described the time when my uncle at age ten discovered his widowed mother (my grandmother) had remarried—as a number three concubine, the ultimate disgrace for an honorable family. The translated version of my uncle's letter read in part:

> *In 1925, I met my mother in Shanghai. When she came to me, I didn't have greeting to her as if seeing nothing. She pull me to a corner secretly and asked me why didn't have greeting to her. I couldn't control myself and cried, "Ma! Why did you leave us? People told me: one day you ate a beancake yourself. Your sister in-law found it and sweared at you, called your names. So...is it true?" She clasped my hand and answered immediately, "It's not true, don't say what like this." After this time there was a few chance to meet her.*

"What!" cried my friends. "Was eating a beancake so terrible?"

Of course not. The beancake was simply a euphemism; a ten-year old boy did not dare question his mother on something as shocking as concubinage. Eating a beancake was his equivalent for committing this selfish act, something inconsiderate of all family members, hence, my grandmother's despairing response to what seemed like a ludicrous charge of gluttony. And sure enough, she was banished from the family, and my uncle saw her only a few times before her death.

While the above may fuel people's argument that Chinese is indeed a language of extreme discretion, it does not mean that Chinese people speak in secrets and riddles. The contexts are fully understood. It is only to those on the *outside* that the language seems cryptic, the behavior inscrutable.

I am, evidently, one of the outsiders. My nephew in Shanghai, who recently started taking English lessons, has been writing me letters in English. I had told him I was a fiction writer, and so in one letter he wrote, "Congratulate to you on your writing. Perhaps one day I should like to read it." I took it in the same vein as "Perhaps one day we can get together for lunch." I sent back a cheery note. A month went by and another letter arrived from Shanghai. "Last one perhaps I hadn't writing distinctly," he said. "In the future, you'll send a copy of your works for me."

I try to explain to my English-speaking friends that Chinese language use is more *strategic* in manner, whereas English tends to be more direct; an American business executive may say, "Let's make a deal," and the Chinese manager may reply, "Is your son interested in learning about your widget business?" Each to his or her own purpose, each with his or her own linguistic path. But I hesitate to add more to the pile of generalizations, because no matter how many examples I provide and explain, I fear that it appears defensive and only reinforces the image: that Chinese people are "discreet and modest"—and it takes an American to explain what they really mean.

Why am I complaining? The description seems harmless enough (after all, the *New York Times Magazine* writer did not say "slippery and evasive"). It is precisely the bland, easy acceptability of the phrase that worries me.

I worry that the dominant society may see Chinese people from a limited—and limiting—perspective. I worry that seemingly benign stereotypes may be part of the reason there are few Chinese in top management positions, in mainstream political roles. I worry about the power of language: that if one says anything enough times—in any language—it might become true.

Could this be why Chinese friends of my parents' generation are willing to accept the generalization?

"Why are you complaining?" one of them said to me. "If people think we are modest and polite, let them think that. Wouldn't Americans be pleased to admit they are thought of as polite?"

And I do believe anyone would take the description as a compliment—at first. But after a while, it annoys, as if the only things that people heard one say were phatic remarks: "I'm so pleased to meet you. I've heard many wonderful things about you. For me? You shouldn't have!"

These remarks are not representative of new ideas, honest emotions, or considered thought. They are what is said from the polite distance of social contexts: of greetings, farewells, wedding thank-you notes, convenient excuses, and the like.

It makes me wonder though. How many anthropologists, how many sociologists, how many travel journalists have documented so-called "natural interactions" in foreign lands, all observed with spiral notebook in hand? How many other cases are there of the long-lost primitive tribe, people who turned out to be sophisticated enough to put on the stone-age show that ethnologists had come to see?

And how many tourists fresh off the bus have wandered into Chinatown expecting the self-effacing shopkeeper to admit under duress that the goods are not worth the price asked? I have witnessed it.

"I don't know," the tourist said to the shopkeeper, a Cantonese woman in her fifties. "It doesn't look genuine to me. I'll give you three dollars."

"You don't like my price, go somewhere else," said the shopkeeper.

"You are not a nice person," cried the shocked tourist, "not a nice person at all!"

"Who say I have to be nice," snapped the shopkeeper.

"So how does one say 'yes' and 'no' in Chinese?" ask my friends a bit warily.

And here I do agree in part with the *New York Times Magazine* article. There is no one word for "yes" or "no"—but not out of necessity to be discreet. If anything, I would say the Chinese equivalent of answering "yes" or "no" is dis*crete*, that is, specific to what is asked.

Ask a Chinese person if he or she has eaten, and he or she might say *chrle* (eaten already) or perhaps *meiyou* (have not).

Ask, "So you had insurance at the time of the accident?" and the response would be *dwei* (correct) or *meiyou* (did not have).

Ask, "Have you stopped beating your wife?" and the answer refers directly to the proposition being asserted or denied: stopped already, still have not, never beat, have no wife.

What could be clearer?

As for those who are still wondering how to translate the language of discretion, I offer this personal example.

My aunt and uncle were about to return to Beijing after a three-month visit to the United States. On their last night I announced I wanted to take them out to dinner.

"Are you hungry?" I asked in Chinese.

"Not hungry," said my uncle promptly, the same response he once gave me ten minutes before he suffered a low-blood-sugar attack.

"Not too hungry," said my aunt. "Perhaps you're hungry?"

"A little," I admitted.

"We can eat, we can eat," they both consented.

"What kind of food?" I asked.

"Oh, doesn't matter. Anything will do. Nothing fancy, just some simple food is fine."

"Do you like Japanese food? We haven't had that yet," I suggested.

They looked at each other.

"We can eat it," said my uncle bravely, this survivor of the Long March .

"We have eaten it before," added my aunt. "Raw fish."

"Oh, you don't like it?" I said. "Don't be polite. We can go somewhere else."

"We are not being polite. We can eat it," my aunt insisted.

So I drove them to Japantown and we walked past several restaurants featuring colorful plastic displays of sushi.

"Not this one, not this one either," I continued to say, as if searching for a Japanese restaurant similar to the last. "Here it is," I finally said, turning into a restaurant famous for its Chinese fish dishes from Shandong.

"Oh, Chinese food!" cried my aunt, obviously relieved.

My uncle patted my arm. "You think Chinese."

"It's your last night here in America," I said. "So don't be polite. Act like an American."

And that night we ate a banquet.

NOTE

1. Edward Sapir, *Selected Writings*, ed. D. G. Mandelbaum (Berkeley and Los Angeles, 1949).

❖ ❖ ❖

Dynamics

1. Evaluate your understanding of the terms "discreet" and "discrete." Work with specific passages from Tan's essay to analyze how Tan creates and makes use of the relationship between these terms. How might these terms both complement and resist each other?

2. Which aspects of the Sapir-Whorf hypothesis appeal to or trouble Tan? Analyze the passages from her essay in which she debates the hypothesis and its implications. What conclusions do you draw about the hypothesis and about Tan's reactions to it?

Critical Tools

1. Tan claims that she has "experienced dramatic cognitive awakenings via the word." Define what you understand this claim to mean. What role does her view of discretion (language as discreet; language as discrete) play in these cognitive awakenings? Use your responses to these questions to evaluate an experience in which new vocabulary or new understandings of a term changed your views or behaviors.

2. How can you use the tension between "discreet" and "discrete" language as an interpretive strategy? Consider some of the new interpretations this tension allows Tan to generate as you explore the "discreet" and "discrete" moments in an argument from another essay. What new insights and responses can you develop by reconsidering the second writer's argument through the lens of discretion?

Draft One/Draft Two

Draft One: Tan suggests that "something enormous is always lost in translation." Explore your response to Tan's statement by examining "translation" within a single language rather than between two languages. Identify some of the "languages" you speak: academic, scientific, vocational, etc. How well do Tan's ideas account for your experience of moving back and forth between—and communicating with—these languages within the language?

Draft Two: Use the ideas you developed in draft one to reconsider a particularly difficult passage from another essay. How might the idea of "translation" help you to discover something new about this passage? As you work through the passage from this perspective, evaluate what you gain and lose through translation. How do your conclusions about Tan's ideas from this exercise compare with your conclusions from draft one?

❖ ❖ ❖

Before Reading Alice Walker. . .

1. In this story Alice Walker is interested in the ways people use their heritage. Think about some people you know who have different relations to their national and ethnic heritage, whether these relations are made visible in clothing and grooming, in political interests, in cultural customs, or in other, less obvious ways. What values do you see at work in individuals who reveal very different relations to their heritage? Where do you place yourself in this matter?

2. If you know anyone who was very much changed by going away for an education, write informally about that process. What happens, and why? What do you think of the results?

Everyday Use

for your grandmama

Alice Walker

I will wait for her in the yard that Maggie and I made so clean and wavy yesterday afternoon. A yard like this is more comfortable than most people know. It is not just a yard. It is like an extended living room. When the hard clay is swept clean as a floor and the fine sand around the edges lined with tiny, irregular grooves, anyone can come and sit and look up into the elm tree and wait for the breezes that never come inside the house.

Maggie will be nervous until after her sister goes: she will stand hopelessly in corners, homely and ashamed of the burn scars down her arms and legs, eyeing her sister with a mixture of envy and awe. She thinks her sister has held life always in the palm of one hand, that "no" is a word the world never learned to say to her.

You've no doubt seen those TV shows where the child who has "made it" is confronted, as a surprise, by her own mother and father, tottering in weakly from backstage. (A pleasant surprise, of course: What would they do if parent and child came on the show only to curse out and insult each other?) On TV mother and child embrace and smile into each other's faces. Sometimes the mother and father weep, the child wraps them in her arms and leans across the table to tell how she would not have made it without their help. I have seen these programs.

Sometimes I dream a dream in which Dee and I are suddenly brought together on a TV program of this sort. Out of a dark and soft-seated limousine I am ushered into a bright room filled with many people. There I meet a smiling, gray, sporty man like Johnny Carson who shakes my hand and tells me what a fine girl I have. Then we are on the stage and Dee is embracing me with tears in her eyes. She pins on my dress a large orchid, even though she has told me once that she thinks orchids are tacky flowers.

In real life I am a large, big-boned woman with rough, man-working hands. In the winter I wear flannel nightgowns to bed and overalls during the day. I can kill and clean a hog as mercilessly as a man. My fat keeps me hot in zero weather. I can work outside all day, breaking ice to get water for washing; I can eat pork liver cooked over the open fire minutes after it comes steaming from the hog. One winter I knocked a bull calf straight in the brain between the eyes with a sledge hammer and had the meat hung up to chill before nightfall. But of course all this does not show on television. I am the way my daughter would want me to be: a hundred pounds lighter, my skin like an uncooked barley pancake. My hair glistens in the hot bright lights. Johnny Carson has much to do to keep up with my quick and witty tongue.

But that is a mistake. I know even before I wake up. Who ever knew a Johnson with a quick tongue? Who can even imagine me looking a strange white man in the eye? It seems to me I have talked to them always with one foot raised in flight, with my head turned in whichever way is farthest from them. Dee, though. She would always look anyone in the eye. Hesitation was no part of her nature.

"How do I look, Mama?" Maggie says, showing just enough of her thin body enveloped in pink skirt and red blouse for me to know she's there, almost hidden by the door.

"Come out into the yard," I say.

Have you ever seen a lame animal, perhaps a dog run over by some careless person rich enough to own a car, sidle up to someone who is ignorant enough to be kind to him? That is the way my Maggie walks. She has been like this, chin on chest, eyes on ground, feet in shuffle, ever since the fire that burned the other house to the ground.

Dee is lighter than Maggie, with nicer hair and a fuller figure. She's a woman now, though sometimes I forget. How long ago was it that the other house burned? Ten, twelve years? Sometimes I can still hear the flames and feel Maggie's arms sticking to me, her hair smoking and her dress falling off her in little black papery flakes. Her eyes seemed stretched open, blazed open by the flames reflected in them. And Dee. I see her standing off under the sweet gum tree she used to dig gum out of; a look of concentration on her face as she watched the last dingy gray board of the house fall in toward the red-hot brick chimney. Why don't you do a dance around the ashes? I'd wanted to ask her. She had hated the house that much.

I used to think she hated Maggie, too. But that was before we raised the money, the church and me, to send her to Augusta to school. She used to read to us without pity; forcing words, lies, other folks' habits, whole lives upon us two, sitting trapped and ignorant underneath her voice. She washed us in a river of make-believe, burned us with a lot of knowledge we didn't necessarily need to know. Pressed us to her with the serious way she read, to shove us away at just the moment, like dimwits, we seemed about to understand.

Dee wanted nice things. A yellow organdy dress to wear to her graduation from high school; black pumps to match a green suit she'd made from an old suit somebody gave me. She was determined to stare down any disaster in her efforts. Her eyelids would not flicker for minutes at a time. Often I fought off the temptation to shake her. At sixteen she had a style of her own: and knew what style was.

I never had an education myself. After second grade the school was closed down. Don't ask my why: in 1927 colored asked fewer questions than they do now. Sometimes Maggie reads to me. She stumbles along good-naturedly but can't see well. She knows she is not bright. Like good looks and money, quickness passed her by. She will marry John Thomas (who has mossy teeth in an earnest face) and then I'll be free to sit here and I guess just sing church songs to myself. Although I never was a good singer. Never could carry a tune. I was always better at a man's job. I used to love to milk till I was hooked in the side in '49. Cows are soothing and slow and don't bother you, unless you try to milk them the wrong way.

I have deliberately turned my back on the house. It is three rooms, just like the one that burned, except the roof is tin; they don't make shingle roofs any more. There are no real windows, just some holes cut in the sides, like the portholes in a ship, but not round and not square, with rawhide holding the shutters up on the outside. This house is in a pasture, too, like the other one. No doubt when Dee sees it she will want to tear it down. She wrote me once that no matter where we "choose" to live, she will manage to come see us. But she will never bring her friends. Maggie and I thought about this and Maggie asked me, "Mama, when did Dee ever *have* any friends?"

She had a few. Furtive boys in pink shirts hanging about on washday after school. Nervous girls who never laughed. Impressed with her they worshiped the well-turned phrase, the cute shape, the scalding humor that erupted like bubbles in lye. She read to them.

When she was courting Jimmy T she didn't have much time to pay to us, but turned all her faultfinding power on him. He *flew* to marry a cheap city girl from a family of ignorant flashy people. She hardly had time to recompose herself.

When she comes I will meet—but there they are!

Maggie attempts to make a dash for the house, in her shuffling way, but I stay her with my hand. "Come back here," I say. And she stops and tries to dig a well in the sand with her toe.

It is hard to see them clearly through the strong sun. But even the first glimpse of leg out of the car tells me it is Dee. Her feet were always neat-looking, as if God himself had shaped them with a certain style. From the other side of the car comes a short, stocky man. Hair is all over his head a foot long and hanging from his chin like a kinky mule tail. I hear Maggie suck in her breath. "Uhnnnh," is what it sounds like. Like when you see the wriggling end of a snake just in front of your foot on the road. "Uhnnnh."

Dee next. A dress down to the ground, in this hot weather. A dress so loud it hurts my eyes. There are yellows and oranges enough to throw back the light of the sun. I feel my whole face warming from the heat waves it throws out. Earrings gold, too, and hanging down to her shoulders. Bracelets dangling and making noises when she moves her arm up to shake the folds of the dress out of her armpits. The dress is loose and flows, and as she walks closer, I like it. I hear Maggie go "Uhnnnh" again. It is her sister's hair. It stands straight up like the wool on a sheep. It is black as night and around the edges are two long pigtails that rope about like small lizards disappearing behind her ears.

"Wa-su-zo-Tean-o!" she says, coming on in that gliding way the dress makes her move. The short stocky fellow with the hair to his navel is all grinning and he follows up with "Asalamalakim, my mother and sister!" He moves to hug Maggie but she falls back, right up against the back of my chair. I feel her trembling there and when I look up I see the perspiration falling off her chin.

"Don't get up," says Dee. Since I am stout it takes something of a push. You can see me trying to move a second or two before I make it. She turns, showing white heels through her sandals, and goes back to the car. Out she peeks next with a Polaroid. She stoops down quickly and lines up picture after picture of me sitting there in front of the house with Maggie cowering behind me. She never takes a shot without making sure the house is included. When a cow comes nibbling around the edge of the yard she snaps it and me and Maggie *and* the house. Then she puts the Polaroid in the back seat of the car, and comes up and kisses me on the forehead.

Meanwhile Asalamalakim is going through motions with Maggie's hand. Maggie's hand is as limp as a fish, and probably as cold, despite the sweat, and she keeps trying to pull it back. It looks like Asalamalakim wants to shake hands but wants to do it fancy. Or maybe he don't know how people shake hands. Anyhow, he soon gives up on Maggie.

"Well," I say. "Dee."

"No, Mama," she says. "Not 'Dee,' Wangero Leewanika Kemanjo!"

"What happened to 'Dee'?" I wanted to know.

"She's dead," Wangero said. "I couldn't bear it any longer, being named after the people who oppress me."

"You know as well as me you was named after your aunt Dicie," I said. Dicie is my sister. She named Dee. We called her "Big Dee" after Dee was born.

"But who was *she* named after?" asked Wangero.

"I guess after Grandma Dee," I said.

"And who was she named after?" asked Wangero.

"Her mother," I said, and saw Wangero was getting tired. "That's about as far back as I can trace it," I said. Though, in fact, I probably could have carried it back beyond the Civil War through the branches.

"Well," said Asalamalakim, "there you are."

"Uhnnnh," I heard Maggie say.

"There I was not," I said, "before 'Dicie' cropped up in our family, so why should I try to trace it that far back?"

He just stood there grinning, looking down on me like somebody inspecting a Model A car. Every once in a while he and Wangero sent eye signals over my head.

"How do you pronounce this name?" I asked.

"You don't have to call me by it if you don't want to," said Wangero.

"Why shouldn't I?" I asked. "If that's what you want us to call you, we'll call you."

"I know it might sound awkward at first," said Wangero.

"I'll get used to it," I said. "Ream it out again."

Well, soon we got the name out of the way. Asalamalakim had a name twice as long and three times as hard. After I tripped over it two or three times he told me to just call him Hakim-a-barber. I wanted to ask him was he a barber, but I didn't really think he was, so I didn't ask.

"You must belong to those beef-cattle peoples down the road," I said. They said "Asalamalakim" when they met you, too, but they didn't shake hands. Always too busy: feeding the cattle, fixing the fences, putting up salt-lick shelters, throwing down hay. When the white folks poisoned some of the herd the men stayed up all night with rifles in their hands. I walked a mile and a half just to see the sight.

Hakim-a-barber said, "I accept some of their doctrines, but farming and raising cattle is not my style." (They didn't tell me, and I didn't ask, whether Wangero (Dee) had really gone and married him.)

We sat down to eat and right away he said he didn't eat collards and pork was unclean. Wangero, though, went on through the chitlins and corn bread, the greens and everything else. She talked a blue streak over the sweet potatoes. Everything delighted her. Even the fact that we still used the benches her daddy made for the table when we couldn't afford to buy chairs.

"Oh, Mama!" she cried. Then turned to Hakim-a-barber. "I never knew how lovely these benches are. You can feel the rump prints," she said, running her hands underneath her and along the bench. Then she gave a sigh and her hand closed over Grandma Dee's butter dish. "That's it!" she said. "I knew there was something I wanted to ask you if I could have." She jumped up from the table and went over in the corner where the churn stood, the milk in it clabber by now. She looked at the churn and looked at it.

"This churn top is what I need," she said. "Didn't Uncle Buddy whittle it out of a tree you all used to have?"

"Yes," I said.

"Uh huh," she said happily. "And I want the dasher, too."

"Uncle Buddy whittle that, too?" asked the barber.

Dee (Wangero) looked up at me.

"Aunt Dee's first husband whittled the dash," said Maggie so low you almost couldn't hear her. "His name was Henry, but they called him Stash."

"Maggie's brain is like an elephant's," Wangero said, laughing. "I can use the churn top as a centerpiece for the alcove table," she said, sliding a plate over the churn, "and I'll think of something artistic to do with the dasher."

When she finished wrapping the dasher the handle stuck out. I took it for a moment in my hands. You didn't even have to look close to see where hands pushing the dasher up and down to make butter had left a kind of sink in the wood. In fact, there were a lot of small sinks; you could see where thumbs and fingers had sunk into the wood. It was beautiful light yellow wood, from a tree that grew in the yard where Big Dee and Stash had lived.

After dinner Dee (Wangero) went to the trunk at the foot of my bed and started rifling through it. Maggie hung back in the kitchen over the dishpan. Out came Wangero with two quilts. They had been pieced by Grandma Dee and then Big Dee and me had hung them on the quilt frames on the front porch and quilted them. One was in the Lone Star pattern. The other was Walk Around the Mountain. In both of them were scraps of dresses Grandma Dee had worn fifty and more years ago. Bits and pieces of Grandpa Jarrell's Paisley shirts. And one teeny faded blue piece, about the size of a penny matchbox, that was from Great Grandpa Ezra's uniform that he wore in the Civil War.

"Mama," Wangero said sweet as a bird. "Can I have these old quilts?"

I heard something fall in the kitchen, and a minute later the kitchen door slammed.

"Why don't you take one or two of the others?" I asked. "These old things was just done by me and Big Dee from some tops your grandma pieced before she died."

"No," said Wangero. "I don't want those. They are stitched around the borders by machine."

"That'll make them last better," I said.

"That's not the point," said Wangero. "These are all pieces of dresses Grandma used to wear. She did all this stitching by hand. Imagine!" She held the quilts securely in her arms, stroking them.

"Some of the pieces, like those lavender ones, come from old clothes her mother handed down to her," I said, moving up to touch the quilts. Dee (Wangero) moved back just enough so that I couldn't reach the quilts. They already belonged to her.

"Imagine!" she breathed again, clutching them closely to her bosom.

"The truth is," I said, "I promised to give them quilts to Maggie, for when she marries John Thomas."

She gasped like a bee had stung her.

"Maggie can't appreciate these quilts!" she said. "She'd probably be backward enough to put them to everyday use."

"I reckon she would," I said. "God knows I been saving 'em for long enough with nobody using 'em. I hope she will!" I didn't want to bring up how I had offered Dee (Wangero) a quilt when she went away to college. Then she had told me they were old-fashioned, out of style.

"But they're *priceless*!" she was saying now, furiously; for she has a temper. "Maggie would put them on the bed and in five years they'd be in rags. Less than that!"

"She can always make some more," I said. "Maggie knows how to quilt."

Dee (Wangero) looked at me with hatred. "You just will not understand. The point is these quilts, *these* quilts!"

"Well," I said, stumped. "What would you do with them?"

"Hang them," she said. As if that was the only thing you *could* do with quilts.

Maggie by now was standing in the door. I could almost hear the sound her feet made as they scraped over each other.

"She can have them, Mama," she said, like somebody used to never winning anything, or having anything reserved for her. "I can 'member Grandma Dee without the quilts."

I looked at her hard. She had filled her bottom lip with checkerberry snuff and it gave her face a kind of dopey, hangdog look. It was Grandma Dee and Big Dee who taught her how to quilt herself. She stood there with her scarred hands hidden in the folds of her skirt. She looked at her sister with something like fear but she wasn't mad at her. This was Maggie's portion. This was the way she knew God to work.

When I looked at her like that something hit me in the top of my head and ran down to the soles of my feet. Just like when I'm in church and the spirit of God touches me and I get happy and shout. I did something I never had done before: hugged Maggie to me, then dragged her on into the room, snatched the quilts out of Miss Wangero's hands and dumped them into Maggie's lap. Maggie just sat there on my bed with her mouth open.

"Take one or two of the others," I said to Dee.

But she turned without a word and went out to Hakim-a-barber.

"You just don't understand," she said, as Maggie and I came out to the car.

"What don't I understand?" I wanted to know.

"Your heritage," she said. And then she turned to Maggie, kissed her, and said, "You ought to try to make something of yourself, too, Maggie. It's really a new day for us. But from the way you and Mama still live you'd never know it."

She put on some sunglasses that hid everything above the tip of her nose and her chin.

Maggie smiled; maybe at the sunglasses. But a real smile, not scared. After we watched the car dust settle I asked Maggie to bring me a dip of snuff. And then the two of us sat there just enjoying, until it was time to go in the house and go to bed.

❖ ❖ ❖

Dynamics

1. Identify several of the cultural artifacts and customs that are mentioned in the story, and describe the relation to heritage that each one embodies for Maggie or her mother and for Wangero. Based on your list and the accompanying descriptions, explain the main ways you see heritage working in their lives. How do you evaluate the different ways?

2. Identify some of the ways the narrator slants the story against Wangero. How do you respond to the passages where she is implicitly critical of her daughter? Do those passages influence your conclusions about the use of heritage?

Critical Tools

1. During the story the narrator mentions several differences between Wangero and her sister, or between Wangero and the narrator. What are these differences, and how much of the story's conflict do they help explain?

2. What words does Wangero use to describe her values? What words do Maggie and the narrator use to describe their values? Are these language differences important? What relevance do you see, for example, in describing a quilt with a word taken from the art world, "priceless"? What do you make of the argument Wangero and the narrator have about naming? What role does language use play in the battle over heritage?

Draft One/Draft Two

Draft One: Assemble a list of the main uses of heritage based on Dynamics #1, above, and apply that list to the events of another text you have read this semester, such as the essays by Rodriguez or Cliff. How does heritage function in the situations of conflict described by these two authors? Use their accounts to extend your theory of the uses of heritage.

Draft Two: Consider one of the texts in this book that offers a critical method, such as the essays by Scholes or Bellah, or the book's introduction. Use the events from Walker's story and from the other text you used in draft one to examine the relation between a critical method and an acceptance of heritage. How, for example, does Scholes's idea of resistance work with or against heritage? What is the significance of your findings?

Invitations to Write

On the following pages you will find a number of "Invitations to Write" about some common aspects of the reading and writing process. Most of these invite you to reflect on and write informally, as if you were talking on paper, about your own approach to the problems of reading, writing, and revising, and they also invite you to try some new strategies that you may find helpful. You should certainly adapt these Invitations to your own circumstance and needs, and feel free to focus your energies on the parts of the Invitations that seem more relevant and helpful to you. They invite you to read and write with greater awareness of the choices you have as an interpreter.

Invitations to Write were first composed by Lou Kelly for her students at University of Iowa's Writing Lab. She also coined the term "talking on paper." We have tried to use several of her pedagogical principles in these Invitations, which were composed for students at Rutgers University by Ken Smith and Dawn Skorczewski. These slightly revised versions are reprinted by permission of Skorczewski and Smith.

What does this have to do with my life?

Choose one of these two invitations to write about for a while:

1. Sometimes a reading or writing assignment seems, at first glance, to be merely academic. This is, it seems to have to do only with the world of the university, never touching the life you have known outside of school. But assignments are far more rewarding if you can look past that first impression to *make* a connection with the life you have witnessed or lived, or the life you hope to live.

    It's very good for a person's morale to be able to make connections between schoolwork and life experience, but that's not the end of it. When you find connections between schoolwork and what you have known outside of school you can start to use the knowledge and experience you bring with you to deepen the value of the schoolwork. You can use your worldly knowledge to illuminate the specialized knowledge of the university.

    Here are some questions that might help you do that. Write for a while about several of these and see what possible connections you can make:

    - Are there any passages in the reading that a person who has lived the sort of life you have lived would be especially able to understand and appreciate? Talk about one of those passages for a while, and how it relates to your experience.

    - What specialized terms are used in discussing this topic? Do you know of any events or facts that help explain one of those terms, or reveal its usefulness? Do you know of any events or facts that challenge or contradict one of those special terms? Talk about this for a while.

    - Are there any experiences you have lived through or witnessed that don't seem to be taken into account by the specialized knowledge contained in the reading or writing assignment? Talk about one or more of those events, and tell what changes might have to be made in the specialized knowledge to take them into account.

2. How does this reading assignment help illuminate my life?

On the other hand, you may feel that the reading or writing assignment says more about your life than your life says about the reading assignment. In that case, write for awhile on one or more of these questions:

- Choose a key passage or idea from the assignment and discuss some of the things it helps explain about the life you have known. After you have said as much as you can about that, consider this: does the passage exhaust the meaning of your experience, or is there more to be said that the passage hasn't touched upon? What additional idea or theory is needed?

- Would a person who knew of this reading and accepted its ideas choose the same paths in life that you have chosen or that you have seen others choose? What would the ideas from this reading do to or for the life of someone you know well? How could these ideas change someone's life?

- Do the ideas of this reading have some special use for a person practicing a certain profession? What difference would these ideas make for someone in that profession?

Getting started on a paper

Write for a while about the ideas or difficulties in your current reading or writing assignment that you want to work on today. Feel free to write as much as you can— ask questions, sum up the arguments in your readings, plan your argument (if you are this far along), spin out ideas and possibilities. Your purpose here is to discover what tools you have available, how you want them to work within the essay assignment, and to determine the most productive path for composing. If you have no idea where to begin, feel free to write down in detail what you do not understand. What is needed is a beginning, a first step in conversation. Pick up your pen and begin writing now...

What is the assignment really asking?

Perhaps this would be a good time to look at your teacher's assignment sheet. Whether you are just starting a paper or trying to get a better revision in order, looking back at the assignment sheet can help a writer take a fresh look at the work to be done.

You might want to write on the assignment sheet itself. For example, you could put a box around part of the assignment that you find most important. Where does the professor actually ask the question that you are supposed to keep in mind as you write? How many questions are there? Which ones have you already thought or written about? Which ones have yet to find their way into your draft or your thoughts about the assignment?

Here are some things you might find useful to do—

- If there are parts of the assignment you haven't yet addressed, write down the question or questions on the top of a sheet of paper and talk on paper for a while about them. What tentative ideas could you offer in response to these questions?

- Does the assignment call for you to quote from sources? What passages in the readings seem to be the best choices for this assignment? Copy down a sentence or two from the reading on the top of a sheet of paper, write down the author and page number, and write informally about it for awhile. What could you say, tentatively, about the quotation? Why is this quotation important for the issues you are writing about in this assignment?

- Does the assignment invite you to draw on the insights of your personal experience? If so, what experiences might be useful to recall and write about here? Take a sheet of paper and write down some tentative ideas about one or two of these experiences.

- How many things does the assignment ask you to do? What parts of your draft or notes or outline address each of those things? Does your draft fulfill the mechanical aspects of the assignment, such as page length, number of sources, and so forth?

These questions are different ways of returning to the assignment sheet for guidance in writing or revising your paper. Not all of them apply to every situation, so think and write about the ones that would help you continue your work at this moment.

Taking a second look at the reading

When writers think about how they are going to approach the essay they're composing, they frequently turn back to the reading they're drawing from to refresh their memories or to generate new ideas. They may notice new ideas or examples or even contradictions in the author's thoughts; they may find quotations they'd like to add to their essays; they may even be surprised at how differently they read an essay the second time around.

Whatever their reasons for turning back to an essay they've already read, writers invariably clarify their thoughts and find material for their own writing when they do. But often their reading strategies are different the second time around.

In order for you to take a second look at the reading, you must believe that what you'll find there will be different this time around. For example, you might not want to begin the essay with its first paragraph, as you did when you first read it.

You may want to turn to a part of the essay that confuses you, or a part of the essay you haven't thought about yet. If you do, take a look at those paragraphs again, then write for a while about what they say and what you might want to say about that. You might begin with a few questions before you make decisions about what you want to say about that part of the essay. For example, if you're having trouble figuring out what the paragraph says, try paraphrasing the difficult sentence in your own words.

Another reading strategy is to begin reading an essay backwards. Try reading the last paragraph, then summarizing it. Then read the previous paragraph, and so on. Do you see something different about the reading when you begin by thinking about where it ends up?

What do the teacher's comments mean?

When a teacher comments on an essay, often he or she has some specific suggestions about how a student might alter a paper to make it more effective. Sometimes, when the comments are on a draft, the student has a chance to try out what the teacher has suggested, or to answer the teacher's questions by writing in response to them.

Often, however, the teacher's comments on an essay are directed toward the writing of future essays. The teacher asks the student to apply something he or she says about the finished essay to the writing of the next essay. Sometimes the teacher's suggestions are easy to apply to another piece of writing. On other occasions, however, it's difficult to know exactly what the teacher is pointing out.

It sometimes helps to try to figure out what the teacher is saying in your own words. There may even be a pattern to the teacher's comments; he or she may say some of the same things on each essay that you write.

Take a few moments to look through the teacher's comments on your most recent essay. In your own words, write what the teacher suggested or asked you to think about. Remember to be specific. If the teacher said three things, you should represent each of them rather than bunching them together. If you find it difficult to say what your teacher is saying to you, try writing a sentence or two of the teacher's comments, then a sentence or two of your own in which you paraphrase what the teacher says.

You may want to categorize your teacher's comments. Does the teacher mention anything about reading, for example? Organizing? Developing your ideas? Using quotations? If you have more than one essay that your teacher has read, talk about the comments on each of them. Are there any ideas or suggestions that appear on more than one of your essays?

After you have paraphrased what your teacher has said, write for a while about how you might apply those thoughts or suggestions to the paper you're working on now.

Asking your own questions

You've probably noticed that your teacher or tutor asks questions about your papers or drafts, rather than merely correcting them. Your teacher may have told you about the purpose of the questions, or you may wonder about that even now.

One reason teachers and tutors ask questions is because they believe that writing a good paper is something like having a conversation. You as a writer have a kind of conversation with the writer of the reading you are responding to, as well as with the teacher or tutor and other members of your class. In this conversation you build a more meaningful understanding of the reading and how it relates to what you already know about the world.

Most professional writers never stop having other people read their drafts and ask these kinds of questions. They also learn to ask the questions themselves, so they do not have to depend entirely on other readers for feedback.

You might want to talk on paper, informally, about the questions we've just asked. Or you may want to turn to your own paper and try to ask some of the same sorts of questions yourself, in the margin, as an aid to your own revision. Compare the questions both you and your readers have written, to see if there are any patterns there.

What sorts of questions have you found most useful in making your own revisions? Recall a few of those that have helped you make a paper stronger, and think about what sort of questions they were. How might a person think of more questions of that kind?

Are there different kinds of questions? Do they serve different purposes? Are some more useful early in the process of writing, while some might be more useful to you later in the process?

Your own independence as a writer will be served or strengthened if you do as professional writers do—continue to use feedback from other readers, but learn to ask the sorts of helpful questions that will allow you to develop your own ideas further on your own.

How is it going?

You have been working for several weeks with your teacher or tutor, and you are writing for one or more of your classes. How has it been going? What parts of your work in the class, in tutoring sessions, and in your work at home have helped you make progress and accomplish some of your goals?

What are your goals at this point in your writing course? At this point in your tutoring enrollment? What would you like to continue working on? What would you like to work on in a different way?

How do you feel about your reading now? Are there certain approaches to reading that are becoming more fruitful? Have you altered your approach to reading in any way?

How do you feel about your writing now? Are you doing new things now as you write? Are certain practices working for you? Are you becoming a different sort of writer?

What part of the class's activities would you like to talk over with the teacher? Have you visited the teacher during office hours? What questions would you ask the classroom teacher if you could?

What questions would you ask your tutor?

Please talk on paper for about 20 minutes about any of these questions, or other things that are on your mind. Take stock of the semester so far, tell your teacher or tutor about it, and explain where you want to go from here.

A Systematic Approach to Error[1]

How do you deal with error?

It will help you to begin working on learning to control your own errors if you describe in detail how *you* deal with errors in your writing. Please talk on paper about as many of these things as you can—

- When you look for errors in your paper, what do you do? And when do you do it? (as you are writing? after you have written a paragraph? after you finish the paper? at some other time?)

- What errors are you most concerned about? What errors do you find the most?

- How do you fix the errors you find? Do you consult reference books or get help from someone else?

- What is the most difficult part of this whole process for you? What parts do you feel confident of already?

- Is there anything else you would like to mention?

Be as thorough and honest as you can be, so you and your teacher can make good judgments about learning how to copyread more effectively.

---

[1]The following Invitations are indebted to Lou Kelly's Systematic Approach to Error, which she developed at the University of Iowa for the Writing Lab.

Tracking a pattern of error

One of the best ways of learning to copyread more effectively begins with a writer's own patterns of error. Most writers eventually discover that they make the same few errors repeatedly, rather than making dozens of different kinds of errors. Once a writer knows the patterns of her own errors, she can learn to copyread much more effectively by systematically looking for those particular errors. This approach can give a writer much more control over the formal correctness of her finished papers.

The easiest way to begin working on your own patterns of error is to ask a teacher or writing center tutor to point out one or two of your most common patterns of error, errors that show up repeatedly in your drafts. Together you can prepare a tip sheet for each error, showing what the error looks like and how it should be corrected, and offering any tips the two of you know for spotting and fixing it more easily. Use these error sheets as a reference when you copyread your papers, and add other sheets as the semester continues, until you have a personal reference guide to most of your patterns of error. By practicing with the teacher or tutor or on your own, you should be able to spot and fix the errors described on the sheets much more effectively by the end of the semester.

Reviewing . . . in your own words

After you have worked on a pattern of error with your teacher, tutor, or feedback partner, you should probably review what you have discovered, in order to make sure that you have really made this new knowledge your own.

Take a few minutes to talk on paper about the pattern of error you have just learned to find and fix. The following questions may help, and adding or changing them to fit your situation may also be useful.

What pattern of error have you worked on? What tips do you have to help find it? How do you go about fixing it? Give a few examples of the error and its correction—use your error analysis sheet to help you, if you wish, but do not simply re-copy it. Try to come up with at least one new example on your own. This is an opportunity for you to use your own words to explain what to do—to help yourself when your memory of the first discussion of this error has faded.

Using your error analysis sheet to copyread a new draft

With the help of your revision partner(s)—your tutor, teacher, or feedback group—
you have discussed how to find a pattern of error that seems to be a habit for you.
Knowing what a habit is is the first step to breaking it. But you also need practice
to realize when you're making that error. Using your error analysis sheets and
whatever notes you've made about your errors, look for places in your new draft
where you have made the error that you have identified as a problem. It might help
to circle "clue words" that you and your revision partners have found around the
error to see if you are making the error again. If you find yourself making the error,
correct it, but also make a note of it on a blank sheet. If you detect any new patterns
of error, make a note of them on a separate page. You may want to discuss your
findings with your revision partners.

If you find no errors in your new piece of writing, it may mean that you have
broken the habit. Or it may mean that you are still having trouble spotting the
error you've worked on. If you suspect that you're making errors but you can't find
them, you might try saying your paper "out loud" in your head, to yourself, to help
you hear the error if it's there. Or you may want to look carefully at your error
analysis sheet again, to decide what you're supposed to be looking for. Either way,
you may want to tell yourself what you're trying to find before you start looking.

A Short Guide to MLA Page Citation

In all of your papers for college, you should show the source of any material you quote. Depending on your major field of study, you might indicate your sources with one of several documentation systems. If your professor does not ask you to use a particular system, you might want to learn and use the system most commonly used in academic journals in your major field. In a course where everyone reads the same texts, the following brief guide to the MLA system may be sufficient. This is a very basic version of the system found in the Third Edition of the *MLA Handbook for Writers of Research Papers*, published in 1988.

The MLA format always requires a page number in parentheses, and sometimes also requires the author's name. This format does *not* include the word "page" or its abbreviation. Here are the most basic guidelines:

1. If your sentence includes a quotation from an author you have named within the last few sentences, give only the page number at the end, in parentheses, before the period:

   Robert Scholes believes that readers make use of "a storehouse of cultural information" when they interpret a text (480).

2. If you haven't named the author within the last few sentences, or if you have been talking about more than one author in your paragraph, give the author's last name and the page number within the parentheses:

   While Barnlund concentrates on barriers to communication, Rosaldo says that social customs are "busy intersections" where a lot of communication takes place (Rosaldo 389).

3. If your sentence ends with a quotation, put the parentheses after the last quotation mark and before the period:

   According to Heath, the community's "literacy activities are public and social" (234).

4. If your quotation is more than four lines long, quote it as a block quotation. Indent a block quotation 10 spaces, without quotation marks, and place the parentheses two spaces after the final period. Like the rest of your paper, the block quotation should be double-spaced. Use long quotations sparingly, only when they are really needed to advance your argument.

Seidler believes that it is difficult for many men to overcome their upbringing and share their emotions:

> In the middle class, men have often grown up to be reticent, even scared, of sharing emotions and feelings, lest they threaten the control which sustains our very sense of masculinity....We fear that others will see us as weak and unmasculine. (494)

This strong but buried sense of masculine fear plays a very important role in Things Fall Apart.

If you need to use other parts of the MLA system, please consult the most recent version of the *MLA Handbook*.